Stern's Guide to the
Cruise Vacation

REVIEWER COMMENTS

Stern's Guide to the Cruise Vacation is an excellent resource for novice and experienced cruisers alike. It offers sound information on the ships as well as the places they anchor. . . . Stern exhibits experience in the complex world of cruises with an ability to combine careful reporting with reasoned opinion.

SHEILA F. BUCKMASTER, SENIOR EDITOR
NATIONAL GEOGRAPHIC TRAVELER

This is the book with which to gain a full and thorough understanding of the wonderful world of cruising. Repeat cruisers and novices alike will gain enormously from the huge volume of features—menus, daily schedules, photos, as well as the details on every cruise ship and port of call throughout the world. This should be the encyclopedia for any cruise aficianado.

SIMON VENESS, EDITOR
WORLD OF CRUISING MAGAZINE

Stern's Guide to the Cruise Vacation is one of the most comprehensive authorities and a must have for both the novice and the seasoned cruiser.

PORTHOLE MAGAZINE

Travelers adrift in a sea of luxury voyage options can get their sea legs with the new edition of Stern's Guide to the Cruise Vacation, *which boasts detailed descriptions of every major cruise ship and port of call around the globe.*

NEW YORK DAILY NEWS

To say this book is thorough is rather like saying your local telephone book provides information. . . . Stern's Guide to the Cruise Vacation *is required reading.*

STATESMAN JOURNAL
SALEM, OREGON

This book probably would be ideal for those going on their first cruise, as there seems to be a little information on just about everything.

CYNTHIA BOAL JANSSENS
CHICAGO TRIBUNE

A softbound review of everything (and I mean everything) you'd ever want to know about taking a sea-faring vacation anywhere in the world . . . Nothing has ever given us the depth of information available in Pelican's offering . . . it would be good insurance of getting exactly what you want from any world cruise long before stepping on the ship.

PETER WAGNER
NORTHWEST IOWA REVIEW

A clever system of awarded stars makes overall judgments easy to make.
INTERNATIONAL TRAVEL NEWS

2010 Edition

Stern's Guide to the
Cruise Vacation

STEVEN B. STERN

PELICAN PUBLISHING COMPANY
GRETNA 2010

First edition, 1974
Second edition, 1984
First Pelican edition, 1988
Fourth edition, 1991
Fifth edition, 1994
Sixth edition, 1995
Seventh edition, 1997
Eighth edition, 1998
Ninth edition, 1999
Tenth edition, 1999
Eleventh edition, 2000
Twelfth edition, 2002
Thirteenth edition, 2003
Fourteenth edition, 2004
Fifteenth edition, 2005
Sixteenth edition, 2005
Seventeenth edition, 2006
Eighteenth edition, 2007
Nineteenth edition, 2008
Twentieth edition, 2009

ISBN-13: 9781589807105

Information in this guidebook is based on authoritative data available at the time of printing. Prices and hours of operation of businesses listed are subject to change without notice. Readers are asked to take this into account when consulting this guide.

Printed in the United States of America

Published by Pelican Publishing Company, Inc.
1000 Burmaster Street, Gretna, Louisiana 70053

Contents

AUTHOR'S RECOMMENDATION

When selecting a cruise, the following steps are those that I personally follow: First, I decide upon the date I wish to sail. Next, I decide in what part of the world to cruise and what ports of call I wish to visit. Then I consult the *Official Steamship Guide,* which lists every cruise ship sailing in every location around the world, as well as their ports of call throughout the year. This allows me to narrow down my search to those ships that are realistic possibilities. For more information, go to www.officialsteamshipguide.com.

Preface

Over the past 40 years, I have had the pleasure of experiencing some marvelous vacations and unforgettable moments aboard cruise ships. I have seen the cruise industry grow from a formal haven for the very rich to a fun-filled, exciting, bargain holiday for a broad cross section of our population. Every year greater numbers of travelers are wisely spending their vacation dollars on a cruise. It has been estimated that the cruise-passenger market has increased 1,800 percent since 1970, when a half million people took a cruise. In 2010, over 12 million North Americans are expected to enjoy a cruise vacation. Since 2000, more than 90 new ships joined the cruise market, and plans to build numerous additional vessels over the next few years have been announced by the various cruise lines. Seventy percent of today's cruisers are between the ages of 25 and 59 and include singles, couples of all ages, families with children, honeymooners, and groups. Undoubtedly, cruising is the most popular and fastest growing segment of the travel industry.

Cruise ships built in the 1960s, '70s, and '80s are quite different from those built today. Today's vessels are generally larger and provide more public areas, larger staterooms with more facilities and amenities, and better trained crews. They offer greater dining options; more menu selections, including healthy cuisine; enlarged buffet-style dining areas on lido decks; upscale, reservation-only specialty restaurants; larger, state-of-the-art fitness centers; sophisticated spas with a bevy of treatment options; more upscale entertainment, including Vegas-quality productions; increased children and teen programs and facilities; and more exotic ports of call.

This guide has been written to familiarize those who have never encountered the delights of the open sea with what they can expect from a cruise vacation, as well as to assist seasoned sailors in making intelligent selections for their next ship and cruise grounds. Chapter 11 offers a detailed description of each major cruise line and the vessels of its fleet. Included are overall ratings for each ship (Star Awards), as well as a description of medical facilities, photographs, sample menus, and daily programs for each cruise line. Chapter 14 summarizes the overall ratings (Star Awards) and goes on to rate ships from each major cruise line in 11 specific categories.

The book also includes a description of the various cruise grounds and ports of call, setting forth points of interest, restaurants, beaches, sports facilities, and what you can cover with only limited time ashore. In chapter 10, cruises on European riverboats and barges are covered. Chapter 12 describes the most expensive, top luxury suites on vessels that offer such accommodations, and chapter 13 is devoted to the popular concept of alternative dining venues aboard ship.

NOTE

Due to the turmoil throughout various areas of the world (including wars, terrorist attacks, and outbreaks of disease, as well as government warnings not to travel to these areas), many cruise lines have found it necessary to change the deployment of their vessels from time to time. Inasmuch as these decisions are made on a frequent basis, it is impossible to be completely up to date when describing itineraries for the various ships. The itineraries we list are based upon the information given to us by the cruise lines prior to publication. Therefore, we strongly suggest that you verify itineraries with the cruise line prior to making your own cruising plans. For more up-to-date itineraries, visit www.officialsteamshipguide.com.

New Ships Coming on Line

With the ever-increasing growth of the cruise industry, the major cruise lines are continuously building new vessels both to expand their fleets and to replace older ships. During the period extending from late 2008 to the end of 2011, the following new vessels are scheduled to enter service:

Aida Cruises:
71,000-ton unnamed—Spring 2010
71,000-ton unnamed—2011

Carnival Cruise Lines:
130,000-ton *Carnival Dream*—Fall 2009
130,000-ton *Carnival Magic*—Summer 2011

Celebrity Cruises:
122,000-ton *Equinox*—Summer 2010
122,000-ton *Eclipse*—Fall 2011

Costa Cruise Lines:
92,700-ton *Costa Deliziosa*—February 2010
114,147-ton unnamed—2011

Cunard Line:
92,000-ton *Queen Elizabeth*—Fall 2010

Disney Cruise Line:
124,000-ton *Dream*—2011
124,000-ton *Fantasy*—2012

Holland America Line:
86,000-ton *Nieuw Amsterdam*—Fall 2010

MSC Cruises:
  92,400-ton *Magnifica*—2010
  92,400-ton *Meraviglia*—2011
  92,400-ton *Favolosa*—2012

Norwegian Cruise Line:
  150,000-ton *Norwegian Epic*—
    Summer 2010

Oceania Cruises:
  66,000-ton *Marina*—2009
  65,000-ton unnamed—2010

P & O Cruises:
  116,000-ton *Azura*—2010

Ponant Cruises:
  10,600-ton *Le Boreal*—Spring 2010
  10,600-ton *L'Austral*—August 2010

Royal Caribbean International:
  220,000-ton *Oasis of the Seas*—Fall
    2009
  220,000-ton *Allure of the Seas*—
    August 2010

Seabourn Cruise Line:
  32,000-ton *Sojurn*—Spring 2010
  32,000-ton unnamed—Summer
    2011

Star Clippers:
  7,400-ton unnamed—2010

Chapter One

The Cruise:
A Complete Vacation

An Introduction to Cruising
(With Four Case Studies)

Lively and exciting, yet serene and relaxing; romantic and glamorous, yet interesting and broadening; elegant and luxurious, yet casual and economical; gregarious and convivial, yet intimate and private. All of these descriptions, although antithetical at first glance, in fact apply to the cruise vacation. A cruise is a truly unique travel experience the ultimate escape from reality that does not lend itself to a simple definition.

Taking a cruise vacation is partaking in a varied program of exciting activities with interesting and congenial fellow passengers from diverse walks of life. It may be indulging in the finest gourmet cuisine prepared by Continental chefs and impeccably served by an experienced crew who cater to your every whim. It is unwinding and relaxing in comfortable, posh surroundings with an impressive variety of facilities and modern conveniences. It is traveling to exotic ports of call, viewing breathtaking scenery, and exploring historic points of interest. It is a cool dip in the pool, breakfast in bed, a relaxing sauna and massage, moonlit walks on deck, costume balls, movies, bridge tournaments, games, entertainment, cocktail parties, shopping, sunning, dancing, romance, companionship, enlightenment, and, best of all, this can be yours for less than you would spend on any comparable vacation.

Although the price of any cruise will vary on the basis of your accommodations, economy-conscious travelers who book minimum cabins can obtain the best possible buy for their vacation dollar. If you reside in the Southeast, for example, you can take a seven-day cruise from Miami stopping at four or five Caribbean ports for as little as $700 to $950. If you live in the Midwest, you can purchase an "air-sea package" (offered by numerous cruise lines), fly to Puerto Rico, and cruise to South America plus five additional Caribbean islands in a seven-day period for as little as $1,200, including your room, all meals and entertainment, round-trip air fare, and transfers to and from the airport and ship. Of course the majority of accommodations aboard ships will cost two to three times more depending on the market category of the vessel. To duplicate these trips flying from place to place by plane and frequenting restaurants and hotels with food and accommodations comparable to those found on the ship would easily cost a great deal more.

On a land vacation, you will have a greater opportunity for in-depth sightseeing and pursuing more time-consuming activities, such as golf and fishing. However, to visit as many varied places and to engage in activities similar to those offered on a cruise would require you to be constantly on the move. One of the most unique characteristics of the cruise vacation is that everything is conveniently located aboard ship. You need not run around seeking out restaurants, nightclubs, hairdressers, laundries, or companionship. It is all right there. Additionally, you are afforded the opportunity to visit many glamorous and diverse foreign countries without the necessity of lugging around heavy baggage, waiting in line at several airports, and constantly changing hotels. After you have spent a busy day in port sightseeing, swimming, and shopping, you can return to your friendly, familiar floating hotel to dine, drink, dance, and be entertained before you finally retire to awake the following morning already delivered to your next exciting port of call.

Cruising has grown impressively in popularity over the past few decades. New modern luxury liners are being built, and older vessels are being remodeled to meet the ever-increasing lure of travelers to the high seas. This demand can be attributed, perhaps, to the fact that today's cruise offers something for just about everyone—young and old, singles and couples, adults and children, gourmets and gourmands, the gregarious and the inhibited, sun-worshippers and those who prefer indoor relaxation. The rich can reserve the most expensive suite aboard and ensconce themselves in the lap of luxury, and the not-so-rich often can enjoy the same food, entertainment, and public facilities while booking a less expensive cabin. Those who desire recreation can participate in a diverse range of events and activities around the clock, while those who wish to relax can sit back and let the experienced staff and crew serve and entertain them. The athletic types can join the exercise class, work out in the gym, jog around the deck, and on shore can swim, play tennis, or catch a fast 18 holes of golf; while the spectator types can watch a movie, attend a lecture, or view the nightly entertainment. The working person can find a cruise that coincides with his or her one-, two-, or three-week vacation, while retired persons can opt to cruise for three or four months around the world.

During the past 20 years, the major cruise lines have introduced numerous state-of-the-art vessels with features not found on ships built in the 1970s and 1980s. These features include an abundance of veranda cabins; specialty, reservation-only fine-dining restaurants; elaborate spas with large, fully equipped gyms; lounges and bars dedicated to wines and champagne, cigar smokers, martini drinkers, sport enthusiasts, etc.; computer cafés; and more extravagant décors. Many of the older vessels pale by comparison. Therefore, if you haven't cruised in several years, you may be pleasantly surprised with the new generation of ships.

Four Case Studies

John and Martha

John, a bookkeeper from Omaha, Nebraska, and his wife, Martha, who have just seen the last of their three children graduate from college, are looking forward to letting loose and having the time of their lives on a very special cruise. They get up early the first morning at sea to watch the sunrise while enjoying some coffee, juice, and rolls on deck. After a few deep knee bends and stretches at the exercise class, they are ready for a hearty breakfast in the dining room with fresh pineapple and melon, smoked salmon, a cheese omelet, sausages, fried potatoes, toast, and pastries.

Following breakfast, they participate in a Ping-Pong tournament and deck games at the pool, followed by a free salsa lesson. After a cool dip in the pool, they are ready for an elegant lunch in the dining room with an opportunity to try some exotic foreign dishes. Sunning and swimming fill up the early hours of the afternoon, still leaving time for the duplicate bridge tournament. A little workout on the exercycle at the gym, followed by a sauna and massage, helps John work off a few of those piña coladas he was sipping all afternoon. He then showers and shaves while Martha is having her hair set at the beauty shop.

John and Martha don their fancy clothes in time to attend the captain's cocktail party and practice the new dance steps they learned earlier. Then comes the "welcome aboard" dinner in the dining room, complete from caviar to crêpes suzette. Martha wants to play a few games of bingo before the evening variety show, and John tries his luck at blackjack and roulette in the casino.

After the evening's entertainment in the main lounge, a few cold cuts, cheeses, and desserts at the midnight buffet just hit the spot; and then it is time to go up to the discotheque to swing with the night owls into the wee hours. Following a leisurely stroll around the deck, our active couple is ready for bed. It was never like this in Omaha!

Michael and Vivian

Michael, an overworked New York attorney, and his wife, Vivian, a harassed primary-school teacher, never had a chance to take a trip when they got married last June. This cruise represents a long-overdue honeymoon. They start their first day at sea by enjoying a leisurely breakfast in bed, followed by some quiet hours soaking up the sun on deck. One shuffleboard game, a short swim in the pool, and a stroll up to the bridge are just enough excitement to help them work up an appetite for a delicious buffet lunch served on deck by the pool.

A little more sun, a few chapters of a good book, a first-run movie in the theater, some tea and cakes on the promenade deck, and our honeymooners are ready for rest and relaxation in their cabin before dressing for the evening. They elect to drink the bottle of champagne their travel agent sent them while enjoying some hot hors d'oeuvres in the lounge; then it's off to the dining room for an eight-course gourmet meal. After the evening entertainment, Michael and Vivian have the first opportunity since their wedding to dance to a romantic orchestra. A chance to gaze at the stars on deck caps off the night. What new marriage couldn't use a day like this?

Joan and Ron

Joan, who works in a Miami insurance office, wants to make the most out of her one remaining week of vacation time. She wants to relax and visit some new places, and she wouldn't object to meeting a tall, dark, handsome stranger if he came along. On the first day at sea, she misses breakfast in the dining room but enjoys some juice, croissants, and coffee served on the deck for the late sleepers. Off comes the cover-up, revealing her new bikini. She takes a stroll around the pool to let all those who are interested know she is aboard.

The eleven o'clock dance class is a must, since it affords her a controlled atmosphere for meeting other passengers. At the class she meets two women from California, and they decide to sit at the same table for lunch. The understanding maître d' arranges a large table for singles, where Joan and her two new friends are joined by another woman traveling alone and four eligible bachelors. The group decides to spend the afternoon at the pool swimming and playing backgammon. Several of the other singles come over to watch, and by the afternoon "singles-only" cocktail party, Joan has already met most of the other single passengers aboard ship.

Ron, one of the eligible bachelors at Joan's table, is an advertising executive from Boston who is recently divorced and in search of some feminine companionship. He initially decides that he and Joan are basically looking for different things; however, her popularity with other single female passengers indicates that she is a good mixer and a potential source of introductions. By participating in the deck games and making frequent trips to the numerous bars, Ron manages to meet a few more women, and those he missed show up at the "singles-only" cocktail party. By dinnertime, he has three or four interesting prospects for the evening. He decides to have a drink with Joan and her friends before dinner; however, he passes up the planned evening entertainment and goes straight to the discotheque where he can dance with all of the other young women he has met.

After dinner, Joan prefers to see the variety show, browse through the shops, and try the "one-arm bandits" before joining the other singles at the discotheque at midnight. By the time she arrives, Ron has already run through a half-dozen possibilities and decided that he really can't relate to any of them. Ron asks Joan to dance, and both feel a strange new chemistry that wasn't evident earlier that evening. Joan and Ron won't give permission to print the rest of the story; therefore, you can select your own ending.

Scotty and Jamie

Scotty, age eight, and his big sister Jamie, age 14, could hardly sleep the night before their mom and dad took them on their first seven-day Caribbean cruise. By sharing a four-berth cabin with their parents, it only cost an extra $375 apiece to bring them along.

The first afternoon aboard ship was exciting. The band was playing, passengers were partying and throwing colorful streamers overboard, and crew members were passing out drinks and sandwiches. Upon arriving at their cabin, Scotty was delighted to find that he had been assigned an upper berth, but Jamie pouted when her dad told her that the other top bunk was hers.

After the ship set sail, Scotty migrated to the electronic game room, where he met numerous other youngsters around his age. After a while, he and a new friend went up on deck to play Ping-Pong and shuffleboard by the pool. At five o'clock, there was a get-together at the disco for teens, which Jamie anxiously attended. A member of the ship's social staff outlined the special events and programs that would be offered throughout the cruise for the teenage set. At the same time, there was a similar meeting for the pre-teens at the ice-cream emporium. Here Scotty learned about the daily movies, bingo, deck sports, pool games, scavenger hunts, masquerade balls, talent shows, and "Coke-tail" parties that would dominate his days aboard ship.

After dinner, Scotty and his new friend went to the movies, followed by pizza and a soda in the special pizzeria restaurant. Jamie attended the first-night-aboard party in the show lounge, where she was introduced to the cruise staff and took part in the audience participation games. After the party, she went to the teen disco, which was already packed to the rafters with enthusiastic young passengers getting to know each other.

Days ashore were especially enjoyable. The varied ports of call offered pristine white-sand beaches, water sports, horseback riding, tennis, historic sights, cute souvenir shops, and scenic drives. Mealtimes were also great fun. Each evening, the dining room was decorated in a different ethnic theme and the attentive waiters were dressed to blend in. Scotty was able to order hamburgers and hot dogs for lunch and a big, fat steak and fries for dinner. Jamie, an aspiring gourmet, elected to sample the more esoteric offerings.

On the last evening aboard, the lights were turned down and all the waiters paraded around the dining room carrying baked Alaskas with sparklers while the passengers sang "Auld Lang Syne." The seven days had passed too quickly and our two young sailors were very sad the morning the ship sailed back into its homeport. They had visited exciting and different islands, made many new friends, and participated in numerous good times. As for Mom and Dad . . . they showed up at dinner, bedtime, and when the youngsters needed quarters for the game machines. When Scotty and Jamie were asked how they liked the cruise, their joint answer was, "Awesome!"

The remaining chapters of this book are designed to familiarize you with the different aspects of the cruise vacation. Chapter 2, entitled "Getting Ready for the Cruise," starts by detailing how to go about planning and booking a cruise and proceeds to set forth objective standards for selecting a ship. The chapter goes on to delineate the factors that will determine the cost of your cabin and list the items you will want to be certain to bring along. Chapter 3 describes your day at sea, depicting the customary facilities found aboard ship as well as the typical program of round-the-clock activities. The dining experience is then portrayed with descriptions of the numerous meals and varieties of cuisine as well as some suggestions relating to multiple sittings and tipping. Chapter 4 analyzes the pros and cons of cruising for singles. The desirability and cost of bringing along your children are explored in chapter 5, together with a description of the events and facilities aboard ships that are designed specifically for their interests as well as the best ships for traveling families. In chapter 6, you will find a summary of the various cruise areas and highlights of the most popular cruise stops, with suggestions on what you can see and do during your day in port. Chapters 7, 8, and 9, respectively, describe where to go in each port to swim, play tennis, and jog.

Chapter 10 describes what to expect when cruising on riverboats and barges in Europe and how they differ from ocean-going vessels. Chapter 11 includes a description of every major cruise line and cruise ship, including my overall ratings (in the form of Star Awards), photographs, sample menus, and daily programs. Chapter 12 describes the most expensive, top-luxury suites on vessels that offer such accommodations, and chapter 13 describes alternative dining specialty restaurants that recently have been added to many ships. Chapter 14 summarizes my Star Awards and goes on to evaluate sample ships of each line in 11 specific categories.

The growing concern of prospective cruisers as to available medical facilities on the various ships is covered in this edition. An analysis of medical care at sea is discussed in chapter two, and the facilities, equipment, and personnel available aboard each ship (as represented by the cruise lines) is included in chapter 11.

Chapter Two

Getting Ready
for the Cruise

Planning and Booking a Cruise

When planning a cruise, you must consider a number of factors. First of all, you must decide at what time of year you will be taking your cruise vacation. If you choose to travel in the late fall or winter, you may prefer cruising in the warmer climate and calmer waters of the Caribbean, South Pacific, Indian Ocean, or Far East. Transatlantic crossings at this time of year can be a bit rough for all but the hardiest seadogs.

On the other hand, a late spring, summer, or early fall cruise in the Eastern Mediterranean to the Greek Islands, Turkish Coast, and Middle East; in the Western Mediterranean to ports of call in Italy, France, and Spain; or in the Baltic, North Sea, and Norwegian Fjords to cities in England, Holland, Sweden, Norway, Denmark, Germany, and Russia, can afford a very interesting opportunity to mingle with passengers from other countries. Transatlantic crossings at these times of year are not necessarily rough, but they are not recommended for your first exploration of the sea. Be aware that ships crossing the Atlantic by the southern route will encounter better weather, permitting more days on deck than those ships taking the northern route.

After you have decided upon the time of the year to go and the general geographic area to see, the next step is to find out which ships will be cruising in that area on the dates you have available. If you are set on cruising on a specific ship, then to determine where you will be sailing at any given time to any given place, I recommend that you consult a copy of the *Official Steamship Guide International*. This magazine is subscribed to by most travel agencies, is updated seasonally, and contains a complete list of prospective cruises for all ships for the upcoming 12-month period as soon as the line makes the dates public. *Ocean Cruise News, Portholes, Cruise Business News, World of Cruising,* and *Cruise Travel* magazines are periodicals that list prospective cruises and include articles describing

18

ships, ports of call, and updates on what is going on in the cruise industry. *World of Cruising Magazine,* the leading cruise magazine in Great Britain, is especially informative, well written, and can be subscribed to in the U.S. Their fax number is 011-44-(0)8704292683 and their Web site is www.woconline.com. Also several Web sites provide information about cruise ships and the latest developments in cruising. Alan Wilson's *Cruise News Daily* sends its subscribers daily information by e-mail. Of course, each of the cruise lines has a Web site where you can obtain specific information about their ships and itineraries.

Over the past few years, numerous travel agencies that specialize in cruising have sprung up. Frequently they can offer deep-discount tickets due to prior arrangements with some of the cruise lines. You will want to check the cruise/discount-fare advertisements in the travel section of your Sunday newspaper, as well as the various cruise periodicals and Web sites. Once you have cruised on a particular line, you will be placed on its mailing list and be provided from time to time with brochures offering special discounted sailings.

When consulting the available guides, you will also have to consider the length of time you have for your vacation. If you have only a week or 10 days, seek out a ship with a correspondingly shorter itinerary. However, if you have two weeks or more, you can also consider the longer cruises.

Now that you have traced the ships that are sailing in the geographic area of your choice during the period you have scheduled for your vacation, you will want to study the credentials and offerings of each of these vessels. Do you prefer French food, Italian service, Scandinavian *joie de vivre,* Dutch hospitality, or British efficiency? Do you wish to storm seven ports in seven days, or do you prefer spending three or four relaxing days at sea? Do you desire the intimacy of a small ship, or is a large superliner your cup of tea? These are the questions that you must ask, and the following section of this chapter, as well as chapters 11 through 14, are devoted to helping you arrive at your decision.

After you have finally selected a vessel, it is desirable to include a second and even a third choice, for now you must determine whether space on the ship you desire is still available. A later section of this chapter on "Costs and Your Cabin" will point out the factors to be considered in choosing accommodations.

When booking reservations for a cabin, you can either go to your travel agent or directly to the cruise line office in your locality or to its Web site. Booking through a travel agent generally has the advantage of having someone else obtain your tickets, make all arrangements, provide you with necessary instructions, and maybe even throw in a bottle of the bubbly when you arrive on ship. However, if your agent tells you that the space you desire is not available, do not give up. Either call another agent, search Web sites, or contact the line directly, request that you be wait-listed, and explain how you are dying to cruise on their ships but can go only at a certain time and for a certain price. Call them up every week or so to check on whether there has been a cancellation. Persistence may pay off because vacationers often change their minds, and there are usually a great number of last-minute cancellations.

To play it safe, you can accept a more expensive room, for example, and ask to be wait-listed for the first cheaper one that becomes available. I do not know for a fact what procedures the various lines follow; however, it is possible that some cruise lines will sell a room that becomes available to a new customer rather than to one who has already accepted another room and has been wait-listed. Therefore, if you are set on obtaining specific accommodations, you may have a better chance if you do not accept a substitute. On the other hand, if you don't, you may be left behind. Here again it will pay off to contact the numerous travel agencies that specialize in cruising since they may have an inventory of pre-purchased accommodations or a little extra clout with the cruise line.

As you would expect, it is more difficult to book cruises for holidays such as Christmas, New Year's, Easter, Thanksgiving, Memorial Day, the Fourth of July, and Labor Day. Everyone wants to go away at these times, and you must book far in advance (as much as six months to a year for a Christmas or New Year's cruise on some ships).

For those who choose to book their cruise through the Internet, cruise lines and travel agencies have established Web sites that provide information on sailings and rates. If you are comfortable with booking travel in this manner, you may find some excellent last-minute bargains. I recommend you go to www.stevensterntravel.com.

I always recommend that cruisers arrive at the port of embarkation at least one day in advance in order to avoid airplane delays and the possibility of "missing the boat." There is nothing more frustrating than trying to catch up with a ship at its next port of call or having to turn around and go home. Although you may have purchased insurance to cover this possibility, it will certainly be a disappointment.

It is generally possible to purchase air through the cruise line, which will have negotiated rates with the airlines. Although the rates can be higher than those on the Internet or those available for advanced purchases through the airlines, the fact remains that the cruise line will have the responsibility of attending to you until they can get you on the ship.

Selecting a Ship

What kind of ship you select will depend upon your feelings about people, food, relaxation, activity, aesthetics, and so on. Whereas one reader may be delighted by a ship that offers a diverse Continental menu of gourmet delights, another may feel dissatisfied because the kitchen staff cannot prepare a thick, juicy sirloin steak. One couple may fall in love with a cruise ship because of the super time they had dancing to good music every evening and taking part in a masquerade ball, but another couple may feel that the same ship was not a good buy because it offered no "big-name" entertainment. The fact that any particular ship may appeal to one does not mean it will appeal to another. Also, the food and service on any given ship can vary from time to time, just as it does in a restaurant or hotel. A change in chefs, for example, can make a big difference.

How, then, can you compare ships and make a selection? To a certain extent, you will rely on the opinions of others. You are encouraged to discuss this with your travel agent as well as with friends (holding similar interests and tastes) who have cruised on the ships you are considering. Acquire all the brochures and other promotional matter printed by the cruise lines. These pamphlets usually contain pictures of the public rooms and cabins, prices, enumeration of facilities, description of ports of call, and a deck plan. If your travel agent does not have the relevant brochure for the ship in which you are interested, you can write directly to the line. Do not hesitate to contact the line about any specific bit of information you may wish to obtain.

To assist you further with your selection, detailed descriptions, per diem fares, and ratings for most cruise ships, as well as photos, sample menus, and activity programs, appear in chapters 11 through 14 of this book.

The following is an analysis of many of the factors that I recommend you consider in comparing potential cruises.

Ports of Call

Check to see at which ports the ship will be calling and then review what each of those ports has to offer (see analysis of ports in chapter 6). Do you prefer spending your days ashore shopping, sunning at a beautiful beach, exploring archeological ruins, hiking through natural scenery, or visiting historic museums? Be certain that the ship stops at a port that will afford you an opportunity to pursue the activities you enjoy.

When sailing the Caribbean, the islands of St. Thomas, St. Croix, and Curaçao are considered to have the most diversified shopping, with the best bargains in French perfume being found in Martinique, Guadeloupe, and St. Martin. The finest beaches for swimming and sunning are found in the Grand Caymans, Bermuda, St. Thomas, St. Croix, St. John, Virgin Gorda, Aruba, Barbados, Antigua, Anguilla, Jamaica, St. Martin, Grenada, the Bahamas, and Cozumel. Archeology buffs will want to visit Cancun, Costa Maya, Guatemala, and the ports of the Yucatán.

Although the beaches of the Mediterranean, Baltic, and North Sea don't compare with those of the Caribbean, the offering of historic points of interest, art, museums, and shopping is far superior in the Mediterranean and northern European ports. Today it is possible to cruise almost anywhere in the world, including such faraway areas as the South Seas, the Far East, Australia, Africa, the Indian Ocean, and even Antarctica.

As mentioned earlier, you will want to determine how many ports are on the itinerary of the cruises you may be considering. For example, some ships visit as many as six ports on a seven-day cruise, whereas others stop at only one or two. Do you prefer a busy itinerary where you are in port almost every day, or do you prefer spending the majority of your days on the open sea?

Next, you should check out the period of time the ship is docked at each port. Too often a ship may be in port for so short a period that there is not time to visit the places you have mapped out. For example, several ships stop in Montego Bay for only five hours, not leaving sufficient time to drive to Dunn's Falls or take the jungle river raft ride down the Martha Brae. Other ships dock at San Juan only in the later afternoon and evening to permit passengers to gamble, while leaving insufficient time to explore the island. There are still other ships that include in their brochures "ports of call" where the vessels dock for merely an hour to pick up passengers. Certain Mediterranean cruises drop anchor at Gibraltar, Cannes, Genoa, and Naples to receive embarking passengers but don't stop long enough to permit any exploration. You should carefully analyze the itinerary of each ship you are considering.

Dining

As pointed out in detail in the next chapter, the dining experience aboard ship is one of the highlights of the cruise. Therefore, a good deal of consideration should be given to the fare offered by the different lines. Although many ships rate far above the average restaurant in this department, the types and varieties of victuals do vary from ship to ship.

Most of the lunch and dinner menus offer an interesting assortment of foods with an emphasis on ethnic dishes that are representative of the nationality of the dining room staff and chef. If you require kosher food, baby food, or have any special dietary restrictions, you should check with the ship line in advance to determine whether the required foods will be available. A very popular concept is the inclusion of alternative specialty restaurants in addition to the main dining room, which affords passengers an opportunity to break up the nightly routine and opt for a more intimate dining experience. These venues generally feature steakhouse, Italian, French, or Asian cuisine. Casual, alternative-dining restaurants are available on almost all of the major vessels. Wine, caviar, and espresso bars, along with pizza parlors, are rapidly being added to many of the ships that have come on line during the past few years. (See alternative dining restaurants in chapter 13.)

In chapter 11, you will find sample menus from ships representing the various lines. Because the menus tend to be similar for ships of the same line, these samples should give you some idea of what to expect. (*Caution:* You will see steak and lobster offered on almost all of the menus, but the quality may vary radically. Beef shipped from the United States and lobster caught off the coast of Maine may be quite a bit more tender than beef picked up in Mexico or lobsters caught in the Caribbean.) In addition, food and dining room service often will be superior on the flagship of each line. Generally, the chefs and waiters earn the privilege of serving on the flagship by working their way up the ladder on the other vessels. The ratings for dining quality found in chapter 14 may assist you in comparing the ships of the various cruise lines.

Service

The quality of service rendered by the dining room staff, the cabin stewards, and social staff can significantly affect your enjoyment of the cruise. A pleasant, efficient waiter can perk up a mediocre meal; an understanding and helpful cabin steward can minimize the inconvenience of a small or otherwise inadequate cabin; and a tactful, perceptive social director can bring together people of common interests and add an additional dimension to your vacation.

Naturally, the quality of service varies from line to line and even among ships of the same line. I have found that ships with European dining room and cabin staffs offer the best all-around service. These waiters and stewards seem to have received the best training, maintain the best attitudes, and are the most anxious to please. I found the mixed European crew on Crystal, Hapag-Lloyd, Regent Seven Seas, Silversea, Oceania, Seabourn, and SeaDream to be superior in these areas. The Greek ships tend to economize and overwork their crews, with the obvious results. Those ships using mixed service crews from the Caribbean islands, South America, India, Indonesia, Philippines, Asia, and Mexico do so as an economy factor. Unfortunately, these people do not have the training or "know-how" of most of the European crews. Many of the cruise lines' predominant use of Indonesian and/or Filipino waiters and room stewards has proved to be some-what of a mixed bag: some cruisers find them charming and attentive, while others have found the service mediocre because of the serious language problem and lack of experience. The all-American crew on several of the U.S. cruise lines are often inexperienced. The nationality of the dining room and cabin crews is indicated in chapter 11.

Service may vary from one year to the next on the same ship, especially when a line is striving to improve this area. Therefore, obtain knowledgeable opinions on the standard of service for any ships you are considering.

Medical Care at Sea

Considering the millions of people of all ages and levels of health who cruise each year to exotic and remote areas where access to state-of-the-art hospitals and well-trained physicians may be limited, one must conclude that the availability and quality of medical facilities and personnel aboard ship should be a major consideration when selecting a particular vessel.

Certainly, a significant segment of the cruising population that opts for longer cruises to more out-of-the-way destinations is retired and getting on in years. Although when encountering an emergency at home, these senior citizens can call 911 and be rushed to a modern hospital, when they find themselves in the middle of the Pacific or docked at a primitive port in New Guinea, the best they can hope for is a decent medical facility and physician aboard ship. Many younger passengers have infirmities that could require special medical attention, while others may suffer accidental injuries either on the ship or during port explorations. Here again, the only available emergency equipment and supplies may be at the ship's medical facility.

Therefore, the experience and specialties of a ship's physician and nurses, the technological equipment and pharmaceuticals available, as well as the x-ray, operating, and emergency facilities, should receive as much consideration by older cruisers and those with pre-existing medical problems as the level of dining, activities, and shore excursions.

Generally, the larger vessels carry more medical staff and are equipped with expanded facilities in anticipation of a greater demand by both passengers and crew members. Many smaller ships have also made ample provision for medical emergencies. However, over the years I have found that ships unwisely economize in this department. Ships sometimes carry too small a medical staff to cope with the passenger/crew load, hire physicians for short durations or who are not trained to deal with multiple emergencies, have limited equipment and supplies available, and tend to downplay their responsibility for passenger health needs.

The American College of Emergency Physicians has published *Guidelines of Care for Cruise Ship Medical Facilities.* Among the numerous recommendations are the following:

1. A medical staff, available around the clock, board-certified in emergency medicine, family practice, and internal medicine, with two to three years of clinical experience, emergency/critical care experience, advanced trauma and cardiac life-support skills, minor surgical skills, and fluency in the major language of passengers and crew.

2. Emergency medical equipment and medications including primary and backup cardiac monitors, primary and backup portable defibrillators, electrocardiograph, wheelchairs, refrigerator/freezer, extrication device, C-collar immobilization capability, trauma cart supplies, airway equipment, volume pumps, ventilators, pulse oximeter, external pacer capability, portable oxygen sufficient until patient can disembark ship, and medications comparable to those required to run two emergency department code carts including advanced cardiac support drugs.

3. Basic laboratory capabilities including x-ray unit, capability to perform hemoglobin, urinalysis, pregnancy, and glucose tolerance tests, a microscope, and a universal crew-blood-donor list.

4. A passenger information program regarding on-board health and safety, a pre-assessment of passengers' medical needs, and a program to meet Physical Disabilities Act standards.

5. A crew screening program covering all communicable diseases and certain other conditions, as well as a crew safety program.

6. Examination and treatment areas and an in-patient holding unit adequate for the size of the ship.

Heads of hospital staff on various cruise lines have suggested that ship doctors be trained in advanced trauma and life support, have broad experience in family and emergency medicine, and be backed up by sufficient registered nurses with similar practical experience to formulate an efficient emergency-response team to deal with cardiac arrest and other serious medical traumas. They advise that when the combined passenger/crew population exceeds 1,000, a second physician is advisable, as well as an expanded nursing staff. Facilities should include a well-stocked computer-controlled pharmacy, a satisfactory range of x-ray facilities, a fully equipped operating theater, biochemistry and full-blood-count equipment, at least one or two intensive-care wards that include a cardiac monitor, EKG machine, and pulse oximetry, and, if possible, a tele-medical facility enabling the shipboard doctor to consult with and obtain advice from hospitals and specialists ashore while giving advice or performing procedures with which he may not be familiar at sea.

We have attempted to elicit information as to the experience of the medical personnel and the extent of the medical facilities, equipment, and systems aboard each cruise ship. However, it would be naive to believe that one could obtain totally honest responses when surveying the various cruise lines as to the quality of the facilities, equipment, and staff aboard their ships. No cruise line would admit to be remiss in any of these areas, although my personal observation leads me to suspect some are inadequately staffed or equipped to handle the passenger and crew load they carry.

Any potential cruiser with a medical problem, in a high-risk group, or with general concerns as to medical facilities aboard a particular ship would be well advised to contact the medical director of the cruise line in advance of booking the trip to determine if the caliber of medical support and facilities he or she may require will be available. Probably, it would be prudent to make a written inquiry and request a written reply so that the party responding is careful to research the matter before making any representations. Similar investigation can be made into the ship's ability to satisfy special dietary needs, as well as possible inoculations that may be advisable. When in doubt, an ounce of prevention is worth a pound of cure, or some such euphemism.

Note: After the short summaries of each ship listed in chapter 11, we have added a code designating the medical personnel, facilities, and equipment that the cruise line has represented is available aboard the vessel. Where the cruise line has not responded to our inquiries, the failure to respond is indicated. I must emphasize that this information was given by an employee of the cruise line, has not been verified by the author or publisher, and may have changed by the time you read this information. A written inquiry made directly to the medical director of the cruise line is your most prudent course.

CODE DESIGNATING MEDICAL PERSONNEL, FACILITIES, AND EQUIPMENT

C	Number of wheelchair-accessible cabins
P	Number of physicians
EM	Certified in emergency medicine
CLS	Certified in advanced trauma and cardiac life support
MS	Ability to perform minor surgical procedures
N	Number of nurses experienced in Emergency Medicine or Critical Care

EMERGENCY MEDICAL EQUIPMENT, LAB EQUIPMENT, AND FACILITIES

CM   Primary and backup cardiac monitors
PD   Primary and backup portable defibrillators
BC   Equipment for biochemistry, full blood count, and urinalysis
EKG Electrocardiograph machine
TC   Trauma cart supplies
PO   Pulse oximeter
EPC External pacer capability
OX   Portable oxygen
WC   At least one wheelchair for 300 passengers and crew
OR   Operating room sufficient for minor surgery (If this is important, you need to obtain details from the cruise line.)
ICU Intensive care unit
X   X-ray unit
M   Microscope
CCP Computer-controlled pharmacy
D   Dialysis equipment
TM   Tele-medical capability
LJ   Life jackets located at Muster Stations (as well as in cabins) sufficient for all passengers. This is not required by SOLA; some cruise lines have a limited number at the Muster Stations. Where "LJ" is included, it indicates that the cruise line has represented to me that it has life jackets sufficient to accommodate all passengers at Muster Stations, in addition to those in the cabins.

Facilities for the Physically Challenged

Cruising is possibly the most convenient way for the physically challenged to visit places of interest around the world. Today, most new ships have increased the number of wheelchair-accessible cabins and have improved public facilities to make them more user-friendly for those with physical impairments.Today the visually or hearing impaired, diabetics, dialysis patients, pulmonary sufferers, and wheelchair users can experience cruising.

The cruise lines and ships that have provided the most facilities and accommodations for the physically challenged are Celebrity, Regent Seven Seas, Norwegian, Crystal, Disney, Princess, Royal Caribbean, Carnival's 100,000+-ton ships, Holland America's newest ships, Star Cruises' new builds, Hapag-Lloyd's *Europa,* and P & O's newer ships. Although there are various sites you can go to online, the most prudent procedure would be to contact the cruise line you are interested in and obtain timely details about the facilities on their ships.

Other Facilities

The facilities will vary from ship to ship, with the most facilities being found on the larger craft. The megaships (more than 70,000 gross registered tons) of

Royal Caribbean, Princess, P & O, Cunard, Celebrity, Disney, Holland America, Costa, MSC Norwegian, Star, and Carnival cruise lines, for example, have just about every facility found in a large resort hotel and then some. However, even the mid-size and smaller vessels make clever use of the area they have, offering passengers almost the same facilities as the larger ships but on a smaller scale. The age of the ship may be a factor here, and if you are considering an older ship, it is important to find out if it has been recently remodeled. Currently, Royal Caribbean's *Voyager*-class and *Freedom*-class ships boast the most impressive facilities at sea, with Princess's *Grand*-class ships, Norwegian's and Carnival's larger ships, and the *Queen Mary 2* running close behind.

Consider and compare the public rooms, swimming pools (number and size), deck areas, restaurant facilities, gymnasium, sauna, deck sports, library, elevators, movie theater, chapel, dance bands, bars, game rooms, hospital, cabins, bathrooms, and so on. Some of the more common facilities are included in the descriptions of the various ships in chapter 11. A better description and pictures of these facilities can be found in the ship's promotional brochures. Be careful! These brochures are like most advertising material; they have a tendency to portray the ship as larger and more beautiful than it may appear on actual inspection.

Activities

Although almost all ships offer a wide range of varied activities, not all ships subscribe to the same program. Golf addicts will want to consider those ships that offer golf clinics and feature excursions to golf courses ashore, joggers should check out which ships afford jogging decks, and amateur chefs may wish to select a ship with gourmet cooking lessons. The vast range of daily activities is more thoroughly described in the next chapter, and chapter 11 contains sample daily programs from ships of most of the major cruise lines.

In general, I have found that the ships offering regular cruises from Florida, California, San Juan, New York, and other U.S. ports have the most activities per day at sea, with the Royal Caribbean, Holland America, Celebrity, Norwegian, Carnival, Crystal, Costa, and Princess lines leading in this department. Ships sailing the Mediterranean and northern Europe seem to offer the least activities (probably because they spend the majority of days in port). Several of the lines offer "once-a-year, special activity" cruises featuring classical or jazz music festivals, gourmet-cooking classes, wine seminars, or Broadway theater.

Today most of the major cruise lines offer "learning at sea" agendas, which may include computer lessons; language lessons; photography and computer technology; lectures on wine, archeology, history, and marine biology; hands-on cooking classes by well-known chefs; musical lessons; painting, weaving, pottery, and other crafts; and numerous other useful courses. We found the Crystal and Princess lines' enrichment programs two of the best.

If you are cruising with children, be sure to note those vessels that offer a special children's program. I was particularly impressed with the children's programs on Norwegian, Royal Caribbean, Princess, Carnival, and Disney cruise

lines, which include special counselors, age-appropriate children's activities, special discos, electronic game rooms, and ice-cream and pizza parlors. Most of the other larger ships also have good facilities and programs for children.

Many of the vessels built after 1990 have special areas and facilities for business meetings and seminars, as well as public computer rooms with instructional classes.

Computers/Internet/E-Mail/Cell Phones

With the growing demand of passengers wishing to send e-mails and check their favorite Web sites, cruise lines have rapidly caught on and are now competing to furnish the most comprehensive computer facilities. Most of the new ships that have come on line during the past few years have quite impressive Internet cafes and computer facilities.

Some cruise lines provide facilities permitting passengers to connect their own personal laptops, while others require you to use the equipment available aboard ship. Most of the major cruise lines have recently expanded their computer facilities and instructional programs. Many of the ships provide wireless access, or WiFi, at various spots throughout the ship, including cabins, so that those who bring their own laptops can access the Internet remotely. One significant benefit is the lower cost of communicating back home by e-mail as opposed to the expensive telephone and fax procedures aboard ships. Since there will be variances among the cruise lines and from ship to ship of the same line as to facilities and charges for Internet access, it would be prudent to check out what is available before sailing.

SeaMobile, which enables passengers to use their cell phones on the ship to both place outgoing and receive incoming calls, is being installed on many ships. You are simply billed a roaming rate by your cell provider. Where this service is available, you will also be able to connect your laptop computer to the Internet.

Accommodations

As previously explained, each ship prints an attractive brochure that includes a deck plan describing the size of each room, number of closets, dresser space, bathroom facilities, type of beds (single, double, or bunk), and general layouts. Thus, it is possible for you to review these facts before booking your cabin. Generally, you will pay more for added space, with the deluxe suites going for two to three times the price of the average cabin. There is often a difference between similarly priced accommodations on different ships. If living quarters are one of your major concerns, then this comparison of rooms will be an important factor in your selection of vessels.

I have been especially impressed with the accommodations in the average room on the *QM2* and the vessels of Carnival, Celebrity, Crystal, Disney, Hapag-Lloyd, Holland America, Regent Seven Seas, Seabourn, Silversea, and Windstar, as well as the newer ships of Princess Cruises, which also include many rooms with outdoor verandas for those who enjoy sitting out on their own private patio overlooking the sea.

Ships built during the past 10 years have put a greater emphasis on providing verandas. Prime examples are the Princess and Silversea cruise lines, the newest ships of Celebrity Cruises, Disney, Holland America, and the Regent Seven Seas cruise lines. The *Seven Seas Mariner* and *Voyager* are the first ships offering verandas in every accommodation throughout the ship. Although cabins with balconies fetch a higher price, many cruisers, after experiencing the joys of a "veranda at sea," find this luxury well worth the extra tariff. Verandas attached to suites tend to be larger and more utilitarian than those adjoining standard cabins, and on a few ships, they include an outdoor Jacuzzi tub.

Price

What do you get for your money? The answer may depend upon whether you are looking for quality or quantity, although it is not necessary to sacrifice either. If you divide the price of the cruise by the number of nights afloat, you will arrive at the average cost per day, which can serve as one standard of comparison. Do not use days afloat because this may be deceptive. A ship that leaves at 7:00 P.M. on a Sunday and returns at 8:00 A.M. on Saturday may be advertised as a "seven-day cruise," when in fact you are spending only six nights and five days aboard.

After you arrive at your average daily cost, determine what kind of cabin this amount of money will purchase on comparable ships. Also compare the miles traveled and the number of ports of call. The existence of the "air-sea package," mentioned earlier and described later, will significantly affect your calculations. If you are comparing two ships and one offers an air-sea package, you must add in the cost of air transportation before making your comparison.

The price of cruising has escalated over the past decade, reflecting the increased demand by travelers as well as the increased cost of food, fuel, and labor. A number of the great "luxury" vessels of the 1960s such as the *France, Michaelangelo,* and *Raffaello* were retired because the French and Italian lines could not afford to keep up the high standard of food and service without losing millions of dollars each year. However, the cruise vacation still represents one of the best bargains around for travelers.

You will find that cruises on the Silversea, Crystal, Cunard, Seabourn, and Regent Seven Seas cruise lines are the most expensive. However, these vessels offer a certain elegance and such a high standard of service that many travelers are willing to pay a little extra. The tariff for the choice cabins on the ships of the Princess, Holland America, Celebrity, Windstar, Disney, and Royal Caribbean lines will run almost as high. A luxury suite on almost any fine cruise ship will cost the most.

Beware of some of the "super-low" rates. When a ship offers a cruise for 50 percent less than another, something has to go (and it usually isn't the ship owner's profits). This does not mean that they will not offer many of the same amenities of the more expensive cruises; however, the food, service, and accommodations will not be of the same quality. One exception would be "loss leaders," offered by lines attempting to open up a new cruise market or attempting to fill their ships to capacity during the off season or during a poor economy. These can be real bargains.

More often than not, brochure tariffs have little or no bearing on the prices passengers actually end up paying. People like to think they are getting a bargain, and by marking up the brochure price and then offering various discounted fares, the cruise lines give the impression that they are providing the customer a good buy. Various discounting vehicles have been employed: lower fares for last-minute bookings; early-purchase discounts (often as high as 50 percent); two-for-one deals where the first passenger pays brochure fare and the second sails free (which is really a 50 percent discount); air-sea fares where air fare to the port of embarkation is offered gratis or at a reduced rate; and special group rates. In addition, numerous travel agencies purchase blocks of space on ships and offer them to their customers at discounted rates. These discount agencies generally advertise in travel sections of newspapers and cruise periodicals. In general, discounted rates and other price-saving deals are greatest well in advance of the sailing and diminish proportionately as the ship fills up.

This practice of charging varying rates at different times can be disturbing because you do not know whether you have received the best reduction until you are aboard ship comparing prices with fellow passengers. However, for better or worse, the practice exists, and those of you wishing to obtain the best bargain have to do your homework.

An emerging trend among the economy, mass-market, and premium cruise lines is to keep the cruise fares competitive while recouping revenues by nickel-and-diming passengers during the cruise for beverages, shore excursions, and expected gratuities. Some observers have predicted that during the next few years, many of the cruise lines will be charging extra for activities and entertainment. On-board revenue is the key to the profitable operation of a ship for the cruise line. Although you may be paying as low as $100 or $150 a day for your cruise, your on-board charges will often equal or exceed this amount. The largest source of on-board revenue is from the sale of beverages. Whether you are ordering an expensive bottle of wine, a martini at the bar, a bottle of beer or a coke, the markup is substantial (as well as the 15 percent gratuity), and opportunities to purchase beverages aboard ship are substantial. The second largest source of revenues is from the markup for shore excursions. Some of the more exotic offerings can run from $200 to $1,000 per person, whereas an average shore excursion is generally from $60 to $100. I have seen some ships charge $40 or $50 to bus passengers to a public beach. Other on-board sources of revenue include purchases of photos from the ship's photographer (these can run from $7 to $30 each), gambling at the casinos and other games of chance such as bingo and horse racing, shops on board as well as rake-offs from shops ashore who are allowed to promote their establishment on the ship, spa and beauty treatments, telephone and Internet charges, and last, but not least, the automatic gratuity that is added on to your shipboard account.

Age of Ship

Unlike a fine wine, ships do not necessarily improve with age. Unless a ship is well maintained and frequently refurbished, it will soon show signs of wear. Fortunately, most lines frequently rebuild and refurbish their crafts so as to prevent deterioration. Chapter 11 indicates the age of the ships as well as the last date they were significantly refurbished. These dates will be of interest to you in comparing the various vessels.

The most exquisite public areas with bright modern décor can be found on the new Carnival, Celebrity, Crystal, Cunard, Holland America, Norwegian, Princess, Royal Caribbean, Regent Seven Seas, and Silversea ships, as well as the *Deutschland, QM2,* and the yachtlike vessels of Seabourn. For a more traditional décor and elegance, you may prefer the public areas of some of the vintage ships; however, do not expect to find the quaint, stately elegance of the old *Queen Mary, Queen Elizabeth,* or *Ile de France.* Sadly, it no longer exists.

By October 1, 1997, all ships were required to meet the standards of "Safety at Sea" (SOLA), an international treaty that addresses the safe operation of ships and has been signed by all seafaring nations who are members of the International Maritime Organization. Most of the standards deal with fire safety and involve refitting cabins with sprinkler systems and smoke detectors. For economic reasons, many of the cruise lines have taken their older ships out of service because of the potential cost to meet these standards. Many of the ships built by the major cruise lines in the 1960s, 1970s, and early 1980s have been sold to smaller and/or emerging cruise lines servicing the economy and foreign markets, renamed, and recycled.

People

People who like people will love cruising. There is no other vacation that affords you as great an opportunity to meet people from all over the world and from all walks of life. This does not mean that you will like everyone you meet any more than you like all of your neighbors or relatives. However, the camaraderie of a cruise offers an ideal climate to make new friends and strike up conversations with people from many different places.

What kind of people will be your fellow passengers? Although there is always a cross section of varied backgrounds, the majority of passengers will be indigenous to the area surrounding the port of embarkation. Passengers from New York and the East Coast will predominate on a cruise emanating from New York. If the cruise departs from California, you can expect a majority of travelers to be from the West Coast and states of the Southwest. Midwesterners tend to leave from Miami, Fort Lauderdale, and the Caribbean; however, today you will find many Easterners and Californians on these cruises. The development of the air-sea package has changed this lineup somewhat, and cruise lines are flying passengers from all over the country to meet their ships.

Cruises commencing in Mediterranean or northern European ports often will have numerous European passengers, with the majority being of the same nationality as the vessel. P & O and Cunard's ships tend to attract more British, Germans, and northern Europeans. Peter Deilmann Cruises, Hapag-Lloyd, and Aida Cruises cater almost exclusively to a German clientele. MSC and Costa's ships, when cruising the Mediterranean, are booked mostly by Italians, and when cruising South America, mostly by South Americans.

Commencing in 2002, many of the major cruise lines repositioned ships to the European market, and many are building new ships to service the expanding cruising interests developing throughout the European population. Carnival, Inc. and RCI, the two largest publicly held cruise companies, have purchased or established various European subsidiaries to attract specific European markets.

Entertainment

As mentioned previously, the opportunity to witness big-name performers is important to many travelers, while others are just as content to dance to good music and make their own fun. The quality of entertainment has vastly improved over the past few years, and many stars and talented artists are now performing on ships. When ships offer big-name entertainers, they will advertise the event. Generally, the cruises on the larger ships leaving from New York or Florida offer the best talent because many of these performers actually rotate ships, staying on the Caribbean circuit. I have found less in the way of talent during European and Pacific cruises.

Some of the best entertainment on ships is of a more informal variety, with emphasis on audience-participation events such as adult games for prizes, dancing, costume balls, gambling, talent shows, and so on. Most ships also offer a wide selection of first-run movies. Several of the Princess, Disney, and newest Carnival ships feature outdoor movies around the pool, accompanied with free snacks and drinks. Many of the more recently built vessels offer closed-circuit television movies or videos in your cabin. The newest high-tech ships feature interactive televisions on which you can select your own videos. If the caliber of entertainment and entertainers is an important consideration, be certain to check out what will be offered on the cruise you are investigating.

Size of Ship

In chapter 11, I have set forth the size of the major cruise ships, including tonnage, length, width, number of decks, passenger capacity, and number of cabins. Thus, you will be able to easily compare the relative sizes of each vessel. The larger ships of the Carnival, Royal Caribbean, Star, Princess, Celebrity, Cunard, Costa, MSC, Norwegian, and Holland America lines tend to offer more facilities, entertainment, dining options, and activities for all age groups, while the smaller vessels are more intimate, friendlier, easier to negotiate, less congested, and can dock at a greater number of ports. Most ships built during the 1970s were in the medium-size category, ranging from 16,000 to 23,000 tons. However, during the 1980s and 1990s the cruise lines introduced many new ships in the 45,000- to 85,000-ton-and-up range, as well as an assortment of small yachtlike vessels. During the late 1990s and into this century, vessels weighing in over 100,000 G.R.T. have become the fad. Although these behemoths may offer endless options not available on other vessels, passengers must be willing to accept long lines, long waits, and long walks. The largest ship built to date, the 220,000-ton, 5,400-passenger *Oasis of the Seas* entered service for Royal Caribbean in late 2009 .

Young children and teens will be better accommodated on the larger ships, where there are more activities and special programs designed to entertain them. This is especially the situation on all of the ships built during the past decade that weigh in over 80,000 tons (Carnival, Disney, Norwegian, Princess, and Royal Caribbean being the leaders in this area).

Nationality of Crew

Chapter 11 also covers the nationality of the service crew for each ship. The nationality of the crew often sets the tone for the cruise, and on European and Mediterranean cruises it may determine the official language spoken. The difference in the nationality of the crew and what it may mean is discussed in this chapter under "Service."

Few ships offer a totally American crew. Chances are that you will take a ship with a foreign crew, and it will be quite like spending time in the country the ship represents. You may find that this makes cruising all the more interesting and educational. You will most likely want to try ships of different nationalities each time you take a cruise vacation. Unfortunately, almost all of the lines have switched to crews of mixed nationalities for economic reasons. Only the top officers reflect the advertised nationality of the ship. This move has destroyed much of the old-country charm and flavor and has created some language barriers.

Shore Excursions

Traditionally, all ships offer a selection of shore excursions that range from less active land and sea sightseeing tours to more active events such as snorkeling, diving, river rafting, horseback riding, and helicopter rides. Over the past few years, the cruise lines have expanded the variety of tours, and the offerings have become increasingly more adventurous. Some of the newer tours include interacting with dolphins; feeding sharks; swimming with sting rays; "canopy tours," where cables are strung from tree to tree and passengers traverse on cable cars from platform to platform above rain forests and jungles (available in Costa Rica, Colon, Panama, and Montego Bay, Jamaica); helicopter rides landing on glaciers and float plane excursions; kayaking, biking, jeep, and dune buggy tours; snuba (a cross between scuba and snorkeling) and power snorkeling; and a host of other offerings geared to appeal to passengers in all age groups. Unfortunately many of these tours can be very pricey, especially for families who must pay on a "per person" basis. This is one of the methods cruise lines use to increase their revenue to compensate for lower fares.

Outstanding Dining, Service, and Luxury

For those who can afford the steep tariffs, the highest standard of food and service and the most comfortable accommodations will be found on the following ships: **Large vessels** (over 50,000 G.R.T.): All of the Crystal ships, *Seven Seas Mariner* and *Voyager,* and "Grill Class" on the *Queen Victoria* and *Queen Mary 2.* **Medium-size vessels** (20,000 to 50,000 G.R.T.): *Seabourn Odyssey, Europa, Seven Seas Navigator, Deutschland, Silver Shadow,* and *Whisper,* the latter two of Silversea Cruises, and *Regatta, Insignia,* and *Nautica* of Oceania Cruises. **Small vessels** (under 20,000 G.R.T.): *Seabourn Pride, Legend,* and *Spirit; Silver Cloud* and *Silver Wind;* and the two *SeaDream* ships. On the larger vessels, you must opt for a suite or deluxe cabin to enjoy the best experiences.

Costs and Your Cabin _____

Given a comparable cabin on a comparable deck during the same season for cruises of similar duration, your tariff on most ships in the same market category (see chapter 14) should not vary more than 10 to 20 percent.

The rates will be higher for single rooms than for rooms shared by two people. Adding a third or fourth person to the room will bring the tariff down even more. Children under 12 sharing a cabin with two full-fare adults will generally pay only half of the minimum fare (the price charged for the least expensive accommodations on the ship).

The more expensive rooms are usually located on a higher deck and are often a little larger. Outside staterooms with verandas, windows, or portholes go for a higher price than inside ones without a view to the sea. This price differential may range from $200 to $2,000 per person on a seven-day cruise. The trend today is to provide balconies in a greater percentage of staterooms. Many cruisers who have experienced this perk now refuse to cruise without one.

Cabins with a double or two lower beds will go for more than those with a lower and an upper bunk. The same room on the same ship will cost more "in season" (mid-December to mid-April in the Caribbean and Pacific; June through September in Europe, with variations) than it will off-season. On transatlantic crossings, you will want to carefully investigate the varying prices for "peak season," "intermediate season," and "low season." You may be able to save as much as 50 percent by sailing eastward in late May rather than mid-June, or by returning westward in early June rather than late July. If your travel agent cannot obtain a discounted rate, he or she may still be able to obtain a cabin upgrade for you if he or she is persistent.

Of course, the longer the duration of the cruise, the more you will pay. This is possibly the only variation that makes real sense. Your per-person cost for a "minimum" room on an average seven-day cruise may range from $850 to $1,750. For 10-day cruises, your average minimum cost may vary from $1,100 to $2,100, and for 14-day cruises from $1,750 to $3,500. Do not be misled by newspaper advertisements publicizing rooms starting at $100 per day, per person. Often there are only a handful of rooms at this modest cost, and they are only available to those who book many months in advance or at the last moment. The average-priced room will be at least 50 percent higher than the minimum-priced one. If your decision as to whether or not to take a cruise is dependent upon the minimum offering, you should start making plans nine months to a year in advance. Several of the luxury-category cruise lines offer free cruises and other perks for loyal customers who have spent the required days at sea with that particular cruise line.

The higher the deck, the more you will pay. Possibly the greatest differential on any given cruise is based upon which deck your cabin is located. Contrary to popular belief, the least motion will be felt in the interior of the lower decks, as long as you are not located over the engines. You do not have to be a student of science to comprehend this principle if you can just imagine a tree blowing in the wind.

The difference in cost between the most expensive and the least expensive cabin on the same ship can vary from 100 percent to 250 percent on the average ship, and up to 500 percent on the super-luxury liners. Although there will exist a difference in area, closet and dresser space, and general accommodations between rooms, all passengers on a cruise enjoy the use of all public facilities, participate in the same activities, and eat the same food. Only your immediate neighbors will know which cabin you occupy, and only snobs will care, so if economy is a major consideration, book the most inexpensive cabin available. However, if you tend toward claustrophobia or feel that lounging around a comfortable room is a prerequisite to enjoying your vacation, then you will have to pay for more expensive quarters. On many of the smaller luxury vessels, all accommodations are junior suites and all go for about the same fare, with a small variance based on which deck you are located.

The price structure on the *Queen Victoria* and *QM2* of Cunard Line is somewhat different from other cruises. Passengers booking the more expensive suites and cabins will eat better food served by more experienced waiters and will enjoy a great deal more pampering.

Before leaving the subject of cost, a final word on port charges and the air-sea package is in order. A universally practiced deception is the tacking on of port charges after quoting the cruise fare. These can run from $60 up to several hundred dollars on longer cruises. Since the cruise line brochures generally quote cabin prices with an asterisk (*) to the effect that port charges will be added, potential customers are often misled as to the total fare. On a more positive note, many of the cruise lines have made arrangements with the private and regularly scheduled air carriers to obtain special package rates for parties who are flying directly to the port of embarkation on the day of the cruise and flying home the day the ship returns to its home port. It works like this: you check in your luggage upon arriving at your home airport; upon landing, you are transported by bus to the dock and your luggage is taken separately from the airport and brought right to your cabin. The airfare is sometimes as low as one-half or even one-quarter of the normal economy rate. In addition, you do save on taxi fares and tips to porters. The value of the air-sea package may vary from season to season on the same ship, and on some cruise lines it is only available to passengers purchasing medium- and higher-priced cabins. Therefore, when considering different cruises, you must carefully check to see the extent to which the air-sea package is available to you for the particular sailing you contemplate taking.

In recent years, the pricing policy of many of the cruise lines has become confusing at best, and possibly deceptive. Many of the companies will offer a few minimum cabins several hundred dollars lower than the other less expensive cabins. This is done in order to advertise the cruise as starting at a price lower than their competitors. When you call to reserve one of these cabins, you are often told that these cabins are all booked and you are quoted cabins at a higher price bracket. In addition, air-sea packages have become complicated in that some lines offer free air or air with a slight add-on (under $100), whereas others merely offer airfares that are only slightly reduced from normal coach fares.

To make matters worse, many of the lines offer an assortment of discounts for early and last-minute bookings. Others discount cabins to tour operators and travel agents guaranteeing to sell a number of cruises. (See the Section on "Prices" above.) Therefore, you will often find that the couple in the adjoining stateroom with identical accommodations is paying a much different price from what you are paying. For those wishing to obtain discounted rates, it would be desirable to check with your travel agent or an agency that specializes in cruises as to which lines are offering early booking discounts as well as last-minute discounts. You may be able to save 25 to 50 percent by booking six months in advance or just a few days before a cruise. Generally, a cruise line with available cabins a few days prior to sailing will offer substantial cabin upgrades at minimum fares in order to fill up its berths.

Because pricing has become so illusory, my division of ships into four price/market categories (in chapters 11 and 14) is not based upon published fares alone. I also take into consideration the cost of items while on the ship (drinks, tours, tipping, etc.) as well as the passenger market the cruise line seeks to attract and actually does attract. Therefore, you may find certain ships placed in categories that do not always correlate with the prices advertised in periodicals and brochures.

What to Bring Along

Due to recent laws, a valid U.S. passport is required for U.S. citizens traveling outside the U.S. To obtain this document, you must apply in person to the Passport Division or passport agencies of the State Department. In some cities this function is handled by the clerk of the federal court or by the federal post office. When making application, you must present a birth certificate or proof that you were either born in the United States or became a naturalized citizen as well as two identical photographs signed by you, together with other identification. Your passport will be good for 10 years from the date issued.

This is an indispensable document abroad and should be diligently guarded. Should you lose it or have it stolen, head for the nearest U.S. Embassy or Consulate to report the loss. For this reason, you would be wise to keep a separate record of your passport number, date, and place of issuance. A passport is your best means of identification in any foreign land when cashing traveler's checks or otherwise establishing credit. It is also wise to bring along your driver's license and a charge card as additional identification.

Certain foreign countries also require visas and/or vaccination certificates. It is best to check with your travel agent or with the cruise line before each trip to determine which, if any, of these documents you may need.

You will want to bring along charge cards and money, of course, and the best way to carry money when traveling is in traveler's checks. Do not forget to keep a record of the check numbers in a separate place from the checks so that you are in a position to report a loss. Personal checks might help in an emergency, but do not count on many places honoring them. Most ships will not cash personal checks, much to the dismay and displeasure of the unwary traveler. You will receive information on ship as to how to change your dollars to local currency upon arriving in a foreign port.

The amount of money you should bring along depends upon the length of the cruise as well as your personal spending habits. Generally, on ship, you will need money for tobacco, cocktails, wine, miscellaneous medicines and sundry items, photographs, stamps, laundry, cleaning, games of chance, and tips. On very few ships you pay as you go, while on almost all there is a compulsory "charge it" system in which you are presented with an itemized invoice of your shipboard charges at the close of the cruise. When in port, you will need money for cab fares, restaurants, shopping, and any other activity you plan to pursue. It would be wise to sit down before you leave and analyze how much the foregoing expenditures may run—then add 30 to 40 percent to be safe.

While on the subject of money and shopping, remember that as a U.S. citizen, you will be permitted to bring back duty-free up to $400 of goods purchased abroad ($600 to $800 from most Caribbean islands), including up to one quart of liquor or wine. Should your ship stop in any of the U.S. Virgin Islands (most Caribbean cruises do), Guam, or American Samoa, you can increase your purchase limit to $1,200 per person and include five liters of wine or spirits (provided your purchases in excess of $400 and one quart of liquor or wine are made on one of these islands). Meats, fruits, vegetables, plants, and plant products will be impounded by U.S. Customs unless they are accompanied by an import license from a U.S. government agency. Americans abroad can also mail home gifts of no more than $10 in value ($20 from the U.S. possessions in the Caribbean and Pacific) to friends and family that are free of duty or tax if the recipient does not receive more than one package a day. These gifts do not have to be declared by the sender. Liquor and tobacco products may not be mailed, however.

When getting ready to pack, be certain that you have sturdy, substantial luggage. Should you rise early on the morning your ship pulls into the port of final disembarkation, you may be shocked to see your favorite Gucci bag being tossed from man to man like a football as it makes its way to the dock. Luggage is frequently damaged while being transported onto and off of the ship, so valuable or fragile pieces should probably be left at home. Be sure to bring along a small traveling bag (about one foot by two feet). These are handy for carrying bathing suits, towels, a change of clothes, suntan lotion, and so on when spending a day ashore.

Your selection of clothes depends to a great extent upon the climate, length of the cruise, and your personal habits. Some travelers prefer to travel light with a few drip-dry garments, while others are not content to wear the same outfit twice. However, on a cruise you are not bothered with having to frequently pack and unpack, and in view of this you may wish to take advantage of the opportunity to display many of your fineries that do not normally make it on your vacations.

On a short cruise (seven days, for example), there are usually only two formal nights, while there are more on the longer cruises. You will find a greater percentage of men wearing a tuxedo on the ships of the Celebrity, Crystal, Cunard, Hapag-Lloyd, Holland America, Princess, Seabourn, and Silversea cruise lines, because these ships tend to attract a wealthier, older, and more formal clientele. Many of the ships now provide tuxedo rentals aboard ship. Although there are always a respectable number of male passengers in plain business suits, this can vary among ships and recently, more and more lines have switched to a country club casual dress code where jackets for men are never required. Azamara, Regent Seven Seas, SeaDream Yacht Club, Star Clippers, and Oceania are prime examples. To be safe, check with the line before leaving.

For the non-formal evenings, the men will wear suits and sport jackets, except for the "casual" evenings in port when no jacket or tie is required. A robe for the shower, sauna, and pool is advisable, although robes are provided on most of the luxury- and several of the premium-market cruise ships. A comfortable pair of deck shoes will get you through the day, and at night you will need dress shoes to coordinate with your suits and jackets. It is generally helpful to stay with one color when possible so you will not need as many different accessories. And don't forget socks, underwear, pajamas, bathing suits, sports shirts, dress shirts, ties, shorts, slacks, a sweater, and a raincoat. The same items you need aboard ship will generally work out for your shore excursions, so a separate wardrobe is unnecessary.

For the women, several of the chic numbers you have been reluctant to wear at home will be right in order. The number of dresses you pack will depend upon how often you wish to change. Again, it will be helpful to coordinate your choices with the same purse, dress shoes, and other accessories so as to cut down on the bulk of items that must be included in your wardrobe. As a rule of thumb, for every seven nights afloat, you can count on needing a dress outfit for two nights, a casual outfit for two nights, and something in between for the other evenings.

During the day, you will need swimming attire, a cover-up, sandals, shorts, skirts, blouses, slacks, a sweater, raincoat, and undergarments. Round this off with your favorite negligee, and you are ready to sail.

Most ships have laundry and cleaning services that vary from moderately expensive to very expensive. Many vessels have self-service Laundromats so you can feel like you have never left home. Frequently, the lines waiting to use these machines are quite long.

Whether to bring along expensive jewelry is a difficult question. Opportunities for theft exist on a ship, and all jewelry and valuables should be kept locked up when not in use. Almost all vessels provide a personal electronic wall safe in your cabin.

You may wish to personally carry aboard your jewelry, cosmetics, and medicines and the clothes you plan to wear the first evening at sea. All too often your luggage will not find its way to your room until several hours after the ship sails. You may feel more comfortable and less panicky if you follow this suggestion.

Some of the miscellaneous items you will not want to forget are sunglasses, suntan lotion, prescription drugs (as well as your prescription for an emergency), a traveling alarm clock, a cell phone (with international access where applicable), and, last but not least, your camera (don't worry about film—all but the most uncommon brands are obtainable). Although most of the ships have their own photographer who will be happy to record your every movement, these pictures can become expensive ($6 each, and up), and they often do not capture you at your best angle. On a cruise, you will experience many beautiful and memorable moments, and you will meet many interesting and often unforgettable people. Don't miss recording them for posterity.

Documents

A valid passport is now required for all travel to or from the U.S. by air, sea, or land. It is possible to purchase a passport card, which is somewhat less expensive than a passport, to facilitate entry into the U.S. by land and at seaports when arriving from Canada, Mexico, the Caribbean, and Bermuda. These cards cannot be used for travel by air. Both documents are valid for 10 years for adults. A new passport costs $100 and a new passport card, $45. For more information go to www.travel.state.gov/passport.

Chapter Three
Your Day at Sea

Although your selection of a cabin will help determine cost, and although the ports of call will elicit "oohs" and "ahs" from your neighbors back home when you exhibit your slides, your daily activities aboard ship as well as your dining experiences will be the decisive factor in forming your overall opinion of the ship.

Most cruise ships make only brief stops in port, permitting just a superficial exploration of the environs—a preview, if you will, for later in-depth visits. Therefore, it is your day at sea that must be given top priority in selecting a cruise.

Facilities and Activities

The facilities and public rooms found on different ships will vary somewhat with the size of the craft and the duration of the cruise. All of the major cruise lines print elaborate color brochures, which you can obtain from travel agents or by writing to the line directly. These brochures will describe and often illustrate the numerous facilities found aboard.

Almost every cruise ship afloat today is fully air conditioned and equipped with the necessary stabilizers to keep the roll and pitch at a minimum. Most ships have radio rooms, providing the opportunity to place calls and fax messages home. Most of the new ships, or those recently renovated, have direct-dial telephones in the private cabins and e-mail facilities somewhere in the public areas. A well-stocked library and cardroom are standard, and you will usually find a ship's hospital and pharmacy with at least one qualified doctor. Hairdresser salons are also available, but make your beauty shop appointments early on formal nights. Most women aboard who have their hair done will want an appointment the day of the captain's dinner.

You will find at least one and as many as four swimming pools. Because of the limited space, however, most pools offer an opportunity, at best, for only a dunk and five or six good strokes. Most ships of the major cruise lines have gymnasiums, and attached to the gym you will often find Jacuzzis, sauna, and massage rooms. In fact, on most of the larger new ships, there are fully equipped health spas offering a variety of treatments. The ships that devote the most area and provide the best fitness and spa facilities are Carnival, Celebrity, Costa, Crystal, Cunard, Disney, Princess, MSC, Norwegian, Regent Seven Seas, and Royal Caribbean ships.

The shops aboard ship will offer clothes, jewelry, and trinkets from numerous foreign ports at bargain prices. The larger ships generally have a variety of shops, while the smaller vessels only have one or two. Liquor, cigarettes, and perfume are generally the best buys. However, if your ship is stopping at a "free port," such as St. Thomas, you may wish to wait and compare prices ashore. Almost all ships provide laundry and cleaning facilities, and many have self-service Laundromats. Some lines feature custom tailors; representatives from the company will take your measurements for shirts, suits, slacks, dresses, etc., and have the items custom made and shipped to your home. Many of the large ships now have facilities for tuxedo rental as well.

For those inclined to try their hand at Lady Luck, most cruise ships have slot machines aboard as well as fully stocked casinos, complete with craps tables, roulette, poker, and blackjack. Again, the larger vessels tend to have the more complete casinos—some of the smaller ships only offer slot machines and one or two blackjack tables.

The usual public rooms consist of two or more grand ballrooms, one or more dining rooms, several smaller lounges, show-lounges, cardrooms, a library, a game room, numerous bars, a movie theater, a discotheque, and a buffet restaurant near the pool with an outdoor grill area. With the popularity of the Internet and e-mail, most ships now have computer facilities available, as well as Internet cafés, some serving coffee, drinks, and snacks. Regular computer classes may also be offered while at sea. Many of the ships built after 1990 have included conference facilities; wine, specialty coffee, and caviar and champagne bars; elaborate Broadway-caliber show-lounges; alternate specialty restaurants; inventive children and teen areas; and a bevy of high-tech accouterments.

Upon rising each morning, you will find a schedule of the day's activities pushed under the door of your cabin. This very important document will indicate what is going on every minute of the day, which movies will be shown in the theater and on your TV, and the dress required for dinner. You will most certainly want to study this publication carefully so you will not miss any activity or happening in which you may wish to participate (see sample programs in chapter 11).

Your ship will have a cruise director and social staff who are there to organize activities, bring the passengers together (especially the singles), give orientation lectures on ports of call, sell shore excursion tickets, and generally act as mentors to the passengers. Some are excellent and can contribute to making your trip a delight. Others vary from indifferent to detrimental, giving wrong information about places of interest in ports or even directing visitors to tourist traps (where they may have a little something going on the side). Be careful to check out the recommendations they may offer on shops and restaurants. It may be advisable to consult your guidebook or one of the tourist magazines that are printed by the tourist boards of the various ports and distributed on ship.

The adventures of John, Martha, Michael, Vivian, Joan, Ron, Scotty, and Jamie described in chapter 1 are just a few examples of the various ways you may elect to spend your days at sea. For those who do not wish just to relax, a cruise also offers a vast range of activities around the clock designed to appeal to every taste. There is probably no resort on earth that offers as much as often.

For the early risers, there are the morning exercise and aerobics classes, walking, jogging, shuffleboard, Ping-Pong, and deck tennis. Many of the larger ships carry a full-time golf pro and offer a morning golf clinic. In addition to the group lessons aboard ship, the golf pro will arrange tours to the local golf courses when ashore. Several lines have occasionally offered a tennis clinic program on some of their cruises that includes daily lessons on the ship and organized games in port. You may wish to attend morning lectures on forthcoming ports of call, especially if you have not been to that port previously. Foreign-language classes in the native tongue of the crew—such as French, Italian, or Greek—are common, as are lessons in bridge, backgammon, blackjack, and chess. A number of the ships offer investment and estate planning seminars, while others offer cooking and needlepoint lessons, wine tastings, musical concerts, trap-shooting, bingo, and deck horse races. Many cruise ships carry a professional dance team that gives complimentary dance lessons each morning.

After lunch there are duplicate bridge, backgammon, and gin-rummy tournaments, as well as first-run movies and bingo. For the children and ambitious adults, there are swimming games at the pool and deck-sport tournaments. In addition to the usual deck sports, a few ships have miniature golf courses and/or golf simulators, and many vessels of the Carnival, Celebrity, Costa, Disney, Princess, Norwegian, and Royal Caribbean lines have basketball courts. At some point in each cruise you are given an opportunity to visit the bridge or tour the kitchen. Late in the afternoon, many passengers squeeze in the hairdresser or a sauna and massage. Many of you will find that just lying out in the deck chair by the pool and soaking up the sun can be one of the nicest experiences during the day. Add music from the ship's calypso band and a rum punch, and it is just like being at a pool on one of the Caribbean islands.

Evenings are usually the most exciting part of the cruise. Even on cruises that hit numerous ports, the majority of evenings are spent at sea. You will probably start out in the cocktail lounges before dinner, where you can sample some hors d'oeuvres, music, and exotic drinks. The captain's welcome-aboard cocktail party is held before dinner, usually on the second night at sea. On this occasion, each passenger is introduced personally to the captain, treated to free drinks, and has an opportunity to meet the other passengers aboard. After dinner each evening, there are several popular quiz show and parlor games such as bingo, Liar's Club, and the Newlywed Game, as well as karaoke. The casinos also are active at this time.

During the majority of evenings at sea, most ships offer a variety or cabaret show. Several of the lines have a policy of offering two completely different shows each evening, one in the main lounge and one later at night in the cabaret or discotheque. These shows feature singers, comedians, magicians, dancers, puppeteers, and more singers. As pointed out in an earlier chapter, the quality of the entertainment has improved in recent years.

One night during each cruise, some ships hold a passenger talent show and, on another night, a passenger costume party. These affairs often afford more laughs than many of the second-rate comedians, magicians, and singers who get paid to perform. Once you get into the spirit of things, you may find that the audience-participation events will leave you with more memorable experiences than the average, run-of-the-mill variety show. For those who prefer something different, most ships offer a first-run movie each evening in the theater. The movies are varied throughout the cruise and generally repeated at least once so you can choose which afternoon or evening you wish to give up some other activity. Outdoor movies by the pool are featured on some of the Carnival, Disney, Princess, and Seabourn ships and on the new builds of several other lines. Closed-circuit television movies or DVDs in your cabin have been introduced on many of the newer vessels. On some ships, these have replaced the movie theater.

Around midnight, most ships offer the midnight buffet, although on some ships this has been replaced by around-the-clock alternate dining facilities, or waiters who go around the public rooms with late-night snacks. Also, later in the evening, things start to swing in the late-night spots, where couples and singles can indulge in some romantic dancing before the traditional stroll on deck. No matter how involved you become in activities, and no matter how tired you may be, you should save a few minutes each night to walk out on deck under the stars and watch the black sea splash against the hull of the ship. Looking out across the sea at such a moment offers a unique opportunity for reflection.

From the foregoing description, it is obvious that there is something for everyone aboard a cruise ship. After a day or two, you should be able to adapt to your own pace and intensity and alternate between playing and relaxing with your usual agility. Chapter 11 includes a sample of daily program schedules for many of the ships.

Dining

Some of your most memorable experiences aboard ships will be your adventures in dining. Over the years, many of the great ships offered some of the finest restaurants to be found anywhere in the world. Dining on many of the vessels with both European kitchen and dining room staffs is comparable to feasting at the best establishments on the Continent. During the past few years, the quality of the dining experience aboard ship has greatly increased.

Can you imagine starting your evening repast with gobs of Beluga caviar, imported Gravlax, a dozen escargots, or perhaps a slice of quiche Lorraine, followed by some onion soup with freshly grated Gruyeres and Parmesan cheeses too thick to cut with a knife? Next comes your fish course of poached salmon or turbot with hollandaise sauce, Dover sole amandine, lobster thermidor, or possibly some trout stuffed with crabmeat.

For your entree, you may decide upon roast duckling à l'orange, steak au poivre, rack of lamb, or Chateaubriand with Béarnaise sauce. The entree may be complemented with some sautéed champignons or truffles. For dessert, why not try a Napoleon slice or other French pastry? Many of the ships have the head-waiters going from table to table each evening, preparing bananas flambé, cherries jubilee, or crêpes suzette. To round things off, you may try an assortment of cheeses from Switzerland, Holland, France, and Italy, followed by some after-dinner mints. Naturally, each course should be accompanied by the proper wine, unless you prefer a shot of vodka with your caviar and Cognac with your coffee.

Although this meal could easily cost $100 to $200 per person in a good French restaurant in Paris or New York, most of these goodies are featured for dinner aboard the vessels of many of the cruise lines at least once or twice during each sailing and nightly on the deluxe vessels. However, many of the ships have been cutting back on the more expensive offerings in recent years.

There no longer exists a purely French vessel. Seasoned cruisers will always miss the incomparable dining room of the *France*, which was taken out of service in 1974. Alas, the days of unlimited champagne and caviar may be gone forever—ship lines are no longer willing to lose millions of dollars each year just to maintain an image of excellence.

There are several ships with Italian kitchens and dining room staffs that offer a wide selection of Italian dishes, including a different variety of pasta with each lunch and dinner. Before the cruise comes to an end, you will have been exposed to spaghetti, macaroni, mostaccioli, rigatoni, cannelloni, lasagna, manicotti, pizza, gnocchi, and a dozen other lesser-known varieties. Among the more popular ships with Italian kitchens sailing from U.S. ports are the vessels of Costa Cruise Lines and MSC Cruises. There are exceptional Italian specialty restaurants on the Crystal, Disney, Hapag-Lloyd, Oceania, Princess, and Regent Seven Seas vessels (see chapter 13). The most ambitious and gastronomic specialty restaurants at sea today can be found on Celebrity's *Millennium*-class ships featuring Continental French-style cuisine. Signatures, on *Seven Seas Mariner* and *Seven Seas Voyager,* are two outstanding French restaurants, possibly the best at sea.

Many recent cruisers have expressed the opinion that today the vessels of the Crystal, Hapag-Lloyd, Oceania, Regent Seven Seas, Seabourn, SeaDream, and Silversea cruise lines have the finest kitchens afloat. The food on these ships is Continental, with the European chefs creating an amazingly diverse range of culinary delights. The dining room staffs are mixed European. I have found the overall dining experience on these ships to be superior to most ships currently sailing. Among the more elegant dining rooms afloat with the most lavish gourmet cuisine are the Queen's Grill and the Princess Grills of the *QM2* and *Queen Victoria.* Unfortunately, these dining rooms are open only to those passengers booking the most expensive suites and staterooms.

A variety of Continental, ethnic, and American dishes are offered on the ships of most cruise lines. Although the quantity and quality of the food on ships is generally satisfactory, service often suffers from the use of mixed crews, including less experienced waiters and stewards from the Caribbean, Central and South America, the Philippines, and Asia. Some of the less widely publicized ships and some of the bargain cruises do not offer the same high quality and vast quantity of food that has come to be associated with cruising. However, most of the major cruise lines now provide an alternate menu available every evening that includes such universally desired items as steak, chicken, fish, and pasta.

If you wish to have special dishes that do not appear on the menu, you must make arrangements with the maître d' at least a day in advance. Generally, he will be anxious to accommodate you, and, of course, you are expected to reciprocate at the end of the cruise with a suitable gratuity. Don't hesitate to ask for any dish that may tickle your palate. A cruise is an excellent opportunity to sample all those special preparations for which you never wanted to splurge in an expensive restaurant. Unfortunately, most ships today are discouraging this practice, and the opportunity to order special gourmet dishes has been completely eliminated on most cruise lines. The corporate policy of most lines to make larger and larger profits has ruled out much of the elegance and special pampering that has long been associated with cruising.

The wine selection aboard many of the ships is perhaps too limited for the tastes of a discerning connoisseur. The prices of wines have escalated in recent years, and the cost of wine on ships is almost as expensive today as the cost in restaurants. Italian and Greek wines are generally the best bargains. On the majority of ships, some of the sommeliers have had too little training, lack the necessary familiarity with and knowledge of wine, and are too harassed to serve it properly. With the ever-growing popularity of wine drinking, this department has greatly improved in recent years. It should be noted that the ships of the Silversea, Regent Seven Seas, SeaDream, and Seabourn cruise lines, many riverboats, and all barges give their passengers free wine with lunch and dinner each day.

Because dining is such an important part of the cruise, you should book your table and choose your sitting carefully. The experienced cruiser will go to the dining steward immediately upon boarding ship to make these arrangements.

Many cruises have both a first and second sitting, which results in two entirely different daily schedules. Should you be traveling with friends, be sure that you all take the same sitting. If your friends take the first sitting and you the second, you may never see them. While you are enjoying cocktails, they may be eating dinner, and while you are having dinner, they may be seeing the first show. While you are watching the second show, they may be dancing, and so on. Ships that provide two sittings also provide two schedules for activities, so all passengers have an opportunity to take part in the various events offered.

When deciding upon whether to take the first or second sitting, you must consider your usual eating habits as well as your dining preferences while on a vacation. If you are an early riser, prefer dinner around six-thirty or seven-thirty, and wish to conclude your evening's entertainment to be in bed by eleven or twelve o'clock, you will prefer the first sitting. If, however, you wish to sleep late, partake in cocktail hour, and not eat until eight-thirty or nine o'clock, then the second sitting is for you. Several of the cruise lines now offer seatings at four different times.

Almost all ships have tables for parties of two, four, six, eight, and 10. If you are honeymooners or second honeymooners and want to be alone, you will prefer a table for two. However, if you have a fight, you're out of luck because it may be difficult to switch tables later. If you feel you will prefer other company, ask the dining room maître d' to make the arrangements. The larger the table, the more people you will get to know, and should one or two at your table not be congenial, there certainly will be others who are.

Upscale vessels such as the ships of SeaDream, Silversea, Regent Seven Seas, Seabourn, and Windstar Sail Cruises have adopted an open-seating policy with no prearranged dining assignments. Several of the premium and mass market cruise ships have adopted an "open-seating, dine when you please and with whom you please" policy, including Azamara, Carnival, Holland America, Norwegian Cruise Line, Oceania, Princess, and Royal Caribbean. However, Carnival, Holland America, Princess, and Royal Caribbean also give passengers the option of traditional, fixed table seating. Other cruise lines can be expected to follow suit, at least in some of their dining areas. Thus, passengers can change table companions as often as they wish. (See chart at end of this chapter.)

Most of the newer ships that have come on line over the past 15 years offer one or more special gourmet dining rooms where a limited number of passengers can enjoy a more intimate upscale dinner on certain evenings. For example, the ships of Crystal Cruises have Asian and Italian restaurants in addition to the main dining rooms; the Celebrity *Millennium-* and *Solstice*-class ships, Regent Seven Seas, Holland America and Cunard feature a French Continental dining room, and the *Europa, Azamara*, Costa, Disney, Oceania Cruise Lines, Princess, and Royal Caribbean ships also have special (advanced-reservation) Italian restaurants. Most cruise lines offer pizza parlors or pizza stations. Exceptional steak and chophouses are also emerging on many of the upscale cruise lines, including Carnival, Oceania, and Princess. Carrying this concept further, the *Seven Seas Mariner* and *Voyager* and the newer ships of Norwegian and Star Cruises feature numerous alternative restaurants. Norwegian's recent new builds not only offer French, Italian, and Asian restaurants, but also a Japanese sushi bar, tappan-yaki rooms, a fusion restaurant, a Hawaiian restaurant, tapas bar, and several more eclectic options in addition to the two main dining rooms. Many of these specialty restaurants feature menus designed by famous chefs. (See chapter 13 for listings of alternative-dining specialty restaurants.)

As mentioned earlier, on the *QM2* and *Queen Victoria* the dining rooms are divided into classifications, and there is a difference in food and service between the Grill Rooms, for those booking the most expensive cabins and suites, and the other dining rooms for those who book the less luxurious accommodations. On other cruise lines everyone is considered to be in one class, and therefore, whether you pay $750 per week or $10,000 per week for your room, you will eat the same food in the same dining room.

All of the cruise ships have adopted the custom of offering numerous feedings in order to give you the impression that you are getting a lot for your money. As a matter of fact, you are, but quite candidly, few of you will be able to attend each gastronomical offering and do it justice.

The first culinary event is the "early bird breakfast," which consists of coffee, tea, rolls, and juice, starting at 6 or 6:30 A.M. Regular breakfast in the dining room commences sometime between 7:30 A.M. and 8:30 A.M. and on many ships is available in your cabin at any time. Breakfast will generally consist of the usual offerings, such as various fruits, juices, cereals, eggs, breakfast meats, rolls, pancakes, and so on. However, on ships where non-U.S. passengers prevail, the food is usually typical of the nationality of the crew.

Traditionally, you could ring for a cabin steward who would bring you a hot breakfast from the regular kitchen or a Continental breakfast from his service kitchen. Many of the ships have eliminated this possibility or varied the routine, requiring passengers who wish breakfast in their cabins to fill out and turn in an order form before going to bed. This has the obvious disadvantage of forcing you to decide in advance what time you want to get up and have breakfast. However, most ships offer a room-service menu available around the clock. Several of the cruise lines even feature multicourse meals from the dining room's evening menu served in your staterooms (at an additional charge). Cunard and Norwegian, the new Princess ships, and some other cruise lines are now offering breakfast in private dining room venues for suite passengers. Many ships with large spas offer spa breakfasts with spa cuisine for spa suite passengers.

Almost all ships have an alternative indoor/outdoor breakfast buffet for the late risers. Having your morning coffee while sitting out in the fresh salt-sea air during a morning at sea is especially delightful.

For those who cannot hold out until lunch, there is a late-morning tea, bullion, cookies, and cakes at about eleven o'clock. Of course, by this time many of your fellow passengers may already be working on their second Bloody Mary or screwdriver. Lunch is generally served in the dining room from twelve to two, depending on your sitting. An indoor/outdoor buffet for those passengers who do not wish to dress to go to the dining room for lunch is generally offered. Buffets on ships are usually quite elaborate and include exotic assortments of cold meats (roast beef, duck, ham, chicken, and venison) attractively displayed with numerous salads, cheeses, several hot dishes, and yummy desserts. Usually, adjacent to the buffet is an outdoor grill offering hamburgers, hot dogs, and other grilled items. When in port, you may find it inconvenient to return to the ship at noon. Some of the ships will furnish you with a box lunch to take with you; otherwise, you may wish to utilize the opportunity to sample some of the local restaurants.

About four or four-thirty in the afternoon, tea, snacks, and sweets are served. You then can partake of cocktails and hors d'oeuvres from six-thirty to eight-thirty. After cocktails comes the pièce de résistance of your gastronomical day—dinner. The variety of ethnic cuisine was discussed earlier. To break up the monotony, many ships adopt a different theme for each dinner meal. There may be Italian night, French night, or Caribbean night, where the cuisine will be indigenous to the country or area that is being featured. Most ships offer numerous courses, and you are encouraged to sample as many dishes as you wish. The appetizers usually include juices, a fruit cup, some form of seafood cocktail, relishes, smoked salmon, and perhaps caviar on special evenings. The next course is soups and pastas. As a rule of thumb, you are best advised to choose a dish from the same country of origin as the chef; that is, the pastas are better on Italian ships, moussaka is best on Greek vessels, and quiche should be prepared by a French chef. The rolls and breads on the Italian and French ships are usually superb and irresistible.

The entrees are generally divided between fish and seafood offerings and meat and fowl preparations. Even if you cannot consume all of this food, you may wish to order a course and share it just to have an opportunity to sample something unusual. Most of the better ships offer a standby such as steak, roast beef, chicken, salmon, and a vegetarian dish every evening for those who are not so adventurous. For those who enjoy wine with the meal, you are best advised to make a selection at lunch or during the prior evening. This will enable the wine steward to have the bottle waiting for you and properly aired. Otherwise, if he is very busy, your wine may not arrive until your dessert. If you do not finish the entire bottle, request that the wine steward store it for you until the following evening.

The desserts are varied, ranging from assorted ice creams and ices to fancy cakes, pastries, and cheeses. As mentioned earlier, many ships have their head-waiters wandering around each night making crêpes Suzette and cherries jubilee so that each table receives these desserts at least once during the cruise. Traditionally, flaming baked Alaska is served on almost every ship on the night of the captain's dinner. This affair generally takes place toward the end of the cruise. Staff and crew alike make every human effort to surpass and outdo all that has preceded the event. The food is the best; the service is even better; there are special decorations; and generally a jovial, festive atmosphere prevails.

Last, but not least, is the midnight buffet. This is the gourmand's delight, where everything that has not been consumed previously on the cruise is refurbished and attractively displayed on a buffet table that often covers the width of the dining room. Many ships go further and prepare some special dishes and fancy desserts for the occasion.

On the ships of most major cruise lines there are pizza stations open in the afternoon and evening and on Disney, Carnival, and Norwegian's latest ships they are open around the clock. Many other ships offer special ice-cream shops, caviar-champagne bars, and wine and coffee bistros.

Recognizing many cruisers' preference for not dressing up each evening, many of the ships are offering a casual dining policy under which all meals are alternatively offered in the buffet restaurant for passengers not wishing to eat in the dining rooms. This seems to have become fairly standard today.

The dress for dinner varies from evening to evening, from casual (no tie or coat required) for evenings in port, to formal attire, which is suggested for the captain's cocktail party, the captain's dinner, and other special occasions. It is, of course, permissible for men to wear a plain business suit and tie on formal evenings; and on the less expensive ships and shorter cruises, most of the male passengers do not bother to bring along a tux. The women, however, generally dress to the hilt, as there is no better place to show off a wardrobe. This does not mean that you will have to run out and spend hundreds or thousands of dollars on clothes in order to enjoy a cruise. Few people do. However, you will want to bring along a variety of your special fineries, depending upon the length of the cruise. An increasing number of cruise lines are opting for country club casual dress throughout the cruise and do not even require men to wear jackets. These cruise lines include Azamara, Disney, Sea Dream Yacht Club, Oceania and Regent Seven Seas, Star Clippers, and Windstar.

The waiters in the dining room will be especially determined to satisfy your every whim because they are hoping to receive a token of your gratitude by way of a tip. You do not tip them at every meal, but wait until the end of the cruise and then place your gratuity in an envelope with a little thank-you note. Most of the ships will indicate the recommended tipping procedures in a bulletin to passengers; on others, you are left on your own. On Silversea, SeaDream, Regent Seven Seas, and Seabourn lines, tipping is not required. Where there is open seating, the cruise lines add a gratuity to your shipboard account.

If in doubt, the chief purser is a reliable source from whom to obtain an explanation of the usual procedures. Although many people adhere to the usual 10 to 15 percent of the passage divided between waiters, cabin stewards, and others who have performed a special service on their behalf, this is not always suitable. Whether your ticket costs $850 or $2,000, you require the same service, and there is a big difference between spreading around $85 and spreading around $200. You will probably be about average if you tip $3.50 to $4.50 per day per person to your waiter and a similar amount to your cabin steward. (Some ships recommend that the busboy be tipped a specified amount in addition to the tip you give the waiter. On others, the waiter shares his tip with the busboy.)

If you are particularly pleased with the service, you may want to tip more, and if the service is unsatisfactory, you should notify the maître d' or the hotel manager early in the voyage so that your trip is not ruined. Don't forget to tip the wine steward, the maître d', the waiters in the bar, and anyone else whom you may call upon for a special service. Their tips will be about the same as you would normally give at home. However, on many ships a 15 percent service charge already has been added to drinks and wine orders.

An emerging policy is to automatically add the tips to your on-board charges with the option to adjust them upward or downward before disembarking. This is the policy on Carnival, Costa, Cunard, Holland America, NCL, Oceania, and Princess cruise lines. Royal Caribbean, Celebrity, Crystal, and Disney still distribute envelopes for passengers to personally disseminate the tips; however, passengers are allowed to charge gratuities to their personal, on-board accounts.

Dining is most certainly one of the biggest highlights of the cruise, and must therefore be given its due importance when selecting a ship. You will find sample menus from many of the cruise ships in chapter 11. Because the quality of food and service varies from year to year on ships as it does in restaurants, you will want to solicit the opinion of your travel agent and anyone you may find who has recently cruised on the ship that you are considering. My ratings for food and service can be found in chapter 14. These are based upon my most recent cruise on each ship and may vary from year to year, depending upon the kitchen and dining room staffs.

The following chart sets forth a summary of dining policies and venues for the major cruise lines:

Cruise Line	Azamara	Carnival	Celebrity	Costa	Crystal
Assigned Seating	N	Y	Y	Y	Y
Open Seating	Y	N	N	N	Y
Dress Code Dressy (D)/ Casual—No Jackets (C)	C	D	D	D	D
Casual Evening Dining Venue	Y	Y	Y	Y	Y
Specialty Steak House Surcharge	Y / Y, but first time free	On Some / Y	N / —	N / —	N / —
Specialty Italian Restaurant Surcharge	Y / Y, but first time free	N / —	N / —	N / —	Y / N
Specialty Asian Restaurant Surcharge	N / —	N / —	N / —	N / —	Y / N
Specialty Continental/ Gourmet or French Surcharge	N / —	On some / Y	Y / Y	On some / Y	N / —
Free Wine & Non-Alcoholic Beverages	N	N	N	N	N
24-Hour Room Service	Y	Y	Y	Y	Y

Cunard	Peter Deilmann/ Deutschland	Disney	Hapag-Lloyd/ Europa	Holland America	MSC
Y	N	Y	N	Y	Y
N	Y	N	Y	Y	N
D	D	C	D	D	D
Y	N	Y	Y	Y	Y
N, part of buffet —	N —	N —	N —	N —	N —
N, part of buffet —	N —	Y Y	Y N	N —	On some Y
N, part of buffet —	N —	N —	Y N	N —	On some Y
Y Y	Y N	N —	N —	Y Y	N —
N	N	Free soft drinks only	N	N	N
Y	Y	Y	Y	Y	Y

Cruise Line	Norwegian	Oceania	P & O	Princess	Regent Seven Seas	Royal Caribbean
Assigned Seating	N	N	Y	Y	N	Y
Open Seating	Y	Y	N	Y	Y	Y
Dress Code Dressy (D)/Casual— No Jackets (C)	C	C	D	D	C	D
Casual Evening Dining Venue	Y	Y	Y	Y	Y	Y
Specialty Steak House	Y	Y	On some	Y	N	Y
Surcharge	Y	N	Y	Y	—	Y
Specialty Italian Restaurant	On some	Y	On some	Y	On some	Y
Surcharge	Y	N	Y	Y	N	Y
Specialty Asian Restaurant	Y	N (Y on *Marina*)	On some	N	On some	N (Y on *Oasis of the Seas*)
Surcharge	Y	—	Y	—	N	—
Specialty Continental/ Gourmet or French	Y	N (Y on *Marina*)	On some	N	On some	N (Y on *Oasis of the Seas*)
Surcharge	Y	—	Y	—	N	—
Free Wine & Non-Alcoholic Beverages	N	N	N	N	Y	N
				—		
24-Hour Room Service	Y	Y	Y	Y	Y	Y

Seabourn	SeaDream	Silversea	Star Clippers	Star	Windstar
N	N	N	N	N	N
Y	Y	Y	Y	Y	Y
D	C	D	C	C	C
Y	Y	Y	N	Y	N
Y	N	N	N	On some	Some nights
N	—	—	—	Y	N
N	N	Y	N	On some	Some nights
—	—	—	—	Y	N
N	N	N (Y on *Silver Spirit*)	N	Y	Some nights
—	—	—	—	Y	N
Y	N	Y	N	On some	Some nights
N	—	Y	—	Y	N
Y	Y	Y	N	N	N
Y	Y	Y	N	Y	Y

Chapter Four

Cruising for Singles

With the growing popularity of the cruise vacation and the onslaught of vigorous advertising, more and more singles are being attracted to the high seas. The image of the elderly passenger propped up in a deck chair, covered with blankets, and sipping tea has given way to the younger, sophisticated single of the modern era.

There is no question that the thought of a cruise should conjure up some romantic visions in the mind of the average single. Imagine watching the sun set over the mountains on a balmy, tropical evening as your ship slowly pulls out of port, or dancing to the melodious tunes of a romantic Italian band until the early hours of the morning, followed by a hand-in-hand stroll on deck to view the moon and stars on a clear Caribbean evening.

Of course, cruising has a great deal more than romance to offer the single. In addition to the numerous activities, exciting ports, and fine cuisine (discussed earlier), the cruise offers the single traveler a planned, organized vacation where most major arrangements have already been taken care of. Who could fail to appreciate not having to constantly tote heavy luggage, tip porters, wave down taxis, arrange itineraries, determine a respectable night spot, or suffer the empty feeling of being alone in a strange land?

What kind of companionship can a single person traveling alone expect to find aboard ship? Generally, it takes a day or so to become familiar with the new surroundings and lose your normal inhibitions. By the second evening at sea, all but the most pretentious bores will have warmed up and gotten into the swing of things. Your fellow passengers may smile and nod as you pass them in corridors, the passengers in the adjoining deck chairs may initiate a conversation, and the couple sitting at the next table in the lounge may invite you to join them. The intimate, often cozy atmosphere of the ship, together with the realization that you are all at the mercy of the high seas and that no one is getting off, stimulates a feeling of togetherness and cordiality.

However, the cruise staff of the ship will not leave you to your own devices to find companionship. The entertainment director and social hostess will stimulate comingling through singles' cocktail parties, group games, dancing classes, bridge tournaments, and similar get-together functions. Of course, no pressure is ever placed upon anyone to attend these activities, and you are free to just relax, cuddle up with a good book, and do your own thing.

Many of the married couples on ship will be very friendly. The unescorted single may find it quite advantageous to strike up a social relationship with several amenable couples so as not to limit his or her companionship just to the other singles aboard. A well-traveled couple may prove to be far more interesting company on a shore excursion than some other single who may not share your tastes or interests. In addition, it is often desirable to have an assortment of other people to join in the ship's public rooms when you are avoiding some other single or do not wish to sit alone.

Often your married companions will insist upon buying you a drink; however, you will want to reciprocate at the earliest possible opportunity so as not to give the impression that you are tagging along for a free ride. When sharing taxis or eating at a restaurant in port, etiquette and common sense dictate that you insist upon paying your own share. Your newfound friends will soon abandon you if it turns out that you have become an expense they didn't include in their vacation budget. The women will be well advised to follow the same principle with regard to any male escort who becomes a semi-regular. He may have bargained on paying for a few drinks and an occasional meal, but he probably did not bring along enough cash to take you on as a dependent.

Having touched upon the existence of the feeling of general camaraderie on the cruise and the desirability of not neglecting married couples as potential shipboard pals, we will now explore the question of what kind of companionship the single can expect from singles of the opposite sex. First of all, it is no secret that singles will be in the minority, as they are at most vacation spots. Most newspaper advertisements for "singles cruises" are misleading. A travel agency or tour operator will pre-book a number of cabins on a regular cruise and attempt to attract a number of single customers through advertising. Second, single females will generally outnumber single males by two to one.

The greatest number of younger singles will be found on the three- and four-day cruises, on the ships of the Royal Caribbean, NCL, and Carnival lines, or on less expensive cruises. Most younger singles on more expensive cruises are traveling with their families.

Longer cruises (15 to 90 days or more) would not be advisable for the single who feels he or she needs good and exciting companionship to make the trip fulfilling. Although you may be fortunate enough to find "Mr. Right" or "Ms. Right" and have the most heavenly time of your life, if you don't you are going to be unhappy for an awfully long time.

Several of the cruise lines feature "gentlemen hosts" who generally are mature gentlemen (ages 55-70) who receive a free cruise in return for acting as dance and bridge partners for women traveling solo. For many years this program has been available on the Cunard, Holland America, Seabourn, Crystal, Regent Seven Seas, and Silversea cruise lines. The program was best satirized in the Jack Lemon-Walter Matthau movie *Out to Sea*.

What, then, is the best cruise for the single? Obviously, you should first select a ship by utilizing the same standards that a couple would consider; that is, food, service, program, ports of call, and so forth. You are still spending your vacation time and hard-earned money, and there is no reason why you should not make your decision with objectivity and discrimination.

However, assuming all else to be equal, the larger the ship, the greater number of singles to choose from as prospective acquaintances and companions. On the other hand, on a very large ship you will find it difficult to become exposed to all of the other passengers early in the trip. It is entirely possible to spend seven days on such a ship without once crossing the path of a fellow passenger who has been on the same ship with you all week. A smaller ship is more intimate, and people warm up more rapidly, but there are fewer people to choose from. You may wish to compare this situation to a small and a large hotel. If you were going to a Caribbean island, would you prefer to stay at a large resort or a smaller, more intimate hotel, assuming similar quality and facilities?

When traveling alone, the cabin price is usually higher and there will be significant savings if you are able to travel with a friend or share a cabin for two. Some of the lines will pair up singles (of the same sex), and others will not. You will have to check with each line in order to determine their current policy. Cabin space in an economy room is limited, and sharing small closets, dressers, and a washroom with even a close friend is often difficult and with a stranger almost impossible. However, if economy is a prime consideration, privacy and comfort may have to be sacrificed. Fortunately, some of the newer ships are being built with a greater number of single occupancy staterooms at rates closer to those charged for each person sharing a double room.

Let me again emphasize that your enjoyment of the cruise vacation does not depend necessarily upon your making friends, finding escorts, or experiencing eternal romance. However, those of you who may be interested in any of these pursuits should consider the following tips:

Let your hair down immediately and freely respond to the fellow passenger's friendly nod or glance. If you insist upon being coy, proper, or aloof, valuable days of the cruise will flee by before you get into the swing of things.

While waiting in the terminal to board ship, survey the prospective group and do not hesitate to introduce yourself to someone who interests you. Inasmuch as you will have to select a table in the dining room as soon as you come on board, this may be as good a time as any to start looking for interesting prospects. (*Note:* Everyone looks a bit dull and seedy when waiting in line to come aboard. Don't worry, they will all look better by tomorrow in different surroundings.)

Upon boarding ships with assigned dinner seatings, go right to the dining room steward and sign up for the late dinner sitting at as large a table as possible. The late sitting gives you time to attend cocktail hour each night, and a large table affords you a greater opportunity to meet a variety of other passengers. Even if some of the people at the table turn out to be bores, you should find at least a few that you can relate to. Seating arrangements may be difficult to change after the cruise starts; therefore, it is best to stack your table with as many desirable companions as possible in the very beginning. As mentioned earlier, the trend among ships today is to get away from assigned seating and to allow passengers to dine when they want and with whomever they want. Here again, the maître d' can be helpful in placing you at a table of other singles.

Force yourself (if necessary) to make friends with whomever you meet when you first board ship. This can best be accomplished in the bars, in the public rooms, or just walking around the decks—everyone is touring the ship at this point. Each person you meet will introduce you to someone else whom he or she has met, all of which has a pyramid effect, exposing you to the greatest number of people possible in the shortest period of time. Once you have been introduced to the eligible singles on the ship, you can start to become selective. However, if you start out being selective, you may never meet enough other singles to permit you to make a selection.

Make friends with married couples because they often are the best matchmakers around.

During the cruise, singles tend to gravitate to the many bars, lounges, and discotheques, and therefore these are often the best locations to meet other singles (who are looking to meet other singles).

Don't miss the singles' get-together cocktail party, which is usually held the first or second day at sea. No matter how corny it may seem to attend this event, the singles' party offers a good opportunity to meet the other singles and to make introductions. Having said this, I must admit that more often than not, very few passengers show up for these parties.

During the first few days, try to attend the card tournaments, dancing classes, deck games, religious services, and other organized events. These social gatherings tend to help break the ice and serve to get the passengers together on a more personal basis.

Stay up for the late, late dancing after midnight. By this time, those not so staunch of heart or steadfast of foot will have retired, the field will be narrowed, and whatever is left is all yours!

Avoid pairing off with one person during the first few days unless you have found a good one. If you panic and grab the first available, the others will think you are taken and you may blow an opportunity to meet all the other singles. On the other hand, if you really have found a good one, hold tight, because you are going to have some stiff competition.

Ladies should not depend too heavily on the crew for companionship. Many are married, some are gay, and 99 percent of the balance aren't very sincere and are interested only in lassoing you and bedding you for the duration of the cruise. This obviously won't do much for your opportunity to meet other interesting passengers.

Fellows, move faster than the crew. Your toughest competition will be the ship's officers and waiters. Although they may not beat out the town idiot ashore, while on ship they appear to be Greek gods. Because they are away from their families for long periods of time, they have become quite adroit at the "quick romance." In fact, acquiring the affections of the more select ladies for the duration of the cruise has become the biggest game in town among the younger officers and members of the crew. However, in recent years this has been forbidden on almost all ships. All is not lost. You have the advantage. You will have the first opportunity to romance the ladies because the crews are usually busy working until the second evening at sea. Stake your claims early. In addition, the ladies will soon realize that the members of the crew are only available at limited times and generally are only interested in one thing. On the other hand, you are available all day and can offer them a little more well-rounded experience.

Pace yourself. Don't wait too long to make your move, or the cruise will be over. On the other hand, the object of your affection may get turned off by someone who is obviously a jerk. On a seven- to 10-day cruise, you can count on the majority of shipboard romances dying midway through the journey. This is because the couples were not well matched and would have broken up after a few dates no matter where they met. Therefore, an attractive candidate who appears to be taken the first day may become very available a little later on.

Don't burn yourself out. Too much sun, food, drink, late hours, and whatever can make you ill and spoil the cruise. You will often stay up until two or three o'clock and still want to get up early because the ship is scheduled to arrive in port later that morning. You will find that a few hours' nap late in the afternoon is revitalizing under such combat conditions.

Those who do find the ultimate mate aboard ship may be interested to know that many of the major cruise lines can arrange weddings when the ship is docked in certain ports; and most of the lines offer special honeymoon packages.

Although the cruising single might not find the same variety of available mates as he or she would at the local singles bar, and although the chance for a lasting romance may be slim, the cruise vacation does offer the single an opportunity to spend a fun and even relaxing vacation, with plenty of companionship while visiting several interesting and exciting foreign ports. (See chapter 14 for how well each ship rates for singles.)

Chapter Five

Cruising with Children

Prior to considering the pros and cons of cruising with children, you must decide whether to take them along on the vacation in the first place. For those of you who embrace the philosophy that a vacation is an opportunity for a second honeymoon—an escape from dishes, housecleaning, commuter trains, and alarm clocks—there exists no argument that could persuade you to embark upon a family sojourn. Certainly, there is no doubt that travel with children requires a degree of sacrifice on the part of the parent.

However, for those of you who feel that vacation time is family time and an opportunity to share some pleasant experiences with your children, consideration of a family cruise should be given top priority on your list of possible holidays.

Although children's requirements and interests vary with age, by and large the preteen crowd is happy swimming, playing, eating hamburgers, and staying up late. Your first reaction may be to take them for a dip in the neighborhood pool, followed by dinner at McDonald's and the late-night horror show. Upon longer reflection, you may conclude that the purpose of traveling with children is not only to show them a good time, but for you to have a good time with them while broadening their intellectual and cultural horizons. Disney World or a family camping trip may prove to be an excellent first endeavor, but the frequent and seasoned traveler will certainly want to move on to more worldly pursuits.

My personal experience would indicate that there exists no more perfect family vacation than a cruise. Where but on a cruise can you find a sufficient variety of delectable foods, entertainment, activities, and events to meet the personal preferences of parent and child alike? Where but on a cruise can your children be royally entertained from morning until night while you just relax?

One of the truly rewarding pluses for a parent is unpacking the luggage only on one occasion while still being able to see a variety of exotic places. Many an adventurous family has been discouraged from taking in several European countries or Caribbean islands because of the hassle of dragging children and baggage from airport to airport and from hotel to hotel. On a cruise, you and the children have the unique opportunity of exploring as many different ports as your time may allow while your hotel floats along with you. On those cruises that offer an air-sea package, you part with your bags upon entering your hometown airport, and then do not see them again until they are brought to your private cabin on the ship.

During the day, a cruise offers a great variety of activities for children. In addition to the standard swimming pools, shuffleboard, deck tennis, Ping-Pong, an electronic game room, and gymnasium, which are open continuously, many cruise ships doing the Caribbean provide counselors and a special program for younger children, including scavenger hunts, arts and crafts, disco parties, supervised shore excursions, costume balls, ice cream and pizza socials, and access to high-tech educational games. In fact, several of the lines have programs in which the children are picked up after breakfast, entertained and fed all day, and not returned until after they have had their evening meal. In addition to the specially designed activities, the children will usually wish to participate in many of the adult-oriented events. During a typical day at sea, most cruises offer such activities as first-run movies, games around the pool, dancing classes, trap shooting, exercise groups, golf instruction, bingo, horse racing, and other parlor games. Don't be surprised if your children have a great deal of difficulty making their selections from the bulletin of the next day's activities that is pushed under your door every morning. Deciding between a bingo game and a Walt Disney movie can be somewhat difficult for a nine-year-old.

Dining on a ship with children is infinitely simpler and vastly more enjoyable than dragging them around from one restaurant to another in hopes of finding a mutually acceptable establishment. Since on many ships you have an assigned table with the same waiter for most of your meals, the waiter will soon learn your children's special needs and be able to efficiently accommodate them. Whether it is a booster chair, chocolate milk, or catsup for the *pommes frites,* you need only ask once and it should be there the remainder of the trip. The waiters are there to please you, and they have been trained to service your entire family in grand style. Although your children will certainly want to sample the numerous international and gourmet offerings, it is possible to arrange for them to have hamburgers, steaks, French fries, or similar "American pie" items at every meal. However, you may be in store for a big surprise when your finicky offspring, who at home insists on having his orange juice strained and the last drop of gravy removed from his meat, orders eggplant Parmesan, Tournedos Rossini, or crêpes suzette.

Most ships offer casual evening dining in the buffet restaurant. Thus, parents can feed their offsprings early if they wish to dine alone later.

There is usually no babysitting problem on a ship. During the day and early evening, most ships provide counselors and/or a children's program. Late in the evening, you may be able to hire one of the cabin attendants to sit with your children for a reasonable price. Some ships provide group babysitting facilities. If your children are not of too tender an age, you may elect to leave them alone in the room. On a ship, you are only moments away from your cabin, and it is convenient to check up on the youngsters frequently without detracting from your own evening. To be safe, it is always advisable to check out the babysitting situation with the cruise line prior to booking your cruise.

In case of an emergency, it is comforting to know that most ships have a hospital, pharmacy, and sailing physician. Contrary to some popularly expressed opinions, ships are as safe a place for children as almost anywhere else. Young children must be cautioned and watched so they do not lean over an open rail or run down wet steps. However, this is certainly no different from preventing them from leaning over an open balcony in a hotel or running around a slippery pool.

It is unlikely that children will be bored. Even before they have an opportunity to search out the many corners of the ship, they will find themselves in port. On most cruises, you will be visiting a different place during a majority of the days afloat. This affords the children an opportunity to stretch their legs and partake in the same activities they would have pursued had you flown to the port rather than sailed. Most ships give lectures and provide you with magazines describing the places of interest in each port prior to your arrival. Thus, there exists ample time and facility to carefully plan your tour of the port so as to include items of interest to the children.

This should not suggest that you must give up your own sightseeing or shopping plans. It is entirely possible in the popular port of St. Thomas to divide your day between shopping for bargains in the wide selection of international stores and then having a leisurely lunch and swim at one of the seaside hotels or magnificent white-sand beaches. Should your ship dock at Montego Bay, your family could raft down an authentic tropical jungle river, climb from the sea up a natural waterfall, ride donkeys through a lush plantation, swim at a clear, palm-laden beach, and take in a native limbo show, all within six to eight hours.

Although almost every cruise will offer most of the activities and programs described above, the best ships for children are probably the larger vessels (over 50,000 tons), because they usually have more facilities, more extensive programs, and more space to move around. The Carnival, Celebrity, Cunard, Disney, Norwegian, Princess, and Royal Caribbean cruise lines have excellent facilities for preschool children. The two 83,000-ton, 2,400-passenger Disney ships that debuted in 1998 and 1999, the *Disney Magic* and *Disney Wonder,* are totally geared and designed for families cruising with youngsters. The 140,000+-ton ships of Royal Caribbean, the *Grand Princess*-class ships of Princess, the post-2000 ships of Norwegian, and the 100+-ton ships of Carnival offer an amazing assortment of activities and facilities that will appeal to teens and preteens alike. Ships of most of the lines have special programs for children during the summer and on holiday cruises. Most of the larger ships also offer special events for teenagers. When selecting an itinerary, you may be well advised to concentrate on the shorter cruises (three to seven days) that travel in calm sunny climes and avoid cruises where the waters could be choppy and the weather inclement. Those Caribbean cruises embarking from U.S. ports and Caribbean islands may be an ideal first venture.

If your children are seven years or older, I would especially recommend taking them on a Mediterranean cruise that visits such historic civilizations as Italy, Turkey, Greece, Spain, France, Egypt, or Israel, or on a Northern European cruise that may dock at such cities as Southampton (Port of London), Le Havre (Port of Paris), Amsterdam, Hamburg, Copenhagen, Oslo, Stockholm, Helsinki, and St. Petersburg. Such Mediterranean and Northern European cruises are marvelous, painless ways to expand your children's education and exposure to foreign lands and cultures. An adult might prefer visiting a different country each year in order to slowly assimilate the culture rather than barnstorming many countries at one time; however, for a child, it is easier to comprehend, remember, and compare the differences when viewed in close proximity—an experience more akin to reading about different countries in a textbook at school.

Probably the greatest argument for cruising with children is the moderate cost. Almost every ship's schedule of fares provides that a child under a certain age (generally 12) sharing a room with two adults need pay only half or less of the minimum fare (the fare charged for the least expensive accommodations aboard). Thus, on a cruise where the fares range from $1,000 to $2,000 per person, it is possible to book a minimum quad (a room accommodating four persons) and pay $1,000 for each adult and $500 for each child. Travelers who desire more sumptuous accommodations can take a room at the more expensive rate and still only pay $500 for any child who may share that room. Should the ship not be completely filled, you may be able to obtain two adjoining double rooms for the same price as sharing a minimum quad. In any event, it never hurts to check with the chief purser or hotel manager upon getting on the ship to see if such an arrangement is available.

The following cruise lines advertise special programs for young children, pre-teens, and teens: Carnival Cruise Lines, Celebrity Cruises, Costa Cruise Lines, Crystal Cruises, Cunard Line, Disney Cruise Line, Holland America Line, Norwegian Cruise Line, Princess Cruises (on most ships), and Royal Caribbean International. All of these lines have special children's facilities, children's menus, reduced rates in a shared cabin, cribs for the cabins, and children's counselors with special programs. Some of them provide private babysitters in the evenings.

I recently compared the programs for tots and teens on the industry's largest vessels. I found that Disney was the most oriented to programs and events for children under 12 years of age, including live Disney musicals, highly supervised programs, and numerous visits and photo opts with the major Disney characters. The 142,000+-G.R.T. ships of Royal Caribbean and the *Grand*-class ships of Princess boast the most expanded and impressive facilities for young children, teens, and adults alike. Their organized children's programs easily rival those of Disney and their facilities may be preferred by teens, especially older teens. The ships of these two cruise lines have equal appeal to adults traveling without children, offering them a more varied cruise experience. Carnival also has numerous facilities and programs for children, and the ships are ideal for family vacations;

however, emphasis appears to be directed to fun-loving, active adults. The newest ships of Norwegian also have very impressive facilities for children and teens.

Of course, every parent knows his or her own children and whether or not they would adjust to the cruise vacation. However, many a parent has been pleasantly surprised at how well-behaved and well-adjusted his children have been on a cruise as compared to their normal behavior at home. Parents often fail to give their children sufficient credit for acquiring maturity. On a cruise, a child for the first time may experience such hedonistic delights as being pampered and waited upon by foreign strangers, tasting the finest culinary creations offered anywhere in the world, witnessing the breathtaking beauty of exotic ports, being lavishly entertained from morning 'til night, and last, but not least, being treated like an adult. Children will more often than not rise to the occasion. Who wouldn't? (See the charts below and chapter 14 for how well each ship rates for children.)

The following chart summarizes the special facilities, activities, and other features you will want to consider when comparing "children-friendly ships." Only the larger cruise lines that promote family cruising are included.

CODE TO CHART

Overall rating of ship for cruising families:
5—Excellent
4—Very Good
3—Good
2—Fair
1—Poor

A. Youth counselors and supervised activities
B. Supervised playrooms with age-appropriate equipment and facilities
C. Designated teen facilities and programs
D. Children's menus in dining rooms
E. Special lower fares for children sharing a stateroom with two adults
F. Evenings when children can dine with youth counselors
G. Group babysitting facilities in the evenings
H. Private babysitting available in cabins
I. Special children's pool or wading pool
J. Children's outside playground
K. Video arcade
L. Basketball court
M. Miniature golf
N. Hamburger, hotdog, and pizza facilities
O. Special program and/or facilities for children on cruise line's private island visits

CRUISE LINES

Carnival Cruise Line: 5+
A; B; C; D; E (special rates for third and fourth guest in a room); F; G; I; J; K; L (on larger ships); M (on some ships); N; O.

Celebrity Cruises: 4
A; B (five age groups); C; D; F; G; H; I; K; L; N.

Costa Cruise Lines: 3+
A; B; C; D; E (sometimes); F; G (ages three and up); I; J; K; N.

Crystal Cruises: 4
A (10 A.M. to noon, 2 P.M. to 5 P.M., and 7 P.M. to 9 P.M.); B (three age groups); C; D; F (on selected evenings); H (rates range from $7.50 to $12.50 per hour based on number of children); I; K; N.

Cunard Line: 4+
A (9 A.M. to midnight, except between noon and 2 P.M. and 5 P.M. and 6 P.M.); B (ages one through seven); D; E (special fares for third and fourth person in cabin); F; G; I; J; N.

Disney Cruise Line: 5+
A (9 A.M. to midnight); B (six different age groups); C; D; E; F; G (infant to three years); I; K; L; N; O.

Holland America Line: 4 (all ships except *Prinsendam*)
A (8 A.M. to noon, 1 P.M. to 5 P.M., and 8 P.M. to 10 P.M.); B; C; D; E; G (ages three and older from 10 P.M. to midnight at $5 per hour); H; I (on *Statendam*-class ships only); K; L; N; O.

MSC Cruises: 3 (post-2000 ships only: *Armonia, Sinfonia, Musica, Opera,* and *Lirica*)
A; B; D; E (in Caribbean); H; I, J, and L (except on *Opera*); K; M; N.

Norwegian Cruise Line:5 (post-2000 ships)
A (sea days 9 A.M. to noon, 2 P.M. to 5 P.M., and 7 P.M.-10 P.M.); B; C; D; E (special fares for third and fourth person in cabin); F (one time per cruise); G; I; K; L; N.

P & O Cruises: 4 (*Oceana, Aurora,* and *Oriana*)
A; B; D (special children's sitting at 5:15 P.M.); E; F; G (six months to five years); I; J; K; L; N.

Princess Cruises: 5+ (all ships except *Pacific Princess* and *Tahitian Princess*)

A; B (three age groups); C; D; E (reduced fares for third and fourth person in cabin); F; G (for children ages three to 12 from 10 P.M. to 1 A.M. at $5 per hour); I; J; K; L; M (on *Grand*-class ships); N; O.

Royal Caribbean International: 5+

A; B (five age groups); C; D; E (special rates for third and fourth person in cabin); F (several nights during cruise); G (10 P.M. to 1 A.M. for $5 an hour for those over three and toilet trained); H (for $8 per hour); I, J, L, M (on most ships); K; N.

Chapter Six

Where to Cruise and How Long

Cruise Grounds; Ports of Call; Points of Interest; and What to Do with Limited Hours in Port

Cruise Grounds

The possibilities for places to cruise are as infinite as the coastal cities found on a map of the world. Today it is feasible to sail about almost anywhere in the seven seas, provided you are endowed with the time, finances, and inclination.

You can board ship at Fort Lauderdale or Miami and sail to Bermuda, the Bahamas, or to any of the tropical islands in the Caribbean. A growing number of vessels provide embarkations for such Caribbean cruises from Palm Beach, Tampa, Port Canaveral, New Orleans, Texas, New York, Baltimore, Philadelphia, Galveston, cities along the Eastern seaboard, and even Puerto Rico, while others include stops in Central and South America.

Should you live near the West Coast, there are numerous cruises leaving from Los Angeles, San Diego, and San Francisco sailing to Mexico, Central America, South America, Hawaii, Alaska, the South Sea Islands, Australia, and the Orient.

If you are traveling in Europe, you can board ship in England, France, Holland, Copenhagen, Sweden, or Germany for cruises traversing the fjords of Norway or visiting ports in the Baltic, northern Europe, and even Russia. Perhaps you would prefer a ship leaving Cannes, Monte Carlo, Athens, Venice, Naples, or Genoa, visiting Southern Spain, Northern Africa, Sicily, the Greek islands, the Turkish Coast, or the Middle East. Dozens of ships based in Pireaus (Port of Athens) offer regular cruises to the myriad of lovely Greek islands as well as to ports in Turkey, Israel, Egypt, and on the Black Sea, and to other Middle Eastern coastal cities. During the spring and summer months, numerous riverboats and barges cruise down the rivers and waterways of France, as well as down the Elbe, Havel, Main, Rhine, and Moselle rivers in Germany, the Danube in Austria and Hungary, the Nile in Egypt, and the waterways of England and Holland.

Several vessels offer "around the world" cruises extending from 40 to 90 days and calling at sample ports in Europe, Africa, Asia, Australia, South America, and various islands along the way. If you do not have time for such a long vacation, it is possible on some of these ships to board and disembark at certain points midway into the cruise. It would be somewhat beyond the scope of this book to cover every conceivable port and every possible itinerary. However, the following sections on "Ports of Call" describe almost all of the popular stops in the more widely traversed cruise areas. The description of each port is not intended to be exhaustive, but is designed to suggest points of interest, scenic places to visit, shopping, beaches, and restaurants for passengers of cruise ships who have from six to 12 hours to spend in port. Current itineraries for the various ships can be found in *Official Steamship Guide International.*

Ports of Call

The U.S., Bermuda, the Bahamas, and the Caribbean
South America
The Mediterranean, Greek Islands, Middle East, and Environs
Northern Europe, the Baltic, the North Sea, the Fjords, and the Rivers of Europe
Cruises from the United States' West Coast, Mexico, the South Seas, Hawaii,
    and the Far East
East Africa and the Indian Ocean
Transatlantic Crossings

Note: In the following descriptions of ports of call there are numerous references to specific restaurants and hotels. It is best to make advance reservations before visiting any of these establishments since some do not welcome cruise-ship passengers, and others may have changed ownership or ceased to operate subsequent to this printing.

The U.S., Bermuda, the Bahamas, and the Caribbean

The lush, blue Caribbean is one of the most desirable areas for the cruise vacation because the waters are calm and the variety of islands is endless. Until the 1970s, the major cruise ships embarked from New York, resulting in several days at the beginning and end of each cruise being spent in the rougher waters of the Atlantic. During the late fall, winter, and early spring, the weather in the Atlantic is often inclement and the ocean is choppy, making it impossible for you to sit out on deck until your ship is well past Cape Hatteras.

Today, most ships positioned in the United States depart from Port Everglades (Port of Fort Lauderdale), Dodge Island (Port of Miami), Tampa, Port Canaveral (Port of Orlando), New Orleans, Palm Beach, or Puerto Rico. However, several of the larger cruise lines are now initiating cruises from numerous other U.S. cities accessible by waterways to the ocean, including Baltimore, Philadelphia, New York, Galveston, Jacksonville, and other ports along the Eastern seaboard. Cruises embarking from the southern U.S. ports offer the traveler instant sun and the time to visit a greater number of islands because the traveling distance has been reduced. Some of the seven-day cruises from these southern ports make as many as six stops, and the 14-day cruises may call on five to 12 different ports.

The islands in the Caribbean area are varied, each with its own individual flavor. The natives of Bermuda, Barbados, Grenada, Jamaica, and the Bahamas still speak with a British accent. French is the official language of Haiti, Martinique, Guadeloupe, St. Barts, and part of St. Martin. The little towns and brightly painted buildings in Aruba, Bonaire, Curaçao, and the other part of Saint Maarten (St. Martin) are reminiscent of Holland, as are the language and restaurants. Spanish is the native tongue in Puerto Rico, Santo Domingo, and Caracas. Although the United States bought St. Thomas, St. John, and St. Croix (the U.S. Virgin Islands) from Denmark in 1917, the Danes left their mark. Some of the streets still bear names similar to the streets of Copenhagen, and Danish smörbrod and beer can still be purchased in a few local restaurants.

Which islands you will enjoy most depends upon your personal tastes and interests. Many of the ships make a point of stopping at least at one island where there is gambling, one island where there is shopping, and one where there is swimming. Most of the islands offer duty-free shopping bargains of one kind or another, and most have beautiful beaches. Rather than running off to a public beach with limited facilities, consider going to a large hotel or resort where you can make a quick change and enjoy the comforts of the hotel's beach, pool, restaurants, and other facilities.

Several of the major cruise lines that deploy numerous ships in the Caribbean own or lease private islands (or parts of islands), offering passengers a one-day beach party. A typical private island will have beach chairs and umbrellas, bathroom facilities, several bars, a dining area or pavilion, a straw market, a boutique, a calypso band, various land and water sport facilities, and hiking paths. Costa Cruises' island, Serena Cay, is located in the Dominican Republic. Disney Cruises' 1,000-acre island, Castaway Cay, lies in the Abaco chain of the Bahamas. Holland America Line's 2,400-acre Half Moon Cay rests southeast of Nassau in the Bahamas. Norwegian Lines' Great Stirrup Cay sits in the Bahama-Berry Islands chain. Princess Cruises' Princess Cay is a 40-acre peninsula on the southern tip of Eleuthra in the Bahamas. MSC's Cayo Levantado is located in the Dominican Public. Royal Caribbean International boasts two private island beaches: Labadee, a 260-acre peninsula on the northern coast of Haiti, and Coco Cay, a 140-acre island in the Bahamas.

The following are the highlights of some of the more popular ports in this area:

ANGUILLA

The most northerly of the Leeward Islands in the eastern Caribbean lies five miles north of St. Martin. Once a part of a federation with St. Kitts and Nevis, Anguilla gained its independence from that association in 1980 and has since been a self-governed British possession. Only 16 miles in length, the island is easily traversed by rental car or taxi.

Anguilla boasts some of the finest resorts in the Caribbean. Malliouhana at Meads Bay is perhaps the most perfect property in the Caribbean, and a marvelous place to spend your day. The beach is among the best on the island. The children's aquatic playground and the state-of-the-art spa/fitness center are extremely impressive. The incredibly charming indoor/outdoor restaurant perched on a cliff overlooking the sea is not only romantic, but features the imaginative French cuisine of the Rostang family. Whether you opt for lunch or dinner, it is one of those uniquely perfect dining experiences that we constantly seek but rarely find.

Cap Juluca at Maundays Bay is a unique Moorish-style retreat spread along a lovely strand of white-sand beach featuring Pimms, an outstanding restaurant, and a new fitness/spa facility. CuisinArt, with its Mediterranean-influenced architecture, is yet another outstanding beachfront resort. If time permits, you will want to visit at least one of these fabulous properties.

The best public beaches are at Shoal Bay and Sandy Ground, where there are some colorful restaurants and small shops. A top choice for a day trip would be a snorkeling expedition to either Sandy Island or Little Cay Bay. Sandy Island, accessible by ferry or motor boat from Sandy Ground, is a tiny islet with a few palm trees surrounded by powder-fine sand and good reefs for snorkeling. The open-air restaurant features barbecued ribs, chicken, and lobster, accompanied by cold beer or rum punch. Little Cay Bay is a picturesque secluded cove accessible only by boat. Island Harbour Restaurant at Scilly Cay is a good choice on the beach. Here you will find a tiny, white-sand beach with turquoise, azure, and verdant green waters—a romantic spot for a private picnic with good snorkeling possibilities.

ANTIGUA

Antigua is a 108-square-mile Caribbean island located about midway between Martinique and St. Thomas and noted most for its numerous white-sand beaches. The travel brochures tout this "Island Paradise" as having 365 beaches—one for each day of the year. The climate is mild, with temperatures varying between the mid-70s and mid-80s.

Your ship will dock at Heritage Quay or at Deep Water Harbor near **St. Johns,** the capital. A small shopping center is located near both piers, with several shops featuring local handicrafts, souvenirs, T-shirts, and a few imported items. Points of interest include English Harbour and Nelson's Dockyard, an 18th-century naval base, St. John's Cathedral, Clarence House, Fig Tree Hill Drive, Devil's Bridge, and Fort Berkeley. There is an 18-hole golf course at Cedar Valley, and nine-hole courses at Antigua Beach Hotel and Half Moon Bay. Casinos are located at the St. James's Club, the Royal Antigua Hotel in Dickenson Bay, Halcyon Cove Beach Resort at Dickenson Bay, King's Casino in St. John, and at the Heritage Quay. The most upscale resorts are Curtain Bluff, Jumby Bay, and Galley Bay. The most popular restaurants on the island include Admiral's Inn (seafood), Chez Pascal (French), Coconut Grove at Dickenson Bay, Le Bistro (French and Seafood), Lobster Pot (Caribbean dishes and seafood), and Alberto's (Italian).

With only six to ten hours in port, I would recommend spending your day at the St. James's Club, Hawksbill Beach Hotel, or at the Rex Halcyon Cove Beach Resort. To visit Curtain Bluff or Jumby Bay you would need to make advance arrangements. These resorts are located on lovely strands of white-sand beach with warm, clear waters. They feature adequate swimming pools, numerous shops, watersports (water-skiing, snorkeling, scuba, and sailing), decent tennis courts, a casino, and picturesque restaurants. The best public beaches are at Pigeon Point, Dickenson Bay, Carlisle Bay, Hawksbill, and Half Moon Bay.

THE BAHAMAS

The Bahamas consist of a stretch of hundreds of islands extending off the coast of Florida down to Haiti. Cruise ships generally stop at **Nassau** or **Freeport,** Grand Bahama, which are the most populous and developed of the Bahamian islands.

Several of the cruise lines have purchased and developed pristine "out-islands" in the Bahamas, where their ships stop for a beach party and snorkeling.

Although the Bahamas have gained complete independence from the motherland, you are constantly reminded of the British influence. In Nassau, you can shop in the native straw market adjacent to the docks at Rawson Square, sample some Bahamian conch chowder at a quaint seaside restaurant, take a horse-and-buggy ride through the streets of town, play tennis at any of the large hotels, swim in the absolutely still-clear waters of the beautiful beaches of **Paradise Island,** or visit the casino and elegant restaurants.

A short excursion to Coral World on Coral Island is worthwhile. Here you can view sea life and fish indigenous to this part of the world, including sharks, stingrays, and giant turtles. Also located here are an open-air restaurant and a snorkeling trail.

Many passengers enjoy spending their day exploring Paradise Island, which is accessible for a $3 charge by motor launches that depart right at the pier between the cruise ships and town. Until recently this was a beautiful pristine island where visitors could walk along miles of white-sand beach and paths running through pine forests past azure lagoons. Unfortunately, the group owning the Atlantis Hotel Complex purchased the majority of the island, knocked down most of the forests, eliminated the lagoons, and constructed glitzy mega-hotels. The Atlantis is an awesome resort with a myriad of pools, beaches, shops, restaurants, bars, a humongous casino, aquariums, sea life ponds and just about everything else you could imagine. It is truly an adult Disney World. The golf course remains on the far side of the island, near the Ocean Club, a more intimate and upscale property. The beaches at Cable Beach Hotel and the Radisson on Nassau are also excellent for sunning, swimming, and watersports, and are accessible by a 10-minute bus ride.

When shopping at Grand Bahama, you will not want to miss the variety of imported merchandise in the colorful international bazaar, where you can stroll down cobbled streets into shops with imports from Scandinavia, Great Britain, Hong Kong, Japan, India, Spain, and France. You also will want to taste some delectable conch fritters and sausages with ale at one of the atmospheric British pubs, try your luck at El Casino adjoining the bazaar, or swim at one of the white-sand beaches in the fashionable Lucaya area.

BARBADOS

Barbados is 21 miles long and 14 miles wide with 260,000 inhabitants who are independent members of the British Commonwealth. They enjoy a dry, sunny climate with temperatures varying from 70 to 80 degrees. The island's British heritage is most evident in the capital, **Bridgetown,** with its quaint houses and its statue of Lord Nelson in Trafalgar Square. Taste the local rum that is reputed to be the best in the world; shop at the Terminal at Bridgeport Harbor or in the Broad Street area for duty-free British woolens, Irish linens, English bone china, French perfumes, Japanese cameras, local black-coral jewelry, and Swiss watches; browse through the local arts and crafts offered for sale at Pelican Village off the Princess Alice Highway; see sugar refined at a local factory; or play tennis, sunbathe, and swim in crystal-clear waters on one of the long stretches of fine sand beach or at one of the large, luxury hotels, such as the Sandy Lane, Glitter Bay, Royal Pavilion, The House and the Coral Reef Club, all of which are located on the west coast, where the waters are extremely calm. There are tennis courts, a golf course, and a beautiful beach at the recently renovated Sandy Lane, one of the Caribbean's most luxurious properties with a world-class spa; however, the hotel is not hospitable to cruise passengers, and arrangements have to be made in advance to enter this and most other hotels. Hotels on the Atlantic east coast enjoy panoramic vistas; however, the sea is frequently not safe for swimming. Public beaches frequented by cruise passengers include Carlisle Bay Beach, which has changing facilities, and the beach adjacent to Sandy Beach Island Resort. Several cruise lines offer pre- and post-cruise options at Accra Beach Hotel, which is located on a nice beach and has good facilities. All of the resorts offer a variety of dining opportunities. The most popular local restaurants outside the resorts include Bagutelle Great House (continental), Carambola (Thai and continental), Sandy Bay (continental), Ile de France (French), Pisces (seafood), Josef's (Scandinavian), Daphne's at The House (hotel), and Fish Pot (seafood). One of the best restaurants on the island, Luna Café, is located atop the Little Arches Hotel. Dining under the stars on the Castilian-style terrace is an extremely romantic experience. Food and service are right up there with the atmosphere.

Other points of interests include Barbados Museum; Flower Forest, an eight-acre floral park; Harrison's Cave, which you tour by electric tram; Barbados Wildlife Reserve; and the oldest synagogue in the Western Hemisphere, dating back to 1654.

BERMUDA

Bermuda is a self-governing member of the British Commonwealth. It covers 21 square miles and has an English-speaking population of 55,000. The people are very British, and the island boasts a mild climate with lovely scenery, pastel houses, and coral-pink beaches. Temperatures vary from 58 to 76 degrees from November through April, and from 65 to 86 degrees from May through October. You can shop for bargains in friendly shops that feature English bone china and woolens, French perfumes, Danish silver, and Swiss watches; visit the botanical gardens, government house, historical society museum, and the completely restored 19th-century fortification at Fort St. Catherine; explore the Crystal Cave, a natural cavern that ranks as Bermuda's most beautiful attraction; play tennis or golf at one of the island's luxury hotels; rent a motorcycle and take a ride across the island; or just swim in the calm, blue waters of a quiet cove along a soft, pink-sand beach. There are some excellent tennis courts at the Southampton Princess and the Sonesta Beach hotels. To the left of the Southampton Princess Hotel is one of the most beautiful stretches of pink-sand beach, inlets, and coves to be found anywhere in the world. You may wish to have your waiter on the ship pack a box lunch with a bottle of wine so you can picnic on this lovely public beach. The Southampton Princess also offers numerous gourmet restaurants, as well as those specializing in seafood and steaks.

If your ship docks at **St. George,** you will find numerous souvenir shops and boutiques right at the harbor. The most interesting and accessible beach is at Tobacco Bay. The mile-and-a-half path that runs along the harbor and ocean between the dock and Tobacco Bay past Fort St. Catherine is scenic and worth exploring.

THE CAYMAN ISLANDS

The Cayman Islands, peaceful little islands lying 100 miles northwest of Jamaica, have a colorful history dating to their discovery by Columbus on his fourth voyage to the West Indies. They are now a crown colony of the United Kingdom, and their favorable tax policy makes these islands one of the world's most attractive tax havens. Several cruise ships tender to **Georgetown** on Grand Cayman to permit their passengers to enjoy a day exploring one of the most beautiful stretches of white-sand beach in the Caribbean. Although **Grand Cayman** is only 22 miles long and eight miles across, it boasts a seven-mile strand of beach lined with pines, palms, and small cottage-like hotel complexes. You can spend your day swimming and snorkeling in the crystal-clear waters; visiting a turtle farm where turtles are bred and raised; playing with stingrays at Stingray City (available by motor launch); golfing at the Britannia or Safe Haven courses; or browsing through the duty-free shops in Georgetown in search of bargains in china and crystal imported from all over Europe, Swiss watches, black coral jewelry, and French perfumes.

Should you be docking in the evening, you can dine at Chef Tell's Grand Old House on a broad veranda and watch the sun set over the beautiful blue waters of the Caribbean while enjoying some of the best food on the island. Hemingway's at the Hyatt Regency; Lantanas at the Caribbean Club; Pappagallo, an Italian and seafood restaurant set in a bird sanctuary overlooking a lagoon; and Ottmars are also excellent. The Ritz-Carlton, Hyatt, Westin, and Radisson are the largest hotels on the island, and each offers tennis courts, a swimming pool, and beaches with full facilities. Those who wish to scuba or snorkel can make arrangements in Georgetown or at any of the larger hotels.

COSTA RICA

Cruise ships traversing the Panama Canal often stop at Central America's most developed democratic republic, which is bordered by Nicaragua to the north and Panama to the south. The beauty of the country is its varied scenery, which includes lush green mountains and valleys, volcanoes, ranches, farmland, rolling hills, lovely streams and waterfalls, jungles, and beaches.

In the center of the country, surrounded by mountains, sits **San Jose,** the capital, where tourists may wish to visit the many parks, the lavish Teatro National (an architectural jewel built in the 19th century that presently offers concerts, ballet, opera, and theater), the National Museum with its archeological and historical artifacts, the Museum of Contemporary Art, the Museo de Oro with its displays of all kinds of gold, the Jade Museum, and the president's home.

Ships call at either the Atlantic port of Limon or the nearby Pacific ports of Caldera and Puntarenas. On the Atlantic side, the best beaches are at the National Park of Cahuita; on the Pacific they are on Nicaya Peninsula. From Puntarenas ferries traverse the gulf of Nicaya to Tambor and Paquera; however, timetables for returns can be unreliable and anyone wishing to visit this area is advised to be certain about the timing of their return. From Tambor or Paquera, you can take a taxi to the beaches and hotels at Playa Tambor, Playa Montezuma, and Cabo Blanco.

Cruise ships generally offer excursions to San Jose, Sarachi (the handicraft town where you can purchase the famous Costa Rican hand-painted oxcarts as well as wine glasses and decanters), and the rain forest at Carrara Biological Reserve and the opportunity to enjoy horseback rides through tropical valleys and forests, river rafting, aerial tram rides, canopy tours, eco-jungle cruises, and visits to an orchid farm, macaw sanctuary, Britt Coffee Plantation, and Poas Volcano National Park. Those venturing out on their own can hire a taxi at the port (maximum four passengers) and for about $150 for three to five hours see the beautiful countryside, visit the Carrara Rain Forest, and explore Jaco, where there is a long stretch of black-sand beach, horseback riding, souvenir shops, and several local restaurants. Unfortunately some of the more popular resort communities cannot be accessed during a one-day visit.

DEVIL'S ISLAND

Lying nine miles off the coast of Guyana are three small islands that were known as the Devil's Islands until 1753, when they were renamed the Salut Islands (islands of salvation).

The largest is L'ile Royale. Saint Joseph to the east is the most beautiful, and Devil's Island to the north is the wildest. These islands were the site of the notorious French penal colony.

Cruise ships send tenders to **L'ile Royale**, where there is a small rustic inn offering limited shopping and cold drinks. Around the island are some of the vestiges of the prison colony, including the prison cells, chapel, death row cells, warden's accommodations, hospital, morgue, and children's cemetery.

L'ile Royale receives a lot of rain and as a result is very lush and verdant. There are numerous paths around the island, rewarding visitors with magnificent views of palms, rocky ocean coastlines, and the two neighboring islands. It is possible to walk or jog around the island. A protected sea area known as the Prisoner's Pool is located directly across the island from the dock. However, the waters in the vicinity are infested with sharks, and I do not know how safe it would be to swim here.

DOMINICA

Dominica is a 291-square mile, mountainous island with lush vegetation, dense rainforests, and over 350 waterfalls. Ships dock at the capital city of Roseau where there are souvenir shops, a local market, and small restaurants and hotels. It is one of the least developed islands in the Caribbean and there are no good beaches. Swimming is possible in rivers under waterfalls. Hiking and mountain climbing are the most popular pastimes. A favorite excursion offered by all cruise ships is a panoramic ride in the rain forest aerial gondolas along with a short hike through the forest over a suspension bridge. Tour guides narrate the excursion pointing out hundreds of varieties of exotic vegetation. Within 20 minutes from town is Trafalgar Falls. Even closer is the Botanic Gardens, with a trail up Morne Bruce, affording a panoramic view of the island. Kayak and snorkel tours are often available.

THE DOMINICAN REPUBLIC

The Dominican Republic shares the island of Hispaniola with Haiti. Although this Spanish-speaking island boasts some majestic mountains and jungle rivers, your ship will probably not dock for a sufficient time to permit you to explore the island. If the ship drops anchor at **Santo Domingo,** you may wish to visit such historical landmarks as Alcazar de Colon, the restored 16th-century palace built for Columbus's son Diego, and the 400-year-old Cathedral Santa Maria La Menor, site of the Christopher Columbus tomb. The National Museum of the Dominican Republic offers some interesting Indian artifacts, while the National Museum of Fine Arts features the work of more recent painters and sculptors. The 445-acre Botanical Gardens at Arroyo Hondo are the largest in all of Latin America and can be toured on foot, by horse carriage, or by boat. The best buys are in amber, which is mined and crafted on the island. You can swim at the pool, play tennis, and gamble at El Embajador Hotel, Jaragua Renaissance, Intercontinental, or the

Sheraton. If time permits, drive out to the Caribbean's largest full-facility resort, Casa De Campo at La Romana, where there are three challenging golf courses, 13 tennis courts, a riding stable, watersports, a picturesque Romanesque-designed artist's village with shops and restaurants, a shooting range, numerous restaurants, and a beautiful beach. Ships of Costa Cruises currently offer beach parties on a private island, with optional excursions to Casa De Campo.

Some ships anchor near Samana and Cayo Levantado Island on the northeast shores of the Dominican Republic. At Samana City and the town of Terrenas there are small shops and restaurants. Whale watching and scuba diving are the main attractions. Visits to El Limon Waterfall and the rainforest at Los Haitises National Park are also worthwhile. There are nice beaches for swimming at Las Terenas, El Portillo, and Playa Popy. However, most cruise ships tender passengers to the picturesque island of Cayo Levantado in Samana Bay. Here there is a large beach with white powdery sand lapped by turquoise waters. Many lounging chairs are spread out on the beach and surrounding the beach are small bars, outdoor barbeque restaurants, and native shops. One can spend an ideal beach day here.

In **Puerto Plata,** there is little to do other than shop for amber in the local market, but if you feel adventurous, rent a horse at the dock and ride through the countryside to the beach. Several new hotels have been built at Playa Dorado, the site of a Robert Trent Jones-designed golf course. Properties with the most facilities include Jack Tar Village, Caribbean Village Club on the Green, and Plaza Dorado Hotel and Casino. The best beach is located 15 miles east of town at Sosua.

THE DUTCH ISLANDS

The Dutch Islands of Aruba, Bonaire, and Curaçao represent the Netherlands in miniature, with gabled, pastel-colored buildings along picturesque streets. Dutch is the official language, although employees in the shops, hotels, and restaurants all speak English. The climate is sunny and dry, cooled by pleasant trade winds with temperatures ranging from a mean of 80 degrees in the winter to 84 degrees in the summer.

In **Curaçao,** you will find a fair selection of merchandise in a number of shops offering bargains in jewelry, watches, china, perfumes, and antiques. Tee shirts and souvenir items are particularly attractive and inexpensive. Willemstad is no longer the shopping haven it used to be. You can see the world-famous floating pontoon bridge in Willemstad swing open to allow ships into the harbor, or from atop the 33-foot-thick fortress walls you can watch the ships sail into the harbor. However, most cruise ships now dock at the new terminal and no longer pass through the bridge. One of the oldest synagogues in the Western world still in use, the Mikve Israel Emanuel Synagogue, is right in town, and on the outskirts of town you can visit the Jewish cemetery, which is one of the oldest Caucasian burial places in the New World. You can sample Curaçao liqueur at the distillery where it is made in Chobolobo, or eat *rijsttafel* (rice with 40 or more exotic complements) at the Rijsttafel Indonesia Restaurant (located outside of town), or you can try *kapucijners* (meat, chick peas, beans, bacon, onions, and sauces) at the historic Fort Nassau Restaurant, a renovated military fort on a hill overlooking the city. Try the French and Swiss cuisine at Bistro le Clochard, a quaint indoor/outdoor restaurant located in the small shopping center between the pier terminal and the pontoon bridge. Astrolab at the Kura Hulanda Hotel is the place for seafood. For tennis or swimming, your best bets are Marriott Beach Hotel and Casino, Hilton Beach Hotel and Casino, or Avila Beach Hotel. The Hyatt Regency Curacao opened in 2008 and a giant Renaissance Complex is under construction in town. Other attractions include Christoffel National Park, Curaçao Seaquarium, Curaçao's Ostrich Farm, Curaçao Underwater Marine Park, and Hato Caves. The best public beaches are Kon Tiki (near the Seaquarium), Blue Bay, and Barbara Beach.

Bonaire boasts 18 miles of reef that surround the island, offering some of the most spectacular scuba diving, spear-fishing, and underwater photography in the Caribbean. At many of the larger hotels, arrangements can be made for these activities, as well as for swimming, water-skiing, sailing, and glass-bottom boat rides. The beaches here are not particularly attractive, and cruise passengers may be better off opting for one of the snorkeling, diving, or sailing excursions offered by the cruise lines. This is also the island of the flamingos, and in the late afternoon bird watchers can see these graceful birds as well as thousands of herons, snipe, pelicans, parrots, parakeets, and others making their way across the blue Caribbean skies.

Aruba's capital is Oranjestad, where you can see many traditional Dutch multicolored houses with red-tile roofs, as well as a charming deep-water harbor. Don't miss the strange Divi-Divi tree and the huge monolithic boulder formations at Casibari. Swim at the beautiful, wide Palm Beach, which services the Aruba Marriott, Hyatt, Radisson, Westin, Holiday Inn, and numerous other large, full-facility hotels, all of which contain casinos and restaurants. For dining, Madame Janette (French and international) is considered the best on the island. Other popular restaurants include: Chez Mathilde near the Renaissance Hotel (continental), Papiamento (Caribbean and seafood), La Dome (French), Flying Fishbone (seafood on the beach), and Chalet Suisse (international, seafood, and steaks). The town is near the harbor and contains numerous shops offering international bargains.

Across from the dock area in the heart of downtown is the Renaissance Hotel with several restaurants, a large casino, a well-equipped gym, a pool, a shopping arcade, and a picturesque, white-sand beach located on a private island with tropical foliage, a bird sanctuary, and a restaurant, accessible by private launch from the hotel lobby.

There are golf courses at the Tierra del Sol Resort and Country Club and at the Aruba Golf Club.

GRENADA

Grenada, which became an independent nation in 1974, is known as the "Spice

Island" because it is here that cloves, mace, cinnamon, ginger, and nutmeg are produced and shipped throughout the world. The 133-square-mile island has a population of 105,000 and an average year-round temperature of 80 degrees. The capital, **St. George,** is often referred to as the most picturesque harbor in the Caribbean, and you will want to climb up one of its quaint cobblestone streets to get a panoramic view of the magnificent waterfront. You may wish to swim at one of the hotels located on the beautiful Grand Anse Beach, such as Spice Island Inn, Coyaba Beach Resort, and Grenada Renaissance. Or you may prefer to drive to Annandale Falls or Concorde Falls to picnic and swim in tropical pools beneath cascading waterfalls. You can visit the nutmeg factories at Gouyave and Grenville and purchase samples of the island's spices either at the factory or almost anywhere in town. Although the island and the beaches are lovely, you will be harassed constantly by vendors and beggars to the point of distraction. The highest-touted restaurants are La Dolce Vita, Coconut Beach (on Grand Anse Beach), La Belle Creole, Canboulay, and Spice Island Inn. LaBelle Creole and Canboulay both serve West Indian cuisine with hillside panoramic views. Spice Island Inn overlooks the beach and sea.

GUADELOUPE

Guadeloupe is a French department made up of two islands separated by a narrow channel—giving the appearance from the air of being a butterfly. Pointe-à-Pitre is in **Grande-Terre,** which is the flat, developed island with fine beaches. **Basse-Terre** is mountainous, with volcanic peaks, tropical green forests, lush vegetation, mountain streams, and waterfalls. The 327,800 inhabitants speak French and live in a basically warm climate that has a great deal of rain from July to November. You may wish to sample some French or Creole cooking at one of the hotel restaurants or in town, or shop for some of the excellent bargains in French perfumes, linens, and wines.

Good beaches include Anse de la Gourde between St. Francois and Pointe des Chateaux, Caravelle Beach near St. Anne, the beachfront at Gosier, and Le Grand Anse north of Deshaies on Basse-Terre; there are nudist beaches at Place Crawen, Pointe Tarare, Illet du Gosier, and Pointe des Chateaux. However, you will find the most facilities at the beautiful, tree-lined, white-sand beach of the Club Med Caravelle Hotel, where you can water-ski, play tennis, and have lunch. You may have to pay to get on the premises. Other large hotels with facilities include La Plantation Ste-Marthe and Le Meridien at St. Francois and La Creole Beach Hotel, Novotel Bas Du Fort, and Auberge de la Vieille Tour, located on the five-mile beach at Gosier. The highest-rated restaurants on Grand Terre include Auberge de la Vieille Tour, Rosini, La Bananier, La Canne a Sucre, La Louisiane, Les Oiseaux, and Le Chateau de Feuilles. In Pointe-a-Pitre try Café Jardin and Sacre-Sale.

If you have enough time, you can drive 40 miles from Pointe-à-Pitre to Basse-Terre and pass through sugarcane plantations, tropical forests at Guadeloupe's National Park, banana trees, beautiful hibiscus, and the high volcanic peaks of La

Soufriére with its waterfalls, lakes, and streams. Crayfish Falls at the National Park is one of the most popular sites on the island.

HAITI

Haiti is a tropical country occupying the western portion of the island of Hispaniola. French is the official language, but the majority of the inhabitants speak a Creole tongue that is difficult to distinguish.

Port-au-Prince is an unusual town with a blend of African and French cultures exhibited in the exquisite native paintings and crafts. You may wish to visit one of the luxury hotels located in the cooler heights of Petionville. Here again, the most facilities will be found at the Club Med; however, you must make advance arrangements to be admitted. You will enjoy tasting some of the French-Creole delicacies as well as the local Barbancourt rum and liqueur. If you have time, you can take a taxi up into the mountains and visit the Barbancourt factory to sample their many different beverages. At night you can dance at a local club, witness a fairly authentic voodoo ceremony, or gamble at the International Casino on the waterfront.

Several ships dock at **Cap Haitien,** 200 miles from Port-au-Prince. This picturesque but poor little city once was the richest colonial city in the French empire. Here you can explore the ruins of the Sans Souci Palace and Christophe's Citadelle atop a donkey, or you can browse through the native market. Whether you are in Port-au-Prince or Cap Haitien, the things to buy are native paintings and sculpture. Much of the arts and crafts sold throughout the other Caribbean islands are produced in Haiti.

ISLES DES SAINTES

Isles des Saintes is composed of a cluster of eight islands off the southern coast of Guadeloupe. Most visitors and cruise ships will stop at Terre-de-Haute, a very scenic island with a panoramic harbor. A short walk across the island from the port will bring you to Plage de Pompierre, a half-moon strand of white sand bordering aqua waters with a backdrop of palms and verdant hills. Anse Crawen is a nudist beach and Plage du Figuier is the best spot for snorkeling. The best hotel is Les Petits Saints. There are numerous small cafes and boutiques near the disembarkation pier in town.

JAMAICA

Jamaica is one of the lushest and most beautiful of the Caribbean islands. It is a land of white-sand beaches, emerald-blue still waters, green forests, jungle rivers, and Blue Mountains. The climate is warm and sunny throughout the year, with little seasonal variation in temperature. Montego Bay, Negril, and Ocho Rios are the fashionable resort areas with numerous fine hotels on long stretches of white-sand beach. Unfortunately, because the attitude and aggressive behavior of some of the citizens have turned off prospective visitors, fewer cruise ships have chosen Jamaica as a port of call.

If your ship docks at **Montego Bay,** you can take a short taxi ride to town and browse through the shops displaying the local crafts, jewelry, watches, and foreign imports. You may wish to tour Rosehall or Greenwood Great Houses, visit Croydin Plantation, take a donkey ride, or go for a swim at Doctor's Cave Beach, Walter Fletcher Beach, or Cornwall Beach, where there is an underwater marine park. You may also wish to take the drive to raft down the tropical Martha Brae River or at Mountain Valley from the Lethe Plantation 10 miles south of town. Perennially, the best resort hotels here have been Round Hill, Tryall Golf, Tennis, and Beach Club, Half Moon Golf, Tennis, and Beach Club, Ritz-Carlton, and Sandals.

Many cruise ships dock at **Ocho Rios.** Within walking distance of the dock are numerous shops, a public beach, and two semi-high-rise hotels that have changed ownership numerous times over the years and are presently operated as the Grande Renaissance Resort. If you wish to spend the day at one of the better hotels or resorts such as San Souci Lido, Plantation Inn, Jamaica Inn, Ciboney, Sandals Dunn's River, Boscobel Beach, or Couples, you must make arrangements in advance because you will have difficulty getting past the front gates.

Probably the most unusual tourist attraction here is Dunn's River Falls, about a five- to 10-minute taxi ride from the port. You can take photos and wander around the park that surrounds these incredible multilevel falls that descend to the sea, or you can experience climbing them with the assistance of a trained guide. Climbing the falls is a sensational experience; however, it is rather dangerous and not advisable for pre-teenage children. Wear a bathing suit and either waterproof athletic shoes or sandals that will not fall off.

From Ocho Rios, you could drive to Kingston via beautiful Fern Gulley and the breathtaking Blue Mountains. This is a beautiful, but somewhat dangerous, drive that should be attempted only if you are not in a hurry. You would need at least ten hours in port at Montego Bay to have sufficient time to raft down the Martha Brae, visit Dunn's River Falls and Fern Gulley at Ocho Rios, and have lunch and a swim at a hotel. If time allows, you may wish to drive in the opposite direction to explore the beautiful beaches at **Negril,** also the location of numerous, full-facility resorts. The most facilities will be found at Negril's all-inclusive resorts such as Grand Hotel Lido, Couples, Beaches, Hedonism II, and Sandals, or the more upscale Poinciana Beach Hotel. Since it may be difficult to camp out at one of these properties, a good choice would be Margaritaville, where you can have a comfortable beach chair and enjoy drinks, lunch, and watersports. You will enjoy walking along Negril's seven-mile beach.

Should you be in Jamaica during the evening, don't miss taking in a native calypso or limbo show at the local clubs or hotels. There are no outstanding restaurants around the island and you are best off dining at one of the better hotels. Best items to purchase are Tia Maria liqueur and the local rums.

KEY WEST, FLORIDA

Key West is not in the Bahamas or the Caribbean, but it is becoming a popular stop for many cruise ships. Technically the southernmost point in the continental U.S., Key West is about 80 miles farther south than the southernmost point in Texas. Lying between the Gulf of Mexico and the Atlantic Ocean, this final vestige of the Florida Keys will remind visitors of the Bahamas, New Orleans, and south Florida rolled into one. Only two miles by four miles in size, the island is easy to navigate on foot or bicycle.

Adjacent to the harbor, visitors can pick up the Old Town Trolley or the Conch Tour Train, both of which provide an excellent overview of the island. Points of interest include Mel Fisher's Maritime Heritage Society Museum; the Ernest Hemingway House, where the famous author wrote many of his novels; the Audubon House, a museum displaying many works of art by the famous artist and naturalist; and the Curry Museum, a turn-of-the-century National Historic Register Museum with three stories of period furnishings. If you elect to walk from the harbor into town (about a mile and a half), you will pass through a lovely residential area.

Arrangements can be made for deep-sea fishing charters (at Mallory Square), glass-bottom boat rides to a living coral reef, snorkeling and scuba tours, and sailboat racing. Golf is available at the 18-hole Key West Golf Club north of town.

Most tourists enjoy browsing through the hundreds of souvenir shops and colorful bars that line Duval and neighboring streets—Sloppy Joe's (Hemingway's favorite bar) and Jimmy Buffet's Margaritaville are the best-known drinking establishments. A two-hour pub tour that visits five pubs and includes four drinks departs daily at 2:30 P.M. There are numerous small restaurants featuring fresh fish and seafood. The most highly touted restaurants are Cafe des Artistes (French Caribbean), Louie's Backyard (fresh seafood), Bagatelle (eclectic), Mangoes (Florida Caribbean and pizza) and Blue Heaven and Pepe's (where the locals go to "see and be seen"). The largest hotels are the Hilton, Hyatt, and the Ritz-Carlton.

MARTINIQUE

Martinique, like Guadeloupe, is a department of France, and its 340,000 inhabitants speak French and a Creole dialect. The weather is generally very warm throughout the year, with considerable rain from July through November. Here, you can see the black-sand beaches that inspired the paintings of Gauguin, visit the birthplace of Empress Josephine at Trois-Ilets, walk through a petrified forest, drive out to the Mont Pelée Volcano and see the lava-drowned town of St. Pierre (sometimes referred to as the Caribbean Pompeii), swim at the hotel beaches on Trois-Ilets or at Anse Mitan, or just stroll around the old, quaint harbor town of Fort de France. You will want to save time to visit the shops along Rue Victor Hugo where you can pick up some excellent bargains in French perfume, Lalique and Baccarat crystal, Limoges china, gloves, and other French imports. However, the town has become quite run down and seedy over the past few years. You can sample French-Creole cooking in town or take a motorboat across the bay to Trois-Ilets/Pointe Du Boute. If time permits, you may prefer to take the 50-kilometer ride to the Club Mediterranean's vacation village at Buccaneer's Creek. Here you will find the island's best beach and watersports. However, you may have great difficulty getting on the premises, so it is best to call before you undertake the long drive. Noteworthy restaurants include Leyritz Plantation at Basse-Pointe (Creole), La Grande Voile in Fort de France (Creole), Le Planteur in Fort de France (French and Creole), Le Verger at La Mentin (French), and La Villa Creole at Trois-Ilets.

MEXICO (EAST COAST)

Cancún is a man-made resort area on the northeast tip of Mexico's Yucatán Peninsula. Ships generally dock at Playa del Carmen, from which it is a 30-minute ride to Cancún, or at the recently built port of Calica, which is 15 minutes farther away. Here you will find 14 miles of white-sand beaches, crystal-clear waters, and an average year-round temperature of 80 degrees. You can spend your day swimming, sunning, snorkeling, or playing tennis at one of the posh resort hotels such as the Ritz-Carlton, Fiesta Americana, Hyatt, or Marriott. You can enjoy 18 holes of championship golf at Pok-Ta-Pok, watersports at Aqua Bay Marina, snorkeling at Xel-Ha River near Tulum, a day of horseback riding through the jungle and beach trails at Rancho Bonita, or the incredible experience of swimming for 30 minutes down an underground river through prehistoric caverns and grottoes at the picturesque Xcaret Archeological Park adjacent to Calica. Xcaret is a unique attraction. In addition to two exotic, underground rivers, visitors can swim with dolphins; snorkel and relax at a picturesque beach; browse through an indoor/outdoor aquarium; visit a wildlife refuge, a bird sanctuary populated with exotic local birds, a butterfly pavilion, an orchard and mushroom nursery, a botanical garden, and many archeological treasures; go horseback riding through jungle trails; and enjoy lunch at one of several restaurants spread around the property.

Most cruises that stop at this area offer optional side trips to **Tulum** or **Chichen Itza** to explore the ruins of these ancient Mayan civilizations.

A newly developed port, a good distance to the South, is Mahahual in the area sometimes referred to as **Costa Maya**. Cruise lines offer tours from here to the archeological ruins at Chacchoben and Kohunlich and to the beach at Uvero. Where once there was little other than a shopping area at the end of the pier and two small beaches, the port was rebuilt following a hurricane in 2007. Now there are a plethora of excursions offered: a zipline tour, a sea trek tour enabling participants to explore the ocean in helmets piped with oxygen, beach and catamaran snorkeling, airboat rides through the mangroves, mountain biking, kayaking, horseback riding, fishing, speedboat adventures, and dune-buggy and ATV safaris.

Cozumel is a small island off the southeastern coast of the Yucatán with fine beaches for swimming, snorkeling, and scuba. The best beach to swim and enjoy a snack or drink is Mia Playa, formerly Playa del Sol, about 10 miles from town;

however, there is an $8 entrance fee. Mr. Sancho, a beach club 1/2%f mile down the road (the original location of Playa del Sol), is more appealing and has no entry fee. For snorkeling, Chankanaab Lagoon Park is only about five miles from town. You can spend the day at Stouffer's Presidente Hotel or Fiesta Americana's Sol Carib, both only a short distance from town with nice pools and restaurants but no outstanding beaches. In town, there are many typical restaurants and art, crafts, souvenir, and jewelry shops. Lunch or drinks at Carlos 'n Charlie's or Senor Frog's is always wild and fun. Many of the cruise lines offer excursions to out of the way beaches via kayaks, small motor boats, or jeeps.

NEW ORLEANS

New Orleans is the home port for Majestic America Line's three riverboats as well as various cruise ships of major cruise lines such as Carnival and American Canadian Caribbean. Passengers frequently opt to spend a few days before or after their sailing in this colorful, historic city. Located at the junction of 19,000 miles of inland waterways created by the Mississippi River, its tributaries, and the Gulf Intracoastal Waterways with access to the Gulf of Mexico, New Orleans has developed into one of the United States' major international sea ports.

Tourists most frequently gravitate to the French Quarter, drawn to its centuries-old buildings with unique ironwork and courtyards and its concentration of fine restaurants, nightclubs, bars, shops, and cafés. When touring this area by foot, you may wish to visit historic Jackson Square to see Clark Mill's equestrian statue of Andrew Jackson; 18th-century St. Louis Cathedral and the Cabildo, which now houses part of the Louisiana State Museum; the Pontalba Apartments, which include the 1850 House and the Le Pétit Théâtre du Vieux Carré; the Manheim Gallery in the old Bank of Louisiana building; Casa Faurie (which houses the famous Brennan's Restaurant); the 1792 Merieult House, location of the Historic New Orleans Collection; picturesque Brulator Court and the Court of the Two Lions; Preservation Hall; Pirates Alley; Père Antoine Alley; Cathedral Garden; Gallier House; and the Haunted House—all located on, or just off of, Royal Street; Soniat House, Beauregard-Keyes House, Old Ursuline Convent, the Pharmacy Museum, and Napoleon House on Chartres Street; as well as the French Market on Barracks Street, where you can sample freshly prepared beignets and chicory coffee, a Louisiana culinary tradition. It would be best to purchase a map of the French Quarter to assist you in your exploration.

Other areas of interest located throughout the city include: the Faubourg-Marigny Historic District, just east of the French Quarter, with its varied collection of 18th- and 19th-century, Creole-style structures built on narrow lots; the elegant Garden District; the Aquarium of the Americas with its underwater walkway; Audubon Park and Zoo; New Orleans Museum of Art in City Park; the National World War II Museum; and the shops and restaurants along the Riverwalk and connecting Ernest N. Morial Convention Center proximate to the cruise ship terminal.

If you wish to stay overnight in the French Quarter, the most highly rated hotels include the Omni Royal Orleans, Royal Sonesta, Hotel Maison de Ville, Holiday Inn French Quarter, and Marriott. Best choices nearer to the Central Business District and convention center include the Fairmont, Hyatt Regency, Hilton, Sheraton, Westin, Radisson, and Windsor Court (the most elegant in the city).

Extraordinary dining is New Orleans' tour de force. Although new restaurants surface from time to time, the traditional establishments are the most reliable and world-renowned. Commander's Palace, set in an 1880s restored building with lush green patios and gardens and a jazz band on Saturdays and Sundays, is a must for visitors seeking typical Creole dishes. Other perennial favorites include Brennan's, Broussard's, Antoine's, Galatoire's, Nola's, Peristyle, Dickie Brennan's Steakhouse, Bacco, Mr. B's Bistro, Emeril's, and Pascal's Manale Restaurant. K-Paul's Louisiana Kitchen, in the French Quarter, is an unpretentious establishment where New Orleans' most famous chef, Paul Prudhomme, dispenses his special interpretations of Creole, Cajun, French, and New Orleans cuisine. For more elegant continental and French dining, you may wish to try Rib Room at Omni Royal Orleans, Sazerac at the Fairmont, and the Grill Room at the Windsor Court. Of course, any respectable tourist would not miss the compulsory pilgrimage to Café du Monde in the French Market for café au lait and beignets.

For nightlife, you will want to stroll through the streets of the French Quarter (especially Bourbon Street) to bar hop, listen to jazz bands, browse through souvenir shops, and experience the after-dark sounds, smells, and exuberant vitality most associated with this city. Many of the larger hotels have quiet piano lounges, as well as music for listening and dancing. Another nighttime possibility would be to take in the riverfront attractions along the Moonwalk and Riverwalk.

New Orleans is also a shopper's paradise where you can search out bargains in antiques or peruse designer shops. The best shopping areas for tourists include Canal Street, the French Quarter, Magazine Street, and the complexes at One Canal Place and Riverwalk.

PUERTO RICO

Puerto Rico is a commonwealth voluntarily associated with the United States. Spanish is the native tongue of the 2,690,000 inhabitants, although many also speak English. The climate is reliably sunny and warm throughout the year. Cruise ships dock at the harbor in **San Juan,** the colorful cosmopolitan capital of the island. During the day, you can explore the quaint, authentically Spanish section of town known as "Old San Juan." Here you walk through cobbled streets surrounded by pretty plazas, Spanish-style buildings, shops, art galleries, restaurants, and museums. Outlet stores with designer discounted merchandise can be found on Cristo Street. You can visit the El Morro Fortress and the San José Church and try some arróz con pollo, paella, asopao, or black bean soup at one of the Spanish restaurants.

In new San Juan, you can visit the sea museum and botanical gardens or just relax, swim, play tennis, or sip a piña colada at one of the large oceanfront hotels.

Perhaps you will have time to drive out to the tropical El Yunqué rain forest and witness the beautiful lush vegetation and impressive variety of birds.

The spectacular El Conquistador Resort is located 31 miles east of San Juan. This mega-resort descends down a cliff and offers an 18-hole golf course, seven tennis courts, several pools, and its own private beach on Palomino Island, a 20-minute motor-launch ride from the hotel marina.

In the evening, you can stroll through Old San Juan, take in top-name entertainment, dance at the many nightclubs, or try your luck at the elegant hotel casinos. In San Juan, there are casinos and nightclubs at the Caribe Hilton, El San Juan, the Ritz-Carlton, the Holiday Inn, the Condado Beach, the Sands, and the Radisson.

ST. BARTHELEMY

Located 15 miles southeast of St. Martin and 140 miles north of Guadeloupe, St. Barts, a political dependency of Guadeloupe, is the most unique of the French West Indian islands. Its predominantly white population is of French and Swedish descent, and the atmosphere is more akin to a small French village on the Côte d'Azur than an island in the heart of the Caribbean.

Most visitors rent jeeps, mokes, or small cars, and enjoy visiting the numerous white-sand beaches, small hotels, guesthouses, atmospheric open-air restaurants, and cafés spread around this eight-square-mile island. **Gustavia,** the capital, is a quaint town with numerous cafés, restaurants, souvenir shops, and boutiques featuring a wide selection of imported goods.

Of the 14 white-sand beaches spread around the island, Baie De St. Jean is the most popular and a colorful strand on which to people-watch or take a stroll. Grand Cul-de-Sac on the northern shore is another local favorite. The most scenic beaches are Anse du Gouverneur, Anse de Grand Saline, and Anse de Colombier. Shell Beach, which is not very attractive, is within walking distance of town.

The two hotels boasting the most facilities on St. Barts are Guanahani at Anse de Grand Cul-de-Sac and Manapany at Anse des Cayes—both offering pools, good beaches, tennis, gourmet restaurants, and expensive exclusivity. In Gustavia, the most highly touted restaurants are Carl Gustav, Sapotillier, La Cremaillère, La Banane, On the Rocks, and Aux Trois Gourmands. Other restaurants of note outside of town include Francois Plantation, Adam, Maya's, La Playa on Plage St.Jean and Le Tamarin.

ST. KITTS AND NEVIS

This two-island nation was an associated state of Great Britain until it chose independence in 1983. St. Kitts covers 65 square miles and has a population of 40,000, while Nevis is only 36 square miles with 9,000 inhabitants. Jets can fly into St. Kitts, but Nevis is only accessible by smaller craft or by a 40-minute ferry ride from its sister island. The islands were first settled by the English and

French in the early 17th century and became important producers of tobacco, ginger, cotton, and sugar, as well as a major hub for slave trading.

Today the islands offer an ideal climate with warm Caribbean sunshine cooled by trade winds. There is sufficient rain to keep the interiors lush, verdant, and tropical.

St. Kitts is dominated by Mt. Misery with its crater lake that rises 4,000 feet amidst rolling hills of sugarcane and palm trees. Cruise ships can dock at Deep Water Harbor, which is only a five-dollar taxi ride or a 30-minute walk from the main town of **Basse-Terre** with its shops specializing in batiks. About three miles from the harbor is Frigate Bay, where there are shops, restaurants, "so-so" Atlantic and Caribbean beaches, and a giant, full-facility Marriott resort with three meandering, free-form pools, one with a swim-up bar, several restaurants, tennis courts, an 18-hole golf course, and a lovely beach. Attached to the resort is the large Royal Beach Casino. Good beaches for swimming on the southern portion of the island include South Friar's Bay, Sand Bank Bay, Turtle Beach, and Cockleshell Bay. A typical, casual place for a seafood lunch or dinner would be Fisherman's Wharf. For West Indian and continental dishes try the restaurants at the Golden Lemon, Ottley's Plantation, the restaurants at the Marriott, and at the Rawlins Plantation hotels.

Points of interest include Brimstone Hill, an imposing fort situated seven hundred feet above the sea affording views of Statia, Saba, St. Martin, and St. Barts; Romney Manor, a 17th-century plantation producing batik handicrafts; and an impressive tropical rain forest. The best beaches are at Banana Bay, Cockleshell Bay, and the Caribbean side of Friar's Bay.

The main town in Nevis, **Charlestown,** is a small, unusually clean Caribbean town with a few guesthouses, small inns and hotels, restaurants, and shops. There is a nice strand of beach about three miles from town that is used by some cruise ships for beach parties.

Nesbit Plantation on the north of the island also has a good beach, a restaurant, tennis courts, horseback riding, and watersports. In the early 1990s, the Four Seasons Hotel chain opened Four Seasons Resort Nevis (one of the most luxurious resorts in the Caribbean), which features an 18-hole Robert Trent Jones II golf course, ten illuminated tennis courts, long stretches of sand on Pinney's Beach, watersports, horseback riding, and several restaurants. From St. Kitts, visitors must take the resort's private shuttle boat from its dock in Basseterre. Three plantation-house hotels, pleasant places for lunch, are Golden Rock Estate, Hermitage Beach Club, and Nesbit Plantation Beach Club.

ST. LUCIA

St. Lucia, an independent member of the British Commonwealth, 21 miles south of Martinique, has a population of 101,000. The climate is dry and sunny in the winter, but a bit warmer and a great deal wetter during the summer months. The capital, **Castries,** is a picturesque town with a beautiful landlocked harbor where you can shop for duty-free bargains in crystal, jewelry, cameras, watches, perfume, and liquor, or sample the island's famous lobsters at a local restaurant. You can drive to Morne Fortuné, one of the two hills behind the town, and at the top explore the remains of Fort Charlotte, a typical 18th-century stronghold. You can take a two-hour voyage by launch to the fishing village of Soufrière, which is located at the base of St. Lucia's famous twin mountains, the Pitons. Here you can drive up Mount Soufrière, the only "drive-in" volcano in the world. You can actually drive right up to the lip of the smoldering crater and look in. Nearby, you can take a dip in sulphur springs, which are said to be therapeutic for sufferers of arthritis and rheumatism.

There is excellent swimming at all the public beaches; however, I would recommend spending the day on one of the hotel beaches at Jalousie Plantation, Sandals St. Lucia and Sandals Halcyon, Anse Chastanet, or at nearby Rodney Bay, the location of Le Sport, The Royal St. Lucien, and the Rex St. Lucien. The restaurants touted to be the best on the island are Green Parrot (seafood), San Antoine (continental), Piton Restaurant and Bar (Caribbean), Dasheene Restaurant and Bar (Caribbean), Capone's (Italian), and Great House (French-Creole).

ST. MARTIN

St. Martin (Saint Maarten) is a 37-square-mile island that was divided by the Dutch and French in 1648. **Philipsburg** is the capital of the Dutch section (Saint Maarten), and **Marigot** is the capital of the French (St. Martin). In addition to Dutch and French, the 14,000 inhabitants also speak English. The climate is dry and pleasant, with temperatures varying from 71 to 86 degrees. In Philipsburg, you can try numerous continental and ethnic restaurants and shop for duty-free bargains in delft and Royal Dutch pewter. In Marigot, you can sample French cuisine and purchase duty-free bargains in French wines, perfume, and gloves. Other than the scenery, there are not many attractions of significant interest to tourists. There are casinos in some of the hotels. Orient is a very colorful beach, a 15-minute drive from Philipsburg. It is reminiscent of Tahiti Beach in St. Tropez, France, and offers topless and nude bathing, as well as numerous small, beachfront restaurants and boutiques. Spartico is an excellent Italian restaurant located on the road between the airport and Marigot. Other good restaurants include LeBec Fin (continental), Oyster Pond Beach Hotel (continental), Le Perroquet (French), Chez Martine (French), Rainbow (continental and West Indian), La Vie en Rose (French), Alizea (French), and L'Auberge Gourmande (French). LaSamanna is the most exclusive resort on the island and is located on Baie Longue, one of the best beaches. If you make arrangements to have lunch at its highly acclaimed restaurant, chances are you can have access to the beach.

ST. VINCENT AND THE GRENADINES

Lying south of St. Lucia, north of Grenada, and west of Barbados in the southern part of Caribbean's Windward Islands is the nation of St. Vincent, which is composed of 32 islands and cays. The largest island is named St. Vincent and is the site of the Caribbean's most active volcano, La Soufrière, which last erupted in 1979.

South of the island of St. Vincent are the islands of Bequia, Mustique, Canouan, Mayreau, Palm Island, Union Island, and Petit St. Vincent, all low-key tourist destinations occasionally visited by cruise ships.

If your ship stops at the island of St. Vincent, two mediocre public beaches for swimming are Villa Beach and Buccament Bay, a black-sand beach on the west coast. A favorite excursion is the boat trip to Baleine Falls, where you can swim in a freshwater pool, climb under the 63-foot falls, and enjoy scenic views of the island. Hotels with the most facilities include Grand View Beach Hotel and Young Island. Young Island boasts the best beach and best resort restaurant and is accessible by a five-minute ride on the hotel's launch from Villa Beach. Arrangements must be made in advance with the hotel.

Nine miles south of the island of St. Vincent is Bequia, the largest island, known for its long stretches of nearly deserted beaches, snorkeling, and diving. The best beaches are at Friendship Bay, Industry Bay, Lower Bay, and Princess Margaret. The picturesque beach and hotel restaurant and bar at Friendship Bay Hotel is a comfortable spot to spend a beach day. Frangipani, overlooking the yacht harbor, is one of the best restaurants on the island.

On Canouan your best bets are the Tamarind Beach Hotel and Yacht Club or Raffles Resort; on Mayreau, Salt Whistle Bay Club and Salt Whistle Bay Beach; on Mustique, Cotton House; and on Palm Island, Palm Island Resort. Petit St. Vincent is a 113-acre private island, the location of one of the Caribbean's highest-rated resorts.

On Mayreau, a tiny one-and-a-half-square-mile cay, there is a steep, mountainous path that runs from the dock and beach at Saline Bay to Salt Whistle Bay, where there is a small, rustic hotel and a pristine beach. Both beaches are panoramic and excellent for swimming. A land taxi or water taxi will provide optional transportation. An occasional ship tenders passengers to a long stretch of so-so beach on Union Island.

SAN FRANCISCO

San Francisco is frequently described by some as the United States' most cultural, European-style city; by others as its most romantic and charming, with picture-perfect backdrops of famous bridges, bay vistas, cable cars and colorful residents; and by still others as its most liberal and hip community. Take your choice, but the fact remains that the San Francisco Bay area is one of the most popular tourist destinations in the world, steeped in history, diversity, and natural beauty.

Possibly the best way to explore the city is on foot. Walking excursions around the various neighborhoods will enable you to absorb the unique flavor of each while visiting the major places of interest. Some of the sites and experiences that are most popular with visitors include:

—Golden Gate Park: San Francisco's answer to New York's Central Park and London's Hyde Park covers 1,000 acres stretching inland from the Pacific Coast at Ocean Beach up to Stanyun Street. On a sunny day the numerous gardens and wooded paths are particularly attractive. Recreational facilities include tennis courts, a golf course, riding stables, fly-casting pools, boat rentals, and baseball, soccer, and polo fields. Within the grounds are the Steinhart Aquarium, the Morrison Planetarium, the Strybing Arboretum and Botanical Gardens, the Natural History Museum, and the Japanese Tea Garden.

—Union Square: This is the center of the city's commercial area with luxury hotels, fine restaurants, galleries, department stores, and upscale boutiques. Chinatown is directly to the north, the Financial District to the east, SoMa to the south, and Nob Hill to the west.

—Fisherman's Wharf: A perennial favorite for tourists are the shopping malls with their overpriced restaurants and shops in this area which include the Wharf, Ghiradelli Square, Pier 39, the Cannery, and the Anchorage.

—Chinatown: A stroll through Chinatown with its colorful markets, shops, and restaurants is a must for every visitor. Pass through the Gateway Arch at Bush Street and Grant Avenue and stroll along Stockton or Grant to Portsmouth Square, which is filled with locals enjoying themselves.

—Other worthwhile and popular sites include the Golden Gate Bridge, Alcatraz Island, Coit tower atop Telegraph Hill, a cable-car ride from Nob Hill to Fisherman's Wharf on the Powell-Hyde line, and a walk through Castro and Haight Ashbury (two of the city's most colorful gay and hippie neighborhoods). Museums include: the Aquarium of the Bay at Fisherman's Wharf, the Asian Art Museum at the Civic Center, the Cable Car Museum at Mason and Washington Streets, the Exploratorium (a science museum in the Marina District), Maritime National Historical Park, Wells Fargo History Museum, the Yerba Buena Center for the Arts and Yerba Buena Gardens(the city's cultural facility similar to New Work's Lincoln Center), the Berkeley Art Museum in Berkeley, and the San Francisco Museum of Modern Art near Union Square.

Along with New York, New Orleans, and Chicago, San Francisco is considered one of the great dining areas of the U.S., boasting some of the country's best restaurants, bistros, and pubs with a cornucopia of cuisine running the gamut from French, Italian, Japanese, and Chinese to Afghan, Moroccan, Vietnamese, Cambodian, and almost every other country around the world. It would be impossible to list all of the dining possibilities.

Only an hour's drive to the north lies the wine country of the Napa and Sonoma Valleys, the location of the United States' most famous wineries. Amid the mountains dipping into grapevine-trellised valleys, you will experience an entirely different environment and climate replete with some of the world's finest wineries and best restaurants. It is possible to book a hot-air-balloon ride over the entire area.

Napa Valley, with its neighboring towns and villages, is the largest and the most commercial of the two towns and has the greater number of wineries, hotels, and restaurants; Sonoma is more laid back. In Napa Valley you will find such world-class properties as Opus One, Robert Mondavi, and Domaine Chandon. The most luxurious retreat, Auberge du Soleil, is set high above a 37-acre vine grove and boasts a world-class spa and marvelous restaurant. Sonoma's more than 35 wineries include Buena Vista, Glen Ellen, Kenwood, and Sebastiani.

SOUTH FLORIDA

The vast majority of cruise ships leaving for the Caribbean and Bahamas embark from either Miami or Fort Lauderdale. Numerous hotels and resorts in these areas can accommodate pre- and post-cruise extensions for almost any pocketbook. In Fort Lauderdale, the three best hotels, all located less than ten minutes from Port Everglades, are Hyatt Pier 66, Marriott's Harbor Beach Resort, and Bahia Mar. The latter two are located on the beach and the Hyatt on the intercoastal surrounded by luxury yachts.

In Miami Beach there are literally hundreds of hotels. Some visitors prefer the art-deco, hip area of South Beach with its stream of cafes, restaurants, discos, and quaint renovated hotels, of which the Delano is the most European and most famous. Joe's Stone Crab, a South Beach icon, is the most famous eatery. Those seeking a golf resort and/or a spa will prefer the Doral Golf Resort and Spa which is inland in Miami not far from Carnival Cruise Line's headquarters.

There are numerous shopping malls, the largest being Sawgrass Mills (a 20 to 30-minute drive) and Aventura Mall, just to the north of Miami and not far from the luxurious Diplomat Hotel in Hollywood. Visitors will enjoy strolling along Las Olas in Fort Lauderdale or Lincoln Road in Miami Beach and visiting the numerous boutiques and restaurants.

An interesting drive would be along AIA, the coastal road from Miami up to Palm Beach, past luxury residential communities. Excursions may include an airboat ride through the Florida Everglades, Miami Seaquarium, Miami's Parrot Jungle, and Butterfly World in Coconut Creek.

TORTOLA, PETER ISLAND, AND VIRGIN GORDA (THE BRITISH VIRGIN ISLANDS)

Several of the cruise ships traversing the Virgin Islands spend a day at **Tortola.** From Tortola, passengers can take a ferry to St. John and to most of the British Virgin Islands. Unspoiled Peter Island Resort and Yacht Harbor is only a 20-minute ride away. There you can sunbathe and swim at one of the resort's lovely pristine beaches, have lunch, play tennis, and participate in numerous watersports.

Your ship will tender you into **Road Town,** the main city of Tortola and capital of the British Virgin Islands. Road Town is not a duty-free port; however, there are bargains on imported British goods and local handicrafts. You can take a taxi ride west to Mount Sage, the island's highest peak, where you will be rewarded with a view of Peter, Salt, Cooper, and Ginger islands. Another excellent view is at Skyworld, a mountaintop restaurant and Tortola's most popular luncheon spot.

There are good beaches with white sand and clear warm water at Smuggler's Cove, Long Bay, Apple Bay (where there is good surfing), and Cane Garden Bay. The last one is the most pristine, and if you spend the day there, you can lunch at the colorful Rhymer's Restaurant. 1748, at Long Bay Beach, is also recommended.

Scuba diving and snorkeling are popular here. The wreck of the *Rhone* is one of the most famous dive sites in the Caribbean and the location for the filming of *The Deep*. The *Rhone* was a British mail steamer that sank in 1867. Snorkelers and divers will want to visit the many reefs that follow the coastal beaches on the north side of the island, Smuggler's Cove being most snorkelers' favorite.

Those not opting to take the ferry to Peter Island can enjoy a day at one of the resorts on Tortola, which include Long Bay Hotel on the north shore and Prospect Reef Resort and Frenchman's Cay Hotel and Yacht Club on Frenchman's Cay, which is connected to Tortola by a bridge.

Virgin Gorda is one of the more picturesque and quaint of the British Virgins. Visitors will enjoy meandering through the shops and pubs in the small town near the harbor, visiting the unique "baths" where they can explore caves and natural pools formed by large boulders while snorkeling in aqua-blue waters, or spending the day at world-famous Little Dix Bay resort with its magnificent beach and lovely grounds. Some ships drop anchor at the opposite end of the island, so passengers can spend the day at Bitter End Resort or nearby Biras Creek.

TRINIDAD AND TOBAGO

Trinidad and Tobago compose a two-island republic nine miles off the coast of Venezuela that became an independent member of the British Commonwealth in 1976. Trinidad is the largest island in the southern part of the Caribbean, having an area of 1,980 square miles and a sunny, pleasant climate. Its more than one million residents are a mixture of African, East Indian, Middle Eastern, and Asian cultures. Trinidad is said to be the birthplace of the calypso, steel band, and limbo, and should your ship be in port during the evening, don't miss an exciting and colorful native show. In **Port-of-Spain**, the capital, there is "in-bound" shopping for numerous duty-free bargains that are sent by the storekeeper directly to your ship. Tobago, which lies 20 miles northeast of Trinidad and is 27 miles long by 7 ½ miles wide, offers sandy beaches, unspoiled rain forests, and coral reefs.

Trinidad boasts beautiful mountains, tropical jungles, lush plantations, and sweeping white-sand beaches. You can drive to Pitch Lake near La Brea, where tons of asphalt are excavated and shipped throughout the world, or you may wish to take the Skyline Highway to the beautiful white-sand Maracas Beach, which is surrounded by palm trees and mountains. (The major hotels are not located near the beaches.) Additionally, you can visit a sugar or coconut plantation, the Caroni Bird Sanctuary, and the Royal Botanic Gardens.

If you wish to dine in Trinidad, you may enjoy the Italian food at Lucianos and Topo Caro, the East Indian food at Gaylords or Mangals, Chinese cuisine at Tiki Village, or French-continental food in the restaurants at the Trinidad Hilton and the Normandie hotels.

In Tobago a nice beach, golf, and tennis are available at Mount Irvine Bay Hotel and Golf Club. Golf is also available at Tobago Plantation Golf & Country Club. The most highly rated resorts are Hilton Tobago located on a 5,000-foot beach surrounded by mangrove forests, Le Grand Courlan near Black Rock set on a sandy beach with a good restaurant, and Coco Reef near Pigeon Point on Coconut Bay. The best restaurants include Dillon's (International near Crown Point), Tamara's (International in the Coco Reef Resort), The Blue Crab (Caribbean/International in Scarborough), Jemmas (local at Speyside), and La Belle Creole (Cajun in the Half-Moon Blue Hotel). The best beach is at Pigeon Point, which is surrounded by Royal Palms and offers food kiosks, craft shops, paddle-boat rides, and a diving concession. The best snorkeling is at Back Bay and at Buccoo Reef off Pigeon Point. There are numerous dive operations all over the island. In the event your ship anchors off of Charlotteville, the only beach less than a two-hour drive is at Blue Water Inn near Speyside.

TURKS AND CAICOS

Although these islands lie at the extreme southeast of the Bahamian archipelago, they have a separate government and are rarely considered a part of the Bahamas. The 500 miles of coral reefs and incredible array of beaches here attract snorkelers and divers; however, there is little tourism apart from the hotels on the Providenciales, commonly referred to as "Provo."

On Provo white-sand beaches abutting crystal-clear waters stretch for 12 miles along the northeast coast. Most of the hotels and restaurants are located on or near Grace Bay Beach between Long Point and Thomas Stubbs Point. Hotels on the beach with good facilities include Beaches Resort & Spa, Grace Bay Club, Point Grace, Club Med Turkoise, Ocean Club, and Royal West Indies Resort. Anacaon at the Grace Bay Club is one of the better restaurants, featuring grilled lobster, fresh fish, and conch chowder. Aqua at Long Point, the trendiest spot, has a terrace overlooking the marina and also specializes in fresh fish and seafood. For a Mediterranean environment with Italian cuisine, Baci near Long Point is also a good choice, as is Coy-abe for continental/Caribbean fare in a tropical garden. Visitors can enjoy 18 holes of golf at the Provo Golf Club. Fishing excursions can be booked through Silver Deep, and sailing, kayaking, and parasailing are offered by B&B Tours at the Leeward Marina. For diving equipment, go to Art Pickering's Provo Turtle Divers, located in front of the Miramar resort, where tennis courts are also available.

Prior to 2006, few ships stopped at Grand Turk, where there was almost nothing of interest save some pristine beaches with few facilities. The best strand was at Governor's Beach in front of the Governor's residence. Some of the finest diving in the archipelagos is around Grand Turk and cruise ships that anchor here generally organize diving and snorkeling excursions. In 2005-2006, Carnival Cruise Line constructed a deepwater dock and a cruise center, with a shopping area, a white-sand beach with umbrellas and sheltered cabanas, and an enormous pool, which is adjacent to a Jimmy Buffet Margaritaville restaurant and watering hole. Many passengers opt to spend the day at this expansive facility. Taxis, buses, and car rentals are available here for shore excursions.

U.S. VIRGIN ISLANDS

The U.S. Virgin Islands were purchased from Denmark in 1917, and they offer the finest shopping and possibly the most beautiful beaches and most desirable climate in the Caribbean. Cruise ships dock at the islands of St. Thomas and St. Croix, and those wishing to explore St. John catch a ferry from the center of town or Red Hook Beach in St. Thomas. (Watch your time here, so you don't miss the ship.) In both St. Thomas and St. Croix, you will want to leave ample time for duty-free shopping at the hundreds of attractive stores that line the main streets. Remember that when purchasing merchandise in the U.S. Virgin Islands, your duty-free allowance increases to $1,400 and your liquor quota increases to five liters.

In **St. Thomas,** you can swim in crystal-clear waters at one of the truly beautiful beaches such as Magens Bay, Coki Point, Sapphire Bay, Red Hook, Morningstar Beach, and Limetree Beach. You may wish to visit Fort Christian, Bluebeard's Tower, and take a glass-bottom boat ride. At night, go to one of the hotels and see a local limbo show. For those who wish to play tennis and swim at one of the outstanding beaches, I would recommend spending the afternoon at the Virgin Grand Resort, which has a pool, private beach, restaurants, and tennis courts and is across the road from the fantastic Coki Beach and Coral World. Marriott recently took over and renovated Frenchmen's Reef, which also has tennis courts and is only a few minutes from where you dock; however, it is located on Morningstar Beach, which is fine for swimming but is not quite as beautiful or unspoiled as the others. The most luxurious resort is the Ritz-Carlton, which has a nice pool and small beach. There are numerous restaurants in town and in the hotels. Many cruisers have indicated that L'Escargot on the waterfront is the best.

Shoppers will enjoy exploring the hundreds of stores lined up for a mile along the main drag in town. I have found the best selections at continental (for crystal, jewelry, imported woolens, and European goods), A. H. Riise (for perfume, china, crystal, watches, jewelry, and liquors), Sparky's (for liquor), and Little Switzerland (for watches and jewelry). Branches of these shops and many others are located in the shopping mall adjacent to where your ship docks. Therefore, it is not necessary to go into town if time is limited.

From **St. Croix** you can sail out to **Buck Island** for some of the best underwater snorkeling in the Caribbean, or you can swim at one of the excellent beaches at the various hotels. The Buccaneer Hotel has a fair beach, a golf course, and excellent tennis courts. Westin Carambola Resort has a lovely beach and good restaurants, and its golf course—four miles from the resort—is considered one of the best and most picturesque in the Caribbean. Don't miss walking through the charming town of **Christiansted,** where Danish architecture is evident in the little pastel-colored homes and stores. Unfortunately, most ships dock at **Fredericksted,** and you must take a long bus or taxi ride to get to Christiansted, which is on the other side of the island.

For those travelers who have already been to St. Thomas and first-time cruisers seeking "heavenly perfection," I recommend spending the day at Caneel Bay Resort or the Westin on the island of **St. John.** To get there, you must take a 30-minute taxi ride from your cruise ship to Red Hook Bay, where you catch a ferry for a pleasant 30-minute boat ride to the island of St. John, followed by another 10-minute taxi or bus ride to the hotels. A few times each day boats leave from the center of town and go directly to St. John. This may sound like a long trip, but it is well worth it. At Caneel Bay, you can explore six virgin horseshoe-shaped, private white-sand beaches studded with palm trees; lie out on a secluded hammock overlooking the sea; swim in clear, warm waters with beautiful tropical fish weaving between your legs; play tennis on one of seven excellent courts; and have a drink and buffet or à la carte lunch in the main building or at Turtle Beach. Joggers will want to scurry down the miles of paths connecting the various beaches, facilities, and cottages; and snorkel enthusiasts will wish to head out for the nearby Trunk Bay, where appropriate equipment can be rented to explore an underwater trail of flora and coral formations. Few resorts in the Caribbean surpass the beautiful grounds of Caneel Bay.

Several smaller vessels now offer regular cruises to St. John as well as some of the more remote British Virgin Islands.

South America

Cruising to foreign lands offers you an opportunity to sample numerous ports to determine whether or not you would wish to return for a longer, in-depth vacation. Just as you can cruise to several Caribbean islands, different countries in the Far East, or various ports in the Mediterranean, so can you cruise to many of the major cities of South America. Because air travel to South America is so expensive, cruising represents an economical yet pleasurable alternative.

Most of the major cities in South America are close enough to the equator to afford year-round sunshine and mild climates. Inasmuch as the seasons are reversed in the Southern Hemisphere, even Buenos Aires has warm weather between December and April.

In recent years, several cruise lines have been tapping the wealthy South American market, promoting trips to many of the major cities, including Rio de Janeiro, Montevideo, and Buenos Aires, as well as cruises up the Amazon River. Each year vessels of the Celebrity, Costa, Crystal, Cunard, Holland America, Seabourn, and Silverseas lines stop at a number of South American ports. It is also possible to explore the Galapagos and the west coast of South America on ships of the Celebrity Cruise Line and Metropolitan Touring. Several cruise lines offer cruises that circumnavigate the continent, while others offer exploration cruises south of Argentina into Antarctica.

AMAZON RIVER CRUISES

The Amazon River, the largest river in the world and estimated to contain one-fifth of all the fresh water on earth, stretches 4,000 miles from its source in the

Andes to the Atlantic Ocean. Although oceangoing ships can navigate inland for some 2,300 miles, many of the regular cruises offering Amazon itineraries enter at Belem, the 200-mile-wide mouth of the river, traverse the Narrows of Breves, stop at Santarem, and conclude their exploration at Manaus. The river is so wide at spots that you will be unable to see the other side; however, when passing through the Narrows of Breves you are treated to miles of beautiful green flora and tributaries located on both sides of your ship. The Amazon hosts 1,500 species of fish, 14,000 species of mammals, 15,000 species of insects, and 3,500 species of birds, although few of these will be visible on your cruise.

Many cruisers opting for an Amazon River itinerary expect to experience a ride up a picturesque jungle river right out of the Tarzan movies. Unfortunately, most cruises do not afford an opportunity to explore the more primitive areas, and most of your time will be spent sailing up a brown-colored river with ever-changing scenery and some unusual, but not fascinating, ports of call.

Belem is situated on Guajara Bay at the gateway to the Amazon and is often the first or last stop for cruise ships exploring the river. The town thrived during the rubber boom of the early 1900s and is still the great trading center of the Amazon.

Your ship will either dock adjacent to the downtown area, where everything is within walking distance, or anchor at Scoraci and tender passengers ashore.

The Hilton Hotel is located in the center of the town and is a good focal point for your explorations. Points of interest include: The Jungle Park, a zoo filled with local animals in their natural habitat; the Goeldi museum, with its extensive collection of Indian artifacts; the neoclassical Teatro de Paz, built in 1874; the Basilica de Nossa Senhora de Nazere, built in 1909 as a replica of St. Peter's; the cathedral in the old colonial section of town, built in the 18th century and restored in 1887; Fort de Castelo; and Ver-o-Peso market on the waterfront.

Numerous little shops offering handicrafts and souvenir items are spread along President Vargas Street between the Hilton and the waterfront.

Many ships also commence or conclude their Amazon River cruises at **Manaus** because its airport can service large planes, affording passengers access to the middle of the Amazon by air. Although it was a thriving commercial metropolis in the late 1800s during the rubber boom, today one might refer to Manaus as the armpit of South America. However, that reference may be unfair to numerous other South American cities that deservedly have received the same accolade, yet by comparison look like Beverly Hills. Rarely can one find a city where every building, street, and sidewalk is in total disrepair and cluttered with garbage.

The city bus tour visits Sao-Sebatiao Square, the 19th-century Palacio Rio Negro, the Opera House that dates back to 1896, the Indian Museum, and the military zoo. Branches of the two largest South American jewelry chains, H. Stern and Amsterdam Sauer, offer transportation from your ship to their shops.

A more interesting option would be the riverboat ride down the Rio Negro to Lake January. Here the boat docks, and you can take a walk on a wooden bridge into a jungle swamp to a pond filled with giant lily pads and an occasional alligator. The night tour to Lake January is dedicated to seeking out alligators by flashlight. Our guide was supposed to wrestle one; however, the match never took place. Although not as picture-perfect as the all-inclusive jungle ride at Disney World, these tours are through an authentic jungle and provide an opportunity to take some unique photographs to show the fans back home. If you are more adventurous, you can attempt to hire your own boat and guide and possibly get deeper into the jungle.

Halfway between Belem at the mouth of the Amazon and Manaus lies the third-largest town in the Brazilian Amazon—**Santarem.** The population grew to 50,000 during the years of the gold rush in the 1920s.

Buses meet ships at the harbor to transport passengers to either the market-place (*mercado*), which lies about a mile and a half downstream, or inland about a mile to the Hotel Tropical, where you can relax by the swimming pool and enjoy a local beer or a *caipirinha,* the traditional drink of the region consisting of smashed lime, sugar, and rum. Santarem is less crowded and in better repair than Manaus and is therefore a more comfortable place to shop for local crafts, many of which can be purchased from the artisans right at the gangway to your ship.

Alter do Chao is a sandy beach 15 miles from Santarem on the Tapajos River. Some ships offer beach parties here.

ARGENTINA–BUENOS AIRES

Most ships that call at Buenos Aires only remain from eight to 24 hours, not permitting sufficient time to explore this cosmopolitan metropolis that is the only place in South America reminiscent of European cities in France, Spain, and Italy. Because your time will be limited, you will want to take an organized morning tour of the city, where you can visit the principal square, Plaza de Mayo; La Catedral, where you can see the tomb of General José de San Martin, the obelisk which is the symbol of the city; the Teatro Colón, an important opera house; La Boca, an Italian district near the old port area; Museo de Art; Jardin Zoologico; the botanical gardens; the Recoleta, a vast-walled complex and site of Evita's tomb; and the residence of the president.

During the afternoon, you will want to stroll down Florida and Lavalle, the major shopping streets, as well as Galerias Pacifico, where you will find excellent bargains on leather shoes and purses in addition to a good selection of European-style boutiques. The quality of the merchandise and inexpensive prices make Buenos Aires the best shopping city in South America. Visitors often enjoy having a steak with all the trimmings and a bottle of local beer or wine at a typical Argentine restaurant. Popular spots include Casa Cruz, Bar Uriarte, La Cabana, La Cabrera, and Bar Sur or El Viejo Almacea for dinner and a Tango show. The best hotels include the Four Seasons, Alvear Palace, and Faena.

BRAZIL

When taking a cruise from **Rio de Janeiro,** you'll want to arrange to stay over in this unique city for a few days at the beginning or end of the cruise. Rio's beauty is due to its natural environs in which green-clad mountains border a city of high-rise apartments and hotels situated across from a string of beaches on the Atlantic Ocean. The hotel-beach-restaurant area starts in the north at the District of Leme and continues south through the districts of Copacabana, Ipanema, Leblon, and Gavea. The best hotels in Copacabana are the Rio Palace, the Rio Othon Palace, the Copacabana Palace, and the Sofitel. In Ipanema, it's the Caesar Park. The Sheraton lies at the intersection of Leblon and Gavea, and the Intercontinental Resort Hotel is still farther away in Gavea. All of these hotels are across the road from the beach and feature private pools, numerous restaurants, shops, and bars. If you desire a resort atmosphere, you will prefer either the Sheraton or the Intercontinental, which are farther away from the main part of the city.

You can eat quite inexpensively at one of the numerous pizzerias that line the beach area, or you can sample local Brazilian and continental dishes at most of the hotel restaurants.

Tennis buffs can rent a court at either the Sheraton or Intercontinental hotels, and joggers can wear out their "New Balance specials" along the walk that stretches for six miles from Leme Beach to the end of Ipanema. Don't miss the samba show at Oba Oba or Plataforma I, nor the picturesque cable-car ride to the top of Sugar Loaf Mountain, where you have a panoramic view of the entire city. A train ride to the top of Corcovada Mountain, where the statue of Christ towers over the entire city, is also a must for all visitors. If time permits, there are organized tours to Tijuca Forest, Paradise, and the Paqueta Islands.

There are many shops and boutiques on Copacabana Avenue, two blocks up from the beach, as well as in the Ipanema area, offering leather goods, jewelry, sportswear, and local handicrafts; however, I found few bargains. Gemstones and jewelry are reputed to be the best buys. H. Stern, the world's leading retail jewelry enterprise, has shops in all the major hotels.

One of the most enjoyable stops is **Salvador** (Bahia), where you can sun on one of the two beautiful beaches at Piata and Itapoa; visit numerous cathedrals and museums throughout the city; shop for silver, jewelry, and hand-carved rosewood at Mercado Modelo, silver at Gerson shops, and arts and crafts at Instituto (Mauá); play tennis at the Hotel Méridien, which has a restaurant at the top that offers the best view of the city; or take an excursion to the island of Itaparica to swim and stroll through a small, charming town filled with parks. You will want to sample the unique Bahian cuisine (combining African and European cooking styles) at Chica da Silva, Yemanja, Lampiao, and Moenda. For French and continental cuisine, the best in town are St. Honore (at the Hotel Méridien) and Chez Bernard. With limited time, you can spend your day at either Hotel Méridien Bahia or Bahia Othon Palace, which offer good pools, shops, and restaurants.

COLOMBIA–CARTAGENA

Located on the Caribbean Coast of Colombia, this 450-year-old city of Spanish heritage has become a popular stop for ships traversing the Panama Canal.

Visitors will want to visit the 17th-century fortress of San Felipe, with its impressive walls, tunnels, and cannons; the old walled city composed of colonial-style buildings with wood balconies and red tile roofs, parks, monasteries, and monuments; La Popa Hill, 500 feet high for a spectacular view of the city; and the new city area of resort hotels, beaches, shops, and restaurants.

The best shopping is at Prerino Gallo Plaza, near the Hilton, where there are several emerald shops, leather stores, craft shops, a disco, and casino.

The beaches are crowded and dirty, and those wishing to sun and swim are best off going to the Cartagena Hilton, where there is a nice pool area, tennis courts, health club, shops, and restaurants.

Walkers and joggers may enjoy the path along the sea that starts at the old city and extends into the new city for three miles or so to the Hilton. Walking or jogging from the port to the old fortress or into the middle of town also is possible because both are only a mile or two from the harbor.

URUGUAY–MONTEVIDEO

In Montevideo you will have the best view of the city from the top of the town hall, where you can also eat lunch at Panormacico Municipal, one of Montevideo's better restaurants. Below town hall is the shopping district, where you can buy leather goods and woolens.

With only one day in port, you can take the city tour and see the obelisk, the La Carreta statue, the flea market, the natural history museum, the cathedral, and the mausoleum of José Artigas; or you can take a taxi out to the resort area of Carrasco, where you will find beautiful homes, restaurants, hotels, and beaches. Those traveling with children may wish to visit the zoological gardens and Rodo Park, an amusement park with rides, ponies, and theaters.

In the evening, there is a tango show and Uruguayan folk music at Tangueria del 40 in the Columbia Palace Hotel, dinner and dancing at El Mirador in the Hotel Oceania, and several discos including Zum Zum, Lancelot, and Ton Ton Metek.

If time allows, Punte del Este is a charming resort town with numerous excellent beaches. L'Auberge and La Posta del Cangrejo are the two best hotels on the beach with good restaurants.

VENEZUELA–CARACAS

The South American port most frequently visited by cruise ships is **La Guaira (Caracas), Venezuela.** This is the richest nation in South America because of its large oil production; however, the economic good fortune of the country has not passed down to the average man in the street, who appears to be living in relative poverty. The shacks of the poor offer a contrast to the opulent residences of the rich. Caracas is a city in a valley surrounded by mountains. The best view is from Mount Avila at its 6,500-foot summit. Check whether the cable car to the top is working—it is almost always out of order. You can also get a good view of the city from atop the Hilton Hotel.

A city tour will visit La Cathedral, with its artistically decorated interior; Santa Teresa Basilica, housing the oldest image of Christ in Venezuela; the capitol building, featuring the paintings of Tovar; Bólivar's birthplace, an outstanding example of colonial architecture; Los Caobos Park; Los Proceres Park; and the Museum of Natural Science, with its collection of stuffed animals.

There is little shopping that is worthwhile. The shops offer a variety of gold jewelry, but there are no bargains. Should you be in Caracas on Sunday, you can attend a bullfight at Plaza de Toros. For tennis or swimming, try the Macuto Hotel in La Guaira. The beach is not terrific, but the hotel has a large pool, shops, restaurants, a disco, theater, nightclub, and many facilities. Many cruisers not wishing to take the hectic tour of Caracas spend the day at the hotel.

Caracas also boasts many good restaurants offering French, Italian, and Venezuelan cuisines.

The Mediterranean, Greek Islands, Middle East, and Environs

Like the Caribbean, the Mediterranean, Adriatic, Aegean, and Black seas are calm, and the weather in the area is generally pleasant, except for certain winter months.

There are probably no cruise grounds that offer as representative a sampling of history, as great a diversity in cultures, or as many varied and exciting places of interest as the Mediterranean. Imagine climbing up to the ancient Acropolis in Athens, standing before the Wailing Wall of Jerusalem, strolling through the famous shopping bazaar of Istanbul, gambling at the posh casinos in Monte Carlo, sunning at the jet-set beaches of the Côte d'Azur or Greek islands, all in seven to 14 days.

For a number of years, various smaller Greek cruise lines have been running regularly scheduled cruises from Piraeus to the Greek islands and to the coastal cities of Turkey. Many of the vessels have seven-day itineraries calling at such ancient and legendary islands as Rhodes, Mykonos, Delos, Santorini, Crete, Corfu, and Patmos, as well as such unusual Turkish ports as Istanbul, Marmaris, and Kusadasi. Some of these ships return to Piraeus between the third and fourth day, permitting passengers with tight schedules to take only half of the itinerary.

Regular cruises to other parts of the Mediterranean and adjoining seas leaving from Genoa, Venice, Naples, Nice, Cannes, Monte Carlo, Athens, or Istanbul have recently been offered by the Celebrity, Club Med, Costa, Crystal, Cunard, MSC, Oceania, Orient, Princess, Regent Seven Seas, Seabourn, Silversea, and Windstar cruise lines. In addition to the aforementioned Greek islands and Middle Eastern ports, these cruises may call in the western Mediterranean at Capri, Sorrento, Palma de Mallorca, Barcelona, Sicily, Malta, Sardinia, Elba, Corsica, or Algeciras; in Africa or off the African coast at Casablanca, Tunis, Dakar, Tangier, Tenerife, Las Palmas, or Funchal; in the Adriatic at Split, Bari, or Dubrovnik; in the Black Sea at Odessa, Yalta, or Sochi; and in the Middle East at Haifa, Israel, Alexandria, Egypt, Beirut, or Cyprus.

Although the majority of these ports have harbors that can accommodate only the smaller vessels, the large ships can drop anchor outside the harbor and transport the passengers ashore in small tenders. Today, a growing number of large luxury liners from the above-mentioned lines are scheduling numerous cruises each summer in the Mediterranean area. These cruises appeal to Europeans as well as to Americans, and have resulted in the development of a highly competitive Mediterranean cruise program paralleling that found in the Caribbean. Unfortunately, terrorism, local wars, and general unrest have caused ships to cancel their itineraries from time to time.

The following are the highlights of some of the more popular cruise stops in this area.

ALGERIA

Algiers, with its population of 900,000, is Algeria's capital; it is a Mediterranean seaport standing on a hillside overlooking the bay. At the bottom of the hill is the modern city, and farther up is the old Moorish section called The Casbah, named for the citadel that stands on the top of the hill. The unique Casbah is an interesting section of crowded, narrow alleys, courtyards, and shops. The climate is varied, with temperatures falling to the 20s in the winter and up over 100 during the summer months. The best season to visit Algiers' "turquoise coast" is between April and November. Worth visiting are several distinguished mosques dating from the Ottoman era, the National Museum of Moslem and Classic Antiquities, the Essai Gardens, and the university. You can take a bus ride, which provides superb views of the city, to the chic residential suburb of El Biar past the palace of the president. Algiers is flanked by several fine beaches on the Mediterranean, where you can swim and snorkel from March through October. The nightlife is limited largely to hotel bars and cabarets catering to foreigners.

CROATIA

Dubrovnik is a small Croatian port with a population of 26,000 located on the Adriatic Sea across from Italy. Its mild climate and medieval architecture have made it a favorite tourist attraction. As you sail into the harbor, you will note its fjord-like coastline. From the harbor you can take a boat across to the island of Lokrum, which is a botanical preserve with interesting foliage, gardens, and a natural history museum. You can drive up Zarkovica Hill for a magnificent view of the city and swim at the beaches at Lapad and Sumratin. The area called the "old town" is completely encircled by a wall built during the 14th century. There are no motor vehicles allowed in the old town, and you will enjoy walking through the main street, Placa, and visiting St. Blaise's Church, Sponza Palace, the colorful market in Gundulic Square, the Rector's Palace, the cathedral, the Trade Union House, the tiny shops on the nearby street called *Ulica od Puca,* and the Fortress Minceta, where you can view the city from atop a circular tower at the highest point on the wall.

At the Dubrovnik President Hotel, a five-minute ride from the harbor, there are numerous bars, a glass-enclosed indoor pool, an outdoor lounge area, both a regular and a nude gravel beach, and an excellent shopping center a block away. Visitors can opt to take a scenic walk or jog back to the harbor from here—it is about two miles, all downhill.

At night you can go to one of the fine local restaurants and taste such native dishes as *borec,* a kind of flaky pastry containing cheese, meat, or fruit; *djuvech,* thin slivers of pork grilled with rice, vegetables, and pepper; *raznici,* a lamb kebab; and *kruskovac,* a pear brandy. After dinner, there are numerous nightclubs, including the outdoor Labyrinth Club at the gate of the old town that offers music, dancing, and a striptease. You can try your luck at the gambling casino, dance at a discotheque, or attend Dubrovnik's summer festival, which features ballets, concerts, and various European artists.

CYPRUS

Cyprus is an island republic in the northeast corner of the Mediterranean, south of Turkey and west of Syria. The island covers 3,500 square miles, and its 650,000 inhabitants are of Greek and Turkish origin. Cyprus has lofty mountain resorts that offer skiing during the winter, some interesting hilltop monasteries and castles, and beautiful forests filled with the regal cedar of Lebanon trees. Cruise ships generally dock at the ports of **Limassol.** Limassol is a resort town bordering the sea with many fine hotels. Le Meridien, Four Seasons, Hawaii Beach, and Amathus Beach hotels offer the most facilities, large pool areas, not-so-nice beaches, watersports, tennis, and restaurants. The entire 10-mile stretch between the harbor and Le Meridien lends itself to walking expeditions with visits to luxury hotels, restaurants, shops, and tavernas. Apart from the resort hotels and sea front, there is little of interest for tourists in this city. The old city of **Famagusta** is surrounded by an impressive wall and fortification containing such sights of historical and architectural interest as the Venetian Palace, Othello's Tower, the Church of St. Peter and St. Paul, and the Cathedral of St. Nicholas. Modern Famagusta, called Varoska, lies a mile to the south of the walled city and is a prosperous Greek community with sandy beaches, shops, tavernas, discos, and bars.

Fifty miles from Famagusta is Nicosia, which is part Greek and part Turkish. Within the walls of the Old City, you can visit St. John's Church (built in 1662) and the Folk Art Museum (formerly a Gothic monastery of the 15th century). There is also the Cyprus Museum, with well-preserved artifacts from archeological excavations. If you drive on the southern coast to the monastery of Stavrovouni, located on the crest of a mountain 2,260 feet above the sea, you can enjoy a breathtaking view of Cyprus, watch the monks at their work, and perhaps break bread with them at lunchtime. Other popular excursions include exploring the Greco-Roman theater at Curium and the wine-producing village of Omodus.

EGYPT

Ships generally dock at either Port Said or Alexandria, both of which are rather dirty, polluted port cities. **Alexandria** is the chief port and second-largest city in Egypt, lying on the northeastern end of the Nile River Delta on a strip of land between the Mediterranean Sea and Lake Mareotis. The temperatures climb from the 50s and 60s in winter to the 90s in summer. The city, which was founded by Alexander the Great in 332 B.C., was a center of Greek culture and learning, but it has lost much of its former importance under the Egyptians. You may enjoy chartering a small boat to take you on a tour of the harbor, or you may prefer to relax on the 20 miles of sandy (so-so) beaches at Montaza, Maamura, or Agami. You can visit the Catacombs of Komel Shuquafa constructed in A.D. 2, the Roman Amphitheater, the Mosque of Aboual-Abaas Mursi, and the Montaza Palace with its beautiful grounds and gardens, which were a former residence of King Farouk and today have been converted to a guesthouse for government officials. The main shopping areas are Mansheya Square, Ramle Tram Station, and the Gold Souk. However, the main reason for your visit is to permit a tour to **Cairo**, Egypt's capital, where you can explore the Egyptian Museum, which houses the most important collection of Egyptian antiquities, including the Tutankhamen treasures; Coptic Museum; Abdin Palace; the Ibn Tulun Mosque; the Sultan Hasan Mosque; the El Ashar Mosque; the "Old Cairo" area (site of numerous ancient Christian churches); or the shops at Kahn al Kahlil and the Musky Bazaar.

Certainly the highlight of any visit to Cairo is the site of the Pyramids of Giza and the legendary Sphinx, located in the Sahara Desert right outside the city. You can tour these magnificent antiquities on foot, on horseback, or by camel. Those not subject to claustrophobia may enjoy walking through the steep, low passages of the interior chambers of one of the pyramids. The Pyramid of Cheops is one of the remaining Seven Wonders of the Ancient World. Built in 2650 B.C., it is still the largest and most massive stone structure in the modern world. A convenient oasis for lunch would be the historic Mena House, a deluxe hotel that was formerly a palatial hunting lodge and is located only minutes from the pyramids. You may prefer one of the river-cruising restaurants along the Nile operated by the Oberoi Hotels group.

Those wishing to visit the antiquities of ancient Egypt will want to consider one of the Nile River cruises from **Luxor** offered by ships of Sheraton Nile Cruises, Sonesta Hotels and Nile Cruises, and Abercrombie & Kent cruise lines. At Luxor, you will want to visit the awesome ruins of Karnak, the largest temple in the world, as well as the temple of Luxor. Across the river on the western bank lies the "city of the dead," with its ornate tombs and artifacts. The ships generally conclude their cruises in **Aswân,** where you can visit the Aswan Dam.

FRANCE (INCLUDING CÔTE D'AZUR AND MONTE CARLO)

Calvi, on the island of Corsica, has recently become a port for some of the smaller cruise ships. For many years an Italian island, Corsica was sold to France in 1786. However, you may find the island more reminiscent of Greece or Italy than France. The small streets that wind around the harbor offer numerous small restaurants, cafés, souvenir shops, boutiques, and food stores. Above the harbor (a five-minute walk) sits the Citadel of Calvi, which dominates the landscape when you approach the town by boat. Walking left from the town will bring you to a long strand of beach surrounded by a pine forest. There are lounges and umbrellas for rent and numerous small bars and snack shops here. Although not well known, Calvi is a charming cruise stop where you can spend a relaxed day at the beach and browsing around the quaint little village.

Cannes and **Nice** on the Côte d'Azur (French Riviera) are the most popular cruise ports in southern France. The climate is warm and sunny throughout the year, except for the winter months, when temperatures at night and in the morning can be quite chilly. You will enjoy walking down the world's most chic promenade, "The Croissette," stopping to browse in smart boutiques or to rest at an outdoor café where you can nibble on cheese and crisp bread while you watch the beautiful French women parade by in their bikinis. The beaches in Cannes and Nice are quite colorful, although not ideal for swimming. You can drive west to **St. Tropez** and sun and swim at Tahiti Beach, which has sand and numerous rental lounges, small restaurants, bars, and facilities, but is not all that much more desirable for swimming. On all the beaches the majority of the women go topless. If your ship stops at St. Tropez, in addition to the beaches, you may enjoy exploring the numerous small boutiques and bistros in town spread along the streets and alleys around the harbor. Some of the cruise lines offer excursions from St. Tropez inland through Provence to visit the wine vineyards.

An interesting side trip would be to the old walled town of **St. Paul-de-Vence,** which rests on a hill terraced with vineyards. This charming little walled city consists of narrow, winding, cobblestone streets lined with quaint shops and villas. You can enjoy lunch and dinner at Chateau du Domaine St. Martin or Le Mas d'Artigny—two of my favorite French inns—or the Colombe d'Or, all of which are located near the city. In the evening in both Cannes and Nice, you may wish to dine at one of the many fine French restaurants, dance at a discotheque, or gamble at the elegant casinos.

The largest hotels in Cannes with the most facilities are the Majestic, the Carlton, the Martinez, and the Grand. My favorite French restaurants on the Riviera are L'Oasis, Moulins de Mougins, the Chanteclair at the Negresco, Eden Rock at Hotel du Cap, and the main dining room at Chateau du Domaine St. Martin, all of which are highly rated and *très cher.*

Monte Carlo, in the principality of Monaco, has become a popular port for smaller cruise ships that can pull right up to the docks in town. The harbor area is colorful with bars and cafés. The main tourist attraction, however, is the main square that is surrounded by the world-famous Casino of Monte Carlo, Hotel de Paris, and Café de Paris. Here you can browse through designer shops, dine at elegant restaurants in Hotel de Paris and the Hermitage, or at the more casual Cafe de Paris, or try your luck at the Casino, and soak up the ultra posh environment. Those preferring American-style gambling can be accommodated at the casino across the square from Hotel de Paris or at the former Loew's Hotel, now the Le

Monte Carlo Grand Hotel. The Palace, its gardens, and an aquatic museum sit on a hill overlooking the harbor, accessible by taxi, bus, car, or a picturesque stroll. Passengers on ships stopping at Monte Carlo or Ville France may wish to take the short drive to the ancient Village of Eze, where they will be rewarded with panoramic views, a quaint, small French town, and various dining options including the acclaimed restaurant at Chateau Chevre d'Or.

GREECE AND THE GREEK ISLANDS

Piraeus is the port of Athens and the busiest cruise port in the Mediterranean area. You will enjoy dining at one of the smaller outdoor restaurants along the waterfront, where you can select your own fish or lobster and watch it cooked to order. It is approximately a five-mile drive into Athens, where you can take in such historic sights as the ancient Acropolis, Hadrian's Arch, the Temple of Zeus, the great marble stadium, the Parthenon, the Byzantine Church of St. Elefterios, and the archeological museum. At the foot of the hill beneath the Acropolis are numerous charming garden restaurants where you can enjoy lunch or a cold drink. Dyogenes is especially enticing.

After a day of sightseeing, you may enjoy shopping for local jewelry, handicrafts, antiques, and designer fashions and furs or taking a short drive to Vouliagmeni Beach, which is a mediocre public beach with decent facilities. In the evening don't miss the impressive sound and light program across from the Acropolis, where the story of ancient Greece is recounted while music, lights, and sound effects bring the story to life. Later in the evening, you will want to visit the charming "plaka" area, where hundreds of tavernas offer authentic *bouzouki* music, Greek dancing, ouzo, and local wines. Most of the tavernas are on or near Mnisikleos Street. On a warm evening, one of the more scenic and romantic experiences in Athens is dining at Orizontas Restaurant at the top of Mt. Lycabettus while watching the sun set over the Acropolis.

If you are spending a day before or after the cruise in Athens, the best hotel is reputed to be the Grand Bretagne on Syntagma Square; however, it is quite run down and not worth the price. I would rather stay at the Hilton or Intercontinental. Only five minutes from the center of town, these hotels feature numerous restaurants along with pool and garden areas. If time permits, your best bet is the extensive resort complex that comprises the Astir Palace in Vouliagmeni, about a half-hour drive from Athens.

If you are driving to Vouliagmeni or staying at the Astir Palace complex, an excellent seafood restaurants with panoramic views is Ithaki, located on a hill about a half-mile before you reach the entrance to the Astir Palace. Ithaki is possibly one of the most romantic restaurants in Greece, serving some of the finest fresh fish and other cuisine with the friendliest, most efficient service—well worth the trip.

When taking a taxi, be certain to obtain some idea of the correct fare before embarking. Often the meters are not working, or when they are, the driver may frequently adjust the meter up as the trip progresses.

Corfu is the northernmost Greek island, located in the Ionian Sea, and has a population of a little more than 100,000. The best weather is in late spring and early fall, with the summers being quite hot. Its 229 square miles are covered with green mountains, beautiful flowers, and millions of gnarled olive trees. Don't miss swimming in the warm, calm Ionian Sea at one of the hotels or taking a horse-and-buggy ride through the quaint little town with its winding streets and interesting people. Places of interest include: the Achilleion Palace, the Archeological Museum, the 14th-century Palaio Frourio (literally old fortress), the royal palace museum complex, and the Esplanade.

You may wish to spend your day at the Corfu Holiday Palace (formerly the Corfu Hilton) overlooking "Mouse Island," two and a half miles from town, or the Astir Palace on Komeno Bay, six miles out of the city. These hotels feature lovely pools, beaches, watersports, and good restaurants. The Corfu Holiday Palace boasts a very picturesque setting. You can spend a part of the day by the pool, then have lunch, followed by a climb down the olive tree-clad hill leading to the azure-blue sea and the bridge over to Mouse Island.

One of the more picturesque areas in Corfu is the beach at Paleokastritsa. It has little grottos, restaurants, and an incomparably beautiful setting. Other nice beaches more suitable for swimming can be found at Glifada on the west coast, Sidari on the north coast, Dassia and Ipsos on the east coast, and Kavos at the southern tip of the island. Those wishing to take a scenic drive, reminiscent of the Amalfi Drive in southern Italy, should start at the beach at Dassia and proceed north to the charming village of Kassiopi, passing through Ipsos, Nissaki, Kalami, and Kouloura.

Crete (Heraklion) is located 81 miles south of mainland Greece between the Aegean and Mediterranean seas. It is the largest and most important of the Greek islands, covering 3,200 square miles and having a population of 483,000. A chain of high mountains divides the island into four distinct regions, each having a different scenery combining to form the impressive beauty of the Cretan landscape. The people are friendly and hospitable and often can be seen in local costumes observing their age-old traditions. The Archaeological Museum of Heraklion has 23 halls that house the remains of the highly developed Minoan civilization, which flourished for more than 2,000 years. If you drive out to Knossos, you can see a maze of ruins, including the remarkable excavation of the partially restored palace of King Minos. You can also drive out to a fishing village in the south and spend a quiet day swimming and sunbathing.

Delos, an uninhabited island 1½ miles southwest of Mykonos in the center of the Aegean Sea, was the legendary birthplace of Zeus's children, Apollo and Artemis, and the most sacred of the Greek islands during Hellenistic times. Under Roman rule, the island grew in stature and wealth, only to be ravaged later by wars and pirate raids. Today, cruise ships dock for a few hours to enable passengers to walk through the ancient ruins, visit the island's small museum, and see the most impressive remains—the lions made of Naxos marble. Delos is considered to be one of the greatest open-air archeological museums in the world.

Katakolan lies 193 miles due west of Athens in the northwest Peloponnese. Cruise ships stop here on the way to Athens to permit passengers to explore the ancient city of Olympia, where the first Olympic races were held in 776 B.C. Set between the Alphios and Kladeos Rivers in a pine-shaded valley is the site of some important archaeological treasures. Places to visit include the Temple of Zeus (456 B.C.); the Temple of Hera (600 B.C.); the Archeological Museum, which houses numerous ancient Greek sculptures; Praxiteles' statue of Hermes; the Head of Hera; Paionios' Winged Victory; and athletic paraphernalia from the ancient games. For visitors wishing to spend a relaxing day by the sea, it is only a 20-minute taxi drive to Aldemar Hotel's Olympic Village complex, which is a large first-class property situated on several miles of brown-sand beach with two inviting free-form swimming pools, tennis courts, a few shops, and a good restaurant to sample Greek specialties for lunch. Also, there are several souvenir shops, boutiques, and tavernas in the town adjacent to the harbor where ships dock.

Situated in the Aegean Sea not far from the coast of Turkey lies **Kos,** a 170-square-mile island with 20,000 inhabitants. It is rich in history, but is best known as the birthplace of Hippocrates, the "father of medicine." Most of the important sites are within walking distance of the harbor; however, many visitors opt to rent bicycles, which of course permit greater mobility for exploring the island. Surrounding the harbor are hundreds of small souvenir shops offering T-shirts, beach attire, leather goods, gold, and pottery, as well as small taverns and restaurants. There are a number of beaches near the town of Kos, including Psalidi, Lambi, and Aghios Fokas. Seven miles west of town is a somewhat better beach at Tinzaki, and two miles farther is a nice sandy beach at Marmari. From the harbor, charter boats offer trips to neighboring islands.

Ancient Kos has two sections. Immediately adjacent to the harbor is the famous Castle of the Knights of St. John, which is a fortress with two enclosures dating back to the 14th and 15th centuries. It is surrounded by a deep moat, and it was originally built as a medical center. Nearby are several Turkish mosques and the famous Hippocrates Tree, reputed to be the oldest tree in Europe and the site where Hippocrates treated the sick.

Southwest of the harbor in the other section of ancient Kos, you can visit impressive ruins, including a vast Roman bath, the Casa Romana, with its well-preserved mosaic floor from the third century A.D. depicting the abduction of Europa by Zeus, the 14-tier Odeon from the Roman period, and the remains of the old Roman Way.

Two miles south of the town of Kos is the sacred shrine of Asklepion, the god of healing. Considered the first medical school in the world, it dates back to the fifth century B.C., when Hippocrates opened the school to encourage the study of medicine. The island was the center of medical practice in ancient times.

Mykonos is the favorite island of the young, bargain travelers as well as the jet set. Here you can stroll through little whitewashed towns with windmills and winding streets, shop for bargains in handmade woolens and jewelry in its small boutiques, buy a designer dress from Galatis at his shop right off the main square, or swim and sun at one of its many excellent sandy beaches on the crystal-clear, blue Aegean Sea. The three best beaches, which can only be reached by taxi or a short boat ride, are the Paradise, the Super Paradise, and the Ilia. The first features nude bathing. Ilia is the most beautiful of the three. There is also a nice beach two miles from town, San Stephanos. The town is known for its windmills on the site of the ancient city, its hundreds of small churches and its mascot, Petros the Pelican, who can be found strolling near the harbor. In the evening you will want to visit the tavernas and cafés bursting with the sounds of *bouzouki* music and fragrant with the aroma of ouzo, coffee, and baklava. The three most upscale restaurants in town are Catrin, Philippi, and Edem.

Nafplion, Greece's first capital after the Greek War of Independence of the 1820s, is located four miles across the Argolic Gulf from Argos, in the Peloponnese area of Greece. The town is known for its three fortresses: the 1714 citadel of Palamidi, which served as a prison until 1980; the Akronalphia fortress, which served as a prison until 1956; and Bourtze, a tiny island fortress 600 yards offshore, which dates back to 1472. This is a big tourist destination for Greeks and other Europeans, with numerous walking streets lined with a mélange of shops and small restaurants. Many of the seaside eateries offer fish and typical Greek fare. The town boasts some of the creamiest gelati in the country, as well as the 18th-century Venetian arsenal that dominates the Plateia Sykntagma. The town is a base for tours to the ancient ruins in Mycenae (site of Europe's oldest monumental structure, the famous Lion's Gate) and ancient Corinth with its archeological wonders of the kingdom of Pelops.

Patmos is in the northern section of the Greek islands, lying close to Asia Minor in the Aegean Sea. This tiny island of only 13 square miles with 2,500 inhabitants is the most sacred of the Greek islands today. It was here that John the Apostle wrote the Apocalypse (the Book of Revelation). The site where St. John saw his prophetic visions is marked by a Byzantine-style church. You can also visit the grotto where he lived or the 11th-century monastery nearby that houses priceless manuscripts and religious works of art. You can walk or ride up to the monastery, which offers some of the most spectacular and beautiful views you may ever experience; or you can swim at one of the colorful sandy beaches— Griko Beach and Dikofti Beach being the most popular.

Rhodes, with its area of 540 square miles and population of 64,000, is located 12 miles off the coast of Turkey in the Aegean Sea. The island's long and eventful history is represented by pre-Hellenic temples, Byzantine churches, mosques and minarets, classical monuments, medieval walled towns, fortresses, and picturesque little villages. This large, fertile island was called "Bride of the Sun" by Homer and "Island of Roses" by more recent poets. In ancient times, it was a prosperous island, and the medieval Knights of St. John of Jerusalem settled here and built a walled, fortified city that is now the best-preserved such town in the Mediterranean area. Rhodes divides into the new and the old town. The new town consists of hotels, boutiques, restaurants, and public beaches; the old town situated near the harbor behind the walls of the Castle of the Knights is a maze of narrow cobbled streets, arched facades, and antiquities. Here you will find hundreds of small tourist shops, tavernas, and restaurants as you work your way up to the historic sights. Sightseeing in the old town of Rhodes should include the 14th-century Castle of the Grand Master, the remarkable Street of the Knights, the mosques built during the Turkish occupation, and the quaint Jewish synagogue.

This is possibly the most developed resort area in the Greek islands, with hundreds of hotels, the most fashionable being the Rodos Palace, three miles from town. All the large hotels feature desirable shops, restaurants, and swimming pools and are situated on beaches. Most of the beaches are dirty, pebbly, and hot; however, the water is clear, warm, and delightful for swimming. There are numerous good indoor/outdoor restaurants near the Grand Hotel in the center of town; and several of the outdoor garden restaurants in the old town area appear inviting.

In the evening, you may enjoy the sound and light performance in the Palace of the Knights or the wine festival at Rodini Park, where you can consume all the wine you can drink for a few drachmas.

Beach enthusiasts will prefer to take the scenic 32-mile drive across the east coast of the island past charming villages set among orchards and olive trees to the town of Lindos, where there are sandy beaches that offer excellent swimming. Here you also can ride a donkey up to the ancient acropolis situated on top of a scenic hill, browse through souvenir shops, and have a beer at a local Taverna.

Santorini, the site of Greece's active volcano, is located on the Aegean Sea, north of Crete and south of Mykonos. The bay on the west coast was once part of the island that sank after a violent eruption of the volcano. Your ship will anchor in the harbor and you can either take a donkey ride or a cable car to the whitewashed town of Thira, with its narrow streets perched on the edge of a steep cliff rising from the sea and offering a superb panorama. An important site is the ancient ruins of Akortiri. The excavations date back to 2000 B.C., when the town was destroyed by earthquakes and volcanic eruptions. Akortiri is one of the best-preserved ruins of a Greek town in existence. You can visit the Boutari Winery, located midway between Thira and Akortiki, where you can tour the winery and taste a selection of Boutari wines. Strolling through the winding streets of Thira, with its small shops, rooftop restaurants, small hotels, and outside cafés overlooking the sea, is a delightful experience. Kastro and Zafora, near the cable-car station, offer a nice selection of Greek dishes and beverages and afford an excellent panorama of the town and harbor. Sphinx, across the walk from Atlantis Hotel, features a continental menu and overlooks the harbor. The two most highly regarded upscale restaurants, Selene and Aris, are only open for dinner. Palia Kameni, to the right of Sphinx, is a small, pleasant al fresco bar, a good choice for a drink with a view.

Skiathos is an incredibly charming, pine-studded island that has not yet suffered the effects of the hordes of European tourists that inundate Mykonos, Rhodes, and Corfu. This beautifully pristine haven in the Northern Aegean boasts colorful shops and cafés that line the waterfront's cobblestone streets, and sandy strands that beckon beachgoers to enjoy the warm waters of the azure sea. The best beach is at Koukounaries, situated at the foot of the Skiathos Palace Hotel, a 20 minute bus or taxi ride from the harbor. Unusual rock formations and a secluded beach can be found at Lalaria, which is accessible by boat. In addition to the beaches, tourists will enjoy strolling through the streets that emanate from the harbor, browsing through the small shops, and having a drink or light meal at one of the numerous outdoor cafés.

ISRAEL

Israel is the small nation on the eastern shore of the Mediterranean founded in 1948 as a homeland for Jews from all parts of the world. The weather is most pleasant in the spring and fall, when the days are warm and the evenings cool. Your ship may dock at **Haifa,** where lovely Mount Carmel descends to the sea. If you only have a short time in port and cannot drive to Jerusalem, you can spend a delightful day in the vicinity of Haifa, where you can visit the Bahai Temple, Elijah's cave, the artist colonies at Ein Hod and Safad, the Druze villages, and a nearby kibbutz (a communal farm where the residents grow the food they eat and lead an industrious, self-sufficient life, seldom leaving their own community). You may wish to relax and have lunch or dinner at the Rondo Grill in the beautiful Dan Carmel Hotel, which offers a spectacular view of the city and harbor, or at the nearby Dan Panorama Hotel. If you have time, take in a local folkloric show with Israeli dancing and singing, and try Israel's delicious answer to the hot dog— a *falafel* sandwich, hummus (mashed chick peas and olive oil), vegetables, and spicy yogurt sauces stuffed into pita bread.

If your ship docks at Ashod or anchors overnight in Haifa, you will have time to drive down the coast to **Tel Aviv,** a modern, industrious Israeli city. There are lovely beaches here and in the nearby suburb of Herzliya. In the evening, you will enjoy walking through the quaint streets and shops in the old town of Jaffa, where there are good continental and Israeli restaurants and nightclubs. The most highly acclaimed French-continental-Israeli restaurants in Tel Aviv are Twelve Tribes at the Sheraton and Mesa, and for typical Middle Eastern specialties, your best bet is Shaul's Inn near the Carmel market. If time allows, you may want to stay overnight at one of the deluxe seashore hotels such as the Hilton, Dan Panorama, Sheraton, Carlton, Hyatt, Intercontinental or Holiday Inn.

You can drive to **Jerusalem** in about an hour from Tel Aviv. Within the walls of the old city are contained some of the holiest sanctuaries of Christianity, Judaism, and Islam. After entering one of the historic gates, you will walk through winding, narrow streets lined with shops and intriguing passageways to the Western Wall or "Wailing Wall," the holiest of Jewish sites and the only remnant of the walls surrounding the temple of biblical times. You can walk down the Via Dolorosa, with its 14 Stations of the Cross, to the Church of the Holy Sepulchre, which stands on Golgotha, the traditional site of the crucifixion of Jesus. The Dome of the Rock nearby marks the spot where Mohammed is said to have ascended to heaven. While in Jerusalem, you may also wish to see the Chagall windows at the Hadassah Hospital, the Kennedy Memorial, Yad Vashem, the memorial to the Holocaust, the Dead Sea Scrolls at the Shrine of the Book, the Knesset building, and the views of the city from the Mount of Olives and Mount Scopus. If you wish to sample typical Middle Eastern dishes in a comfortable atmosphere, you will enjoy Minaret Restaurant at Eight King David Street, where four generations of Abo Salah's family have entertained locals, tourists, and dignitaries since 1960. Start off with a tasting of mixed salads including hummus, tahina, baba ganush, and several other varieties followed by a sampling of grilled meats and poultries on skewers. Currently popular French-continental restaurants include Arcadia, Mishkenot Sha'anim, Katy's, Darna (Moroccan/French/Kosher), and Ocean (seafood); however, in Israel many upscale restaurants frequently come and go. The best hotel facilities are at the King David Hotel, which is a centrally located hotel with a great deal of old-world charm; the Hilton next door; Laromma; the Sheraton; and the Hyatt, which sits on Mount Scopus near Hadassah Hospital overlooking the old city.

Bethlehem is only a short drive from Jerusalem, and you can continue on to the famous Dead Sea. Here you can float in hot water so dense with salt that it is impossible to sink. If time allows, you will want to visit historic **Masada,** the recently uncovered ruins of the mountaintop fortress where an entire city of Jews made a last stand against the Romans in A.D. 70, all preferring to take their lives rather than surrender. Continuing back to Haifa, you can take a lovely drive past the Sea of Galilee, Tiberius, and the Golan Heights.

ITALY

Civitavecchia Port of **Rome:** The crowded port at Civitavecchia has become a popular choice among cruise lines for embarking and disembarking passengers because of its proximity to Rome's international airport. Just as Rome wasn't built in a day, it is probably impossible to adequately explore this expansive metropolitan city in a day. Therefore, many cruise lines offer pre- and post-cruise land options in the eternal city. Should this only be a one-day stopover, and you have never visited Rome, you probably are best off taking one of the ship's organized tours. However, for those who have been there before or who have opted for the pre- or post-cruise stay over, there is a plethora of possibilities to discover.

Although one would have to spend a week here to thoroughly explore the environs, given limited time, the following would be the most important, "don't miss" points of interest: St. Peter's Square and the Vatican, home of the Pieta by Michelangelo, as well as the Vatican Museum and the Sistine Chapel with the paintings of Michelangelo; the Roman Forum and the nearby Colosseum; the Pantheon, the most intact building from ancient Rome located near the Piazza Navona; the Catacombs of the Appian Way; the Piazza di Spagna (Spanish Steps) leading up to the Borghese Gardens and the famous Galleria Borghese with its numerous Italian masterpieces; the cafes and shops along the Via Veneto; Trevi

Fountain; Galleria Nazionale d'Arte Antica, which is located in the Palazzo Barberini, with paintings from the 13th to 16th century; Michelangelo's statue of Moses located in the Church of San Pietro in Vincoli; and the old Jewish Ghetto near Campo de'Fiori and the Theater of Marcellus.

Serious shoppers will prefer the designer boutiques that line the streets that are across from the Piazza di Spagna, including Via Borgognona and Via Condotti. Other major shopping streets would include Via del Corso, Via Francesco Crispi, Via Frattina, Via Sistina, Via Vittorio Veneto, and Via Barberini. Although it would be difficult to picture the following suggestion without a map, a walking tour that would cover most of this would start at the Spanish Steps, visiting the shops on the streets across from the bottom of the steps, then ascending to the top and following Via Sistina to Piazza Barberini and continuing on to Via Vittorio Veneto, and ending at the Via Veneto, where you can stop for a beverage or lunch at an outdoor café. After this pause you can continue on to the Borghese Gardens. After exploring Galleria Borghese, you can proceed through this colorful park and end up back at the Spanish Steps. With a map, this will not be as difficult as it sounds.

There are hundreds of hotels and restaurants in Rome, as in any large city. Your best bet for lunch is to opt for one near where you're touring that looks appealing and has a menu in your price range. There are a concentration of restaurants on the Piazza Navona, on the Via Veneto, and in the Trastevere area. The most expensive hotels, including Hassler, Lord Byron, Eden, and Excelsior, all boast excellent restaurants. However, there are many fine moderately priced restaurants as well.

Elba is a small Italian island with 91 miles of coastline lying in the Mediterranean between Corsica and mainland Italy, and is best known as Napoleon's place of exile in 1814. His residence in Portoferraio and country home in San Martino are still open today as museums for visitors. Ships dock at the capital, Portoferraio, a busy, not-so-beautiful port town with a few shops, restaurants, a fortress, and a decent public beach (with pebbles and no sand). For those not venturing out from town, La Ferrigna is touted to be the place for lunch to try Elban cooking with emphasis on fresh fish and seafood.

After taking a tour around the island, which should include Napoleon's country home in San Martino, the port town of Porto Azzurro, and the fishing village at Marciana Marina, you may wish to have lunch and spend the afternoon at the beach areas at Procchio, Marina di Campo, or the Bay of Biodola. The Bay of Biodola is only a 10-minute drive from port and has a long strand of brown-sand beach, a lovely setting, and numerous upscale hotels with private beach areas, pools, and restaurants. The Heritage is probably your best bet.

Genoa, Portofino, Cinque Terre, and **Environs:** Genoa is Italy's largest port and ranks second in size only to Marseilles among Mediterranean ports. Few ships stop at Genoa as a port of call unless they are embarking from that city. Most ships anchor off of Portofino and tender into its charming, picturesque harbor.

It has been said that Genoa is a city of layers or levels: the lowest level is the noisy and dirty harbor area, with its ships, dance halls, and bars; the middle level contains large hotels, shops, good restaurants, cinemas, the opera house, and the Via Garibaldi, with its chain of late Renaissance palaces; and the upper level is a series of hills, winding streets, and funiculars. Genoa lies in the middle of Italy's two Rivieras, and you can drive to such seaside resort towns as San Remo, Rapallo, Santa Margarita Ligure, Portofino, La Spezia, and Viareggio.

With only limited time, your best bet is to drive to Portofino, 50 miles southeast of Genoa. As previously mentioned, the vast majority of ships visiting this area of Italy tender passengers directly into the horseshoe-shaped harbor of Portofino. Here you can explore small boutiques, souvenir shops, and small outdoor cafes. Since the entire town is so small, your exploration will take only a few hours. You may wish to take the uphill climb to the fashionable Splendido Hotel, a yachtsmen's rendezvous perched on the side of a mountain overlooking the harbor. Here you can enjoy lunch or a drink with a panoramic vista. The hotel recently built an annex right on the harbor where the tender leaves you off, appropriately named Splendido Mare. An alfresco lunch here is also excellent and memorable. Another possibility would be to take the 10-minute bus ride or 50-minute walk from Portofino to the neighboring town of Santa Margarita Ligure. This is also a colorful village with more hotels, shops, and restaurants than you will find in Portofino.

The coastline towns commonly referred to as the Cinque Terre lie five miles east of Genoa and are set among olive and chestnut groves on a steep, rocky terrain overlooking the sea. They include the communities of Monterosso, Vernazza, Corniglia, Manarola, and Riomaggiore. Most cruise ships anchor off the coast of Portovenere, which is adjacent to these communities. The best way to explore the area and enjoy the landscape is by excursion boat. For the more hearty (Olympic types), 14 walking trails are available for wandering from town to town. The easiest, shortest, and most popular scenic walk is between Riomaggiore and Manarola. The only sandy beach is a crowded strand in Monterosso. Typical restaurants for Lingurian seafood abound in each of the communities.

Livorno Port for **Florence:** Since Florence is not located on the sea, ships call at Livorno to enable passengers to take overland trips to Florence, Pisa, and Siena. Usually the ships will offer expensive bus tours to Florence; however, it is possible to take an hour-and-a-half train ride from Livorno for as little as $11 round trip. Although Florence is one of Italy's largest cities, it is possible to get around by foot while covering all the major points of interest. The distance from the train station to the famous Ponte Vecchio (old bridge) is only a bit over a mile.

Your sightseeing should include visits to the Galleria dell'Accademia, home of Michelangelo's famous statue of David (be prepared for a very long wait to get in); Galleria degli Uffizi, one of the world's outstanding museums and Italy's finest collection of art; the Cathedral of Santa Maria del Fiore (Duomo), with its unique bell tower designed by Giotto; Santa Croce, a Franciscan Gothic church with frescoes by Giotto, as well as the tombs of Michelangelo, Machiavelli, Rossini, and Galileo; the 13th-century Palazzo Vecchio with its 308-foot tower, once home to the Medici; and the colorful area surrounding the Ponte Vecchio, spanning the Arno River, surrounded by shops and small trattorias. The shops on the bridge carry exquisite jewelry by some of Italy's great designers.

Florence also offers numerous designer boutiques, the best of which are located on Via dei Tornabuoni, Via Vigna Nuova, and Via Porta Rossa. Some of the city's most excellent restaurants include Enoteca, I Quattro Amici, Alle Murate, and Sabatini's. For a less expensive meal, try Cavallino, Buca dell'Orafo, or Le Fonticine. Many tourists enjoy sipping a cappuccino or other beverage on Piazza della Signoria, one of the country's most dramatic squares. For a splendid panorama of the city, you can cross the Arno and climb up a small hill to Piazzale Michelangelo, where a bronze copy of Michelangelo's David dominates the square.

Naples, Sorrento, Capri, Amalfi, and **Positano:** Many ships visit Naples or Sorrento on their way to and from Rome. Accessible from both ports are the ruins of Pompei, the island of Capri, and the romantic villages of Positano and Amalfi that sit along the picturesque Amalfi Drive.

If your ship stops in Naples, it is quite easy to take the one-hour hydrofoil ride to the island of Capri, or to take the 15-mile drive to Pompei. If you wish to visit the towns along the Amalfi Drive, you must first take a 30- to 60-minute drive to either Sorrento or Salerno, where you gain access to this fantastically beautiful and breathtaking coastal road that winds around cliffs and passes through quaint little seaside towns. Recently, ships more frequently tender in to Sorrento because it is more accessible for exploration of the Amalfi coast and it only takes 20 minutes to travel by hydrofoil from here to Capri.

Tours to Pompei include an explanation of the well-preserved ruins of this ancient city destroyed by the eruption of Mount Vesuvius in 79 A.D. The crater of Mount Vesuvius can be ascended by chairlift. In the city of Naples, you can visit the National Museum to see its valuable art collections and relics from Pompei. Also worthwhile are the Aquarium of Naples, the San Carlo Opera House, and many of the beautiful churches and castles.

If you do not take an organized tour along the Amalfi Drive, it is possible to rent a car or hire a taxi for the day. You will want to explore the quaint seaside towns of Amalfi and Positano and drive up to Ravello for an exquisite view of this entire area. Positano, with its pedestrian path lined with shops and boutiques that winds down the cliff from the main road to the sea, is the most frequented town for tourists. Two outstanding and romantic resorts in Positano are San Pietro and Le Sirenuse, both excellent places to stop for lunch or dinner. Next 2 is also a highly touted restaurant. In Amalfi, another charmer is the Santa Catarina. Those wishing to stop here for lunch will take an elevator from the main hotel through the cliff to an outdoor terrace surrounded by citrus trees, overlooking the sea and the pool. In Palermo, the best place for lunch with an awesome view of the other towns and sea is the terrace of the Hotel Palumbo, where the proprietor will serve you wine from the hotel's own vineyards.

From either Naples or Sorrento you can take the hydrofoil (*aliscafi*) to the beautiful, floral Isle of Capri, where you will be dropped off in a pretty little harbor.

You must then purchase a ticket to take the short ride up the funicular railway to the main square, where you can sit at an outdoor café and watch one of the world's most colorful assortment of tourists pass by. There is a pebbled beach at Marina Piccolo, but it is probably not worth the effort if your time ashore is limited. The best hotel in Capri is the Grand Quisisana, which sits at one end of the path that leads from the town square. Lunch by the pool here or dinner at Restaurant Quisi in the hotel are truly rewarding experiences. There are many designer shops that line the path from the main square to Hotel Quisisana, as well as on the path that leads from the hotel toward the point where tourists go to take photos of the Faraglioni Rocks. Other options include a short bus ride up to Anacapri, another town that sits at the top of the mountain where there are additional hotels, restaurants and shops, and panoramic views down to Capri Town and the sea, as well as a boat ride from the main harbor to the famous Blue Grotto or around the island.

This area south of Naples (Amalfi, Positano, Sorrento, Ravello, and the Isle of Capri) is possibly the most beautiful part of Southern Europe and should not be missed.

Sardinia: If your ship visits Port Cervo on the Costa Smeralda area of this Mediterranean island, you will tender into a harbor with a large concentration of luxury yachts. You can browse through boutiques and shops that surround the harbor and are located in the nearby Hotel Cervo, play 18 holes of golf at the Robert Trent Jones-designed Pevero Golf Club, or spend the day at a beach. Since all the beaches are public, you may wish to visit the beach adjoining the luxury resort Cala di Volpe (about a 10-minute taxi ride from the harbor). If you are willing to pay the price, you can join the resort's affluent clientele for an extremely lavish lunch buffet. Other luxury resorts located nearby include Romazzino and Pitriccia.

Sicily is an Italian island off the coast of Italy with an area of 9,900 square miles, making it the largest island in the Mediterranean. Its 4,800,000 inhabitants live in a mild climate, with the average temperature ranging from 45 degrees (F) in the winter to 80 degrees (F) in the summer. Cruise ships stop either at Palermo or at the port cities of Naxos, Messina, or Catania for visits to Taormina.

In Palermo, you can browse through the fine shops on the Via Liberta, Via Roma, and Via Ruggero Settimo and visit the old Royal Palace, which contains a lovely chapel well known for its mosaics and marble floors. You can take a taxi to the sanctuary on Monte Pellegrino at 2,000 feet above sea level, offering a striking view of the island. From Palermo, you can drive to Syracuse to see a classical production at the ancient Roman amphitheater. You can drive to Mondello, where there are pleasant beaches and fine seafood restaurants; or you may prefer spending the day at Citta Del Mare in Terrasini, 20 miles away, which is a Club Med-style resort village complete with 11 tennis courts, a miniature golf course, an Olympic-size pool, a series of water slides leading down to the sea, a cinema, a discotheque, and several restaurants and bars.

If your ship docks at a port on the east coast of the island, you can take a tour, a taxi, or public bus to the resort town of Taormina. This picturesque village winds in and out of hills, then drops to the sea. Any stop at Taormina should include a visit to the Greek-Roman Theater, an illustrious monument built by the ancient Greeks and rebuilt by the Romans. The shops and better restaurants are located in the center of the city, which lies high up in the hills. If time permits, a nice place to visit and have lunch is the San Domenico Palace. This is an old monastery converted to an elegant hotel, replete with hundreds of original antiques and Renaissance paintings. The gardens here are beautiful and afford a breathtaking panorama of the coast and sea below. The craggy coastline is dotted with European-style beaches, (not particularly attractive), where you can rent chairs and purchase snacks and drinks. There is little shopping on the beaches, and the restaurants that line the streets, by and large, are mediocre.

Above Taormina is the world-famous volcano Mount Etna. Rising 10,784 feet from the sea, it is the highest volcano in Europe. You can take a tour to the 6,000-foot level and have lunch, then continue up to the observatory at 9,000 feet.

Venice: This most unusual and fabled city on the Adriatic, lying on a cluster of small islands divided by canals, has been the subject matter of many novels and the photogenic centerfold for countless cruise and travel brochures. Most of the larger cruise ships dock at the maritime terminal near the railroad station, a 10-minute Vapori (motorboat bus) ride, or an hour's walk from the city's main plaza, Piazza San Marco. However, some smaller vessels and riverboats pull up on the Grand Canal, about a 15-minute stroll in a westerly direction to San Marco.

In this famous piazza (square), surrounded by shops and restaurants with outdoor cafés, inundated with swarms of pigeons, is the Palace of the Doges, with its Italian Gothic-style architecture and priceless collection of paintings, linked by the Bridge of Sighs to an infamous prison; the Basilica di San Marco, a fine example of Byzantine architecture; and the Campanile, an old bell tower that dominates the city's skyline, with an elevator to the top for a birds-eye view of the city. From late afternoon, throughout the evening, tourists swarm to the numerous outdoor cafés that line the square for an espresso or other beverage while listening to romantic Italian bands. The two most famous and most pricey cafes are Quadri and Florian. You may remember this as the sight where Rossano Brazzi picked up Katherine Hepburn in the 1950's movie *Summertime.*

In front of the Piazza you can charter a private gondola for a ride through the winding canals that compose the streets of Venice. Directly behind the Piazza, you can embark on your journey through the narrow streets lined with shops and restaurants that meander across picturesque stone bridges to the famous 16th-century Rialto Bridge. Spanning the bridge, and in this general area, you will find outdoor shopping stalls with inexpensive souvenirs and "knock-off items." The better shops are located in the streets between San Marco and the Rialto Bridge. Items indigenous to Venice are the decorative paper mache masks and, of course, the world-famous Venetian Glass, which is manufactured on the nearby island of Murano. There are tours to Murano to visit the factory and watch the artisans blow the glass into varied designs.

Those wishing to dine ashore can wander into countless small trattorias, not all of which are that rewarding, in spite of their appealing appearance. The best restaurant within easy walking distance of San Marco is Do Leone in the Londra Palace Hotel. Other excellent choices are the rooftop restaurant at the Royal Danieli and the restaurants on the Canal at the Gritti Palace and Bauer Grunwald. These are also the best hotels for a pre- or post-cruise overnight, the Londra Palace being the less expensive, more intimate gem. Many tourists (of which I am not one) feel it is a must to visit the famous Harry's Bar, immediately to the west of San Marco. For a special treat, have lunch by the pool or dinner overlooking the Canal at the Hotel Cipriani on Giudecca Island, a five-minute ride by the hotel's private water taxi from the dock, also immediately to the west of San Marco. This is the best full-facility resort in Venice and one of the most luxurious in Italy.

The most famous art museums are Accademia, featuring Italian masters spanning the 14th to the 18th century, and Collezione Peggy Guggenheim at Venier dei Leoni, with its comprehensive modern-art collections, including works of Picasso, Chagall, Pollock, and Dali.

For those who have already explored Venice, I suggest an optional excursion to the island of Lido, a 20-minute Vapori ride from San Marco or a 30-minute Vapori ride from the maritime station. This is a clean, floral island with a nice assortment of restaurants, shops, and hotels, as well as a casino. The largest hotels with piers and sand beaches are the Grand Hotel des Bain and the Excelsior Palace.

MALTA

Malta, an island located in the Mediterranean between Italy and Africa, previously part of the British Commonwealth, is today a self-governing constitutional monarchy. The climate is mild during the winter and dry and hot in the summer. After your ship pulls into the port city of **Valletta,** you can charter a horse-and-buggy and ride into the main section of town. You will find some fine examples of baroque and Renaissance art and architecture if you visit the Palace of the Grand Masters, the Royal Malta Library, or the Cathedral of St. John. Other attractions include the view from the Upper Barrakka Gardens, the fortified peninsulas of Vittoriosa and Seneglea, the town of Cospicua and the Mediterranean Conference Center's audiovisual production about Maltese history. You may enjoy stopping for lunch at the venerable Phoenecia Hotel (now a Meridien), adjacent to town, or take a 20-minute drive to the Malta Hilton or the Westin hotels. Lace, homespun cotton clothes, and wool rugs are the best buys; however, shopping is not particularly attractive here. In the evening you may wish to stroll through the area referred to as "The Gut," with its dives, honky-tonks, beer parlors, and cabarets.

MOROCCO

Casablanca is a major port in North Africa, with more than a million inhabitants enjoying a mild, warm climate. Some of the more popular tourist attractions include the tiny old Medina near the harbor, which is a historical relic and site of the earliest settlement; the new Medina on the eastern side of town, where you can watch cases being tried at the local courts; and the United Nations Square, which is surrounded by tropical gardens grouped around government buildings. At United Nations Square, you can walk through the local shops and find bargains in ancient and modern carpets, leather, jewelry, and local crafts. You can stop in a Moroccan restaurant and try kabobs, *harira* (a type of chicken soup), *pastia* (layers of filo leaves stuffed with chicken, eggs, cinnamon, and exotic spices), *tajin* (a type of stew), and some local wine. If you wish to relax at a beach or pool, you will prefer to take a leisurely ride along the corniche to Anfa and Ain Diab. If time permits, you will want to travel to the ancient city of **Marrakesh,** driving through this colorful town in an open, horse-drawn carriage. The best restaurants in Marrakesh are Casa Lalla and Palar's Jed Mahal.

PORTUGAL

Overlooking a broad bay, **Lisbon** lies on Portugal's west coast, about seven miles from the Atlantic Ocean. The city's 820,000 inhabitants enjoy an ideal climate where temperatures average in the 50s in January and in the 70s in July. Although once considered one of Europe's most picturesque cities, today it appears a bit worn and dirty. Of greatest interest are the numerous monuments, churches, and museums. You will want to walk through the Baixa, the colorful, downtown section of the city, with its pavements of black and white mosaics in checked patterns or forming scenes that recall outstanding events from Lisbon's history. The narrow streets are lined with so-so shops and cafés. Start at Placa do Comercio and proceed up Rue Agusto to Rossio Square. Shoppers will wish to consider the handmade shoes, decorative glazed tiles, beautiful pottery, copperware, and leather goods. Colombie, located in the Benefice district, is a large shopping mall, the largest in Portugal. You may wish to stroll through the historic Alfama area, with its maze of cobblestone streets, lanes, Moorish and medieval buildings, and old castle enclosed by moats with reedy waters filled with ducks, fish, and flamingos. Nearby, you can visit the 12th-century Romanesque Sé Cathedral and the King's Fountain.

The top hotels include the Ritz, Avenida Palace, Sheraton, and Alpha Lisboa. Recommended restaurants include Gabrinius (fish and seafood), Veranda at the Ritz (international), Casa do Leao (Portuguese cuisine with a view), Oterraco (gourmet with a view), Casa de Comida (continental and Portuguese), and Al Fana Grill at the Sheraton (Portuguese and international). A pleasant alternative way to spend your day would be to take the 20-minute train ride to Estoril and Cascais, the resort area north of the city. In Estoril there are numerous hotels, a casino, several sandy beaches, boutiques and restaurants. Cascais is a most charming village with cobble streets, a medieval fortress, shops and an abundance of cafés, seafood restaurants, and pizzerias. My favorite is the romantic courtyard at Pizzeria Lucullus where you may wish to try the gazpacho, sangria, and delicious, crusty pizza. This excursion is definitely the best choice for repeat visitors.

Funchal is the port of the Portuguese Madeira Islands, which lie in the Atlantic 500 miles off the coast of Lisbon. These volcanic islands enjoy a mild, sunny climate, with temperatures ranging from the 60s in winter to the 70s in summer. As you approach port, you will notice the rocky coastline studded with quaint lighthouses, fishing ports, and whaling villages. As you disembark, you will be greeted by the natives in rowboats filled with fruit, baskets, and embroideries welcoming you to this island covered with flowers, bushes, trees, and other vegetation.

Funchal is a resort town with a lazy holiday atmosphere, and you will enjoy walking through the main square, stopping to visit the Jesuit church, town hall, and the bishop's palace. You can browse through quaint shops for antiques as well as for beautiful embroideries on Irish linens and French silks, or you can stroll through the open-air market. You can sip some famous Madeira wine and relax at one of the hotel pools overlooking the cliffs, since the beaches have volcanic black pebbles and are not desirable for swimming. If time allows, you can drive to Cabo Girao to visit the vineyards, to Curral las Freiras to visit a village monastery hidden from view by rocks, or to Comacha to see the house where Madeira baskets are made. You can enjoy a great view from Cabao Girao, Europe's second-highest cliff, 1,800 feet above the ocean. Reid's Hotel is a famous, elegant hotel that dates back to 1891 and is presently managed by Orient Express. Both the Royal and Savoy Hotels offer restaurants, bars, swimming pools, tennis courts, spas, and gardens.

SENEGAL

Dakar is an Atlantic port and the capital of Senegal in western Africa; it has a hot climate and much rain during the summer. The city itself reflects a great deal of European style and French influence, but the people have a definite African character. Some of the more interesting sights include the graceful Presidential Palace; the elegant new Parliament Building; the university; the teeming Sandaga Market; the Ifan Museum, with its magnificent collection of West African carvings, pottery, cloth, and musical instruments; and the medina, with its colorful, cluttered market. There are nice beaches for swimming at N'Gor and Bernard Inlet. If possible, try to attend a native *mechoui,* which is a colorful feast including the barbecue of a sheep or goat. At the Craftsman's Village at Soumbedioune, you will find bargains on native jewelry, leatherwork, pottery, filigree, and woven goods.

SPAIN

Algeciras is a port in southeastern Spain across the bay from Gibraltar. From this town, you can take an overnight boat train to Madrid, a 2½-hour ferry ride to **Tangier** in **North Africa,** or a several-hours' drive to the Costa del Sol area and visit the picturesque towns of Marbella, Malaga, Torremolinos, and Porto

Banus. On the Costa del Sol, you will find numerous resort hotels, beaches, boutiques, shops, good restaurants, night spots, and tourists from all over Europe. The best resorts with the most facilities are Marbella Club and Puente Romano, both located in Marbella. The most colorful harbor area is at Puerto Banus, a 10-minute ride from Marbella. Here you can stroll along the waterfront filled with giant yachts and visit some of the best shops and small ethnic restaurants to be found in Spain.

The famous Rock of Gibraltar, at the western entrance to the Mediterranean, is located in the British colony of Gibraltar. If your ship stops here, you can ascend the Rock by cable car, visit St. Michael's Cave (a natural grotto), Apes' Den (inhabited by wild Barbary apes), and meander through duty-free shops and pubs on Main Street.

If your ship docks in the harbor of Malaga, you will be able to take the tour to Granada and visit the famous Alhambra Castle and charming surrounding parks and attractions. On your way, you may wish to stop for lunch or a drink at the magnificent La Bobadilla Resort, which is built on a hillside in the style of a Moorish village. If you prefer, about an hour's drive along the coast to the west will permit visits to Torremolinos, Marbella, and Porto Banus.

Barcelona is located on the Mediterranean coast of northern Spain, not far from France. This busy city with more than two million inhabitants is the largest Spanish-speaking port in the world after Buenos Aires. You will be able to capture the Spanish flavor by taking in the traditional bullfight, enjoying a flamenco show, or having some gazpacho and paella at a typical Spanish restaurant. You can visit the historic cathedral known as "La Seu" in the old town as well as the interesting building nearby; drive or take the cable car up to the top of the hill of Tibidabo, from the heights of which you can see the Pyrenees; visit the National Museum, the museum of Catalan Art in the Palacio Nacional, the Miro Foundation in Montjuïc Park, and the Picasso Museum; stop by Gaudi's famous Cathedral of the Holy Family; or walk down the Paseo de Gracia or the tree-lined Ramblas Avenue with its colorful flower stalls and shop for leather goods, linens, and souvenirs. The best restaurants in town are La Dama (gourmet French Catalan), Talaia Mar (Spanish and French food and a good view of the city), Jaume de Provenca (Spanish and continental food in a lovely setting at reasonable prices), Botafumiero (seafood), and Via Veneto (continental menu in a grand environment—expensive).

The 44-story, full-facility Hotel Arts managed by the Ritz-Carlton chain is Barcelona's most prestigious residence, located in Marina City next to a long strand of sandy beach and a small-craft marina. This is an excellent pre- and post-cruise option.

Ships call at the port city of Cadiz (Europe's oldest city) to enable passengers to visit the historical city of Seville, the capital of the region of Andalusia. About five to ten minutes from the marina in Cadiz is Plaza de San Juan Dias and Plaza de la Cathedral. Most of the shops and restaurants are located on small streets emanating from these plazas. About an hour away is Jerez de la Frontera, the center of Spain's sherry industry. Here you can visit the vineyards and tour the wine-producing facilities, as well as visit the surrounding estates and opulent churches.

The bus ride to Seville takes about an hour and a half. Steeped in history, Seville is one of the loveliest cities in Spain with a wealth of fascinating styles of architecture spanning various centuries. Entering the city you will enjoy driving down Avenue de la Palmeras to view the dozens of international pavilions constructed for the 1929 Latin American Exposition. Stop at Plaza Espagne and Plaza America, two photo-friendly squares with impressive early 20th-century Andalusian architecture. At Plaza America is an archeological museum.

Walking tours would be the best way to enjoy the city's most important sites. Commence at the Gardens of Murilla, site of the monument to Columbus, and proceed through the Santa Cruz area, which was the posh, residential sector originally inhabited by Seville's Jewish population during the 12th and 13th centuries prior to the Spanish Inquisition. Soon you will wind your way to the impressive Cathedral of Seville and its Giralda Tower. The third largest cathedral in the world, it was built as a mosque during the 12th century and expanded in the 16th century when it became a Catholic church. Directly to the south is the famous Alcazar Palace and gardens, the oldest operational palace in Europe, a fine example of Mudejar architecture. Numerous souvenir shops and small restaurants line the streets and alleys surrounding the church and palace. A short distance away is Plaza Nueva with its banks, hotels, and designer shops. Other interesting sites on the banks of the river that runs through the town are the 13th century Tower of Gold, now a maritime museum and the baroque Maestranza Bullring.

The **Canary Islands** are a group of seven Spanish islands in the Atlantic Ocean 60 miles off the coast of northwest Africa. The islands are mountainous and have a mild climate with temperatures ranging from the 60s in winter to the 70s in summer. Most cruise ships stop at either **Las Palmas** on the Grand Canary Island or **Santa Cruz** on the island of Tenerife. The islands are volcanic, resulting in several black-sand beaches. Although there are no famous restaurants, you will want to try the fish and seafood as well as some of the local rice dishes. At Las Palmas, you can shop at a number of attractive, duty-free stores; explore the narrow streets and plazas of the old part of the city by horse and carriage; watch the sunset at an open-air café; swim at the beaches of Las Canteras, Alcaravaneras, or La Laja; or witness a cockfight.

Santa Cruz is a lively town that may seem to be more beautiful than Las Palmas. Here you can visit the archeological and anthropological museum, the 17th-century Carta Palace, and the historical relics of the Church of the Concepción. There are beaches at Las Tereitas and Las Gaviotas. Tourists often take an excursion from Santa Cruz through the town of La Laguna, followed by a beautiful drive to Orotava and Porto de la Cruz, passing by beautiful coastlines, tropical flowers, and foliage. From Orotava, you ascend the Teide Mountain, which includes a funicular railroad ride to the volcano's cone, where you can witness a panoramic view of all the Canary Islands. On the way back to Santa Cruz, you may wish to swim in the warm waters and lounge on the fine sand of El Medano Beach. Another attraction is Siam Park, a water park with a restaurant, a beach club, and several amusement park rides and attractions. There are good dining possibilities around Plaza de las Americas, Los Cristianos, and Arona. At Costa Adeje there is a 27-hole golf course and driving range.

Palma is the main resort area and port of Majorca, one of the Spanish **Balearic Islands** lying in the Mediterranean 120 miles south of Barcelona. Tourists from all over the world pour into Palma each year to enjoy its mild winters and beautiful summers. In town, there are numerous Spanish-style restaurants (El Patio is among the best) and excellent shops where you can obtain bargains in pearls and leather goods. The best shopping area is along Jaime III, General Mola, and Paseo de Borne streets. The larger hotels in Palma are not on the ocean, and you will have to travel away from the city to bathe in the sea. A worthwhile trip that will take an entire day would include a visit to the Drach caves at Porto Cristo, followed by a trip to Formentor. The Drach caves are the largest in the world, with magnificent stalagmites and stalactites and a natural underground lake and auditorium where you can witness a truly unique concert. The drive up a mountain and down to the hotel at Formentor is breathtaking. Here you can enjoy a delicious lunch complete with sangria; swim at a sheltered, pine-studded bathing beach; play tennis on modern courts; and go horseback riding in the mountains. The best resorts near the town of Palma are the Son Vida, a delightful choice for an outdoor lunch by the pool, and Arabella Golf Hotel, a sister hotel on a scenic golf course.

Some cruise ships call at ports on other Balearic Islands. Most ships visiting the island of **Menorca,** anchor or tender to the port of **Mahon** (Mao). Here there is little of interest other than taking a picturesque walk along the harbor where you will find small cafés and a few souvenir shops, or walking up the stairs near the main harbor to the town where you can explore charming little streets and visit additional shops and restaurants. There are beaches located around the island accessible by taxi. **Ibiza** is a more interesting cruise stop and a major vacation destination for the British and Germans. Right off the harbor are narrow streets lined with restaurants and souvenir and leather shops. You will want to visit the fortress and castle that sit above the harbor and one of the colorful beaches (some of which include nude bathing). Salines is the most popular beach and only a short bus ride from the town.

TUNISIA

Your ship will dock at **LaGoulette** or **Bizerte,** the ports for Tunis and Carthage. Your best choice will be to take an organized tour that transports you to Tunis and visits the ruins of ancient Carthage dating back to 814 B.C. You will probably stop at the National Archeological Museum; the pretty suburb of Sidi Abon Said, with its white buildings and cobbled streets; and the interesting Casbah, with its mosques and numerous *souks* (shopping streets) featuring Oriental rugs, brass trays, gold jewelry, linens, and souvenirs.

TURKEY

Turkey has become a very popular stop for Greek island and Mediterranean cruises. Traditionally, the three ports most often visited are Istanbul, Izmir, and Kusadasi. However, several ships now offer stops at the more scenic coastal resort towns of Marmaris and Antalya.

Istanbul, formerly Constantinople, is the city of legend and history where East and West meet. This great commercial seaport is the largest city in Turkey, stretching along both the European and Asiatic sides of the Bosporus, which connects the Sea of Marmara with the Black Sea. You will not want to miss the Grand Bazaar in the heart of the old city, which is one of the most unique shopping areas in the world. Here you can browse through four thousand tiny shops spread along 92 winding streets and see bargains in gold, copper, ceramics, jewelry, rugs, leather, suedes, handicrafts, and just about anything else you could imagine. There are a number of stores both in the bazaar and nearby where you can have leather and suede outfits made to order while you wait. You will want to visit the famous Topkapi Museum, formerly the Palace of the Sultans, where today you can view some of the world's most valuable and beautiful works of art, rare stones, jewels, ancient weapons, furnishings, other antiquities, and the harems of the Sultans.

One of the most unique sights when sailing into Istanbul is the skyline filled with beautiful mosques with their domes, semidomes, and minarets. The most famous is the Blue Mosque or Sultan Ahmed Mosque located near the Topkapi Museum. You will also want to visit St. Sophia, which was built by Emperor Justinian in the sixth century as a Christian church, altered to a mosque, and later turned into a museum with its magnificent architecture, important mosaics, and unusual chandeliers. Aghia Sophia (as it is now called) is said to be the world's finest example of Byzantine architecture. You can stop at a restaurant where the locals eat in the Cicok Pasaji, Kumkapi area, or atop the 14th-century Galeta Tower, not far from the pier, for simple versions of Turkish appetizers and salads, fish, seafood, shish kebab, baklava, and coffee; or you may wish to have a drink or dine at one of the magnificent Istanbul hotels such as the Ciragan Palace, Hilton, Four Seasons, Intercontinental, or Conrad. All of these make excellent pre- or postcruise headquarters with central locations, panoramic views, numerous restaurants, large health clubs, and pools. The top epicurean dinner restaurants in Istanbul include Ulus 29, Safron at the Intercontinental and Körfez for seafood, accessible by a short ferry ride.

Some ships stop at the small port town of **Dikili** to enable passengers to take the short drive through rolling hills, pine trees, and vineyards to Bergama and the ruins of Pergamon. Pergamon was an ancient Greek city in Asia Minor that dates back to the third century B.C. The city was built on terraces of steep mountains and is composed of an acropolis with ruins of several temples and a sanctuary to the god of medicine. After the tour, you can wander through the small shops and outdoor markets near the harbor or enjoy fresh fish right off the boat at a local restaurant.

Izmir and **Kusadasi** are other ports in Turkey where cruise ships often stop. Izmir is an important, colorful port and the headquarters for the NATO

Command guarding the eastern Mediterranean. Kusadasi is a summer resort town where you can swim at small beaches, ride a camel on the sand, or shop for gold, jewelry, rugs, leather, suede, and antiques at one of its many stores. Bargains on leather are probably among the best in the world. Kusadasi has several excellent resort hotels with lovely pool areas, including the Fantasia, Onur, and Koru-Mar. The Koru-Mar is only a mile away from the harbor and affords picturesque views of the city and sea. **Ephesus** is inland from Izmir or Kusadasi. This ancient city, uncovered by Austrian archeologists, has some of the most impressive archeological ruins in the world, including a mile-long marble road, restored buildings, the Arcadian Way, Temple of Hadrian, the Library, the Odeon, the public toilets, the ruins of the Temple of Diana, the site of the Temple of Artemis (considered one of the Seven Wonders of the World), and the Last Abode of Mary. There are numerous restaurants spread throughout the town, most specializing in fresh fish and seafood.

Once a tiny sleeping village leveled by a devastating earthquake in 1057, **Marmaris** has been resurrected as Turkey's most beautiful, upscale resort area and yacht haven. Fringing a protected bay surrounded by rugged pine-forested mountains, the town has a floral beach walk that meanders along the harbor and bay past numerous hotels, posh resorts, restaurants, tavernas, and shops. The harbor where the cruise ships generally dock is dotted with private yachts and sailing vessels and is only a 10-minute walk from the town center, where you will find dozens of restaurants, bars, and tavernas reminiscent of St. Tropez and Puerto Banus. In the town center, there is also a covered bazaar that offers many of the same bargains in gold, jewelry, leather goods, carpets, and other merchandise as found in the Grand Bazaar of Istanbul or in the shops of Kusadasi, except in a less crowded, more pleasant surrounding. Extending for about five miles from the town center is the beach walk mentioned above. The most beautiful resort is the Marmaris Palace, which has private bungalows and hotel rooms with pools, restaurants, and lush grounds that run down pine-clad hills to the beach area. The clientele is mostly German. Other nice beach resorts in the area include Mares Marmaris and Grand Azur. Side trips can be taken to the typical Turkish seaside villages of Icmeler, Tarunc, and Kumlubuk, and tours are also offered to the graves of Likya and the ruins of Caunos.

Antalya, set on a majestic coastline of beaches and rocky caves, is a very attractive resort city with shady, palm-lined boulevards, a picturesque marina, and an old quarter called Kaleici with narrow, winding streets and quaint, old wood houses next to the city walls. Places of interest include the Archeology Museum, the clock tower, Hadrian's Gate, Hidirlik Tower, Kesik Minaret complex, and the Turban Kaleici Marina. There are several full-facility resort hotels, the Sheraton Voyager being the most upscale. Other choices overlooking the sea include Talya, Falez, and Cender. The beaches, although picturesque, are pebbly and uninviting. Excursions away from the city may include the upper and lower Dudden waterfalls, the restored archeological ruins at Perge, or the archeological sites and beaches at Patara. Golfers may wish to opt for the 24-mile drive to the National Golf Club in Belek, where they will find both a nine-hole and a championship 18-hole course situated amongst shady pine forests near pretty beach areas.

UKRAINE, RUSSIA, BULGARIA, AND BLACK SEA PORTS

A number of ships cruise the Black Sea, stopping at such Ukrainian ports as Odessa, Sevastapol, and Yalta; the port of Sochi; and the Bulgarian port of Nessebar.

Odessa, located in the south central Ukraine, is called "the pearl of the Black Sea," with its picturesque seascape, streets, and marketplaces. To the landlocked Russian, this is a town of sun, golden-sand beaches, and green parks. However, to the western visitor it is a town in total disrepair. You can stroll from one end of the seafront to the other, visiting the Potempkin steps, Pushkin Statue, the Opera House, the Vorontsov Palace, the Square of the Commune, and the archeological museum. The main shopping is along Deribasovskaya Street. You may wish to visit one of the city's beaches at Arcadia, Luzanovska, and Chernomorka. Other points of interest accessible by taxi are Shomrei Shabbos Synagogue, the old main Synagogue on Yevreyskaya Street, Gargarin Palace, Tolstoy Palace, the Russian Byzantine-style Uspensky Cathedral, and the Museum of Fine Arts.

Sochi, Russia, is the largest seaside resort in the former U.S.S.R., protected from cold winds and sudden temperature changes by the Caucasus Mountains. There is a large central pebble bathing beach as well as many smaller beaches with adjoining *sanatoria* (non-luxurious Russian health resorts with clinics, solarium pools, beaches, public rooms, and sports facilities). You may wish to visit the famous Dendrarium Botanical Gardens, containing fountains, statues, subtropical flora, and trees and shrubs from all over the world. A visit to Stalin's Dacha is interesting, as are the mineral springs and spa at Matsesta and the Dagomy Tea Plantation.

Yalta, Ukraine, is a Black Sea port on the southern coast of the Crimean Peninsula at the southern foothills of the Yaila Mountains. The city is also sheltered by mountains and enjoys a temperate climate. This seaside resort town that ascends up the mountain slopes is surrounded by evergreen forests and parks, vineyards, and fruit farms where pear, almond, peach, apple, and apricot trees are grown. It is the most beautiful of the Black Sea cities and is reminiscent of Greek islands and Mediterranean ports. There are three main beaches and numerous sanatoria. You can walk along the Lenin Quay, where you will find the main shops, hotels, cafés, and restaurants. Places and points of interest include the Ethnographic Museum (devoted to Eastern art), the Tchekhov Museum (which was once the author's house), Yuri Gagarin Park, Livadia Palace, the summer residence of the Tsar Nicholas II and sight of the Yalta Conference in 1945, Alupka Palace and art museum, Massandra Palace, Park and Combine (famous for its wines), the Alexander Nevsky Cathedral with its onion-shaped domes, and the Nikitsky Botanical Gardens.

The principal shopping area extends along the Roosevelt and Lenin Quays; however, items of interest would be limited to Matryoshkea dolls, lacquer boxes, traditional embroideries, amber jewelry, caviar, and vodka. Swallow's Nest, precariously perched on a rock overlooking the sea, was built in 1911 to resemble a medieval castle and offers a lovely panorama. This is a major tourist attraction and some ship tours utilize the location for a typical Crimean-style lunch.

Sevastapol, Ukraine, sits on a group of hills forming a natural amphitheater overlooking Bakhtiarsky Bay on the Crimean Peninsula. The city offers charming gardens, attractive squares and boulevards, numerous monuments, and museums. From the port you can take a ten-minute walk through a park to a local beach (concrete) to see the locals at leisure. Points of interest would include Vladimir Cathedral, the archeological site of Chersonesus, where the last Greek colony existed on the Northern Black Sea, the adjoining museum, the 16th-century Khans Palace, the eighth-century Uspensky Maonastery, and the Sevastopol Aquarium.

Nessebar, Bulgaria, is also located on the Black Sea. Your ship will dock only minutes away from the picturesque, charming old quarter of town situated on the Nessebar Peninsula, an architectural/archeological reserve, dating back to the 10th and 11th centuries. North and South of the peninsula are small strips of beach. The town is composed of colorful, winding streets lined with stone and timber houses, restaurants, and shops.

Also in town you can visit the Archeological Museum, several medieval churches, and the walls and towers of Hellenistic and Byzantine fortresses (fifth to 15th century).

You may wish to shop for bargains on "knock-off" designer sunglasses, perfumes, and other items (not close to the quality of the real thing), local souvenirs, local art, and embroidered linens. An especially desirable crystal shop is located at 20 Mitropolitska Street. It specializes in unique hand-painted and individually blown table crystal. Tours also visit the vineyards at Promerie wine center.

Northern Europe, the Baltic, the North Sea, the Fjords, and the Rivers of Europe

During the late spring and summer, a number of ships offer cruises to northern European ports in the Baltic and North Seas as well as up to the picturesque fjords of Norway and down the rivers of Germany, Austria, Hungary, and France. Although the climate may not be as ideal as in the Caribbean or Mediterranean, the weather is generally mild enough at these times of year to permit you to sit out on deck and take in the magnificent sights and scenery.

The cruises are generally longer (at least 10 to 14 days) and more expensive than those found in the Mediterranean; however, they afford you an opportunity to visit a large number of interesting ports while sampling a variety of cultures all in one trip without the inconvenience of flying from place to place.

These cruises usually initiate from Southampton, Dover, Tilbury, Stockholm, Amsterdam, Hamburg, or Copenhagen, and the ships either sail up the coast of Norway to the fjords and "Land of the Midnight Sun," circumnavigate the British Isles, or stop at such interesting northern European ports as Amsterdam, Oslo, Helsinki, Stockholm, Copenhagen, Hamburg, Gdynia, Tallinn, Visby, and St. Petersburg.

The ships of most major cruise lines cruise these areas.

For a totally different experience, seasoned cruisers will enjoy a leisurely river-boat trip on the Rhine, Mosel, Danube, Elbe, Seine, Saône, or Rhône Rivers with visits to historic cities and charming villages.

The following are the highlights of some of the more popular northern ports:

BELGIUM

Cruise ships visiting Belgium dock at Zeebrugge, a seaside resort and fishing port linked to the historic metropolis of Brugge by a 7.5-mile canal. Train service is available to Brugge (15 minutes), Ghent (one hour), and Brussels (two hours). Flemish is spoken in the northern part of Belgium and French in the southern.

Brugge is one of the most charming cities in Europe with its ten-mile net-work of canals filled with swans and ducks, flowing under small bridges surrounded by parks and attractive buildings built over the centuries in Romanesque, Gothic, Neo-gothic, Baroque, and Renaissance styles. The market square, located in the center of town, is dominated by the 14th-century Belfry, a 275-foot medieval tower where 47 bells chime every 15 minutes. The square is surrounded by Flemish buildings and numerous restaurants, bistros, and shops. Nearby is the Burg, a medieval square and site of the 14th-century Town Hall and the Basilica of the Holy Blood. Other points of interest include the cathedral with a Michelangelo statue of Mary and child, Groeninge Museum with its fine collection of Flemish primitive painters, the Chocolate Museum, and the Diamond Museum.

Alternative ways to explore the city would be by motorboat tours on the canals or by horse and buggy. Brugge is famous for its chocolates, mussels, and beer. The major shopping streets are Steenstraat and Katelynestraat, where you can shop for Belgian lace, chocolates, ceramics, crystal, linen, and pewter.

DANUBE RIVER

The Danube River emanates in the southeast portion of Germany and passes through eight European countries before it connects with the Black Sea. Most riverboats embark passengers in **Passau**, a quaint town with a romantic setting located at the confluence of three rivers: the Danube, Inn, and Ilz. Quite close to the point where the rivers converge is the old town area, where you can walk through narrow cobblestone streets and alleys. Visit St. Stephan's Cathedral, with its baroque stuccoed ceiling, Gothic architecture, and frescoes. During the summer you can hear a classical concert at noon on the world's largest church organ. Make sure you see the town hall and the 13th-century Castle Oberhaus—the location of a museum, art gallery, and observatory. You can rest along the way at an outdoor café overlooking the river and sample a local beer, ice cream, or pastry. Blauer Bock, set in a 14th-century building with a riverside terrace, would be a good choice. The main shopping streets off Ludwigsplatz are quite colorful, with numerous shops and small cafes.

The stretch of the river extending between Passau and Vienna is the most picturesque, meandering through verdant hills and symmetrical forests. Each evening, passengers are mesmerized by the sunset over the smooth waters of the Danube, creating the appearance of a bright orange ball melting into the river.

After Passau, your boat will pass through the **Wachau** region, a wine-producing area with vine-clad rolling slopes. The round towers of fortified churches and the battlement turrets of ancient castles frequently emerge as the river winds its way through Austria.

Prior to reaching Vienna, most boats visit **Dürnstein,** a charming Austrian village dominated by the beautiful baroque tower of an early-18th-century convent. You can visit the cathedral, stroll the narrow streets of the town as they wind up a hill, taste wine at a local vintner, have a coffee and pastry on an outdoor terrace overlooking the river, or walk along the paths bordered by vineyards that follow the river. You can even enjoy the panoramic view from the 12th-century castle that sits on a steep hill, 520 feet above the town, and is connected by an ancient wall. This castle is where King Richard the Lion-Hearted was said to have been incarcerated. Between Passau and Durnstein lies the Village of Melk, where you can visit the Melk Abbey, one of the finest baroque buildings in the world.

The next major stop is one of the highlights of any cruise on the Danube, Austria's famous capital, **Vienna.** From the river, you will want to take a taxi or the metro (train No. 1) to Stephansplatz, which is in the middle of the historic and commercial core of the city, as well as the site of the soaring St. Stephan's, an impressive Gothic cathedral with a steeple that rises 450 feet. In this area are numerous traditional Viennese coffeehouses, outside cafés, and pedestrian-only shopping streets, the Kartnerstrasse being the liveliest. Within easy walking distance are the 700-year-old, 2,600-room Hofburg Palace (about two dozen rooms are open to the public, as is the crown jewel collection); the Museum of Fine Arts; the State Opera House; the 1,441-room early-17th-century Schonbrunn Palace; and the city park with its statue of Johann Strauss.

There are highly rated, more formal restaurants in the deluxe hotels such as the Bristol, Sacher, Hilton, and Imperial. Less expensive typical Viennese restaurants are spread throughout this area. I especially enjoyed lunch on the protected patio of the Sacher Hotel dining room, where Viennese specialties reach top gourmet level, embellished by the excellent service staff. Two other highly esteemed dining establishments for fine Viennese cuisine and charming atmosphere are Drei Hussarin, located on Weihburggasse right off Kartnerstrasse not far from St. Stephan's Square, and Steiereck. If you do not have time for a meal, a must is sampling a coffee and pastry, or at least an Austrian beer, in a coffeehouse. Although a version of Sacher Torte is available throughout the city, purists can enjoy a slice of the rich chocolate delight in the café connected to the Sacher Hotel.

On your way back to the river in the evening, you can visit the amusement park at the Prater, where a Ferris wheel with large enclosed gondolas offers a scenic 10-minute ride affording the best views of the city. Another spot to enjoy the view of the city while having a coffee is the café that revolves 590 feet above ground on the Danube Tower.

Another port of call on most itineraries, **Bratislava, Slovakia,** is of interest to tourists mostly due to its political history and the evolution of its varied governments. The Bratislava Hrad (castle) houses a historical museum and sits on a hill overlooking the city above the old town. Other scenic views of the town and river are possible from S.N.P. Bridge and Tower. The Danube is a fairly new, modern hotel on the river; however, the best luxury hotel is the Carlton, now managed by Radisson and located across from the Opera House and Philharmonic Concert Hall at the top of the Promenade, one of the colorful main thoroughfares in the city center. Emanating north from the Promenade are several other streets lined with shops, restaurants, and cafes. Follow the streets and you will find yourself at the town square, locale of a historical museum and Café Mayer and Café Roland, two of the best indoor/outdoor people-watching cafes in which to enjoy a drink or meal.

The shorter cruises that do not extend to the Black Sea generally turn around at **Budapest,** one of the most picturesque and interesting cities along the Danube. The capital of Hungary with a population of three million is actually composed of two cities, Buda and Pest, which are connected by a series of bridges that span the river.

The most popular tourist areas on the Buda side are Castle Hill and Gellert Hill. Castle Hill was the center of Buda during the Middle Ages; today it is composed of small souvenir shops, cafés, restaurants, the Hilton Hotel and Casino, the 13th-century Matthias Church, and the Royal palace, which houses a historical museum and national art gallery and numerous statues and structures of historical interest.

Although Castle Hill is an excellent location from which to look across to the Pest side of the city and the Houses of Parliament, the panoramic vista of the Danube from 770 feet above on Gellert Hill is the most awesome. The Citadel on Gellert Hill was built in 1849 as a prison and is now a tourist attraction with restaurants, shops, and nightclubs. Also located here is Liberty Statue. Visible throughout the city, it was built as a tribute to the Soviet liberators.

On the Pest side are many of the larger hotels, restaurants, and pedestrian shopping streets, as well as the Houses of Parliament, St. Stephan's Basilica, the statues and monuments at Hero's Square (constructed in 1896), the oldest synagogue in Europe, and several museums. The Atrium Sofitel Intercontinental and the Marriott enjoy excellent locations and provide many facilities, making them excellent choices for pre- or post-cruise overnight stays. Other top hotels include the Hilton, Kempinski, and Forum.

Margaret Island, which is connected by a bridge to both Buda and Pest, is a large, attractive park with tennis courts, soccer fields, children's playgrounds, small restaurants, a public swimming pool, a garden theater, and the Grand Hotel, another good choice to overnight. The park is a very popular recreational area for the citizens of the city.

Gundel's, which occupies a palatial mansion in City Park, is the home of "pancakes Gundel," offers one of the finest dining experiences in Budapest, and is the place to see and be seen. Other atmospheric Hungarian restaurants include Matya's Pince and Belcanto (near the opera house).

Some of the more popular multilingual riverboats cruising on the Danube include the elegant 212-passenger M/S *Mozart* (for Peter Deilmann Cruises), the 150-passenger *Amadeus Classic* and *Amadeus Symphony,* the 88-passenger *River Cloud,* the *Prussian Princess,* and the vessels of A-Rosa, Viking, and Uniworld cruise lines. There are many other companies with riverboats cruising this area; however, most are sold as a charter or exclusively to the German-speaking market.

If you are heading in the opposite direction from Passau, your riverboat may make two additional stops on the upper Danube at Regensburg and Nurenburg.

Regensburg, one of Germany's best-preserved cities, dates back to A.D. 77 as a Celtic settlement. The Romans took over in A.D. 179 and remnants of the Roman occupation can be seen in the ancient Porta Praetoria behind the cathedral, with its huge stones piled in front of an arched gateway and the 16-arch Steinerne Brucke (the oldest bridge in Germany). Regensburg flourished in the 12th and 13th centuries as Germany's wealthiest town and a major center of trade and commerce. The best example of Gothic architecture in Bavaria is the cathedral located in the heart of the Old Town area where the famous boy's choir performs on Sunday mornings. Visitors will also enjoy touring the magnificent palace and monastery of the family Thurn and Taxis. Those wishing to experience a taste of Bavaria may enjoy coffee and pastry at the historic Princess Konditorei, wurst and sauerkraut at the Salzstadt building below the Steinerne bridge, or a full meal at the Ratskeller or Rosenpalais Restaurant and Bistro.

Almost all major attractions, hotels, and restaurants in **Nurenberg** lie in a one-mile area stretching between the main railway station to the south and the medieval Kaiserberg Castle atop a hill at the northern edge of the Altstadt (the Old City). Within this area you may wish to visit the Hauptmarkt, the central market square; the Town Hall; Handwerkerhof, near the railway station, a craft mall in a medieval castle setting; Justizgebaude, where the Nurenberg trials were held; the Albrecht Durer House, the only completely Gothic house in the city devoted to the life and works of the 15th/16th-century artist Albrecht Durer; Germanisches Nationalmuseum, the largest museum of German art and culture, covering the entire historical spectrum of German craftsmanship and fine arts; Kaiserburg Castle, residence of kings and emperors with portions built in the 12th, 14th, and 15th centuries; Spielzeug Museum, with exhibits of toys dating back over the centuries; St. Lorenz Church, built between the 13th and 15th centuries; and St. Sebaldus Church, an example of transition from Romanesque to German Gothic styles. You can shop for children's toys at Obletter, at Kistner for antique books, prints, and engravings from the masters, and at the aforementioned Handwerkerhof for local handicrafts, glassware, pewter, woodcarvings, and toys.

The top hotels are Le Meridien Grand, Maritim, Atrium, and Durer. Essigbratlein, in a house dating back to 1550, serving French/continental cuisine is touted as the best restaurant in town along with Goldenes Posthorn, featuring a Franconian menu along with wines dating as far back as 1889. Heilig-Geist-Spital is the city's largest historical wine house. It is over 650 years old, featuring 100 vintages of wine along with Franconian cuisine. For an inexpensive bratwurst, kraut, and beer try Bratwurst-Hausle, Historische Bratwurst-Glocklien, or Herrenbrau at the Hauptmarkt.

DENMARK

Copenhagen, the capital and chief port of Denmark, is a friendly, charming, cosmopolitan city with some of the finest restaurants and shops in Europe. From the Raadhuspladsen, the main square with its towering town hall, you can walk (or ride a rented bicycle) down the winding Strøget street toward Kongens Nytorv and the harbor area of Nyhavn. On the Strøget, you can browse through such famous shops as Illums Bolighus (modern design center), Georg Jensen (silver), Royal Copenhagen (china), and Birger Christensen (furs). From Nyhavn, you are only a short distance from Langelinie Pavillion, where you can have an outdoor lunch or dinner in a park overlooking the *Little Mermaid,* a statue inspired by Hans Christian Andersen's fairy tale that gracefully sits on a rock overlooking the harbor.

If you head in the opposite direction from the main square (Raadhuspladsen), you can visit the Glyptothek Museum, with its excellent collection of French paintings and Egyptian sculpture, and the fantastic Tivoli Gardens, with its flowers, open-air theater, concert hall, amusement rides, restaurants, nightclubs, and nightly fireworks. You may also enjoy visiting the lovely Copenhagen Zoo, Rosenborg Palace with its crown jewels, the National Art Museum, or the Carlsberg Beer factory. You will want to try one of the delicious open-face sandwiches called *smörbrod,* as well as the great Tuborg and Carlsberg beers.

Inside the Tivoli Gardens are numerous excellent restaurants in which to sample *smörbrod.* Ida Davidson's (formerly Oscar Davidson's) at Store Kongensgade 70 has been the most famous establishment for *smörbrod* since 1888. For fish and seafood, you will want to try Krogs, Fiskekaelderen, and DenGlydne Fortun. Gourmets will enjoy Kommandanten; Kong Hans Kaelder; Lenore Christine, Les Etoiles, or one of the exceptional restaurants in the Royal, Plaza, D'Angleterre, Kong Frederik, Scandinavia, and several other hotels. Actually, it would be difficult to have anything but a good meal in Copenhagen, wherever you might stop.

Possible excursions would include visits to Frilandsmuseet, an open-air museum set in the pastoral countryside to the north, where there is a display of Danish farmhouses from various regions set in their natural environs; a visit to Kronborg Castle at Helsingor, famous as the setting of Shakespeare's *Hamlet* and 45 minutes north of Copenhagen; or Denmark's National History Museum, housed in Frederiksborg Castle in Hillerod, where you can boat on the castle's lake.

ESTONIA

Tallinn is the major port city with a population of 500,000. Dating back nine centuries, almost every building in the Old Town has some historic or architectural interest. Cruise ships on their way to Helsinki and St. Petersburg have found this a convenient stop where passengers can stroll through cobblestone streets while viewing Gothic architecture, a variety of churches and museums, numerous historic sites, and lovely parks.

It is recommended that visitors tour Tallinn by foot in order to take full advantage of the many places of interest. You may wish to start your tour at Toompea, the upper town, which is situated on a hill that affords a panoramic view of the city and harbor. Here you can visit the 16th-century Cannon Tower, Toompea Palace, St. Alexander Nevski's Cathedral, the 13th-century Dome Church, and take a walk through narrow Kohter Street to the observation platform, where you will enjoy the best view of the lower Old Town. There are several souvenir shops here and refreshments can be purchased at the café adjacent to the Virgin's Tower.

In the lower town you can visit the Town Hall constructed at the beginning of the 15th century; the homes and guild halls along Pikk Street; the 13th-century spire of St. Olan's Church, which dominates the Tallinn skyline; and the Maritime Museum housed in the 16th-century Cannon Tower known as Fat Margaret.

Tours are generally offered to farms in the countryside. The largest hotel in town is the Viru Hotel, which is located near numerous restaurants and shops. Shuttle buses from your ship will generally leave you off in front of this hotel.

FINLAND

Helsinki is the capital, largest city, and chief port of Finland, and it lies on the southern coast on the Gulf of Finland. Tourists will find this a refreshing, clean city with its new buildings, lovely parks, and spacious walks and streets. You will enjoy shopping for Finnish-designed household items, reindeer slippers, boots, clothing, Marimekko, ceramics, and furs, either at Stockmann's (Helsinki's largest department store) or at one of the many friendly shops at the Forum Shopping Center, the Senate Center, or along the Esplanade. In the morning, there is an open-air market right at the harbor with numerous stalls featuring flowers, vegetables, fish, wearing apparel, and handicrafts. Behind the market is the Esplanade that not only is lined with shops and boutiques, but also is the location of numerous restaurants and outdoor cafés. Places of interest include the Finnish Design Center, the cathedral, the State Council Building, and the university library in Senate Square, the monument to Sibelius, Temppeliaukio Church built into solid rock, the town hall, the Empress Stone Obelisk, and the Fountain of Havis Amanda in the Market Square. Other excellent places to visit are the parliament house, the national museum, the National Art Gallery, the magnificent new Finlandia Concert Hall, the botanical gardens and their water tower, Linnanmäki (Helsinki's permanent amusement park); and the Open-air Museum of Seurasaari, which contains specimens of various types of wooden houses built by the Finns over the centuries. You will want to try a Finnish sauna as well as a Finnish smörgasbord, which will include many native Finnish dishes in addition to the usual fare. A list of the best restaurants in Helsinki will include Motti, Karl König, Havis Amanda Fish Restaurant, Savoy, and Esplanadikappeli.

FINLAND-STOCKHOLM CAR FERRY CRUISES

Several large cruise ships with capacity to carry automobiles offer overnight cruise experiences between **Stockholm, Sweden,** and either Helsinki or Turku, Finland. The largest and most upscale ships with this itinerary include *Silja Europa* (Silja Line, 3,000 passengers, entered service 1993), *Silja Symphony* (Silja Line, 2,700 passengers, entered service 1991), *Cinderella* (Viking Line, 2,500 passengers, entered service 1989), *Mariella* (Viking Line, 2,500 passengers, entered service 1985), *Amorella* (Viking Line, 2,480 passengers), *Gabriella* (Viking Line, 2,420 passengers), and *Isabella* (Viking Line, 2,214 passengers). Most passengers utilize these ships as a means of transportation from one country to the other, and many take their families and automobiles. These ships offer numerous alternative restaurants and dining is generally not included in the cruise fare. There are theaters, live entertainment, casinos, and an array of facilities on these ships where passengers party into the wee hours. Departures are generally in the late afternoon and arrivals early the following morning. Do not expect the quality of comfort, food, service, or entertainment found on most cruise ships.

FRANCE

Your ship may dock at **Le Havre,** an important French harbor at the mouth of the Seine River on the English Channel. From here, you can take a train to **Paris,** where you will want to visit as many of the following sites as time allows: the colossal Arc de Triomphe; the famous Eiffel Tower, standing a thousand feet high; the magnificent Théâtre de l'Opéra; the fashionable Champs-Elysées; the beautiful Place de la Concorde; the Tuileries; Notre-Dame de Paris; the world-famous Louvre, home of the *Mona Lisa, Winged Victory,* and the *Venus de Milo;* l'Orangerie Art Museum; the Left Bank area with its small cafés, artists, and colorful crowds; the basilica of Sacre Coeur on the top of Montmartre; the palace at Versailles; and a boat tour down the Seine on the *bateaux mouches.* You can shop for crystal at Lalique and Baccarat; jewelry at Cartier and Boucheron; menswear at Pierre Cardin, Givenchy's, and Laroche's; handbags at Morabito and Gucci; gloves at Hermes; and French perfumes at most department stores, shops, and *parfumeries.* You can also visit one of the couture houses such as Balenciaga, Yves Saint Laurent, Givenchy, Pierre Cardin, Balmain, Carven, Courreges, Guy Laroche, Jean Patou, Lanvin, Madeleine de Rauch, and Nina Ricci.

You will not want to miss having a meal at a French restaurant in Paris. The most famous and most expensive gastronomic palaces are the Tour d'Argent, Lucas Carton, Jamin, Rostang, Taillevant, Le Pré Catelan, Laurent, Amboissie, Apicius, Jacques Cagne, Jules Verne (on the Eiffel Tower), Maxim's, and Lasserre; however, there are many excellent, less expensive establishments where you can obtain a meal in the true French fashion. Later in the evening, you may wish to take in the Folies Bergère, the lavish production at the Lido, the Moulin Rouge, one of the many other night spots in the Montmartre area, or one of the many discotheques, jazz spots, or cabarets along the Saint-Germain-des-Pres.

If time allows, an overnight or several-day trip to the Burgundy country between Paris and Lyon or the Château country in the Loire Valley could prove to be a most charming and rewarding experience. I would recommend staying at one of the charming French inns that are owned and run by today's great chefs of France. My favorite is George Blanc's in Vonnas. Other superior choices would be Château d'Esclimont (only a short drive from Paris), Auberge des Templiers (Les Bèzards), Les Crayères (Reims), Château d'Artigny (Tours), La Côte Saint-Jacque (Joigny), and Domaine des Hauts de Loire (Onzain).

RHÔNE AND SAÔNE RIVERS

Numerous riverboats offer cruises up and down the Rhône and Saône Rivers and visit some of the more interesting and historic cities and villages along the way. These cruises afford excellent opportunities to visit the famous vineyards of the Rhône and Burgundy regions as well as some of the most famous restaurants in France. (See chapter 10.)

Arles is a charming town, originally inhabited by the Greeks and Romans. It boasts numerous imposing ancient ruins including a Roman amphitheater that seats 21,000 spectators and the Theater Antique, both of which were constructed in the late first century. The quaint "Old Town" area includes art museums and Romanesque cathedrals, as well as bars, bistros, restaurants, and shops. Arles was the site for many Van Gogh works, including his masterpiece, *Pont de Trinquetaille* (The Bridge). The ancient Roman cemetery at Alyscamps was the subject matter of paintings by both Van Gogh and Gauguin. There are numerous small shops specializing in colorful linens, place mats, and souvenirs in the colors and designs of Provence.

Avignon is another quaint city surrounded by three miles of totally preserved ancient ramparts with their original seven entrances and 39 protective towers. Inside these walls are shops, restaurants, hotels, apartments, and such famous historic monuments as the 14th-century Pope's Palace, one of the largest medieval palaces in the world and residence of numerous popes during the Renaissance period, when the papal seat was moved here from Rome. In the evening, your boat or barge may pass by the remains of the St. Beneget Bridge, made famous by the song "Sur le Pont d'Avignon" and a marvelous vantage point from which to view the Pope's Palace and ancient walls. You may wish to visit the vineyards of Chateauneuf-du-Pape, which are only a short drive from the city. The most famous restaurants here are Hiely and Christian Etienne, both located in the center of town. The most famous hotels are Hotel d'Europe and La Mirande, an 18th-century mansion.

Viviers is a small medieval village rich in history, typical of many French towns in the countryside. Visitors can walk narrow cobblestone paths past restored buildings and ancient gates to the interesting Cathedral of Viviers, which was built in the 12th to 15th centuries in a combination of Romanesque, classical, and Gothic styles. From the top of the hill behind the cathedral, you have a panoramic view of the region. You can take a tour that drives through the rolling hills, green valleys, and vineyards of the Ardéche countryside with a visit to the nearby vineyards of Côte Vivarais for a wine tasting.

Tournon is a small village that sits across the Rhône from the famous vineyards of the Hermitage. Here you can explore such wine houses as Chapoutier and Jaboulet. Your boat will dock across the road from the historic 14th-century castle, and you can stroll or cycle along the river Doux, a tributary of the Rhône. You can visit the Romanesque former Abbey of Saint-Philibert. Also from Tournon, you can take a two-hour train ride on a turn-of-the-century steam train along the Doux and Ardéche valleys.

Vienne is yet another historic city founded by the Roman legions in A.D. 50. Of interest are the Gothic Cathedral of St. Maurier, dating back to 1200; the excavations at St. Romain en Galle; the old Amphitheater; the Pyramid; and the Temple of Augustus. Nearby are the vineyards of Côte Rotie, considered the very finest wine of the Rhône region. In town, across from the Pyramid, is the famous restaurant of Ferdinand Pointe, who was the teacher for many of the best chefs in France. Pointe died many years ago, and although the restaurant is excellent, it no longer receives the same acclaim as in the past.

Lyon, the second-largest city in France, is set along the Rhône and Saône Rivers and has much to offer its visitors. Stroll through one of the lovely parks or through the cobbled streets of old Lyon on the right bank of the Saône, with its numerous shops, boutiques, restaurants, and bistros.

Musée des Beaux-Arts is France's second-largest fine arts museum with an outstanding collection of 19th- and 20th-century paintings. Musée de la Civilisation Gallo-Romaine, which is built into the Fourvière Hill, has ancient Roman relics and is located next to the old Roman Theater—the oldest in France—built in A.D. 19. Another Roman amphitheater is located at Croix Rousse.

The region of Lyon is a gastronomic paradise and gourmet heaven, being the location of many of the very best restaurants in France. In the city, you can dine at the famous Leon de Lyon and Orsi (both *Michelin* two-star establishments). Only minutes from the city is the world-famous restaurant of Chef Paul Bocuse in Collange Mount d'Or (*Michelin* three-star). Within an hour's drive are George Blanc in Vonnas, Troisgros in Roanne, and Alain Chappel in Mionney.

Some of the cruises go up to **Macon,** in the heart of the Burgundy region, where a short drive will bring you to all of the famous vineyards of the Côte de Nuit, Côte d'Or, Beaujolais, Maconnais, and Chablis wine regions.

St. Malo is set on the English Channel in the middle of Brittany, on the northwest coast of France. This is a convenient port of call for ships cruising between Great Britain and Spain. The major attraction is the charming walled town, known as Intra-Muras, filled with 17th- and 18th-century buildings, winding cobblestone streets, shops, bistros, restaurants, museums, and cathedrals. You can walk the ramparts around the entire city, which afford spectacular views of the Brittany coastline. Among the numerous excellent restaurants, several of note include La Duchesse Anne, Le Chalut, Le Chasse Maree, Abordage, and Etrave.

The specialty in all restaurants is fresh fish and seafood, especially mussels. The most popular tour from St. Malo is the drive to the picturesque island fortress of Mont St. Michel with its Benedictine abbey and gothic buildings.

Normandy is the area in the northwestern portion of France, a portion of which abuts the English Channel. Cruise ships most often visit the charming seaside fishing village of Honfleur, located at the mouth of the Seine River, connected to Le Havre by a recently constructed span bridge. The town, with its narrow cobbled streets lined with timbered buildings dating back to the 15th and 16th centuries, is best explored on foot. You can stroll along "Vieux Bassin," the horseshoe-shaped 17th-century harbor, with its numerous restaurants, cafes, shops, art galleries, and museums. Points of interest include Musée Eugene Boudin housing paintings by Boudin and other impressionists, Musée du Vieux Honfleur, and the timbered Saint Catherine's Church and bell tower, with its vaulted roof reminiscent of a ship's hull.

Honfleur is the place to sample Calvados liqueur, such great cheeses of Normandy as pont l'eveque, camembert, and liverot, mussels, and fresh fish and seafood. There are numerous small restaurants that surround the old harbor, the most highly rated being Terrace et L'Assiette (one star *Michelin*), L'Absinthe, and Entre Terre el Mer.

A 12-mile drive from Honfleur through the French countryside will bring you to Deauville, site of the annual American Film Festival. The environs surrounding the casino and Hotel Normandie with its designer shops is one of the most sophisticated, elegant areas in France. Avenue du Lucien Barrier, leading from the casino to the promenade bordering the beach, is the place to see and be seen. On the expansive beach, you can rent an umbrella or cabana named after a famous American movie star, and you can linger over a coffee or drink served in an outdoor cafe. Nearby, the Pleasure Harbor filled with sailboats and yachts is surrounded by restaurants, bistros, and small boutiques.

GERMANY

Bremerhaven, located on the North Sea between Denmark and Holland, is the outer port of Bremen, which is one of Germany's largest ports, with excellent harbor facilities. In Bremen, you may wish to visit the Old Town, which lies on the right bank of the Weser, with its historic old Gothic buildings, the Roland Monument, St. Peter's Cathedral, and the Rathaus. You can try a German meal at the Rathskeller, Essighause, St. Petrus Weinstuben und Flett, and the Atles Bremer Brauhaus.

You can drive to **Travemünde,** a Baltic beach resort with sandy dune beaches, surrounded by thick pine forests. There you can visit its casino, nightclub, and restaurant. You can also take the short trip to **Hamburg** and visit the Renaissance Rathaus with its tall clock tower, the Kunsthalle, the Stadtpark, the Musikhalle, the Historical Museum, the Schnapps Museum, the Bismarck Monument, and St. Michael's Church. Here you may wish to browse through the shops along Jungfernsteig, Grosse Bleichen, Neuer Wall, and Ballindamm; take an hour-long boat ride on the beautiful Lake Alster; eat in one of its many excellent restaurants; or partake in the city's roaring nightlife along the Reeperbahn (undoubtedly the naughtiest street in the world). Some ships travel down the Elbe River and dock at Hamburg. During the evening, the two-hour twilight boat ride around Lake Alster and its tributaries is especially enjoyable. Afterwards, a typical Hamburg dinner at Friesenkeller (opposite the Lake Alster dock) is a good bet, or one of the outdoor restaurants along the Colonnaden. For fine dining, the best-known restaurants include Landhaus Sherrer, Landhaus Dill, the dining rooms at Vier Jahreszeiten and Louis Jacob Hotels, Le Canard, and Fischereihafen.

Some ships stop at **Lübeck,** which has been an important port and city of trade since the 12th century. If you do not opt to take the one-hour drive to Hamburg, you may wish to browse through this somewhat quaint town. Places of interest include St. Mary's Church, the third largest in Germany, housing the world's largest mechanical organ; the Town Hall, featuring Gothic and Renaissance styles; and St. Anne's Museum, an old monastery that displays local handicrafts. Schiffergesellschaft is a very atmospheric, typical German restaurant housed in a 16th-century sailor's guild house, an excellent choice for lunch ashore.

RHINE AND MOSELLE RIVERS

Numerous riverboat cruise lines offer cruises down the Rhine or Moselle Rivers, passing castles and vineyards and stopping at little villages and cities along the way. These riverboats are considerably smaller than most cruise ships, and they offer fewer activities and amenities. However, on the first-class vessels, the food and service are continental and impeccable. On all the ships, each public room and cabin is designed to permit a panoramic view of the scenery as your boat lazily sails along the river. (See chapter 10 for a description of riverboat cruise lines.)

The Rhine River is one of the longest in Europe, flowing from its source in the Swiss Alps to the North Sea at Rotterdam. The Moselle has its source in the Vosges Mountains in France and flows through Luxembourg into Germany until it converges with the Rhine at Koblenz. Most of the Rhine cruises travel between Amsterdam or Rotterdam in the Netherlands and Basel, Switzerland, stopping at Düsseldorf, Cologne, Speyer, Braubach, Rüdesheim, and Heidelberg in Germany and Strasbourg in France. The most scenic area of the Rhine is the portion extending between Rüdesheim and Koblenz, which offers the greatest concentration of historic castles and fortresses, as well as the legendary Loreley cliff. Moselle River itineraries run between Koblenz at the mouth of the Moselle and the ancient village of Trier, with stops at such villages as Alken, Cochem, Beilstein, Zell, and Bernkastle-Kues. Some riverboats also continue on to Luxembourg. Overall, the Moselle itinerary is the more scenic and romantic.

Basel is a moderately large cosmopolitan city in northern **Switzerland,** a short distance from both the French and German borders. You will want to visit the Kunstmuseum of art, Münster (cathedral), Tinguely Museum, zoo, university, and shops and restaurants in the old town area. Although the Drei Könige is the best hostelry in town, if you are only staying overnight waiting to board your boat, you may prefer the Hilton, which is modern, very comfortable, has a pool and sauna, and is right near the harbor and railroad station. Hans Stucki's Bruderholz Restaurant vies for top honors in Switzerland and is a good choice for excellent haute cuisine.

Strasbourg is a charming French town on the Rhine that is definitely affected by the German influence of its neighbor. Its Gothic cathedral is one of the most impressive in existence, and the area around the cathedral is perfect for having a drink in an outdoor café, people watching, and browsing through shops. There is an impressive collection of Picasso, Dali, and Kandinsky at the Museum of Modern and Contemporary Art. One of the best ways to see Strasbourg is from a canal cruise. For a special treat, you can have lunch or dinner at the world-famous Beuerehiesel Restaurant, which sits in the middle of the lovely Orangerie park and commands three stars from *Michelin*. A *Michelin* two-star favorite here is Au Crocodile. At Au Crocodile, amiable Monique and Emile Jung will escort you through a degustation of Alsatian specialties and fine wines. Although reputed by authorities to have one of the finest wine cellars in the world and to offer one of the best all-around dining experiences in France, Emile, Monique, and their dedicated staff are gracious, humble hosts who make their guests feel welcome and special. This is a must for every aficionado of fine dining. Joggers and hikers will want to run or walk along the quay of the river (to the right as you disembark from the ship) for about a mile to Orangerie and run along the paths of the park past a children's zoo, pretty lake, and outdoor musical performances.

Heidelberg is a picturesque university town with lovely old homes and buildings built on hills along the banks of the River Neckar. The old town area consists of shops, hotels, and restaurants surrounding the university. It is quite atmospheric and dates back to the Roman era. Have lunch or a drink at the historic Ritter Hotel, which exemplifies Heidelberg in the days of *The Student Prince.* Performances of this operetta in English as well as concerts are performed on the grounds of the famous 14th-century Heidelberg Castle, which is located directly above the town overlooking the Neckar. This is also the site of the largest wine cask in existence. Riverboats offerings tours to Heidelberg generally dock at Speyer. When exploring Speyer, the major attractions include the Kaiserdom, one of the finest Romanesque cathedrals in the world; the Historical Museum of the Palatinate; the old Jewish synagogue with its well preserved mikva, or ritual baths; and the Technik Museum with its large collections of locomotives, aircraft, vintage automobiles, and automatic musical instruments, as well as a historical 420-ton U-boat. Two atmospheric restaurants are the Ratskeller in the city hall and Wirtshaft zum Alten Engel.

Rüdesheim is in the middle of the Rheingau wine area. You will want to visit the gardens and impressive monastery at Eberbach that date back to 1136. Here you can enjoy a tasting of wines from the Rheingau and explore the ancient Gothic chapel, cloisters, and wine cellars. The most interesting attraction in the city is the Siegfried's Music Museum with its fascinating display and demonstrations of mechanical musical instruments from the past hundred years. In the evening, you can wander through the numerous typical restaurants, inns, wine and beer halls, and shops located up and down the streets along the river. The most activity will be found along Drosselgasse. A good choice to dine or have a drink along with music would be Breuer's Rudesheimer Schloss. This is one of the best towns in Germany to partake of the colorful nightlife. Many of the wine gardens have orchestras specializing in folk dancing. This is the spot to watch (and join) the people having fun. Next to where the boat docks are tennis courts, a park, and a giant swimming pool. You will also enjoy the scenic 10-minute cable-car ride to Niederwald Monument.

Cologne is a lovely historic city with a picturesque vista of the Rhine. Dominating the center of town stands the beautifully preserved cathedral, which is the largest Gothic building in the world. If you are able to negotiate the 360-step climb up a spiral staircase to the top of the cathedral, you will be rewarded with a splendid view of the city. The Museum Ludwig contains a large collection of Picassos as well as works by Dali, Lichtenstein, and Warhol. Among the top-rated restaurants are Die Bastei, located in an elevated, glassed-in, three-quarter-circle building jutting out over the waters of the Rhine; the elegant Stüben House at the Excelsior Ernst Hotel; Le Moissonnieer (French), the Schweizer Stübe, a Swiss eatery near the cathedral; and the Alt Köln and Sion, which feature typical German fare. The most interesting area in which to take a walk or stop for a drink is located between the three bridges on the west bank of the river. Immediately behind the river walk are several streets filled with shops and outdoor shopping stalls. Located nine miles from Cologne is the Grandhotel Schloss Bensberg, a restored baroque castle that houses excellent French and Italian restaurants.

You can take an organized bus tour around **Düsseldorf**, a large, modern metropolis with tall buildings, elegant shops, and a good mass-transportation system. You will enjoy roaming around the colorful old town section, where you will find hundreds of little bars, shops, restaurants, and discotheques. Riverboats generally stop here only in the evening to permit passengers to partake of the nightlife in the old town area. The most highly rated restaurant in Düsseldorf is Im Schiffchen (French). For German cooking, try Aalschokker and Victorian.

Koblenz, a charming city at the confluence of the Rhine and Moselle Rivers, dates back to the Roman era and contains numerous historic landmarks. You will want to visit the Deutsches Eck monument (19th century) at the point where the rivers meet; the pillars, towers, balconies, and dormer windows of the Balduin Bridge (14th century); the Elector's Palace (18th century), a neoclassical building; the "Plan," a square with shops and restaurants surrounded by old mansions; the Florinsmarket in the old town with its old buildings, alleyways, and wine taverns; Stolzenfels Castle (19th century); the Church of Our Lady, a combination of Romanesque, Gothic, and baroque architectural styles; St. Castors Church (12th century); and of course, the little restaurants and taverns along the riverfront.

Cochem enjoys an enviable position in the heart of the Moselle wine country and is the most inundated with tourists. Many of the day boats stop here, and it is an excellent place to bed down for the night for those exploring the area by car. You can try Hotel Alte/Thorschenke (a historic inn from the 14th century), Lochspeicher, or the Landenberg. Cruise boats stop here to allow passengers to explore Reichsburg Castle and the many shops, restaurants, wine stores, bars, and guesthouses along the river. Excursions to the famous Eltz castle emanate from here also.

Bernkastel-Kues is undoubtedly the most charming, picturesque village on any of the rivers. When you step off the boat and take in the river filled with ducks and swans beneath the old bridge and the gingerbread-timbered houses and colorful dormers and steeples with a backdrop of green forests and steep vineyards as far as the eye can see, you will believe that you have just entered the world of *Hansel and Gretel.* This is also the site of the famous Bernkasteler-Doktor vineyards, and bottles of what is possibly the best of the Moselle wines can be purchased in shops here for far less than they are offered throughout the rest of the world. You will enjoy visiting the Moselle wine museum, Castle of Landshut ruins, market square; strolling down the cobblestone streets and through the shops; sampling the wine; and dining in one of the old inns or taverns.

Trier, a 2,000-year-old Roman town, sits near the end of the Moselle River, right after the junction of the Ruwer and before the Moselle splits into the Saar and tapers off. This is an important center of the Moselle wine industry and is surrounded by vineyards. You will want to visit the Roman amphitheater, the Basilica, Imperial thermal baths, Porta Nigra, the ancient black gate, the birth home of Karl Marx, and the Landesmuseum (wine artifacts) and take a stroll down one of the wine-paths (weinlehrpfad) that pass by numerous vineyards. Moselle River cruises either embark or terminate in Trier, and there are several restaurants immediately above the dock, including Pfeffermuhle, one of the best in the city. Two conveniently located restaurants in the middle of town are Zum Christophel and Romisher Kaiser. Overnight accommodations are available at the Europa Park Hotel, Holiday Inn, or Hotel Petrisberg.

GREAT BRITAIN

Your ship may dock at **Southampton,** where you will board a train to **London,** the capital and great historical city of Britain. Some ships dock at **Tilbury** or **Dover.** Smaller ships can negotiate the Thames and dock right near the Tower Bridge. Since there are hundreds of points of interest here, you will have to budget your short time in port carefully. Places of interest, history, and importance include: Westminster Abbey, where kings and queens are crowned and important personages buried; the Houses of Parliament, Big Ben, and the Palace of Westminster; Piccadilly, which is the Times Square of London; the fine shops on Bond Street, Oxford Street, and Regent Street; Trafalgar Square, with its statue of Nelson and the National Gallery; St. Paul's Cathedral, built by Sir Christopher Wren; the historic Tower of London, which now houses the crown jewels; Grosvenor Square, which is the site of the American embassy and Roosevelt Memorial; the fashionable Mayfair area, with its fine homes, hotels, and shepherd's market; beautiful Hyde Park; the law courts and Inns of Court; the British Museum; the Wax Museum; the restaurants and clubs in the Soho district; Kensington Palace; the artists' area of Chelsea; and Buckingham Palace, with its changing of the guard.

There are many well-known, excellent restaurants in London, including La Gavroche, Tante Claire, Chez Nico, the Chelsea Room and Rib Room at the Hyatt, Connaught Grill, Gordon Ramsey at Hotel Claridge, and the Savoy Grill. At lunchtime, you may enjoy trying one of the atmospheric local pubs or perhaps the historic Cheshire Cheese, built in 1667. In the evening, you may wish to take in a play or a musical at one of London's many theaters, dine and dance at one of the fine nightclubs, or gamble at a gaming club (you must arrange in advance for membership). London also offers several world-famous department stores, including Harrod's in Knightsbridge, Selfridge's on Oxford Street, and Fortnum and Mason in Piccadilly.

A short distance from Southampton, 90 miles south of London, near New Milton, is England's most charming and luxurious resort, Chewton Glen. You will enjoy dining at this uniquely beautiful and elegant country manor house and taking a stroll around its magnificent parks, nearby forests, and seaside. Another rewarding deviation, a 30-minute drive from London, is Michel Roux's Waterside Inn at Bray, which sits on one of the more picturesque section of the Thames. This is considered by many to be Great Britain's finest dining establishment. This is definitely a "do not miss" experience.

HOLLAND

Amsterdam is the capital and largest city in the Netherlands and one of the chief commercial ports of Europe. This city is made up of numerous islands surrounded by circular canals with bridges that connect the islands. You can obtain a good overall picture of the city by taking one of the glass-roofed boat tours of the canals. This is a charming, colorful city with friendly people, and you will enjoy exploring many of the areas on foot. You can visit the Royal Palace, the Tower of Tears, Rembrandt's House, the tropical museum, the Van Gogh Museum, the Amsterdam Historical Museum, the Jewish Historical Museum, Anne Frank House, and the world-famous Rijksmuseum, which houses many Dutch and European masterpieces, including Rembrandt's *The Night Watch*. You will want to shop for fine porcelains, pewter, delft, jewelry, and the antiques on Kalverstraat, Rokin, and the Leidsestraat.

There are several good cabarets and nightclubs and numerous fine Dutch and cosmopolitan restaurants. On the various narrow streets that emanate from the Leidseplein and Leidestraat, you will find hundreds of excellent ethnic restaurants including French, Italian, Greek, Argentinean, Indian, Indonesian, and even a Hard Rock Cafe. For something different, try *rijsttafel* at one of the Indonesian restaurants such as Sahid Jaya, Djawa, Samba Sebo, Speciaal, or Tempo Doeloe. Other venerable Dutch/continental eateries around town include the Silver Spoon (De Silveren Spiegel), the Five Flies (D'Vijff Vlieghen), De Roode

Leeuw, and the Black Sheep (Swarte Schaep). La Rive is a *Michelin*-rated French restaurant. After dinner you may enjoy the numerous jazz clubs or the discos in the hotels. Or you may wish to explore Amsterdam's notorious red light district near the Ouderkerksplein, where ladies of the evening of all nationalities are perched in windows luring customers. The city is also well-known for its coffee houses that specialize in offering marijuana to their patrons.

NORWAY

Norway is a long, narrow country on the northwestern edge of the European continent whose coastline is marked by long, narrow inlets called "fjords." The northern part of the country lies above the Arctic Circle and is called the "Land of the Midnight Sun" because it has long periods every summer when the sun shines 24 hours a day. Many cruise ships traverse the rocky western coast of Norway, where there is surprisingly mild weather due to the warm North Atlantic current of the Gulf Stream.

Bergen sits on the natural harbor of a sheltered fjord where mountains rise majestically around a valley. This is Norway's second largest city, where you will want to visit the colorful fish, flower, and fruit markets along the quay, Rosencrantz Tower, Bryggen (a group of wooden medieval-style warehouses along the wharf), the Hanseatic Museum, the new aquarium, Lungegardsvann (a lake surrounded by trees and flowers), Trollhaugen (the home of composer Edvard Grieg), and the Bergenhus Fortress and Haakon's Hall. A must for every visitor (when weather permits) is the funicular railway ride up 1,000 feet to the top of Mount Floyen where you can enjoy a spectacular panorama, have a snack, and hike on mountain trails. You can shop and have lunch at Bryggen or the Galleriet shopping center. The best buys are Norwegian-style sweaters. The best restaurants are the Bellevue, which has excellent views, service, and cuisine; Enfjorinen, a wharfhouse specializing in fish and seafood; To Kokker, next door; Fiskeroyen; Augustin; and Bryggestuen. For a traditional Norwegian evening, you will enjoy Fana Folklore for dining, dancing, and singing.

Stavanger is an interesting town where the major industries are sardine exporting and shipbuilding. Its marketplace is a colorful spot where peasants come from miles around to shop for fish, vegetables, and fruits. Nearby is the famous Lysefjord, thought to be one of the most spectacular fjords in the country, with its towering mountains, farms, and Pulpit Rock, which hangs 1,800 feet above the fjord. Two good restaurants are Restaurationen and Prinsen.

Trondheim is a delightful colonial city where you may want to visit the famous Nidaros Cathedral, which is one of Europe's finest Gothic buildings; the Stiftsgarden, which is a royal residence dating from the 18th century and made of wood; the Bishop's Palace; and the Museum of Music at Ringve, with its remarkable collection of musical instruments. Try the restaurant at the Britannia Hotel.

Hammerfest is one of the most northerly cities in the world, lying north of the Arctic Circle in the Land of the Midnight Sun. Here the sun does not set from May through July. From Hammerfest, your ship will proceed to Skarsvog, the North Cape, and Honningsvaag.

Oslo, located in the southern part of the country, is the capital and the largest city in Norway. Here you will want to walk down the charming main street, Karl Johansgate, to the Royal Palace, past the National Theater, the University of Oslo, the statues of Ibsen and Björnson, the cathedral, and the National Art Museum. This street is also home to the principal shopping district. You may also wish to visit the town hall, Akershus Castle (dating back to A.D. 1300, rebuilt in the 17th century), Frogner Park (scene of 150 groups of bronze and granite sculptures by Gustav Vigeland), Edvard Munch Museum, the Viking Ship Museum, and the Kon Tiki Museum at Bygdøy. At lunchtime, you will want to stop at a Norwegian restaurant and partake of the *koldtbord* (cold table), featuring fish, seafood, cheeses, meats, and salads. The Norwegians also serve *smörbrod* (open-face sandwiches) in many varieties. You may wish to shop for local handicrafts in ceramics, woven textiles, and carved woods, as well as in silver, pewter, and glass. You can see a permanent exhibition of Norwegian arts, crafts, and furniture at the Forum and at the Norwegian Design Store. The restaurants in the Grand, Scandinavia, and continental hotels are all excellent, or you can try one of the outdoor cafes or restaurants along the waterfront at Aker Brygge.

PASSENGER AND CAR FERRY SERVICE BETWEEN EUROPE AND NORWAY

Since 1990, the cruise ships of Color Line have provided transportation between Europe and Norway on comfortable vessels that accommodate both passengers and automobiles. Cabins vary greatly in size, price, and creature comforts. The least expensive are generally located below the car deck, can accommodate up to four persons in upper and lower berths, and have wash basins but no shower or toilet. The most expensive luxury suites include small lounge areas, desks, mini-bars, televisions, radios, telephones, full bathrooms with robes, and hair dryers.

Public areas on all ships include vast duty-free shops, several bars, show lounges, indoor pools, saunas, movie theaters, children's playrooms, Internet cafes, and a variety of restaurants ranging from cafeterias and coffee shops to Norwegian buffets and continental à la carte restaurants. Meals are not included in the cruise fare.

Service between Hirtshals, Denmark, and Kristiansand, Norway, which takes 4½ hours, and to Oslo, Norway, which takes 8½ hours, is offered on either the *Color Festival* (entered service 1985; 34,314 G.R.T.; carrying 2,000 passengers in 588 cabins, 340 cars), the *Skagen* (entered service 1975; 12,333 G.R.T.; carrying 1,238 passengers, 430 cars), or the *Christian IV* (entered service 1981; 15,064 G.R.T.; carrying 2,000 passengers, 530 cars).

Service between Kiel, Germany, and Oslo, Norway, which takes 19 hours, is offered daily on the *Prinsesse Ragnhild* (entered service 1981 and renovated in 1992; 38,500 G.R.T.; carrying 1,875 passengers, 770 cars).

Service between Newcastle, Great Britain, and Bergen, Haugesund, and Stavanger in Norway, which takes about 23 hours, is available three times each week on the *Color Viking* (entered service 1975 and was stretched and renovated in 1989;

20,581 G.R.T.; carrying 1,250 passengers in 420 cabins, 320 cars). Cost-conscious passengers can spend the night in a reclining airplane-style chair instead of a cabin (not recommended).

The 75,000-ton, 2,750-passenger *Color Fantasy* entered service in 2004, operating between Oslo and Kiel. It is the largest and most expensive ferry every built. A similar ship, *Color Magic,* entered service in 2007. Both vessels have a passenger capacity of 2,700 in 1,016 cabins and can carry 550 cars on the car decks. These two ships have large show-lounges with cabaret shows, Internet cafés, casinos, boutiques, playrooms and water parks for children, discos, conference centers, spas and fitness centers, numerous bars, and restaurants.

During the summer season, these ships can be quite crowded with families. The primary purpose of the line is to provide transportation for tourists, families, and those on automobile vacations with numerous diversions during the crossings. You cannot compare the level of comfort with cruise ships where passengers come to relax and luxuriate.

The general agents in the United States are Bergen Line at 405 Fifth Avenue, New York, NY 10022, telephone: (800) 323-7436.

Bergen Line, Inc. also markets Norwegian Coastal Voyages, a company that has been operating for more than 100 years and calls at 34 Norwegian ports daily. The line presently has 11 ships, most of which were built since 1993, with passenger capacities between 169 and 674. Each ship has lounges, dining rooms, 24-hour cafeterias, and souvenir and sundry shops. The newer vessels have children's playrooms, conference facilities, elevators, and cabins for disabled passengers. Fares for outside cabins range from $120 to $230 per person per day, with suites costing more and inside cabins less. (See chapter 11 for details on ships.)

The ships offer cruises six days southbound, seven days northbound, and 12 days round-trip. Itineraries include the cultural cities of Bergen and Trondheim; small arctic towns such as Tromso, Oksfjord, and Hammerfest; and passages through narrow straits and past magnificent fjords.

The newest ships of the line, the 16,053-ton *Trollfjord* and *Midnatsol* entered service in 2002 and 2003 respectively. The ships have 290 cabins and 19 suites and can accommodate 822 passengers. Public areas include numerous dining venues, a conference area, a children's area and arcade, a library, and several lounges. The ships cruise round trip from Bergen, Norway, to Kirkenes in 11 days.

POLAND

Gdynia is the Polish port where most cruise ships stop, and it is only a few miles from the popular seaside resort of Sopot, with its beautiful beaches and festivals. Here you can sun, swim, and dance. The weather is generally moderate, with temperatures ranging from the 30s in the winter to the 70s in the summer. You are also only a short distance from **Gdansk** (Danzig), the hub of the Polish shipping industry. Here you can see a rebuilt city that was nearly destroyed during World War II, and you can try one of the several good restaurants where you can consume sausages, cabbage, *czarzy chleb* (coarse rye bread), *bigos* (sauerkraut and smoked meats), *barszcz* soup, and some delicious pastries and wash it all down with one of the domestic beers.

SCOTLAND

The smaller cruise ships can dock at Leith, which is a couple of miles from the center of Edinburgh. Larger ships anchor off shore and passengers must take an hour bus ride into town. Places of interest include: Edinburgh Castle, Palace of Holyroodhouse, National Gallery of Scotland, Scottish National Gallery of Modern Art, Princess Street Gardens, and the shops along Princess Street, George Street, and Royal Mile. The Witchery by the Castle is one of Edinburg's most well-known restaurants.

SWEDEN

Stockholm is the beautiful capital of Sweden, built on more than 14 islands connected by bridges. You can walk through the cobbled, winding streets of the old town, with its ancient buildings crowded together in medieval fashion and the site of the Royal Palace and Museum. Here you can also visit antique shops, fashionable boutiques, cellar bars, and nightclubs. You will want to shop in the modern department stores such as Nordiska Kompaniet, Paul U. Bergström, and Ahlen, where you will find quality furs, Orrefors and Kosta Swedish crystal, and beautiful silver and stainless steel. You will also want to visit the town hall, one of the major architectural works of our time; Drottningholm Castle; the home of Swedish sculptor Carl Milles, filled with his own works of art; the National Museum, with its huge collection of Swedish and foreign art; and the Opera House.

You may enjoy a short trip to **Skansen,** with its zoological and botanical gardens, its charming old homes, concerts, restaurants, nightclubs, discotheques, and open-air dancing on warm summer evenings. There are opera and ballet performances at the Royal Opera and concerts at the Stockholm Concert Hall. Some of the local restaurants offer Swedish *smörgasbord,* with its large variety of fish, meat, and cheese courses. This is most often accompanied by Swedish, Danish, or German beer. Operakällaren has been considered the outstanding restaurant in Stockholm for decades. Other distinguished establishments include Restaurant Riche, the restaurants at the Grand Hotel, and the Stalmästaregarden, Diana, Kallaren Aurora, Fem Sma Hus, and Stortorgskallaren.

FERRY SERVICE FROM SWEDEN

Birka Lines, headquartered in Mariehamn, Aland Islands, offers cruises from Stockholm to Helsinki-Turku-Talinn and other Baltic countries. The 34,728-ton, 1,800-passenger *Birka Paradise* entered service in 2004. The *Birka Paradise* has many amenities similar to large cruise ships. Most of the 734 accommodations have four beds and there are some suites, including duplex suites. Public areas include a Caribbean-themed lido area, known as Paradise Beach, with a sliding glass roof, a swimming pool, two Jacuzzis, artificial palms, and artificial sunlight solar fixtures. At night the pool is covered with an automatic sliding dance floor and the area converts to a nightclub with Latin rhythms. In addition there are three saunas, a spa with five treatment rooms, numerous lounges, bars, and dance venues, duty-free shops, two main buffet restaurants, and an upscale á la cart restaurant.

FORMER U.S.S.R. (NORTH)–RUSSIA

Most of the ships that cruise to the northern European capitals stop for several days at **St. Petersburg**, formerly Leningrad, offering Western tourists an opportunity to look at the lifestyle of the Russians. St. Petersburg is the second-largest city in Russia, lying on the Baltic Sea at the eastern end of the Gulf of Finland, 400 miles northwest of Moscow. This city was built by Peter the Great in the 18th century and originally called St. Petersburg, then renamed in 1924 after V. I. Lenin, the founder of the Communist party, and then returned to its original name after the breakup of the U.S.S.R. Most of the city is on the southern bank of the Neva River, but it also covers many islands spanned by more than one hundred bridges. St. Petersburg is a city noted for its splendid palaces, fountains, parks, monuments, and 18th- and 19th-century baroque and neoclassical architecture.

The main part of the city is divided by three long avenues that meet at the Admiralty Building, which stands in the center of the city and dominates the skyline. Close to the Admiralty stands the Winter Palace, which was built in the baroque style during the 18th century and served as a winter residence for the czars until 1917. Today, it is part of the Hermitage Museum and houses many famous masterpieces from the ancient Greeks, the Italian Renaissance, and the French moderns. Nearby you can also see the Alexandrovskaya column, commemorating the Russian victory over Napoleon; the massive St. Isaac's Cathedral, with its 112 monolithic columns and 300-foot gilt cupola; and the monument to Peter the Great known as the Bronze Horseman.

In addition to the many stores, restaurants, and cafés that line the principal thoroughfare, Nevsky Prospekt, you will also want to see the Smolny Monastery and Institute, built in the nineteenth century, the Kazansky Cathedral (which now houses a museum), the Pioneer Palace (a children's recreational center), the Russian Museum, the public library, and the Kirov Theater. You may also wish to visit the Park of Culture and Rest, the Leningrad Mosque, Peter-Paul Cathedral, and Kirov Stadium. Or you can take a short drive to Petrodvorets, the summer residence of Peter the Great, where there are a number of beautiful palaces, parks, pavilions, fountains, and statues created during the 18th and 19th centuries.

On Nevsky Prospekt is the Grand Hotel Europa, a very clean, elegant European-style hotel with numerous restaurants. This is a desirable place to stop and break up your tour.

Seventeen miles south of St. Petersburg is an area formerly known as the Czar's Village and the site of the Catherine Palace, named in honor of Peter the Great's wife, Catherine I. Nearby is the town of Pushkin, where the noted poet Alexandra Pushkin studied in the early 19th century. On your return, you could visit Pavlovsk, one of Russia's most beautifully restored palaces.

Although Russian restaurants are a far cry from those of Western Europe, you may wish to stop in and soak up some local atmosphere while drinking vodka and sampling some caviar, borscht, *kasha,* or *zakouski* (highly seasoned hot hors d'oeuvres). Don't drink the water, and be prepared for very slow service. Recommended Russian restaurants include Astoria, St. Petersburg, and the restaurants in the Grand Hotel Europa. If your time is limited, you may be wise to book a tour through St. Petersburg's "Intourist" travel service. They will supply you with a car and an English-speaking guide who will escort you through all of the above sites while offering some local history along the way. With the massive changes taking place in East-West relations, you can expect vast improvements in this part of the world as a tour destination.

Cruises from the United States' West Coast, Mexico, the South Seas, Hawaii, and the Far East

To accommodate potential cruisers living on the West Coast and in the southwestern states, a number of cruise lines have based their ships in Los Angeles. Vessels of most of the major cruise lines offer a variety of cruise vacations departing from Los Angeles or San Francisco.

A number of the cruises follow the southwestern coast, calling at such Mexican ports as Cabo San Lucas, Mazatlan, Manzanillo, Puerto Vallarta, Zihuatanejo-Ixtapa, and Acapulco. Many of the ships extend their itineraries through Central America, crossing through the Panama Canal, cruising in the Caribbean, and terminating at either San Juan, Puerto Rico, or Port Everglades, Florida. During the spring and summer months, most of these same ships shift their itineraries, sailing to Canada and Alaska.

Several ships of Norwegian Cruise Line provide regular weekly cruises around the Hawaiian Islands, stopping at the islands of Oahu, Hawaii, Maui, and Kauai.

Several of the lines have scheduled longer cruises from California that stop at such exotic South Sea islands as Tahiti, Bora Bora, Moorea, Tonga, Samoa, New Caledonia, Vanuatu, and Fiji. Many of these ships go on to New Zealand, the Great Barrier Reef, and Australia, and even as far as Japan, Hong Kong, the Philippines, Indonesia, and Malaysia. The Celebrity, Crystal, Cunard, Oceania, Princess, Regent Seven Seas, Renaissance, Royal Caribbean, and Silversea cruise lines offer several cruises each year in the Far East. Star Cruises, based in Singapore, is a relative newcomer to the cruise business, specializing in diverse Asian itineraries geared for an Asian clientele. Several cruise lines offer regular cruises in French Polynesia. P & O Australia and Princess have itineraries emanating from Australia.

The following are the highlights of some of the more popular Alaskan, Mexican, Hawaiian, South Pacific, and Far Eastern ports:

ALASKA

Alaska and British Columbia have become cruise grounds for a number of ships departing from the West Coast.

Juneau, the capital of Alaska, is also the third-largest and one of the most colorful cities in the state, with a history dating back to the discovery of gold in 1879. You will enjoy cruising the myriad of fjords, straits, sounds, and passages of the Tongass National Forest, with its unsurpassed scenery and abundant wildlife. Other points of interest include the aerial tram ride that takes visitors from the cruise terminal to the top of Mt. Roberts, the incomparable Glacier Bay National Park, the Mendenhall Glacier, the Alaska State Museum, and the Golden Creek Mine Town. Most ships offer a variety of tours to Mendenhall Glacier, to the Golden Creek Mine Town, and to an Alaska salmon bake to sample the area's most famous delicacy. Other shore excursions offered by many of the cruise ships include a rafting trip down the Mendenhall River, a helicopter flight over the Mendenhall Glacier and other glaciers with a landing on an ice field, and a float plane ride to Taku Lodge through the glaciers to a wilderness habitat where visitors can gorge themselves with barbecued salmon and take a nature walk. Most ships cruising this area meander into Glacier Bay. This affords passengers an opportunity to photograph both the mirror-like blue waters with bobbing ice formations, all surrounded by jagged wilderness, mountain peaks, and fjords interlaced with gleaming white glaciers.

Ketchikan is known as Alaska's first city because it is the first major community travelers see as they journey north. The city is located on a large island at the foot of Deer Mountain with fishing, timber, and tourism comprising the major industries. The city is known for its outstanding collection of native totem poles located at Totem Heritage Center, Totem Bight Historical Park, and Saxman Village. Excursions include tours of the town and totem poles; a visit to Saxman Village to explore a native community and to view totem carvers at work and folk-loric performances; a float plane ride to Misty Fjord National Monument, a 2.2-million-acre wilderness area, home to brown and black bears, mountain goats, moose, and bald eagles; a hike up the three-mile trail from town to the top of Deer Mountain to enjoy a spectacular panorama of the harbor and wilderness; a mountain-bike tour along the shore of the Inside Passage; canoe and kayak tours; and sport fishing for salmon.

Sitka is a picturesque little city reflecting the early Russian influence of its first European settlers. You will see harbors filled with little fishing boats, roofs lined with gulls, and a backdrop of snow-peaked mountains. In the summer you can take a three-hour jet boat cruise past little islands to view bald eagles, sea otters, and humpback whales. You may wish to visit the Sitka National Monument to see its museum, totem poles, craft shops, and spruce forest paths; the Alaska museum; and St. Michael's Cathedral; or see the scenic Harbor Mountain or Mt. Verstovia and the Mt. Edgecumbe Crater. The helicopter tour, weather permitting, is a good way to see many of these sites. Possible options include a catamaran tour of Sitka's islands combined with motorized raft rides to a wildlife sanctuary, the scenic Silver Bay Cruise, or a fishing charter.

Skagway, dating back to the Gold Rush days of Alaska, is presently a tribute to that era. From the pier where your cruise ship docks, you can walk to downtown Skagway, or you can take a horse-drawn carriage or antique bus on a tour. Options for tourists include a spectacular helicopter ride landing on a glacier, a glider ride over ice fields and Glacier Bay with a float trip through a bald eagle preserve, a city and historical tour on a streetcar, a tour to an 1898 gold miners' camp, a cruise on the *Glacier Queen* to Smuggler's Avenue and the old Gold Rush town of Dyea, a bicycle or horseback ride on the Dyea Plains, a railroad tour to White Pass Summit, or a hike from town to Upper Dewey Lake.

AUSTRALIA

Australia is a young, growing country. Its location south of the equator results in the seasons being reversed, with the best weather coming in September through April. Many cruise ships dock at **Sydney,** where you will pull into a magnificent harbor and see the Sydney Harbor Bridge, the largest arch bridge in the world. You may want to browse through the shops at Centrepoint Shopping Center and look for woolens, Australian opals, jewelry, and kangaroo furs, followed by lunch or dinner at its revolving tower restaurant, which affords a spectacular view of the city and surrounding area.

Perhaps you would prefer to test your skills at surfing and skin-diving at one of the many beautiful beaches. There are numerous small, sheltered, romantic coves hemmed in by high rocky cliffs, as well as wide strands of white-sand beaches with magnificent surf. Bondi Beach, five miles south of town, offers good surf, restaurants, a pavilion, and swimming pool; Manly Beach is a resort with a lovely park, pool, and numerous restaurants reached via a 20-minute ferry ride; and Palm Beach, the most beautiful of all, is an hour-and-a-half drive north from the city. You can see the koala and the duckbill platypus at the famous Taronga Park Zoo or visit Parliament House, the botanic gardens, Hyde Park, Randwick Racecourse, and the unusually designed Sydney Opera House.

If you have time, you can take a trip through the Blue Mountains to the limestone caverns and wildlife sanctuaries at Jenolan Caves. You can go down to Circular Quay in the harbor and take a boat trip, or visit "The Rocks," an atmospheric, old town area with pubs, restaurants, souvenir shops, and art galleries. In the evening, you may want to see the theaters, bars, and nightlife in the King's Cross area, or take in a concert, opera, play, or ballet at the Sydney Opera House.

Several ships traverse the Whitsunday Islands area near Cairns and the **Great Barrier Reef.** Generally, passengers participate in organized tours on smaller crafts to see the reef. If time allows, you would enjoy visiting Hayman Island Resort, located on its own private island and considered one of the most exclusive properties in this part of the world. Visitors fly into Hamilton Island Airport and are transported to Hayman Island by one of the resort's private launches.

BRITISH COLUMBIA

Vancouver, with a population of more than one million, is Canada's third-largest and most scenic city, as well as her busiest and most famous seaport. Located just 25 miles from the U.S. border, Vancouver is the center of Canada's fishing, mining, and lumber industries. The mild climate is due to the protective mountains and warm winds from the Pacific. Places of interest to the tourist include spectacular Stanley Park, the 1,000-acre-wilderness woodland set on a peninsula with its famous zoo, aquarium, totem poles, children's amusements, and Evergreens, 5½-mile seawall path ideal for long walks, jogging, cycling, and in-line skating, and the 1½-mile walking/jogging path around lovely Lost Lagoon; Chinatown along Pender Street; the historic gaslight district known as Gastown; shops, restaurants, and cafés on Robson Street; the botanical gardens and arboretum in Queen Elizabeth Park; the fountain display in front of the City Courthouse, with its changing patterns of water and lights; and the skyride up to the top of Grouse Mountain, where there is a restaurant with a beautiful view of the environs. Shop for English woolens, china, and imports. The best shopping center is the Pacific Center Mall and boutiques on the adjoining streets.

The best hotels are Four Seasons, Pan Pacific, Sutton Place, and Hyatt for luxury and proximity to the business district where the cruise ship docks at Canada Place. However, those opting for a pre- or post-cruise stay may prefer Westin Bayshore at the entrance to Stanley Park, where the tower rooms enjoy spectacular views of the park, harbor, and snowcapped mountains. Although there are numerous restaurants featuring cuisine from around the world, for a very special gastronomic dinner, Chartwell's at the Four Seasons is a don't-miss. Here preparation, presentation, ambiance, and service blend to offer a world-class experience.

Victoria, the capital of British Columbia, is the largest city on Vancouver Island. It can be reached only by ferryboat from Vancouver. Vancouver Island is the largest island on the Pacific Coast of North America, lying directly west of Vancouver and the state of Washington. Victoria is often referred to as Canada's most British city, with its flower gardens, narrow winding streets, Parliament buildings, Provincial Museum, and Empress Hotel (an excellent choice for an Indian buffet lunch). Lumbering is the city's chief industry, and you will see beautiful forests of fir, cedar, and hemlock on mountain slopes. You may wish to see the 35-acre Butchart Gardens; one of the tallest totem poles in the world at Beacon Hill Park; numerous other totem poles at Thunderbird Park; Oak Bary Marina and Sealand; Dunsmuir Castle; the Pacific Undersea Gardens, a natural aquarium with an undersea theater; The Royal London Wax Museum; or Chaucer Lane, with its replicas of Shakespeare's and Ann Hathaway's English cottages.

BORNEO

Borneo is the name of the large island located south of the Philippines and northeast of Indonesia that is surrounded by the South China, Sulu, and Java Seas. The southeast portion of the island, known as Kalimantan, is a province of

Indonesia. The northwest section is made up of the tiny Sultanate of Brunei, which is bordered by the Malaysian states of Sabah to its north and Sarawak to its south.

Cruise ships most commonly visit Kota Kinabalu, the capital city of Sabah, or Brunei. Known as Jesseltown prior to 1968, Kota Kinabalu has a population of approximately 150,000 people of Chinese, Malay, Filipino, and Indonesian origins. Your tour of the city should include the State Mosque with its 216-foot-high minarets and lavish furnishings, the Sabah Museum, the outdoor market at Kampong Ayer Square, the 30-story cylindrical tower of the Sabah Foundation, the view of the town and offshore islands from Signal Hill, and the resort area at the Tanjung Aru Beach Hotel.

Excursions outside the city may include a visit to a tribal community at Mengkabong water village, where thatch-roofed homes built on stilts over the sea are inhabited by the Bajous. Penampang Village is where the Kadagan tribe lives today in modern stilt houses furnished with electricity, water, and hi-fi's. Here you will also see skulls wrapped in palm leaves hung from living room ceilings like wine bottles as heirlooms of the families' head-hunting ancestors. A popular all-day tour will take you to the National Park to view hundreds of varieties of wild orchids and other flora, as well as birds, monkeys, deer, a rain forest, and the famous Mt. Kinabalu, which towers 13,455 feet above the sea and is the tallest mountain in Southeast Asia.

Beach people will enjoy spending a perfect day at the lovely Tanjung Aru Beach Resort, 10 minutes from town. At the hotel, visitors can sunbathe and swim in the sea or in a large, picturesque pool, play tennis and golf, sample excellently prepared Malaysian and Chinese cuisine, and visit one of the unspoiled pristine islands that sit in the bay. For approximately $8.00 per person, the hotel's motor launch will transport you to Sulug, Memutik, Gaya, Manukan, or Sapi. These islands, reminiscent of the Yasawa Group off Fiji, boast white-sand beaches, lush tropical forests, rare varieties of sea shells, clear waters, good swimming and snorkeling, and few, if any, other visitors.

Brunei gained its independence from Great Britain in 1983 and today is an independent Islamic sultanate covering only 2,230 square miles. Most of its Malay and Chinese population enjoy a somewhat higher standard of living than their neighbors due to the large production of oil and gasoline in this country.

From the port of Muara at the mouth of the Brunei River, you can take the 17-mile drive to the capital city of Bandar Seri Begawan (BSB), or you can take a boat up the river past mangrove swamps and tie up at a wharf in the city. Across from the center of the city, connected by water taxis, is Kampang Ayer, the water village of stilt houses that encircles the Omar Ali Saifuddin Mosque, one of the largest mosques in Asia. The golden dome of the mosque dominates the view of BSB.

You will want to include a visit to the Churchill Memorial and museum; the billion-dollar Sultan's Palace, with its minarets, extensive grounds, 2,000 rooms, and 1,000 servants; and the ruins of the Stone Fort at Kota Batu, once the palace of the sultans. The Sheraton is the deluxe hotel in BSB, and you will find numerous good Malay, Chinese, and Indonesian restaurants around town. An interesting 45-minute boat ride will take you to visit a communal long house in the Temburong district, where Iban tribal people will greet you with dancing, and where you can see shrunken heads hanging from roofs.

THE FIJI ISLANDS

The Fiji Islands consist of more than five hundred scattered islands northeast of Australia in the South Pacific, with temperatures ranging from the mid-80s during the day down to the low 70s at night, and with much rain from June through October. Fiji was a British Crown Colony until 1970, when it became independent. The population of approximately 550,000 is 40 percent native Fijians (originally from Africa), 10 percent miscellaneous, and 50 percent descendants of laborers brought to the island from India. Most of the islands were formed by volcanoes and have high volcanic peaks, rolling hills, rivers, tropical rain forests, and coral reefs.

Your ship will dock at the largest island, **Viti Levu,** at either Suva or Lautoka, the port nearest to Nandi. The towns themselves are of little interest, and the real beauty is in the scenery and beaches. Depending upon your time limitations, you may wish to take a boat ride to one of the lovely, unspoiled outer islands in the Mamanuca group that lies off the coast of Lautoka. One-day trips can be arranged to Plantation, Mana, Beachcomber, Castaway, or Treasure islands, all of which offer watersports and small resorts with facilities.

If your time is more limited, you will want to spend your day at either The Fijian, Westin Denarau Island, or Sheraton Fiji Resorts. The Fijian offers a lovely beach, tennis, horseback riding, golf, numerous shops, restaurants, and other facilities. The two Sheratons are newer, more lavish, have nice pool areas, and are closer to Nandi; however, the beaches are not as desirable and they have fewer facilities. In the evening, you may enjoy attending a Fijian *mangiti,* where meats, vegetables, and seafood are wrapped in banana leaves and steamed in an oven of hot stones in the ground. After dinner, you will be entertained by native dancers in a *meke* performance (all of which is similar to the Hawaiian luau).

The most picturesque and pristine outer islands are in the Yasawa group, which includes Turtle Island and Sawa-I-Lau cave, where the movie *Blue Lagoon* was filmed. Presently, Blue Lagoon Cruises and Seafarer Cruises, Ltd., offer three- and four-night cruises to the Yasawas from the dock at Lautoka; and Captain Cook cruises from the marina at the Westin Denarau Resorts. These are very small boats on which the accommodations, food, and service were historically a far cry from your usual cruise ship; however, newer more upscale vessels were built in the 1990s and offer more comfortable surroundings.

For a very special, tropical-island experience before or after your cruise, the Wakaya Club and Vatulele Island Resort, each located on its own private island, offer the ultimate in casual luxury.

THE HAWAIIAN ISLANDS

Hawaii, composed of more than 20 islands and atolls 2,300 miles southwest of California, has a total population of approximately 800,000 and a year-round average temperature of 75 degrees. Cruise ships dock at the harbors of Honolulu in Oahu, Hilo, and Kona on the big island of Hawaii, Nawiliwili in Kauai, and Lahaina in Maui.

In **Honolulu,** on the island of **Oahu,** you will want to walk along the famous Waikiki Beach, lined with giant hotels and crowds of sunbathers, swimmers, and surfers. You can shop for your *muumuu* and other items in the mall at the Ala Moana Shopping Center, and later sail out to the *Arizona* Memorial at Pearl Harbor. If you drive past Diamond Head to the posh Kahala section, you can see beautiful homes and landscaping and finally stop at the lovely Kahala Hotel & Resort for a cool drink, a dip in the ocean, or just to watch the feeding of the dolphins and tropical fish in the hotel lagoon. If time allows, attend a luau at one of the large hotels or drive around the island to the Polynesian Cultural Center, where you can see exhibits, clothes, dances, and crafts, as well as sample foods from six different Polynesian islands. There are many exceptional restaurants on Oahu, including Hoku's at the Kahala, La Mer at Halekulani, Micheles at the Colony Surf, and Nicholas Nicholas. The most upscale resorts in Oahu are Kahala Resort, Halekulani, and Ihilani, the latter located in the Ko Olina development. All three are only 20-minute drives from the airport.

When your ship pulls into the town of **Hilo** on the big island of Hawaii, you can rent a car at the airport only 10 minutes' drive from town and purchase a map of the Hilo area. If you take Hawaii Highway 19 north for a 15-minute drive, you will reach Akaka Falls, where you can take a half-hour walk through banyan trees, ti plants, ginger plants, and other tropical vegetation to view two different waterfalls. On your drive back toward Hilo, look for the "Hawaiian Warrior Marker" on Waianunue Avenue, which will direct you to the lookout above the Rainbow Falls that flow into the Wailuku River gorge. Early in the morning you can see a rainbow on the mist of the falls.

At the north end of Banyan Drive, you can visit the 30-acre replica of Japanese gardens. If you drive for 30 miles on Hawaii Highway 11, you will arrive at Hawaii Volcanoes National Park, where you can have lunch overlooking the crater of Kilauea, an active volcano that periodically pours out molten lava. Head back by way of Chain of Craters Road to Hawaii Highway 130, following the Kalapana coastline to Kaimue black-sand beach (near where Hawaii Highway 130 intersects Hawaii Highway 137). Here there is a small cove dramatically lined with a dense grove of tall coconut trees. On the way back to Hilo on Hawaii Highway 11, you can visit the macadamia nut factory.

If you are in the area of **Kona,** on the West side of the island, you can visit coffee plantations and the Parker Ranch (second largest in the United States), or partake of the famous buffet lunch at the Mauna Kea Beach Hotel near Kamuela (a 45-mile drive north of Kona) or at its sister property, Hapuna Beach Hotel. At these hotels you can play tennis on championship Lay-Kold courts, golf at the Robert Trent Jones-designed championship course, or sun and swim in the crystal waters of the two best beaches on the island. Nearby is the equally excellent Mauna Lani Resort, which also boasts a lovely beach, pool, tennis courts, golf courses, a diversity of good restaurants, and lovely grounds. The Hilton Waikoloa features one of the most exotic swimming-pool complexes in the world, as well as vast facilities and excellent restaurants. Four Seasons Hualalai is perhaps the most elegant resort in the Kona area and offers golf, tennis, a health spa and fine dining. All over the island you will be able to see the towering peaks of the Mauna Kea and Mauna Loa mountains. There is shopping in Kona at the Kona Inn Shopping Village and Akona Kai Mall. There are a number of short cruises offered that explore the Kona coast, such as Capt. Bean's sunset cruise or moonlight cruise, the *Capt. Cook VII* glass-bottom boat cruise, and the Fairwind Tours' 50-foot trimaran (snorkeling) cruise. There is a beach at Kahaluu Beach Park, four miles south of Kona.

Kauai is the lushest and greenest of the islands. Here you will want to drive up to the top of Waimea Canyon, which is reminiscent of the Grand Canyon in Arizona; body surf at Poipu Beach; take a boat down the Wailua River to visit the famous Fern Grotto; and swim at Lumahai Beach, possibly one of the more picturesque golden-sand beaches in the world. The finest resort on the island is the Hyatt Regency Kauai near Poipu Beach. The pool complex and health spa are awesome, as are the setting and decor. Another good choice is at Princeville on Hanalai Bay.

On the island of **Maui** you can visit the Halekala Crater, which is the largest dormant volcanic crater in the world; see the 2,000-foot Iao Needle, which rises from the beautiful Iao Valley; walk through the historic and charming whaling village of Lahaina, with its shops, pubs, and restaurants; swim, golf, play tennis, and shop at the hotels in the posh Kaanapali area, such as the Hyatt, Sheraton, Westin, and Royal Lahaina; or take the picturesque, winding drive to heavenly Hana, stopping to explore the Waianapanapa Cave and black-sand beach, the unique Hana Ranch Hotel, Hamoa Beach, and the Seven Sacred Pools. Excellent resorts with full facilities include the Hyatt Regency Maui in Kaanapali, the Four Seasons and Grand Wailea in Wailea, and Kapalua Bay Resort and the Ritz-Carlton in the Kapalua area.

Although ships do not presently visit Lanai, this small island, proximate to Maui, is the home of two of Hawaii's finest resorts and golf courses. The Lodge at Koele and Manele Bay are two upscale properties with reciprocal privileges that offer the ultimate vacation experience for the well-heeled traveler.

INDIA

Bombay, (now officially known as Mumbai) India's major harbor city and one of the largest ports in the world, sprawls over seven islands linked by causeways and bridges. The city is an industrial and commercial center and the country's film capital. Your ship will dock in the Fort District near Victoria Terminus train station, the Gateway of India arch, and the famous Taj Mahal Intercontinental Hotel. This is an extremely crowded and dirty city and most streets and walks are in bad condition, which results in very slow traffic. Allow yourself plenty of time when venturing out on your own.

Major tourist attractions include The Prince of Wales Museum with its fine display of Asian art, archeology, porcelain, and jade; the Jahangir Art Gallery; Rajabai Clock Tower, a semi-Gothic monument rising 260 feet; Crawford Market, erected in 1867, where cloth, meat, fish, and vegetables are sold; Javeri Bazaar; the Jewelers Market; and Chor Bazaar, the flea market; Victoria Museum and Victoria Gardens, where elephant, camel, and pony rides are available. The Aquarium, the elegant residences, Hanging Gardens, and Kamala Nehru Park are all on Malabar Hill, an excellent locale to observe a panorama of the city, especially at sunset.

Excursions from Bombay could include Elephanta Island, six miles across Bombay Harbor. There you can view caves with impressive displays of early Hindu religious art, including the 18-foot-high panel of Siva Trimurti (a three-headed statue depicting the triple aspect of Hindu divinity); the Kanheri Caves, located in a national park 28 miles from the city, where more than 1,000 caves were carved between the second and 15th centuries. Or you can take a two-hour flight to Agra for a visit to the world-renowned Taj Mahal, built in the 17th century by the Mogul emperor Shah Jahan in tribute to his wife.

When dining in Bombay, you will want to sample authentic Indian curries (spicy stews), prawn patia (a combination of prawns, tomato, and dried spices), Dahi Maach (fish in a yogurt-ginger sauce), Biriani (saffron rice with chicken or lamb), tandoori (clay-oven prepared chicken marinated in yogurt and seasonings), and tandoori naan bread (leavened bread cooked in a clay oven). All of the better hotels, such as the Oberoi and Taj Mahal Intercontinental, have excellent Indian-style and continental restaurants. My favorite for tandoori Indian cuisine with a great view is the Kondahar on the second floor of the Oberoi.

You may enjoy bargaining in the shops for gold and silver jewelry, precious stones, marble from Agra, embroidered silks, leather goods, pottery from Jaipur, Tibetan-style carpets, and Mogul paintings reproduced on silk. The shopping arcade at the Oberoi Hotel offers several floors of shops in a clean environment away from the clamor of the streets and markets. Bargains abound and prices are as cheap as can be found anywhere in the world for this type of merchandise.

Madras (known as Chennai since 1997), is India's fourth-largest city, featuring an abundance of squalor, pollution, dense street traffic, and aggressive, annoying vendors and taxi drivers. Although this is a most disappointing port of call, many ships still visit Madras on extended world cruises because it is one of the only options en route to break up the journey from Bangkok or Singapore to the Middle East and Africa.

The city's maze of streets is easy to get lost in. You are best advised either to take an organized tour or hire your own taxi. There are three upscale hotels in the city in which to have lunch or to use as your headquarters: the Taj Corman-dal, Park Sheraton, and Chola Sheraton. Although there are shopping emporiums, you will not find the selection that exists in Bombay and Delhi. If you wish to take a walk, the least-polluted area is along Marina and Elliot's Beach, which are located about a mile to the left (south) of the harbor. You will pass by the War Memorial, Madras University, Senate House, the Moorish-style Cepauk Palace, Presidentia College, the Auna Memorial, and the Marina Swimming Pool and Aquarium.

Tours outside of Madras should include the ruins at Mahabalipuram, which date back to the seventh century A.D. and include the "Rathas" carved out of rocks in the form of temple chariots decorated with pillars, stone elephants, and guardian animals. If you prefer to spend your day at a beach resort, Taj Fisherman's Cove on Covelong Beach and V.G.P. Golden Beach Resort can be accessed south of the city on the road to Mahabalipuram.

INDONESIA

Indonesia is the world's largest archipelago, consisting of 13,677 volcanic ver-dant islands straddling the equator, 900 of which are settled.

Beautiful Bali, one of Indonesia's islands, is a tropical land with lush vegetation, rice paddies, soaring volcanic peaks, sandy seacoasts, and dense jungles of palms, bamboo, rattan, and banyan trees. The best time to visit Bali is during the dry summer season or in very early fall before the monsoons. On your tour of the island, you will want to include a visit to the most sacred Balinese temple, Pura Besakih, on the slopes of Mount Agung; the village of Ubud for paintings and the Museum of Modern Balinese Art; the village of Mas for woodcarvings; the village of Celuk for gold and silver work; the village of Klungkung for wood and bone carvings; and the Nusa Dua Beach area, with its shops and resort hotels (the Bali Grand Hyatt, Sheraton, Bali Hilton, and Nusa Dua Beach being the largest).

If your time is limited, you may wish to use one of these hotels as the focal point of your visit. Each is a lovely hotel capturing the Balinese atmosphere, offer-ing an interesting pool area, tennis courts, a sandy beach, beautiful grounds, rep-resentative shops, and an outdoor dining area where in the evening you can watch Balinese dancers and sample such Indonesian cuisine as rijsttafel (numerous dishes of meats, vegetables, and condiments with rice), satay (meat or chicken barbe-cued on skewers with peanut-coconut sauce),babi guling (baked pig), and nasi goreng (Indonesian fried rice). From here you can take side tours to the various vil-lages to shop for native crafts.

You will want to witness a performance of the Balinese dances. The "Kejak-monkey dance," where groups of nearly 200 men sit in concentric circles and act out a Balinese mythological story, is performed most evenings in several villages. There are also the "Legong," performed by three girls; the "Djoged Bumbung"; and the colorful "Barong," with its costumed characters portraying the fight between good and evil. I found the Barong dance to be the most interesting. If you prefer to spend your day at a uniquely picturesque luxury resort, there are six exquisite choices: The Four Seasons and Ritz-Carlton at Jimbaran Bay, Amandari or Four Seasons-Sayan near Ubud, Amanusa above Nusa Dua Beach, and Amankila on the east side of the island. These are possibly the most unique, romantic luxury properties in the world.

JAPAN

Off the coast of Asia, Japan consists of a group of islands with a population of more than 100 million people in an area about the size of the state of California. The weather is similar to the central United States, with cold winters, rainy springs, hot summers, and lovely autumns. Ships dock at **Yokohama,** the port of Tokyo, where you will disembark and then proceed to **Tokyo,** a modern, busy, crowded, energetic city. The best values are Japanese cameras, binoculars, transistor radios, watches, jewelry, and pearls. Be sure to bring along your passport to take advantage of the fact that many items are sold tax free to tourists, although there are few real bargains today, and most of the Japanese goods can be purchased for less in Hong Kong. The best shopping can be found in the department stores located along the Ginza area or in the arcades of the large hotels.

You will want to try such traditional Japanese dishes as *sukiyaki* (meat and vegetables sautéed in soy sauce and *sake*), *teriyaki* (slices of beef marinated in soy sauce), *tempura* (seafood or vegetables dipped in batter and deep-fried), *yakitori* (bits of chicken barbecued on a skewer), *oil-yaki* (steak broiled in oil), *shabu-shabu* (beef and vegetables cooked in a hot broth), and, of course, *sushi* and *sashimi.* All of these can be washed down with *sake* (rice wine) or Japanese beer. If you prefer, there are also excellent Italian, German, Chinese, and French restaurants in Tokyo. All food, especially beef, is outrageously expensive in restaurants. Plastic models of the food served in the restaurants are displayed outside the window of each establishment.

You may wish to attend a geisha party, where local geisha girls in kimonos serve dinner and drinks, play guitars, sing, and entertain; or you may enjoy a Noh performance, which is a historical Japanese play with music and dancing where the actors wear masks; or perhaps you will want to try a Japanese bath, where a pretty Japanese girl guides you through the ritual of steam bath, water bath, and massage, the best being at the Tokyo Onsen.

Getting around in Tokyo is difficult because many of the streets have no names or street numbers. Therefore, it is best to take a tour or have a local draw you a map with landmarks. Places of interest to visit in Tokyo include the Imperial Palace, Yasukuni Shrine, the Tokyo Tower, Shinjuku Gyoen Gardens, Zojoji Temple, Sengakuju Temple, and National Museum; or drive out 30 miles to Kamakura and visit the Hachiman Shrine and the site of the great 700-year-old bronze Buddha, which stands 42 feet high and is considered one of the world's great sculptural masterpieces. If time permits, you may wish to take a train to the Fuji Lake area and see Mount Fujiyama and one of Japan's summer resort districts offering good fishing and hunting, or you may wish to proceed on to Kyoto and visit its beautiful gardens, parks, palaces, and shrines.

Cruise ships often stop at Kagoshima. Located on the southernmost of Japan's four major islands, Kagoshima was the first city to introduce western civilization to Japan, serving as the gateway for trade and exchange between Japan and the world. The city looks out across Kinko Bay to the silhouette of Sakurajima, an active volcano. Visitors often take tours to Senganen, a serene Japanese-style landscape garden constructed in 1660, the Shuko Shuseikan Museum, and the car ferry over to Sakurajima Island to view the lunar-like landscape and lava fields created by past eruptions. The Arimura Lava Observatory, located on a small hill, is an excellent vantage point from which to observe the volcano. Excursions from Kagoshima may include the castle town of Chiran, best known for its well-preserved samurai street, and the Satsuma Peninsula with its hot springs, subtropical flora, beaches, and rocky coastlines. Here you will have views of Mt. Kaimon, a 3,000-foot-high volcano, and you can visit the famous hot springs resort of Ibusuki.

Nagasaki is another city frequently visited by cruise ships. Points of interest include the Nagasaki Peace Park and the Peace Memorial Statue, the Atomic Bomb Museum, Glover Garden, an open-air museum, and the town of Narita, the birthplace of Japanese ceramics, where you can view master works from various Japanese historical periods and make purchases to take back home.

MALAYSIA

The country of Malaysia as we know it today was formed in 1963. Its 11 million inhabitants, living in 11 states that constitute the Federation of Malaya, Sabah, and Sarawak, are made up of Malays, Chinese, and Indians. It is a country with a warm, tropical climate, much rain, and lush forests where palms, rubber trees, orchids, and hibiscus abound.

Many ships stop at the lovely topical island of Penang, which offers wide expanses of golden-sand beaches with calm, warm waters, dense forests, excellent tourist resort hotels, and a relatively high standard of living for its residents. This is one of the major resort areas in Asia. Tourist attractions include the Buddhist Temple, the Snake Temple, Botanic Gardens, a visit to a batik factory, and a ride on the funicular railway up Penang Hill. You may enjoy spending the day at the Rasa Sayang Hotel, which contains most of the facilities and amenities of luxury-class Caribbean resort hotels, including a beautiful beach with all watersports; two pools; four tennis courts; a putting range; a disco; Japanese, Malay, and continental restaurants; shops; and lovely grounds. Similar facilities can be found nearby at the Golden Sands Hotel or at the Matiara.

Some ships also dock at Port Kelang, 28 miles from Kuala Lumpur, the capital of Malaysia, where you can drive to the outskirts and visit rubber estates, palm plantations, and tin mines. Seven miles north of the city are the Bata Caves, where you take a funicular cable car to see some excellent limestone caverns with illuminated stalagmites. On your drive into the city, you can visit the beautiful Blue Mosque and gardens. In and around the city you can visit the National Museum, with displays relating to Malaysian history, arts, crafts, and commerce; the Sri Mahamariamman, a large, ornate Hindu temple; the National mosque; the Lake Gardens; Chinatown; the gambling casino at Genting Highlands; the Selangor pewter factory (the largest in the world); the PETRONAS Twin Towers, one of the tallest buildings in the world and largest shopping malls in Southeast Asia; and the Selayang batik factory. You will want to sample the many different types of Chinese cuisine as well as native Malay food, especially the delicious Malaysian satay. Satay is beef or chicken grilled on bamboo skewers with a hot sauce made from peanuts, coconut milk, and hot peppers. There are excellent continental, Chinese, and Malay restaurants in the Hilton, Shangri-La, Marriott, Mandarin Oriental, and Regent hotels. When shopping for Malaysian handicrafts, silks, batik, and pewter, you will find the best selections (but no bargains) at the TDC Bukit Nanas Handicraft Center at Jalan Raja Chulan, the Sundie Wang Shopping Complex across from the Regent Hotel, and the Sunday Market in the heart of Kumpung Bharu.

The cluster of 104 unspoiled islands that comprise the archipelago of **Langkawi** lies off the northwestern tip of Malaysia. Many cruise ships spend a day at the largest island, Pulau Langkawi, with its mountainous interior, long sandy beaches, wildlife, marine national parks, lush vegetation, and duty-free shopping. You will enjoy spending a portion of your visit at one of the large hotels or resorts, most of which are located on lovely beaches and afford opportunities to taste Malaysian dishes at their seaside restaurants. A good choice would be the Pelangi Beach Resort, only a ten-minute drive from the port with acres of grounds, beach, and exotic pools, as well as the Tanjung Rhu, located on a vast expanse of white-sand beach overlooking interesting caves and rock formations. The Datai, located on the northwest tip, is a most unique property, with large bungalows set in a tropical forest that leads down to a beach, and the island's largest golf course is nearby. However, the attitude at Datai is very snobbish, and they do not permit nonguests to roam around the property.

(For a discussion of the Malaysian region of Sabah and Kota Kinabalu see Borneo above.)

MEXICO (WEST COAST)

Mexico is as historically interesting and as culturally different as any country in Europe or Asia. The Spanish-speaking inhabitants can trace their origins to the ancient Aztec Indians, who were conquered by Spain in the 16th century. Today you can see this blend of culture against a background of breathtaking landscapes, picturesque little villages, and a sophisticated range of entertainment. The most popular cruise stops on the west coast are Cabo San Lucas, Acapulco, Mazatlan, Puerto Vallarta, Manzanillo, and Zihuatanejo-Ixtapa, which are all seacoast towns with warm winters and hot summers. Although you will be able to sample such Mexican dishes as nachos, carne asada, tacos, enchiladas, and flautas at most places, the majority of the better restaurants and hotels specialize in continental, French, and Italian cuisine.

For many years **Acapulco** has been a favorite tourist attraction of both the jet set and the average tourist because of its guaranteed good climate; large selection of hotels, restaurants, and nightclubs; and informal atmosphere. You can eat, drink, dance, sun, swim, play tennis, and golf at a number of the superdeluxe hotels. The Fairmont Acapulco Princess, built in the design of an Aztec pyramid, offers four imaginative, picturesque swimming pools, an 18-hole golf course, outdoor and indoor air-conditioned tennis courts, parasailing, water-skiing, horseback riding, seven restaurants, a state-of-the-art fitness center and luxury spa, and a discotheque. For romantics, you cannot beat the villas with private pools overlooking Acapulco Bay at Las Brisas. Other deluxe hotels with good facilities are the Mayan Palace, Camino Real, Villa Vera, Acapulco Hyatt Regency, and the Fairmont Pierre Marques. You can shop in town for native crafts in leather, pottery, wood, and silver. You can ride a parachute high in the sky behind a speedboat (parasailing), and on Sundays during the winter months, you can watch a bullfight.

A late-afternoon lunch at the open-air Paradise Restaurant on the beach (near the El Presidente Hotel) is a must. Here you can snack on grilled snapper and shrimp, sip exotic tropical drinks, dance to a lively band, haggle with vendors, and watch the locals pass by. For dinner, Acapulco boasts numerous fine restaurants, including Baikel (continental), Carlos 'n Charlie's (eclectic), Hacienda (Mexican) at the Fairmont Princess, Tabachins (gourmet) at the Fairmont Pierre Marques, Bella Vista (continental) at Las Brisas Hotel, Madieras (continental), located about a half-mile from Las Brisas, Kookaburra (seafood), Casanova (Italian), Coyuca 22 (steak and seafood), and Le Jardin Des Artistes (French). At 8:15, 9:15, 10:30, and 11:30 each evening from the nearby El Mirador Hotel, you can watch the divers at La Quebrada leap 150 feet off a cliff past jagged rocks to the sea. The Flying Pole Dancers of Papantla perform nightly at 10:30 P.M. in a huge garden next to the Hyatt Regency Hotel. Still later in the evening, disco is in full swing at Baby O's, Carlos's Chili'n Dance Hall, Hard Rock Cafe, Madara, Siboney, Palladium, and Salon Q. There are variety shows at most of the larger hotels and at Acapulco Centro Entertainment Complex.

Cabo San Lucas is a small village in Las Cabos at the tip of Baja California. Ships generally stop here for only a few hours. Tenders will drop you off in front of open-air shopping stalls that offer T-shirts, serapes, Mexican-style dresses, jewelry, and most of the same items you saw in the other Mexican ports. There are several hotels within a mile of the harbor: the Melia and the Hacienda, which have the best swimming beach and tennis courts; the Finistera, which sits atop a steep hill; and the Solar, which is fronted by a dramatic beach on the Atlantic that is not safe for swimming. Many visitors take the boat ride around "Los Arcos" to obtain a better view of these picturesque rock formations, the pelicans, and seals. There are also small boats that will transport you to and from the pristine beach that abuts the rocks and offers an ideal place to snorkel, picnic, and get away from it all. Recommended restaurants include Macambo (seafood), Mi Casa (Mexican), Ruth's Chris (steakhouse), and Giggling Marlin (wild and eclectic). If time permits, the best resort complex with golf, tennis, restaurants, pools, and a beach is Las Ventanas, a 20- to 30-minute drive from Cabo San Lucas; however, you need to make arrangements well in advance to gain admittance. Other full-facility upscale resorts include Pamilla, Four Seasons, Esperanza, Sheraton, and Westin.

Manzanillo is a busy Mexican port with fine beaches. If your ship docks here for a day, you may wish to take a 10-minute drive to Las Hadas. This ultraposh resort was built in 1974 for $60 million by Bolivian tin magnate Antenor Patino. Here you will find 204 charming villas and rooms built in Moorish, Mediterranean, and Mexican styles, with minarets and domes on top of all-white buildings, set off by colorful tropical plants and bougainvillea. The resort complex includes a king-size, lagoon-like pool with its own island, suspension bridge, waterfall, and swim-up bar, ten tennis courts, an 18-hole golf course, four restaurants, six bars, and a long strand of beach. This is where the movie *10* was filmed. Another excellent luxury resort also a short drive from where you dock is the luxurious Grand Bay Resort.

Mazatlan is the world's sportfishing capital, where you can charter a boat and fish for marlin and sailfish. You can take a horse-drawn *araña* along the shoreline drive or to the historic plaza and cathedral. As your ship pulls into the harbor, you can see the 515-foot El Faro lighthouse, which is the second-highest lighthouse in the world. You can shop for silver, jewelry, leather, Mexican pottery, and crafts at the numerous shops along the Golden Zone and at Mazatlan Arts and Crafts Center. In the Golden Zone is the stadium where you can watch the open-air performance by folkloric dancers followed by the aerial acrobatics of the famed Papantla Flyers, who twirl around a 75-foot pole. If you wish to spend the day using hotel facilities, you may wish to try El Cid or Camino Real. El Cid is the largest hotel, offering a large, picturesque pool, 15 clay tennis courts, an 18-hole golf course, water-skiing, parasailing, and numerous restaurants. If you proceed south from El Cid, you will pass by numerous shops and restaurants. For lunch, try the Shrimp Bucket, Casa Loma, or Señor Frog, a very happening place to chill out on margaritas.

Puerto Vallarta has been described as a sleepy little village, ruggedly beautiful, and romantically placed on a superb beach. The Gringo Gulch area consists of houses inhabited by wealthy foreigners. The heart of the shopping area is Juarez Street, where you will find bargains in sandals, silver, jewelry, embroidered works, colorful skirts, and dresses. You may want to swim at the beaches at the hotels, which are located a few minutes' walk from where your ship docks, and utilize their other facilities. You can try some excellent Mexican specialties while lunching at the outdoor restaurants at these hotels, or you may enjoy Las Palmas, Señor Frogs, Blue Shrimp, Café des Artistes, Thierry Blouet, and Carlos O'Brian's in the middle of town. Mismaloya, a more protected beach with a backdrop of verdant hills, is located six miles south of downtown. La Jolla de Mismaloya, an upscale hotel, is located here, as well as several secluded beaches only accessible by boat from Mismaloya Beach. Marina Vallarta, north of the harbor, in the direction of the airport, is a recently developed 445-acre resort condominium complex consisting of numerous shops, restaurants, a 400-berth marina, a 6,500-yard golf course, and numerous new hotels including the Marriott, Melia, and Villas Quinta Real. The most luxurious resort with all facilities is the Four Seasons, Punta Mita; however, it is over an hour's drive from the cruise dock.

Many of the cruise lines offer mountain bike excursions, horseback riding, kayaking, and jungle canopy adventures, as well as sailing, snorkeling, diving, and dolphin encounters.

Zihuatanejo-Ixtapa is a picturesque, pristine, unspoiled fishing village surrounded by mountains on a sparkling, protected bay. The clear waters, perfect for scuba diving and snorkeling, reveal pink coral and interesting underwater life. The brilliant flowers scent the air with a delightful fragrance, and coconut palms line the shore, where peaceful fishermen sit making their daily catch. You can spend the day at one of the numerous resorts with lovely beaches in Ixtapa, or you can take a trip by boat to the uninhabited Ixtapa Island, where you can swim, sun, and snack on a sheltered beach facing the mainland. The hotels with the most facilities are the Camino Real, Krystal, Omni, and Sheraton. There are numerous shops across from the strip of hotels in Ixtapa and there are craft shops and boutiques near the dock in Zihuatanejo. If you are in port for dinner, in addition to the hotel restaurants, you may wish to try Bogart's or the local branch of Carlos 'n Charlie's.

MYANMAR (FORMERLY BURMA)

Situated at the crossroads of Asia with India and Bangladesh on its western border and China, Thailand, and Laos to the east, this 261,000-square-mile country is a conglomeration of people and traditions. Eighty percent are Buddhists, and visitors will view Buddhist monks in yellow-orange-colored robes walking around the country.

The capital city, Yangon (formerly Rangoon), is connected to the sea by a 20-mile stretch of the Yangon River, which can be navigated by smaller cruise ships, while others transport passengers by ferryboat. The most famous site is the golden-domed, jewel-studded Shwedagon Pagoda, one of the most dynamic and important Buddhist shrines in Southeast Asia, situated on Singuttara Hill near Royal Lake and Gardens about two miles north of the city center. This is an awesome conglomeration of temples, shrines, statuary, and Buddhist architecture that you must explore barefoot. You may also enjoy visiting Sule Pagoda, a shrine believed to be built in the third century B.C. and said to contain a single hair from Buddha; the National Museum; Peoples Park; and the shopping center in town. Yangon is noted for lacquerware, fine gemstones, and jewelry including blood rubies, sapphires, and jade. Beware of fakes, and although prices are higher and less flexible in government-controlled tourist stores, they may be the safest.

The Strand is the traditional, colonial hotel reminiscent of Raffles, and the Inya

Lake and Thamada are two additional first-class hostelries. Visitors often opt for lunch at either the Royal Garden or Karaweik restaurants, both colorful structures that give the appearance of native boats floating on Royal Lake overlooking Shwedagon Pagoda.

NEW CALEDONIA

New Caledonia is an archipelago in Melanesia, southeast of New Guinea and northeast of Australia. Captain Cook discovered these islands in 1774 when the people still practiced cannibalism. France took possession in 1853 and created a penal colony where convicts were sent to mine nickel deposits. In 1956, New Caledonia became a French Overseas Territory, and in 1998, there was a referendum for self-determination. Possessing 44 percent of the world's reserves of nickel together with an abundance of other minerals, these islands are among the most prosperous in the South Pacific and are the last stronghold of white colonialism in Melanesia.

Nouméa is the capital of the main island of Grande Terre, which is 250 miles long, 30 miles wide, and protected by reefs with picturesque coastal beaches and many ridges of craggy mountains in the interior. The town is near the harbor where you may wish to visit the public market, Place des Cocotiers with its flaming royal poincianas, New Caledonian Museum for native art, St. Joseph Cathedral, and the old town hall. A more scenic itinerary would include a walk commencing at Le Meridien Hotel along the waterfront at Anse Vata, past the small aquarium to the beach at Baie de Citron.

Those wishing to spend a day at a resort can choose among Kuendu Beach Resort to the south or Le Meridien, Club Med, and Park Royal, all on Anse Vata. Two upscale (and expensive) French seafood restaurants on Anse Vata are Miratti Gascon behind the Park Royal and LaCoupole near the aquarium.

Ile des Pins, lying to the south of Grande Terre, is a lovely pine-studded island with chalk-white beaches popular with divers and sun-worshippers. You can arrange an outrigger canoe trip to the secluded beaches and warm shallow waters of Baie d'Upi and Baie d'Oro on the east coast or many of the little surrounding sandy atolls. Most cruise ships tender into Baie de Kuto, where there is an exceptional, long strand of beach lapped by aqua-blue waters. Immediately behind is Baie de Kanumera, which is more isolated and even more picturesque. Nearby are wooded forests, nature villages, camping grounds, and Hotel Kou-Bugny, a small but impressive conclave of roundevals with a pool and a restaurant a few yards off the beach at Kuto. This is one of the finest beach islands in the South Pacific.

NEW ZEALAND

New Zealand is an unusual country with green fields, tropical foliage, fjords, and snowcapped mountains. Your ship will pull into beautiful Waitemata Harbor at **Auckland,** the country's chief port, which is as far south of the equator as San Francisco is north, with similar weather, but reverse seasons. In Auckland, you can visit the crater of an extinct volcano at the top of Mount Eden, see the rare flightless kiwi bird at the zoo, look out at the city from the Intercontinental Hotel's rooftop restaurant, or take a sightseeing tour along the city's picturesque Waterfront Drive, up through the residential suburb of Tamaki Heights, and then on to Ellerslie Race Course. The best beach is Takapuna, four miles north of the city. Shoppers can purchase natural lambswool products at the duty-free shop near the harbor.

If you drive up to the fishing village of Russel, you can take a cruise through the **Bay of Islands,** passing through beautiful little islands, inlets, remote farms, beaches, and game-fishing waters. You will not want to miss taking the trip to Waitomo Caves to see the unique Glowworm Grotto, which is a huge cavern illuminated solely by the bluish glow of millions of tiny glowworms affixed to the rocky ceilings. If you fly or take a bus to **Rotorua,** you can see spectacular, steaming geysers such as Pohutu Geyser at Whakarewarewa, the hot waterfalls, colored pools, and deeply gashed craters at Waiotapu, the geysers at Wairakei near a resort complex adjoining Geyser Valley, or take the one-hour tour to Waiora Valley. Here you may wish to visit the Agrodome to watch a sheep-shearing demonstration, learn how sheep are raised, and purchase lamb's wool products.

If your ship stops at **Christchurch** you can fly, drive, or take a bus tour of the Southern Alps, visiting Mount Cook, Franz Joseph Glacier, and Milford Sound, with its waterfalls and fjords. At **Queenstown** near the southern tip of New Zealand, you can take a cable car up a mountain to view Whakatipu Glacier Lake and the Southern Alps or you can take a "jet boat" ride down the rivers past waterfalls and picturesque countryside.

PEOPLE'S REPUBLIC OF CHINA

Beijing, the grand capital of the People's Republic of China, occupies a vast, sprawling area of several thousand miles. Located in the center of the city is Tiananmen Square, the world's largest public square and the site of the Mao Zedong Memorial Hall and tomb. Across the road from the square is the entrance to the Forbidden City of the Ming Dynasty, 175 acres of elegant palaces, pavilions, courtyards, and gardens, the largest palace complex in the world.

Other important places to see and things of interest to do within the city include: a visit to the Beijing Zoo, which boasts more than 5,000 animals including its most famous residents, the pandas; a rickshaw ride through Hutong's ancient city alleys bordering courtyards where local families reside in contrast to the more modern high-rise apartments; and a performance of the unique Beijing Opera. Outside the city, you will want to visit the Sacred Way and Ming Tombs, the Badaling Hills, the best-preserved sector of the fabled Great Wall of China, and the magnificent Summer Palace, a 700-acre garden and complex of lakes, ponds, and pavilions.

Composed of 236 islands and home to five million inhabitants, **Hong Kong,** a former British crown colony and now a part of the People's Republic of China, is possibly the most exciting and fun cruise stop in this part of the world. Most of the population, industry, and commerce are concentrated in the city of Kowloon and on neighboring Hong Kong Island. These teeming metropolises are separated by lovely Victoria Harbor, which can be crossed in seven minutes on the local *Star Ferry* at a cost of approximately 15 cents. You can capture the magnificence of the harbor with its imposing skyline of high-rise buildings while crossing on this ferry or from the top of Victoria Peak, which is accessible by an eight-minute ride up the "Peak Train" (located on Hong Kong Island a mile from the ferry station). The weather is best during the dry season from July to March. In the summer, temperatures vary from the mid-70s to the high 80s, but winter temperatures are usually in the 50s and 60s.

You can arrange for various sightseeing tours that visit the floating city of Aberdeen (where the floating "Jumbo" restaurants of Hong Kong are located), where people live on junks and sampans; panoramic Victoria Peak and Peak Tower amusement and shopping complex (there the best places to eat are Cafe Disco Bar and Grill and Zens); the Zoological and Botanical Gardens; a so-so beach and semi-resort area at Repulse Bay; Ocean Park (a good family destination); and the New Territories, with their industrial complexes, farming villages, and skyscraper towns. Within a five-minute walk from Ocean Terminal in Kowloon where your ship docks are the Hong Kong Center for the Performing Arts, the Space Museum, which is a large planetarium, Kowloon Park, the *Star Ferry* terminal, and a giant indoor shopping mall. For an interesting view across to Hong Kong Island, as well as an opportunity to sample the flavor of Kowloon, take the walk along the promenade that borders the harbor and extends from where your ship docks at Ocean Terminal, past the Clock Tower, Space Museum, and luxury waterfront hotels, and ends at the post office.

With most visitors, however, sightseeing generally plays a subordinate role to the main order of the day: shopping and bargaining. Nowhere in the world can one find as vast an array of shops and quality merchandise at such competitive prices (sometimes one-third to one-half of the prices in the United States). No matter where you are, you will find shopping centers with an assortment of shops that make the major shopping malls in the United States seem like dime stores. The shops in the side streets that intersect Nathan Road (Kowloon) are touted to offer the best bargains, although you may find it easier to maneuver in the shopping centers that are found in the large office buildings and hotels, adjacent to the *Star Ferry* (Kowloon side), or those connected to the New World Hotel. On Hong Kong Island, the Admiralty Complex comprises four shopping centers connected by elevated walkways including the popular Pacific Place. The best bargains are in gold, jewelry, European designer clothes, ivory, oriental furniture and antiques, cameras, optical goods, linens, watches, pearls, jade, and leather. If you have a few days, many tailor shops will provide you with a tailor-made suit or shirts at a reasonable price (the fabrics are quality but the tailoring is not).

If all of this shopping drains your energy, you can rejuvenate at one of Hong Kong's thousands of fine restaurants, which offer cuisine from every country of the world and every region of China. Western-style steakhouses, fast-food franchises, and gourmet continental establishments also abound here. It would be impossible to list all of the good restaurants; however, if I had to pick the two best (and most expensive) with imposing panoramas, I would recommend Petrus on top the Island Shangri-La as the best French restaurant in Hong Kong, and perhaps all of Asia, where you will be treated to exquisite French cuisine accompanied by an impressive variety of international wines, and Man Wah's at the top of the Mandarin Oriental. It has an established tradition for gourmet northern Chinese dishes with a view. Other restaurants of note include: in Kowloon—Yu (seafood) and Spoon (French) at the Intercontinental; Gaddis (French), Felix (continental), and Spring Moon (Cantonese) at the Peninsula; Margaux (French) and Shang Palace (Chinese) at the Kowloon Shangri-La. On Hong Kong Island—Cafe Too (international) at the Island Shangri-La; Toscana (Italian) at the Ritz-Carlton; Isola at the International Finance Center (Italian with a view); and Grissini (Italian) at the Grand Hyatt.

There are many excellent luxury hotels, the largest and best being the Mandarin Oriental, Ritz-Carlton, Four Seasons, Island Shangri-La, Grand Hyatt, Conrad, and Marriott on Hong Kong Island and the Intercontinental, Peninsula, Shangri-La, Hyatt Regency, and Nikko on Kowloon. We found the Island Shangri-La outstanding in all areas including decor, room comfort, service, dining, and amenities.

If time allows, you may wish to arrange a one- or two-day side tour to the Portuguese territory of Macau or to other border cities of the People's Republic of China.

Kuangchow (Canton), lies on the Pearl River 113 miles from Hong Kong (accessible by a three-hour train ride or hoverferry). Autumn is the best time of year to visit, with the least rain and temperatures in the 70s. Summers are somewhat hotter, and in the winter the temperatures vary from the high 40s to the low 60s.

Few of the six million inhabitants of Kuangchow and its environs speak English well enough to answer your questions. Therefore, getting from place to place is very difficult, and you will see more on an organized tour. Do not depend on the taxi drivers, hotel attendants, or service people in the restaurants to understand English. If you go off by yourself, have the name of the place you are visiting as well as the name of the place to which you plan to return written out in Chinese letters. Taxis are the best means of transportation, and they are relatively inexpensive.

Although Kuangchow is reputed to be one of the gastronomic capitals of Chinese cuisine, you will find the food in all the restaurants a far cry from the Cantonese food you have eaten at home, in Hong Kong, or in other Asian cities. You can shop for Chinese arts and handicrafts in the Friendship Stores or the People's Department Store.

In Kuangchow proper, you will want to visit the "Temple of the Six Banyan Trees" and the neighboring nine-story-high "Flowering Pagoda," the Canton Zoo, which is the home of the Chinese panda, the Guangzhou museum in Yuexiu Park, Guangxiao Temple, Dr. Sun Yat-Sen Memorial Hall, the Cultural Park, the South China Botanical Gardens, and the Orchid Garden. If you are in Kuangchow in the fall or spring, you can visit the Kuangchow Export Trade Fair.

Scenic spots to be found outside the city are Seven-Star Crags, 70 miles west, with cliffs, caves, lakes, and Chinese pavilions; Conghua Hot Springs, 50 miles northeast, a tourist health resort; Xiqiao Hill scenic area, 40 miles west, with 72 peaks, stone caves, waterfalls, and springs; and Foshan City, 17 miles southwest, famous for its artistic porcelain, pottery works, art, crafts, and its 900-year-old Ancestral Temple.

During the past several decades, **Shanghai** has established itself as one of the major ports of call in mainland China. The shopping and dining options here are every bit as attractive as Hong Kong, as are the numerous districts of the city, each with its own unique characteristics. Any exploration of the city should include the Bund, a broad waterfront boulevard lined with stately European-influenced buildings and upscale restaurants and shops; the Pudong New District, site of the futuristic Oriental Pearl TV Tower and the incredible Jin Mao Building (the fourth-tallest in the world), which houses offices, shops, and the Grand Hyatt Hotel; the Old Town, a vibrant marketplace surrounding the unique, beautiful YuYuan Garden with its exquisite rockeries, dragon walls, pavilions, and towers. Be sure to also visit the shops along Nanjing Lu street; People's Square and People's Park; the Shanghai Museum with the country's premier collection of art and artifacts; and the Jade Buddha, a six-and-a-half-foot high, 455-pound seated Buddha constructed of white jade. Shanghai boasts some of Southeast Asia's most modern and magnificent hotels, as well as a plethora of fine-dining possibilities with cuisines from the various regions of China as well as from countries around the world.

Many visitors include the historical city of **Xian** on their way to a Yangtze River cruise. Encircled by a complete ancient city wall with deep moats and draw bridges, the wall stretches for nine miles. Within the city, points of interest include the Bell Tower, Drum Tower, and China's greatest archeological treasure, the Qin Mausoleum, housing one of the eight wonders of the ancient world, the Terra Cotta Army. Here more than 7,000 life-size terra cotta warriors in full battle gear standing in formation were buried along with Emperor Qin Shi Huang over 200 years before the common era. A great place to overnight would be the Sofitel in Xian, one of the more modern and posh hotels in China. In the evening, the exceptional dinner and the Vegas-style song and dance performance at the Tang Dynasty Restaurant is a must.

Many visitors to China opt for a **Yangtze River** cruise since the river is surrounded by some of the world's most spectacular landscapes: mist mountains, breathtaking gorges, and serene lagoons. Key ports along the way include Chongqing, the gateway for downstream Yangtze River cruises and a large, bustling city; Fengdu, a 40-minute drive from the one-mile-long Snow Jade Cave with its limestone formations; the Shibaozai Temple, a 12-story red pagoda perched on a sheer cliff built in the 17th century; the renowned Three Gorges with the misty green mountains of Wu (Witches) Gorge and the Twelve Peaks; the remarkable canyons of the Lesser Three Gorges on the Daning River, where sheer cliffs and steep mountains rise on either side and clear water flows between towering peaks covered with lush greenery; Sandouping, the site of the five-state locks of the Three Gorges Dam, the world's largest; and Wuhan, the gateway from upstream Yangtze cruises and the location of the Hubei Provincial Museum. Since most of the riverboats only have Chinese doctors and Chinese medicines, travelers on these cruises would be well advised to bring along their own antibiotics, cold medicines, and any other drugs they may need should they become ill.

PHILIPPINES

The Philippines is a mountainous country with fertile plains, tropical vegetation, and dense forests. After 350 years of Spanish rule, it became a U.S. possession and was given its independence in 1946. The official languages are English, Filipino, and Spanish. Most of the people speak a dialect of English that is very difficult to understand.

The country is composed of more than 7,000 islands, the principal city of **Manila** being located on the island of Luzon. Your tour of the city should include the Ayala Historical Museum; the Cultural Center; the National Museum; the Nayong Filipino, a showcase of the country's six major regions exhibiting typical living quarters and handicrafts; the wealthy residential area of Forbes Park; and the walled city at Intramuros, the site of the first Spanish settlement.

Although shopping in Manila does not compare with shopping in Hong Kong, Singapore, or Bangkok, there are bargains to be found in handicrafts, rattan, sarongs, embroideries, ladies' bags, and rings. The best shopping areas are in the Ermita district, along Roxas Boulevard and the Makati Commercial Center. Those wishing to try their luck at craps, roulette, blackjack, baccarat, and fan tan can be accommodated 24 hours a day at a large casino in the Philippine Village Hotel. Most of the major luxury hotels and restaurants are located in the Ermita and "reclaimed area" districts along Manila Bay. The Philippines Plaza Hotel and Shangri-La are large hotels that command impressive views of the bay and offer a wide range of amenities.

Typical Philippine food includes *lechon* (pig on a spit), chicken and pork *adobo* (a spicy dish), *lumpia* (a crêpe-like food combining coconut, pork, shrimp, and vegetables in a tissue-thin wrapping), various fresh local fish, and delicious pineapple, bananas, mango, and papaya. Although the food is not as tasty, colorful, or well-prepared as Chinese food, the local San Miguel beer is one of the richest, most tasty brews I have come across. Western-style foods (continental, French, Italian, steaks, and so on) and token Filipino fare can be found at restaurants and in all the major hotels, where you will also find nightclubs and discos for dancing.

If your time is not too limited, the real beauty of the islands is to be found outside of the densely populated, dirty cities. A two-hour drive to Pagsanjan Falls will take you past native villages, green-clad mountains, and beautiful palm forests to an interesting river and waterfall. Here you can rent a canoe with two skilled paddlers and "shoot the rapids." The trip up and down the river takes about one-and-a-half to two hours, during which you wind through tall hills covered with giant palms. Parts of the river are calm, with water buffalo lazily bathing in the sun, while other portions contain strong currents and rapids.

The half-day trip to Hidden Valley is one of the most rewarding excursions I have ever experienced in my travels. Here you can hike down a one-mile trail through a forest of countless varieties of tropical trees, past natural pools to a picturesque waterfall. The first pool you encounter provides one of the most satisfying treats for the senses you could imagine. The setting is that of two blue-green pools separated by a tiny waterfall surrounded by hills laden with tropical trees and vegetation. The water is clear and warm and the area smells of fragrant flowers. Swimming in that pool is an occasion you will never forget and never equal. The price of about $7.50 per person to enter Hidden Valley includes lunch, soft drinks, and full use of the facilities.

The excursion to Hidden Valley can be combined with a trip to Pagsanjan and can be completed in about nine hours.

SAMOA

Samoa consists of 16 islands in the South Pacific, the six most easterly ones being owned by the United States. The 192,000 people are mostly Polynesian. The temperature is hot and humid, getting up to the 90s during the day. There is a great deal of heavy rain in the winter months. Most of the restaurants serve American-style food. You can attend a tribal feast that is called *fia-fia* and is similar to the Hawaiian *luau,* the Tahitian *tamaaroa,* and the Fijian *mangiti,* featuring pig, chicken, or fish steamed over a hot stone oven. American Samoa's main island, **Tutilla,** consists of volcanic formations surrounded by coral reefs, with green tropical forests and small villages.

The main village, Pago Pago (pronounced "Pango Pango"), is adjacent to the harbor, contains a few craft shops, grocery stores, and K-mart-style department stores. The only hotel, the Rainmaker, is a five-minute walk from where your ship docks, and contains two hundred rooms. It is located on a peninsula jutting out into the bay and includes a small pool, an area to swim in the bay, a restaurant, and a souvenir shop. If you take a drive along the South Coast, you will pass a few small villages, the airport, numerous small churches, native huts called *fares,* and eventually arrive at Amanave Beach, which is somewhat picturesque but has no changing facilities and too many rocks to permit serious swimming. The organized tours afford an opportunity to sample typical island food and folklore shows. You may wish you had passed up the food. Golfers can play the nine-hole course near the airport.

SINGAPORE

The island of Singapore is situated at the southern extremity of the Malay Peninsula, only 85 miles north of the equator, with a hot and humid climate varying from 75 degrees at night up to 90 degrees during the day. The country is only 26 miles long by 14 miles wide and was a British colony for 140 years. In 1963, it became part of the Federation of Malaysia, but tensions between Malays and ethnic Chinese led to Singapore becoming a separate nation two years later. Its population of 2½ million is 76 percent Chinese, 15 percent Malay, and 9 percent mixed English, Indian, and Pakistani. You will find it to be the cleanest, most modern country in Eastern Asia.

Your sightseeing tour of Singapore should include the lush botanic gardens, an excellent venue for walking or jogging, the golden Hindu temple of Sri Mariamman, China Town, the Arab District, Asian Civilizations Museum, Singapore History Museum, Marina Square, Zoological Gardens and Night Safari Park, the food stalls in the street markets, the Jarong Bird Park, Raffle's City, and the panoramic cable-car ride from Mt. Faber to Sentosa Island.

Sentosa Island lies directly across from the World Trade Center, and those not opting for the cable-car ride can take a five-minute ferryboat or a bus. The best way to obtain a feel for the island is to take the free monorail excursion. The beaches here are beautiful, and a good destination is the Rasa Sentosa Resort, which lies on a palm-lined, white-sand protected beach across from the Underwater World Oceanarium and monorail stop. Other attractions here include: Volcanoland Theme Park; Fountain Gardens; the Coralarium; Asian Village; a wax museum, Fort Siloso; and several historical museums.

Although prices are somewhat higher than in Hong Kong, Singapore offers good free port shopping. You will find large varieties of cameras, watches, radios, antiques, leather goods, jewelry, ivory, and carpets. The major shopping areas are Change Alley, Raffle's City and Raffles Hotel Arcade, the numerous large shopping centers along and near Orchard Road, Singapore Handicraft Center, Tanglin Shopping Center, Far East Plaza, Shaw Center, Lucky Plaza, Tangs, Scotts, Tong Building, and Wisma Atria.

Singapore boasts numerous restaurants with excellent Western, Chinese, Thai, Malasian, and Indian cuisine. Many of the hotels offer elaborate inter-national buffets enabling guests to sample all of these varied cuisines at one sitting. Mezza Nine at the Grand Hyatt features menus from nine different countries and may be a good choice for lunch. Some of the more highly recommended Chinese restaurants include: Jiang Nan-Chun at the Four Seasons, Chang Palace at the Shangri-La, Li Bai at the Sheraton Towers, and Chang Jiang at the Goodwood Park. Other popular restaurants, featuring a variety of international cuisine, include: Les Ami in the Botanical Gardens, Blu on top of the Shangri-La, Oscars at the Conrad, L'Aigle d'Or at the Duxton, Tandoor at the Holiday Inn Park View, Nadaman at the Shangri-La, Compass Rose at the Westin, Michaelangelo, and Indochine. The famous Raffles Hotel has been restored and is the "in place" for high tea. Although less appealing, you can inexpensively sample a variety of all the foods of Eastern

Asia in the food stalls at Newton Circus and at Rasa Singapura behind the Hand-icraft Center and on Sentosa Island.

There are Asian cultural shows offered with dinner at many of the larger hotels, as well as at nightclubs, discos, and supper clubs. The luxury hotels offering the most facilities, restaurants, and entertainment are the Shangri-La, Ritz-Carlton Millenium, Four Seasons, Westin, Oriental, Marina Mandarin, Pan Pacific, Conrad, and Grand Hyatt.

SOCIETY ISLANDS—FRENCH POLYNESIA (BORA BORA, HUAHINE, MOOREA, RAIATEA/TAHAA, AND TAHITI)

French Polynesia, or the Society Islands, is a group of 14 inhabited islands in the South Pacific, 4,200 miles southwest of San Francisco, that enjoys an ideal climate and trade winds with temperatures ranging from a low of around 70 to the upper 80s. December through April can be humid and rainy.

The islands are administered as an overseas territory of France, and French is the official language. Life is quite informal, and jackets and ties are seldom seen.

I found the Tahitian people working in the hotels, restaurants, and shops to be unhelpful, impatient, and generally rude. This gives one a feeling of annoyance when visiting these otherwise lovely islands.

Although there are numerous French-style restaurants in the hotels and in Papeete (Tahiti), none approach the quality of French restaurants in Europe or in the United States, and service is generally disappointing considering the high prices. Shopping is limited to souvenirs, T-shirts, *pareos* (native skirts), and a few French imports. If possible, you will enjoy attending a *tamaaroa,* a native feast similar to a *luau,* at one of the hotels, where a pig or chicken will be roasted over hot stones and served with vegetables, fruits, and coconut.

The largest of the islands, but—contrary to popular belief—not the prettiest, is **Tahiti,** with its main town of Papeete. Here you can stroll down a picturesque waterfront looking out at the island of Moorea, shop for a few French imports, dine at several so-so French restaurants, or take a drive around the island and visit the Gauguin Museum, the blowhole at Arahoko, the Cascade of Vaipahi, the water grotto of Maraa, and the waterfalls and rapid streams that cut into the steep mountains. There are no great beaches on the island of Tahiti; however, there are three "first-class" (not deluxe) hotels that have pools and beaches, and will arrange deep-sea fishing, water-skiing, or a tour of the lagoon. The Intercontinental (formerly the Tahiti Beachcomber Parkroyal) is about four miles from Papeete (your best bet). Other possibilities include Le Meridien, about nine miles from Papeete, and the Outrigger, only a few minutes from town. You can try the restaurants in the hotels, or La Chaumiere or Belvedere up in the mountains (a short taxi ride away), which offer a good view of the island. The Lotus, situated on the lagoon at Tahiti Beachcomber Parkroyal, offers the most picturesque setting, along with an impressive French menu. L'eau a la Bouche, in town, is reputed to serve up some of the best cuisine, and Coco's is currently the place to see and be seen.

Bora Bora is a small, unspoiled dream island with haunting mountains and some of the most beautiful palm tree-lined, snow-white beaches in the world. The waters surrounding the main island (which is only 20 miles in circumference) are protected by a coral reef that creates miles of a beautiful aqua-colored lagoon containing tiny pristine islets where you can sun on virgin beaches and swim in crystal-clear waters.

The main town of Vaitape is composed of small grocery stores, a hospital, and a few souvenir shops. In the lagoon, set on their own private islands are the Bora Bora Lagoon Resort, Le Meridien Bora Bora, and Pearl Beach Resorts where you may wish to make arrangements to have lunch and spend the day. These properties are as close to paradise in the South Seas as you will find. Other possibilities to spend your day in port include Hotel Bora Bora, three miles from town, and the Intercontinental (formerly Moana Beach Parkroyal Hotel), a mile farther down the road. All of these hotels are quite posh by Polynesian standards, with excellent restaurants and lovely white-sand beaches. There is snorkeling in the waters in front of all the hotels.

There is only one road that circles 17 miles around the island. You can navigate around this road and explore the island by renting a Jeep "funcar," moped, or bicycle.

Probably the most spectacular experience to be had in Bora Bora is watching the sun set slowly over the lagoon and mountains, followed by the illumination of the sky and sea to a bright orange and purple.

Huahine is located approximately 110 miles from Tahiti. The islands' population of 5,400 is spread along two separate islands measuring 28 square miles. Huahine Nui (Big Huahine) to the north and Huahine Iti (Little Huahine) to the south are connected by a small bridge. The island's rugged landscape and blue bays provide a colorful setting for the myriad of archeological and historical sites.

Places of interest include the small museum and cultural center at the 16th-century Fare Pote'e; a restored ancient temple, Matairea-Rahi, on Matairea Hill; Marae Manunu, a Polynesian religious temple that rises up between the sea and lagoon on Oavarei Motu; the blue- and green-eyed sacred eels, measuring 16 to 23 feet, at the village of Faie; and the typical south sea village of Fare with its so-so boutiques, snack bars, and copra warehouses. From Fare you can take the Te Tiare Beach Resort's motor launch to this lovely, secluded resort with a small white-sand beach, pool, restaurant, bar, and 41 garden, beach, and overwater bungalows. This is the most enjoyable way to spend your day. Another possiblity is the Hotel Sofitel, which also is situated on a beach.

Moorea is another incredibly lovely, lush, tropical island somewhat larger than Bora Bora, only 12 miles from the island of Tahiti, accessible by launch or air taxi. Here there are numerous needle mountain spires (including the fabled Bali Hai), green valleys, and white-sand beaches bordering a protected lagoon. You can take the 37-mile drive around the island by car or motor scooter. The most picturesque spot is Belvedere, about a 15-minute drive west of the airport. Here you proceed up a road through pineapple fields, coconut palms, and numerous varieties of tropical vegetation to a lookout point where you have a magnificent view of Cook's Bay, Papetoai Bay, and Moorea's jagged mountain peaks. You can swim, snorkel, water-ski, take a sailboat ride, play tennis, and have lunch at any of the three largest hotels on the island: Club Med (about a 35-minute drive west of the airport, but this may be closed), Club Bali Hai (about a 10-minute drive west of the airport), and Kia Ora (about a five-minute drive south of the airport). The most upscale resort on the island is the Intercontinental (formerly Moorea Beachcomber Parkroyal), an excellent place to spend a few days before or after your cruise. A branch of Dolphin Quest is located at the resort.

There is no special shopping center, only an occasional boutique offering native dresses, *pareos,* T-shirts, and wicker baskets. On the road behind Club Med are shops and small restaurants. The Plantation and L'Aventura located here are excellent choices for a French dinner in charming island settings.

Rangiora in the Tuamotu Archipelago in French Polynesia, located 200 miles northwest of Papeete, is composed of a series of islands and motus surrounding a blue lagoon. The one major hotel, Kia Ora, is composed of beachfront and overwater bungalows, a restaurant, and a so-so beach. Unless you opt for snorkeling, diving, or a glass-bottom-boat excursion, the only other choice is a scenic walk along the lagoon on the Pacific side of the island.

Raiatea and **Tahaa**—these two mountainous islands, located immediately to the south of Bora Bora, 125 miles northwest from Tahiti, share a common coral foundation and a protected lagoon filled with small white-sand motus. Mt. Tefateaiti, rising 3,333 feet, dominates Raiatea, and Mt. Ohiri at 1,935 feet is the highest point on Tahaa.

There are no respectable beaches on either island, but snorkeling, scuba diving, and swimming opportunities are offered on sailing excursions to the motus. A popular way to explore Raiatea is a tour that commences in a motorized outrigger canoe along the perimeter of the island and up the jungle Faaroa River, followed by a Jeep ride back along the single road that stops along the way to explore small coconut and vanilla plantations, waterfalls, and the base of verdant mountains. A boat shuttle operates between Raiatea and Tahaa. The few small hotels have no beaches and are not worth visiting. Points of interest include the vanilla plantations, Polynesian petroghes carved in basaltic stone in the Mitimitiaute and Haapapaara Valleys, the Taputapuatea archeological site, and the tiare-lipetechi, a rare white flower found on Temehani Mountain.

SOUTH KOREA

Cruise ships visiting South Korea dock in the port city of **Inch'on.** Sites in Inch'on include the Inch'on Landing Hall, the Yeonan Pier Fish Market, and the Jayu Freedom Park. From this port city it is necessary to take a three-quarter- to one-hour drive to the capital city of Seoul. Peeking out from mega-modern high-rises and scattered among the 12-lane highways and the Han Gang River are traces of the city's 5,000-year history: temples, city gates, palaces, and gardens. Visits to this city should include the new national Museum of Korea, the world's sixth-largest museum and the premier institution of Korean National Culture exhibits; the Namdaemum Market, a traditional market for shopping and bargaining; a few of the well-preserved palaces located within the city; Namsan Park; a Zen meditation service and tea ceremony at the Jogyejong Buddhist Temple; the Korean Folk Village; the DMZ (Demilitarized Zone) and the Third Tunnel. Deluxe hotels scattered around Seoul include the Grand Hyatt, Ritz-Carlton, Swiss Grand, Westin Chosun, Hilton, and Grand Intercontinental.

TAIWAN

Surrounded by mountains and crisscrossed by rivers, **Taipei,** the center of government for the Republic of China, is a modern, cosmopolitan city infused with ancient culture and tradition. From the port city of **Chilung** where ships dock, it is a 30- to 40-minute drive to Taipei. The most important sites include the National Palace Museum, which houses an important art collection of 700,000 items of jade, bronze, porcelain, lacquers, and ancient Chinese paintings and prints; Martyrs' Shrine, a memorial to those who sacrificed their lives in founding the Republic of China, with plaques detailing the past 150 years of the country's history; the Chiang Kai-shek Memorial set in 63 acres of parks and landscaped gardens; Sun Yat-sen's Memorial; Taipei 101, the world's tallest building; and Yangmingshan National Park with its butterfly corridor, bird watching trail, hot springs, volcanic hollows, mountains, and cherry blossoms.

THAILAND

Bangkok, the capital of Thailand (known as Siam until 1939), with its six million inhabitants, 94 percent of whom are Buddhists, is a city of contrasts. At first glance, it appears to be a noisy, polluted city with hundreds of hotels, massage parlors, shops, poverty, and horrendous traffic jams. Further exploration reveals a fascinating, well-preserved Asian culture represented by its beautiful temples, palaces, and the more primitive way of life to which many of its people still cling.

Any visit to Bangkok must start with an early-morning cruise down the Chao Phraya River (River of the Kings) to the "floating markets." The trip will start at the dock next to the Oriental and Shangri-La hotels and will take you past the huts and junks of the "river people," past numerous Buddhist temples (called "Wats"), and past the marketplace where the river people come in their dugout canoes to buy and sell their wares. Before you return, your boat will visit one of the most famous and colorful Wats, The Temple of the Dawn. You can also take an afternoon tour into the adjoining countryside on the "Rice Barge Cruise" to view rural family life along the canals.

In the city, you will want to tour the magnificent Grand Palace and the adjacent Wat Phra Keo housing the chapel of the Emerald Buddha, which is 31 inches high, carved out of emerald-colored jasper, and adorned with gold and jewels. You will also want to visit Wat Traimitr, the temple of the famous Golden Buddha, which is 5½ tons of solid gold, Wat Pho, the Temple of the Reclining Buddha, the National Art Gallery, and the National Museum.

An interesting afternoon tour outside the city goes to the Rose Garden, where energetic young Thais entertain you with an excellent cultural show that includes Thai boxing, sword fighting, classical and folk dancing, and elephants at work.

The six most posh hotels with pools, restaurants, entertainment, and other facilities are the Oriental (which is considered by many to be the "best hotel in the world"), Shangri-La, Regent, Peninsula, Ritz-Carlton, and Dusit Thani. The best French-style restaurant is the Normandie, which sits on top of the Oriental Hotel, overlooking the River of the Kings. This ultra-posh, romantic, and expensive dining room features gourmet French cuisine with menus created by acclaimed French chefs. Angelini, the Italian restaurant at the Shangri-La, is also excellent, as is Mezzaluna.

You can try authentic, spicy, Thai food at numerous restaurants throughout the city. It is best to get a recommendation from a local resident. Several tourist-oriented Thai restaurants provide a fixed menu of toned-down Thai dishes, together with Thai dancing. These include the Thai restaurants located on the river at the Oriental and Shangri-La Hotels, as well as the Spice Market at the Regent. Sala Rim Naam at the Oriental is exceptional and its lunch buffet provides an opportunity to sample a large variety of Thai dishes. Dinner cruises up and down the River of the Kings are also widely available. In the evening, many visitors enjoy exploring the notorious Patpong Road (a few blocks from the Dusit Thani Hotel) with its massage parlors and live sex shows.

The stores offering the best variety of Thai silks, handicrafts, paintings, and jewelry are located in the shopping centers adjacent to many of the hotels; however the best bargains are found in the stalls along the streets.

Some ships dock near the resort town of **Pattaya**, 85 miles from Bangkok. This is a rather crowded strip of resort hotels, souvenir shops, restaurants, massage parlors, and mediocre beaches. The largest and most secluded hotel with the best beach, pool, tennis courts, and restaurants is the Royal Cliff, which occupies some impressive acreage on a cliff overlooking the Bay of Thailand.

Ko Sumui is one of the most scenic islands in Thailand's 80 small-island archipelago. Places to visit include Wat Phra Yai, a temple housing the giant golden "Big Buddha," Safari Elephant Camp for an elephant show, Namuang Waterfall, as well as a rice field to watch a buffalo show or coconut and rubber plantations. Other choices may include elephant trekking through tropical jungles or relaxing on one of the numerous white-sand beaches. Chaweng Beach is lined with numerous hotels and is the most populated stretch of the island. Central Samui Beach Resort offers the most facilities in this area. Royal Meridien is a luxury resort with a pristine beach near the port area; however, prior arrangements must be made to gain entrance.

Phuket is a small island south of the mainland in the Andaman Sea. The beaches here are among the best in the world. Amanpuri Resort is situated on a coconut plantation on Pansea Beach and is one of the most romantic and exotically beautiful resorts in the world—as well as an excellent choice for lunch and a refreshing swim in warm, crystal-clear waters. The Dusit Laguna, Sheraton Grand Laguna, Allemanda, and the luxurious Banyon Tree resorts are located at the Laguna Phuket Resort complex on Bang Tao Beach. This is the best place to experience an elephant ride. At Banyon Tree there is a full-scale spa facility with an 18-hole golf course and the most lavish pool villas in the world. A cruise around Phang Nga Bay is a must. Here you will find a labyrinth of forested limestone pillars rearing out of the Andaman Sea. You can explore caves, caverns, mangrove-lined tropical rivers, and the island where the James Bond movie *Man with the Golden Gun* was filmed. Half-day cruises to numerous pristine islands and excellent diving and snorkeling locations are also available, including excursions to the Surin Islands, Similan Islands, Rok Nok, Khai Nok, Krabi and Phi Phi Islands. Other sights of interest include the Nan Tok Tone Sai Waterfall in Khao Phra Taew Park, a national forest and wild-life preserve; the Marine Station, with its display of more than 100 species of fish; the temple of Wat Chalong; Phuket Fantasea theme park on Kamala Bay, Thai Cultural Village for a performance of Thai dancing, sword fighting, boxing and elephants at work, and Phuket Town. Shopping for Thai silk and batik fabrics, precious stones and silver, gold, copies of designer watches, souvenirs, and lacquerware items is best along Patong Beach, a colorful area lined with hotels, restaurants, and shops, which is located across from Phuket's most populated public beach.

VANUATU

This Y-shaped archipelago of 82 islands covering 400 miles in the Melanesia area of the South Pacific, northwest of Fiji, north of New Zealand, and east of Australia, gained its independence from a combined French and English rule in 1980 when it was known as New Hebrides. There are two main islands, Espiritu Santo and Efate.

Luganville, or **Santo,** as it is locally called, is the only large town on Espiritu Santo, where 100,000 U.S. servicemen were stationed during World War II. Today there is little of interest in town save the open-air farmers' market by the river or a stroll along the paths separating the native homes. Possible tours include snorkeling at Million Dollar Point, an outrigger canoe ride on the Sarakata River, or a tour around the island to see some historic points from World War II.

Port Vila on Efate Island is the administrative, commercial, and tourist center lying on a sleepy lagoon bordered by vibrant tropical jungles. Here you can take a glass-bottom boat ride circumnavigating Port Vila's harbor, snorkel and swim in a secluded bay, spend the day at two of the island's larger resorts—Le Meridien or Le Lagon Parkroyal (which are only five minutes from town), or take a helicopter ride and view dense, impenetrable jungles, breathtaking waterfalls, clear rivers, and blue lagoons. The 15-minute drive to Mele Maat is a must. Here you can climb up a jungle mountain path over a succession of charming pools fed by cascading waterfalls.

VIETNAM

Wedged between China, Laos, Cambodia, and the South China Sea, this historic, war-ravaged country, about the size of Norway but with a vastly larger population, has become a favorite visit for cruise ships traversing Southeast Asia.

Ho Chi Minh City (formerly **Saigon**), with a population of more than five million, is the largest, most dynamic of the Vietnamese cities and the center of culture and commerce. In the middle of the commercial section, not far from the harbor, are Saigon Square and Dong Khoi Street, an area with numerous hotels, shops, art galleries, and restaurants. The Rex Hotel gained public notice during the Vietnam War; however, several more modern hotels have recently been built, including the Sofitel, Hyatt, Marriott, continental, and Caravelle. Nam Kah is the best seafood restaurant in the city. Points of interest include Reunification Hall (formerly the Presidential Palace), the Museum of Vietnamese History, the view from the top of the new modern trade center, and Choulan, the bustling Chinese quarter. A don't-miss attraction is the superb water-puppet show, a unique Vietnamese art form. Another enjoyable experience is the performance of traditional Vietnamese musical instruments offered throughout the day at Reunification Hall.

Da Nang, located in the center of the country, is another favorite port of call. Sightseeing should include visits to the former trade center of the country in Hoi-An, where today you can visit art galleries and silk factories; a climb to the top of Marble Mountain, the sight of many battles during the Vietnam War, and which today offers an excellent panorama of the surroundings; and the modern, five-star Furama Hotel that sits in the middle of famous China Beach. Tours are generally offered to the imperial city of Hue, to the Ho Chi Minh Trail, and the Cham Museum, which houses the world's best collection of art from the Cham civilization. Lunch by the pool at the Furama Hotel is a delightful experience and affords an opportunity to sample a variety of Asian cuisine.

Hanoi, the capital of Vietnam, a two- to three-hour drive from the port of Haiphong (or a one-hour helicopter ride), is less cosmopolitan and less colorful than Ho Chi Minh City. The hordes of bicycles and motorcycles that do not stop at intersections, or for pedestrians, make it a real challenge to cross streets. (This is also true throughout the country.) The main tourist attractions include the grandiose, Stalinist-style mausoleum of Ho Chi Minh, the country's most revered leader; his former homes with their surrounding gardens and ponds; the Ho Chi Minh Museum; the One Pillar Pagoda; the Temple of Literature, a well-preserved example of Vietnamese architecture housing 82 stone tablet artifacts; and the 36 streets in the old quarter of town, where each street is named after the merchandise offered, i.e., "Fish Street," "Meat Street," "Vegetable Street," "Basket Street," etc.

East Africa and the Indian Ocean

Well-traveled cruisers looking for new and exotic cruise areas are beginning to explore the eastern coast of Africa and the unusual islands in the Indian Ocean that stretch from the southern tip of Africa to India.

For decades, most of the superliners offering world cruises visited the ports of Durban, Madagascar, Mombasa, Zanzibar, Mauritius, Reunion, and the Seychelle and Maldive group of islands. Recently, several of the more upscale vessels have begun offering a series of seven- to 14-day cruises in this area and provide passengers a pre- or post-cruise option to enjoy a safari experience at game preserves in Kenya and Tanzania.

COMOR'ES ISLANDS

Anjouan, Grande Comore, Mayotte, and Moheli—the four islands in the Comores—are located between Madagascar and Mozambique, Africa, in the Indian Ocean. The islands have a long history. During the 19th century, they were ruled by sultanates, and the major industries were the export of spices and slaves. Slavery was abolished in 1904, and in 1912 the four islands became French colonies. In 1975, all of the islands except Mayotte became independent. Having wisely voted to retain the French influence, Mayotte is the only island in the Comores with a decent standard of living and not suffering from overpopulation and poverty. The people of the Comores speak French, Arabic, and a native dialect. They are mostly Moslems, and many practice polygamy.

Most cruise ships stop at **Anjouan** because it is the most scenic of the four islands with verdant hills, mountains, and valleys covered with towering palms, banana trees, and tropical forests dotted with waterfalls and streams—all looking down to the blue waters of the Indian Ocean. The port town of Mutsamudu is dirty, crowded, and of little interest. You will want to drive out into the country to the scenic point at Mt. Ntingui to a factory that processes oil from the ylang-ylang flower used in French perfumes or to one of the picturesque beaches. The best beach is at Moya Plage, where there is a nice hotel; however, it takes 90 minutes to drive there. One mile from town is a small, scenic white-sand beach connected to Comotel Al-Amal, where there is also a small pool, bar, and restaurant.

The largest of the Comores is **Grande Comore**. In town, you can stroll through a clutter of homes and narrow alleys reminiscent of Greek island villages (but much dirtier). You can drive out to see the Karthala Volcano, which has the largest crater in the world. The best beach is at Maloudja, also the location of the best hotel. Other choices may include Novotel Ylang-Ylang and Istranda Palace.

Mayotte, the least impoverished of the four islands and still a French colony, is surrounded by a coral reef. Many private yachts anchor at the beach at Soulou to shower and picnic at the waterfall located there. The best beach for swimming and snorkeling is at N'Goudja, where there is also a decent hotel. **Moheli** has little development; however, there are good beaches at Miremani, Sambadjon, Sambia, and Itsamia.

KENYA

Kenya, an independent republic within the British Commonwealth, intersected by the equator, is possibly the destination that offers the greatest variety of attractions for visitors to Africa. You can visit Nairobi, East Africa's most cosmopolitan city, then go on safari through some of the best game reserves in the world, or relax at a beach resort along the clear, blue waters of the Indian Ocean.

One day to explore this country is not nearly sufficient. Therefore, many cruise ships, when calling at **Mombasa**, the port city of Kenya, generally arrange overnight or two- to four-day pre- and post-cruise excursions. Because you will want to make the most of your time, I suggest that you make arrangements with a reliable tour organization to plan and conduct your tour. Abercrombie & Kent (A & K) and Micato Safaris are deservingly the favorites of the major cruise lines. Micato has been owned and operated for more than 40 years by the Pinto family. Their itineraries include a warm, personalized orientation dinner at the home of Felix and Jane Pinto, high atop Lavington Hill, overlooking the twinkling lights of Nairobi; excellent professional English-speaking tour guides in modern, air-conditioned safari vehicles; and guaranteed reservations at Kenya's best hotels, lodges, and tent camps. A & K is well-known around the world and offers a comparable safari experience. United Touring is another large operator in the area.

If your cruise commences or ends in Kenya, you will fly in or out of Nairobi's international airport. The best hotels in Nairobi include the venerable Norfolk, Nairobi Safari Club, Hilton, Serena, and Intercontinental. Windsor Hotel and Country Club is situated 30 minutes from Nairobi and 20 minutes from the airport in a suburb surrounded by parks, woodlands, and coffee plantations. This is the most comfortable choice for a few days of rest, relaxation, and possibly a few rounds of golf.

For dining in Nairobi, your best bets are the Grill Room at the Norfolk (continental), Tamarind (seafood), and Carnivore (unique game). You will want to visit the National Museum and Aviary to view its collection of tribal ornaments, native wildlife, and Dr. Louis Leakey's exhibit on prehistoric man; Karen Estates, former home of Baroness Karen von Blixen, who wrote *Out of Africa* and other literary works under the pseudonym of Isak Dinesen; Giraffe Manor, where you can hand-feed giraffes; and Nairobi National Park with its lion population and animal orphanage.

Of course, the greatest attraction in Kenya is a camera safari to one of the country's game reserves. If you only have time for one such reserve, the largest concentration of game to be observed is at the Masai Mara Park, which borders the Serengeti in Tanzania. Game that abound here include giraffes, elephants, lions, baboons, zebra, gazelles, impalas, and wildebeests. Masai Mara Sopa Lodge, located near a native Masai village, enjoys an enviable elevated location with breathtaking views of Olooliumutia Valley and the Mara plains. Other lodges in the Masai include Mara Serena Safari Lodge and Kakrok. For those wishing to "rough it" at a modernly equipped tented camp, the best of the lot are Mara Intrepids Camp, Gouvenor's Camp, Sarova Mara, Siana Springs, and Kichwa Tempo.

Other top safari destinations include mountain lodge Treetop Hotel in Mt. Kenya National Park, where you can view a multitude of animals when they come to drink at a waterhole around which the lodge is built. While in this area, you may want to spend a day or two relaxing at the world-famous Mt. Kenya Safari Club, set in a lovely park in the foothills of snow-capped Mt. Kenya and surrounded by the world's most famous game conservation park. The resort was once owned by the late William Holden, but is now owned by Lonrho Hotels. The private game reserve and animal orphanage adjacent to the resort are owned by actress Stephanie Powers and the renowned conservationists Don and Iris Hunt.

Still other excellent national parks in which to view game include Samburu, Amboseli, Tsavo, and Aberderes. At Amboseli National Park, preferred camps are Tortilis Camp and Amboseli Serena Safari Lodge.

The port city of **Mombasa,** an old town rich in history, is located largely on an island that connects to the mainland by causeway. The airport is on the mainland, but the port and city are on the island. Of interest is Fort Jesus, built by the Portuguese at the turn of the 16th century, which dominates the harbor and the old town itself. The two best hotels are the Castle in the middle of town and the Outrigger Hotel at Ras Liwatoni on the beach. Numerous beach hotels stretch out to the south and north of mainland Mombasa, and there is a national marine park and scuba diving at Malindi. Traditional African dance can be observed at Giriami Villages.

Lamu Island, a small Kenyan island that sits off the coast with an exclusively Muslim population, is a place that appeals to some tourists for an "away-from-it-all" holiday. Several cruise ships make a short visit here after Mombasa. Lamu is often referred to as the Katmandu of Africa and was popular with the hippies in the 1960s and early 1970s. It is a rather dirty town with not much of interest other than the museum with its display of a traditional Swahili house and models of various types of *dhow,* the unique wood boat that is the major method of transportation (other than donkey) around the island. If you have a few hours, the best bet is to take the 45-minute walk along the coast, or a short *dhow* ride to Shela Village, using Peponis' Hotel as your home base. The beach extending for several miles past Peponis' is a magnificent stretch of light sand, dunes, and small palms lapped by the warm waters of the Indian Ocean. Here you can also wander around the small Islamic Village and have a cold beer or snack at Peponis'.

MADAGASCAR

Madagascar, the fourth-largest island in the world, is thought to have geologically split off from Africa. It was not inhabited until A.D. 500, when it was settled by Indonesians and Malaysians. In 1500, the Portuguese came to settle and colonize, and they were followed by the Dutch, British, and French. The country was a French colony from 1896 until it gained its independence in 1960. The population of 11 million is Malagasy, a mixture of black Africans, Indonesians, and Arabs. The language is French; however, France and most of the Western world lost interest in Madagascar after its independence, and today it is a poor, overpopulated country that experiences very little tourism.

Most cruise ships visit Nose Be and Nose Komba, two small tropical islands that lie off the northwest coast of the main island. This is a very picturesque area, one where the sea is generally calm and picture-postcard little islands peek out of the water with green peaks surrounded by blue sky and low-hanging, puffy cumulus clouds.

From the dock at **Nose Be,** you can either walk about a half-mile or take the shuttle bus into town. If you walk, you will pass by the large colonial-style homes built by the French in the early 1900s, which are now dilapidated. In town, there is an open marketplace and a few craft and souvenir shops. You can take a 45-minute drive across this verdant island of rolling hills, rivers, towering palms, sugarcane, coffee, and banana and ylang-ylang trees to Audilana Beach. On this beautiful tan-sand beach covered with tall palm trees, you can bathe in the very warm, clear waters of the Indian Ocean. This is also the location of a Club Med.

Nose Komba is a tiny island best known for its rare lemur sanctuary. Your tender will leave you off on a picturesque brown-sand beach with coral reefs for snorkeling, surrounded by hills covered with deep-green tropical flora. You can walk through a secluded, self-sustaining native village to an area that is the rare lemur's habitat. If you bring bananas, the friendly primates will jump on your shoulder and consume the bananas out of your hand. It's messy, but fun. The natives of the village are very friendly, the children are darling, and if you wish, you can purchase seashells, primitive handicrafts, or linens.

The beach is excellent for snorkeling, but you need to wear plastic sandals if you are venturing out in the water for a swim.

The port town of **Antsiranara** (formerly Diego Suarez), is set on the northeastern tip of Madagascar. The town, with its 50,000 inhabitants, is about ¾ of a mile from the dock area, both of which are quite dirty, in total disrepair and not of much interest. Ramena Beach, the best and most popular beach in this area, lies 18 miles from the city. It would be a 60-minute drive to the southward to visit Ambre National Park, with its volcanic mountains and beautiful crater lakes. In the same direction is Roussettes Waterfalls and Rainforest.

MALDIVE ISLANDS

Referred to by Marco Polo as "the flower of the Indies," the Maldives lie 450 miles southwest of Sri Lanka and consist of 1,190 tiny, palm-decked coral islands in 26 atoll clusters that trail down the Indian Ocean and overlap the equator. Only 220 are inhabited by a population totaling 270,000, which consists of a mixture of Sri Lankans, Indians, Indonesians, Malayans, Arabs, Africans, and Europeans. The Maldives broke away from Great Britain in 1965 as an independent Islamic republic. Twenty-five percent live in Male, the capital, where most of the inhabitants fish for a living. More than 80 islands have opened small hideaway resorts, the nearer ones in the north and south Male atolls being accessible by motorboats or water taxis called "dhoni." The others can be reached by helicopter and seaplane from the airport that sits on a small island near Male.

There is not much of interest in Male other than the Sultan's Park, the National Museum, and a few souvenir shops. The real reason for visiting the Maldives is to witness the beauty of the hundreds of pristine islands and underwater life. The waters are crystal clear—ideal for swimming, snorkeling, and diving.

Most of the resorts offer extensive diving programs and are frequented by scuba-diving enthusiasts. However, in recent years several luxury resorts have opened that feature not only great diving programs, watersports, and incredible fine-white-sand, palm-studded beaches and lagoons, but also sumptuous beach-front and over-water bungalows, good dining, and upscale service. Four Seasons on Kuda Huraa Island and Banyon Tree on Vabbinfaru Island are both in the north Male atoll, only a 25-minute motorboat ride from Male or the airport. Another popular resort accessible by motorboat is the Island Hideaway at Dhonakulhi.

Some ships visit the Maldives because they are directly on the route between Africa and India, as well as to other Asian countries. Be certain that the ship intends to provide a tour of the islands, assist you with your own arrangements to book transportation to an island, or at least hold a beach party on one of the islands; otherwise, stopping here is not very rewarding.

MAURITIUS

Lying 480 miles east of Madagascar and 3,600 miles to the west of Australia, in the Indian Ocean, lies the Republic of Mauritius, a volcanic island best known for its picturesque beaches, water activities, and colorful melange of cultures. Its 1.1 million population is half Hindu (the descendants of indentured Indian laborers), and the other half a mixture of African, Chinese, French, and British. At various times a possession of the Dutch, French, and British, this tiny island gained its independence from Britain in 1968 and became a republic in 1992. The hottest months are during the rainy season from January through April, and the coolest extending from early July through September. Sugar cane is a major export and tourism an important source of revenue.

Port Louis, on the northwest coast, is the major commercial center. Here you can visit the Natural History Museum, Jummah Mosque, the city market, Pere Laval's Shrine, Fort Adelaide, the Casela Bird Park, and take the 15-minute drive to view exotic plants and palm trees in the botanical gardens at Pamplemousses. The best hotel here is Labourdonnais on the waterfront, and nearby are numerous restaurants, bars, a casino, and cinemas.

Beach resort areas include: Trou aux Biches, Choisy and Grand Baie to the north of Port Louis, Flic en Flac to the south of Port Louis, and Pointe de Flac, Trou d'Eau Douche, Ile Aux Cerfs, Belle Mare, and Blue Bay all on the eastern coast. All forms of boating and watersports are available at the myriad of luxury resorts. Numerous companies offer deep-sea fishing and diving. Walking and trecking are popular in the mountains and valleys of the island's interior. Other places of interest include: Black River Gorge National Park, Chamarel Falls, and the crater at Trou Aux Cerfs.

Mauritius boasts many exotic luxury resorts, each with extremely comfortable accommodations, a diverse range of restaurants, beautiful beaches, every imaginable watersport, and lovely landscapes. The most popular on the east coast are St. Geran at Pointe de Flacq, Touessrok at Trou d'Eau Douche, and the more exotic Le Prince Maurice at Poste de Flac. On the west coast, the Oberoi at Baie aux Tortues, Royal Palm at Grand Baie, and the Sugar Beach Resort are your best choices. If you do not elect to utilize one of these hotels, a pleasant beach day can be spent at Ile aux Cerfs, a public beach-park with a blue lagoon, a white sandy beach, restaurants, bars, souvenir shops, and watersports.

OMAN

Oman is the oldest of all of the established Arab countries. Muscat, known as the "capital region," is made up of three distinct cities, separated geographically by hills and ridges, each with its own particular identity. Muscat is the old port area and the location of most of the places of interest; Matrah, to the northwest, is the main trading district and the country's most important harbor; Ruwi, a few miles inland, is a modern commercial and administrative center. The coastline is dynamic, with jagged rocky cliffs rising above picturesque, whitewashed towns with mosques and minarets.

Visitors will want to tour the old city of Muscat to view the spectacularly beautiful Al-Alam Palace and gardens flanked by two 16th-century Portuguese forts, Jalali to the east and Mirani to the west. Another impressive Portuguese 16th-century fort sits atop a cliff near the harbor in Matrah and affords a good panorama of the city.

Sightseeing in Oman should also include a visit to the Natural History Museum as well as the Oman Museum, which houses old manuscripts, local arts and crafts, and displays of Omani architecture and design. Bargaining at the souks in Muscat and Matrah are popular tourist priorities. Here you will find antique jewelry, souvenirs, sandals, colorful textiles, gold, silver, spices, and incense.

Dining is best and safest at one of the better hotels such as Al-Bustan Palace Intercontinental, a five-minute drive past Muscat, where you will find a long strand of beach, a pool, tennis courts, numerous restaurants, and a good example of Arabian opulence.

Those wishing to take a long walk or jog will especially appreciate the corniche, the road and path along the gulf extending from the harbor in Matrah to the town of Muscat, a distance of about two miles.

REUNION

Lying 480 miles east of Madagascar, southeast of Mauritius in the Indian Ocean, this overseas department of France boasts breathtaking landscapes, volcanic peaks and verdant gorges. Originally settled by the French during the 17th century, today its population of approximately 700,000 is 40 percent Creole, 20 percent Indian, and a 40 percent mixture of French, other Europeans, and Chinese. French is the national language, although most residents speak Creole. The French franc is the official currency. Few residents speak English.

The prime attraction for visitors is trekking the volcanic peaks and valleys. Beach resorts with an abundance of watersports are available; however, nearby Mauritius is far more popular with the sun-worshiping crowd. The island, dominated by two major mountain ranges, is 120 miles in circumference with hot, rainy summers, extending from October through March, and cool, dry winters from April through September. Cyclone activity is possible in February and March.

Ships generally drop anchor near Le Port, which is midway between the capital city of St. Denis, and the most popular beach area of St. Gilles-Les Bains; both are accessible by a 30-minute taxi or bus ride. (Taxis are outrageously expensive).

St. Denis is the lively capital city with a population of 130,000. The most interesting area is Le Barachois, located at the western end of the waterfront. It is composed of bars, sidewalk cafés, shops, and the city's largest hotel, Le St. Denis. Attractions include the Musee Leon Dierx, an art museum; Jardin l'Etat, a botanical garden; the Hindu Temple; the Grande Mosque; and the handicraft market. The better shops and boutiques can be found on Rue du Marechal and Rue le Clerc.

St. Giles-Les Bains is the most popular beach resort area, easily accessible by an hour bus or taxi ride from St.Denis and a half-hour from Le Port. The most upscale hotel is St. Alexis, located near the locals' favorite beach at Bocan Canot. You can have lunch at one of the seafood restaurants or pizzerias located at the harbor-beach area at St. Gilles. I especially enjoyed the pizza, pastas, and salads on the second level of Quai de la Pasta, a delightful spot overlooking the harbor and beach. Surfing, scuba, deep-sea fishing and numerous watersports are available; however, shark incidents have occurred here. Golf and horseback riding can also be arranged.

SEYCHELLE ISLANDS

These unique, dynamically beautiful tropical islands that encompass a 75-square-mile archipelago are located in the Indian Ocean near the equator, a thousand miles east of Kenya and a thousand miles away from any other land mass. The islands were uninhabited until the mid-18th century, when France took possession. Over the years, the 115 islands (80 of which are still deserted) were settled by Europeans, Africans, and Asians, and today the 70,000 inhabitants speak Creole, French, and English.

These islands are geologically unique in that they are of solid-granite origin rather than volcanic rock, with dramatic cliffs that rise from the sea, carpeted with lush vegetation and interesting boulder formations that are the debris of gigantic movements of the earth's crust thousands of years ago. The Seychelle beaches are the very best in the world, and the warm seas surrounding the islands offer countless opportunities for swimming, watersports, scuba, and snorkeling. Several of the islands are home for rare species of sea birds and plant life found nowhere else in the world. The weather is hot, humid, and sometimes windy during the monsoon seasons. December and January are the worst months, and May through October are the best.

There are several international airplane flights each week into **Mahé**—the largest of the islands. The harbor at Mahé's largest city, Victoria, is the port of call for many cruise ships. Ninety-five percent of the population of the Seychelles lives on Mahé. It is here that you will find the major hotels, the best restaurants, and the best shopping, as well as 68 beautiful beaches. The most pristine and picturesque beaches are Anse Royale on the southeast coast and Anse Intendence on the southwest coast; the most popular, but not the most beautiful, is at Baie Beau Vallon, where numerous hotels are located.

The capital town of Victoria, which sits near the harbor, is very clean but not terribly interesting. There are a number of shops and boutiques, as well as several restaurants. The better hotels, resorts, and restaurants are located around the island and not in Victoria.

Presently, the two first-class resorts on the island are Banyon Tree and the Plantation Club at Baie Lazare, which offers lovely grounds, very comfortable accommodations, and many amenities. A number of luxury hotel chains are in the process of developing resorts on this island. Other hotels with facilities are Meridian at Barbaron, Sunset Beach, Meridian Fisherman's Cove, Berjaya Beau Vallon Bay Beach Resort, Notholme, and Coral Strand, all on Beau Vallon Bay. All of these hotels have beaches, pools, tennis courts, shops, and good restaurants. The best restaurants are Chez Plume at Anse Boileau, La Perle Noire at Beau Vallon, and Le Corsaire and LaScala at Bel Ombre.

To really appreciate this incredibly lush island, you should rent a car or mini-moke or hire a taxi to drive you around Mahé. Nowhere in the world can you witness such incredible beauty.

Praslin lies to the northwest of Mahé and is a 2½-hour ferryboat ride or 15-minute propeller flight. Here you can enjoy the one-mile walk through the 450-acre Valley-De-Mai, a lovely forest and the home of the botanical rarity, the coco-de-mer palm, as well as such rare birds as the black parrot, blue pigeon, and bulbul. This seven-mile-long island is surrounded by a coral reef and boasts numerous silver-white-sand beaches. Cote d'Or and Anse Volbert make up a 2½-mile stretch of white-sand beach lined with palm trees only five or six miles from the pier where your tender docks. Here you can swim, snorkel, and have lunch or a snack at one of the small hotels or restaurants located along the beach, including Berjaya Praslin Beach Hotel, Paradise Hotel, and Acajou.

A few miles farther down the road you will experience one of the most idyllic beaches in the world, the incomparable Anse Lazio. The setting of palms, pines, seagrapes, and flowers is breathtaking; the powder-white sand is firm and excellent for strolling and jogging; and the absolutely crystal-clear warm waters are the very finest for swimming. Adjacent to this extraordinary beach is an equally extraordinary semi-open-air restaurant, Richelieu Verlaque's Bon Bon Plume, which features exceptional fresh fish, seafoods, Creole dishes, French wines, and other beverages and overlooks the panorama of Anse Lazio. Those opting to spend their day ashore at Anse Lazio and Bon Bon Plume will be rewarded with one of the most exquisite island experiences they may ever encounter.

The best resorts on the island are the ultra-deluxe, Lemurea at Anse Kerlan near the airport, and La Reserve, L'Archipel, and Acajou, all located on the east coast. At Lemurea there is an 18-hole golf course. If you are in Praslin in the evening, the two best restaurants, other than those at Lemurea, are the charming semi-open-air restaurant sitting on an over-water jetty at La Reserve and the elegant Tante Mimi, situated in a colonial-style building above the casino and serving continental cuisine.

La Digue, a 30-minute boat ride from Praslin or three hours from Mahé, is the most beautiful, pristine, and photographed of the Seychelle Islands. The breathtakingly scenic Anse Source D'Argent, in my opinion, is the most picturesque beach setting in the world. Here, warm turquoise waters with the mildest of currents lap silver-white-sand beaches and tiny private coves interspersed with geometric gray boulder formations, palm trees, and other tropical flora and green hills in the background. This is the scene that appears most often on postcards and brochures depicting the Seychelles. The island is surrounded by a coral reef, and opportunities to snorkel and swim are abundant.

From La Passe, where your boat or tender docks, you can walk or rent a bicycle or oxcart for the two-mile trek through town, past La Digue Lodge (a small hotel) and L'Union Estate, to Anse Source D'Argent. Select any of the private coves to leave your towel and snorkel gear. After you have strolled along the mile or so of sandy paths, rock formations, and coves, and taken some of the most scenic photos imaginable, you will want to settle down and enjoy the sun, soothing warm waters, and picturesque surroundings. This is the perfect romantic hideaway. If you have no one with whom to share romance, it is a great place to sit and reflect.

There are many other spectacular beaches on the island, including Grand Anse and Petite Anse (two magnificent half-mile-long expanses of white sand beach with crystal-clear waters and heavy waves and current), as well as Anse CoCo, Anse Fourmis, Anse Banane, Anse Patates, and Anse Gaulettes. If time permits, you can ride a bicycle around the island, although there are some places where you will have to proceed by foot. The winds and currents can be rather strong from May through October, and generally the safest place to swim is at Anse Source D'Argent. Places to visit include Black Paradise Flycatcher Reserve, a 37-acre shaded woodland where these rare birds make their home; and L'Union Estate, an old coconut plantation with a traditional colonial house, shipyard, colony of giant tortoises, and horseback riding.

Aride, a nature reserve, is two hours by boat from Mahé. Wardens, who live on the island, will take you on a tour of nature paths to view the beautiful Wright's gardenia, other flora indigenous to the island, and the largest collection of sea birds in the world, including the roseate sooty and bridled tern, the lesser and common noddy, and the white-tailed tropic bird. The pure white-sand beach in front of the wooded area is very beautiful, but swimming and snorkeling can be a bit dangerous when the waves are high.

Curieuse is a small island two miles long that is a half-mile from the north coast of Praslin. Here you can take a rather rugged nature walk across a steep hill to a swamp to view a colony of 100 giant Aldalra tortoises. The long stretch of white-sand beach is picturesque and borders clean, warm waters ideal for swimming and some of the best snorkeling in the Seychelles. Several cruise ships offer barbecues or picnics here.

Cousins is a 70-acre island bird reserve sanctuary for the rare Seychelle ground doves, weaver birds, toc toc, and thousands of other species. There is a half-mile expanse of beach, but the water is generally pretty rough and snorkeling is only fair. **Bird Island, Desroches,** and **Poivre** are three islands offering good game fishing.

UNITED ARAB EMIRATES

Dubai, which lies 100 miles down the coastal road from Abu Dhabi, is really two cities divided by an inlet from the Persian Gulf known as "The Creek." On the north side of The Creek is the village of Deira and on the south, Dubai. Your ship will dock at Port Rashid on the Dubai side, two miles from the center of town. With a half-million inhabitants, it is the second largest of the seven emirates, offering the visitor a distinctive blend of modern city and timeless desert.

There are many deluxe hotels, including Burj Al Arab, Jumeirah Beach Hotel, Madinat Jumeirah, Grand Hyatt, Hyatt Regency, and JW Marriott. At these establishments you will be rewarded with fine dining, shops, panoramic views, and a good home base for your exploration. You will want to sample Arabian specialties such as hummus (a chickpea and sesame seed puree), *taboule* (cracked wheat salad with tomatoes, mint, and parsley), and the variety of spicy lamb dishes, fish, and seafood indigenous to the region. In the small restaurants, the traditional repast is *shawarma,* grilled slivers of lamb or chicken mixed with salad and stuffed inside pita-bread pockets. Several hotels and tour organizations feature "desert safari dinners," where guests enjoy a barbecue dinner under the stars while seated on a carpet under a canopy.

You will want to browse the traditional souks and tiny shops of the old town core and test your skills at bargaining. The famous Gold Souk in Dubai has hundreds of shops and gold is sold by its weight. Persian carpets here are considered the best buys outside of Iran. Also, there are modern multilevel shopping malls at Al Rega Road, Karama, Al Dhiyafa Road, and Bani Yas Square.

Dubai is home to the annual PGA Desert Golf Classic and the only 18-hole golf course in the emirates with real greens. Swimming and watersports are available at Jumeirah Beach Park and Al Mimzer Park, south of the port.

A fun way to cross The Creek is on a shared water taxi called abras. The Creek offers a picturesque glimpse of the city's trading heritage.

Places of interest include Al Fahide Fort, renovated in 1970 to house an archaeological museum; the view from the top of the World Trade Center; Dubai Zoo;

Dubai World Amusement Park, site of the *QE2*; the camel racetrack; the shops and restaurants at Holiday Center; the Textile Souk on Al Fahidi Street; the Spice Souk; the Gold Souk; Majlis Gallery; and Juneira Mosque, a spectacular example of modern Islamic architecture.

ZANZIBAR ISLAND, TANZANIA

Known as the "Spice Island," Zanzibar has been ruled at one time or another by Egyptians, Indians, Chinese, Portuguese, Persians, Dutch, Arabs, and English. The island reached prominence during the 19th century as the hub of the slave-trading industry and as a major grower and exporter of spices—especially cloves, which are grown on plantations around the island. Ninety percent of the island's inhabitants are Muslims, and Arab influence is present in the architecture, numerous ruins, and customs.

If you do not opt to take an organized tour, you can readily hire an English-speaking taxi driver for about seven to ten dollars an hour. You may wish to explore the labyrinth of narrow winding streets with whitewashed coral houses, shops, restaurants, and public buildings in the "Old Stone Town" area. Attractions here include two former sultans' palaces, a Portuguese fort built in 1700, a mosque, several cathedrals, a museum, the old slave market, and the indoor/outdoor public market, where produce, fish, and meats are sold. The favored restaurant amongst tourists in the Old Stone Town is Fisherman's Restaurant, which features fresh fish, lobster, and other seafood.

To appreciate the tropical splendor of Zanzibar, you must drive out to the beaches, native villages, and spice plantations. Zanzibar is a major producer of cloves. A lovely spot to spend a few hours is Mawimbine Club Village, on the west side of the island where you dock, about a 15-minute drive from town. This is a charming tropical resort with sixty-four thatched bungalows set in lush gardens with a pool, bar, restaurant, and a nice strand of white-sand beach. watersports and deep-sea fishing can be arranged here. Down the road is a small native village and spice plantation that can be visited in combination with the drive to Mawimbine.

There are a number of fine beaches on the opposite (east) side of the island at Jambiani and Bwejuu, but you probably will not have enough time to get there.

Transatlantic Crossings

When planning your European vacation, why not plan to sail at least one way? Prior to the jet age, cruising to and from Europe was considered by many as "the only way to go." Today, however, the relaxed luxury of sailing abroad has given way to the desires of the typical traveler who wishes to take in as much as he can in as short a time as possible. Those of you who find it difficult to immediately unwind at the beginning of a vacation may find that a five-day ocean crossing is just what the doctor ordered. Others who have been exhausted from the hustle and bustle of a whirlwind European tour may prefer to take a relaxing cruise home to rest up before going back to the demands of everyday life.

As the cruise lines are scheduling a greater number of cruises in the Caribbean and Mediterranean, their ships are making fewer transatlantic crossings. Whereas 30 years ago a traveler leaving for Europe had numerous vessels to choose from, today only a few ships make regularly scheduled trips. However, it is possible to cruise on numerous lines when they are repositioning their vessels between the United States and Europe in late spring and early fall.

Some ships make a few crossings by the southern route. This route takes from five to 15 days, depending on your point of embarkation and ports of call. Typically, the ships stop at a few of the following ports: Lisbon, Algeciras, Barcelona, Cannes, Genoa, Naples, and Piraeus.

The *QM2* (Cunard Line) has a number of regularly scheduled crossings by the northern route to such ports as Southampton, Le Havre, and Bremerhaven, which take from five to seven days.

As pointed out earlier in the book, when sailing transatlantic, you will find that the seas are rougher than in the Caribbean or Mediterranean, and that the southern route will allow more sunny days on deck than the northern route.

However, don't let these factors discourage you. Sailing on a modern luxury liner is an unforgettable experience. If your vacation plans will not permit a longer cruise and Europe is on your agenda, treat yourself to a transatlantic crossing for at least one leg of your trip.

Length of Cruise

How long a cruise should you take? The answer, of course, depends upon how much time you have available, as well as what length vacation you may prefer. If you are the type that becomes fidgety after having spent a week at a vacation spot, you also probably will become restless should you spend longer than a week at sea. On the other hand, if it takes you a week just to unwind and longer vacations are your preference, a longer cruise will appeal to you.

The duration of a cruise can vary from a one-or-two-day journey to "nowhere" to an around-the-world cruise that may take from 90 to 120 days. If you have only a short time to spend afloat, you may wish to consider cruises to "nowhere" from New York, Miami, Fort Lauderdale, Orlando, or Los Angeles, which are offered by a number of the cruise lines. On these outings, the ships merely sail out into the ocean for one or two days, giving the passengers a sample of life aboard a cruise ship at sea. One or two ships of Carnival, Celebrity, Royal Caribbean, Disney, and Norwegian offer short-duration cruises (three or four days) from Florida to the Bahamas. Several ships offer three- and four-day cruises from Piraeus to the Greek islands and Turkish Coast. In addition, there are a few short cruises running from time to time from Los Angeles and between islands in the Caribbean.

If you can spend a week, there are numerous seven-day cruises offered by the major cruise lines. Cruises to Bermuda and the Bahamas are run on a regular basis out of New York. Years ago, the Norwegian Caribbean Line (renamed Norwegian Cruise Line in 1988) pioneered the concept of regular seven-day cruises from Florida to the Caribbean, and today every major cruise line offers regular seven-day Caribbean cruises from Florida. If you prefer a seven-day cruise from a California port to ports in Mexico, you can be obliged by ships of the Carnival, Celebrity, Royal Caribbean, Princess, and other cruise lines. Several ships that offer three- and four-day cruises to the Greek islands and Turkish coast also have seven-day itineraries. Most lines offer regular spring, summer, and early fall cruises in the eastern and western Mediterranean. Many of the lines offering cruises from Florida also make weekly trips from Puerto Rico to a variety of Caribbean islands. Almost all other major cruise lines offer a number of seven-day cruises from time to time in various seas of the world, but not on a regular basis. Thus, the traveler with only seven days to spend has a great variety of ships and cruise areas from which to choose.

These seven-day cruises are of three basic types. There are the barnstorming cruises that make as many as six or seven stops in seven days, giving you maximum exposure to a number of different ports for your dollar but affording little time to catch your breath. Then there are certain cruises that hit only a few ports and let you spend most of your time playing and relaxing on ship. The third type of seven-day cruise makes short trips, such as from New York to Bermuda and Nassau. These ships dock in one port several days, acting as your hotel and leaving you plenty of time to explore the island.

There are a number of cruises with eight- to 13-day durations, but the 10-day to 14-day cruise has become extremely popular because it coincides with many travelers' two-week vacations and offers plenty of time to call on a large number of ports while still leaving several relaxing days at sea. Many of the previously mentioned lines offer regular 10- or 14-day itineraries traversing the Panama Canal, or leaving from Florida to the Caribbean, from Los Angeles to Mexico or Alaska, as well as from various Mediterranean ports to other ports on the Mediterranean.

If you wish to cruise to the Hawaiian Islands, the South Pacific, the Far East, South America, or the Northlands, your cruise, by necessity, will be of a longer duration, unless you can arrange to fly part of the way and take only a portion of the itinerary. Ships of the Cunard, Regent Seven Seas, Silverseas, Crystal, Holland America, and Seabourn lines specialize in long cruises that call on ports in several continents and sometimes circumnavigate the globe. Some of the super-liners (such as the *QM2*) and the Crystal and the Holland America ships make one or more of these "longer" or around-the-world journeys each year. Princess, Regent Seven Seas, Seabourn, Silversea, Holland America, Crystal, and a number of other cruise lines feature fascinating itineraries for some of their vessels in the Far East, visiting such exotic ports of call as Bali, Singapore, Bangkok, Phuket, Vietnam, Bombay, and Hong Kong. Many of the other cruise lines have indicated they will be entering this market in the near future.

Although it is always dangerous to generalize, one can say that the majority of passengers on the longer cruises are usually over 55, retired, semi-retired, or of independent means, since the everyday working man seldom can afford to take so much time off for a vacation. The first-time sailors tend to gravitate toward the seven- to 14-day cruises that offer the larger sampling of ports. It would be difficult to make any additional generalizations. Most other categories of cruise vacationers will select cruises with durations and itineraries matching their personal tastes. However, there is often a geographical proximity between the cruiser's hometown and the ports of embarkation.

If you are contemplating a longer cruise, you may wish to avoid too small a vessel, since you will want more space to move around. Although it may be intimate and even cozy to frequent the same public rooms of a small ship on a seven- or even 14-day cruise, after a month or so you could be climbing the walls. The larger vessels offer more space, facilities, and public rooms, as well as a greater variety of people to meet.

In conclusion, I feel that however long your vacation, however extensive or limited your budget, wherever it is you prefer to cruise, and whatever your preference in ships, there exists a cruise vacation meeting your requirements—and a cruise vacation is one experience in life that should not be missed.

Chapter Seven

"Beaching It" When in Port

Since childhood, I have retained fond memories of romping about on a beautiful beach. I recall the total experience—the smell of the salt water, the tingling of spray from the waves, the hot sand on the bottom of my feet, the warm sun on my shoulders, and the exhilaration of a cool dip. Those who share this nostalgic identity with the sea may feel that a vacation is not complete unless it includes staying at a beach resort. However, it is possible to combine "cruising" and "beaching."

Most every ship cruising the Caribbean, Mexico, and Hawaii spends the majority of days in ports where beach aficionados can dawdle away lazy hours on a variety of lovely beaches. Just pack a small bag with a beach towel, change of clothes, and suntan lotion and head out to your favorite watering hole.

Several of the major cruise lines that deploy numerous ships in the Caribbean own or lease private islands (or parts of islands), offering passengers a one-day beach party. A typical private island will have beach chairs and umbrellas, bathroom facilities, several bars, a dining area or pavilion, a straw market, a boutique, a calypso band, various land and watersport facilities, and hiking paths. Costa Cruises' island, Serena Cay, is located in the Dominican Republic. Disney Cruises' 1,000-acre island, Castaway Cay, lies in the Abaco chain of the Bahamas. Holland America Line's 2,400-acre Half Moon Cay rests southeast of Nassau in the Bahamas. Norwegian Lines' Great Stirrup Cay sits in the Bahama-Berry Islands chain. Princess Cruises' Princess Cay is a 40-acre peninsula on the southern tip of Eleuthera in the Bahamas. MSC's Cayo Levantado is located in the Dominican Republic. Royal Caribbean International boasts two private island beaches: Labadee, a 260-acre peninsula on the northern coast of Haiti, and Coco Cay, a 140-acre island in the Bahamas.

Although there are countless beautiful virgin strands, many are unsafe for swimming and offer no facilities for changing clothes or purchasing a cold drink. Therefore, I generally prefer selecting a beach with facilities adjoining a resort hotel. Often, these are among the most beautiful on the island. The following is an alphabetical list of my favorites:

Africa and Indian Ocean

KENYA

Along Kenya's shoreline, there are long strands of beach with numerous hotels that stretch both to the north and south of Mombasa. In addition, there is also a good sand-dune beach on Lamu Island at Shela Village past Peponis' Hotel.

NOSE BE (MADAGASCAR)

The best beach is at the Audilava Beach Hotel, where there is also a pool, tennis court, and other facilities.

SEYCHELLES

The islands of the Seychelles boast the finest beaches in the world. On Mahé the best beaches are at Anse Royale, Anse Intendence, and Grand Anse, on Praslin at Anse Lazio and Anse Volbert, and on La Digue at Anse Source D'Argent, Grand Anse, and Petite Anse. Actually, every beach in these islands is incredible. The beaches offer the most idyllic settings and warmest water. They are incomparable.

TANZANIA

If your ship stops at Zanzibar Island, a 15-minute drive from port will take you to Mawimbine Club Village, where there is a good beach for swimming in the warm Indian Ocean.

Australia

There are numerous large, sandy beaches in the suburbs of Sydney, described earlier in chapter 6. All of the islands around the Great Barrier Reef boast lovely beaches for swimming, including Lizard Island and Hayman Island.

The Caribbean and Atlantic

ANGUILLA

The beach at Malliouhana is the best and least windy on the island. The beaches at Cap Juluca, Shoal Bay, and Sandy Island are also very picturesque and enjoyable.

ANTIGUA

You can't go wrong at any of the alleged 365 beaches. My preference is to spend the day at the beaches at St. James's Club, Dickenson Cove, or Halcyon Cove, because of the additional facilities.

ARUBA

Your best bet is Palm Beach, the long stretch of white-sand beach fronting the strip of deluxe hotels that includes the Aruba Sheraton, Aruba Caribbean, Americana, Holiday Inn, Concorde, and Hyatt. All of these hotels have swimming pools, tennis courts, and informal poolside dining. The water is usually quiet and warm and without waves or surf. The hotels are located less than 10 minutes from the harbor.

For a special beach experience, visit the private tropical island with its protected white-sand beach accessible by motor launch from the lobby of the Aruba Renaissance Hotel in town. Some cruise ships offer excursions here; otherwise, arrangements have to be made at the hotel.

BAHAMAS

Abacos—Here you will find miles of virgin beach on Treasure Cay or Guana Cay. These are among the most beautiful unspoiled beaches in the Caribbean.

Grand Bahama (Freeport/Lucaya)—The beach in front of the Holiday Inn Hotel in Lucaya is unquestionably the best on the island; however, it involves an expensive twenty- to thirty-minute taxi ride from the harbor. Most cruisers utilize the beach across from the former Xanadu Princess. The beach is crowded and the sea often too shallow for serious swimming.

Nassau—The best beaches are at Cable Beach and on Paradise Island. The most pristine, unspoiled strand is lined with pine trees and fronts the posh Ocean Club. To get there, cross over the toll bridge to Paradise Island, go straight to the sea, turn right, and walk about three blocks. If you turned left, you would be at a very nice beach in front of what formerly were the Paradise Island and Britannia Beach hotels and now is the Atlantis Hotel complex. All of these hotels have large pools, tennis courts, changing facilities, and informal outdoor restaurants.

BARBADOS

The best beaches can be found on the Caribbean side at Sandy Lane, Glitter Bay, Royal Pavilion, and Paradise Beach Club. All of these hotels are less than an hour's ride from the harbor. The beach at Sandy Lane is one of the best in the Caribbean; however, you would have to sneak on, unless you can make prior arrangements with the hotel.

BERMUDA

One of my personal favorites is the several miles of pink-sand beach directly to the left of the Southampton Princess Hotel. Here you will find little coves, shady hills, and warm, clear water. The Southampton Princess is only a 15- to 20-minute ride from the harbor.

CARACAS (VENEZUELA)

The only beach is at the former Macuto Sheraton, now the Macuto Hotel, in La Guaira. It is not very beautiful and not worth the special trip unless you are going to the hotel for other reasons. The pool at the Macuto is much nicer than the beach.

CARTAGENA

Your best bet is the public beach in front of the Hilton. At the Hilton, there are tennis courts, an outdoor bar, and several restaurants.

CAYMAN ISLANDS

Many consider the seven-mile stretch of beach on Grand Cayman Island to be one of the most beautiful in the Caribbean. This is the favorite of scuba divers and snorkelers. A five-minute taxi ride from town will take you to the Hyatt Regency Grand Cayman, the largest and best hotel on the island. Go down to the beach, turn left (or right), and walk for miles on an unspoiled, white-sand beach lined with pines and palms. The Hyatt, Treasure Island, Westin, and Ritz Carlton are the only hotels here offering a pool, tennis, a restaurant, snorkeling gear, and a large private beach area.

CURAÇAO

There are nice beaches at the Marriott, Hilton, and Avila Beach hotels.

DOMINICAN REPUBLIC

If your ship stops at Santo Domingo, the nearest beach is at Boca Chica. There are hotel pools in town in El Embajador, the Ramada, and the Sheraton. If time allows, go to the beach at Casa de Campo in La Romana. This is one of the best beaches on the island, and Casa de Campo is possibly the most complete resort in the Caribbean. Costa ships stop at their private beach at Serena Cay.

FORTALEZA (BRAZIL)

Within seven miles of town, there are lovely beaches at Iracema, Meirelles, Mucuripe, de Futuro, and Caca e Pesca.

GRENADA

Grand Anse Beach in front of the Grenada Beach Hotel and Spice Island Inn is convenient because it is only a short taxi ride from town and offers the most facilities. This is a long, fine, white-sand beach with warm, deep-blue waters. However, the constant stream of hawkers and peddlers that aggressively approach you with beads and spices is so annoying that it is difficult to relax. Most of the other hotels with beaches are a great deal farther away, and the taxi rides can be prohibitively expensive.

GUADELOUPE

My favorite is the picturesque beach at the Club Med Caravelle. You will have to make advance arrangements and pay a fee to get through the gates. Sneaking onto the property also is possible if this doesn't make you uncomfortable. There are also nice beaches, pools, and tennis courts at the Frantel, La Creole Beach, and Meridien-Guadeloupe.

HAITI

Port-au-Prince does not have a decent beach. The Club Med at Montrouis is about the best, but it is 1½ hours from town. There are swimming pools at El Rancho, Castel Haiti, Holiday Inn, and the Splendid Hotels.

JAMAICA

Ocho Rios—If your time is limited, you may wish to settle for a beach at the foot of Dunn's Falls after climbing the most important scenic attraction in Jamaica. If you prefer a private beach, pools, tennis courts, and other amenities, you can try any of the larger hotels, such as San Souci and Ciboney. So-so beaches and pools can be found at the Renaissance Hotel, which is located near where your ship docks.

Montego Bay—Most cruisers end up at the public strip known as Doctor's Cave Beach or Cornwall Beach, where there is an underwater marine park. Those wishing a private beach with tennis, pools, restaurants, and other facilities should try Round Hill, Tryall, the Half Moon, or the Holiday Inn.

Negril—The best beaches in Jamaica are at Negril; however, it takes several hours to reach this area from Montego Bay, and this would prevent you from exploring any other part of the island.

MARTINIQUE

The best beach is at Club Med—Buccaneer's Creek. However, this is a several-hour drive from Fort-de-France, and advance arrangements would have to be made here as in Guadeloupe. You may prefer to take a twenty-minute motor-launch ride from Fort-de-France to Pointe du Bout, where the former Meridien and Bakoua Hotels are located adjacent to each other. Both hotels offer mediocre, "partially topless" beaches, tennis courts, a swimming pool, and French-Creole restaurants.

PUERTO RICO

The beaches in Puerto Rico contain darker sand and lack the pristine beauty of the beaches on many of the other islands. If your time is limited, the closest beach with facilities would be at the Caribe Hilton Hotel, which is only five minutes by taxi from the harbor. The beaches at the Sheraton, Ritz Carlton, and El San Juan are also nice. The full-facility, El Conquistador Hotel, a one to one-and-a-half hours drive from San Juan, has its own private island beach with numerous water-sport facilities, a shop, and a restaurant.

RECIFE (BRAZIL)

You can choose from Pina or Boa Viagem beaches in the city, with its five-mile ocean promenade lined with coconut palms, or from the more pristine beaches at Piedade, Venda Grande, Candeias, or Borra de Jangadar—all a 10- to 20-mile drive away.

RIO DE JANEIRO (BRAZIL)

The city is lined with a long stretch of beach that is most noted for its local color. The most populated beach is Copacabana. Ipanema runs a close second. The only hotel directly on a beach is the Sheraton, which is at the juncture of Ipanema and Gavea.

ST. BARTS

The best beaches are at Grand Cul-de-Sac and St. Jean.

ST. LUCIA

Renuit Beach is very nice, easily accessible, and fronts several nice hotels. There is a white-sand beach at the Hilton Jalousie Plantation and another scenic beach at Anse Chastanet.

ST. MAARTEN

The beach at La Samana is magnificent; however, you would have to make special arrangements with the hotel. Orient Beach, about a 15-minute ride from Philipsburg, is reminiscent of Tahiti Beach in St. Tropez, France, with topless and nude bathing and numerous small beach restaurants and boutiques.

TOBAGO

The best beach is at Pigeon Point.

TRINIDAD

The nearest beach is 14 miles from the capital at Maracas Bay. There are no facilities here. You may be better off settling for the pool at the Trinidad Hilton.

TURKS AND CAICOS

The best beach on Provo is Grace Bay Beach and on Grand Turk, Governor's Beach (though it has no facilities) and at the new port facility, with a nice beach, gigantic pool, a restaurant, and shops. There are many hotels on Grace Bay Beach.

VIRGIN ISLANDS

St. Croix—There are nice beaches, tennis courts, and informal restaurants at the Carambola and the Buccaneer Beach Hotel. Buck Island would be the best choice.

St. John—The several horseshoe-shaped, private beaches at Caneel Bay Resort are possibly the loveliest in the Caribbean. A day in port at this resort is a must whenever possible. The tennis courts are excellent and usually empty, and the paths running through the acres of vegetation are a jogger's dream. The Westin is also exquisite; however, the beach is not as desirable as those at Caneel. Trunk Bay is the best choice for snorkelers or those seeking a public beach.

St. Thomas—Magen's Bay is deservingly reputed to be one of the top beaches in the world. I personally prefer spending the day at the Virgin Grand Resort and taking my dip at "nearby" Coki Beach. There is also good swimming at Marriott's Frenchman's Reef on Morningstar Beach, only a five-minute taxi ride from the harbor.

Tortola—There are several fine beaches, but the best bet is Sugar Cane Bay, which is a long strand with facilities and a colorful restaurant. Snorkelers should head out to Smuggler's Cove.

Virgin Gorda—The Baths is an attraction with unique boulder formations that visitors can climb and explore, all adjacent to a nice strand of white-sand beach. Many cruise ships offer excursions here. Possibly one of the very best beaches in the Caribbean is at Little Dix Bay Resort; however, visitors must make arrangements with the hotel.

Europe

Because there are not many "great beaches" in Europe, I will mention just a few that make up in local color what they lack in pristine beauty. Some of the best strands can be found on the island of Ibiza and at Hotel Formentor on the Spanish island of Majorca. Other sandy beaches include Lido Beach near Venice, the numerous beaches in Mykonos and Skiathos, Tahiti Beach in St. Tropez, the beach resorts in Kusadasi and Marmaris (Turkey), and the main beach in Tel Aviv. Some colorful beach resort areas with little sand include the beaches of Capri, Cannes, Nice, Corfu, Rhodes, Costa del Sol, and the Italian Riviera.

On the island of Calvi, there is a long strand of beach surrounded by a pine forest to the left of the main part of town. In Cannes, the best place to spend the day is at one of the various beach clubs and restaurants with beach facilities that line the sea in front of the major thoroughfare. Here you can walk in all directions to take advantage of the exotic human scenery. The beaches in Marbella are widely frequented, but you will probably prefer the pools at the various hotels.

Far East

There are a number of great beaches in the Far East. The best "resort beach" areas can be found at Phuket, Ko Samui, the various islands in the Andaman Sea, and Pataya in Thailand; Penang, Langawi, and Sabah in Malaysia; and Bali in Indonesia. Repulse Bay in Hong Kong is just so-so. The small uninhabited islets a short boat ride from the Tanjung Aru Beach Resort in Sabah and those in Phuket and its neighboring islands offer some of the most beautiful beaches and best swimming in the world.

Mexico

ACAPULCO

Although none of the beaches in Acapulco compare with those in the Caribbean or Cancún, the best of the lot is in front of the Princess and Pierre Marques hotels. The myriad of pools at the Princess is interesting and exciting. For local color try Caleta Beach.

CABO SAN LUCAS

The best beach for swimming is in front of the Hacienda Hotel, five minutes from where you disembark from your tender. The beach fronting the Solmar and Finistera hotels is more picturesque, but too dangerous for swimming. Lover's Beach, accessible only by boat, is the most picturesque.

CANCUN

There are 10 miles of beautiful white-sand beach stretching in front of the all of the hotels in the hotel area. Here the water is clear but the waves can be too strong for safe swimming. If your ship docks at Calica, don't miss the beaches and underground-river swimming at Xcaret.

COZUMEL

Playa del Sol and Mr. Sanchos, about a 20-minute drive from town, offer the best sand, swimming, and facilities.

MANZANILLO

The beaches at Las Hadas and Grand Bay Resorts are very nice, as are the picturesque pools.

PUERTO VALLARTA

The beaches in Puerto Vallarta, as in Acapulco, are not exceptional. The hotels with beaches closest to the harbor are the Posada Vallarta, Fiesta Americana, and the Holiday Inn. For local color go to Los Muertos.

ZIHUATANEJO-IXTAPA

The beach that runs along the stretch of high-rise hotels in Ixtapa and the more private beach at the Camino Real are the best. In Zihuatanejo go to Playa la Ropa.

Middle East

Sandy beaches can be found in Herzelia, Eilat, and Tel Aviv in Israel; Kusadasi and Marmaris in Turkey; and in Cyprus; however, they are nothing to write home about. For those cruising the Greek islands, the beaches are best at Mykonos and Skiathos. The beaches at Lindos in Rhodes, Corfu, Kos, and Crete are decent.

Pacific

FIJI

The best beach on the big island of Viti Levu is found at The Fijian Resort. There are lovely, pristine beaches in the Yasawa Islands group and on Mana Island, Beachcomber Island, Plantation Island, Treasure Island, and Turtle Island. These also are among the best in the world.

HAWAII

For those cruising the Hawaiian Islands, you will want to consider the following beaches:

Oahu—The best strand is in front of the Kahala Mandarin Oriental, 15 minutes from Waikiki, and at Ihilani. The beaches in Waikiki are too crowded with tourists; however, the beach in front of the Hilton Hawaiian Village is the best of the lot.

Maui—The beach in Kaanapali fronting all the hotels, the beaches at Wailea, or the beach at Kapalua Bay resort are your best bets.

Kauai—One of my favorite beaches in the world is Lumaha Beach, where *South Pacific* was filmed. Although this involves an hour-and-a-half drive, you will be rewarded with witnessing as much as Mother Nature can provide. There are no facilities here, and swimming is dangerous in the winter months. If you do not have time to visit Lumaha, then bodysurfers will want to go to Poipu, between the Sheraton and Hyatt resorts, and nonsurfers will prefer the facilities at the beach fronting the Kauai Marriott at Kauai Lagoons. The Hyatt Regency Kauai, with its pool complex and protected beach, is your most exotic locale.

Hawaii—If your ship docks at Hilo, you will enjoy the scenic black-sand beach at Kaimu. This may be too dangerous for swimming. At Kona, the best beaches can be found at the Mauna Kea Beach, Hapuna, and Mauna Lani Hotels. Nearby at Hilton Waikoloa is one of the most extensive and imaginative pool complexes in the world.

NEW CALEDONIA

Ile des Pins is a lovely pine-studded island with numerous chalk-white beaches ideal for swimmers, divers, and sun worshipers.

TAHITI

Bora Bora—In Bora Bora, there are numerous little islets with nothing but palms, sandy beaches, and crystal-clear waters sitting in a very large protected lagoon. The half-mile of crescent-shaped beach at the Hotel Bora Bora and Intercontinental Le Moana Resort on the mainland offer some good snorkeling close to the shore. Romantics may prefer the setting at Bora Bora Lagoon Resort on Motu Toopua, Bora Bora Pearl Beach Resort, or Meridien Bora Bora, all of which can be reached by the resorts' private launches.

Moorea—In Moorea, the best beach with facilities is at the Club Med, where there is snorkeling and countless watersports. There is also a beach with watersport facilities at the Bali Hai, Kia Ora Hotels, and Intercontinental Moorea Beachcomber Parkroyal.

Tahiti—On the big island of Tahiti, your best bets are the unique sand-bottom pools and lagoons at the Intercontinental Tahiti Beachcomber Parkroyal and the Meridien. These are by far the best places to swim and sun.

Chapter Eight

Cruising for Tennis Buffs

Many of my friends who are ardent tennis buffs have avoided cruising because they could not conceive of taking a vacation without playing tennis. Being somewhat of a tennis aficionado myself, I have always managed to include tennis with my cruises. Because it is possible to play tennis in almost every Caribbean, Mexican, and South American port of call, I merely select ships with multiport itineraries. Ships offering three ports in four days, six ports in seven days, or 11 ports in 14 days will permit ample opportunity to keep your game from getting rusty.

From experience, I would not recommend public tennis courts or tennis clubs. It is far easier and less time-consuming to play at the courts in the various hotels, which are also usually maintained in better condition. Because many hotels do not permit nonresidents to use their facilities, it is often necessary to represent yourself as a guest. If this slight bit of deception offends you, the alternatives are to make arrangements with the management or offer the person in charge of the courts a fee.

The following list contains those tennis facilities I have found to be the most desirable and most accessible from where your ship may dock:

Acapulco: Acapulco Princess Hotel or the Pierre Marques (a 20-minute ride from port), or the Acapulco Plaza (a five-minute ride from port).

Anguilla: Malliouhana Hotel and Cap Juluca.

Antigua: St. James's Club, Halcyon Beach Resort, Curtain Bluff.

Aruba: Hyatt, Holiday Inn, Sheraton, Americana, Aruba Caribbean, or Concorde.

Barbados: Sandy Lane, Glitter Bay, or Royal Pavillion.

Bermuda: Southampton Princess.

Cabo San Lucas: Las Ventanas.

Cancun: All hotels on the strip.

Curaçao: Marriott or Hilton.

Eastern Mediterranean: On Corfu, at the Corfu Holiday Palace; in Limassol (Cyprus) at the Amathus Beach Hotel, Four Seasons, or Le Meridien; in Tel Aviv (Israel) at the Hilton; in Jerusalem (Israel) at the Hyatt or King David; in Kusadasi (Turkey) at the Fantasia and Onur; in Athens at Astir Palace complex in Vouliagmeni; in Rhodes at The Rhodos Palace or Dionysos; and in Skiathos at the Skiathos Palace.

Fiji: Westin Denarau, the Fijian Resort, or the Hyatt.

Grand Cayman Island: Hyatt Regency Grand Cayman, Westin, or Ritz-Carlton.

Great Barrier Reef: Hayman Island and Lizard Island.

Grenada: Grenada Beach Hotel.

Guadeloupe: Club Med Caravelle or Le Meridien.

Haiti: At Port-au-Prince, the Club Med, Holiday Inn, or El Rancho.

Hawaii: In Oahu, the public courts at the foot of Diamond Head, the hotel courts at the Kahala Resort, or the Ihilani; in Maui, Kapalua Bay, Four Seasons, Grand Wailea, the Maui Hyatt, or the country club at Wailea; in Kauai, the Hyatt; in Kona, Mauna Kea, Mauna Lani, or Hilton Waikoloa.

Jamaica: In Montego Bay, Round Hill, the Half Moon, Holiday Inn, or Intercontinental; in Ocho Rios, the Renaissance, San Souci, or Syboney.

Kenya: Windsor Hotel and Country Club near Nairobi and Mt. Kenya Safari Club.

Malaysia: In Penang, at the Rasa Sayang; in Sabah, at the Tanjung Aru Beach Resort; in Langkawi, at the Four Seasons, Radisson, Sheraton, or Datai.

Martinique: Bakoua Beach, the Meridien, or Club Med.

Nassau: Atlantis or Ocean Club (both located on Paradise Island).

Peter Island: Peter Island Resort.

Puerto Rico: In San Juan, the Caribe Hilton, Holiday Inn, Sheraton, or El San Juan; or drive out to the lovely El Conquistador (a 40-mile drive from port).

Puerto Vallarta: Melia Posada Vallarta, Fiesta Americana, or Holiday Inn.

Rio de Janeiro: Sheraton or Intercontinental hotels.

Santo Domingo: El Embajador, the Sheraton, or Casa de Campo (a two-hour drive).

St. Barts: Guanahani.

St. Croix: at Carambola or Buccaneer.

St. John: Caneel Bay.

St. Lucia: Hilton or Sandals.

St. Maarten: La Samanna, or Little Bay Beach.

St. Thomas: The Frenchmen's Reef, Virgin Grand, Lime Tree, or Ritz-Carlton.

Seychelle Islands: On Mahé, at the Sheraton Plantation, Banyan Tree, and other resorts; and on Praslin, at Lemuria.

Singapore: Shangri-La and Rasa Sentosa.

Tahiti: On the big island, the courts at Meridien or Intercontinental Beachcomber Parkroyal; in Bora Bora, at Bora Bora Lagoons or the Hotel Bora Bora; and in Moorea, at the Intercontinental Moorea Beachcomber Parkroyal, or the Kia Ora Moorea Hotel.

Thailand: In Pataya, at the Royal Cliff, in Bangkok at the Oriental or Shangri-La, or in Phuket at Amanpuri or Banyon Tree.

Virgin Gorda: Little Dix Bay Resort or Bitter End.

Western Mediterranean: On Capri, at the Luna or Grand Quisisana; in Cannes, at Montfleury; in Cap Antibes at Hotel du Cap; in Majorca, at Formentor, Arbella, or Son Vida; in Marbella, at Puente Romano or Los Monteros; in San Remo, at the Grand; in Lake Como at Villa d' Este; in Taormina, at the Holiday Inn; in Venice, at Grand Hotel des Bains, the Excelsior Palace, or Cipriani.

Several cruise lines have introduced tennis programs on many of their cruises. Well-known tennis pros give group lessons aboard ship, then organize tennis matches while in port. These programs have met with enthusiastic approval by tennis-oriented cruisers. Hopefully, more of these tennis programs will be offered on cruise lines in the future.

Chapter Nine

Cruising for Joggers

Like so many health-oriented travelers, I have become addicted to the sport of jogging as a program for staying fit and trim. The widely held notion that on a cruise one pigs out and adds a quick ten pounds has frightened away many weight-conscious joggers. If you are one of this dedicated breed, allay your fears. It is possible to run (or take a long walk) every day on the vast majority of cruises.

Just as the inveterate gambler will choose a ship that either has its own casino or visits ports that offer gambling, so a dedicated jogger (or walker) will want to select a ship that provides a jogging track or one that makes sufficient stops to afford him or her ample opportunity to follow the regular program.

In recent years, most of the large- and middle-size ships have provided special areas for jogging. Often this involves romping around the circumference of an outside deck, or running back and forth in a horseshoe path. Although the giant vessels of Carnival, Costa, Crystal, Cunard, Norwegian, Royal Caribbean, and Princess offer the longest, uninterrupted expanse, most of the others have designated deck space to accommodate those wishing to walk off meals or jog. The dimensions for most ships sailing can be found in chapter 11.

Whenever possible, most seasoned joggers (and walkers) prefer a straight open path in sufficiently beautiful or interesting surroundings to break up the innate boredom of their daily routine. In those ports where there is insufficient time to seek out an ideal stretch of ground, I have settled for running through the main commercial areas, using this as an opportunity to sight-see and obtain the lay of the land. Although it is feasible to jog in almost every port, some offer more desirable options than others. (Forrest Gump may have jogged across the U.S., but sometimes I feel like I have jogged around the world.) The following are some of my personal recommendations in alphabetical order:

Acapulco (Mexico): The beach that fronts the Acapulco Princess, Pierre Marques, and Mayan Palace hotels is ideal. If you wish to remain closer to port, your only choice is to run along the sidewalks that border the main hotels on Acapulco Bay. The beach itself is too congested for jogging.

Alaska: On most stops in the inland passage, you can jog from the dock into town.

Amsterdam (Holland): If you walk out from the Marriott Hotel (in the center of town), turn right, and proceed for one block, you will find the entrance to a lovely park. You can run for several miles around this park, or you can exit at the opposite end. Several blocks from this exit (to your right) is a long stretch of park that leads to the zoo. A map of the city will help you find the exact locations.

Anguilla: Wherever you spend the day, there are roads and trails along which you can jog and enjoy the scenery, which includes goats and sheep. Those who prefer running on the beach will enjoy the stretch between Malliouhana and Cocolobo or in front of the villas at Cap Juluca.

Antigua: Jogging along the beach at any of the major resorts is a treat. If you start at Halcyon Cove, you can head toward town and go for miles.

Aruba: You can run for several miles along the beach or the road bordering the Sheraton, Aruba Caribbean, Concorde, Americana, Hyatt, and Holiday Inn hotels.

Athens: The botanical gardens in the middle of town is the most desirable locale; however, along the waterfront in Piraeus or at Vouliagmeni is also picturesque.

Bahamas: In Nassau, the addition of Atlantis destroyed many of the more scenic paths. Presently, your best option is to jog from the bridge down the road to your right, which leads to the Ocean Club resort, and continue back by the beach, circling around Atlantis, and then continue on the path up to Club Med and back to the bridge. Because this involves several zigzags, a map of Paradise Island would prove helpful. Other options include the five-mile, round-trip jaunt from the harbor across two bridges to Coral Island, where Coral World is located; and jogging along the sidewalks emanating from Cable Beach. In Freeport, there are numerous quiet beach roads that front the hotels. In the Abacos, you can enjoy an uninterrupted, several-mile run on the beaches.

Bali (Indonesia): If you are in the Nusa Dua area, there are numerous sidewalks between the various resorts, and you can either run along these sidewalks that border the main road or along the beach.

Bangkok (Thailand): Since this is such a polluted city, your best bet is the two-mile run around colorful Lumpini Park, in front of the Dusit Thani Hotel.

Barbados: If you spend the day at Sandy Lane, there are numerous roads starting from behind the tennis courts near the golf course. Otherwise, you can try the beaches on the Gold Coast.

Barcelona (Spain): From where your ship docks in the main harbor, you can turn right and run for several miles on the walk that surrounds the sea. The marina and beach walk in front of the Hotel Arts is your best choice.

Bermuda: The doorman at the Fairmont Southhampton will give you directions for a three- to five-mile romp that takes you behind the golf courses and lighthouse (to the right of the hotel) and permits you to return on the cliff road overlooking the sea. As an alternative, you can run in the opposite direction along the various beaches, starting at Horseshoe Beach.

Bora Bora (French Polynesia): The main island is 20 miles in circumference and has only one road that encircles the island in clear view of the lagoon. You can run for as many miles as you wish on the road from any point, or you can go the entire 20-mile distance around. If you start from the center of town at Vaitape, it is about 3½ miles to Hotel Bora Bora. A more scenic run would start at Hotel Bora Bora and extend in the opposite direction from town past the new Club Med.

Buenos Aires (Argentina): If time permits, the botanical gardens and surrounding parks offer the best scenery and least congestion.

Cabo San Lucas: You can jog along the road where the tenders disembark for about a mile and a half to the Hacienda Hotel.

Cancún (Mexico): Because the sand is really too soft to permit running along the beach, you are better off jogging along the sidewalks that abut the road that connects all the major hotels.

Cannes (France): For the most local color, you will want to jog down the long stretch of walk known as "The Croissette," which is adjacent to the beach across from all the hotels.

Capri: Alas, this lovely island is so broken up with villas, walks, and hills that there is no level stretch of road that lends itself to jogging. The best I could do was to take the path that is located to the right as you walk out of the Grand Quisisana Hotel. It extends for a mile or so to the Punta Tragara Hotel. (Watch out for dog droppings.)

Caracas (Venezuela): If you spend part of the day at the Macuto Sheraton Hotel in La Guaira, you can run along the roads that line the sea (to your right as you walk out of the hotel). Otherwise, you will be relegated to the seedy harbor area next to your ship, where it is possible to run along a sidewalk for several miles (to your right as you leave the dock).

Cartagena: You can run along the sidewalk along the waterfront all the way from the old town to the Hilton. As an alternative, you can jog from your ship to town or to the ancient fortress, both being about a mile from the harbor.

Cayman Islands: Unquestionably, one of the best runs I have experienced is along Seven-Mile Beach. You can run for several miles in either direction if you start at the Hyatt.

Copenhagen: It is possible to run from the middle of town west on Sonder Boulevard and N.Y. Carlsberg Vej to the zoo, past the Carlsberg Beer Factory. Another interesting itinerary would be to head out from the middle of town north on Vester Farimagsgade and Norre Farimagsgade to the botanical gardens and nearby Rosenborg Castle and continue north along Oster Volgade to the Langelinie Pavilion, the site of the *Little Mermaid* statue. Locals seem to prefer to jog along the canal that starts behind the Sheraton Hotel and extends for about two miles toward Langeline.

Corfu: Although you can easily jog through the town that is in front of the harbor, you may prefer the dirt roads and countryside commencing at the Holiday Palace, or the beach at Paleokastritsa.

Cozumel (Mexico): You can run along the side of the main road that follows the sea commencing in the middle of town and extending out past all the hotels and villas. If you go out to the Playa del Sol or Mr. Sanchos, you can run for several miles in either direction along this picturesque strand of beach.

Curaçao: Starting at the hotel complex near the Hilton, you can run for several miles on a road next to the sea that goes into Willemsted.

Cyprus: The 10-mile stretch of walkways along the beach between the harbor and Le Meridien Hotel offers numerous possibilities.

Dominican Republic: From Santo Domingo, there is a path running for miles along the sea in the direction of the airport. The best jogging trails are at Casa de Campo or the Club Med at Punta Cana.

Dubrovnik: The downhill jog from the President Hotel to the harbor is easy and picturesque.

Fiji: The jogging track along the golf course overlooking the ocean at The Fijian Resort is your most picturesque choice. You can also jog along the beach at the Sheratons for several miles in either direction.

Great Barrier Reef: Many ships offer passengers the opportunity to spend the day at Hayman Island, where there are picturesque trails behind the resort.

Grenada: Starting at the Grenada Beach Hotel, you can run for several miles in either direction along the beach road. There are also roads leading from the harbor toward Grand Anse Beach.

Guadeloupe: Starting at the Club Med Caravelle, you can run along the main road in either direction.

Hawaii: In Oahu, the best stretch for jogging is around the park at the foot of Diamond Head or the paths along the beaches at Ihilani; in Maui, it is along the golf course and stretch of hotels and condos in the Kanapaali area or along the sea at Wailea; in Kauai, it is on the road from Breneke Beach to the Sheraton or the Hyatt, or around the golf course and lagoons at the Marriott Kauai.

Helsinki: The route from the harbor to the Esplanade is a colorful one.

Hong Kong: There is no ideal place to jog in this crowded city. The only open stretch extends on the harbor walk between the railroad station and the *Star Ferry* on the Kowloon side. It is also possible to jog in Kowloon Park.

Ibiza: You can run for several miles on the walks that surround the harbor where your ship docks.

Ile des Pins, New Caledonia: This island is ideal for jogging on expansive beaches.

Israel: In Tel Aviv, you can proceed for miles down the scenic beach path behind the Hilton, Sheraton, and Dan hotels, or run through the resort area of Herzelia. In Jerusalem, you will enjoy running anywhere, taking in the exotic sights. A scenic run would start at the Hyatt past the University to the Intercontinental.

Istanbul (Turkey): This city is so crowded, that there is really no good place to run. You just do the best you can on the streets. It is possible to follow the path along the harbor from where your ship docks. As you exit the terminal, turn right and continue toward Ciragan Palace and Casino.

Ixtapa: You can jog along the sidewalk that runs in front of the string of high-rise hotels.

Jamaica: In Montego Bay, you may enjoy running from the harbor along the main road toward the airport past the main hotels; and in Ocho Rios you can run from the harbor toward Dunn's Falls.

Kota Kinabala: From Tanjung Aru Beach Resort, proceed along the beach or beach road toward the airport.

Kuangchow (People's Republic of China): I preferred jogging in Luihua and Yuexiu parks adjacent to the Dong Fang Hotel or the paths inside the Canton Zoo. For a different experience, you can run alongside the people cycling on special paths to and from work.

Kusadasi (Turkey): As you exit the harbor facing the town, you can turn left and run along the coast for several miles past the Koru-Mar Hotel.

Lisbon: Although you can follow the walk adjoining the harbor, a more desirable area is Estoril.

London: The best place for jogging is either around Hyde Park or through Green Park and St. James Park, where you can take in Buckingham Palace, Westminster Abbey, and Parliament.

Majorca: The best jogging is along the pine-studded paths leading out from Hotel Formentor, on the far tip of the island. You can also run along the waterfront near the harbor or along the road that encircles the Son Vida property.

Manila (Philippines): Starting at the Philippine Plaza Hotel, you can proceed for miles along Manila Bay on a clear path without venturing into the crowded city.

Manzanillo: There are good jogging paths at Las Hadas and Grand Bay Resort.

Marbella: You can run along the beach from the Punta Romano Resort into town.

Marmaris, Turkey: From port you can proceed indefinitely along the harbor past scenic hotels and resorts until it is time to turn around.

Martinique: The best path is on the road behind the Meridien and Bakoua Beach hotels.

Mazatlan: You can run for miles on the road that extends along the waterfront from town past the various hotels.

Moorea (French Polynesia): You can jog in any direction along the road that runs 37 miles around the island; it has a beautiful blue lagoon on one side, and palm trees and green-clad mountain spires on the other.

Moselle and Rhine Rivers (Germany): You will have a truly unique experience if you jump off your riverboat while it is going through a lock and meet it when it pulls into the next town. Anyone who runs a 10-minute mile or better should arrive before the boat. If this does not appeal, you can run along the riverbank at almost every port of call.

Mykonos: You can jog on the road leading out to the beach, San Stefanos, to the right of the main square (as you face the sea).

Nairobi: The paths extending along the golf course and entrance to Windsor Golf & Country Club are the best.

Nice: Running from the harbor along the walk adjacent to the beach, across the road from the hotels and apartment buildings is the most colorful, but it is also very crowded.

Oman: The road along the Corniche from the harbor to Al-Bustan Palace is very picturesque.

Palermo (Sicily): If you don't make it out to Citta del Mare or the beaches at Mondelo, your best bet is running along the "smelly" waterfront for several miles to the right (facing the sea) of where your ship docks.

Paris: Running down any street of the city is colorful, but the most picturesque expanse would be adjacent to the River Seine on the Left Bank. I also enjoyed running around the Tuileries Gardens early in the morning (about three-quarters of a mile around) or along the paths in the Bois de Boulogne.

Penang (Malaysia): Starting at the Rasa Sayang Hotel, you can jog along the beach up to the Casuarina Beach Hotel.

Phuket: You can jog along any of the beaches or the roads behind the beaches.

Portofino: Although somewhat dangerous due to traffic, you can run from the town of Portofino to Santa Margarita and back.

Puerto Rico: From the harbor, near the old town where your ship docks, it is possible to jog along the waterfront to the Caribe Hilton Hotel for about three miles.

Puerto Vallarta (Mexico): You can run down the main road from the harbor past the Posada Vallarta, Holiday Inn, and Fiesta Americana hotels (with considerable pollution), or along the beach.

Rhône and Saône Rivers (France): Here again you can run along the riverbank at almost every port of call.

Rhodes: You can run along the expansive harbor into Rhodes Town or on walks anywhere in the city.

Rio de Janeiro (Brazil): You can run for miles along the black-and-white mosaic walks that border Copacabana and Ipanema beaches, commencing at the Meridien Hotel and continuing as far as the Sheraton.

Rome: The most charming area in which to jog is the Borghese Gardens; however, it is possible to jog around the entire city. Those wishing to combine their sightseeing with exercise can jog from the Forum and Coliseum along the Tiber River to the Vatican.

St. Barthelemy: You can run along the road where the cruise ships dock in a semicircle, or in the direction of Shell Beach, or along the beach and beach road at Baie de St. Jean.

St. Croix: There are picturesque trails along the sea at Carambola Resort or at Buccaneer.

St. John: On the grounds at Caneel Bay Resort are numerous paths that will take you past lovely trees, flowers, and tropical plants.

St. Lucia: You can jog along any of the beaches or country roads. Renuit Beach offers the best jogging possibilities.

St. Martin: You may wish to jog up and down Oriental Beach and take in the human scenery or you can jog on the road behind the beach.

St. Petersburg, Russia: You can proceed for miles along the harbor, or venture out into Nevsky Prospekt.

St. Thomas: You can jog along the road by the Virgin Grand Hotel, Magens Bay Hotel, or Lime Tree Beach Hotel. If time is a factor, you can jog from the harbor where the ship docks into the main part of town along the waterfront.

Seychelle Islands: Jogging on any of the silver-white-sand beaches is excellent. Generally, the sand is firm. My favorites for jogging were Anse Lazio and Anse Volbert on Praslin, Grand Anse on Mahé, and Grand Anse on La Digue (or jogging from town to Source D'Argent).

Shanghai: Although crowded, the boardwalk along the harbor in the Bund area is quite picturesque and offers interesting views to joggers.

Singapore: The botanical gardens offer the most picturesque possibility in this lovely city. The paths on Sentosa Island are also ideal for joggers.

Stockholm: You can run from the harbor into town and follow the sea to the amusement park area.

Sydney (Australia): Hyde Park, which runs through the center of the city, and the Botanical Gardens near the Sydney Opera House are the best areas for jogging here.

Tortola: The beach at Cane Garden Bay offers the most desirable jogging possibility. Otherwise, the roads along the harbor will accommodate.

Vancouver, B.C.: Running through Stanley Park is an extraordinary experience.

Venice: The walk bordering the Adriatic in the Lido Beach area is the most picturesque and least-interrupted jogging area in Venice. You can start at the Grand Hotel de Bains and proceed for several miles past the Excelsior. An alternative is along the Grand Canal, past the parks about one mile to the left of San Marco, near where the cruise ships dock.

Chapter Ten

European Riverboats and Barges

For those who appreciate a cruise vacation but for diversion would enjoy a more intimate, low-key experience sailing down scenic inland waterways and visiting non-coastal European cities, a riverboat or barge may be the perfect solution.

Numerous riverboat companies operate in Europe, traversing the Rhine, Main, Moselle, Elbe, Havel, Danube, Seine, Saône, Rhône, and Volga Rivers, as well as waterways in Russia, Holland, and other countries. Unfortunately, the majority of these companies are not marketed in North America and are best known to European vacationers. The companies that own their own riverboats and seek to interest passengers outside of Europe include AMA Waterways, Avalon Waterways, Grand Circle Cruises, Luftner River Cruises, Sea Cloud Cruises, Vantage Cruise Tours, Viking River Cruises, and Uniworld. (See full descriptions in Chapter 11.)

Many of the riverboats are also promoted through package-tour operators such as Abercrombie and Kent (Oak Brook, IL), European Cruises (Ft. Lauderdale, FL), Exclusive Tours (Toronto, Ont.), and Global Quest (Mineola, NY).

Although there are many differences from one riverboat to another, typically they are long and narrow, with two or three passenger decks, plus a sun deck atop the vessel. The boats are designed to accommodate rivers with low bridges and numerous locks, the limitations of which dictate the dimensions of the vessels.

Passenger cabins generally emulate average size cabins on cruise ships, although on non-luxury boats they tend to be a bit smaller. Recently built vessels generally provide two twin beds convertible to a double bed arrangement, whereas those boats built prior to 2000 tend to have twin beds on opposite sides of the cabin where one or both beds fold up and convert to a couch during the daytime. Most have large picture windows, wardrobes, dressers, televisions, telephones, air conditioning, and small bathrooms with a toilet, vanity, and shower. The more upscale riverboats provide hairdryers, writing desks, glassed-in shower stalls, robes, refrigerators, and private safes in the cabins, and generally offer some junior suites. Some of the newer boats even sport French doors that open to small balconies.

Public areas on all riverboats include a large main dining room, a lounge with a bar and section for a musical entertainer, a reception area sometimes adjoining a small shop, library and/or hairdresser and a sun deck with lounge chairs. Other facilities that can be found on some (but not all) riverboats include a gym, sauna, small pool or whirlpool, additional bars atop ship, laundries, and outdoor dining areas.

In the past, little entertainment has been offered on riverboats other than piano music in the evenings, port lectures, and local musicians, entertainers, or dance groups that are occasionally brought aboard ship while in port. This may be changing as the riverboat companies seek to attract a more diverse and younger clientele. A recent entry into the market, the four A-Rosa vessels (now a Carnival brand), provide a more active Club Med-style environment with expanded facilities and indoor and alfresco, buffet dining. However, these ships are sold exclusively in the German market.

The main thrust of riverboat travel is watching the passing scenery and the shore excursion options. Itineraries on all rivers feature the major cities and villages that would be of interest to tourists. The boats visit one or more different destinations daily and offer tours to major attractions and points of interest. Most of the cruise lines do not charge for the majority of these tours.

A typical itinerary on the Danube would include such cities as Nuremberg, Regensberg, and Passau in Germany; Melk, Durnstein, and Vienna in Austria; Bratislava in Slovakia; and Budapest in Hungary. Rhine cruises generally stop at Basel, Switzerland; Strasbourg, France; Heidelberg, Rudesheim, Koblenz, and Cologne in Germany; and Amsterdam, Netherlands. Some may extend into the Moselle to visit Alken, Cochem, Zell, Bernkastler-Kues, and Trier. Cruises in France either run up the Seine from Paris to Honfleur or on the Rhône and Saône Rivers between Arles or Avignon and Lyon or Beaune. Elbe River cruises often emanate from Hamburg or Berlin down to Dresden or Bad Schandau with optional excursions to Prague. Riverboats also ply the waterways between St. Petersburg and Moscow in Russia, from Budapest to the Black Sea and between Amsterdam and Brussels.

While cruising, passengers enjoy the scenic sites along the rivers such as castles, vineyards, small villages, and ancient cathedrals.

Usually breakfast is laid out buffet style with an array of continental offerings such as salmon, herring, pâtés, cold cuts, and cheeses in addition to the more traditional eggs, breakfast meats, fruits, juices, cereals, and pastries. Lunch is often a combination of salads, cold meats, and cheeses from the buffet complemented by warm offerings from the kitchen. Multi-course dinners are common; however, on most ships there is either a fixed menu or one offering two choices for the appetizer and main course. Do not expect the variety of selections found on oceangoing cruise ships.

Several companies, including Viking River Cruises, Victoria Cruises, and Uniworld (all covered in Chapter 11), offer river cruises on the Yangtze River in China.

Viking River Cruises' two new riverboats are quite upscale and comfortable.

Barges, on the other hand, traverse smaller rivers, canals, and waterways not accessible to riverboats due to the low water levels and numerous locks. They operate all over France and Holland as well as in parts of Great Britain. The major barge companies offering charters of the whole boat and/or individual accommodations are European Waterways, French Country Waterways, and Grand Circle Cruise Tours. Some of these barge companies, as well as many smaller enterprises, are represented by tour operators who sell bookings, the largest with the most options being Abercrombie and Kent. (See chapter 11.) Other agencies specializing in barge cruise sales include Exclusive Tours (Toronto, Ont.), European Barging (Houston, TX), Springer Cruises (Bellevue, WA), and The Barge Lady (Chicago, IL).

In general, barges contain four to eight cabins, each with a small private bathroom. They are not lavishly furnished but are utilitarian and provide adequate storage space for the journey. The condition of the plumbing and air conditioning can be a problem on some of the older vessels if they have not been well maintained. Public areas consist of a main, all-purpose lounge with a well-stocked complimentary bar, a dining area adjacent to the lounge and a small outside deck for sunning, dining, enjoying a coffee or drink, or just watching the scenery.

Some barges, such as *La Bonne Amie, Renaissance,* and *Le Bon Vivant,* are quite lavish with large staterooms and bathrooms akin to a first class hotel and beautifully decorated public areas. The barges of French Country Waterways, though not quite as lavish, are also very nice, as are those of European Waterways. (See chapter 11.)

Barges are generally sold in six-night segments or are chartered to families or groups for other time periods. Many barges require a charter of the entire boat and will not accept individual passengers. Prices tend to be quite steep and can run from $2,000 up to $6,000 per person for a six-night sojourn.

Dining is generally superb on the vessels of the companies mentioned above. Since there are only a few passengers, a barge provides a private, yacht-like experience where the individual passengers can be catered to. The barge carries an experienced chef who prepares gourmet meals using fresh products purchased daily. When cruising in France, wines and cheeses indigenous to the region will be described and offered at each meal. Special requests are often honored and wines, soft drinks, and alcoholic beverages are included in the fare.

During the day, the barge sails slowly down picturesque waterways, allowing passengers to enjoy the passing scenery. Bicycles are provided, enabling passengers to exit the barge at a port or lock for a leisurely ride and meet their boat at its next stop. Shore excursions to vineyards, wineries, farms, castles, churches, and other points of interest are offered daily. Passengers are transported to these destinations by a minivan that accompanies the barge along its journey. Barges travel only during the daylight hours and hunker down each evening at some village. Some of the barge companies offer a dinner ashore at least once during the cruise. French Country Waterways and some of the ships of European Waterways include dining at a one-, two-, or three-star *Michelin*-rated restaurant.

There are many other barge companies that will charter small barges without a crew. The cost may be somewhat less, but this experience will be best enjoyed by those experienced in handling some other form of watercraft and who do not mind assisting in the opening and closing of locks along the way.

The foregoing descriptions may not entice those cruisers who enjoy expansive facilities, large suites, nightly entertainment, gambling, and diverse dining options. However, for seasoned cruisers who prefer a more intimate, laid-back experience and the opportunity to visit cities, villages, and scenic areas not available to oceangoing vessels, a riverboat or barge experience will prove most rewarding.

Note: The larger riverboat and barge companies are covered in Chapter 11, while ports-of-call along the Danube, Rhine, Rhône, Saône, and Moselle Rivers are described in Chapter 6.

Chapter Eleven

The Cruise Lines and Their Vessels

In this chapter, you will find a section describing every major cruise line, including photographs for those we were able to obtain them from, a dinner menu, and a daily program for most of the ships of each line. The synopsis at the beginning of each section lists the vessels currently sailing, their former names, the date they entered service, the date they were refurbished, gross tonnage, length and width, maximum passenger capacity, number of cabins, nationality of officers and crew, usual itineraries, and my overall ratings, i.e., "Star Awards." (An explanation of the significance of the Star Awards is given in chapter 14.) Briefly, the ships are divided into four market categories based on per diem prices for average cabins, on-board costs, and the economic class of passengers the cruise line seeks to attract:

Category A	(black stars) being the most expensive—Deluxe.
Category B	(crisscrossed stars) being the next most expensive—Premium.
Category C	(diagonal stars) being the middle-priced market—Standard.
Category D	(white stars) being the least expensive—Economy.

The ships are then rated on a six-point system, six+ stars being the highest. Only oceangoing cruise ships are rated. No ratings are given for barges and most riverboats.

In the text of each section, you will find a brief history of the cruise line, a description of the physical makeup of each ship, including cabins, inside and outside public areas, dining, service, pricing, usual itineraries, and my opinion of the strongest points.

The intent of this chapter is to provide readers with as much information as possible in a succinct, organized fashion, so as to enable them to make their own intelligent selections for their cruise vacation. For a summary of ship statistics, ratings, and current itineraries, visit www.stevensterntravel.com.

THE CRUISE LINES AND THEIR VESSELS

ABERCROMBIE & KENT

AIDA CRUISES

AMA WATERWAYS

AMERICAN CANADIAN CARIBBEAN LINE, INC.

AMERICAN CRUISE LINES

AVALON WATERWAYS

CARNIVAL CRUISE LINE

CELEBRITY CRUISES, INC.

CLUB MED CRUISES

COSTA CRUISE LINES

CRUISE WEST

CRYSTAL CRUISES

CUNARD LINE, LTD.

PETER DEILMANN CRUISES

DISNEY CRUISE LINE

EUROPEAN WATERWAYS

FRED OLSEN CRUISE LINE

FRENCH COUNTRY WATERWAYS, LTD.

GRAND CIRCLE CRUISES

HAPAG-LLOYD

HOLLAND AMERICA LINE

HURTIGRUTEN

METROPOLITAN TOURING'S GALAPAGOS CRUISES

MSC CRUISES

NOMADE YACHTING

NORWEGIAN CRUISE LINE

OCEANIA CRUISES

P & O CRUISES

P & O CRUISES AUSTRALIA

PRINCESS CRUISES

REGENT SEVEN SEAS CRUISES

RESIDENSEA MANAGEMENT, LTD.

ROYAL CARIBBEAN INTERNATIONAL

SEABOURN CRUISE LINE

SEA CLOUD CRUISES

SEADREAM YACHT CLUB

SILJA LINE

SILVERSEA CRUISES, LTD.

SONESTA NILE CRUISE COLLECTION

STAR CLIPPERS, INC.

STAR CRUISES

UNIWORLD

VICTORIA CRUISES, INC.

VIKING RIVER CRUISES

WINDSTAR CRUISES

MISCELLANEOUS CRUISE LINES

ABERCROMBIE & KENT
1411 Opus Place
Executive Towers West II, Suite 300
Downers Grove, Illinois 60515
(800) 323-7308; (630) 725-3400
(630) 725-3401 Fax
www.abercrombiekent.com

ALOUETTE: entered service 1986; refurbished 2008; 98' x 17'; 4-passenger capacity; 2 cabins; cruises on Canal du Midi in France.

AMARYLLIS: entered service 2002; refurbished 2007; 129' x 17'; 8-passenger capacity; 4 cabins; cruises on various routes in France, including Burgundy, Beaujolais, and France-Comte.

ANJODI: entered service 1983; refurbished 2006; 100' x 16.5'; 8-passenger capacity; 4 cabins; cruises Canal du Midi, Provence, and Camargue in France.

ECLIPSE: entered service 1999; 210' x 41'; 48-passenger capacity; 26 cabins; cruises in the Galapagos.

ELISABETH: entered service 1988; refurbished 2008; 100' x 17'; 6-passenger capacity; 3 cabins; cruises Canal du Nivernais and Burgundy in France.

ENCHANTE: entered service 2008; 100' x 16.5'; 8-passenger capacity; 4 cabins; cruises Canal du Midi and Provence and the Camargue in France.

FLEUR DE LYS: entered service 1986; refurbished 2006; 129' x 17'; 6-passenger capacity; 3 cabins; British officers and mixed crew; cruises in the Burgundy in France.

HIRONDELLE: entered service 1994; refurbished 2008; 128' x 17'; 8-passenger capacity; 4 cabins; cruises Loire Valley, Burgundy, and France-Comte in France.

LA BELLE EPOQUE: entered service 1995; refit 2006; 126' x 16.5'; 13-passenger capacity; 7 cabins; British and French officers and crew; cruises in Burgundy and Chablis in France. **(Category B—Not Rated)**

L'ART DE VIVRE: entered service 1998; 100'x 17'; 8-passenger capacity; 4 cabins; French and English officers and crew; cruises in Burgundy and Canal du Nivernais in France.

LA NOUVELLE ETOILE: entered service 2002; 129' x 18'; 8-passenger capacity;

4 cabins; cruises in Holland; northern Burgundy, Champagne, and Alsace-Lorraine in France; and Moselle region in Germany.

LE PHENICIEN: entered service 1959; completely refurbished 2002; 127' x 16.5'; 18-passenger capacity; 9 cabins; cruises in Provence, the Camargue, and Languedoc in France.

LIBELLULE: entered service 1996; 128' x 17'; 20-passenger capacity; 10 cabins; French and British officers and crew; cruises in Southern Burgundy and Beaujolais.

L'IMPRESSIONNISTE: entered service 1996; refurbished 2007; 129' x 16.5'; 13-passenger capacity; 7 cabins; British and French officers and crew; cruises Central Burgundy in France.

LORRAINE: entered service 1985; refurbished 2007; 128' x 17'; 22-passenger capacity; 11 cabins; cruises in Burgundy and Alsace-Lorraine regions of France.

MAGNA CARTA: entered service 2001; 117' x 16.5'; 8-passenger capacity; 4 cabins; cruises River Thames in England.

MARE AUSTRALIS and *VIA AUSTRALIS*: entered service 2002 and 2005, respectively; 236' x 44'; 129-passenger capacity; 64 cabins; cruises fjords of Patagonia from Ushuaia around Cape Horn and Straights of Magellan to Punta Arenas Chile. (See Cruceros Australis under Miscellaneous Cruise Lines.)

MARJORIE II: entered service 1998; 129' x 16.5'; 12-passenger capacity; 6 cabins; cruises in Holland and northern Burgundy in France.

MEANDERER: entered service 1992; refurbished 2008; 123' x 17'; 6-passenger capacity; 3 cabins; cruises the Upper Loire in France.

MINERVA (formerly *Explorer II* and *Minerva*): entered service 1996; 12,500 G.R.T.; 436' x 65.5'; 300-passenger capacity but limited to 199 passengers in 108 outside cabins; 197 actual cabins; European officers and Filipino crew; cruises in Antarctica, Falkland Islands, South Georgia, and the South Atlantic. (See Swan Hellenic Cruises.)

NAPOLEON: entered service 1990; refurbished 2008; 129' x 17.5'; 12-passenger capacity; 6 cabins; cruises in Vallee du Rhône and Provence, France.

NILE ADVENTURER: entered service 1990; refurbished 2001; 64-passenger capacity; 32 cabins; Egyptian officers and crew; Nile River cruises.

PROSPERITE: 128' x 16'; 8-passenger capacity; 4 cabins; cruises in central Burgundy.

RENAISSANCE (formerly *La Bonne Humeur*): entered service 1997; refurbished 2006; 126' x 16'; 8-passenger capacity; 4 cabins; cruises in western Burgundy and Upper Loire.

RIVER CLOUD: entered service 1996; 361' x 37'; 90-passenger capacity; 45 cabins; European officers; Danube River cruises through Holland, Germany, Austria, and Hungary. (See Sea Cloud Cruises.)

RIVER CLOUD II: entered service 2001; 338' x 32'; 88-passenger capacity; 43 cabins; European officers and crew; cruises on Danube and other rivers in central Europe. (See Sea Cloud Cruises.)

ROAD TO MANDALAY: rebuilt in 2009; 330' long; 82-passenger capacity; 43 cabins; cruises the Ayeyarwady River in Myanmar.

ROI SOLEIL: entered service 1999; renovated 2009; 98' x 16.5'; 6-passenger capacity; 3 cabins; cruises in Burgundy, Provence, Camargue-Languedoc, and the Canal du Midi in France.

SAFARI EXPLORER: entered service 1998; refurbished 2008; 145' x 36'; 36-passenger capacity; 18 cabins; cruises round-trip from Juneau, Alaska, including Glacier Bay.

SAFARI SPIRIT: entered service 2001; refurbished 2004; 105' x 24.5'; 12-passenger capacity; 6 cabins; cruises between Juneau and Petersburg, Alaska.

SAFARI QUEST: entered service 1993; partially refurbished in 2005, 2006, and 2007; 120' x 28'; 22-passenger capacity; 11 cabins; cruises Alaska's inside passage and Sea of Cortez, Mexico.

SAROCHE: refurbished 2007; 128' x 16.5'; 6-passenger capacity; 3 cabins; cruises in Central Burgundy, Provence, and the Camargue in France.

SCOTTISH HIGHLANDER: entered service 2000; refurbished 2006; 117' x 16.5'; 8-passenger capacity; 4 cabins; cruises in Scotland on Caledonian Canal.

SHANNON PRINCESS II: entered service 2003; refurbished 2008; 105' x 20'; 10-passenger capacity; 5 cabins; cruises in Ireland on the River Shannon and Lough Derg.

SUN BOAT III: entered service 1993; and refurbished 2005; 200' x 34.5'; 36-passenger capacity; 18 cabins; Nile River cruises.

SUN BOAT IV: entered service 1996; refurbished 2006; 236' x 42'; 80-passenger capacity; 40 cabins; Nile River cruises.

VOLGA DREAM: entered service 2007; 320' x 50'; 111-passenger capacity; 58 cabins; cruises on the Volga-Baltic Waterway in Russia.

YANGZI EXPLORER: refurbished 2008; 300' x 52'; 124-passenger capacity; 58 cabins; cruises on Yangtze River, China.

Abercrombie & Kent is one of the largest tour operators in the world, specializing in the upscale travel market. Many of its tours include sailing on cruise ships, riverboats, and barges. Although the various vessels (other than the *Sun Boats*) are independently owned and operated by several companies, A & K markets them and in many situations has chartered the entire ship or boat for its tours. (Many of the above-described vessels are described in more detail, including those under European Waterways and Sea Cloud Cruises.)

A & K has offered barge and river cruises since the '60s. Today, it represents 38 vessels with itineraries in the Burgundy, Provence, Champagne, Alsace, and Loire Valley regions of France; on the River Thames in Great Britain; on the River Shannon in Ireland; on the Caledonian Canal in Scotland; the Inside Passage as well as remote areas of Alaska. Its vessels cruise the South Atlantic and the fjords of Patagonia. As well as tours to China, Antarctica, and the Galapagos Islands, A & K offers river cruises through the canals and rivers of France, Austria, Germany, Hungary, Slovakia, Holland, Belgium, Egypt, and Myanmar, as well as the Yangtze in China.

Most vessels have a dining room, lounge, and outdoor observation area. Most are small, intimate vessels offering a unique experience for six to 12 passengers, with the emphasis on the scenic regions visited and sampling the cuisine and fine wines and cheeses indigenous to the regions.

The more upscale barges such as *Prosperite, Renaissance* (formerly *La Bonne Humeur*), and *Amaryllis* have large, very comfortable accommodations, whereas some of the others have smaller, more compact quarters. However, dining, service, tour guides, and overall ambiance prevail on most of the barges. The barges are marketed as deluxe or luxury, with per diem prices ranging from $350 to $1,200 per night, per person. Prices usually include all meals, wine, open bar, transportation, local transfers, and guided sightseeing.

Riverboats are quite different from the barges, offering a mini-cruise experience with large dining rooms, lounges with some entertainment, and accommodations and cabin amenities more comparable to average cabins on cruise ships. Prices vary from one riverboat company to the next, as does the quality of dining, service, and amenities included in the fare. The *River Cloud* and *River Cloud II* are two of the more upscale and elegant riverboats traversing the Danube and rivers in central Europe, superior in food, service, and decor to most of the other riverboats. (See chapter on Sea Cloud Cruises.)

A & K is also marketing Antarctica, Falkland Islands, and South Georgia expedition cruises on the *Minerva* (formerly *Explorer II* and *Saga Pearl*). On its Antarctica sailings, the *Minerva* carries 199 passengers in 108 outside cabins that range in size from 140 to 360 square feet. At other times, the ship has a capacity to carry 350 passengers in 197 cabins. The ship has frequently been chartered by various cruise lines and is again owned by Swan Hellenic Cruises.

The *Road to Mandalay* is owned by London-based Orient Express Hotels, Trains & Cruises, which put this 330-foot-long river cruiser into service in 1996 to ply the waters of the Ayeyarwady River. The northbound itinerary departs from Bagan and goes upstream to Mandalay, and the southbound does the reverse. Only portions of two days are spent sailing, and the riverboat spends most of its time as a riverfront hotel at either end of the line, permitting passengers easy access to the points of interest in Myanmar (formerly Burma), including the famous Shwedagon Pagoda in Yangon (formerly Rangoon). The vessel has 43 cabins accommodating 82 passengers and includes a restaurant, piano bar, boutique, beauty salon, small library, and a spacious lounge. Breakfast and lunch are served buffet style, and an open-seating, four-course, set-menu dinner is offered nightly. Orient Express also has an ownership interest in the *Alouette, Amaryllis, Fleur de Lys, Hirondelle,* and *Napoleon* barges operating in France.

A & K also offers extensive tours to popular and remote destinations around the world and utilizes cruise ships from several upscale cruise lines for portions of these journeys.

Strong Points:

Intimate, elegant, scenic, as well as educational experience, with good food and beverages on a variety of barges, riverboats, and small cruise ships, packaged with land arrangements by one of the most successful tour operators.

Author and La Belle Epoque, *courtesy Abercrombie & Kent*

Renaissance, *courtesy of Abercombie & Kent*

Courtesy Abercrombie & Kent

AIDA CRUISES
Am Strande 3d L 18055
Rostock, Germany
+49(0) 381 444-0
+49(0) 381 444-8888 Fax
www.aida.de

AIDAAURA: entered service 2003; 43,289 G.R.T.; 665.5' x 92.2'; 1,582-passenger capacity (1,266 double occupancy); 633 cabins; German officers and Filipino and Chinese crew; cruises in Western Mediterranean and Caribbean. (Category C—Not Rated)

AIDABELLA and *AIDADIVA:* entered service 2008 and 2007, respectively; 68,500 G.R.T.; 817' x 106'; 2,500-passenger capacity (2,050 double occupancy); 1,025 cabins; German officers and Filipino and Chinese crew; cruises in Mediterranean, Baltic, Northern Europe, Caribbean, and other destinations. (Category C—Not Rated)

AIDACARA (formerly *AIDA*): entered service 1996; 38,531 G.R.T.; 634.2' x 90.6'; 1,230-passenger capacity (1,186 double occupancy); 593 cabins; German officers and Filipino and Chinese crew; cruises in Mediterranean and Baltic. (Category C—Not Rated)

AIDAVITA: entered service 2002; 42,289 G.R.T.; 665.5' x 92.2'; 1,582-passenger capacity (1,266 double occupancy); 633 cabins; German officers and Filipino and Chinese crew; cruises in the Caribbean and Mediterranean. (Category C—Not Rated)

Originally owned by Deutsche Seereederei and Seetours, the company was acquired by P & O/Princess Cruises in 2000. P & O/Princess Cruises was then acquired by Carnival Corporation in 2003. In 2007, Carnival entered into a joint venture with TUI, Germany's largest tour operator, wherein Carnival owns 75 percent and TUI 25 percent.

The cruise line describes itself as "a fun/club product especially tailored for the German market." Actually, its target group is families and the younger German market (under 50)—possibly described as a German version of Club Med at Sea. Certainly it is a contrast to such other German-market vessels as the *Deutschland* or *Europa,* which appeal mostly to an older, more sophisticated demographic. The trademark of the ships is the red lips and blue eyes painted on the bow. The accent is on a casual environment, many activities on board, and active shore excursions. Few passengers come from nations other than Germany, Austria, and Switzerland.

AIDABlu, the former *Crown Princess,* which sailed for the AIDA Cruises brand from 2005 until 2006 was transferred to Ocean Village.

AIDACara, the former *AIDA,* has 391 ocean-view cabins (including 44 with balconies, 12 junior suites, and four full suites). There are 202 inside cabins and eight cabins that are wheelchair accessible. The smallest measures 145 square feet and the four suites increase to 377 square feet, share a common balcony, and include a bathtub and stocked minibar. In the remaining accommodations, storage space is limited, but there are hair dryers in the living area, TVs, and a refrigerator. For dining, guests have a choice of two self-service buffet restaurants with large selections or a more intimate à la carte, reservation-only dining room. The ship features an extensive fitness, wellness, and sports program including a large, full-facility spa.

The 42,400-ton, 1,266-passenger *AIDAAura* and *AIDAVita* (1,582-passenger capacity with every berth occupied) offer 422 outside cabins and 211 inside, four wheelchair-accessible cabins, and 60 cabins and suites with balconies. Accommodations range in size from 145 square feet to the 344 square-foot suites. They are similar in facilities to the *AIDACara.* Similarly there are two self-service buffet restaurants, as well as a reservation-only, à la carte dining room, extensive fitness, wellness, and sports programs, and spas offering many treatments. Typical of many German ships, these have a nude sun bathing deck and bicycles for shore excursions, but no casino.

The 68,500-ton, 2,050-passenger *AIDADiva* entered service in 2007, followed by its sister ship, *AIDABella,* in 2008. Of the 1,025 accommodations, 666 face the sea and 439 have balconies. There are 18 suites. Public rooms are atop ship and staterooms are on the lower decks. All accommodations have TVs, Internet access, safes, and hair dryers. There are seven restaurants, four of which are self-service. Diners at Rossini, Buffalo, and Sushi Bar pay an extra charge. The central common area, the Theatrium, is a combination atrium and show lounge spanning three decks. Other public areas include a disco, spa, gym, two-deck-high pool with a sliding glass roof, and relaxation area with water beds, hammocks, and a large Jacuzzi. Additional facilities include two more pools, three more Jacuzzis, a golf driving range, a volley ball court, a squash court, a climbing wall, a jogging track, and several lounges. There are dedicated play areas, facilities, and programs for children ages four to seven and eight to 13.

An additional 68,500-ton sister ship will enter service in 2009. In 2010, 2011, and 2012, three additional 71,000-ton, 2,174-passenger ships are scheduled to join the fleet.

Strong Points:

These ships are ideal for families and younger German-speaking cruisers looking for a casual atmosphere and many activities.

Courtesy AIDA Cruises

Courtesy AIDA Cruises

Courtesy AIDA Cruises

Courtesy AIDA Cruises

AMA WATERWAYS
21625 Prairie Street
Chatsworth, California 91311
(800) 626-0126; (818) 428-6198
(818) 772-7335 Fax
www.amawaterways.com

MS *AMACELLO,* MS *AMADAGIO,* MS *AMADANTE,* MS *AMADOLCE,* MS *AMALEGRO,* MS *AMALYRA,* and MS *AMABELLA:* entered service in 2008, 2006, 2008, 2009, 2007, 2009, and 2010, respectively; 360' x 38'; 148-passenger capacity; 77 cabins; international officers and crew; cruises on the Danube, Main Canal, Rhine, Moselle, Rhone, and Saone as well as waterways of Belgium and Holland. **(Category B—Not Rated)**

MS *AMADOURO:* 77.85m x 11m; 130-passenger capacity; 65 cabins; international officers and crew; cruises on the Douro River Valley in Portugal and Spain. **(Category B—Not Rated)**

MS *LA MARGUERITE:* entered service 2009; 235' x 41'; 92-passenger capacity; 46 cabins; international officers and crew; cruises on the Mekong River. **(Category B—Not Rated)**

MS *SWISS PEARL:* entered service 1993; 360' x 37'; 124-passenger capacity; 64 cabins; international officers and crew; cruises on Rhone and Saone Rivers in France.

MS *TOLSTOY:* entered service 2005; renovated 2006; 360' x 41'; 160-passenger capacity; 73 cabins; international officers and crew; cruises on Rivers of Russia.

In 2002, Rudi Schreiner, former president of Viking River Cruises, and Jim Murphy, former owner and CEO of Brendan Worldwide Vacations, launched Amadeus Waterways. Subsequently the line changed its name to AMA Waterways. From 2006 through 2009, the company introduced six new deluxe riverboats designed to traverse the various rivers and waterways of Europe. Additionally, the cruise line leases or charters four riverboats that offer cruises on the rivers of Russia, France, the Douro River Valley in Portugal and Spain, and the Mekong River in Southeast Asia.

The 148-passenger MS *Amacello,* MS *Amadagio,* MS *Amadante,* MS *Amadolce,* MS *Amalegro,* MS *Amalyra,* and MS *Amabella* are sister ships that entered service between 2006 and 2009 and are among the newest and most modern vessels cruising on the rivers of Europe. Two additional sister ships are scheduled to enter service in 2010.

Seventy-three of the cabins on these ships measure 170 square feet, and the four junior suites on each ship measure 255 square feet. Of the accommodations, 82 percent sport French balconies and each includes two twin beds convertible to queen size, plush bedding, down duvets, a cozy sitting area, a safe, terrycloth bathrobes, a hair dryer, flat-screen TVs with English-language stations, satellite telephones, and Internet access. The junior suites have larger sitting areas and a bathtub and shower.

Public areas include a well-appointed, panoramic, open-seating dining room with complimentary wine, beer, and soda with dinner and complimentary cappuccino and espresso with all meals; a lounge and bar with panoramic river views; a library; a glassed-in wellness area encompassing a fitness center, sauna, and massage and beauty salon; a sun deck with whirlpool lounges and a walking track; and bicycles for passengers wishing to explore the cities and villages in this fashion.

All-inclusive shore excursions are conducted by knowledgeable English-speaking tour guides. About 70 percent of the passengers are from the U.S. or Canada, and the rest are from Australia, New Zealand, and other parts of the world. The ships offer varying itineraries on such European rivers as the Danube, Main, Rhine, and Moselle. Prices range from $1,700 per person for a seven-night cruise in a standard stateroom to $8,800 per person for a 30-night cruise and land package.

The 130-passenger MS *Amadouro* cruises exclusively on the Douro River through Spain and Portugal. There are 38 double cabins with private balconies and the remaining 27 have large picture windows. All measure 135 square feet. On sun deck atop ship are two Jacuzzis and a pool.

The 92-passenger MS *La Marguerite* is a very modern riverboat with spacious accommodations. Of the 38 226-square-foot deluxe staterooms 30 have balconies. The six 284-square-foot suites also have balconies, and the two 443-square-foot suites have both balconies and whirlpool tubs. Common areas include a panoramic restaurant, lounge and library, business center, sundeck with lounges, whirlpool and bar, lobby-reception area, small fitness room, spa for treatments, and beauty salon. Beer, soft drinks, spirits, bottled water, coffee, and tea are all complimentary. This is the first and only modern riverboat plying the waters of the Mekong River, which flows through Vietnam, Laos, and Cambodia.

The 160-passenger MS *Tolstoy* is one of the most modern riverboats offering cruises on the waterways of Russia. Spacious public areas include lounges, bars, library, movie hall, sun deck, smaller patio deck, indoor swimming pool with a sliding sun roof and pool bar, sauna, beauty salon, and souvenir shop. Standard cabins measure 110 square feet with large picture windows that open. For higher fees, there are seven deluxe 220-square-foot cabins with two twin beds (that cannot be joined), a sitting area, and two picture windows. There are also six 330-square-foot suites with three picture windows, a day room with TV, a refrigerator, and a separate bedroom.

Strong Points:

The six (soon to be eight) riverboats owned by the cruise line and built during the past four years are among the most modern, comfortable, and upscale vessels to offer cruises on the European waterways. The MS *La Marguerite* offers some of the most spacious accommodations of any riverboat in service. The other vessels operated by AMA offer exotic itineraries best explored in the comfort of these riverboats.

Courtesy AMA Waterways

Courtesy AMA Waterways

Courtesy AMA Waterways

Courtesy AMA Waterways

AMERICAN CANADIAN CARIBBEAN LINE, INC.
461 Water Street
P.O. Box 368
Warren, Rhode Island 02885
(800) 556-7450
(401) 247-2350 Fax

GRANDE CARIBE: entered service 1997; 98 G.R.T.; 183' x 40'; 98-passenger capacity; 49 cabins; American officers and crew; cruises through Chesapeake Bay, Erie Canal, Saguenay River, Intracoastal Waterway, Maine, New England islands, fall foliage, and Canada. **(Category C/D—Not Rated)**

GRANDE MARINER: entered service 1998; 98 G.R.T.; 183' x 40'; 98-passenger capacity; 49 cabins; American crew; cruises to Panama and Belize, through Erie Canal, Intracoastal Waterway, Gulf South, Great Lakes, New England islands, fall foliage, and Canada. **(Category C/D—Not Rated)**

NIAGARA PRINCE: entered service 1994; refurbished and resumed service in April 2009; 99 G.R.T.; 175' x 40'; 66-passenger capacity; 34 cabins; American crew; cruises to Mississippi and mid-American waterways, Hudson River, Lake Champlain, Intracoastal Waterway, Erie Canal, and Great Lakes. **(Category D— Not Rated)**

(Medical Facilities: There are no healthcare or handicap facilities aboard these vessels. There are stair lifts.)

The owner and designer of the ships of ACCL, Luther H. Blount, founded the cruise line in 1966. It is now managed by his daughter, the president of ACCL, Nancy Blount. These uniquely designed smaller ships specialize in destination cruises to out-of-the-way ports of call that larger vessels cannot navigate throughout the Caribbean, New England, the Great Lakes U.S., Erie Canal, Mississippi River, Chesapeake Bay, U.S. Intracoastal Waterway and Canadian east coast rivers and canals, Caribbean, and the Panama Canal/Central America.

Public areas include one dining room that accommodates all passengers in a single seating and one lounge used for receptions and lectures. (On *Niagara Prince* the dining room and lounge are in the same area on sun deck.) Historical and cultural programs are conducted by historians, scientists, and local guides. Some staterooms have upper and lower berths, while others have two lower berths and some can be made into a double bed. All have small private facilities (similar to those found on RVs) and limited storage.

Grande Caribe and *Niagara Prince* were refitted in 2009 with a nautical theme and updated lounges and dining areas. Some cabins now have a separate shower. *Gande Mariner* is scheduled for a similar refit in 2010.

The line advertises itself as "the original small ship cruise line . . . no-frills, informal, unpretentious, casual and friendly . . . with an emphasis on the destination, not the ship . . . no room service, no glitz and 'bring-your-own-bottle bar policy' . . . we offer unpretentious adventure for the mature, experienced traveler. . . ." Prices start at $250 per person per night, with most itineraries averaging about 11 days.

Courtesy American Canadian Caribbean Line, Inc.

Courtesy American Canadian Caribbean Line, Inc.

Courtesy American Canadian Caribbean Line, Inc.

Courtesy American Canadian Caribbean Line, Inc.

AMERICAN CRUISE LINES
741 Boston Post Road, Suite 200
Guilford, Connecticut 06437
(800) 814-6880
(203) 453-0417 Fax
www.americancruiselines.com

MV *AMERICAN EAGLE:* entered service 2000; 180' x 40'; 4 decks; 31 state-rooms; 49-passenger capacity; American officers and crew; 6-, 7-, and 14-night cruises along East Coast of U.S. from Maine to Florida. (**Category B/C—Not Rated**)

MV *AMERICAN GLORY:* entered service 2002; 180' x 42'; 4 decks; 31 state-rooms; 49-passenger capacity; American officers and crew; 6-, 7-, 10-, and 14-night cruises along East Cost of U.S. from Maine to Florida. (**Category B/C—Not Rated**)

MV *AMERICAN SPIRIT:* entered service 2005; 2,000 G.R.T.; 225' x 45'; 4 decks; 51 staterooms; 100-passenger capacity; American officers and crew; 6-, 7-, and 14-night cruises along East Coast of U.S. from Maine to Florida. (**Category B/C—Not Rated**)

MV *AMERICAN STAR:* entered service in 2007; 2,000 G.R.T.; 225' x 45'; 4 decks; 51 staterooms; 100-passenger capacity; American officers and crew; 6-, 7-, 10-, and 14-night cruises along the East Coast of U.S. from Maine to Florida. (**Category B/C—Not Rated**)

MV *INDEPENDENCE:* entered service 2010; 3,000 G.R.T.; 54 staterooms; 100-passenger capacity; American officers and crew; 6-,7-,10-, and 14-night cruises from Maine to Florida. (**Category B/C—Not Rated**)

(Medical Facilities: Each ship has two wheelchair-accessible staterooms; P-0; N-0; EM-1; CM; PD; TC; PO; EPC; OX; WC; TM; LJ.)

American Cruise Lines was founded in 1974. In the years since its inception, the company has operated several vessels, including the original MV *Eagle,* MV *Independence,* MV *America,* MV *Charleston,* MV *New Orleans,* and MV *Savannah.* Today it operates four modern vessels and is introducing a new MV *Independence* in 2010.

Each vessel is specifically designed to allow travel in unique inland water-ways, secluded coves, and hidden harbors where larger vessels cannot go. Itiner-aries include six-, seven-, 10-, and 14-night cruises emanating from Providence, Rhode Island; New York, New York; Baltimore, Maryland; Bangor, Maine; Charleston, South Carolina; and Jacksonville, St. Augustine, and Sanford, Florida.

Prices on a seven-night cruise range from $3,295 per person (double occupancy) to $4,265 for cabins with balconies on the higher deck. Single cabins start at $4,685. Early booking discounts are available.

All staterooms face outside with large opening windows and measure from 180 to 254 square feet. Six on the *Eagle,* 14 on the *Glory,* 25 on the *Spirit,* and 26 on the *Star* have private balconies. The staterooms on the *Independence* measure from 220 to 400 square feet, and 42 have private balconies. All staterooms include twin- or king-size beds, private bathroom facilities, hair dryers, satellite TV, DVD players, and private climate control. Public areas include a sun deck atop ship; sports and fitness facilities; exercise equipment, including a treadmill, stair machine, and bicycle; a glass-enclosed, three-meals-a-day, single-seating dining room with panoramic views; an elevator to all decks; multiple lounges; Internet access; and a library. The dress aboard is resort casual. Special features include complimentary cocktails before dinner, complimentary wines with dinner, and onboard lecturers and naturalists. There are no phones; however, cell phones will work throughout the ship while underway as well as in port or ashore. Cabin service is available only in the morning.

Available activities on-board the various ships include guest speakers, naturalists, Audubon specialists, and chef demonstrations. Entertainment includes piano players, singers, string trios, comedians, magic acts, theme parties, and game tournaments.

The 104-passenger MV *Independence* will debut larger and more technically advanced then the other vessels, with larger staterooms and private balconies.

Strong Points:

Small, intimate ships providing a comfortable cruise experience and opportunity to explore cities, villages, and waterways along the East Coast of the U.S.

Courtesy American Cruise Lines

Courtesy American Cruise Lines

Courtesy American Cruise Lines

Daily Activities
Sunday, July 15, 2007

Weather Forecast
Sunny, not a cloud in the sky – temperature 78°

6:30 a.m. Depart Bucksport, ME for Bar Harbor, ME

Enjoy a delightful day of cruising through the serene waters of Maine's most scenic waterways including Eggemoggin Reach, Blue Hill Bay to Frenchman Bay. Join our onboard naturalist on the top deck to learn and discover more about this areas fascinating wildlife including whales, puffins, and eagles.

Early Riser's Coffee, Tea, Juice, and Pastries in the Nantucket Lounge

7:30 – 9:00 a.m. Passenger "Breakfast to Order" in the Dining Salon

10:00 a.m. "Go Fly a Kite" on the Observation Deck – join the fun!
Outrageous Cookies in the Nantucket Lounge
"Let's Play Bingo" in the Nantucket Lounge

12:00 p.m. Arrive in beautiful Bar Harbor, ME

12:30 p.m. Passenger Luncheon Service in the Dining Salon

2:00 p.m. Tour Bar Harbor – Enjoy a spectacular one and a half hour "Mansions and Mountain" tour including Acadia National Park with a stop at Cadillac Mountain. The park encompasses 47,633 acres of granite-domed mountains and ocean shoreline. Evidence suggests that native people first lived here at least 5,000 years ago. It likewise is a haven for wildlife and varied plants. You will find the history and opulent mansions of Bar Harbor fascinating while getting a taste of true Down East accent, humor and flavor.

OR

Enjoy an afternoon of strolling and shopping along Bar Harbor's picturesque Mt. Desert and Cottage Street with its eclectic specialty shops and galleries.

5:30 p.m. Complimentary Evening Cocktails and Hors d'Oeuvres and an oyster and crab shucking feast in the Nantucket Lounge

6:30 p.m. Passenger Dinner Service in the Dining Salon

8:00 p.m. Join our guest speaker Sam Ladley in the Nantucket Lounge. Mr. Ladley will entertain you this evening with great stories and history of the quaint and charming seaports of Maine.

Ice Cream Sundaes and Root Beer Floats served in the Nantucket Lounge

* If you would like to visit one of Bar Harbor's magnificent sites that are not listed on today's itinerary, please ask your Cruise Director to help you arrange a tour that better fits you.

Courtesy American Cruise Lines

AMERICAN
CRUISE LINES

Dinner Menu – Saturday, July 27, 2007

Appetizers

Seared Fresh Ahi Tuna drizzled with Wasabi Vinaigrette
over a bed of Micro Mustard Greens tossed in White Truffle Oil

Or

Fresh Caesar or Field Greens Salad

Or

French Onion Soup topped with a Baked Parmesan & Gruyere Crouton

Entrées

Filet Tenderloin Steak finished with
Creamy Peppercorn Cognac Sauce
Accompanied by Wild Mushroom Risotto and Baby Carrots

Or

Seared Diver Scallops with a drizzle of Saffron Aioli
Accompanied by Lobster Risotto and Fresh Steamed Broccoli

Or

Fresh Grouper topped with a Citrus Mango Salsa
Accompanied by Lime Infused Texmati Rice and Steamed Broccoli

Or

Grilled Portabella Mushroom Cap Stuffed with Sun Dried Tomatoes, Roasted Red
Peppers and Red Onions
Drizzled with a Balsamic Sherry Glaze

Desserts

Decadent Raspberry Chocolate Terrine

Or

Fresh Berry Tart
Raspberries, Blueberries and Blackberries
Lightly coated with a port wine reduction

Or

A choice of Butter Pecan, Pistachio, Mint Chocolate Chip, Chocolate, Vanilla or Sugar
Free Vanilla Ice Cream

Courtesy American Cruise Lines

AVALON WATERWAYS
P.O. Box 2639
Warminster, Pennsylvania 18974
(877) 380-1544
www.avalonwaterways.com

AVALON AFFINITY, AVALON CREATIVITY, AVALON FELICITY, AVALON LUMINARY, and *AVALON SCENERY:* entered service 2009, 2009, 2010, 2010, and 2008, respectively; 361' long; 138-passenger capacity; 69, 68, 65, 65, and 67 cabins, respectively; international officers and crew; cruises on rivers of Europe. **(Category B—Not Rated)**

AVALON IMAGERY, AVALON TRANQUILITY, and *AVALON TAPESTRY:* entered service 2007, 2007, and 2008, respectively; 443' long; 170-passenger capacity; 85, 85, and 82 cabins, respectively; international officers and crew; cruises on rivers of Europe. **(Category B—Not Rated)**

AVALON POETRY and *AVALON ARTISTRY:* entered service 2005 and 2004, respectively; 426' long; 180-passenger capacity; 89 cabins; international officers and crew; cruises on rivers of Europe. **(Category B—Not Rated)**

This cruise line, a part of the Globus family of brands, commenced service on the waterways of Europe in 2004 with the introduction of the *Avalon Artistry.* Seven additional riverboats were added by the close of 2009. With its oldest vessel cruising for only five years, the line boasts the youngest fleet of riverboats plying the waters of the Rhone, Saone, Rhine, Moselle, and Danube Rivers or the Main Canal and waterways in Belgium and Holland.

Staterooms measure 172 square feet, whereas suites are 258 square feet, unusually large for a riverboat. Most accommodations have floor-to-ceiling sliding glass doors with French balconies. All have European-style duvets, flat-screen satellite TV and radios, minibars, hair dryers, safes, writing desks, and nice-size closets. There are two suites on the *Scenery, Creativity, Tapestry,* and *Artistry* and four on the *Affinity, Imagery,* and *Poetry.* There are elevators on the *Scenery, Creativity,* and *Affinity.*

Public areas include a sky deck with deck chairs, navigation bridge and onboard camera, reception area, main lounge and bar, hairdresser, and restaurant. The riverboat also offers Internet access and a small fitness center. On the three newest ships there is a small whirlpool on the sky deck. There is nightly piano music, complimentary wine with dinner, and turn-down service each evening.

Parent company, Globus, also offers Nile cruises on the *Royal Lotus,* Yangtze River cruises on the *Victoria Anna* and *Victoria Jenna,* and Galapagos Island cruises on the *Santa Cruz* and *La Pinta.*

Strong Points:
A modern riverboat line with spacious accommodations.

Courtesy Avalon Waterways

Courtesy Avalon Waterways

Courtesy Avalon Waterways

CARNIVAL CRUISE LINES
3655 N.W. 87th Avenue
Miami, Florida 33178
(800) CARNIVAL

CARNIVAL CONQUEST, CARNIVAL GLORY, CARNIVAL VALOR, CARNIVAL LIBERTY, and *CARNIVAL FREEDOM:* entered service 2002, 2003, 2004, 2005, and 2007, respectively; 110,000 G.R.T.; 952' x 116'; 3,700-passenger capacity (2,974 double occupancy); 1,487 cabins; Italian officers and international crew; 7-day Caribbean itineraries from Galveston, Texas, for *Conquest;* from Port Canaveral, Florida, for *Glory;* and from Miami, Florida, for *Valor. Carnival Liberty* operates 7-day cruises from Miami; *Carnival Freedom* operates 12-day European cruises and 6- and 8-day Caribbean cruises from Fort Lauderdale.

☆☆☆☆☆

(Medical Facilities: C-27; P-1, EM, CLS, MS; N-4; PD; BC; EKG; TC; PO; EPC; OX; WC; OR; ICU; X; M; LJ.)

CARNIVAL DESTINY: entered service 1996; 101,353 G.R.T.; 893' x 116'; 2,642-passenger capacity; 1,321 cabins; Italian officers and international crew; 4- and 5-day cruises to western Caribbean from Miami.

☆☆☆☆☆

CARNIVAL DREAM: entered service 2009; 130,000 G.R.T.; 1,004' x 158'; 3,646-passenger capacity (4,631 with every berth filled); 1,823 cabins; Italian officers and international crew; 7-night eastern and western Caribbean itineraries from Port Canaveral.

☆☆☆☆☆ +

CARNIVAL SPLENDOR: entered service 2008; 113,300 G.R.T.; 3,006 passenger capacity (double occupancy); 1,503 cabins; Italian officers and international crew; 7-night Mexican Riviera cruises from Long Beach, California.

☆☆☆☆☆

(Medical Facilities: C-27; P-1, EM, CLS, MS; N-4; PD; BC; EKG; TC; PO; EPC; OX; WC; OR; ICU; X; M; LJ.)

CARNIVAL SPIRIT, CARNIVAL PRIDE, CARNIVAL LEGEND, and *CARNIVAL MIRACLE:* entered service 2001, 2001, 2002, and 2004, respectively; 88,500 G.R.T.; 960' x 105.7'; 2,124-passenger capacity; 1,062 cabins; Italian officers and international crew; *Carnival Spirit* offers 8-day Mexican Riviera cruises from San Diego, California, and 7-day Alaskan itineraries from Seaward/Anchorage, Alaska, and Vancouver, Canada; *Carnival Pride*'s 6-,7-, and 8-day sailings commence from Baltimore, Maryland, and cruise the Bahamas and Florida; *Carnival Miracle* offers 8-day sailings from New York and Fort Lauderdale, Florida, to the Caribbean; *Carnival Legend* offers 7-day cruises from Tampa, Florida, to the Caribbean.

☆ ☆ ☆ ☆ ☆

(Medical Facilities: C-16; P-1, EM, CLS, MS; N-3; CM; PD; BC; EKG; TC; PO; EPC; OX; WC; OR; ICU; X; M; TM; LJ.)

CARNIVAL TRIUMPH and *CARNIVAL VICTORY:* entered service 1999 and 2000, respectively; 102,000 G.R.T.; 893' x 116'; 2,758-passenger capacity; 1,379 cabins; Italian officers and international crew; *Carnival Triumph* offers 4-, 5-, and 7-day cruises in western Caribbean from New Orleans; *Carnival Victory* offers 7-day sailings from San Juan to the southern Caribbean.

☆ ☆ ☆ ☆ ☆

(Medical Facilities: C-27; P-1; EM, CLS, MS; N-4; CM; PD; BC; EKG; TC; PO; EPC; OX; WC; OR; ICU; X; M; LJ.)

CARNIVAL ECSTASY and *CARNIVAL FANTASY:* entered service 1991 and 1990, respectively; *Carnival Fantasy* renovated 2005; 70,367 G.R.T.; 855' x 103'; 2,052- and 2,056-passenger capacity; 1,026 and 1,028 cabins; Italian officers and international crew; 4- and 5-day cruises from Mobile, Alabama, to the Caribbean on *Carnival Fantasy* and 4- and 5-day cruises from Galveston, Texas, to Mexico on *Carnival Ecstasy.*

☆ ☆ ☆ ☆

(Medical Facilities: C-20; P-1; EM, CLS, MS; N-3; CM; PD; BC; EKG; TC; PO; EPC; OX; WC; OR; X; ICU; M; LJ.)

CARNIVAL SENSATION, CARNIVAL FASCINATION, CARNIVAL IMAGI-NATION, CARNIVAL INSPIRATION, CARNIVAL ELATION, and *CARNIVAL PARADISE:* entered service 1993, 1994, 1995, 1996, 1998, and 1998, respectively; *Carnival Fascination* and *Carnival Sensation* renovated 2006 and 2009, respectively; 70,367 G.R.T.; 855' x 103'; 2,052-passenger capacity; 1,020 cabins; Italian officers and international crew; *Carnival Sensation* operates 3- and 4-day cruises from Port Canaveral, Florida, to the Bahamas; *Carnival Fascination* operates 4- and 5-day Key West/Bahamas sailings from Jacksonville, Florida; *Carnival Imagination* offers 3- and 4-day Bahamas/western Caribbean cruises from Miami; *Carnival Inspiration* operates 4- and 5-day cruises from Tampa to western Caribbean; *Carnival Elation* operates 3- and 4-day cruises from San Diego to Baja, Mexico; *Carnival Paradise* operates 3- and 4-day cruises from Long Beach to Baja, Mexico.

⭐ ⭐ ⭐ ⭐ +

(Medical Facilities: C-20; P-1; EM; CLS, MS; N-3; CM; PD; BC; EKG; TC; PO; EPC; OX; OR; WC; ICU; X; M; LJ.)

Note: Passenger capacities listed are based on double occupancy.

These ships are rated in 11 separate categories in the second half of chapter 14.

Carnival's founder, Ted Arison, started the company in 1972 with the purchase of the *Empress of Canada* from the Canadian Pacific Line. After a refurbishing, it entered the Caribbean market as the *Mardi Gras.* This was followed by the purchase and refurbishing of the sister ship, *Empress of Britain,* which commenced service in 1976 as the *Carnivale.* The former *S.A. Vaal* of the Union Castle Line, refurbished for more than $30 million and renamed the *Festivale,* was added in 1978. Major advertising and promotion of these vessels as the "Fun Ships," together with attractive air-sea packaging, quickly made Carnival one of the most financially successful cruise lines in the industry.

This led to the construction of the *Tropicale* for more than $100 million, designed to be the forerunner of the cruise line's updated, full-capacity "Fun Ships" of the 1980s. It entered service in 1982 with Mexican Riviera cruises from Los Angeles. In February 2001, the ship was transferred to Carnival's sister company, Costa Cruises.

Continued financial success and belief in the future of the American cruise market led to the construction of three new vessels in the 46,000- to 48,000-ton category. The *Holiday* entered Caribbean service in 1985, followed by the *Jubilee* in 1986, and the *Celebration* in 1987. With the addition of these newer ships with expanded passenger capacity on seven-day Caribbean itineraries, the aging *Mardi*

Gras and *Carnivale* were relegated to three- and four-day runs from Florida to the Bahamas. Subsequently, the *Mardi Gras* and *Carnivale* were sold to the now-defunct Epirotiki Lines and the *Festivale* to the now-defunct Dolphin Cruise Line. The *Jubilee* was transferred to Carnival's P & O Cruises Australia in 2004. The *Celebration* and *Holiday* were transferred to one of Carnival's sister companies, Ibero-Cruceros, in 2008 and 2009, respectively.

Today, Carnival is one of the leading cruise lines in the middle-cruise market, with ships that have the capacity to put more than 50,000 passengers afloat each week in lower berths. (If you include sailings for less than a week's duration, this figure is somewhat higher.) By fall, 2009, the Carnival fleet numbered 22. The casual, amusement-park environment, plethora of activities and entertainment, round-the-clock partying, and attractive packaging have interested a new generation of younger cruisers—singles, couples, and families. This is one of the few major cruise lines where 70 percent of passengers are under 55 years old, with 30 percent under age 35. During the summer and the holidays, a large percentage of passengers are families traveling with children.

Carnival contracted to build eight 70,000+-ton sister cruise ships with $225 million-plus price tags in the 1990s: the *Carnival Fantasy* commenced service in March 1990, the *Carnival Ecstasy* in June 1991, the *Carnival Sensation* in November 1993, the *Carnival Fascination* in 1994, the *Carnival Imagination* in 1995, the *Carnival Inspiration* in 1996, and the *Carnival Elation* and *Carnival Paradise* in 1998. The 101,353-ton *Carnival Destiny*, with more than 1,300 cabins, entered service in 1996. Sister ships to the *Carnival Destiny*, the 102,000-ton *Carnival Triumph* and *Carnival Victory*, entered service in 1999 and 2000, respectively. Five additional 110,000-ton ships named *Carnival Conquest, Carnival Glory, Carnival Valor, Carnival Liberty,* and *Carnival Freedom* entered service in 2002, 2003, 2004, 2005, and 2006, respectively. The 88,500-ton *Carnival Spirit* entered service in the spring of 2001, the *Carnival Pride* in December 2001, *Carnival Legend* in August 2002, and *Carnival Miracle* in 2004. Eighty percent of the staterooms on these four ships offer a sitting area and ocean views, and approximately two-thirds have balconies.

The *Fantasy, Ecstasy, Sensation, Fascination, Imagination, Inspiration, Elation,* and *Paradise* are very similar in layout and design; however, they differ in decor, and with each new ship there have been innovations and improvements. Joe Farcus, interior architect for all of the Carnival ships, attempts to create a "fantasy vacation environment." The later entries have less dazzle, are a bit more traditional in decor, and, in my opinion, are more tasteful.

Each of these ships measures a little over 70,000+ tons, extends approximately 855 feet in length, has 1,026 cabins that accommodate 2,052 double occupancy, and 2,606 if all of the upper berths are filled. Standard cabins measure 183 to 190 square feet, featuring twin beds that convert to double beds, closed-circuit color televisions, private safes, telephones, moderate closet and drawer space, and bathrooms with large showers but limited storage space. Forty percent of the cabins are inside; however, they are very similar to the outside accommodations, except that they have no windows or portholes and are 10 to 20 percent smaller.

Some have upper and lower berths. The 28 most expensive suites have verandas, refrigerators, a small sitting area, a small walk-in closet, and a combination Jacuzzi tub and shower. The 26 demi-suites are a bit larger than the standard cabins and include a very small sitting area and a narrow veranda. The full suites measure 350 square feet, with 71-square-foot balconies.

The focal point of each ship is a spectacular grand atrium rising seven decks to an immense skylight, with two glass birdcage elevators traversing between top and bottom. The majority of the cabins except the demi- and veranda-suites are located on the four lower decks, with the public rooms and two dining rooms on the upper levels of the ship.

Public rooms include a multilevel, state-of-the-art show lounge with a turntable stage and several more intimate lounges that feature a variety of nightly entertainment, ranging from discos with neon arcs and copper lightning bolts to variety acts, comedians, and other entertainers. Extending into the wee hours, there is something nightly for everyone.

The casinos offer numerous blackjack, roulette, craps, and Caribbean poker tables as well as dozens of slots. The library and cardrooms are more traditional and offer a quiet respite. The boutiques at the Galleria Mall feature jewelry, logo items, T-shirts, men and women's cruise and formal wear, liquor, and sundries.

Sports and health enthusiasts will appreciate the padded jogging tracks, the pool-deck areas, and the spa/health clubs that include an aerobics room, gymnasium with weights, cardiovascular and exercise equipment looking out to sea, men and women's locker rooms with sauna, steam and multi-nozzled showers, hairdressing salon, and an area featuring numerous beauty and massage treatments normally found only at fancy spas.

Beginning in 2006, the *Fantasy*-class ships were refurbished and received various additions, including new comfort bedding and flat-screen TVs in the staterooms, remodeled bathrooms, a new atrium bar and Internet café, expanded children's facilities, a new teen center, a nine-hole miniature golf course, and a patisserie/coffee bar. Over the next few years, the *Fantasy*-class ships will receive additional innovations, such as part of the line's $250 million "Evolutions of Fun" refurbishment program, new Caribbean-resort-style pool and lido areas and Carnival Water Works, sporting the longest, most elaborate waterslides at sea (four-deck-high, 300-foot-long cascading waterslide and an 82-foot-long dual racing waterslide). New, too, will be the Serenity adults-only deck area, with outdoor deck space furnished with plush chaise lounges, chairs, and oversized umbrellas. These areas include a large sheltered area, two whirlpools, and bar service. In addition, the spa facilities will be renovated and enhanced. Thus far, four of the eight *Fantasy*-class ships have been retrofitted with the full Evolutions of Fun amenities with the remaining four ships scheduled to be completed over the next few years. In early 2009, 98 balcony staterooms were added to the *Carnival Sensation*.

The *Carnival Destiny* was the first cruise ship to exceed 100,000 tons. She carries a crew of 1,050 that can service 1,321 staterooms, with a potential passenger capacity of 3,400; however, double occupancy capacity is 2,642. Upon entering the ship, you will be overwhelmed by the huge central atrium with its birdcage elevators traversing the numerous decks of the ship. No less impressive are the three-level, 1,500-passenger-capacity Palladium show lounge; the two bi-level elegant dining rooms featuring numerous intimate booths; the full-facility spa/fitness center; the giant outdoor lido area with four pools, the longest waterslide at sea, Jacuzzis, and magradome; a plethora of bars, lounges, shops, and facilities for children of all ages; and the alternative-dining restaurant on lido deck, with eclectic offerings, including numerous food stations featuring pizza, a salad bar, frozen yogurt and ice cream, Asian specialties, and a New York-style deli. All stateroom accommodations include direct-dial telephones, remote-control televisions with a large selection of stations, private room safes, generous storage, showers, and hair dryers. Four hundred thirty-two accommodations have balconies, and there are 40 suites and eight penthouse suites. About 30 percent of the cabins are inside. For passenger convenience, there are Laundromats on each deck. (It will cost a total of $5.25 to wash and dry one load with detergent.) For cruisers who enjoy the extra facilities and options found on megaships, the *Carnival Destiny* will surely fill the bill. The *Carnival Triumph* and *Carnival Victory* are sister ships with similar facilities.

In 2005, the *Carnival Destiny* received a multimillion-dollar renovation that included a new teen club, a renovated lido restaurant, children's pool, casino, and updated suite accommodations. In 2008, the ship was equipped with a 270-square-foot outdoor LED screen on lido deck.

The 110,000-ton, 2,974-passenger *Carnival Conquest, Carnival Glory, Carnival Valor, Carnival Liberty,* and *Carnival Freedom* entered service in 2002, 2003, 2004, 2005, and 2007, respectively. Similar in design and facilities to the *Destiny*-class ships, they are 60 feet longer and have expanded children and teen facilities and programs as well as elegant supper clubs. Sixty-one percent of the staterooms face the sea and 37 percent have balconies. When every berth is filled, they can accommodate 3,700 passengers.

Carnival Valor was the first ship in the fleet (and world) to feature 100 percent, bow-to-stern wireless Internet access in all staterooms and public areas. This new Wi-Fi system complements the ship's Internet café. If you do not wish to bring your own laptop, you can rent one while aboard. The program was subsequently extended to *Carnival Liberty* and *Carnival Freedom* with the remainder of the fleet offering Wi-Fi Internet access in virtually all public rooms and areas.

Carnival Liberty and *Carnival Freedom* were the first ships in the cruise line to introduce the Carnival Seaside Theater, a 12-foot-high, 22-foot-wide LED outdoor movie screen located on lido deck. The theater features movies, sporting events, concerts, and various programs while guests relax in lounge chairs and enjoy drinks, popcorn, and other typical movie fare. This technology will be extended to other ships in the future.

During 2008, *Carnival Destiny, Carnival Triumph,* and *Carnival Liberty* spent time in dry dock and 48 additional 230-square-foot staterooms were added to each vessel. *Carnival Liberty* received two new 750-square-foot deluxe staterooms.

The 113,300-ton *Carnival Splendor* entered service in July 2008. Sixty percent of the 1,503 staterooms have sea views and 60 percent of these sport balconies. The spa facilities were expanded to 21,000 square feet, spanning two decks, with a thalasso pool, thermal suites, and 68 spa staterooms. For the younger set there are 5,500 square feet of children's playroom space across two levels as well as extensive water park facilities.

The 130,000-ton, 3,646-passenger *Carnival Dream* entered service in September 2009 as the largest ship in the Carnival fleet. A sister ship, *Carnival Magic,* is scheduled to enter service in June 2011. In addition to all of the facilities found on the 110,000-ton ships, this new generation ship has several innovations: Ocean Plaza, a new concept for the line with an indoor/outdoor café and live music; a huge waterworks park for families, with scenic whirlpools that extend over the ship's beam; an 11-deck-high atrium with a cantilevered bandstand atop a massive dance floor on the ground level; an expansive 23,750-square-foot Cloud 9 spa, the largest and most elaborate on any Carnival ship to date; a half-mile, open-air promenade encircling the ship on its fifth level with four scenic whirlpools cantilevered out over the sea; and some deluxe staterooms featuring two bathrooms.

Dining standards on the Carnival ships have significantly improved over the years. The line now offers a variety of dining possibilities with varied menus. The two main dining rooms serve all three meals. Five-course dinners are featured, which include a variety of appetizers, soups, salads, pasta entrees, and desserts, with steak, chicken, and health-conscious options always available. The large indoor/outdoor lido restaurants offer a mediocre breakfast buffet, but on the larger ships, exceptional lunch and dinner buffets include salad bars, freshly made pasta, hamburgers, jumbo hot dogs, pizza hot from the oven, self-serve frozen yogurt and ice cream available 24 hours a day, New York-style delis, Asian-cuisine stations, specialty seafood venues, and a rotating variety of ethnic favorites from around the world. New gourmet-style Spa Carnival fare (healthy cuisine) was first introduced on *Carnival Freedom* and thereafter was extended fleetwide. In 2009, Carnival inaugurated "Your Choice Dining" where passengers select between early and late seating or "Your Time" seating, which allows diners to eat wherever they choose at any time between 5:45 P.M. and 9:30 P.M. When approaching the dining room for a reservation passengers are given a pager, which beeps when the table is available. This procedure will be adopted throughout the fleet by the summer of 2010.

In addition, a larger percentage of passengers are availing themselves of the casual alternative dinner service in the Seaview Bistro/lido restaurants. The more recent Carnival ships (including all the *Spirit-* and *Conquest*-class ships) and the *Carnival Splendor* and *Carnival Dream* include an elegant, reservations-only Supper Club offering prime steaks, lobster tails, escargot, caviar, and other upscale cuisine with all the trimmings, as well as dynamic desserts. Each course is imaginatively presented and impeccably served. There is a $30-per-person surcharge to eat here. Other dining options include patisseries, sushi bars, and 24-hour cabin service.

Although the food preparation, presentation, and variety are uniformly quite good, service throughout the entire ship is not up to the same quality. There appear to be too few crew members and supervisors to do the jobs efficiently, and the service procedures in the dining rooms and housekeeping are geared to using less personnel, rather than to satisfying passengers' needs. Most of the crew seem to be focused on carrying out a "short list" of tasks and are reluctant to go beyond that list or exercise any imagination.

The line features three different children's programs—Camp Carnival for ages 2-11, Circle "C" for 12 to14 year olds, and Club O2 for ages 15-17—on all the ships. Additionally, the ships offer children's menus, youth counselors, and video-game rooms. Through a partnership with Elite Golf Cruises, LLC, Carnival's guests have the opportunity to play top golf courses and receive personalized instruction both aboard ship and during golf outings ashore. Activities and entertainment seem designed to appeal to single and married young to middle-age adults (under 50). Of course, many of the activities will also appeal to older cruisers as well.

Commencing in 2004, captains on Carnival ships are licensed to perform wedding-vow renewal ceremonies. In 2005, Carnival upgraded stateroom amenities with a new Carnival Comfort Bed, which includes custom pillows, fine quality duvet covers, pillow cases, and a spring mattress set. Commencing in 2007, a new water balloon-themed attraction, Water Wars, located near the main pools, was installed throughout the fleet. All Carnival ships now offer cell phone service and wireless Internet access.

Although Carnival Cruise Line is certainly comfortable with its dominant position in the mass-market category of cruise lines, the spacious outside cabins and quality cuisine in the various restaurants rival the parent corporation's premium-cruise category brands. Carnival Cruise Lines is the flagship company of Carnival Corporation & plc, a multiline cruise conglomerate (traded on the New York and London Stock Exchanges). In addition to Carnival Cruise Lines, the corporation owns AIDA Cruises, Costa Cruises, Cunard Line, Holland America Line, IberoCruceros, Ocean Village, P & O Cruises, P & O Cruises Australia, Princess Cruises, and the Yachts of Seabourn, all of which are operated and promoted as separate products.

In 2007, Carnival entered into a joint venture with Iberojet Tours of Spain, wherein Carnival acquired 75 percent of Iberojet Cruises, which owned two ships, the 47,000-ton *Grand Mistral* and the 25,000-ton *Grand Voyager*. The new venture was named "IberoCruceros." Carnival Corporation & plc transferred the 1,486-passenger *Celebration* and the 1,452-passenger *Holiday* from its Carnival Cruise Lines brand to the new venture and it is anticipated that Carnival may transfer additional ships in the future.

Carnival frequently changes the deployment of its vessels, so it is best to consult the cruise line and not rely on any but the most recent brochures.

Strong Points:

Glamorous, newer ships, a variety of daytime and evening activities and entertainment, a casual lively atmosphere, fine dining, and plenty of fellow passengers from 20 to 55 years old. An excellent choice for active families and good value for the money. Truly the "Fun Ships" as advertised.

Courtesy Carnival Cruise Lines

Courtesy Carnival Cruise Lines

Captain's Welcome Dinner

The Master Summons All Who Sail with Him to Dine as Royal Guests in a Spectacular Celebration of the Seagoing Life.
All Aboard are to Heed the Captain's Wishes of Making Merry on this Special Occasion.
The Captain has Ordered the Very Best of Everything for His Guests, For on His Night, He Salutes Each of You

Bon Appetit!

Starters

Carpaccio of Fresh Pear and Citrus Segments
Thinly Sliced Pears, Orange and Grapefruit Wedges Marinated with Campari and Lime Juice

Black Tiger Shrimp Cocktail
Served with American Cocktail Sauce

 ### Baked Stuffed White Mushrooms
Spinach, Romano Cheese and Fine Herbs

Minestrone Milanese
Italian Vegetable Soup with Plum Tomatoes, Beans and Pasta

West Indian Roasted Pumpkin Soup
Gently Roasted in the Oven, Blended with Chicken Broth and a Touch of Cream

Strawberry Bisque
Chilled Creamy Strawberry Soup with Fresh Mint

Salads

Wilted Spinach and Portobello Mushrooms with Fresh Bacon Bits
Walnut and Blue Cheese Dressing

Caesar Salad
Hearts of Romaine Lettuce Tossed with our Caesar Dressing
Freshly Grated Parmesan Cheese and Herb Croutons

These Items are Lower in Calories, Sodium, Cholesterol and Fat. Salads are prepared with
Diet Dressing. Calorie Count and Fat Content can vary up to 10%.

Chilled Supreme of Fresh Fruit
Melons, Kiwi, Mango and Papaya
[100 Calories, 0 grams of Fat, 0 grams of Trans-Fat]

Iced Baby Spinach Leaves, Watercress and Alfalfa Sprouts
Served with Fat Free Italian Dressing [30 Calories, 0.5 grams of Fat, 0 grams of Trans-Fat]

Chicken Roulade with Butternut Squash Essence
Served with Grilled Vegetables and Berries
[310 Calories, 2 grams of Fat, 0 grams of Trans-Fat]

D72A_0307

GEORGES BLANC SIGNATURE SELECTION

SIGNATURE SELECTION

It is with special pride that we offer our guests the culinary masterpieces of French master chef Georges Blanc. We're honored that we are the only cruise line that can offer the unique recipes and guidance of this legendary master chef, restaurateur, wine connoisseur and bestselling cookbook author. Once you have savored the unparalleled creations of our signature chef —paired with superb wines chosen from his own collection— you will appreciate why Georges Blanc has achieved such international fame.

Main Courses

Spaghetti Carbonara
Tossed with a Creamy Bacon, Cheese and Garlic Sauce
Also available as Starter

Grilled Fillet of Fresh Victorian Perch
Grilled Beefsteak Tomato Salad, German Lentil Stew and Potato Pancake

Broiled Lobster Tail with Melted Butter
Mushroom Risotto and Broccoli Florets

 ### Supreme of Hudson Valley Duck
Pink Seared Duck Breast, Onion and Tomato Tart
Apple Crisp, Sweet Turnip Puree and Snow Peas

Roasted Prime Rib of Aged American Beef
Baked Potato, Balsamic Glazed Tomatoes, Sautéed Green Beans and Roasted Cauliflower

Chili Rellenos
Tomato and Broccoli Stuffed Pepper, Baked with Aged Cheddar and Manchego Cheese

Alternative Selections

Fresh Fruit Cocktail

Broiled Fillet of Fresh Pacific Salmon
Served with Vegetables of the Day

Grilled Breast of Corn Fed Chicken
Served with Vegetables of the Day

Premium Black Angus Jumbo Burger
Served on a Freshly Baked Bun with Traditional Garnish and Golden Fries

Grilled New York Sirloin Steak
Served with Vegetables of the Day and Red Bliss Potatoes

Baked Idaho Potatoes, French Fries or Steamed White Rice

Assorted Steamed Vegetables

D72B 0307

GEORGES BLANC SIGNATURE SELECTION

Desserts

CARAMELIZED APPLES ON PUFF PASTRY
Served with Vanilla Cream and Caramel Sauce

CHERRIES JUBILEE
Dark Cherries in our own Sauce, Flamed with Cherry Brandy
Served over Vanilla Ice Cream

DIET BANANA GATEAU
Diet Banana Sponge Cake, Filled with a Low Calorie Banana Cream
Dessert is Prepared with a Sugar Substitute

Alternative Selections

WARM CHOCOLATE MELTING CAKE
Served with Vanilla Ice Cream

FRESH TROPICAL FRUIT PLATE

*Ice Creams

VANILLA • CHOCOLATE • STRAWBERRY • BUTTER PECAN
Sugar-Free Ice Cream is available upon request

Sherbets

ORANGE • PINEAPPLE • LIME

Cheeses

PORT SALUT • BRIE • GOUDA • IMPORTED SWISS • DANISH BLEU

Beverages

FRESHLY BREWED COFFEE, REGULAR OR DECAFFEINATED • MILK • SKIMMED MILK
HOT CHOCOLATE • ICED, HOT AND HERBAL TEAS • ESPRESSO • CAPPUCCINO

Liqueurs

SAMBUCA • KAHLÚA • GRAND MARNIER
AMARETTO DI SARONNO

Cognacs and Brandies

HARDY V.S.O.P. • HENNESSY V.S.O.P. • COURVOISIER V.S.
FUNDADOR BRANDY

Dessert Wines and Ports

RIESLING, ZELTINGER SONNENUHR, SPÄTLESE SELBACH OSTER
DOW'S LATE BOTTLED VINTAGE • GRAHAM'S SIX GRAPE
QUADY ELECTRA, CALIFORNIA

Denotes Master Chef Georges Blanc Signature Selection

DE72.1206

ACTIVITIES SCHEDULE

Find out about all the entertainment & activities happening onboard.

Good Morning Valor TV Show

8:30am .... Channel 16 on your Stateroom TV

Library Open

9:30pm-11:30pm .... Iliad Library. Deck 4

Trivial Pursuit Trivia

10:00am .... Lido Deck

It's in the Bag Scavenger Hunt!

11:00am .... Ivanhoe Theatre

Be sure to bring a bag full of crazy, different stuff for this game!

Pool Volleyball

11:30am .... Lido Deck

Brain Teaser Trivia

12:00pm .... Lido Deck, aft

Survivor!

1:00pm .... Lido Deck

Horesracing!

2:15pm .... Ivanhoe Theatre

Library Open

2:30pm-4:30pm .... Iliad Library. Deck 4

7 Game Pajama Bingo (7 games on ONE card)

2:45pm .... Ivanhoe Theatre

Sea Fued

4:00pm .... American Lobby

Friends of Bill W Meet

5:00pm .... Heroes' Club, Deck 4

Basketball & Volleyball Courts open

until 6pm .... Deck 12

Shuffleboard Court open

24hrs .... Verandah Deck , aft

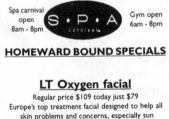

Spa carnival open 8am - 8pm   **S · P · A**   carnival   Gym open 6am - 8pm

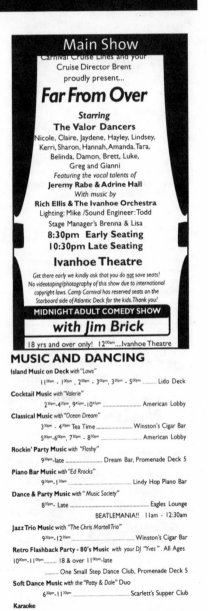

Main Show

Carnival Cruise Lines and your Cruise Director Brent proudly present...

Far From Over

Starring

The Valor Dancers

Nicole, Claire, Jaydene, Hayley, Lindsey, Kerri, Sharon, Hannah, Amanda, Tara, Belinda, Damon, Brett, Luke, Greg and Gianni

Featuring the vocal talents of

Jeremy Rabe & Adrine Hall

With music by

Rich Ellis & The Ivanhoe Orchestra

Lighting: Mike /Sound Engineer: Todd

Stage Manager's Brenna & Lisa

8:30pm Early Seating

10:30pm Late Seating

Ivanhoe Theatre

Get there early we kindly ask that you do not save seats!
No videotaping/photography of this show due to international copyright laws. Camp Carnival has reserved seats on the Starboard side of Atlantic Deck for the kids. Thank you!

MIDNIGHT ADULT COMEDY SHOW

with Jim Brick

18 yrs and over only! 12⁰⁰am ....Ivanhoe Theatre

MUSIC AND DANCING

Island Music on Deck with "Laws"

11⁰⁰am - 1⁰⁰pm , 2⁰⁰pm - 3⁰⁰pm, 3³⁰pm - 5⁰⁰pm _____ Lido Deck

Cocktail Music with "Valerie"

2³⁰pm-4³⁰pm, 9⁴⁵pm-10⁴⁵pm .... American Lobby

Classical Music with "Ocean Dream"

3³⁰pm - 4³⁰pm Tea Time .... Winston's Cigar Bar

5⁰⁰pm-6⁰⁰pm, 7³⁰pm - 8³⁰pm _____ American Lobby

Rockin' Party Music with "Flashy"

9³⁰pm-late .... Dream Bar, Promenade Deck 5

Piano Bar Music with "Ed Rrocks"

9³⁰pm-1³⁰am _____ Lindy Hop Piano Bar

Dance & Party Music with " Music Society"

8³⁰pm- Late .... Eagles Lounge

BEATLEMANIA!! 11am - 12:30am

Jazz Trio Music with "The Chris Martell Trio"

9³⁰pm-12³⁰am _____ Winston's Cigar Bar

Retro Flashback Party - 80's Music with your DJ "Yves ". All Ages

10⁰⁰pm-11⁰⁰pm........ 18 & over 11⁰⁰pm-late

.... One Small Step Dance Club, Promenade Deck 5

Soft Dance Music with the "Patty & Dale" Duo

6³⁰pm-11³⁰pm _____ Scarlett's Supper Club

Karaoke

9:30pm-11pm All ages/11pm-late 18 & up ...... Paris Hot

THINGS TO KNOW

Camp Carnival

9:00am	Camp Carnival Opens	Deck 12, fwd.
1:00pm	Family Story Time	Deck 12, fwd.
5:45pm	Kid's Dinner	Rosie's Restaurant
9:30pm	Teen (12-17) Disco	Caboose

Club O$_2$ (15-17yrs)

Please check your O$_2$ caper for a full listing of today's activities

12:00pm	Volleyball	Ball Courts
3:00pm	Scavenger Hunt	Club O$_2$ @ the Caboose
11:30pm	Formal Party (15-17's)	Club O$_2$ @ the Caboose

Wake Up Calls

Dial 37 and the military version of the time you would like to receive the call. For example, if you would like an 800am call, simply dial 37 then 0800. Or, for 800pm, dial 37 then 2000. To remove unwanted wake up calls, dial * then 37.

Infirmary Hours

In case of emergency – please dial #911. Over-the-counter items such as Tylenol and Band-Aids are available at the Purser's desk and from Room Service. Services are charged to your Sail & Sign card.

Infirmary Open 8:00am-8:00pm

Doctor's Hours 8:15am-11:00am & 3:00pm-6:00pm
Deck 0 , fwd

Phoning Home

Featuring even lower satellite calling rates. Calls to the U.S., Canada and the Caribbean are only $6.99 per minute! International calls are only $9.99 per minute. You can call anywhere in the world directly from your stateroom. Consult your stateroom directory for dialing instructions.

Swimming Pools/Whirlpools

"No Lifeguard on duty, so swim at your own risk"

8:00am-8:00pm	Main Pool/Whirlpools/Spa Carnival
8:00am -10:00pm	Aft Pool
8:00am-12:00am	(Adults Only) Whirlpool Lido Deck ,Aft
Waterslide 10:00am - 5:00pm	Sports Deck, Fwd

Beach Towels

Fresh beach towels will be placed in your stateroom the night before each port of call. Please use these towels while ashore and on the ship's open decks. Please return the towels to your Stateroom Steward when you are finished with them. A charge of $22 will be billed to your Sail & Sign account for each towel not returned.

Carnival Valor is Non-smoking except for...

Casino, Casino Bar, Paris Hot, Lindy Hop, One Small Step Dance Club, Winston's Cigar Bar, Deck 9 Main Pool area midship, starboard side & Deck 9 aft by the bar only when Skydome is OPEN. Lobby Deck 3 starboard side (right side, outside balcony deck) Deck 10 is smoking. *Cigar smoking* is not permitted in the Casino or anywhere else except in the Winston's Cigar Bar or Outer Deck 10, starboard side .

"Carnival's Goal Is To Be The Industry Leader For Environmental Excellence"
Report Environmental Compliance Concerns 4ENV (Dial Direct From Carnival Cruise Lines Ships)
1-888-290-5105 (North America) 1-305-406-5863 (International) www.carnivalcompliance.com

Today-At-A- Glance

Time	Activity	Location
6:00am	Gym open	Spa Deck 11, fwd
7:00am	**Good Morning Valor Show**	**Channel 16**
8:00am	Spa & Salon open	Spa Deck 11, fwd
	Yoga Class ($10 fee)	Spa Deck 11, fwd
	Funship Airbrushed Tattoos	Lido Deck, poolside
9:00am	Casino Slots Open	Shogun Club Casino
	Duty-FREE Gift Shop open	Promenade Deck
	Camp Carnival opens	Deck 12, fwd
	Spinning Class ($10 fee)	Spa Deck 11, fwd
9:30am	Activities Desk/Library open	Deck 4
10:00am	OPC Slot Tournament Rd 2	Shogun Club Casino
	Photo Gallery open	Atlantic Deck 4
	Formalities Shop open	Promenade Deck 5
	Sea Miles Desk Opens	Promenade Deck fwd
	Trivial Pursuit Trivia Quiz	Lido Deck
	BODY Symmetry Stretch & Relax Class	Spa Deck 11, fwd
10:30am	Gold Learning Center open	Deck 11, aft
	Couples Massage Seminar	Spa Deck 11, fwd
	Eyes Like Diamonds Workshop	Spa Deck 11, fwd
11:00am	It's In the Bag Scavenger hunt!	Ivanhoe Theatre
	Island Music on Deck	Lido Deck
11:30am	Pool Volleyball	Lido Deck
12:00pm	Shore Excursions Desk open	Lobby Deck 3
	Wine Tasting	Scarlett's Supper Club
	Brain Teaser Trivia	Lido Deck, aft
12:30pm	Art Auction Preview	Eagles Lounge, Deck 5 aft
1:00pm	Survivor!	Lido Deck
	Family Story Time	Deck 12, fwd
1:30pm	Art Auction begins	Eagles Lounge, Deck 5 aft
2:00pm	$500 Slot Tournament begins	Shogun Club Casino
	Formalities Shop open	Promenade Deck 5
	Put on weight this cruise? Detox Seminar	Spa Deck 11,
	Sea Miles Desk Opens	Promenade Deck fwd
	Island Music on Deck	Lido Deck
	Magic Makeover Workshop	Spa Deck 11, fwd
2:15pm	Horseracing!	Ivanhoe Theatre
2:30pm	Activities Desk/Library open	Deck 4
	Cocktail Piano Music	American Lobby
2:45pm	7 game Bingo on ONE card!!	Ivanhoe Theatre
3:00pm	The Great Diet Debate-seminar	Spa Deck 11, fwd
3:30pm	Tea Time with Classical Music	Winston's Cigar Bar
	Island Music on Deck	Lido Deck
4:00pm	Pilates class ($10 fee)	Spa Deck 11, fwd
	Sea Fued	American Lobby
4:30pm	Formal Portraits	Lobby & Promenade Decks
5:00pm	$500 Slot Tournament begins	Shogun Club Casino
	Aerobics Class ($10 fee)	Spa Deck 11, fwd
	Photo Gallery open	Atlantic Deck 4
	Friends of Bill W Meet	Heroes' Club
	Classical Music	American Lobby
5:45pm	Kid's Dinner	Rosie's Restaurant Deck 11
6:00pm	Shore Excursions Desk open	Lobby Deck 3
	Fitness Fantasia (14-21yrs)	Spa Deck 11
6:30pm	Soft Dance Music	Scarlett's Supper Club
7:15pm	Formal Portraits	Lobby & Promenade Decks
7:30pm	Classical Music	American Lobby
8:30pm	**Showtime "Far from Over"**	**Ivanhoe Theatre**
	Dance & Party Music	Eagles Lounge
	Port Shopping Desk Open	Promenade Deck 5
9:30pm	Formal Portraits	Lobby & Promenade Decks
	Karaoke-late	Paris Hot Lounge
	Piano Bar Music	Lindy Hop Piano Bar
	Jazz Music	Winston's Cigar Bar
	Party Music-late	Dream Bar, Promenade Deck
	Teen Mock-Tail Party(12-17yr)	The Caboose
9:45pm	Cocktail Piano Music	American Lobby
10:00pm	Flashback retro-80's Party	One Small Step Disco
10:30pm	**Showtime "Far from Over"**	**Ivanhoe Theatre**
11:30pm	OPC Cash Raffle Draw	Shogun Club Casino
12:00am	Adult "R" Rated Comedy Show	Ivanhoe Theatre

Food & Drink Showcase

Breakfast

6:00am	Continental Breakfast	Rosie's Restaurant
8:00am-10:30pm	Breakfast on Deck	Rosie's Restaurant
8:00am-12:00pm	Breakfast for late risers!	Rosie's Restaurant, fwd
8:00am-10:00am	Open Seating	Washington Dining Room

Lunch

12:00pm - 2:30pm	Lido lunch & salad bar	Rosie's Restaurant
12:00pm - 2:30pm	Seafood Fare	Fish & Chips Deck 10
12:00pm - 2:30pm	Asian Corner	The Oriental
12:00pm - 6:00pm	The Grill	Rosie's Restaurant, aft
11:00am - 11:00pm	The Deli	Rosie's Restaurant
12:30pm-2:00pm	Open Seating	Washington Dining Room

Taste of the Nations
Today's Feature: **American**

Dinner

**"Formal" is the recommended attire
for this evenings meal.**

All three restaurants are smoke free environments.

Main Seating

5:45pm	Washington Dining Room	Lobby Deck 3, aft
6:15pm	Lincoln Dining Room	Lobby Deck 3, fwd

Late Seating

8:00pm	Washington Dining Room	Lobby Deck 3, aft
8:30pm	Lincoln Dining Room	Lobby Deck 3, fwd

Seaview Bistro

6:00pm - 9:30pm		Rosie's Restaurant

Festivale Gala Buffet

11:30pm - 1:30am		Rosie's Restaurant

Photo Session 11:30pm - 12:15pm - Dining Pleasure 12:30am - 1:30am

Togo Sushi Bar

5:00pm - 8:30pm		Promenade Deck, midship

Available 24 hours

Pizzeria		Rosie's Restaurant
Coffee/Tea/Ice Cream		Rosie's Restaurant

The United States Public Health Service has determined that eating uncooked or partially cooked meat, poultry, fish, seafood or eggs may present a health risk to the consumer particularly those that may be more vulnerable.

BEVERAGE SERVICE

TODAY'S DRINK SPECIAL
"Yellow Bird"
Only $2.95 regular glass or $6.25 with Souvenir Glass!
Morning Drink Special
10am - 12pm: Mimosa, Bloody Mary, Screwdrivers $2.95! Lobby, Casino & Pool Bars
ICED MARTINI PARTY
5:30pm-8:30pm -Casino Bar, Deck 5

Winston's Fine Cigar Bar

Relax and light up one of our many fine cigars, including: Macanudos, Paragas, Cuban-seeds and others. For the perfect night, pair it with a delicious drink from the bar. Located on Atlantic Deck, Aft.

Scarlett's Supper Club

Wine Tasting at 12:00pm!
Welcome to a world of award winning chefs, extraordinary cuisine & fine service at a nominal charge. Open daily from 6:00pm-9:30pm. Reservations needed - phone 1078 between 12:00pm - 10:00pm today. Please allow at least 2 hours to enjoy a complete dining experience. Book early to avoid disappointment. *Music & Dancing Nightly!*

Java Cafe'"Coffee Shop Company"

We also have tasty pastries, milkshakes & ice cream sundaes. All for a nominal charge.
8:00am-1:00am   Promenade Deck 5
8:00am-5:00pm   Rosie's Restaurant, Lido Deck

CELEBRITY CRUISES, INC.
CELEBRITY CRUISES
AZAMARA
1050 Caribbean Way
Miami, Florida 33132
(305) 539-6000
(800) 437-3111
(800) 437-9111 Fax

AZAMARA JOURNEY and *AZAMARA QUEST* (formerly *R-6* and *R-7* of Renaissance Cruises): entered service 2000; 30,277 G.R.T.; 598' x 95'; 694-passenger capacity (double occupancy); 347 staterooms; Greek officers and international crew; cruises Bermuda, Caribbean, South America, Asia, Mediterranean, Northern Europe, Baltic, and various waters around the world.

CELEBRITY CENTURY: entered service 1995; renovated 2006; 70,606 G.R.T.; 815' x 105'; 1,750-passenger capacity; 875 cabins; Greek officers and international crew; offers Caribbean, Mediterranean, and Northern European cruises and 4- and 5-night cruises from Miami, Florida, during the winter months.

CELEBRITY CONSTELLATION: entered service 2002; 91,000 G.R.T.; 964.6' x 105.6'; 1,950-passenger capacity; 975 cabins; Greek officers and international crew; cruises from San Juan to southern Caribbean, in the Mediterranean and Northern Europe, transatlantic crossings, and Canada/New England.

CELEBRITY INFINITY: entered service 2001; 91,000 G.R.T.; 964.6' x 105.6'; 1,950-passenger capacity; 975 cabins; Greek officers and international crew; Panama Canal cruises between Florida and California, South American cruises, Hawaiian Island cruises, and Alaskan cruises from Vancouver.

CELEBRITY MERCURY: entered service 1997; renovated 2007; 77,713 G.R.T.; 866' x 105'; 1,870-passenger capacity; 935 cabins; Greek officers and international crew; cruises throughout the Caribbean, Mexican Riviera from San Diego and San Francisco, and Alaskan cruises from Seattle.

CELEBRITY MILLENNIUM: entered service 2000; 91,000 G.R.T.; 964.6' x 105.6'; 1,950-passenger capacity; 975 cabins; Greek officers and international crew; cruises from Fort Lauderdale to eastern Caribbean, 11- and 12-night Mediterranean cruises, and transatlantic crossings.

CELEBRITY SOLSTICE, CELEBRITY EQUINOX, and *CELEBRITY ECLIPSE:* entered service 2008, 2009, and 2010, respectively; 1,033' x 121'; 122,000-G.R.T.; 2,850-passenger capacity; 1,425 cabins; Greek officers and international crew; cruises in Caribbean and Mediterranean and transatlantic repositioning. **(Category B—Not Rated)**

CELEBRITY SUMMIT: entered service 2001; 91,000 G.R.T.; 964.6' x 105.6'; 1,950-passenger capacity; 975 cabins; Greek officers and international crew; 10- and 11-night Caribbean cruises from Fort Lauderdale; Panama Canal cruises; 7-night Alaskan cruises from Vancouver and Seward; Hawaiian Island cruises from Los Angeles.

CELEBRITY XPEDITION: entered service 2004; 2,329 G.R.T.; 296' x 43'; 98-passenger capacity; 49 cabins; Ecuadorian officers and crew; 7-night Galapagos cruises. **(Category B—Not Rated)**

(Medical Facilities: C-8 on *Century, Galaxy,* and *Mercury;* and C-26 on *Millennium, Infinity, Constellation,* and *Summit;* C-6 on *Journey* and *Quest;* P-2, EM, CLS, MS; N-3; CM; PD; BC; EKG; TC; PO; EPC; OX; WC; ICU; X; M; LJ.)

These ships are rated in 11 separate categories in the second half of chapter 14.

In 1990, Chandris created a new Celebrity Cruises division to compete in the premium-cruise market while continuing its Fantasy Cruises division at the budget end of the market. For its new Celebrity Cruises division, Chandris rebuilt, lengthened, redesigned, and refurbished the former *Galileo* in 1989, renaming her

Meridian, and built *Horizon,* which entered service in 1990, and *Zenith,* which entered service in 1992. The two divisions promoted their ships like separate companies and did not advertise the Chandris name. In 1994, the name of the U.S. company was changed to Celebrity Cruises, Inc. In 1995, 1996, and 1997, Celebrity introduced three 70,000+-ton innovative high-tech vessels, *Century, Galaxy,* and *Mercury.* In 1997, *Meridian* was sold. During the summer of 1997, Royal Caribbean Cruises, Ltd. acquired Celebrity and now operates Celebrity Cruises as a separate brand.

In 1999, Celebrity announced plans to construct four 91,000-ton ships to enter service over a three-year period. The first of the new class, appropriately named *Millennium,* entered service in the spring of 2000 offering varied European itineraries. The ship was repositioned to Fort Lauderdale in November to commence Caribbean sailings. The second vessel, *Infinity,* entered service in the spring of 2001; the third, *Summit,* in the fall of 2001; and the fourth, *Constellation,* in the spring of 2002, giving Celebrity over 16,000 lower guest berths at sea.

The *Horizon* and *Zenith* were cleverly conceived ships for the 1990s and later updated for the new millennium. In October 2005, the *Horizon* was transferred to Island Cruises, a joint venture between Royal Caribbean and British-based package operator First Choice Holidays. In 2007, *Zenith* was transferred to Pullmantur, a subsidiary of Royal Caribbean. At the same time, the former *R-6* of Renaissance Cruises was transferred to Celebrity and renamed *Celebrity Journey.* In 2007, the former *R-7* of Renaissance Cruises and *Blue Moon* of Pullmantur also was transferred to Celebrity and renamed *Celebrity Quest.* Subsequently in 2007, the Azamara brand was created and the ships were rebranded and renamed *Azamara Journey* and *Azamara Quest.* These ships offer longer cruises to destinations around the world, calling at ports not often visited by other Celebrity ships. Upon transfer to Celebrity the ships underwent a revitalization to redecorate and refurbish 32 new veranda suites on each ship, providing new bedding and soft goods; carpeting, flooring, and art work throughout the ships; expansion of the casino; and the addition of such Celebrity signature facilities as the Martini Bar, Cova Café, Michael's Club, AquaSpa by Elemis, Acupuncture at Sea, and online facilities.

There is a high ratio of service staff to passengers (1:2) on all Celebrity ships. Service in the dining rooms, staterooms, and various lounges is among the best in the premium market, and the ships carry a large number of social and entertainment staff. The diversity and presentation of food offerings in the dining rooms have been exceptional for ships in the premium-class category.

In December 1995, Celebrity introduced the 70,000+-ton, 815-foot, 1,750-passenger *Century,* followed by the 77,713-ton, 866-foot, 1,870-passenger *Galaxy* in December 1996 and its sister ship, *Mercury,* in November 1997. The vessels are equipped with a sophisticated array of entertainment options and interactive audio, video, and in-cabin entertainment systems. These high-tech amenities include a fully equipped, state-of-the art conference center with electronic voting chair pads and broadcast capabilities; a 921-seat, multilevel, amphitheater-style show lounge designed to accommodate Broadway-scale productions with its revolving stage, hydraulic orchestra pit, and sophisticated special-effects capability; a revolutionary high-tech-equipped lounge and disco; and in-cabin interactive televisions featuring the Celebrity Network, an innovation that permits guests to order room service, select their dinner wine, purchase shore excursions, gamble at casino games charged to their personal accounts, review their shipboard account, and purchase pay-for-view movies. *Galaxy* and *Mercury* are very similar in physical layout to *Century*, but with different decor and various innovations, including martini bars, magradomes that slide over the rear pool areas when the weather is inclement, family staterooms that hold up to five persons, computer equipment with classes, and larger verandas in the Sky Suites.

All of the 875 staterooms on *Century* and the 935 on *Galaxy* and *Mercury* include ample closet and drawer space, convertible twin beds, dressing table and mirror, direct-dial telephones, minibar-refrigerators, electronic safes, hair dryers, waffle robes, interactive television systems, and nice-size bathrooms with showers, sinks, and storage more generous than on most ships. The eight 537-square-foot, spacious Royal Suites, with 94-square-foot verandas, and the 20 Sky Suites, with even larger verandas, include video systems, marble baths with whirlpool jets, champagne, personalized stationery and business cards, afternoon tea and snacks, nightly hors d'oeuvres, and 24-hour butler service. Eleven additional deluxe cabins also have verandas. The two penthouse suites, which are 1,219 square feet, include a master bedroom with its own bathroom, living room, dining room, kitchen pantry, powder room, large balcony with an outdoor Jacuzzi, a sophisticated security system, and can be combined with the adjoining suite to accommodate two additional guests. Comfort and service in the suites emulate that found on more expensive ships that compete in the deluxe-category cruise market. Cruisers who demand luxurious suites, personalized butler service, and gourmet cuisine but who also require ships offering an abundance of activities and entertainment will find the "suite life" on all Celebrity vessels viable alternatives to many of the more expensive deluxe cruise ships. There are also a number of wheelchair-accessible staterooms on the three larger ships, and the design of these vessels is especially well adapted for the handicapped. These ships also have "concierge-class" staterooms with the amenities described earlier.

The ships are attractively furbished in contemporary/Art Deco designs with outstanding, multimillion-dollar art collections originally assembled by Christina Chandris. The two-tiered Grand Restaurants feature majestic staircases, a piano balcony where soft dinner music is played by a quartet, two-story picture windows looking out to the sea, and continental menus and wine lists. Complimentary room service is available around the clock in all staterooms, while suites also feature service such as full breakfasts served in the suite. Casual, buffet-style breakfasts and lunches, which feature four separate buffet areas and a sushi café, are offered atop ship in the lido cafés. Celebrity has created the atmosphere of a European bistro in the lido, a backdrop for casual dinners served most evenings. For additional variety, there are hamburger/hot dog grills and pizza ovens by the pool, martini, wine and espresso bars, and caviar and champagne bars.

The ships also offer AquaSpa, one of the more complete health spas at sea, operated by Elemis, Ltd. In addition to a large, fully equipped exercise and aerobics room with dozens of cardiovascular machines, a hair salon, his and hers dressing rooms with showers, steam rooms, and saunas, there also is a marvelous thalassotherapy pool and a bevy of beauty, health, relaxation, and massage treatments available. AquaSpa packages may be booked in advance and range in price from $200 to $699. The thalassotherapy pool was removed from the *Century* during its renovation in 2006 and replaced with a Persian Garden offering steam, sauna, and a variety of showers.

Other public facilities on each of these three ships include 7,500-foot casinos; impressive observation lounges that convert to discos at night; cabaret-style nightclubs; advanced technology, supervised children's playrooms, and numerous electronic game facilities; three-story "Grand" foyers that rise from the marble main lobbies and feature extensive shopping galleries; lido decks with two attached swimming pools, four whirlpools, designated sport areas, small jogging tracks, and several bars; and libraries, Internet cafés, and cardrooms.

During the spring of 2006 the *Century* went into dry dock and received $55 million in renovations, which included 14 new Sky Suites; 10 new staterooms; 314 new verandas; new bedding; flat-screen TVs and wireless Internet access in the staterooms; a 66-seat specialty restaurant, Murano (similar to those on the *Millennium*-class ships); a sushi bar; the Ocean Grill, a casual limited-menu restaurant atop ship open in the evenings as an alternative to the dining room; a Cova Café; expansion of the AquaSpa; addition of the Acupuncture at Sea program; a new spa café; a new martini bar; a teen lounge with a jukebox, dance floor, and video arcade; expanded Internet facilities and computer classes; and an updated and expanded fitness center. Similar renovations were done on the *Mercury* in 2007 and on the *Galaxy* in 2008. However, later in 2008, the *Galaxy* was transferred to a new venture between Royal Caribbean and TUI of Germany. She was positioned to capture the German cruise market looking for a compromise between the luxury ships of Hapag-Lloyd and the mass—market/economy ships of Aida.

The 1,950-passenger, 91,000-ton *Millennium* entered service in the late spring of 2000 boasting numerous innovations and facilities not available on the other vessels, as well as providing 80 percent ocean-view accommodations with verandas in 74 percent of those staterooms and suites. Two almost identical sister ships, *Infinity* and *Summit,* came on line during 2001 with an additional sibling, *Constellation,* during the spring of 2002. The smallest inside cabin measures a generous 170 square feet and includes a sitting area with a sofa and an entertainment tower with a private safe, minibar, interactive television, and DVD player; radio; direct-dial telephone; hair dryer; and robes. Premium ocean-view staterooms (including verandas) are 232 to 513 square feet, and the suites (including verandas) range in size from 308 feet for the Sky Suites, 467 feet for the eight Celebrity Suites (no verandas), 733 feet for the very spacious and desirable Royal Suites, and 1,432 feet for the two ultra-deluxe penthouse suites (with additional 1,100-foot wraparound verandas). These two charmers, two of the largest suites afloat, include all the features of the penthouse suites described above on the *Century*, plus a baby grand piano, exercise equipment, fax machine, enlarged master bathroom with a deep-soaking whirlpool tub surrounded by bay windows looking out to sea and a separate jet-spray shower, two state-of-the-art audiovisual entertainment systems with large televisions, flat-screen PC with Internet access and printer, expansive veranda with an outdoor whirlpool, wet bar and lounge seating area, and lavish decorations such as a foyer with mosaic floors.

Another innovation on *Millennium* is the first specialty restaurant in the Celebrity fleet, named the Olympic, after the RMS *Olympic*, the sister ship to the *Titanic*, which was launched in 1911. The decor, which includes the original walnut paneling from the *Olympic*, expresses the elegance and romance of the turn-of-the-century transatlantic liners. A 206-label wine cellar, as well as suggested wines by the glass to accompany each course, enhance this gourmet experience. The other three *Millennium*-class ships also include artifacts and themes from classic ocean liners. The name of the specialty restaurant on the *Infinity* is United States, on the *Summit*, Normandie, and on the *Constellation*, Ocean Liners. These are four of the finest gourmet specialty restaurants at sea. A similar specialty restaurant was added to *Century* during her renovation, and comparable restaurants may be added in the future to the other ships in the fleet.

The 25,000-square foot AquaSpa fitness facility is considerably expanded (twice the size as on the *Century*-class vessels), boasting some of the largest and most extensive spa facilities afloat, including a spacious, outdoor (but glassed-in and heat-controlled) thalassotherapy pool surrounded by day-use cabanas on *Infinity, Summit,* and *Constellation*. The 14,467-foot shopping mall, the Emporium, with its interesting diversity of shops; all indoor and outdoor public areas; and facilities for the physically challenged have also been greatly enlarged and expanded. *Millennium* was the first cruise ship to incorporate gas-turbine technology, which reduces exhaust emissions up to 90 percent and curtails noise and vibration.

Other facilities available include: the AquaSpa Café, offering heart-healthy spa cuisine al fresco; a martini bar and a champagne bar serving caviar; Michael's Club, the comfortable English-Georgian-style piano bar and fine liqueurs lounge; a piano bar; Cova Café, a coffee bar offering freshly baked pastries, signature coffees, and teas formulated from the original Cova Cafeteria and Pastry Shop in Milan (it converts to a wine bar in the evening); the three-deck, 901-seat Celebrity Theater, venue for production shows; the 18-station Internet café with e-mail and on-line access for 95 cents per minute (and passengers have Internet access in all staterooms aboard *Infinity, Constellation,* and *Summit*); music and traditional book libraries; a 300-seat cinema/conference center; five additional meeting/function rooms; a conservatory with botanical gardens; a resort/pool deck with two pools, four whirlpools, expansive lounge areas, and an adjacent fitness center (with 40 pieces of equipment), and the AquaSpa, offering 20 exotic and rejuvenating treatments as well as a choice of nine facial treatments and a beauty salon; sport facilities, including basketball, paddle tennis, volleyball, quoits, a running/jogging track; a Fun Factory and video-game arcade for children; a giant casino; a glass-enclosed observation lounge atop ship with nightly entertainment for dancing; and numerous other lounges, bars, and areas designed for guests to socialize and enjoy a variety of amusements. The ships also offer massages and fashion shows by the pool and an "acupuncture at sea" as part of their new "wellness program." The four *Millennium*-class vessels are virtually similar except for variations in decor.

Celebrity has added a new premium category on *Millennium*-class ships and on *Century* known as "concierge class," the category below "suite class." Concierge class on the four *Millennium*-class ship staterooms measure 191 square feet with 41 square feet of balcony and include a complimentary bottle of champagne, fresh flowers, a selection of fruit, upscale bedding and pillows, afternoon canapés, personalized stationery, additional room amenities, a special room-service breakfast menu, priority shore excursion bookings, and early embarkation and debarkation, as well as special concierge services.

All of the Celebrity vessels feature an option for casual dining on most nights of every cruise. The menu includes a fresh fruit cocktail, Caesar or lettuce salad, lasagna al forno, broiled salmon steak, spit-roasted chicken, grilled sirloin steak, a variety of pizzas, Key lime pie, and Black Forest cake. Twenty-four-hour room service is available with a comprehensive menu, as well as hot pizza delivered to all staterooms by uniformed delivery persons.

In the summer of 2004, Celebrity entered the small-ship/expedition market with the introduction of it new 2,329-ton, 98-passenger *Celebrity Xpedition*. The ship offers seven-night itineraries in the Galapagos with pre- and post-cruise stay-overs in Quito, Ecuador. Both *Celebrity Journey* and *Celebrity Quest* were to be operated under the Celebrity Xpeditions brand, specializing in cruises to less frequented cruise destinations; however, in 2007, the cruise line decided to establish the new Azamara brand and rename the ships *Azamara Journey* and *Azamara Quest*. These two ships are positioned somewhere between the upper end of the premium cruise market and the luxury cruise market, offering more amenities, longer and more exotic itineraries, and a higher degree of pampering in a smaller, more intimate environment.

There are 12 categories of accommodations, including four Penthouse Suites, four Royal Suites, 32 Sky Suites, 199 veranda staterooms, 80 ocean-view rooms, and 26 inside staterooms. The suites range in size from 266 square feet with 60-square-foot verandas in the Sky Suites to 501 square feet with 156-square-foot verandas in the Penthouse Suites. The staterooms range in size from 158 square feet for an inside stateroom to 175 square feet with a 40-square-foot veranda for the veranda category staterooms. Six accommodations can accommodate wheelchairs.

Every accommodation offers butler service and includes twin beds convertible to queen size, flowers, fresh fruit, Elemis toiletries, Frette cotton robes, slippers, plasma flat-screen TVs, European bedding, refrigerators with minibars, in-room safes, hand-held hair dryers, and in-room movies through pay-per-view. A gratuity of $12.25 per person per day is added to passenger shipboard accounts. The butlers perform some of the same services normally rendered by the cabin attendants and room service.

Dining options include an open-seating main dining room; Windows' Café offering a buffet-style breakfast and lunch with casual dining at dinner time; Prime C specialty steakhouse restaurant; Aqualina restaurant featuring a gourmet menu with Mediterranean overtones; bar surrounded by tables overlooking the lobby atrium serving specialty coffees, pastries, wine, champagne, martinis, snacks, and other beverages (similar to Cova Café on Celebrity ships); pool grill; and 24-hour room service. Suite guests receive two free dinners in the specialty restaurants, whereas stateroom guests only receive one. Additional visits to these restaurants require a $25 surcharge. There are no formal nights and resort-casual wear is acceptable in all restaurants.

Other public areas include a cabaret lounge, several additional bars and lounges, Internet café, casino, photo shop, three boutiques, spa, well-equipped gym, comfortable outdoor pool/lido area, guest relations and excursion desks, and medical facility. There are no formal children's programs or youth staff. A no-smoking policy prevails throughout the ship, except in two designated areas.

Acupuncture at Sea, a program staffed with professional acupuncture practitioners, has been added to all of the ships. Captains on both Celebrity and Azamara ships can now marry couples legally at sea. In 2006, the cruise line entered into an arrangement with Leap Frog School House to provide multisensory, educational learning tools for their children's programs.

In the fall of 2008 the 122,000-ton, 2,850-passenger *Celebrity Solstice* came on line. Two additional *Solstice*-class ships, *Equinox* and *Eclipse,* followed in 2009 and 2010, respectively, with two more in 2011 and 2012 scheduled to join them. Ninety percent of the staterooms face the sea and 90 percent of these sport private balconies. An average standard cabin will measure 215 square feet (somewhat larger than on other Celebrity ships). New for Celebrity, 130 veranda staterooms are designated "aqua-class staterooms." Located in a separate area, occupants have unlimited use of the spa's Persian Gardens, priority times for spa therapies, and a private healthy-fare restaurant named Blue. There are 10 dining options, including the two-level Grand Epernay; three-meal-a-day main dining room; Tuscan Grill steakhouse; Silk Harvest featuring Asian fusion cuisine; Murano, the elegant continental-dining restaurant featured on the *Celebrity Century;* Blue, the healthy-fare restaurant; and several other casual venues. The ship Lawn Club boasts a half-acre of real grass where passengers can picnic or play croquet and bocce ball.

Celebrity frequently varies its itineraries; therefore, it is best to obtain their most recent brochures before making your travel plans. Celebrity is currently focusing on Caribbean, Bermuda, Alaskan, Hawaiian, Panama Canal, South American, Mediterranean, and Northern European destinations.

Strong Points:
Celebrity Cruises' ships have been well received by their guests, travel writers,

and travel agents. The spacious, full-amenity staterooms and suites, fine dining, concerned service, dedication to passenger satisfaction, innovative entertainment options, and vast array of facilities make Celebrity one of the better buys and one of the top contenders in the premium cruise market. The ships offer good all-around cruise experiences, with the option to purchase suites as sumptuous as those offered on the more expensive luxury cruise ships. The new Azamara brand ships offer a more intimate cruise experience to exotic ports that many larger ships cannot reach on longer itineraries.

Courtesy Celebrity Cruises

Dining room, courtesy Celebrity Cruises

Six-star award plaque from Stern's Travel Guides, Ltd., courtesy Celebrity Cruises

Sky suite, courtesy Celebrity Cruises

Royal suite, courtesy Celebrity Cruises

Pool deck on Summit, *courtesy Celebrity Cruises*

Quest Discoveries

Appetizers

Shrimp Cocktail,
Bloody Mary Sauce, Celery Sticks

Duck Rillettes,
Sourdough Bread, Beet Salad

Morel & Black Trumpet Mushroom
Ragôut en Croute, White Truffle Oil

Pan Fried Chicken Potstickers,
Spicy Mustard, Soya & Black Vinegar

Caviar

OSETRA OR SEVRUGA
Warm Brioche Points,
Russian Service
(Market Price)

Soups

Yukon Gold Potato & Spinach Soup

Classic French Onion Soup
with Gruyere Cheese

Chilled Carrot-Cardamom with Lobster

Salads

Hearts of Romaine, Pink Grapefruit, Avocado and Pumpkin Seeds

Red & White Endive, Frisée, Green Apples and Candied Walnuts

SELECTION OF DRESSINGS:

Cilantro-Lime Dressing   Red Wine Vinaigrette   Ranch

Entrees

SINGAPORE NOODLES
BBQ Pork, Shrimp, Asian Vegetables & Curry

CRISP SEARED CHILEAN SEA BASS
Quinoa, Ratatouille Vinaigrette

ROASTED CHICKEN BREAST
Ragôut of Asparagus, Fingerling Potatoes, Olives, Pearl Onions and Thyme

PORK MEDALLION OSCAR
Crabmeat & Asparagus topped with Lime-Jalapeño Hollandaise

BEEF TENDERLOIN WITH MARROW CRUST
Potato Pancake, Slow Cooked Shallots, Truffle Jus

VEGETARIAN OPTIONS
Please inquire with your server

Classic Dinner Favorites

Azamara Fruitini

Shrimp Cocktail with Traditional Cocktail Sauce

Caesar Salad with Parmesan and Garlic Croutons
Chicken or Shrimp optional

Grilled Filet of Salmon, Wild Rice and Herb Butter

Lemon Marinated Roasted Chicken, Garlic Mashed Potatoes, Grilled Asparagus

Pan Seared New York Strip Steak, Twice Baked Potato, Broccoli Gratin

Selection of French and American Cheeses, Artisan Bread, Quince Paste

Tahitian Vanilla Crème Brulee

০৪৪০

Azamara Cellars

Our highly skilled Cellar Master has selected the following wines to complement tonight's
Master Chef Selection:

White

CHARDONNAY, BENZIGER, LOS CARNEROS, CALIFORNIA

This full bodied wine will pair beautifully with a creamy dressed salad, pork and seafood.

Red

PINOT NOIR, DOMAINE DROUHIN, WILLAMETTE, OREGON

*The premier grape of Burgundy, this wine is well-suited to pair with chicken, beef and pork
and will play well with creamy sauces and spicy seasonings.*

By the Glass

CHAMPAGNE BRUT, TAITTINGER "LA FRANÇAISE", FRANCE

Crisp and Refreshing yet well rounded and creamy, this sparkling wine is the perfect aperitif.

WHITE: SAUVIGNON BLANC, WENTE, LIVERMORE, CALIFORNIA

*A friendly food wine, sauvignon blanc can use its high level of acidity to balance rich food
or sauces on our palate or uses its aromas to play well with fragrant ingredients.*

RED: PINOT NOIR, FIVE RIVERS, SANTA BARBARA, CALIFORNIA

*Pinot noir has a structure that gives it great diversity. Go beyond the obvious wine and
pair this wine with beef broth soups or even a fish.*

Courtesy Azamara Cruises

Metropolitan Restaurant

Appetizers

Shrimp Cocktail

Caribbean Tropical Fruit in a Coconut-Flavored Rum Sauce

Supreme of Chicken Terrine

Veal Sweetbread with Crisp Potato Pancake

Soups

Cream of Asparagus

Petite Marmite "Henry IV"

Chilled Berry and Cumin Yogurt

Salads

Caesar
Tossed Romaine Lettuce, Parmesan Cheese and Croutons

Panache of Crunchy Mixed Greens

OUR HOMEMADE DRESSINGS TONIGHT ARE:

Tarragon   Red Wine Vinaigrette   Caesar   Spicy Tomato

Entrees

GEMELLI WITH DUCK CONFIT
Boneless Duck Leg cooked in the Traditional Style, served over Pasta with
Sautéed Mushrooms and Diced Zucchini, enhanced with a delicate Sauce

DARNE OF SALMON
Pan-Seared, presented on a Bed of Chunky Fruit, Lychee and Fennel Chutney,
accompanied by Steamed Potatoes

BROILED LOBSTER TAIL
Lobster Tail, Flavored with a Frothy Tarragon and Shallot Butter, Served with Drawn Butter

GRILLED QUAIL
Marinated Grilled Quail with Shiitake and Button Mushrooms, Pomme Fondant,
served with Sauce Devil

PRIME RIB OF BEEF
The Finest Cut of Roast Beef
presented with Baked Potato, Natural Juice and Creamed Horseradish

Desserts

Baked Alaska   Irish Coffee Torte with a Spirited Whisky Sauce   Venetian Napoléon

Bittersweet Chocolate Cake   Low-Fat Orange-Pumpkin Sherbet with Lemon Coulis

No Sugar Added Pastry Cigar

An Array of Petit Fours, with the Chef's Compliments

Vanilla, Chocolate, Cinnamon, Blueberry or No Sugar Added Ice Cream   Pear and Vanilla Sherbet

A Selection of Domestic and Imported Cheeses served with Crackers and Biscuits

STAND'06/D#13

Courtesy Celebrity Cruises

Daily Dining Choices

This Evening's Dress Code: Formal
Gentlemen: Tuxedo, dinner jacket, or dark suit and tie.
Ladies: A dressy outfit. Formal Gown or Cocktail Dress.

X Metropolitan Restaurant Deck 4/5 Aft

8:00am – 10:00am	Open Seating Breakfast
12 Noon – 2:00pm	Open Seating Luncheon
6:00pm	Main Seating Dinner
8:30pm	Late Seating Dinner

*The Metropolitan Restaurant entrances are on Decks 4 & 5.
At dinner time, punctuality is appreciated and the doors
will be closed 30 minutes after the listed Dinner Seating.*
Evening Music by the Accord Quartet

X Casual Dining Boulevard Deck 10 Aft

5:00pm – 8:30pm	Sunset Happy Hour with Music & Savories – Ocean Café Bar, Aft
5:30pm – 9:30pm	Sushi Café
6:00pm – 10:00pm	Alternative Dining

*By Reservation. Please Call Ext. 4312.
Suggested gratuity $2.00 per person.*

12 Noon – 1:00am	Home made Pizza

*The Dress code is casual every day. Although in all other areas
the dress code of the evening applies. We kindly ask for your
cooperation and consideration for your fellow guests.*

X Ocean Café Deck 10 Aft

24 Hours	Coffee & Tea Available at Starboard, Midship
7:00am – 11:00am	Waffles and Pankcakes Freshly Made, Aft
7:00am – 11:30am	Breakfast Buffet
7:00am – 1:00pm	Eggs and Omelette Corner
12 Noon – 2:30pm	Lunch Buffet
12 Noon – 10:00pm	Frozen Yogurt & Homemade Ice Cream
12 Noon – 3:00pm	Sandwich plus Hot Soup Bar, Aft
12 Noon – 1:00am	Freshly Tossed Pasta & Salad Bar
4:00pm – 5:00pm	Casual Afternoon Tea

X Riviera Grill Deck 10 Poolside

12 Noon – 7:00pm	Hamburgers, Hotdogs & Daily Specials

X Cova Café & Patisseria Deck 5 Atrium

8:30am – 11:00am	Taste of Europe – Croissant & Danish
3:00pm – 5:00pm	Taste of Europe – Pastries
5:00pm – 8:30pm	Cova Cafe & Wine Bar-Savories Served

X AquaSpa Café Deck 10 Forward

7:30am – 10:00am	Light and Healthy Breakfast
12 Noon – 8:00pm	Healthy Choice All Day Dining

X Olympic Restaurant Deck 3 Midship

6:00pm – 10:00pm	A la Carte Dining

*For Guests wishing to dine in the Olympic Restaurant, reservations
can be made daily 9:00am – 6:00pm by dialing ext. 4707.
A per person cover charge will be added directly to your SeaPass
Account. Charges will be explained upon entry. (Formal nights a tie &
suit, dinner jacket or tuxedo is required. All other evenins, the ships
dress code will be followed). Guests must be 12 years or older. As you
enjoy this fine dining experience, **Anna Lisa** will entertain you with
beautiful harp music. Cancellation of reservation 24 hours in advance
is requested.*

X Late Night Gourmet Bites All Public Lounges

12 Mid – 1:00am	Gourmet Bites

Activities & Events

8:30am	**Walk-A-Thon.** A great way to start the day with the Activities Staff .... Mast Bar, Port Side 11 Fwd
9:00am	**Catholic Mass** with Father O'Connell .... Cinema 3
9:00am	**Computer Class:** Beginning Windows/Email .... Computer Center 6
9:00am	**Fortunes Casino** Slots open. At 12 Noon Tables are open . Fortunes Casino 4
9:00am – 5:00pm	**Poolside Massages** are available upon request. Call the AquaSpa for an appointment ext. 4751. (charges apply.) .... by appointment
9:00am – 12 Noon	Planning your next Celebrity Cruise? See advantages of booking onboard with **Cruise Sales Mgr Humberto.** (See pg 4 for other hours). ..... Grand Foyer, 3 Stbd
9:15am	**Shuffleboard** with the Activities Staff. .... Sunrise Deck 11 Port
10:00am	**Morning General Trivia** with the Activities Staff .... Cosmos Nightclub 11
10:00am	**Complimentary Lifestyle Seminar: Detox for Weight Loss...** Aqua Spa 10
10:00am	**50% off Selected Jewelry** outside the Jewelry Store . . Emporium Boutiques 5
10:00am	**The 5 Minute Make Over.** Free application .... Aqua Spa 10
10:00am	**Big Golf Seminar** with PGA Golf Pro Ryan .... Gamma Rm 3
10:00am	**Acupuncture at Sea Lecture:** Introduction to Oriental Medicine .... Cinema 3
10:30am	**Catchphrase!** Put it in your own words with the Activities Staff .... Cosmos Nightclub 11
10:30am	**Savor The Caribbean Cooking Demonstration** with Chef Johnny Vinczencz .... Rendez-Vous Lounge 4
10:30am	**Table Tennis Tournament** with the Activities Staff ..... Resort Deck 10 Port
10:30am	**Computer Class:** Download Digital Images & Organise . . Computer Center 6
10:45am	**Golf Putting Tourney** with the Activities Staff .... Poolside 10
10:45am	**How to fight IBS the easy way** .... Aqua Spa 10
11:00am	**Paddle Tennis!** The Activities Staff show you how. The court is open until 2:00pm .... Sports Deck 12
11:00am	**Art Seminar:** 30,000 years of Art History from Caveman to Picasso .... Emporium Art Gallery 5
11:00am	**"Highlights of San Juan & St. Thomas"** One Time Only! Get your VIP Cards, new Savvy Traveller Guides and maps. ... Celebrity Theater 4
11:30am	**Diamond & Tanzanite Seminar** with raffle prize draw . . Emporium Boutiques 5
11:30am	**Honeymooners & Anniversary Party** – Celebrate your special occasion with your Cruise Director Derek ..... Cosmos Nightclub 11
11:45am	**Secrets to Aging with Beautiful Skin.** Learn the art of having beautiful skin .... Aqua Spa 10
12 Noon	**Digital Photography lecture:** Camera Hints & Program Overview ..... Cinema 3
12 Noon	**Mastering the Art of Mixology** - Perfect Cocktails .... Poolside 10
12:30pm	**Frontliners** play live music by the pool until 1:15pm .... Poolside 10
12:45pm	**Arts & Crafts.** "Ribbon Roses" with the Activities Staff . Cosmos Nightclub 11
1:00pm	**Acupuncture at Sea Lecture:** Arthritis Relief with Acupuncture ...... Cinema 3

Bingo
Snowball Jackpot Bingo

Join Cher & the Activities
Staff for the first bingo
session of the cruise.

3:45pm
Cosmos Nightclub, 11

*Cards on sale 30 minutes before
the game*

Celebrity Cruises proudly present

Savor the Caribbean
Culinary Demonstration
with
Guest Chef
Johnny Vinczencz
10:30am
Rendez-Vous Lounge, 4

Activities & Events

1:00pm	**Preview for today's Champagne Art Auction.** $5000 fine art raffle and free artwork for attending. Auction to follow @ 2:00pm . . Rendez-Vous Lounge 4
1:00pm – 6:00pm	**Golf Lessons and Simulator time** are available. Come meet your Golf Pro Ryan . . . . Golf Simulator 11
1:15pm	**Movie Theme Trivia** with the Activities Staff . . . . Poolside 10
1:45pm	**Fruits and Vegetable Carving.** Come marvel at our carvers . . . . . Poolside 10
2:00pm	**Cosmetic Seminar** with Korina . . . . Emporium Boutiques 5
2:00pm	**Casino Blackjack Tournament:** $25 to enter . . . . Fortunes Casino 4
2:00pm	**Volleyball** with the Activities Staff . . . . Sports Deck 12
2:00pm	**Complimentary Life Style Seminar: Burn Fat Faster** . . . . Aqua Spa 10
2:00pm	**Movie:** 'Elizabethtown'. 123 Minutes. Rated PG-13. Starring: Orlando Bloom & Kirsten Dunst . . . . Cinema 3
2:15pm	**Bridge Players** meet up for a game with your fellow guests . Cova Card Rm 5
2:30pm	**Wine Appreciation** with our Sommeliers and Wine Expert. ($10 fee per person) . . . . Metropolitan Restaurant 5
2:30pm	**Merengue Dance Class** with Celebrity Dancer Daniel . . Cosmos Nightclub 11
2:30pm	**Computer Class:** Adobe Photoshop Elements I ($20) . . . . . Computer Center 6
2:30pm	**Poolgames! Fun in the Sun** with the Activities Staff . . . . Poolside 10
3:00pm	**Basketball Open Court** for your fellow guest . . . . Sports Deck 12
3:15pm	**Battle of the Sexes 1** with the Activities Staff . . . . Cosmos Nightclub 11
3:30pm	**Watch Seminar** with Mark in the Boutique C . . . . . . Emporium Boutiques 5
3:30pm	**Select & Elite Member – Captains Club Event** . . . . Olympic Restaurant 3
3:45pm	**Snowball Jackpot Bingo** with your Activity Manager, Cher. Your chance to win dinner for 2 in the Olympic Restaurant Cards on sale at 3:15pm . . . . Cosmos Nightclub 11
4:00pm	**Computer Class:** Download Digital Images and Organise . . Computer Center 6
4:00pm	**Enjoy our Roman Glass Selection** . . . . Emporium Boutiques 5
4:00pm	**Paddle Tennis Court** is open until 5:30pm . . . . Sports Deck 12
4:00pm	**Robert** plays great guitar music until 5:00pm . . . . Poolside 10
4:30pm	**Free Swarovski Prize Draw** outside Jewelry store . . Emporium Boutiques 5
5:00pm	**Friends of Bill W. & Lois** meet in the . . . . Beta Rm 3
5:00pm	**All Members – Captains Club Event** . . . . Fortunes Casino 4
5:15pm – 6:15pm	**Ron Van Dyke** play an early set of cocktail music . . . . Cova Café di Milano 5
5:15pm – 6:15pm	**The Blueseas Quartet** play an early set of cocktail music . . . . Rendez-Vous Lounge 4
5:30pm	**Soccer.** Team up and play with your fellow guests . . . . Sports Deck 12
6:15pm	**Movie:** 'Elizabethtown'. 123 Minutes. Rated PG-13. Starring: Orlando Bloom & Kirsten Dunst . . . . Cinema 3
6:15pm – 7:15pm	**Robert** plays guitar music for your listening pleasure . . . . Ocean Café Bar 10 Aft

Activities & Events

6:45pm – 7:30pm	**Ron Van Dyke** plays the piano for your pre-dinner enjoyment. . . . . Cova Café di Milano 5
6:45pm – 7:30pm	**The Blueseas Quartet** plays for your enjoyment . . . . Rendez-Vous Lounge 4
7:45pm – 8:45pm	**Robert** plays more guitar music and entertains you at the . . . . Ocean Café Bar 10 Aft
7:45pm – 8:45pm	**Ron Van Dyke** plays more beautiful piano music for your enjoyment . . . . Cova Café di Milano 5
7:45pm – 8:45pm	**The Blueseas Quartet** plays music to entertain you . . . . Rendez-Vous Lounge 4
8:00pm	**Rat Pack Hour** with **D.J. Lenny** until 9:00pm . . . . Cosmos Nightclub 11
8:00pm – 9:00pm	Come by the desk to get your free 1 carat blue Sapphire Card from **David**, your **Discover Shopping Guide** . . . . Deck 4 Port
8:00pm	**Friends of Dorothy** meet in the . . . . Martini Bar 5
8:30pm	**Movie:** 'Elizabethtown'. 123 Minutes. Rated PG-13. Starring: Orlando Bloom & Kirsten Dunst . . . . Cinema 3
8:30pm	**Captain's Welcome Gala Toast.** . . . . **Celebrity Theater** **4 & 5**
8:45pm	**Celebrity Cruises presents the Celebrity Singers & Dancers** in "**Spectacle of Broadway**" . . . . **Celebrity Theater** **4 & 5**
9:00pm	**Divine Diva Hour!** Join **D.J. Lenny** in the . . . . Cosmos Nightclub 11
9:45pm	**Acappella Sensation The Coverdales** provide you with harmonic music . . . . Cova Café di Milano 5
9:45pm	**Frontliners** play dancing music until 10:30pm . . . . Rendez-Vous Lounge 4
9:45pm – 10:30pm	**Ron Van Dyke** continues the musical atmosphere . . . . Cova Café di Milano 5
10:00pm – 12:30am	**Dancing Through the Decades.** Dance the great sounds of the past. Music by **D.J. Lenny** . . . . Cosmos Nightclub 11
10:15pm	**Ensigns & Teen Coketails** . . . . Cosmos Nightclub 11
10:30pm	**Captain's Welcome Gala Toast.** . . . . **Celebrity Theater** **4 & 5**
10:45pm	**Celebrity Cruises presents the Celebrity Singers & Dancers** in "**Spectacle of Broadway**" . . . . **Celebrity Theater** **4 & 5**
10:45pm – 11:45pm	**Frontliners** continue to play dancing music . . . . Rendez-Vous Lounge 4
11:00pm – 11:45pm	**Robert** plays a set of great music for your listening pleasure . . . . Cova Café di Milano 5
11:00pm	**Movie:** 'Elizabethtown'. 123 Minutes. Rated PG-13. Starring: Orlando Bloom & Kirsten Dunst . . . . Cinema 3
11:45pm	**Acappella Sensation The Coverdales** provide you with harmonic music . . . . Cova Café di Milano 5
12 Mid – 1:00am	**Frontliners** play a late set for your enjoyment . . . . Rendez-Vous Lounge 4
12 Mid	**Robert** plays a late set until 12:45am . . . . Cova Café di Milano 5
12:30am – ???	**D.J. Lenny** plays into the wee hours . . . . Cosmos Nightclub 11

Captain's Gala Toast

*The Master,
Captain Michael Karatzas
cordially invites all guests to
join him for a
Bon Voyage Gala Toast
in our Celebrity Theater.*

*8:30pm – Main Seating
Guests
10:30pm – Late Seating
Guests
Music provided by
The Celebrity Orchestra.*

Dancing Through The Decades

Join
D.J. Lenny
as he plays great music
from the past to present.

10:00pm–12:30am
Cosmos Nightclub, Deck 11

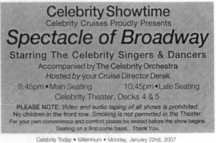

Celebrity Showtime
Celebrity Cruises Proudly Presents

Spectacle of Broadway

Starring The Celebrity Singers & Dancers
Accompanied by The Celebrity Orchestra
Hosted by your Cruise Director Derek

8:45pm • Main Seating   10:45pm • Late Seating
Celebrity Theater, Decks 4 & 5

PLEASE NOTE: *Video and audio taping of all shows is prohibited.*
No children in the front row. *Smoking is not permitted in the Theater.*
For your own convenience and comfort please be seated before the show begins.
Seating on a first come basis. Thank You.

Courtesy Celebrity Cruises

CLUB MED CRUISES
75 Valencia Avenue
Coral Gables, Florida 33134
(800) CLUB MED
(800) 258-2633 or (305) 925-9000

Club Med II: entered service 1992; 14,000 G.R.T.; 614' x 66'; 392-passenger capacity; 196 cabins; European officers, international crew, and international Club Med social staff; cruises in the Caribbean and Mediterranean.

Club Med's first cruise venture, *Club Med I,* initiated service in February 1990. *Club Med II* followed in 1992. At 542 feet, these two graceful ladies represented the cruise industry's largest sailing vessels, carrying five masts and seven computer-controlled sails. *Club Med I* was sold to Windstar Cruises in 1998 and now sails as the *Wind Surf.* During the fall, winter, and early spring, *Club Med II* sails in the Caribbean, but in the late spring and summer, she shifts to the Mediterranean, offering cruises that vary between three and 12 days to islands and ports around the Mediterranean.

Prices for U.S. passengers start at $2,700 for a seven-day cruise but are somewhat higher for a suite and single occupancy. Reasonable air/sea packages including land options at Club Med Villages are available.

All of the spacious ocean-view cabins measure 195 square feet and are located on the bottom three decks. There are also six suites that measure approximately twice as much. Thirty-five of the cabins can accommodate passengers, and six can accommodate four. All cabins have twin beds that can be converted to king size, and every stateroom includes a telephone, four-channel television, radio, refrigerator, minibar, private safe, large mirrors on showers, large sinks and vanities, separate toilet compartment, numerous shelves, and bathrobes and beach towels.

The ship carries its own sailboats, scuba gear, windsurf boards, wake boards, water skis, snorkel equipment, launches, sports platform, and expert staff to give lessons. All sports are free except diving. There are two saltwater swimming pools. A spa with three treatment rooms, massages, saunas, and facials are offered, and a well-equipped fitness center is located atop the ship.

Two open-seating restaurants provide a variety of dining options, from lavish Club Med-style breakfast and lunch buffets (with both indoor and outdoor seating available in the top-deck restaurant) to more formal waiter service in the middeck. On a recent Mediterranean cruise, I found freshly baked bread, rolls, fresh fruits, and cheeses especially outstanding. There are very acceptable French house wines provided *gratis* at lunch and dinner, as well as an à la carte wine list. A no-tipping policy prevails, as at other Club Meds. Room service and minibars in the rooms are available.

The ship also offers four bars, including a piano bar and lounge and pool bars. Other public facilities include a boutique, hairdresser/beauty salon, and a small meeting/cardroom. After dinner, the G.O.s (genteel organizers/social staff) provide you with typical Club Med-style entertainment, followed by late-night dance music in the disco. Club Med provides a very good cruising experience with maximum time spent in each port of call; however, I found that activities and entertainment are not as well developed as those found on more conventional cruise ships.

Strong Points:

An upscale Club Med experience at sea, offering comfortable cabins and great watersports, French food, and the opportunity to visit tropical islands and great beaches in the Caribbean or some unusual ports in the Mediterranean.

Courtesy Club Med Cruises

Courtesy Club Med Cruises

Menu

"SAINT GERMAIN" SOUP (Pea Soup)
or
ICED CAROTTS CREAM SOUP WITH ORANGES

****

SMOKED SALMON WITH GRAPEFRUITS
or

SHRIMPS AND FRESH MUSHROOMS SALAD WITH COGNAC

****

FROG LEGS IN "PROVENCALE" STYLE
WITH PUREE OF TOMATOES WITH BASIL
or
SWEETBREADS IN "PERIGOURDINE"STYLE

****

GRILLED BEEF RIBEYE WITH "BORDELAISE" SAUCE
or
DUCK FILLET WTIH SHERRIES
or
BROCHETTE OF LEG OF LAMB WITH HERBS

****

CHEESE BOARD

****

SABAGLIONE WITH CHAMPAGNE

or

FRUITS WITH THE 2 SHERBETS

Courtesy Club Med Cruises

COSTA CRUISE LINES

200 South Park Road, Suite #200   Costa Cociere S.P.A.
Hollywood, Florida 33021   Via XII Ottobre 2
(954) 266-5600   16121 Genoa, Italy
(954) 266-2100 Fax

www.costacruises.com

COSTA ALLEGRA (formerly *Alexandra*): entered service 1969; totally rebuilt 1992 and refurbished 2001 and 2006; 28,500 G.R.T.; 616' x 84'; 1,000-passenger capacity; 399 cabins; Italian officers and international crew; cruises Southeast Asia during spring and Mediterranean during summer and fall. (**Category C/D— Not Rated**)

COSTA ATLANTICA and *COSTA MEDITERRANEA:* entered service 2000 and 2003, respectively; 86,000 G.R.T.; 960' x 106'; 2,114-passenger capacity; 2,680-passenger capacity when full; 1,057 cabins; Italian officers and international crew; *Costa Atlantica* cruises the Caribbean during winter and spring, Northern Europe during summer and Canada/New England in fall; *Costa Mediterranea* cruises the Mediterranean during summer and fall and South America during winter and spring.

★ ★ ★ ★ ★

COSTA CLASSICA: entered service 1991; refurbished 2001 and 2005; 53,000 G.R.T.; 722' x 102'; 1,308-passenger capacity; 654 cabins; Italian officers and international crew; cruises throughout the Far East.

★ ★ ★ ★

COSTA CONCORDIA, COSTA SERENA, and *COSTA PACIFICA:* entered service 2006, 2007, and 2009, respectively; *Costa Concordia* and *Costa Serena* 114,000 G.R.T.; *Costa Pacifica* 114,500 G.R.T.; 951'x116'; 3,780-passenger capacity (3,000 double occupancy); 1,500 cabins; Italian officers and international crew; *Concordia* cruises South America during winter and spring and Mediterranean during summer and fall; *Serena* cruises eastern Mediterranean during summer and fall and Canary Islands during winter and spring; *Pacific* cruises the Mediterranean.

★ ★ ★ ★ ★

COSTA EUROPA (formerly *Westerdam* and *Homeric*): entered service 1986; lengthened 1990; refurbished 2003 and 2005; 55,000 G.R.T.; 798' x 101'; 1,494-passenger capacity; 733 cabins; Italian officers and international crew; cruises winter and spring alternating between Dubai and eastern Mediterranean and during summer and fall cruises in the eastern Mediterranean. (Leased to Thompson Cruises in 2009.)

COSTA FORTUNA and *COSTA MAGICA:* entered service 2003 and 2004, respectively; 103,000 G.R.T.; 893' x 125'; 3,788-passenger capacity (2,720 double occupancy); 1,358 cabins; Italian officers and international crew; *Costa Fortuna* cruises eastern Mediterranean during summer and fall and eastern Caribbean during winter and spring; *Costa Magica* cruises northern Europe and the Mediterranean during summer and fall and South America during winter and spring.

COSTA LUMINOSA and *COSTA DELIZIOSA*: entered service 2009; 92,600 G.R.T.; 2,828-passenger capacity (2,264 double occupancy); 1,132 cabins; Italian officers and international crew; *Costa Luminosa* cruises in Dubai during winter and spring, northern Europe during summer, and Canary Islands in fall; *Costa Deliziosa* cruises in Dubai during winter and spring, northern Europe during summer, and eastern Mediterranean during fall.

COSTA MARINA: entered service 1969; rebuilt 1990; refurbished 2002; 26,000 G.R.T.; 616' x 84'; 776-passenger capacity; 383 cabins; Italian officers and international crew; cruises the Mediterranean.

COSTA ROMANTICA: entered service 1993; refurbished 2003; 53,000 G.R.T.; 722' x 102'; 1,356-passenger capacity; 678 cabins; Italian officers and international crew; cruises the Indian Ocean during winter and spring and Far East during summer and fall.

COSTA VICTORIA: entered service 1996; renovated 2004; 75,000 G.R.T.; 828' x 105.5'; 1,928-passenger capacity; 964 cabins; Italian officers and international crew; cruises South America during winter and spring and eastern Mediterranean during summer and fall.

(Medical Facilities: Cruise line indicated there is one physician and two nurses aboard each ship but furnished no additional information.)

Note: **Passenger capacity reflects double occupancy except where otherwise indicated. Ships are capable of carrying more passengers.**

These ships are rated in 11 separate categories in the second half of chapter 14.

Until 1997, when Costa Cruises was acquired by Carnival Corporation and Airtours, the controlling owners were the Costa family, whose business ventures date back to 1854. In 2000, Carnival bought out the interest of Airtours. Costa made its entrance into the cruise industry in 1947, when it introduced Italy's first air-conditioned passenger ship, the *Anna C,* which carried clients between Italy and South America. During the 1950s, '60s, and '70s, the company added eight more vessels, some named after the grandchildren of its president, the *Federico C, Franca C, Carla C, Andrea C, Enrico C, Eugenio C, Giovanni C,* and *Flavia.* From time to time, it chartered other ships, including the *Leonardo da Vinci* and *Amerikanis,* as well as the *Daphne* and *Danae.* In recent years, Costa has sold its older ships, renovated others, and embarked on a program of new builds, offering transatlantic cruises as well as cruises in the Caribbean, North Cape/fjords/ Baltic/Russia, South America, the Mediterranean, Dubai, Suez Canal and Egypt, the Far East, Canada and New England, and the Indian Ocean.

The first of the Costa new builds, the 53,000-ton, 1,308-passenger *Costa Classica,* entered service in 1991, followed by *Costa Romantica,* a sister ship, in 1993, and the 75,000-ton, 1,928-passenger *Costa Victoria* in 1996. The 53,872-ton *Costa Europa,* formerly *Westerdam* of Holland America Line and *Homeric* of Home Line, joined the Costa fleet in 2002 and was refurbished in 2003. In 2006, six new suites with balconies were added and 48 staterooms were completely redesigned. In 2009 she was transferred to Thompson Cruises on a long-term lease. With the introduction of the magnificently designed and decorated *Costa Atlantica* in 2000, the cruise line moved up several notches against the competition. This ship and her sister ship, *Costa Mediterranea,* are far more attractive vessels with more impressive facilities, more verandas, and larger staterooms than their Costa predecessors. Costa's next step was the order of two new 103,000-ton ships, *Costa Fortuna* and *Costa Magica,* which entered service in 2003 and 2004, respectively. Opting for larger ships with greater passenger capacity, Costa's parent company, Carnival Corporation, ordered still bigger ships for the future, and in 2006 the 114,000-ton, 3,780-passenger (3,000-passenger double occupancy) *Costa Concordia* entered service, followed by a sister ship, *Costa Serena,* in 2007. In the summer of 2009, *Costa Pacifica,* a 114,500-ton, 3,780-passenger (3012-passenger double occupancy) sister ship to the *Costa Concordia* and *Costa Serena,* made her debut, to be followed by two other 114,500-ton ships in 2011 and 2012. Also in 2009, the 92,600-ton, 2,828-passenger (2,264 double occupancy) *Costa Luminosa* entered service with a sister ship, *Costa Deliziosa,* due in 2010.

The keynote for Costa is Italian ambiance and spirit. On all the ships, you will find friendly Italian officers, romantic Italian orchestras, and helpful cruise directors and social staff. The officers and others holding important positions are Italian; however, the waiters, cabin attendants, and remainder of the crew are recruited from India, Goa, the Philippines, and other areas around the world and have varying cruise experience. Generally, you do not find big-name entertainers, and the dining experience both in the main restaurants and the buffets is inconsistent. However, the wine list offers an excellent selection of Italian wines at reasonable prices.

The ships with Caribbean itineraries follow the pattern of other cruise ships in the Caribbean mass market but carry many Spanish-speaking passengers as well as Italian and European families who have crossed the sea to enjoy a warm Caribbean winter cruise. When sailing in the Mediterranean, you will have mostly Italian and a smattering of other European shipmates. On all ships, you will hear announcements in Italian, French, English, German, and Spanish. The food, entertainment, and activities are somewhat more geared to the European clientele. Management advises that recently enhancements have been made in the food and service departments. Most of the stage productions are performed in English. For those wanting a cosmopolitan experience, these cruises offer a unique opportunity to sail "Italian style" with Italians and passengers from around the world on a more intimate basis. In the past, a less formal, less service-oriented, and more party-focused atmosphere prevailed; however, management advises that this is changing. During Christmas holidays and the summer months, you will find many young adults and families traveling with children, as well as on-board activities to accommodate them. Available on both Mediterranean cruises (April through October) and on Caribbean cruises (November through April) are special programs and counselors for children three to 12 and a Costa Teens Club for teenagers.

In the summer of 1990, Costa introduced the *Costa Marina,* a 26,000-ton rebuilt container ship that accommodates 1,005 (776 double occupancy) passengers in 388 cabins.

In early 1991, the *Costa Classica* entered service, the first totally new ship built by Costa since the *Eugenio C.* At 53,000 tons, with a capacity to accommodate 1,764 passengers (1,308 double occupancy). Two-thirds of the cabins are outside, and 20 percent have double or queen beds. All cabins and the 10 veranda suites include radio, cable television, telephone, private safes, hair dryers, and good storage space. In addition to the main restaurant, there is a pizzeria, a pastry and coffee shop, and an indoor/outdoor lido restaurant. There is also a health spa with a fitness center including exercise equipment, sauna, steam room, whirlpools, massage, and other body treatment facilities; a gambling casino; and a 1,500-square-foot conference center for business meetings. In 2005 she was refurbished. She presently offers cruises in the Far East. An almost identical sister ship, *Costa Romantica,* entered service in November 1993. All cabins are larger than on the older Costa ships, and the suites offer additional space, comfort, amenities, and privacy. The clientele includes many Italians.

In December 1992, *Costa Allegra* was added to the fleet. At 28,500 tons, the ship can accommodate 1,072 (820 double occupancy) passengers in 399 cabins, more than half of which are outside. The interior design is composed of skylights, transparent tiles, glass-roofed atriums, greenhouse domes, bold colors, flowing waterfalls and streams, and art and murals by some of Europe's leading artists. Public facilities include a meeting center; imaginative lounges, bars, and showrooms; a circle of shops; a casino; a large restaurant; a disco; a pool; an indoor/outdoor café; and a Romanesque spa featuring exercise equipment, aerobics, free weights, whirlpools, steam/sauna rooms, massage, and a beauty parlor. A special low-calorie spa menu is also offered in the dining room, as it is on all Costa ships. In 2006, the ship received a 12 million redesign, which included enlar gement of the gym and spa, expansion of the shopping area, redecoration of staterooms, and the creation of four new specialty restaurants. She sails in Southeast Asia from Shanghai during spring and the Mediterranean during summer and fall.

The 75,000-ton, 2,464-passenger (1,928 double occupancy) *Costa Victoria* entered service in the summer of 1996. She cruises South America during the winter and spring and offers eastern Mediterranean cruises during the summer and fall. The ship features a grand atrium spanning seven decks, extending to a crystal dome at the top. Public facilities include an Italian-style spa and fitness center that houses an indoor pool, sauna, steam room, whirlpool, and exercise room with a limited number of cardiovascular machines and other equipment; a walking/jogging track around deck 6; a lido area with two outside pools, four whirlpools, basketball, shuffleboard, and one miniature tennis court; two main dining rooms, a four-station buffet restaurant with an outdoor area overlooking the sea, pizzeria, and poolside grill; a two-deck show lounge; a tri-level lounge for dancing and other entertainment; a disco; a large fully stocked casino; and several lounges and bars. The decor of the ship is austere compared to most large ships built in the 1990s and does not include the expensive art found on the post-2000 Costa ships or on Celebrity, Princess, Royal Caribbean, and Holland America vessels, nor the glitz and spectacle of the Carnival line. Cabins—though functional, with adequate storage, private safes, minibars, hair dryers, and remote-control televisions—are relatively small, having no sitting areas. In 2004, 242 cabins and four mini-suites were fitted with balconies. The limited number of suites and mini-suites are not as large or as posh as those on many of Costa's competitors; however, the availability of two extra beds in the large walk-in closet areas makes them a viable alternative for families. The ship features an alternative specialty restaurant, Ristorante Magnifico with cuisine by Ettore Bocchia.

The 86,000-ton, 2,680-passenger (2,114 double occupancy) *Costa Atlantica* entered service in 2000, followed by a sister ship, *Costa Mediterranea,* in 2003, representing a giant leap forward for the cruise line in terms of creating more elegantly designed and decorated ships. On the *Atlantica,* the public areas, with their eclectic Italian theme honoring the films of Federico Fellini, are magnificent and include over 400 original works of art and a replica of Venice's Café Florian, a landmark in St. Mark's Square. The décor on the *Mediterranea* is even more spectacular. Architect and designer Joseph Farcus has created a floating palazzo in which Italian art, frescoes, murals, and statuary adorn all of the common areas and exquisite granite, marble, and woods enhance every cabin and public room. Many Costa repeat passengers prefer this ship to the line's other vessels.

The 1,057 staterooms and suites on both ships are far more attractive and comfortable than on the earlier Costa new builds. Two-thirds have ocean views, verandas, and measure 210 square feet (which includes a 30-square-foot veranda). Twenty percent are located in the interior of the ship and measure 160 square feet. Every accommodation features a refrigerator/minibar, remote-control television, hair dryer, personal safe, dresser with a makeup area, small sitting area, and adequate-sized bathroom. Although the six grand suites (measuring 650 square feet including large verandas) are the most desirable, the 34 360-foot (with veranda) panorama suites are also extremely comfortable with enormous storage and closet space, Jacuzzi tub/shower combinations and double vanities in the bathrooms, separate dressing/makeup areas, and large verandas.

Public areas are uniformly exquisite and include two-level restaurants serving all three meals in two sittings. The buffets and pizzerias, attractively furnished, are alternative casual venues with multiple food stations and both inside and outside tables. There are also hamburger/hot-dog grills. Club Atlantica and Club Medusa, elegant, glass-enclosed observation lounges, serve both as alternative specialty restaurants (with menus designed by Gualtieri Marchesi) in the evening and late-night spots for romantic dancing. Other public areas include imaginative Greek/Roman-style spa centers with multiple levels of state-of-the-art exercise equipment, hair salons, his and hers locker rooms with steam and sauna, and numerous treatment rooms offering a full therapy program; three central swimming pools, one with a retractable magradome; children's pools; whirlpools; jogging tracks; basketball areas; shopping streets with upscale boutiques and signature item/sundry shops; conference facilities; casinos; cardrooms; Internet café/libraries; children's facilities; impressive three-deck-high theaters, the locale for production shows; two-level discos; several additional lounges for various entertainments; and the above-mentioned Café Florian on the *Atlantica.* Eastern Caribbean itineraries on both ships include a visit to Costa's private beach on Catalina Island on the coast of the Dominican Republic.

The 103,000-ton, 2,720-passenger (3,788 with every berth occupied) *Costa*

Fortuna also joined the fleet in 2003, followed by her sister ship, *Costa Magica,* in 2004. Five hundred and twenty-two of the 1,358 cabins and suites on each ship have balconies, and 27 can accommodate the physically challenged. An inside cabin measures 160 square feet; an ocean view with balcony 210 square feet, a suite with balcony 360 square feet, and the Grand Suite with veranda 650 square feet. The décor of the *Fortuna* incorporates the style and design of the grand ocean liners of the past. The décor on the *Magica* pays tribute to the most beautiful and magical Italian locales. These are beautifully decorated ships; however, the traffic pattern is a bit complicated due to the location of the dining rooms. Facilities on each ship are similar to the *Atlantica* and *Mediterranea,* except somewhat expanded, and include a nine-deck-high atrium; 11 bars; a three-deck theater; three swimming pools, including one covered by a retractable magradome; a children's pool and a children's play area; a casino; a disco; an enormous, elegant ballroom; an internet café; a business/conference center; a two-deck gym and spa; unusually comfortable, spacious changing rooms with large sauna, steam, and shower facilities; two two-story main dining rooms; a buffet and pizzeria; and a combination specialty restaurant and observation lounge. The *Fortuna* cruises the eastern Mediterranean during the summer and fall and the eastern Caribbean during winter and spring, while *Costa Magica* cruises northern Europe and the Mediterranean during the summer and fall and Brazil during the winter and spring.

The 114,000-ton *Costa Concordia,* with a 3,780-passenger capacity (and 3,000 lower berths), entered service during 2006, followed by a sister ship, *Costa Serena,* in 2007. Sixty percent of the cabins have ocean views, and 50 percent have balconies. Unique features on these ships not presently on the other Costa vessels include two pools with sliding-glass roofs, one of which has a 200-square-foot video screen; five Jacuzzis; the Samsara Spa, a 20,000-square-foot wellness and relaxation center spanning two decks and including a gym, an indoor thalassotherapy pool, treatment rooms, a Turkish bath and solarium, and a specialty health restaurant; and 55 staterooms and 12 suites that have direct access to the spa and special spa amenities; Club Concordia, a specialty restaurant with cuisine by *Michelin*-rated chef Ettore Bocchia; 13 bars; and a theater spanning three decks. There are numerous venues for listening and dancing in the evenings. Another sister ship, *Costa Pacifica,* arrived in 2009 at 114,500 tons with six additional cabins and 16 additional verandas. The Samsara Spa was expanded to 23,000 square feet and there are two pools, one with a retractable magradome and the other with a giant outdoor movie screen. Two identical siblings are scheduled for 2011 and 2012.

The 92,600-ton, 2,828-passenger (2,260 double occupancy) *Costa Luminosa* and a sister ship, *Costa Deliziosa,* entered service in 2009 and 2010, respectively, boasting verandas in 68 percent of the staterooms and a new golf simulator with 37 virtual golf courses. *Costa Luminosa* cruises in Dubai during the winter and spring, Northern Europe during the summer, and the Canary Islands in fall. Costa Deliziosa cruises in Dubai during the winter and spring, northern Europe during the summer, and the eastern Mediterranean during the fall.

Guests booking 120 days in advance can take advantage of early booking fares that can result in up to a 50 percent savings.

Strong Points:

Fun-oriented full-facility ships with Italian themes affording an opportunity to travel with numerous Italian and international passengers; special appeal for Spanish- and Italian-speaking passengers; an abundance of families and children's activities during holidays and summer months; good value for your cruise dollar.

Mediterranea *veranda suite, courtesy Costa Cruise Lines*

Costa Atlantica, *courtesy Costa Cruise Lines*

Costa Atlantica, *courtesy Costa Cruise Lines*

NIGHT ENTERTAINMENT

DRESS CODE: FORMAL / GALA

URBINO THEATER

deck 3 Raffaello, deck 4 Michelangelo, deck 5 Leonardo

9.15pm
1st Sitting Guests

11.00pm
2nd Sitting Guests

YOUR CRUISE DIRECTOR
MAX
presents

Magic Moments

with the singers
**Allison McAreavey, Ian Fraser
Natalie Makepeace, David Austen**
and the Costa Magica Dancers

For the safety of the performers, the protection of their personal image and to
guarantee the quality of the special effects, the use of photography and video
cameras is not permitted. Please switch off your mobile phones
before the beginning of the show. Thank you.

**8.30pm - Grand Bar Salento,
deck 5 Leonardo
GUESS THAT TUNE!!**
with the Cruise Staff
and Duo Blue Note

**9.45pm-10.30pm - Spoleto Lounge,
deck 5 Leonardo
SPECIAL BRASIL**
Bossa Nova - Samba - Popular Brazilian Music
with Duo Farenight

**10.30pm - Grand Bar Salento deck 5 Leonardo
THAT'S AMORE**
with the Cruise Staff and the Duo Blue Note

**11.00pm-11.30pm - Spoleto Lounge, deck 5 Leonardo
A TRIBUTE TO ELTON JOHN**
with Maurizio

11.15pm-1.00am - Capri Lounge deck 5 Leonardo

Sock-Hop
60's-70's Boggie Night

At midnight **TWIST CONTEST**
with the Rocking Cruise Staff & the Night Out Band
followed by 80's Music.
and party continues in the Disco...

**12.30am Grado Disco, deck 4 Michelangelo
DISCO FEVER!!**
Saturday Night Fever
Music from the 60's & 70's
with your Cruise Staff and DJ Emme

INFORMATION

Credit Card registration
By registering your credit card (Visa, MasterCard, American Express) at the beginning of the cruise, all payments will be automatically debited to your account. Registration of the credit card can be done at the Guest Service, deck 3 Raffaello, open 24 hours. Please do not forget to bring along your credit card coupon which you received together with your cruise ticket. Please do not forget to bring along your credit card coupon which you received together with your cruise ticket and your Costa Card. We remind you that it will not be possible to change the type of account settlement chosen (from Credit Card to cash or from Cash to Credit Card) during the last 2 days of the cruise.

Safety in your cabin
Please be informed that Candles, Irons Fans and Multiple Plugs are not permitted in the cabin for safety reasons. We also urge you to use the ship's hairdryer rather than your personal one. Please read the flyer "Before anything else, safety" placed in your cabin. Thank you for your co-operation.

Deck Chairs
We would like to inform you that it is not allowed to reserve deck chairs with personal belongings. If you go away, please make sure you take everything with you. The lost and found objects will be delivered to the Customer Service on deck 3 Raffaello. Thank you for your co-operation.

Lifts
Children under the age of 12 may not use the lifts unsupervised.
For safety reasons please make sure that children do not place their hands on the lift doors: the doors slide open and children might not realise.
We kindly ask all guests if using our on board lifts by making sure you press the correct button and not the two at the same time. Thank you.

Smoking / Non Smoking
We kindly remind you that it is forbidden to smoke in the theater, in the restaurants (including indoor areas of the Buffet Restaurant), in the area in front of the elevators, in the elevators, in the corridors and on the stairs. We have designated smoking areas in the public lounges. The Cigar Bar L'Aquila on deck 5 is the only reserved area for pipe or cigar smokers. The Bar Spoleto on deck 5 is non smoking area. Thank you for your co-operation.

Honeymooners
Honeymooning Couples and those celebrating wedding anniversaries please contact Customer Service on deck 3 Raffaello.

Important: Pool
We inform all our guests that the swimming pool Positano, on deck 9, (backside) is for adults only. The swimming pool reserved for children is located on deck 12. We would like to inform you that the pools on board do not have guard rails. For your own security please be careful whilst around the pool area as it can become very slippery. Diving is prohibited! We remind you that the parents should look after their children whilst using the pools, and respect the other guests.

World News
Depending on the satellite reception, every day a fax-newspaper containing the principal information on world events will be delivered to your cabin.

BEAUTY SALON

Reshape your body...in 1 hour!
Do you battle with diet and exercise?!
Then IONITHERMIE is for you: only 120 $
Courses of 3 ionithermie: 300 $

AGE CAN BE A BEAUTIFUL THING!
Defy the ageing process!
Experience "LT Oxygen Lifting facial":
a unique treatment that uses scientific
technology combined with pure nature to
help achieve a perfectly balanced skin. This
specializes in 3 specific areas: deep
cleansing, hydrating and anti-ageing.
50 min. only 99 $!

Gym, deck 11 Tiepolo
10.00am: POWER PILATES ($ 11)
5.00pm: POWER YOGA ($ 11)

PHOTO SHOP

Your embarkation photos
are now available!
It is easy to find with the ticket.

Special video offer:
the ship, the excursions,
the cruise, only 75 $.
Book the video of the cruise and our
videographer will be pleased include
your images taken at your table
during tonight's Gala dinner.

This morning digital products for sale.

Photo Gallery, deck 4 Michelangelo
Photo Kiosk, deck 5 Leonardo

DUTY FREE BOUTIQUE

For your Gala night

Cocktail Rings
Special Offer: 2 rings for $ 39,99
and...
Swarowski jewellery
at duty free prices!

"Beverly Hills" gold 50% off
big unveilling with champagne
at noon in the shops

deck 5 Leonardo

CASINO - BINGO

Noon - Grand Bar Salento, Deck 5
8.00pm - Grand Bar Salento, Deck 5

SUPER BINGO

with Eugenio
You can win US$ 1600 with the first
46 numbers drawn!

10.00am: slot machine tournament
2.00pm - Pool, deck 9: horse racing
3.30pm: Black Jack tournament
(only 20 $ to enter and 20 $ to re-
enter, third re-entry for free.
Final at aprox. 5.30pm)
Minors under 18 are not allowed to play in the Casino

YOUR DAY ONBOARD

Your friendly Cruise Staff invite you to take part in the following daily activities:

8.30am	Walk - a - Thon Meeting point at Pool Lido Maratea deck 9 Giotto
9.00am	Perfect ABS class Club Salute Saturnia, deck 11 Tiepolo
9.15am	Morning Gym Pool Lido Maratea deck 9 Giotto
9.30am	General knowledge trivia Grand Bar Salento, deck 5 Leonardo
9.45am	Fuzball tournament Pool Lido Maratea deck 9 Giotto
10.00am	Seminar La Therapie: Revealing the latest in treating sun damage, age spots, scaring and wrinkles Club Salute Saturnia, deck 11 Tiepolo
10.00am	Dance Class Ballroom: Merengue with our Guest Dance Instructors Tommy and Carolyne Grand Bar Salento, deck 5 Leonardo
10.30am	Bridge lecture with our Bridge Instructor Darlene Card room, deck 5 Leonardo
10.30am	Dance class: Cha Cha Cha Lido Maratea deck 9 Giotto
10.45-11.45am	Arts & Crafts: Let's paint Lido Positano deck 9 Giotto
11.00am	Show Quiz Grand Bar Salento, deck 5 Leonardo
11.00am	Seminar Aromastone Therapy: learn the healing and de-stressing effects of balinese stones and aromatherapy Club Salute Saturnia, deck 11 Tiepolo
11.00am	Old Mc Donalds Farm Game: Cows VS Pigs Lido Maratea deck 9 Giotto
11.30am	Let's dance Lido Maratea deck 9 Giotto
2.00pm	Seminar seaweed secrets: Learn the secrets to naturally de-toxify and nourish your body Club Salute Saturnia, deck 11 Tiepolo
2.00pm	Friends of Bill W. Grado Disco deck 4 Michelangelo
2.00pm	Let's play Volleyball Tennis court deck 12 Mantegna
2.30pm	Arts & Crafts: Paper Flowers Lido Positano deck 9 Giotto
2.30pm	Italian lesson: "Buongiorno Italia" Capo Colonna Lounge deck 5 Leonardo
2.45pm	Dance lesson: Mambo Lido Maratea deck 9 Giotto
3.00pm	Seminar: How to achieve a flat stomach Club Salute Saturnia, deck 11 Tiepolo
3.30pm	**Emergency boat drill**
4.00pm	Game: Tic, Tac, Toe Pool Lido Maratea deck 9 Giotto
4.15pm	History quiz Grand Bar Salento, deck 5 Leonardo
4.30pm	Let's dance Pool Lido Maratea deck 9 Giotto
5.00pm	Total body work out Pool Lido Maratea deck 9 Giotto

Pool Lido Maratea deck 9 Giotto
from 1.00pm to 2.00pm & from 5.30pm to 6.30pm

Spice Islanders Calypso Band

Mini & Maxi Club   (3-12 years)

All daily activities can be found in the "fun@sea" program, available in the SQUOK CLUB.
deck 12 Mantegna.

TeenZone   (with Sabrina & Laura) (13-18 years)

11.00am	Ping-pong tournament - Teen surfboard, Pool, deck 9 Giotto
5.00pm	Basket tournament - Tennis court, deck 12 Mantegna
11.00pm	MTV Competition - Disco Grado, deck 4 Michelangelo

MUSICAL ENTERTAINMENT

Restaurant Portofino
Duo Badi: 5.30pm-6.00pm, 8.30pm-9.00pm
Restaurant Costa Smeralda
Vincenzo: 5.45pm-6.15pm, 8.45pm-9.15pm
Atrio Italia Magica, deck 3 Raffaello
Roberto: 5.00pm-6.00pm, 7.00pm-8.00pm,
9.15pm-10.30pm
Pasquale: 6.00pm-7.00pm, 8.00pm-9.15pm,
10.30pm-11.30pm
Vincenzo: 11.30pm-12.30am, 12.45am-1.30am
Grand Bar Salento, deck 5 Leonardo
Duo Blue Note: 5.00pm-6.15pm, 8.30pm-9.45pm,
11.30pm-12.30am
Trio Tringali: 7.00pm-8.00pm, 9.45pm-11.00pm,
12.30am-1.30am
Capri Lounge, deck 5 Leonardo
Night Out Band: 9.45pm-1.30am

Piano Bar Capo Colonna, deck 5 Leonardo
Alex: 5.00pm-6.00pm, 8.00pm-9.15pm,
10.30pm-midnight
Duo Badi: 6.45pm-7.45pm, 9.15pm-10.30pm,
midnight-12.30am
Antonio: 12.30am-1.30am
Ballroom Spoleto, deck 5 Leonardo
Maurizio: 6.30pm-7.15pm, 8.30pm-9.30pm,
11.00pm-midnight
Duo Farenight: 7.30pm-8.30pm, 9.45pm-11.00pm,
midnight-1.00am
Club Vicenza, deck 11 Tiepolo
Antonio: 6.30pm-.....
Disco Grado deck 4 Michelangelo
from 11.30pm with DJ Emme

Courtesy Costa Cruise Lines

Captain's Gala Dinner

APPETIZERS

Cocktail di gamberetti
Shrimp Cocktail

Prosciutto di parma con perle di melone
Prosciutto Ham with Melon Balls

Melanzane alla parmigiana
Eggplants with Parmesan cheese and tomato sauce

SOUPS

Crema di pomodoro rustica
Rustic Tomato Soup

Consommé di anatra
Duck Consommé Beijing

Crema fredda di albicocche al miele
Chilled Apricot and Honey

SALADS

Insalata del giorno
Tossed Crunchy Romaine Lettuce, Radicchio with Caesar Dressing and Cherry Tomatoes

Insalata mista
Crisp Heart of Lettuce with Cucumber, Red Bell Peppers, Italian Parsley and shaved Parmesan

ITALIAN TRADITION

May we suggest eating your Pasta Dish prior to Main Course, as Italians do.

Risotto royale allo champagne
Risotto With Champagne

Lasagne alla bolognese
Lasagna with Meat Ragout

ENTREES

Pesce wahoo al forno
Broiled Wahoo placed on a Bed of Zucchini Spaghetti and Sautéed Tomatoes with
Lemon-Garlic Parsley Sauce and Steamed Potatoes

Quaglie farcite servite con salsa al lambrusco
Tender Quails partially boned and Stuffed with a Savory Country Filling,
served with a Lambrusco Wine Sauce

Aragosta al forno
Broiled Lobster with a Delicate Tarragon and Shallot Butter

Costata di manzo al sugo naturale
America's favorite cut of Beef served with its own Juices and Creamy Horseradish

MEATLESS

Polenta con verdure all'aglio
Polenta with Garlicky Greens individually molded, then topped with Freshly Sautéed Spinach Leaves,
Sliced Red Onions, Mushrooms and Slivered Golden Garlic

*Some products may be frozen. We inform you that this food is defrosted observing the strictest procedures
that do not change the properties of its taste in any way.*

dinn_06_051203.don

Desserts

Bomba vesuviana
Baked Alaska on Parade

Torta di zucca agli amaretti
Pumpkin Cake with Amaretti Biscuits

Gelato malaga, alla fragola o alla vaniglia
Rum Raisin, Strawberry or Vanilla

Sorbetto al limone o alla pesca
Refreshing Lemon or Peach Sherbet

Gelato senza zucchero
No Sugar Added Ice Cream

Formaggio
An Assortment of International and Domestic Cheese
Served with Crackers and Biscuits

Frutta fresca di stagione
Fresh Seasonal Fruit Basket

Dessert Wines

	US$
Veuve Clicquot Ponsardin Brut	65.00
Asti Spumante Martini	20.00
flûte	4.50
Moscato d'Asti Bosc dla Rey Batasiolo	20.00
flûte	4.50
Ruby Port Sandemann	4.50
Harvey's Bristol Cream	4.50
Baglio Florio Marsala	4.50
Vecchioflorio Riserva Marsala	4.50

Please be advised that a 15% Service charge is added to the bill

CRUISE WEST
2301 Fifth Avenue, Suite # 401
Seattle, Washington 98121
(888) 851-8133
(206) 441-8687
(206) 441-4757 Fax
www.cruisewest.com

PACIFIC EXPLORER: entered service 1995; remodeled 1998; 185' long; 100-passenger capacity; 50 cabins; Costa Rican officers and crew; cruises in Costa Rica and Panama. (**No Category—Not Rated**)

SPIRIT OF ALASKA (formerly *Pacific Northwest Explorer*): entered service 1980; renovated 1998; 97 G.R.T.; 143' x 28'; 78-passenger capacity; 39 cabins; American officers and crew; cruises in Alaska and British Columbia. (**No Category—Not Rated**)

SPIRIT OF COLUMBIA (formerly *New Shoreham II*): entered service 1979; renovated 1995; 98 G.R.T.; 143' x 39'; 78-passenger capacity; 39 cabins; American officers and crew; cruises in Alaska and British Columbia. (**No Category—Not Rated**)

SPIRIT OF DISCOVERY (formerly *Independence* and *Columbia*): entered service 1976; renovated 1992; 94 G.R.T.; 166' x 32'; 84-passenger capacity; 43 cabins; American officers and crew; cruises on Columbia and Snake Rivers and in Alaska. (**No Category—Not Rated**)

SPIRIT OF ENDEAVOUR (formerly *Newport Clipper* and *Sea Spirit*): entered service 1983; renovated 1999; 95 G.R.T.; 217' x 37'; 102-passenger capacity; 51 cabins; American officers and crew; cruises Alaska, Pacific Northwest, and British Columbia. (**No Category—Not Rated**)

SPIRIT OF GLACIER BAY (formerly *Nantucket Clipper* and *Spirit of Nantucket*): entered service 1984; 1,471 G.R.T.; 207' x 37'; 102-passenger capacity; 51 cabins; American officers and crew; cruises in Alaska. (**No Category—Not Rated**)

SPIRIT OF '98 (formerly *Pilgrim Belle, Colonial Explorer,* and *Victorian Empress*): entered service 1984; renovated 1995; 96 G.R.T.; 192' x 40'; 96-passenger capacity; 48 cabins; American officers and crew; cruises Columbia and Snake Rivers, Alaska, and British Columbia. (**No Category—Not Rated**)

SPIRIT OF OCEANUS (formerly *Renaissance V, Sun Viva,* and *Megastar Sagittarius*): entered service 1991; remodeled 2001; 4,500 G.R.T.; 294.5' x 50'; 120-passenger capacity; 57 suites; international officers and crew; cruises Alaska, Bering Sea, Russia, Asia, and South Pacific. (**No Category—Not Rated**)

SPIRIT OF YORKTOWN (formerly *Yorktown Clipper*): entered service 1988; refurbished 2007; 2,352 G.R.T.; 257' x 43'; 138-passenger capacity; 69 cabins; American officers and crew; cruises to California's wine country, Mexico's Sea of Cortez, and Alaska's Inside Passage. **(No Category—Not Rated)**

West Travel, the parent company of Cruise West, was established in 1973 by Chuck West, founder and former owner of Westours. Commencing in 1989, the company embarked upon a program to acquire small cruise ships and currently owns and operates eight vessels and leases the *Pacific Explorer.* It has itineraries in Alaska and British Columbia, along the Columbia and Snake Rivers, in Mexico's Sea of Cortez, and to Costa Rica, Panama, Asia, the South Pacific, Europe's Danube River, the Galapagos, and Antarctica. Per person, per diem, prices range from $343 to $1,677 for an owner's suite depending on the vessel, cabin category, and itinerary.

Typically, these are small, intimate destination-oriented vessels with public areas that include a small sun deck, a dining room, and a lounge. Accommodations are pristine by today's standards. Most ships have a few upscale cabins or suites with television, refrigerator, queen bed, and more space. The majority of accommodations are quite small but ample and comfortable. However, the *Spirit of Oceanus* (the former *Renaissance V*) is composed of all spacious suites, several with verandas.

In 2006, the cruise line purchased the *Nantucket Clipper* and the *Yorktown Clipper* from Clipper Cruise Line. The *Nantucket Clipper* is now named *Spirit of Glacier Bay* and offers Alaskan cruises. The *Yorktown Clipper* was renamed *Spirit of Yorktown* and refurbished in 2007, creating four balcony cabins.

These ships do not offer entertainment or activities, but rather emphasize enrichment lectures, land tours, and the small-ship, cruise-destination experience.

Strong Points:

A small-vessel experience with emphasis on close-up exploration of small ports of call and remote, narrow waterways where larger vessels cannot navigate. The *Spirit of Oceanus* is an especially comfortable vessel.

Courtesy Cruise West

Courtesy Cruise West

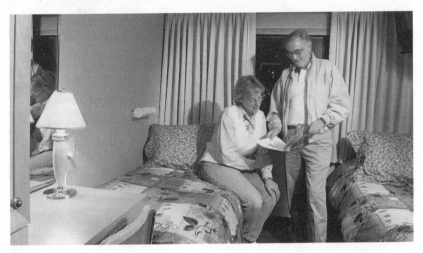

Courtesy Cruise West

Courtesy Cruise West

Spirit of Endeavour Menu

Appetizers

Carpaccio of Beef
Paper-thin slices of beef tenderloin
on a hot mustard emulsion and
dressed with extra virgin olive oil,
Reggiano cheese and freshly
cracked black pepper

Crab-Stuffed Portobello
Dungeness crab stuffing with a
roasted red bell pepper coulis

Soup

**Clam Chowder
'Endeavour'**
A fire roasted tomato based
chowder flavored with juniper
berries and gin

Salads

Mesculan with Toasted Walnuts
Pt. Reyes Original Farmstead
California blue cheese,
red and green seedless grapes and
an aged Balsamic vinaigrette

'Endeavour' House Salad
Mixed greens, tomato wedges,
shredded carrots and black olives,
with your choice of dressing

Freshly Baked Breads

A selection from artisan bakers
located in Sonoma, California

Entrée Selections

*All entrées are served with the
Chef's Daily Selection of fresh seasonal
vegetables, rice or potato
(Baked Idaho potato is available upon request)*

Grilled Venison Gran Venur
Two seared medallions served
with a classic red currants and
port wine demi-glaze.
Served with a wild rice pilaf

Cornish Game Hen
One-half a hen roasted and served
with an orange and brandy jus

Spanish Style Rockfish
A fresh fillet poached in a saffron
court bouillon and topped with a
tomato, olive, pearl onion and herb
relish. Accompanied by parsley
baby red potatoes

**Grilled Vegetable
Napoleon**
Grilled seasonal vegetables
stacked and presented with
an Israeli cous cous and
a sweet pea and California
goat cheese pesto

CruiseWest
Up-close, casual and personal.

CRYSTAL CRUISES
2049 Century Park East, Suite 1400
Los Angeles, California 90067
(310) 785-9300

CRYSTAL SERENITY: entered service 2003; renovated 2008; 68,870 G.R.T.; 820' x 105.6'; 1,070-passenger capacity; 535 staterooms; Norwegian captain and international officers, European hotel and dining staff, and international crew; cruises South Pacific, Australia/New Zealand, Europe, Black Sea, Mediterranean, Canary Islands, Caribbean, Panama Canal, transatlantic, and other destinations around the world.

CRYSTAL SYMPHONY: entered service 1995; renovated 2004 and 2006; 51,044 G.R.T.; 781' x 99'; 922-passenger capacity; 461 staterooms; international officers, European hotel and dining staff, international crew; cruises South America, Panama Canal, Europe, Baltic, Antarctica, transatlantic, Asia, Canada/New England, east coast of U.S., Mexican Riviera, Caribbean, and other destinations around the world.

(Medical Facilities: C-7 on *Symphony* and C-8 on *Serenity;* P-1; EM, CLS, MS; N-2; CM; PD; BC [but not full blood count]; EKG; TC, PO; OX; WC; ICU; X; M; LJ. M; TM; LJ—telemedicine is limited to fax and e-mail of digital photos.)

Note: Six+ black stars is the highest rating given in this edition to ships in the deluxe market category.

These ships are rated in 11 separate categories in the second half of chapter 14.

Crystal Cruises, a subsidiary owned by Nippon Yusen Kaisha (NYK) of Japan and based in Los Angeles, launched its first luxury-class ship, *Crystal Harmony,* in the summer of 1990, followed by *Crystal Symphony* in 1995. With construction costs of $200 million and $250 million, respectively, these are two of the largest, most spacious ships competing in the luxury cruise market. Both ships recently received multimillion-dollar overhauls and renovations. These sleek vessels boast some of the largest luxury penthouses afloat, with outdoor verandas in all penthouses, as well as in more than 80 percent of the staterooms. Average staterooms are among the most desirable at sea. *Crystal Harmony* was transferred to the Japanese parent company in late 2005 and now sails as *Asuka II.* In 2003, the 68,870-ton, 1,070-passenger *Crystal Serenity* joined the fleet, with all the features found on the first two vessels plus numerous additional facilities. Eighty-five percent of the accommodations on *Crystal Serenity* sport verandas.

The 461 staterooms on *Symphony* are composed of the two 982-square-foot Crystal Penthouses, 19 additional penthouse suites measuring 491 square feet, 44 penthouses at 367 feet, 214 outside deluxe staterooms with verandas, and 182 additional outside staterooms. All penthouses and staterooms have twin beds that convert to queen- or king-size beds, 100 percent Egyptian cotton sheets, plush duvets, sitting areas, stocked mini-refrigerators, hair dryers, robes, makeup mirrors, private safes, showers and bathtubs, large closets, writing-makeup desks, voice mail, 14-channel color TV/DVD, and radio systems that include CNN, TNT, Fox News, CNBC, and ESPN. All accommodations at every price level are tastefully decorated with light woods and soft pastels, and patrons are supplied with fresh fruit daily, as well as 24-hour room service. All non-veranda cabins on *Symphony* have large picture windows, and all bathrooms have double vanities. A "pillow menu" allows guests to select from four different kinds of pillows to fit their individual requirements. The Crystal Penthouses feature butler service, over-sized Jacuzzis, Jacuzzi-tub-showers, an additional enclosed shower stall, 35-inch flat-screen color television, DVD, CD, stereo equipment, and walk-in closets. Describing the accommodations on these ships is more akin to describing the accommodations at a luxury resort rather than on oceangoing vessels.

During its renovation in 2004, *Crystal Symphony* received a new Feng Shui-designed spa and fitness center, expanded computer facilities, and a new Vintage Room that accommodates 12 to 14 guests for the cruise line's exclusive Wine-Makers dinner. Additional renovations in 2006 included redecorating and adding 20" LCD flat-screen TVs to all staterooms, reconstructing the bathrooms, adding a new nightclub, and redesigning the casino, Bistro Café, specialty restaurants, Computer University at Sea, and shops.

The 535 staterooms and suites on *Crystal Serenity* are composed of four 1,345 square-foot Crystal Penthouses (one can really spread out here), 32 538-square-foot penthouse suites, 72 403-square-foot penthouses, 82 269-square-foot penthouse staterooms (spread over two decks), 274 269-square-foot deluxe staterooms with verandas, and 70 226-square-foot outside deluxe staterooms. Again, 87 percent of the accommodations have private verandas. In 2007, 20 additional third-berth accommodations were added, bringing the total to 165. Each category is considerably larger than on other ships of this size. All the features found on the *Symphony* can be found on this ship as well. All penthouse accommodations include butler service, complimentary fully stocked bar in room upon embarkation, complimentary soft drinks and bottled water in room throughout the cruise, complimentary shoeshine service, and numerous other amenities.

The central focus of both ships is the magnificent Crystal Plaza atrium lobby. Leading off this area are a casino; disco; piano bar; 202-seat Hollywood Theater; bistro offering an assortment of international coffees, wines, pastries, and gourmet snacks; and a 3,000-square-foot shopping area (3,692 square feet on *Crystal Serenity*). A number of lounges, bars, and showrooms (including the observation lounges) afford 270-degree views. The Crystal Casino features slot machines, craps, baccarat, poker, and roulette tables. Elaborate Broadway-style productions are offered throughout the cruise, in addition to cabaret entertainers, classical concerts, and several dance bands. Crystal offers the best entertainment in the luxury cruise market.

The recently expanded Crystal spas offer yoga, Pilates, aerobics, personal training, indoor cycling classes, and state-of-the-art Kineses strength-training equipment (coordinated by a full-time fitness director) as well as an assortment of exercise equipment (treadmills on *Serenity* have individual TVs), saunas, and steam rooms. Featured at Feng Shui-designed Crystal salons are a new range of innovative face and body treatments including facials; massages; makeup instruction; eye, hair, and scalp treatments; manicures; and hairstyling. There are two swimming pools on *Symphony:* the Seahorse pool, with two adjacent Jacuzzis, and the Neptune indoor/outdoor pool, with a swim-up bar serving all beverages, hot dogs, hamburgers, pizza, ice-cream creations, and deli sandwiches. Additionally, a full promenade deck winds around the ship, and there is an outdoor track above the pool for jogging or walking, a paddle-tennis court, skeet shooting, and shuffleboard.

Additional facilities found on *Crystal Serenity* include a sushi bar, casual evening restaurant on deck, larger spa and more treatment rooms, expanded gym and aerobics studio, two outdoor whirlpools, second indoor/outdoor pool covered by a magrodome roof, second paddle-tennis court, golf driving range, The Studio—home of the line's Creative Learning Institute—and an expanded Computer University at Sea classroom.

The Creative Learning Institute features educational classes in foreign languages, estate planning, wine appreciation, gourmet cooking, interior design, skin care, beginner keyboard lessons, makeup artistry, jewelry design, tai chi, sewing and pattern making; wellness enrichment lectures by historians, celebrities, and financial experts; recently released and classic movies; dance classes; and numerous other activities offered daily. The abundance and variety of upscale/sophisticated activities, especially on sea days, is possibly the most impressive in the industry.

Crystal has introduced a more extensive children's program to attract family travelers. Additional third berths have been added to all categories of staterooms and suites; a designated children's playroom is available; and supervised, age-appropriate programs for guests ages 17 and under are also featured. On select cruises, children 11 and under sharing accommodations with two adults travel free.

Crystal was the first cruise line to offer alternative dinner restaurants at no extra charge. In addition to luxurious main dining rooms, passengers can opt for the superb Italian cuisine in the romantic Prego Restaurants on both vessels, which now feature dishes of the critically acclaimed Valentino Restaurants in Los Angeles and Las Vegas. World-class master chef Nobuyuki "Nobu" Matsuhisa has designed the menus and added his touch of excellence to two specialty restaurants, Silk Road and the Sushi Bar, also on both ships. Dining at the specialty restaurants is complimentary; however, a seven-dollar per person gratuity is suggested. During each cruise, special Wine-Maker dinners are offered in the Vintage Room for four to 14 guests at a charge of $180+ per person depending on the wines chosen.

Casual breakfast and lunch buffets are offered both indoors and alfresco at the Lido Café near the pools. On some days at sea, lavish theme buffets are attractively presented by the pool. On select evenings, special dinners are also offered poolside. All meals, as well as snacks, are available around the clock through extensive room-service menus. Penthouse guests can order room service from the specialty restaurants as well as from the dining room. Smoked salmon and other expensive delicacies are offered at the buffets, and hot and cold hors d'oeuvres are served each evening in the lounges. The breakfast buffet includes freshly made omelets, Belgian waffles, delicious pastries, fresh fruits, and other standard items, while the luncheon buffets offer numerous eclectic dishes, freshly made pasta, Caesar salad, and a variety of delectable desserts. Tastes, just outside the Lido Café, offers specialty comfort food for lunch and dinner when weather permits. The Bistro provides specialty coffees, other beverages, and attractive gourmet snacks throughout the day—ideal for those who miss breakfast or lunch, or just feel like visiting over a cup of cappuccino. Afternoon tea with appropriate teatime fare is offered each afternoon at the Palm Court along with musical entertainment. Passengers ensconced in the penthouses enjoy an initial setup of complimentary liquors, nightly hors d'oeuvres and/or caviar trays in their rooms, free pressing, shoe shines, personalized stationery, and personal butler services.

Since 2004, special low-carb dishes have been offered in all restaurants, including the specialty dining rooms and Lido Café. Guests requiring kosher-prepared cuisine must notify the cruise line 90 days in advance of sailing. In addition, Crystal Cruises offers its own proprietary label, "C Wines," which includes cabernet sauvignon, chardonnay, and merlot premium and reserve selections. In 2007, Crystal became the first cruise line to be trans-fat free.

Other special features available to all passengers include 24-hour front-desk service, two European-trained concierges to assist with travel and land arrangements, a Crystal Ambassador (gentleman) host program for the mature ladies, self-service launderettes throughout the ship, satellite telephone service, descriptive videos of all shore excursions, and access to private business offices equipped with computers, tele-faxes, and secretarial services on request. The ships often feature on-board enrichment programs. Both vessels offer Computer University at Sea, an extensive program enabling passengers to take group and private lessons on using a computer, accessing the World Wide Web, designing and publishing a Web site, editing digital videos, and sending e-mails. Over 30 computers are available around the clock for cruisers who wish to send e-mails or surf the Internet. In 2006, additional wireless Internet and cell phone service was added, allowing passengers to use their laptops, cell phones, and smart phones while at sea. However, certain areas of the ships such as restaurants and theaters are designated cell phone free. In 2009, Crystal introduced technology concierges, a complimentary service offered through the Computer University at Sea, to educate guests about the various gadgets they travel with, such as the iPod, iPhone, BlackBerry, Garmin, and Colorado 400c navigation device.

A pre- and post-cruise hotel program features luxury hotels in 22 embarkation/debarkation cities and includes such world-famous properties as the Hassler in Rome, Cipriani in Venice, Hermitage in Monte Carlo, Bel Air in Los Angeles, Dorchester in London, and Mandarin Oriental in Hong Kong.

During the year, numerous theme cruises are offered: classical music, ballroom dancing, jazz and big bands, tai chi, yoga and Pilates, wine and food, golf, and arts/antiquities.

Crystal's ships visit 185 ports worldwide. Over 1,500 Crystal Adventures shore excursions are offered, including customized off-ship adventures. *Crystal Serenity* also offers a 100+-day, around-the-world itinerary (able to be purchased in segments).

Crystal offers a uniquely excellent cruise experience that combines the impeccable service, gourmet dining, and spacious accommodations found on the small, luxury, yacht-like vessels with the state-of-the-art facilities and high-caliber entertainment and activities offered on the major ships of today's most popular cruise lines.

Prices average about $500 per day, per person for a deluxe outside stateroom. Crystal Penthouses run over $2,000. However, lower tariffs are offered frequently on select cruises.

Strong Points:

A large variety of sophisticated activities including excellent educational programs, excellent dining and service, spacious and comfortable accommodations in all categories, special pampering for penthouse category occupants, and the ultimate in luxury on large, full-facility ships. The line is considered by many reviewers, surveys, and seasoned cruisers to be the best of the large luxury ships afloat.

Courtesy Crystal Cruises

Courtesy Crystal Cruises

Courtesy Crystal Cruises

Courtesy Crystal Cruises

Courtesy Crystal Cruises

Courtesy Crystal Cruises

Courtesy Crystal Cruises

Courtesy Crystal Cruises

CAPTAIN'S GALA

Captain's Gala Welcome Dinner

Saturday, September 1, 2007
Crystal Dining Room, Crystal Serenity
At Sea, en Route to Civitavecchia (Rome), Italy

Maître d'Hôtel **Leo Assmair**   Executive Chef **Tamas Toth**

I would like to extend a warm welcome to all our guests aboard Crystal Serenity for this joyous occasion. I am pleased to celebrate this Gala Evening with you. Bon Voyage and Bon Appétit.

Captain Glenn Edvardsen, Commander

VEGETARIAN SELECTIONS

Selected Fruits presented in a Pineapple Boat, Sprinkled with Grand Marnier

Wild Forest Mushroom Soup "Cappuccino Style"

Maple Glazed Sweet Potato Soufflé
With Grilled Asparagus & Parsnips and Red Wine Reduction

Crunchy Vanilla Mousse with Fudge Sauce

ON THE LIGHTER SIDE

Crystal Cruises responds to today's trend toward dishes lighter in cholesterol, carbohydrates, fat and sodium by offering these special selections:

Captain's Salad
Selected Bouquet of Fresh Garden Lettuce with Cherry Tomatoes,
Cucumbers, Fresh Mushrooms, Sprouts and Aubergine Chips,
Served with Walnut-Balsamic Dressing

Broiled Fillet of Atlantic Halibut
Served on a Bed of Steamed Spinach with Baby Vegetables
Topped with Plum Tomato and Olive Ragoût

Freshly Frozen, Nonfat German Chocolate Yogurt

HEAD SOMMELIER'S SUGGESTIONS

Champagne by the Glass:
Billecart Salmon Rosé, Brut, Mareuil-Sur-Ay, France NV $19.00

White Wine
By the Bottle: Chardonnay, Far Niente Winery, Napa Valley, California 2005 $85.00
By the Glass: Chardonnay, Grgich Hills Cellars, Napa Valley, California 2004 $16.00

Red Wine
By the Bottle: Insignia, Joseph Phelps Vineyard, Napa Valley 2001 $198.00
By the Glass: Cabernet Sauvignon, Cuvaison Estate Wines, Napa Valley 2004 $10.00
For our complete selection of fine wines by the glass, please ask your Sommelier.

CRYSTAL CRUISES

APPETIZERS

Iced Malossol Caviar with Sour Cream, Chopped Eggs and Onions,
Accompanied by Melba Toast and Buckwheat Blinis

Pâté de Foie Gras with Port Wine Jelly and Toasted Brioche

Fresh Fine Claire Oysters
Served on Crushed Ice with Red Wine Shallot Vinaigrette and Cocktail Sauce

Selected Fruits presented in a Pineapple Boat, Sprinkled with Grand Marnier

SOUP AND SALAD

Wild Forest Mushroom Soup "Cappuccino Style"

Clear Oxtail Soup
With Sherry, Wild Rice, Vegetables and Chester Sesame Sticks
Low-sodium soups are available upon request

Captain's Salad
Selected Bouquet of Fresh Garden Lettuce with Cherry Tomatoes, Cucumbers, Fresh
Mushrooms, Sprouts and Aubergine Chips, Served with Walnut-Balsamic Dressing
Traditional favorite dressings available, plus today's specials:
Fat-Free Honey Lime or Low-Calorie Carrot Cucumber Dressing

PASTA SPECIAL

Spinach Tagliatelle Tossed with Alfredo Sauce
Sun-Dried Tomatoes, Chanterelles and Fava Beans

SHERBET

Refreshing Passion Fruit Bellini Sherbet

SALAD ENTRÉE

Beef Tenderloin Salad
Bouquet of Garden Greens tossed with Sherry-Walnut Vinaigrette, Topped with
Sliced Beef Tenderloin, Sprinkled with Pecan Nuts and Served with Crisp Lavosh

MAIN FARES

Broiled Fresh Lobster from Maine with Melted Butter or Sauce Hollandaise,
Served with Steamed Green Asparagus and Truffled Leek Risotto

Pan-Fried Fillet of Atlantic Halibut on a Potato Galette,
Served with Baby Squash and Champagne Beurre Blanc,
Topped with Plum Tomato-Saffron Confit

Châteaubriand – Sliced Black Angus Beef Tenderloin with Port Wine Gravy,
Served with Baby Vegetables and Duchesse Potatoes

Marinated, Baked Quail with Porcini Stuffing, Honey Braised Summer Cabbage,
Thyme-Roasted Artichokes, Glazed Baby Carrots and Madeira Sauce

*Upon your request, these **Traditional Main Fares** are also available:*
Grilled Black Angus New York Cut Sirloin Steak with Baked Potato, Spring Vegetables and Green Peppercorn
Hollandaise or Plain Grilled Chicken Breast with Mashed Potatoes, Asparagus Spears and Natural Gravy

SIDE ORDERS

Champagne-Honey Braised Cabbage   Asparagus Spears   Assorted Vegetables
Truffled Leek Risotto   Herb Potatoes   Spaghetti with Tomato Sauce

Upon request, dishes are available without sauce, and main courses can be served as half portions.
Vegetables are also available steamed, without butter or salt.

CRYSTAL CRUISES

Courtesy Crystal Cruises

Daytime Activities

Good Morning

TIME	EVENT	PLACE	DECK
7:00am – 4:00pm	**Crystal Today** with Cruise Director Gary Hunter. Repeated until 4:00pm.	TV Channel 53	
7:30am ★	**Morning Walk On Water with the WALKVEST®** with Sports Director David.	Promenade Deck Aft	7
8:00am ★	**Fitness Class: *Stretch and Relax*** with Fitness Instructor Alwyn.	Fitness Center	13
8:00am	**Catholic Mass** is celebrated by Msgr. Joseph Bixenman.	Hollywood Theatre	6
8:30am – 12 Noon	**The Library is Open** to check out books, games, CDs & DVDs for your enjoyment. Drop by to pick up the daily quiz and/or sign-up for the afternoon games get-together.	Library	7
9:00am	**Captain's Update.** The latest weather and navigation information.	PA System & Channel 68	
9:05am	**Interdenominational Service** is conducted by Msgr. Joseph Bixenman.	Hollywood Theatre	6
9:05am ★	**Yamaha Passport to Music, Class A** with instructor Debbie Skinner. All guests are welcome.	The Studio	7
9:30am	**Salon Seminar: Barbering** with Spa Therapist Jeffrey. Learn about the various treatments we have just for men as well as barbering services we offer on board.	Spa/Salon	13
10:00am	**Crystal Visions Enrichment Program.** Military Historian Dr. Conrad Crane presents "From Rome to Nagasaki: Bat Bombs, A-Bombs, and Other Notable Air Operations of WWII." *(Repeated from 1:00pm to 7:00pm on TV Ch. 54, alternating with 11:00am lecture)*	Hollywood Theatre	6
10:00am	**Beginners' Bridge Class:** "All Hands on Deck" with Instructors Andy & Cheryl Halpern.	Bridge Lounge	7
10:00am ★	**TaylorMade® Golf Clinic:** "The Full Swing: Swing Motion and Posture" with PGA Professional Roberto Borgatti. *(The golf nets are located on Deck 6 Aft, accessible down the stairwells on Deck 7 Aft.)*	Sports Area	6
10:00am	**Paddle Tennis Open Play** with Sports Director David and fellow guests. For your safety, please wear proper tennis shoes.	Wimbledon Court	13
10:30am	**Team Trivia** with the Entertainment Staff.	Stardust Club	6
10:30am	**Spa Seminar: Ionithermie** with Spa Therapist Melissa. Europe's #1 treatment. Find out how to increase circulation, firm and tone the skin and improve skin texture.	Avenue Saloon	6
11:00am	**Crystal Visions Enrichment Program.** Memory Expert Dr. Fred Chernow discusses "Simple Tips for Remembering Names." How to quickly match the face with the name when being introduced. Also strategies for remembering the names of their family members, home towns, and occupations. *(Repeated from 1:00pm to 7:00pm on TV Ch. 54, alternating with 10:00am lecture)*	Hollywood Theatre	6
11:00am ★	**Berlitz Conversational Italian, Class A** with Instructor Martha Rodriguez. All guests welcome.	The Studio	7
11:00am	**Intermediate Bridge Class:** "Cruising into Successful Slams" with Instructors Andy & Cheryl Halpern.	Bridge Lounge	7
11:00am	**Scarf Tying Lesson** with Activities Hostess Naomi.	Lido Café Aft	12
11:00am	**Fitness Seminar: *Detox for Weight Loss*** with Fitness Instructor Alwyn.	Fitness Center	13
11:30am	**Shuffleboard** with Sports Director David and fellow guests.	Promenade Deck	7
11:30am – 12:30pm	**Thomas Daniels** plays the Crystal piano for your midday cocktail pleasure.	Crystal Cove	5

★ Indicates Creative Learning Institute activity.

Good Afternoon

Time	Activity	Location	Deck
12 Noon – 1:00pm	**Complimentary Gaming Lessons** with the Casino staff.	Crystal Casino	6
12:30pm – 1:30pm	**Enjoy Poolside Music** with The Crystal Sextet. *(weather permitting)*	Seahorse Pool	12
1:30pm	**Crystal Visions Enrichment Lecture.** Special Interest Lecturer, "Renaissance Man" Fred Plotkin discusses "Cinema Italiano: Italy's Greatest Films and Stars" followed by the Oscar-nominated 1958 Italian film "Big Deal on Madonna Street (*Soliti ignoti, I*). at 2:30pm. *(Repeated from 7:00pm to Midnight on TV Ch. 54.)*	Hollywood Theatre	6
1:30pm ★	**Yamaha Passport to Music, Class B** with Instructor Debbie Skinner. All guests welcome.	The Studio	7
1:30pm	**Complimentary Dance Class** with Instructors Balin Kolbig and James Stout, and the Ambassador Hosts. Learn the **Salsa.**	Palm Court	12
1:30pm – 6:00pm	**The Library is Open** to check out books, games, CDs and DVDs for your enjoyment.	Library	7
2:00pm	**Free Slot Tournament.** Come and try your luck in the casino.	Crystal Casino	6
2:00pm ★	**Computer University@Sea Class**: "Introductory Computing using Vista" with Instructor Erin Manning. *(For pre-registered guests)*	CU@Sea	7
2:00pm	**Spa Seminar: 5-minute Make-over** with Spa Therapist Gillian. Discover how this natural bronzing powder leaves you with healthy glow.	Avenue Saloon	6
2:00pm – 2:30pm	**Needlepoint Hand-Out** with Activities Hostess Naomi. Beginner's class will be held on the next sea day, September 5. *(Guest must be present to receive a kit; one kit per person.)*	Lido Café, Port	12
2:15pm (Preview) (2:45pm Auction)	**Champagne Art Auction** with Art Director Tim. We have an exceptional display of modern masters showcased here today including hand signed works by Picasso, Dali, and Chagall. Experience the fun and excitement of a live art auction with savings of up to 85% below gallery retail prices. Complimentary champagne will be served and somebody must win a $1000 work of framed art at the main event of the afternoon with your Art Director Tim.	Crystal Plaza	5
2:30pm	**Duplicate and Social Bridge** with Instructors Andy & Cheryl Halpern.	Bridge Lounge	7
2:30pm	**Paddle Tennis Open-Play** with Sports Director David and fellow guests. For your safety, please wear proper tennis shoes.	Wimbledon Court	13
2:30pm ★	**TaylorMade® Golf Clinic** with PGA Golf Professional Roberto Borgatti. "The Full Swing: Turn and Weight Shift." *(The golf nets are located on Deck 6 Aft, accessible down the stairwells on Deck 7 Aft.)*	Sports Area	6
2:30pm	**Movie: Big Deal on Madonna Street (Soliti ignoti, I).** 1958 Italian flim directed by Mario Monicelli, featuring Vitorrio Gassman, Renato Salvatori, Memmo Carotento. Peppe, formerly a boxer, organizes the break-in of a pawnshop. NR; 1:46.	Hollywood Theatre	6
3:00pm ★	**Berlitz Conversational Italian, Class B** with Instructor Martha Rodriguez. All guests welcome.	The Studio	7
3:00pm	**Black Jack Tournament.** Come and try your luck in the casino.	Crystal Casino	6
3:00pm ★	**Odyssey Art at Sea: Venice Motifs** with Instructor Sylvia Hallgren. Roman Holiday. Try a simple sketching technique using watercolor pencils to capture an impression of Rome. All guests welcome.	Lido Café, Aft	12
3:15pm ★	**Computer University@Sea Class**: "Basic Digital Photo Finishing" with Instructor Erin Manning. *(For pre-registered guests)*	CU@Sea	7
3:30pm – 4:30pm	**English Colonial Tea Time** with the Crystal Trio.	Palm Court	12
4:00pm	**Table Tennis Open-Play** with Sports Director David and fellow guests.	Sports Area	6
4:00pm ★	**Fitness Class: Circuit** with Fitness Instructor Alwyn.	Fitness Center	13
4:00pm ★	**Yamaha Passport to Music, Level 2** with Instructor Debbie Skinner.	The Studio	7
4:00pm – 10:00pm	**Crystal Tonight** with Cruise Director Gary Hunter.	TV Channel 53	
4:30pm ★	**Computer University@Sea Lecture:** "Digital Photography 101: Take Better Pictures in a Snap!" with CU@Sea Instructor Erin Manning	Hollywood Theatre	6
4:30pm ★	**Fitness Class: Stretch and Relax** with Fitness Instructor Alwyn.	Fitness Center	13
4:30pm	**Bingo** with the Entertainment Staff. Cards on sale at 4:15pm.	Stardust Club	6
4:30pm ★	**Afternoon Walk On Water with the WALKVEST®** with Sports Director David.	Promenade Deck Aft	7
5:30pm	**Friends of Bill W.** meet in...	Pulse	6

Evening Entertainment

Good Evening

Time	Event	Venue	
5:30pm – 6:15pm & 7:45pm – 8:30pm	**Thomas Daniels** entertains at the Crystal piano. Enjoy cocktails while you listen in the...	Crystal Cove	5
5:30pm – 6:15pm & 7:45pm – 8:30pm	**John Mentis** plays your favorites in our cozy bar. Enjoy cocktails while you listen in the...	Avenue Saloon	6
5:30pm – 6:15pm & 7:45pm – 8:30pm	**Dance to the sounds of The Crystal Sextet** playing for your dancing and listening pleasure. Join the Ambassador Hosts.	Palm Court	12
7:30pm – 11:00pm	**The Library is open** to check out books, CDs & DVDs for your enjoyment during the cruise.	Library	7
8:30pm (one show only)	**Movie: *Pirates of the Caribbean: At World's End*.** Featuring Johnny Depp, Orlando Bloom, and Keira Knightly. Yo ho ho, its our last bottle of rum. When Captain Jack gets taken literally to the end of the world, Will, Elizabeth and Captain Barbossa band together to bring him back in this fun filled adventure. The crew must then employ the help of the nine pirate lords in a final stand against Beckett, Davy Jones and the East India Trade. Rated PG-13; 2:48.	Hollywood Theatre	6
9:30pm – 10:30pm	**Thomas Daniels** entertains at the Crystal piano. Enjoy cocktails while you listen in the...	Crystal Cove	5
9:30pm – 12:30am	**Dance to the sounds of the Crystal Sextet.** Join the Ambassador Hosts.	Palm Court	12
9:30pm – 12:30am	**John Mentis** plays your favorites in our cozy bar.	Avenue Saloon	6
11:00pm – Late	**Late Night Dancing** to the latest hits of today with D.J. Maxi.	Pulse	6
11:15pm – 11:45pm	**The Crystal Trio** plays music in the...	Crystal Plaza	5

8:45pm and 10:30pm • Galaxy Lounge

IN TOWN TONIGHT

Crystal Cruises proudly presents

an opening perfomance by Australian Dance Champions

Balin & James

followed by Headline Entertainer

Dynamic West End Star Philippa Healey

The Voice of an Angel

Accompanied by **The Galaxy Orchestra** under the direction of **Raphaël Derkson**

Crystal Serenity • Monday, September 3, 2007

Courtesy Crystal Cruises

CUNARD LINE

In U.S

24303 Town Center Drive, Suite 200
Valencia, California
(800) 7-Cunard
(661) 753-1000

In U.K.

Richmond House, Terminus Terrace
Southampton, England SO14 3PN
0044 8450710300
0044 2380657018 Fax

www.cunard.com

QUEEN MARY 2: entered service 2004; 150,000 G.R.T.; 1,132' x 135'; 2,592-passenger capacity (3,090 with every berth filled); 1,296 cabins; British officers and international crew; cruises to various areas around the world, including transatlantic crossings between Great Britain and New York, New England/Canada, world cruises, South America, Caribbean, Norway, and Europe.

Queens Grill

Princess Grill

Britannia Restaurant

(Medical Facilities: C-30; P-2; EM, CLS, MS; N-2; CM; PD; EKG; TC; PO; EPC; OX; WC; OR; ICU; X; M.)

QUEEN VICTORIA and *QUEEN ELIZABETH:* entered service in 2007 and 2010, respectively; 90,000 and 92,000 G.R.T., respectively; 964.5' x 106'; 1,980-passenger capacity (2,534 with every berth filled); 1,007 cabins; British officers and international crew; cruises to various areas around the world.

Queens Grill

★ ★ ★ ★ ★ ★ +

Princess Grill

★ ★ ★ ★ ★ ★

Britannia Restaurant

(Medical Facilities: Same as *QM2,* except 20 wheelchair-accessible cabins.)

These ships are rated in 11 separate categories in the second half of chapter 14.

Cunard Line was founded back in 1840 by Samuel Cunard, a merchant from Nova Scotia. His original plan was to provide transatlantic mail service while carrying a few passengers at the same time. The first ship, *Britannia,* was a 1,150-ton paddle-wheel steamer that made the crossing between continents in 14 days.

Over the years, the Cunard flag has flown on such well-known vessels as *Aquitania, Mauretania, Lusitania, Caronia, Franconia, Queen Mary,* and the original *Queen Elizabeth.* Ironically, Cunard Line not only originated transatlantic passenger service nearly 170 years ago but also presently, via *Queen Mary 2,* is the last major cruise line offering regular transatlantic crossings.

Cunard, as a wholly owned subsidiary of the British conglomerate Trafalgar House, was acquired by the Norwegian construction and engineering firm of Kvaerner in 1996 and was resold to Carnival Corporation in May 1998. Carnival Corporation then merged Cunard with Seabourn Cruise Line (a company organized in 1987) to form Cunard Line. One hundred percent of the new cruise line is now owned by Carnival Corporation. Seabourn and Cunard continue to operate as separate brands and Cunard's offices have been divided between California and Southampton, England.

Cunard purchased *Sea Goddess I* and *II* in 1986 and in 1994 acquired *Royal Viking Sun* and all rights to the Royal Viking logo. At the time of the merger with Seabourn, the two *Sea Goddesses* and *Royal Viking Sun* were transferred to the Seabourn brand and renamed *Seabourn Goddess I, Seabourn Goddess II,* and *Seabourn Sun.* Subsequently, the two *Seabourn Goddesses* were sold to the former owner and CEO of Seabourn and renamed *SeaDream I* and *II,* and in April 2002 the *Sun* was transferred to Holland America Line, another subsidiary of Carnival Corporation, and renamed *Prinsendam.*

In the mid-1970s, Cunard built *Princess* and *Countess,* two 17,000-ton ships designed to accommodate the then-emerging mass market of first-time and more economy-minded cruisers. Both of these ships were sold off in the 1990s. In 1983, it acquired *Sagafjord* and *Vistafjord* (subsequently renamed *Caronia*) from the now-defunct Norwegian America Cruises. The *Sagafjord* ceased operating for Cunard in 1996 and the *Caronia* in 2004. Both ships presently sail for Saga Cruises.

In the early 1990s, Cunard acquired the following ships of Crown Cruise Line: *Crown Monarch, Crown Dynasty,* and *Crown Jewel.* However, all of these vessels were subsequently transferred to other cruise lines.

Queen Elizabeth 2 entered service in 1969 and was the flagship of the fleet until the introduction of the *Queen Mary 2.* After she underwent numerous renovations and refurbishments, bringing her into the 21st century, the cruise line finally decided to retire her in 2008, and she is now permanently located as a floating hotel in Dubai at Dubai World Amusement Park.

In January 2004, *Queen Mary 2,* formerly the largest ship in service (prior to Royal Caribbean's *Freedom*-class and *Genesis*-class ships), debuted at approximately 150,000 G.R.T., 1,132 feet long, with a 131-foot beam, accommodating 2,592 passengers. The ship operates transatlantic crossings as well as regular cruises, similar to the itineraries formerly operated by *QE2.* The accommodating crew is composed of more than 50 different nationalities and is no longer mostly British.

In December 2007, *Queen Victoria* made its debut. Although she is somewhat smaller than *Queen Mary 2*, at 90,000 tons, 964.5 feet long, with a 106-foot beam, accommodating 1,980 passengers, she has similar staterooms, suites, restaurants, and common areas to those of the former vessel, but on a smaller scale. *Queen Elizabeth*, with similar dimensions, entered service in October 2010.

Queen Victoria, Queen Mary 2, and *Queen Elizabeth* are unique ships in their continuation of a system whereby passengers paying more for their cabins are entitled to an escalating scale of cabin facilities and different dining rooms, all offering a higher caliber of service and gourmet options. Thus, it is possible to travel less expensively in a small cabin and dine in the Britannia Restaurant or cruise in grand luxury in a suite on both ships and enjoy meals in one of the elegant Grill dining rooms. Irrespective of which category you book, you will have access to the same ship facilities and participate in the same activities and entertainment.

On *Queen Mary 2*, the least expensive cabins start at 157 square feet with the five most expensive Grand Duplex suites coming in between 1,566 and 2,249 square feet and spanning two levels (featuring three baths and giant balconies). Other top-of-the-line accommodations include four forward suites, the Queen Elizabeth and Queen Mary Suites with private elevators (at 1,194 square feet), the Queen Anne and Queen Victoria Suites at 796-square-feet, six 758-square-foot penthouse suites, and a plethora of additional junior and full suites ranging in size from 381 to 506 square feet. Deluxe and premium balcony staterooms measure 248 square feet. Seventy-seven percent of the accommodations have ocean views and three-quarters of these boast balconies. All Queens Grill suites come with butler service, walk-in closets, flat-screen TV, entertainment systems, selected beverages, and spirits and wines. Grill Room guests have access to a special concierge center and exclusive cocktail lounge.

The spa, beauty salon, and wellness and fitness facilities on board, with 24 treatment rooms and a staff of 51, are operated by the prestigious Canyon Ranch. The facilities are beautiful and among the very best at sea. There is a daily charge of $35 for non-spa treatment guests entitling them to use the changing rooms, showers, steam room, sauna, and magnificent aqua therapy center. Although the gym is gratis to all guests, there are no changing rooms or showers other than those at Canyon Ranch. Body and therapy treatments at the spa run from $109 to $239.

The onboard enrichment program, Cunard Insights, introduces guests to stimulating experts and accomplished visionaries who reflect the line's heritage of prestige and the quest for oceangoing adventure. Through a series of lectures, Q&As, debates, social gatherings, and workshops, guests will connect with personalities who have achieved notable distinction in areas including history, world affairs, science, politics, entertainment, the arts, and literature.

QM2 also offers an enrichment program known as "ConneXions," with seven classrooms offering a diverse range of educational courses and dozens of computers with e-mail capabilities. Other innovations include a $5 million art collection; planetarium, the site for a variety of constellation shows, movies, and lectures; British nannies for infant care; kennel for your favorite pet; and interactive televisions (capable of sending and receiving e-mails) in each accommodation.

The passengers booking the most luxurious accommodations have a separate lounge and a separate sun-deck area, and they dine in the Queens Grill and

Princess Grill, while the others dine in the two-seating, 1,351-seat Britannia Restaurant. In 2006, a new "Britannia Club Class" designation was given to 46 deluxe staterooms on deck, 12 of which entitled the occupants to a special single-seating arrangement in an annex to the Britannia Restaurant similar to that in the Grill Rooms. King's Court, a buffet restaurant for breakfast and lunch, transforms into four dining venues featuring Asian, Italian, English Grill, and Chef's Galley. At Chef's Galley, guests watch shipboard and guest chefs prepare their meals with a how-to commentary prior to consumption of culinary treats accompanied by appropriate wines. This is an evening's entertainment for aspiring gourmets. Other alternative dining venues include the outstanding Todd English Restaurant, serving contemporary Mediterranean cuisine, with menus designed by world-famous chef and television personality Todd English. Two more casual options are the Golden Lion Pub, offering traditional British pub favorites, and Boardwalk Café, for hamburgers, hot dogs, fries, and other snacks (weather permitting).

Starting at the top of the ship, on deck 12, you will find a pool area with a sliding-glass roof, the Boardwalk Café, kennels, and some junior suites. Most of the other suites are located on decks 9 through 11. A library, bookstore, beauty salon, some staterooms, and the upper level of the Canyon Ranch SpaClub are on deck 8. The lower level of the spa (including the changing rooms and aqua therapy center), a large three-room gym, and a lounge, as well as the Grill Rooms and buffet restaurants, can be found on deck 7. On deck 6 are numerous staterooms and the children's areas and pool. Additional cabins are on decks 4 and 5. Most public areas (including the remaining restaurants, the show lounge, theater, shopping arcade, casino, numerous bars and lounges, and the main lobby) are located on decks 2 and 3. The various public indoor and outdoor deck areas are somewhat fragmented and not accessible by all elevators. It takes a bit of exploration to become familiar with navigating around the ship. The outdoor lounges and pools are spread among several decks and there is no single central pool/lido/deck chair area, as on many ships. On deck 7, the promenade deck, passengers can walk or jog around the entire deck or lounge in teak deck chairs. The Pets on Deck program provides 12 kennels. For a $300 to $500 fee your puppy receives fresh-baked biscuits at turn down, a choice of beds and blankets, a *QM2* logo coat, name tag and food dish, and a personalized cruise card.

The 90,000-ton, 2,014-passenger (2,504 with every berth filled) *Queen Victoria* joined the fleet in December 2007, well in time to replace the retiring *QE2*. *Queen Victoria* is a beautifully appointed vessel with public areas exuding style and elegance. As on the other Cunard ships, guests booking the most expensive accommodations dine in the Queens or Princess Grill Rooms with expanded menus and pampered service, while the remaining passengers dine in the larger, two-seating Britannia Restaurant, with a somewhat more limited menu, or in the buffet restaurant in the lido area. The Grill Room passengers share a private bar and lounge with their own concierge and alfresco dining courtyard and can sun in exclusive privacy on their own terrace atop ship.

Eighty-six percent of the 1,007 guest accommodations have ocean views and 71 percent sport balconies while 20 are wheelchair accessible. All include twin beds that convert to queens, flat-screen TVs, stocked refrigerators, hair dryers, private safes, a combination desk/makeup furnishing, and a seating area. As you move up from category to category in price, the size, furnishings, storage space, and amenities increase proportionately. The 143 least expensive inside cabins range in size from 152 to 207 square feet and the 146 ocean-view cabins vary from 180 to 197 square feet and feature a small sitting area. In all of the Britannia-category staterooms, storage space is limited and bathrooms are rather small. However, in 2008, drawers were added under the beds to provide extra storage. The 591 balcony cabins measure 249 square feet, including a nice-sized balcony. Those occupying the 61 Princess Grill staterooms enjoy 367 square feet with balcony, enlarged bathrooms with tub, and lounging areas. Most of the luxurious 60 Queens Grill suites vary from 508 to 771 square feet and include large marble bathrooms with whirlpool bathtubs, expansive balconies, and a butler. For the big bucks, you can book one of the two 1,100-square-foot Master Suites or one of the four 2,097-square-foot Grand Suites.

Outdoor deck space includes a midship pool and an aft pool, each with two whirlpools and comfortable lounging chairs. Numerous areas on multiple levels provide more than adequate lounging space. Sport facilities include a deck-tennis court, golf nets, and shuffleboard.

In the spa/fitness center you will find a large, very well-equipped gym where cardio machines have their own TVs, an adjoining aerobic area, a thermal suite, a hydrotherapy pool, an aroma spa, a laconicum, a caldarium, a relaxation area (a daily fee applies for non-treatment guests), a men and women's salon, and treatment rooms offering a bevy of spa treatments and rituals.

The classic-style, multilevel Royal Court Theater seating 830 features reservation-only private boxes where for $25 per person, guests can enjoy preshow dessert, coffee, and champagne in a private lounge. The two-deck Queens Room is the spot for traditional English afternoon tea and evening ballroom dancing. For those wishing to imbibe, there are 13 bars, including the stylish Clicquot Champagne Bar serving caviar, a whiskey bar, a wine bar, and the English pub-style Golden Lion Pub featuring typical English fare, music sing-alongs, and TV sports. In addition to a large Internet café, there is a computer-learning center offering classes throughout each cruise.

At the Royal Arcade there are 4,000 square feet of shops featuring upscale merchandise. The two-story, traditionally styled English library features 6,000 books (second largest at sea, only exceeded by the 8,000-book library on QM2). Nearby is a well-stocked bookstore offering bestsellers and nautically themed books.

Other public areas include several elegant observation lounges atop ship; a cigar room; card, game, and meeting rooms; children's playrooms; a large casino; a floating museum showcasing Cunard memorabilia; and numerous quiet lounging areas.

The reservation-only, alternative dining restaurant, Todd English, provides innovative, gourmet cuisine for a $20 surcharge at lunch and $30 at dinner. Café Carinthia offers pastries and specialty coffees and teas, and English pub food is available at lunchtime at the Golden Lion Pub.

The dress code on Cunard ships is a great deal more stringent than on other cruise lines. Men are expected to wear jackets to dinner, except on occasional casual evenings, and for several evenings each week formal attire is suggested.

A new 90,000-ton, 2,092-passenger ocean liner, *Queen Elizabeth,* will enter service in October 2010. She is named after Cunard's first *Queen Elizabeth,* the ship launched in 1938 as the world's largest liner. Although different in décor and featuring various innovations, the ship's layout is quite similar to that of the *Queen Victoria.* Beneath the Garden Lounge (with a vaulted glass ceiling which creates a conservatory feel) guests can enjoy supper clubs and mix dining with dancing under the stars. The Games Deck will offer paddle tennis, croquet, and traditional British bowls under a canopy shielding guests from the sun. The aft outdoor space on deck 9 will be the venue for a new concept of entertainment with garden parties reminiscent of those held at British country houses. In addition to the Queens and Princess Grill rooms for the top-suite passengers, the Britannia Club, having first debuted aboard *Queen Mary 2,* features a private dining room with single seating dining for those guests in the top balcony staterooms.

Strong Points:

These are grand ships that exude class and tradition with great facilities, loads of entertainment, and fine dining. For those who can pay the price, the Grill rooms allow passengers to enjoy greater stateroom comfort, better dining, more pampering, and an especially elegant, sophisticated experience. Those that believe "bigger is better" will adore *QM2,* while those who don't will find very similar amenities on the smaller *Queen Victoria.*

Queen Victoria, *courtesy Cunard Cruise Line*

Queen's Grill on QM2, *courtesy Cunard Line*

Exterior of QM2, *courtesy Cunard Line*

Princess Grill, courtesy Cunard Line

DAILY PROGRAMME

THE MOST FAMOUS OCEAN LINERS IN THE WORLD℠

CAPTAIN PAUL WRIGHT, MASTER
ROBERT HOWIE, HOTEL MANAGER
RAY ROUSE, CRUISE DIRECTOR

QUEEN MARY 2
THURSDAY 3RD MARCH 2005
SUNRISE 6:22AM SUNSET 6:16PM

VOYAGE STATS

Caribbean Adventure Cruise

The Dress for tonight is Formal: Tuxedo (alternatively a dark suit) for gentlemen. Evening gown or other appropriate attire for the ladies. Dress Codes will be enforced in the Britannia and Grill Restaurants.

Wine Tasting

For more details, see the 'New Horizons' page or ask your Sommelier.

Horse Racing & Auction

Bets open at 2:00pm and the race followed by the auction at 2:30pm.
Terrace Bar Deck 8 Aft.

Cocktail of the Day
'Piñacolada'
Cool & smooth
Only $3.95!
White Rum, Coconut Cream & Pineapple Juice.

Martini of the Day
'Karma Electra'
Only $4.25!
Absolut Mandarin, Midori, Chambord, Orange Juice & Sprite.

Martini Mixology
&
Cocktail Mixology
For more details, see the 'Shipboard Information' page!

Celebrity Guest
Mickey Rooney

**At 12:15pm
in the Royal Court Theatre**
Interview with Mickey Rooney

At 4:00pm in Illuminations
Mickey Rooney introduces his film
"Strike Up the Band"

Today's Highlights...

Royal Court Theatre Decks 2 & 3
11:00am Port & Shopping Advisor Jamie Sage: " Curaçao & Bonaire."

Illuminations Deck 3 Forward
9:30am Enrichment Lecturer Dr. David Pasta: "When Will the World Run Out Of Oil?"

10:30am Maritime Historian Bill Miller: "Sailing to the Sun: Tales of the Great Cruise Ships."

2:45pm Enrichment Lecturer Myles Standish: "CalTech's Jet Propulsion Laboratory."

ConneXions Room 2 Deck 2
3:00pm Travel Writer & Fellow Guest Steven Stern: Question & Answer Session and Booksigning.

Spectacular Showtime
The Royal Cunard Singers & Dancers
'Zing Went the Strings'
8:45pm & 10:45pm
in the Royal Court Theatre
presented by your Cruise Director Ray Rouse

This is an original production show, which is an affectionate tribute to the songs, films and life of one of the most adored divas of our time. It is an acknowledgement of the contribution and influences Judy Garland made to many of today's greatest stars.

Cruise Director Ray's quote of the day - Courtesy of Mickey Rooney
You always pass failure on the way to success.

Environmental Compliance HOTLINE 1 (888) 290-5105 (North America) | environmental@carnival.com

OH WHAT A NIGHT!

Showtime Spectacular

Presented by your Cruise Director,
Ray Rouse
8:45pm & 10:45pm

presenting

'Zing Went the Strings'

starring

The Royal Cunard Singers & Dancers

Music by the Royal Court Theatre Orchestra
under the direction of Musical Director
Patrick O'Neil.

Ballroom & Latin Dancing

10:00pm - 12:15am
Dance to the music of the Queens
Room Orchestra with vocalist Paul
Ritchie.

Pianist Manon Robert

7:30pm - 8:30pm
10:00pm - Midnight
Join Manon at the piano.

Movie Matinee

'Strike Up the Band'

4:00pm A Musical/Comedy starring
Mickey Rooney and Judy Garland.
2hrs, Cert: Not rated

**Introduced by our Celebrity Guest
Mickey Rooney.**

This Evening's Movie

'Shall We Dance'

8:00pm & 10:30pm A Romantic
Comedy starring Richard Gere,
Jennifer Lopez and Susan Sarandon.
1hr 46mins, Cert: PG-13.

Pianist Paul Madden

5:00pm - 6:00pm
Paul plays some melodies for you.

Jazz In The Pub

7:45pm - 8:45pm
9:45pm - 11:00pm
Unwind with cool jazz sounds.
Sing your favourite song!

Karaoke

11:00pm - Late
Come and be a singing sensation!

Pre-Dinner Cocktails

At 5:30pm, Enjoy pre-dinner drinks

Pianist Paul Madden

7:45pm - 8:30pm
Join Paul at the piano.

Harpist Ellen Smith

5:15pm - 6:15pm
Beautiful melodies with Ellen.

Pianist Paul Madden

6:30pm - 7:15pm
Paul entertains you at the piano.

Barrington (Barty) Brown

7:30pm - 8:30pm
9:45pm - Late
Words and music by Irving Berlin, The
Gershwins, Cole Porter, and more of
your favourites.

DJ Smudge

10:00pm - 10:45pm

Groovy 70's

11:45pm - 12:15am
DJ Smudge takes you back in time to
the fab & groovy 70's. Yeah baby!!

1:30am - Late
Dance the night away in the G32. No
persons under the age of 18 are permitted after Midnight.

Show Band Xtasea

10:45pm - 11:45pm
12:15am - 1:30am
Enjoy all your favourite hits.

Con Fuoco String Quartet

9:45pm - 10:45pm
Join the quartet in the lobby.

TODAY AT A GLANCE

8:00am	CR Life Skills Conditioning
	- *Knightsbridge Room Deck 1*
8:30am	Catholic Holy Mass - *Illuminations Deck 3 Fwd*
9:00am	Beginners Bridge Class - *Atlantic Room Deck 11*
	Golf Simulator Open until 5:00pm
	- *The Fairways, Pavilion Pool Area Deck 12*
	CR Yoga For Everyone - *Knightsbridge Room Deck 1*
9:30am	Enrichment Lecturer: Dr. David Pasta
	- *Illuminations Deck 3 Fwd*
	Crossword Puzzles and Brainteasers available
	- *QM2 Bookshop & Library Deck 8*
9:45am	Line Dance Class - *Queens Room Deck 3*
10:00am	Creative Arts Class: Verla Brown $35 fee for
	Watercolour Supplies - *Chelsea Room Deck 1*
	CR Pilates Matwork - *Knightsbridge Room Deck 1*
10:15am	Shuffleboard Competition
	- *Starboard Side Courts Deck 12*
	Informal Card Play - *Beside the Royal Court*
	Theatre Deck 2 Starboard Side
10:30am	Bingo Cards go on Sale - *Queens Room Deck 3*
	Art Preview - *Winter Garden Deck 7*
	Maritime Historian: Bill Miller
	- *Illuminations Deck 3 Fwd*
	Napkin Folding - *Champagne Bar Deck 3*
	Intermediate Bridge Class - *Atlantic Room Deck 11*
11:00am	Bingo Commences - *Queens Room Deck 3*
	Art Auction - *Winter Garden Deck 7*
	Port & Shopping Lecture: Jamie Sage
	- *Royal Court Theatre Decks 2 & 3*
	Quoits Competition
	- *Starboard Side Courts, Deck 13*
11:30am	Pub Team Trivia - *Golden Lion Pub Deck 2*

Noon	Planetarium Films "Infinity Express" (Noon,
	12:35pm, 1:05pm & 1:40pm)
	- *Illuminations Deck 3 Forward*
12:15pm	Interview with Mickey Rooney
	- *Royal Court Theatre Decks 2 & 3*
	Dance Class - *Queens Room Deck 3*
	Pub Lunch Melodies - *Golden Lion Pub Deck 2*
	Lunchtime Melodies - *Chart Room Deck 3*
12:30pm	Show Band Xtasea - *Terrace Bar Deck 8 Aft*
	Harpist Ellen Smith - *Winter Garden Deck 7*

1:00pm	Interest Corner: Friends of Dorothy
	- *Commodore Club Deck 9*
2:00pm	Horse Bets Open - *Terrace Bar Deck 8 Aft*
	Duplicate Bridge - *Atlantic Room Deck 11*
2:15pm	Informal Card Play (repeat of 10:15am)
2:30pm	Horse Races & Auction - *Terrace Bar Deck 8 Aft*
	Table Tennis Competition - *Pavilion Deck 12*
2:45pm	Enrichment Lecturer: Myles Standish
	- *Illuminations Deck 3 Fwd*
	Cocktail Mixology - *Pavilion Bar Deck 12*
3:00pm	Wine Tasting - *Britannia Restaurant Deck 2*
	Martini Mixology - *Commodore Club Deck 9*
	Q & A Session and Booksigning with travel
	writer and fellow guest Steven Stern
	- *ConneXions Room 2 Deck 2*
	Queen Mary Reunion - Guests who sailed on
	Queen Mary 1936-67 - *Chart Room Deck 3*
	CR Lower Body Conditioning
	- *Knightsbridge Room Deck 1*
	Interest Corner: Friends of Bill W.
	- *Boardroom Deck 9*
3:15pm	Ice Carving - *Terrace Bar Deck 8 Aft*
	Men's Darts Tournament
	- *Golden Lion Pub Deck 2*
4:00pm	Matinee Movie: "Strike Up The Band" Introduced
	by Mickey Rooney - *Illuminations Deck 3 Fwd*
	FREE '44y Pitching' Competition
	- *The Fairways, Pavilion Pool Area Deck 12*
	CR Dance Aerobics - *Knightsbridge Room Deck 1*
4:30pm	Wipe Out Quiz - *Golden Lion Pub Deck 2*
5:15pm	CR Restorative Yoga - *Knightsbridge Room Deck 1*

Everything you wanted to know about cruising
and were afraid to ask!

Steven Stern, author of *Stern's Guide to the Cruise Vacation* and *Stern's Guide to the Greatest Resorts of the World* will be conducting a Booksigning and Informal Q&A in ConneXions Room 2 Deck 2 at 3:00pm this afternoon!

Knightsbridge Room - (1 Deck) C Stairway;
Chelsea Room - (1 Deck) B Stairway;
Interest Corners - Un-hosted social get-togethers;
CR - Canyon Ranch SpaClub.

Courtesy Cunard Line

BRITANNIA RESTAURANT

Dinner
Wednesday 28th January 2004

APPETIZERS AND SOUPS

Braised Chicken & Roasted Artichoke Barigoule
Char Grilled Bell Peppers With Humus & Italian Flat Bread *(V)*
$^{C}_{R}$ Arugula Salad with Roasted Tomatoes & Parmesan Cheese 95/5/3 *(V)*
Marinated Shrimp, Sweet Soy Dressing & Creamed Wasabi Puree
White Cheddar Cheese Soup
Clear Oxtail Essence, Sherry Wine, Chester Stick

SALADS

Baby Spinach, Oak Leaf With Aged Balsamic Dressing
Potato, Egg & Scallion Salad, Crispy Pancetta

$^{C}_{R}$ Indicates dishes created and recommended by Canyon Ranch SpaClub   Nutrition Key : Calories / Fat Grams / Fiber Grams   *(V)* Indicates dishes suitable for Vegetarians

BRITANNIA RESTAURANT

ENTRÉES

Braised Beef Ravioli, Tomato Sauce, Toasted Garlic & Fresh Oregano

Poached Scottish Salmon, Braised Vegetables, Parsley Nage

C_R Raspberry Mustard-Crusted Chicken Breast with Fig Balsamic Vinegar 440/11/6

Double Cut Lamb Cutlets, Herbes de Provence Natural Jus

Slow Roasted Beef Rib, Braised Onion Confit & Fondant Potato

Aubergine Mushroom Lasagna, Mushroom Foam Jus *(V)*

DESSERT MENU

Baklava with Pistachio Anglaise and Cinnamon Ice Cream

Iced Grand Marnier Souffle, Warm Chocolate Sauce

Cherry Jubilee with Vanilla Ice Cream

C_R Apple Strudel 160/4/2

Sugar Free - Raspberry Chocolate Cake

Banana and Vanilla Ice Cream with Blueberry Frozen Yogurt, Kiwi Sauce

Cheese Selection with Port Salut, Goat's Cheese, Danish Blue, Edam Cheese

Courtesy Cunard Line

PRINCESS GRILL

Dinner
Wednesday, 2nd March 2005

CANYON RANCH SPA SELECTION
Appetizer — Cold Sesame Noodle Salad 125/5/2 *(V)*
Entrée — Grilled Basa with Green Tomato Relish & Grits Cake 250/13/4
Dessert — Pecan Tart 150/8/1

APPETIZERS AND SOUPS
Seared Pheasant & Foie Gras, Shiitake Mushrooms, Truffle Dressing
Asparagus Risotto with Truffle Emulsion & Mascarpone
Three Mushroom Cream Soup, Parmesan Croutons
Red Lentil Broth with Chicken Dumplings
Chilled Roasted Tomato & Pepper Soup, Basil & Pineapple *(V)*

SALADS
Belgium Endive Leaves, Truffle Dressing
Beefsteak Tomato & Avocado Salad, Flat Parsley & Tarragon Vinaigrette

PRINCESS GRILL

ENTRÉES

Roasted Monkfish Tail, Chorizo, Mussel & Saffron Risotto

Sauteed Jumbo Shrimp & Champagne Cream, Parmesan Pilaf and Basil Oil

Magret of Duck, Creamy Polenta, Wild Berry Sauce

Slow Roasted Prime Rib Of Beef, Fondant Potatoes, Natural Gravy

Caramelised Leek & Goat Cheese Tart, Citrus and White Truffle Oil, Mesclun Salad *(V)*

DESSERT

Layer of Pistachio and Almond Biscuit with Hazelnut Sauce

Raspberry Cointreau Mousse with Fresh Berries and Mango Mirror

Hazelnut Crème Brûleé

Chocolate Mousse with Hazelnut Sweet Dough, Vanilla Rum Raisin Sauce, Citrus Sorbet

Sugar Free — Mango Royal Crusted with Passion Fruit Sauce and Litchis

Cookies n'Cream and Vanilla Ice Cream with Mocha Frozen Yogurt, Cherry Sauce

Nutrition Key : Calories / Fat Grams / Fiber Grams   *(V)* Indicates dishes suitable for Vegetarians

Courtesy Cunard Line

PETER DEILMANN CRUISES
1800 Diagonal Road, Suite 170
Alexandria, Virginia 22314
(800) 348-8287; (703) 549-1741
(703) 549-7924 Fax
www.deilmann-cruises.com

M.S. *DEUTSCHLAND:* entered service 1998; refurbished 2008; 22,400 G.R.T.;
574' x 82'; 513-passenger capacity; 264 cabins; German officers, German and
international crew; itineraries all over the world.

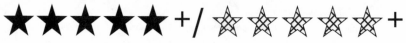

(Medical Facilities: C-2; P-1; EM, CLS & MS; 2N; CM; PD; BC; EKG; TC; PO;
OX; WC; OR; ICU; X; M; CCP; D; TM; LJ.)

This ship is rated in 11 separate categories in the second half of chapter 14.

Peter Deilmann Reederei is the owner of the M.S. *Deutschland* and until the
summer of 2009 also operated nine river vessels. The clientele on the *Deutschland*
is predominantly from German-speaking countries. Until financial problems
resulted in the loss of the company's riverboat fleet, these vessels were considered
among the best plying the rivers of Europe.

The *Deutschland* is a traditional oceangoing cruise vessel offering exotic itineraries (able to be purchased in segments) around the world. The *Deutschland* is one
of the most beautifully appointed ships in service and makes efforts to attract English-speaking passengers to complement its predominantly German clientele. On
the *Deutschland* all announcements and most written material—including daily
programs, shore-excursion information, and menus—are offered in English as well
as in German.

Entering service in 1998, the 22,400-ton *Deutschland* accommodates up to 513
passengers in 264 staterooms serviced by a largely European crew of 260. The
exterior design is classical with a large funnel, reminiscent of ships built in the
mid-1900s. The interior boasts an extremely elegant, tasteful decor with an abundance of burled woods, brass, marble, etched glass, and soft pastels adorning
every nook and cranny. Early 1900s-style furnishings and accents include crystal
chandeliers, sconces, etched-glass doors, brass balustrades and hardware, potted
palms, wooden deck chairs, and a variety of art work. This Art Deco/grand hotel
theme is carried into all staterooms, bathrooms, and hallways, making the *Deutschland* one of the most lovely and extravagantly furnished cruise ships in service.

Of the 264 cabins on the *Deutschland,* 206 are outside with full-size picture windows, and all include radios, telephones, bathrobes, slippers, hair dryers, minibars,
and safes. They vary in size from 125 square feet for some inside cabins, 160 square

feet for an average outside cabin, up to 240 square feet for a junior suite, 324 square feet for a full suite, and 400 square feet for the most expensive suite. Only the two largest suites have private balconies. Although the lower-priced and standard cabins are not as spacious as those found on other deluxe- or premium-market vessels, the bedroom and bathroom furnishings, appliances, and decor are exquisite.

Atop ship on deck 9 is the lido deck, composed of the midship outdoor pool; a lido bar; the lido terrace, a combination observation lounge, library, and venue for continental breakfast and afternoon tea; and the casual buffet-style lido restaurant and grill, with adjoining outdoor umbrella-sheltered tables. This restaurant is tastefully and comfortably furnished, a pleasant change from the typical poolside buffet facility.

The suites and more expensive staterooms are found on deck 8, together with the cinema/conference auditorium. Most of the remaining inside and outside cabins are located on decks 4 and 5, along with the reception/shore-excursion desk and the library.

Public rooms found on decks 6 and 7 include the exquisitely designed, two-level Emperor's Ballroom, where passengers sit in comfortable lounge chairs with adjoining small cocktail tables and view the entertainment and gala events; the elegant two-seating Berlin Restaurant; the more intimate, romantic, 104-seat, reservation-only Four Seasons specialty restaurant; the stylish Lili Marleen Lounge; a fitness center that includes a small gym with several treadmills, Exercycles, and step machines and connects to an impressive, dual-gender, clothing-optional sauna, steam, shower complex; a boutique and beauty salon; a photo gallery; and the Old Fritz, a warmly furnished, atmospheric, German-style pub.

At the bottom of the ship, on deck 3, is a small indoor pool surrounded by a sauna, steam room, sun-bed solarium, massage rooms, showers, and dressing area. The area serves as the focal point of the vessel's extensive wellness program, which includes such services as thalassotherapy, Ayurveda treatments, and heat therapy. The ship's hospital is also located on this deck.

The ship has no casino or promenade deck where passengers could enjoy an uninterrupted stroll around the entire circumference of the ship without tripping over other guests. There is limited e-mail access through assigned private e-mail accounts.

Dining selections at all meals in all restaurants are numerous, with an emphasis on German-style cuisine, including an abundance of game dishes. Service is continental and efficient, and dining is at a more leisurely pace than on most other ships. Dining in the Four Seasons specialty restaurant is by reservation only. There is no cover charge and participation is not limited.

Activities and entertainment are conducted in German, geared mostly to German tastes, and are not nearly as abundant as on ships catering to North American or British clientele. Two television stations offer English-language movies, while the others are in German. Although English-speaking passengers are in a conspicuous minority, the captain, hotel manager, and entire staff are most attentive and make special efforts to accommodate their needs and preferences. The number of passengers from countries other than Germany has been growing each year.

Strong Points

The *Deutschland* is an upscale, state-of-the-art, beautifully appointed vessel offering exotic itineraries throughout the world. It appeals to those interested in out-of-the-way places and is especially ideal for sophisticated German cruisers.

Deutschland, *courtesy Peter Deilmann Cruises*

Deutschland, *courtesy Peter Deilmann Cruises*

Deutschland, *courtesy Peter Deilmann Cruises*

Deutschland, *courtesy Peter Deilmann Cruises*

DEUTSCHLAND

Captain Jungbluts
Farewell-Gala-Dinner

At sea, 8 November 2000

Wine recommendation

1998 Chablis Premier Cru Montmains	69,00
Joseph Drouhin	
Côte d'Or	
1993 Château Rausan Ségla	124,00
Margaux	
Schloßabzug	

Carpaccio of salmon with scallops, lime oil, red peppercorns

or

Terrine of venison and wildboar loin
with vinegar cherry's and rucola

～

Wild mushroom soup with sherry amontillado, ravioli

～

Gratin of wild coast rock lobster
with orange-mustard-sabayon, champagne risotto

～

Passion fruit sherbet with Peter Deilmann Cuvee

～

"Beef Wellington"
Oven roasted whole tenderloin wrapped in puff pastry
Madeira sauce, with assorted vegetables and chateau potatoes

or

With lemongrass stuffed quail
on soy-plum sauce with ginger, bacon, egg noodles
artichokes, sugar carrots, chinese cabbage, spring onions

～

Australia King Island Brie

～

Grand Ice Parade MS Deutschland
in the Restaurant

～

Mocha-coffee
Pralines and truffles

Courtesy Peter Deilmann Cruises

HEUTE

Das Tagesprogramm auf Ihrer Reise mit der Deutschland

Ausgabe Nr. 822   Wednesday, 8 November. 2000

At sea

Sunrise: 5.58 am
Sunset: 6.31 pm

COCKTAIL OF THE DAY
Amber Jack
Jack Daniel's
Amaretto
Sugar
Lemon juice

Good Morning DEUTSCHLAND

07.30 am	wake up with some nice music and news from the bridge on channel 8
07.30 am	**"Yoga-Stretching"** - with Hannelore, meeting point is the pool at the LIDO-Deck
09.15 am	In the cinema at the ADMIRALS-Deck **Morning service** with pastor Walter Grunwald
09.30 am	**"Walk-a-Mile"** - walk a nautical mile, 1852 m, with Oksana, one of the "Five Star Dancers". Meeting point is the pool at the LIDO-Deck.

10.00 am	In the Kaisersaal **_"Mikrokosmos Inseln"_** Lecture about islands, settlement and ecology with Dr. Gerhard Beese (in German)
11.00 am	At the POOL-Bar on the LIDO-Deck **_"Frühschoppen" with free beer_** **with Billy Mo and the orchestra Evergreen Juniors** In the foyer on Deck 6 in front of the Kaisersaal **Display of wine**. Our head wine stewardess Christiane Henze will gladly take your order and will give you information and advice until 12.30 pm.
11.30 am	**"5 Tibeter"** – relaxing exercise with Hannelore Basner-Wiencke in the Kaisersaal
11.45 am	**Passengers choir of MS DEUTSCHLAND** Meet Prof. Binge in the cinema at the ADMIRALS-Deck
12.00 pm	In the LIDO-Gourmet **_"Aus deutschen Landen"_** Lunch buffet and musical entertainment with the Hanse-Swing-Trio
01.00 pm	**Passengers choir of MS DEUTSCHLAND** The rehearsal with Prof. Günter Binge takes place in the Kaisersaal.
02.30 pm	In the cinema at the ADMIRALS-Deck **"Orthomolekulare Therapie – Vital Plus-Therapie"** Lecture with Dr. med. Joachim Dietz (in German)
03.30 pm	**Tea, coffee and pastry** in the LIDO-Gourmet and LIDO-Terrasse
04.00 pm	**Skeet shooting** Meet at the reception desk. 10 shots cost DM 20.-.
04.30 am	In the Kaisersaal **_"Straße der Wölfe"_** Reading with Dr. Gabriele Krone-Schmalz (in German) **Bingo** – with Tommy in the LILI MARLEEN salon. 1 card costs DM 5.-.
05.30 pm	**Table reservation for the restaurant "VIERJAHRESZEITEN"** Chief steward Richard Nikolaus will gladly take your reservation in the foyer on the KOMMODORE-Deck until 06.00 pm. **Cocktail hour** with the Hanse-Swing-Trio in the LILI MARLEEN salon We serve hot snacks. **Sundowner** with Christian Güntert in front of the "Alter Fritz" pub

DEUTSCHLAND

| 07.30 pm | In the Kaisersaal |

Captain's cocktail party

Captain Andreas Jungblut would like to say good-bye
and invites you for a farewell cocktail into the Kaisersaal.

After dinner in the salon LILI MARLEEN and in the ADLON-Lounge:
Irish Coffee with Irish whisky, sugar and whipped cream

| 08.30 pm | **Musical entertainment** with the Hanse-Swing-Trio in the LILI MARLEEN salon and Christina Güntert on the piano in front of the "Alter Fritz" pub |

| 09.00 pm | **Dance music** with the orchestra Evergreen Juniors in the Kaisersaal |

| 09.30 pm | In the Kaisersaal |

"From classic to jazz"

with Christian Güntert on the piano

| 09.50 pm | **Dance music** with the orchestra Evergreen Juniors in the Kaisersaal |

| 10.00 pm | In the cinema on ADMIRALS-Deck **"The Birdcage"** (in German) |

| 10.15 pm | In the Kaisersaal |

Farewell Show

with the artists and the orchestra Evergreen Juniors

Afterwards dance music with the orchestra Evergreen Juniors in the Kaisersaal

| 11.30 pm | **Galley buffet** Executive Chef Bernhard Zorn and his team prepared a very special buffet for you. The entrance to the main kitchen is located in the restaurant BERLIN. |

Courtesy Peter Deilmann Cruises

DISNEY CRUISE LINE
P.O. Box 10210
Lake Buena Vista, Florida 32830
(888) 325-2500; (407) 566-3500
(407) 566-3541 Fax
www.disneycruise.com

DISNEY MAGIC: entered service 1998; renovated 2008; 83,000 G.R.T.; 964' x 106'; 2,700-passenger capacity; 877 staterooms; European officers and international crew; Mediterranean and Baltic cruises during summer and alternate seven-day Caribbean cruises to eastern and western Caribbean rest of year.

✮✮✮✮✮ +

DISNEY WONDER: entered service 1999; renovated 2006; 83,000 G.R.T.; 964' x 106'; 2,700-passenger capacity; 877 staterooms; European officers and international crew; three- and four-day cruises from Port Canaveral.

✮✮✮✮✮ +

(Medical Facilities: C-12; P-2, CLS, MS; N-4; CM; PD; BC; EKG; TC; PO; EPC; OX; WC; OR; ICU; X; M; LJ.)

These ships are rated in 11 separate categories in the second half of chapter 14.

The state-of-the-art, unique, 83,000-ton *Disney Magic,* designed to be reminiscent of the classic ocean liners and capable of accommodating 2,700 passengers, entered service in July 1998, followed by *Disney Wonder* in August 1999.

The 877 larger-than-average staterooms range in size from 184 square feet up to the 1,029-square-foot Disney suites. Seventy-three percent of the accommodations are outside and almost half have verandas. All sleep at least three persons, while some accommodate four or five. All staterooms include tubs and showers (721 out of 877 have split bathrooms), remote-control televisions, private safes, hair dryers, phones with voicemail message service, and privacy dividers separating bedrooms from the sitting areas that convert to pull-down beds and sofas for the children. In addition, there are two luxurious Royal suites and two 945-square-foot two-bedroom suites that can sleep seven, as well as 16 614-square-foot one-bedroom suites, 14 of which sleep five and four that are wheelchair accessible. The suites rival those on luxury-category ships. The line offers a dozen stateroom categories, air-sea packages, early booking discounts, and land packages that include visits to Walt Disney World Resort. Cabins, staterooms, and suites in all categories are a good deal larger and include more amenities than on most other cruise ships; however, they are designed to accommodate more passengers. The availability of a tub and shower in a split bathroom design in the lower-cost categories is unusual in the cruise industry.

All cruises departing from Port Canaveral include a visit to Castaway Cay, Disney's privately developed 1,000-acre island in the Bahamas, where guests will enjoy a protected lagoon for watersports, shops, dining pavilions, bicycles, and separate adults-only, family, and teen beaches. The ships are able to dock at the island and avoid time-consuming tender service. Programs exclusively for teens and tots are also featured. Among the special activities available for all passengers is Castaway Ray's Stingray Adventure, a supervised, interactive experience with the rays.

The dining experience aboard these vessels is unique in that it permits guests to move to a different theme restaurant each night. Dinner companions and their wait staff move together to three different locations, including Lumiere's, a more traditional, Art Deco-motif dining room; Parrot Cay, sporting a colorful, tropical decor; and Animator's Palate, a totally unique restaurant that transforms over the course of the evening from a room decorated solely in black and white to a kaleidoscope of lights and colors. On the *Disney Wonder*, Lumiere's has been replaced with Tritons, a seafood restaurant with an "under the sea" theme. Dining in these three venues is pleasant and much improved from the cruise line's inception, and the cuisine could be described as eclectic with continental offerings as well as hearty American fare.

Palo is a 138-seat alternative, adults-only, Italian specialty restaurant located atop ship, with windows out to the sea. This is definitely the choice for adults traveling without children. Reservations are required and it is advisable to book immediately upon coming on board. It is also possible to make reservations online at www.disneycruise.com. Here I found the dining experience top-notch, with gourmet Italian cuisine, an impressive wine list, and excellent presentation and service. Champagne brunches offered here on days at sea are awesome. High Tea is also served here on days at sea. In addition, families can opt for an indoor/outdoor café serving all three meals, snacks, and a buffet lunch and dinner for children; a hamburger, hot dog, and pizza grill near the pool; and an ice cream bar—Goofy's Galley—offering fresh fruit, salads, wraps, Panini, and sandwiches as well as ice cream. Room service is available around the clock.

Public areas (which are traditional and nautical in décor with numerous Disney-character and Art Deco accents) and activities include an entire deck devoted to children and featuring age-specific supervised programs, a children's pool, game arcade, special teen club, play areas, and a full complement of children's counselors and state-of-the-art kids' area; three outdoor pools—one for families, a supervised children's pool fashioned in the image of Mickey Mouse with an impressive waterslide, and a third with adjoining whirlpools exclusively for adults; a 977-seat theater for musical productions and a 290-seat cinema for Disney classics, first-run releases, and live entertainment (3-D technology was added in 2008); a state-of-the-art, jumbo outdoor movie screen for poolside movies; dinner and deck parties with fireworks; shopping opportunities with emphasis on signature Disney items; several themed nightclubs and lounges; a teen club atop ship; a 9000-square-foot, ocean-view, equipped gym and Steiner health spa; and a promenade deck for jogging and walking. There is no casino, in keeping with the Disney family image. However, the separate adult pool; private beach on Castaway Cay; lounge areas; spa villas with indoor treatment rooms, outdoor verandas, hot tubs, lounge chairs, and open-air shower; Internet/specialty coffee café, and the excellent, upscale, specialty adults-only Italian restaurant afford some sanctuary for cruisers traveling without children or wishing a few hours' respite. Activities directed to adult singles, couples without children, or older teens are not as extensive as those on other larger cruise ships.

Over the past few years, various renovations were made to the ships, including the addition of an LED movie screen over the family pool for outdoor movies, expansion of the spa and fitness center, a new toddler pool, a sports pub, an updated conference center, and a new, adults-only specialty-coffee lounge.

In early 2007, Disney placed an order to build two new 128,000-ton, 1,250-stateroom vessels scheduled for delivery in 2011 and 2012. The first will be named *Disney Dream* and the second, *Disney Fantasy.*

The two present ships offer a traditional Disney-style experience at sea that will appeal to families who enjoy a Disney vacation and wish to combine a short cruise with visits to the theme parks. Activities and entertainment are definitely directed to families and the younger set. Different activities are scheduled for the various children's age groups. However, each year there is an increasing emphasis on adult-only facilities. These ships are presently receiving very positive passenger feedback, especially from families experiencing their first cruise. Many improvements have been made in entertainment, service, dining, and activities since the inception of the cruise line.

Strong Points:

This is an excellent family-oriented cruise for parents with young children, pre-teens, and early teens, as well as Mickey Mouse junkies. Efforts are made to provide something for all members of the family.

Disney Magic *and* Disney Wonder, *courtesy Disney Cruise Line*

Kid's Pool on Disney Magic, *courtesy Disney Cruise Line*

Veranda Suite, courtesy Disney Cruise Line

Apéritifs

Kir Royal
Sparkling Wine with a touch
of Crème de Cassis. $5.25

Alizé Passion
Crafted from Cognac, Passion
Fruit Juice, and Vodka. $4.50

Smoothies

Delicious, rich Ice Cream blended with
your favorite flavors. Choose from
Chocolate, Strawberry, Vanilla,
Peach, or Banana. $3.50
With Rum or Vodka. $4.50

Featured Wines

Mumm Cordon Rouge, Champagne
A great celebration bubbly, this versatile
Cuvee is fruity, subtle, and refined.
$11.00 Glass $52.00 Bottle

Delaporte Sancerre, Loire
This classic Sancerre features a floral and
slightly grassy bouquet with mineral
notes and is excellent with seafood.
$8.00 Glass $37.00 Bottle

**Louis Jadot Pouilly-Fuissé,
Burgundy**
Pouilly-Fuissé is America's favorite
French Chardonnay.
$8.75 Glass $42.00 Bottle

**Louis Jadot Beaujolais-
Village, Burgundy**
Bright Raspberry and Cherry flavors accent
a fruity finish in this lightest of all reds.
$5.25 Glass $25.00 Bottle

Chateau Phelan-Segur, St. Estephe
This Bordeaux is a forceful example of how
blending Cabernet Sauvignon, Merlot, and
Cabernet Franc can produce a wine for
consuming with flavorful meats and pastas.
$14.50 Glass $69.00 Bottle

Our Special Layered Liqueur of the Night

French Flag
Grenadine, Crème de Cacao,
and Blue Curaçao. $4.50
In our specialty glass. $6.50

*We offer a complete array of cocktails,
a full bar, and an extensive wine list.*

Courtesy Disney Cruise Line

Starters

⋄ **Deep Fried Camembert**
with a Marinara Sauce

Shrimp Medley
served with Cocktail Sauce

Pearls of Seasonal Melon
with Port Wine

⋄ **Escargot**
with Diced Mushrooms and Garlic Butter

Cream of Cauliflower Soup

Mixed Garden Salad
tossed with Red Wine Vinaigrette and topped with
Goat Cheese Croutons

Main Course

Cheese Ravioli
served with a Tomato-Basil Sauce

Garlic-roasted Beef Tenderloin
served with Mashed Potatoes and a Green Peppercorn Sauce

Herb-crusted Sea Bass
with Sautéed Spinach and Champagne Sauce

Braised Lamb Shank
served with Portobello Polenta and a Red Wine Sauce

⋄ **Roasted Duck Breast**
with Sautéed Parsnips and an Orange Sauce

Chef's Vegetarian Selection of the Day

*Additional selections of Sirloin Steak,
Grilled Chicken Breast, fresh Fish, or "Lighter Fare"
are available. Kindly ask your server.*

Desserts

Chocolate Mousse Cake
served with Rum-Caramel Sauce

Caramelized Apple Tart
with Vanilla Sauce

Grand Marnier Soufflé
with Chocolate Sauce

⋄ **Crème Brûlée**

Chef's Sugar-free Dessert

⋄ **Restaurant Specialty**

DISNEY MAGIC

ACTIVITIES & ENTERTAINMENT

6:00am - 12:00am	**Goofy's Pool** is open for use. Deck 9, Midship.
6:00am - 12:00am	**The Quiet Cove Pool** is open for use. Deck 9, Forward. *(Guests 18 and older)*
6:00am - 10:00pm	**Mickey's Pool** is open for use. Deck 9, Aft.
8:00am - 12:00am	**Quarter Masters Arcade** is open for your enjoyment on Deck 9, Midship.
8:00am - 4:00pm	**Bridge, Cards & Games,** Fantasia Reading & Game Room, Deck 2, Midship.
8:00am	**Stretch & Relax,** Vista Spa, Deck 9, Forward.
8:30am - 9:00am	**Toddler Time:** Explore the Oceaneer Club with your Toddler, Deck 5, Midship.
9:00am - 6:30pm	**Mickey's Slide** is open for use. Deck 9, Aft *(Height and age restrictions apply).*
9:00am - 12:00pm	**Shore Excursion Desk:** Your last opportunity to reserve excursion tickets for St. Maarten, Deck 3, Midship.
9:00am - 11:00am	**Disney Vacation Club:** Stop by to learn the benefits of membership. Deck 4, Midship.
9:00am	**Walk a *Smile* Mile:** Join us for a stroll around Deck 4. Meet in Preludes, Deck 4, Forward.
9:30am	**Ballroom Dancing:** Learn the basics of the Foxtrot & Waltz Rockin' Bar D, Deck 3, Forward.
10:00am	**Sign Up Sheets** for Family & Adult Talent Show, limited space available. Sign up at the Shore Excursion Desk, Deck 3, Midship.
10:00am	**Team Trivia:** Join your Cruise Staff in the Promenade Lounge Deck 3, Aft.
10:00am	**Bridge, Cards and Tournaments** in the Fantasia Reading & Game Room, Deck 2, Midship. *(Sign-up sheets available)*
10:00am	**Disney's Art of Entertaining:** "Dazzling Desserts" Our expert chef showcases dessert tips and tricks in Studio Sea, Deck 4, Midship. *(Guests 18 and older)*
10:30am	**Shuffleboard Challenge for Families,** Deck 4, Aft, Port Side.
10:45am	**Jackpot Bingo!** Win Cash Prizes! (First game begins at 11:00am). Rockin' Bar D, Deck 3, Forward.
11:00am - 4:00pm	**Island Music:** Enjoy the sounds of Kool Breeze. Pool Side Gazebo Deck 9, Midship.
11:30am	**Secrets to Beautiful Hair,** Vista Spa, Deck 9, Forward.
11:30am - 12:30pm	**Disney Vacation Club Presentation:** A fun, informative Virtual Open House, Studio Sea, Deck 4, Midship.
12:00pm	**Voice from the Bridge:** A navigational update from the Captain. *(PA System)*
12:15pm	**Family Mini Olympics:** Join the Cruise Staff for fun & games, Sports Deck, Deck 10, Forward.
12:15pm	**Singles, Single Parents or Traveling alone** meet for an informal lunch with the Cruise Staff, Parrot Cay, Deck 3, Aft.
12:30pm	**Island Magic Stage Show** showing in the Buena Vista Theatre, Deck 5, Aft.
1:00pm - 2:00pm	**Disney Vacation Club:** Stop by to learn the benefits of membership. Deck 4, Midship.
1:30pm	**Snorkel Demonstration:** Join the Recreation Staff to learn the basics Goofy Pool, Deck 9, Midship.
1:45pm	**Mickey 200 Sign Up:** first 18 teams to sign up will make a racing car from vegetables for this wild & wacky race, The Off Beat Club, Deck 3, Forward.
2:00pm	**Island Magic Stage Show** showing in the Buena Vista Theatre, Deck 5, Aft
2:00pm	**The Best "Disney Legs" Contest:** Join your Cruise Staff for this fun game, Goofy Pool, Deck 9 Midship.
2:00pm - 3:00pm	**Disney's Navigator Series:** The Making of the Disney Magic and charting her course. Rockin' Bar D, Deck 3, Forward. *(Guests 18 and older)*
2:00pm - 3:00pm	**Disney's Art of Entertaining:** Innovation, Fun & Creativity in Tablescaping. Studio Sea, Deck 4, Midship.
2:00pm - 3:00pm	**Mickey 200:** Let the racing begin, May the FASTEST VEGGIE WIN! The Off Beat Club, Deck 3, Forward.
2:00pm - 4:00pm	**Shore Excursion Desk:** Your opportunity to reserve excursion tickets for St.Thomas. Deck 3, Midship.
3:00pm	**Jackpot Bingo!** WIN Cash Prizes! (First game begins at 3:15pm). Rockin' Bar D, Deck 3, Forward.
3:00pm	**Back Care Seminar:** Vista Spa, Deck 9, Forward.
3:00pm - 4:00pm	**Stem to Stern Wine Tasting** with our Cellar Master. Sessions, Deck 3, Forward. Reserve your spot at Guest Services $12.00. *(Guests 21 and older)*
3:00pm - 6:30pm	**Disney Vacation Club:** Stop by to learn about benefits of membership. Deck 4, Midship.
3:30pm	**High Tea in Palo:** Space is limited, reservations required. Palo, Deck 10, Aft. *(Guests 18 and older)*

Disney Character Appearance   Disney's Navigator Series   Shore Excursion

Disney's Art of Entertaining   Disney's Behind-the-Scenes   Guests 18 & Older

---

Character Appearances
Meet some of your favorite Disney Friends:

12:30pm - 1:00pm
Buena Vista Theatre, Deck 5, Aft.

2:00pm - 2:30pm
Buena Vista Theatre, Deck 5, Aft.

3:00pm - 3:30pm
Mickey Pool, Deck 9, Aft.

5:30pm - 6:20pm
Atrium Lobby, Deck 3, Midship

7:00pm - 7:30pm
Atrium Lobby, Deck 3, Midship.

7:30pm - 8:20pm
Atrium, Deck 3, Midship.

10:00pm - 10:30pm
Atrium Lobby, Deck 3, Midship.

Movies
Deck 5, Aft

Island Magic Stage Show
12:30pm - Running Time :30
Island Magic Stage Show
2:00pm - Running Time :30
Pearl Harbor (PG13)
3:15pm - Running Time 3:03
102 Dalmations (PG)
6:30pm - Running Time 1:40
102 Dalmations (PG)
8:30pm - Running Time 1:40
Castaway (PG)
11:15pm - Running Time 2:23

FAMILY MAGIC QUEST

Join your Cruise Staff for the wildest & wackiest game on the seven seas!
7:45pm
Studio Sea, Deck 4, Midship.

FAMILY KARAOKE

Join us for some singing FUN!
9:45pm
Studio Sea, Deck 4, Midship

Create your own
COOL Smoothie! $3.50

Family Activities

Team Trivia
10:00am
Shuffle Board Challenge
10:30am
Jackpot Bingo!
10:45am & 3:00pm
Family Mini Olympics
12:15pm
Magic Quest
7:45pm
Cabaret Show Time
7:45pm
Family Karaoke
9:45pm
Family Dance Music
11:00pm - 11:30pm

🃏 Trading Cards

Join in on the fun of collecting various trading cards unique to the *Disney Magic* and *Disney Cruise Line*.

Anywhere you see the "card" icon on your *Personal Navigator*, a trading card will be distributed to our younger cruisers.

*Note: A different card is available at each designated time!

That's the fun of trading cards, don't miss out!

🎴 Island Magic Stage Show 🎴

Don't miss this *FUN* filled stage show featuring some of your favorite Disney Friends.

Captain Mickey takes us on a Magical adventure to Disney's Castaway Cay.

12:30pm & 2:00pm, Buena Vista Theatre, Deck 5, Aft

🎵 SESSIONS 🍷

7:30pm - 8:30pm
Joy Wright
Entertains at the piano.

9:30pm - 12:30am
Joy Wright
weaves her musical magic at the piano.

Beat Street - Deck 3, Forward
(Guests 18 & older)

Disney Vacation Club

Welcomes its members and all Guests to a fun & informative,

Virtual Open House, 11:30am - 12:30pm
Studio Sea, Deck 4, Midship
If you believe in Magic, you belong!

Stem to Stern

"Wine Tasting"

Sample fine wines from around the world
3:00pm - 4:00pm Sessions, Deck 3, Forward.
Reverve your place at Guest Services $12.
(Guests 21 and older)

ADULT ACTIVITIES

Disney Navigator Series
2:00pm
Stem to Stern Wine Tasting
3:00pm - 4:00pm
Rock the House
9:30pm - 10:00pm
Who's the Boss?
9:45pm
Dueling Pianos
10:15pm & 11:15pm
Rock and Roll Night
11:00pm
Dance Party
11:45pm - 2:00am

Courtesy Disney Cruise Line

3:30pm	**Disney's Navigator Series Ship Tour:** Join us for this walking tour, as we highlight several public rooms illustrating the ship's designing of Disney culture, theming & artistry, The Off Beat Club, Deck 3, Forward.
4:00pm	**Hi/Low Aerobics:** Vista Spa, Deck 9, Forward.
4:00pm - 5:00pm	**Family Basketball Time:** Meet at the Wide World of Sports for informal play. Deck 10, forward.
4:30pm	**Friends of Bill W.** will be meeting in Fantasia Reading & Game Room, Deck 2, Midship
4:30pm	**Seaweed Secrets:** Learn benefits of detoxification for arthritis. Sessions, Deck 3, Forward.
4:30pm	**Mixed Doubles Ping Pong Tournament:** Meet at tables. Deck 9, Forward, Port Side.
5:15pm	**Castaway Club Members:** A special reception for all our returning Disney Cruise Line Guests. Rockin' Bar D, Deck 3, Forward (please bring invitation)
5:15pm - 6:00pm	**Promenade Lounge** presents the smooth & sassy music of *Del & Lynn*, Deck 3, Aft.
5:30pm - 6:30pm	**Family Time:** Explore Disney's Oceaneer Club and Lab, Deck 5, Midship *(Adult accompaniment please).*
5:30pm - 6:30pm	**Portraits** taken in the Atrium Lobby, Deck 3, Midship.

3:15pm, 6:30pm & 8:30pm — Disney Cruise Line proudly presents

C'est Magique
Deck 4, Forward
As a courtesy to all Guests we kindly advise that the saving of seats is not permitted in the Walt Disney Theatre.

7:30pm - 8:30pm	**Pin Trading:** Collect and trade with your fellow guests & Senior Officers in the Atrium Lobby, Deck 3 Midship.
7:30pm - 8:30pm	**Your Shopping in Paradise Guide** *Shelby* is available to answer questions regarding St. Maarten and St. Thomas Duty Free Shopping. Deck 3, Midship, Starboard Side.
7:30pm - 8:30pm	**Sparkling Moments:** Enjoy fine wines and Champagne, available for purchase, Atrium Lobby, Deck 3, Midship.
7:30pm - 8:45pm	**Portraits** taken in the Atrium Lobby, Deck 3, Midship.
7:30pm - 9:00pm	**Disney Vacation Club:** Stop by to learn about benefits of membership, Deck 4, Midship.
7:30pm - 12:30am	**Sessions** presents Joy Wright entertaining at the piano. Deck 3, Forward. *(Guests 18 and older)*
7:45pm	**Cabaret Show Time** with the Comedy & Music of *Dan Riley*, Rockin' Bar D, Deck 3, Forward. *(Everyone Welcome)*
7:45pm	**Magic Quest:** Join your Cruise Staff for the wildest & wackiest game on the seven seas for the entire family! Studio Sea, Deck 4, Midship.
7:45pm	**ESPN Sports Trivia Challenge** with the Cruise Staff, ESPN Skybox, Deck 11, Midship.
7:45pm - 8:15pm	**Family Pianos:** Craziness for the Kids & You! The Off Beat Club, Deck 3, Forward. *(Everyone Welcome)*
9:30pm - 10:30pm	**Promenade Lounge:** Bring the family and dance to the music of *Del & Lynn*. Deck 3, Aft.
9:30pm - 10:00pm	**Rock the House** with Double Trouble. Rockin' Bar D, Deck 3, Forward. *(Guests 18 and older)*
9:45pm	**Who's the Boss?** Join your Cruise Staff to find out which gender RULES! The Off Beat Club, Deck 3, Forward. *(Guests 18 and older)*
9:45pm	**Disney Behind the Scenes:** Question & Answer session with the Walt Disney Theatre Cast. Walt Disney Theatre, Deck 4, Forward.
9:45pm - 11:00pm	**Family Karaoke:** It's a casting call for all family members in Studio Sea, Deck 4, Midship.
10:00pm - 10:30pm	**Character Family Portraits:** Have your portrait taken with Mickey, Minnie, Goofy & Pluto for this one time only opportunity in the Atrium Lobby, Deck 3, Midship. (No Autographs Please)
10:15pm	**Cabaret Show Time** with the Comedy & Music of *Dan Riley*, Rockin' Bar D, Deck 3, Forward. *(Guests 18 and older)*
10:15pm - 11:00pm	**Dueling Pianos Tribute:** The Beatles & British Rock Invasion. The Off Beat Club, Deck 3, Forward. *(Guests 18 and older)*
10:30pm - 12:00am	**Promenade Lounge Presents:** Smooth & Sassy music of *Del & Lynn*. Deck 3, Aft.

Rock & Roll Night!

11:00pm	**Rock Around the Clock"** with your Cruise Staff & Double Trouble, Rockin' Bar D, Deck 3, Forward *(Guests 18 and older)*
11:00pm - 11:30pm	**Family Dance Music:** Our DJ plays todays hottest hits, Studio Sea, Deck 4, Midship.
11:15pm - 12:00am	**Dueling Pianos Sing Along:** Raise your voices & your spirits in the Off Beat Club, Deck 3, Forward. *(Guests 18 and older)*
11:45pm - 2:00am	**Dance Party** with *Double Trouble & Frankie J*, Rockin' Bar D, Deck 3, Forward. *(Guests 18 and older)*

EUROPEAN WATERWAYS—GO BARGING
35 Wharf Road, Wraysbury, Middlesex
TW19 5JQ, England
(UK) 44(0)1784482439
(US) (800) 394-8630
(AU) 1-800-771278
(UK) 44(0)1784483072 Fax
www.gobarging.com

ALOUETTE: entered service 1986; refurbished 2001; 98' x 17'; 4-passenger capacity; 2 cabins; British officers and crew; cruises on Canal du Midi.

ANJODI: entered service 1983; refurbished 2006; 100' x 16.6'; 8-passenger capacity; 4 cabins; British and French officers and crew; cruises on Canal du Midi and Provence in southern France.

ATHOS: entered service 1982; refurbished 2006; 103' x 18.3'; 10-passenger capacity; 5 cabins; French and British crew; cruises on Canal du Midi.

ENCHANTE: entered service 2009; refurbished 2009; 100' x 17'; 8-passenger capacity; 4 cabins; British officers and crew; cruises in Camargue and Provence in southern France.

HIRONDELLE: entered service 1993; 128' x 17'; 8-passenger capacity; 4 cabins; British officers and crew; cruises in Burgundy and Franche-Comte.

LA BELLE EPOQUE: entered service 1995; refurbished 2006; 126' x 16.6'; 13-passenger capacity; 7 cabins (a/c); British and French officers and crew; cruises in Burgundy. **(Category B—No Rating)**

LA DOLCE VITA: entered service 2005; 65' x 16.4'; 6-passenger capacity; 3 cabins; Italian and British officers and crew; cruises in Venice and Brenta River in Italy.

L'ART DE VIVRE: entered service 1998; refurbished 2006; 100' x 16.6'; 8-passenger capacity; 4 cabins; French and British officers and crew; cruises on Nivernais Canal in Burgundy.

L'IMPRESSIONNISTE: entered service 1996; refurbished 2006; 126' x 16.6'; 13-passenger capacity; 7 cabins; British and French officers and crew; cruises the Burgundy Canal.

LA REINE PEDAQUE: entered service 1985; 128' x 15'; 8-passenger capacity; 4 cabins; French officers and crew; cruises the Burgundy Canal.

MAGNA CARTA: entered service 2002; 117' x 16.6'; 8- to 10-passenger capacity; 4 to 5 cabins; British officers and crew; cruises lower Thames in England.

NAPOLEON: entered service 1992; refurbished 2001; 129'x 17.5'; 12-passenger capacity; 6 cabins; cruises in Vallee du Rhone and Provence.

NYMPHEA: entered service 1980, refurbished 2003; 80' long; 6-passenger capacity; 3 cabins; British and French officers and crew; cruises in Loire Valley, France.

RENAISSANCE (formerly *La Bonne Humeur*): entered service 1997; refurbished 2006; 128' x 17.6'; 8-passenger capacity; 4 cabins; British and French officers and crew; cruises western Burgundy and the Upper Loire.

SAVOIR FAIRE: entered service 1932; 130' x 16.6'; 12-passenger capacity; 6 cabins; British officers and crew; cruises in Champagne and Burgundy in France, western Belgium, and western Holland.

SCOTTISH HIGHLANDER: entered service 1999; refurbished 2006; 117' x 16.6'; 8-passenger capacity; 4 cabins; cruises in Scotland on Caledonian Canal.

SHANNON PRINCESS II: entered service 2003; 107' x 20'; 10-passenger capacity; 5 cabins; Irish crew; cruises in Ireland on the River Shannon.

European Waterways has owned and represented luxury hotel barges since 1974. All of the vessels they own or represent have been recently built or completely refurbished throughout with wood paneling, carpeting, and a blend of antique and traditional decor. All have central heating and most are fully air conditioned.

With a capacity ranging from six to 13 passengers, each vessel has a combination salon, bar, and dining area with large windows for viewing the countryside and a partially covered or umbrella-tabled sun deck lined with brightly colored flowers. Some vessels have on-deck spa pools.

Accommodations range from 280-square-foot twin- and double-bedded staterooms to smaller suites with sitting areas. All have small windows, closets, drawers, and tiled bathrooms that include shower and sink; some have tubs.

Each barge carries a fleet of bicycles for passengers to use along the waterway paths, as well as a library of books, games, and audio tapes.

Dining is the highlight of each cruise, where highly trained chefs skilled in the tradition of regional cuisine prepare epicurean meals for guests, with emphasis on the fabulous local cheeses, vintage wines, and fresh produce. Commencing in 2008, the cruise line has enhanced the barge experience by treating guests to a gourmet meal on shore at a *Michelin*-starred restaurant. Passengers on a *La Belle*

Epoque cruise in Burgundy will have lunch or dinner at L'Esperance; passengers on *L'Impressionniste* in Burgundy will dine at the Abbaye de la Bussière; and those on the *Renaissance* at Auberge Les Templiers (one of the all-time favorites).

Captains are not only technically qualified to operate the entire vessel, but are also knowledgeable tour guides ashore.

Included in the price that ranges from $3,100 to $6,490 are accommodations, all meals with wines, champagne welcome, open bar, sightseeing, and other facilities. Air fare and hot-air ballooning is not included.

During the day, passengers are offered tours to points of interest along the route, which could include medieval villages, museums, magnificent chateaux, abbeys, wine cellars, and colorful open markets. Paths along the canals and waterways offer opportunities for long walks, jogging, and bicycle excursions.

Personally, I have had exceptional sojourns on these riverboats. Most recently I cruised on the *Renaissance,* which is comparable to a private river yacht that you share with three other couples. The accommodations are spacious, impeccably decorated, with large bathrooms similar to a hotel rather than a riverboat. The cuisine is outstanding and the entire experience was one of the most charming and relaxing imaginable. Previously I had cruised on *La Belle Epoque,* which was also enchanting, with an incredibly knowledgeable captain and a master chef.

Strong Points:

An intimate, tranquil cruise/barge experience with fine dining and excellent, friendly service. This is a must for experienced cruisers seeking something different, intimate, and charming.

Courtesy European Waterways

Courtesy European Waterways

Courtesy European Waterways

Courtesy European Waterways

LA BELLE EPOQUE
MENU

LUNCH

CONTAL CHEESE AND MUSTARD MARINATED
TOMATOES IN A PASTRY CRUST
COUSCOUS SALAD
MARINTATED CABBAGE WITH SHALLOTS AND
PARSLEY
PROSCIUTTO WRAPPED MELON
CHEESES:
PAPILLON ROQUEFORT. DELICE DE BOURGOGNE

DINNER

WILD MUSHROOMS IN PUFF PASTRY
DUCK BREAST IN A CASSIS SAUCE WITH CARROT
PUREE AND BRAISED ENDIVE
MIXED GREENS
CHEESES:
GAPARON, BUCHONS DE CHEVRE
ICED HAZELNUT MOUSSE WITH RASPBERRY COULIS

Courtesy European Waterways

FRED OLSEN CRUISE LINE

In U.S.
c/o Borton Overseas
5412 Lyndale Avenue S
Minneapolis, Minnesota 55419
(800) 843-0602
(612) 822-4755

In U.K.
Fred Olsen House
White House Road
Ipswich 1P1 5LL
England
Tel. 01473292200

www.fredolsencruises.com

BALMORAL (formerly *Crown Odyssey* and *Norwegian Crown*): entered service 1988; 34,242 G.R.T.; 614' x 92.5'; 1,104-passenger capacity; 552 cabins; Norwegian officers, British cruise staff, and Filipino crew; cruises to Caribbean from Miami, to the Mediterranean from Rome, and to the Baltic and northern waters from UK. **(Category C—Not Rated)**

(Medical Facilities: C-2; P-1; N-1; CM, OX, WC.)

BLACK WATCH (formerly *Royal Viking Star*): entered service 1972; renovated 1998; 28,492 G.R.T.; 630' x 83'; 798-passenger capacity; 427 cabins; Norwegian officers, British cruise staff, and Filipino crew; cruises in North Sea, Baltic, Canary Islands, and around South America and Caribbean. **(Category C/D—Not Rated)**

(Medical Facilities: C-4; P-1; N-2; CM, EKG, OX, WC, OR, X.)

BOUDICCA (formerly *Royal Viking Sky, Superstar Capricorn, Birka Queen,* and *Grand Latino*): entered service in 1973; 25,000 G.R.T.; 593' x 84'; 836-passenger capacity; 420 cabins; Norwegian officers, British cruise staff, and Filipino crew; cruises to be announced. **(Category C—Not Rated)**

BRAEMAR (formerly *Crown Dynasty* and *Norwegian Dynasty*): entered service 1993; renovated 2001; 19,089 G.R.T.; 537' x 74'; 821-passenger capacity; 377 cabins; Norwegian officers; British cruise staff and Filipino crew; cruises in North Sea, Baltic, Arctic Circle, Mediterranean, Canary Islands, and Caribbean. **(Category C—Not Rated)**

(Medical Facilities: C-4; P-1; N-2: DM, EKG, OX, WC, OR, X.)

This family-owned, Norwegian-heritage cruise line dates back 150 years. Today, it services a largely British clientele offering a full-scale, no-frills cruise experience, traversing exotic ports around the world at bargain rates.

The *Black Watch* was born in the early 1970s as the luxurious *Royal Viking Star,* and it continues to display much of the wood, brass, and class of the ships of that era. Accommodations are not up to those of the ships built in recent years; however, they are comfortable and livable. Ninety percent of the cabins have portholes or windows. Inside cabins measure up to 140 square feet and escalate in size up to 200 square feet for a superior outside cabin on lido deck. Junior suites measure 240 feet, deluxe suites 260 feet, the six marquee suites are 440 feet, and the three premier suites come in at 550 feet. All accommodations have a television, hair dryer, and bathroom with shower. Superior cabins have picture windows and bathtubs and the suites include refrigerators and sitting areas. If you require a veranda, your only options are the premier and marquee suites.

There are two main indoor restaurants as well as a casual indoor/outdoor café. Other public areas include numerous lounges; a cabaret show lounge; a fitness center with a gym, sauna and treatment rooms; a casino; Internet facilities, a cardroom; a launderette;, a beauty salon; a swimming pool; a splash pool; and outdoor Jacuzzis.

Prices range from $178 per person per night for the least expensive accommodation up to $470 per person for the premier suite.

The 19,089-ton, 821 passenger *Braemer* was built in 1993 and formerly sailed as the *Crown Dynasty* and the *Norwegian Dynasty*. After being acquired by Fred Olsen Cruises it received numerous cosmetic changes in 2001, including a wraparound promenade deck for walkers and joggers. Public facilities include a traditional two-seating restaurant and a casual buffet-style café; a show lounge for nightly cabaret entertainment and several smaller bar/lounges; a swimming pool/lido area with Jacuzzis; a fitness center with a gym, massage, and treatment area and sauna; a library; a cardroom; an Internet center; a shopping arcade; a children's playroom; a game arcade; and a small casino. Several of the most expensive suites have balconies.

In 2005, the cruise line purchased the 800-passenger *Grand Latino*, formerly *Royal Viking Sky*, from Iberojet Cruceros and renamed her *Boudicca*. The ship is similar to the *Black Watch* (formerly *Royal Viking Star*). In 2006, the line acquired the former *Crown Odyssey* from Norwegian and renamed her *Balmoral*. She commenced cruising for the line in January 2008 after a refit.

Strong Points:

Great itineraries at reasonable prices with a full-cruise experience on older, non-state-of-the-art vessels. The ships are very popular in the UK.

Courtesy Fred Olsen Cruise Line

Braemar, *courtesy Fred Olsen Cruise Line*

CHEF'S RECOMMENDATIONS

Asparagus Fricassée
Green asparagus fricassée presented warm in a puff pastry basket

Chilled Strawberry Soup
Chilled strawberry soup flavoured with Champagne

Corn Fed Chicken Suprême
A corn fed breast of chicken presented in a creamy mushroom sauce,
served with red cabbage, green peas and duchesse potatoes filled with tomato concasse

Chocolate and Cappuccino Mousse Cake
Layers of chocolate sponge and cappuccino mousse, served with apricot purée and cherries

LIGHTER BITES

Melon Pearl Cocktail
Ripe melon pearls served with melon sorbet

Beef Consommé "Celestine"
Clear beef soup, served with pancakes julienne

Roasted Greek Salad
Thyme and garlic scented roasted vegetables with light feta cheese, black olives,
lemon juice and balsamic vinegar

Beef Tenderloin
Whole roast beef tenderloin cooked to your liking, presented with seasonal
steamed vegetables, jacket potato and a red wine glaze

Please ask your waiter for today's low fat/calorie dessert

| **APPETISERS** | * | **Melon Pearl Cocktail** |
| | | Ripe melon pearls served with a melon sorbet |

                    * **Asparagus Fricassée**
Green asparagus fricassée presented warm in a puff pastry basket

SOUPS   * **Carrot Soup**
Cream of carrot soup served with tomato concasse

Consommé "Monte Carlo"
Beef consommé, served with crêpes filled with goose liver pâté

    * **Chilled Strawberry Soup**
Chilled strawberry soup flavoured with Champagne

SALADS   * **Today's Mixed Salad**
Served with a choice of garlic cream dressing or Greek
vinaigrette

    * **Roasted Greek Salad**
Thyme and garlic scented roasted vegetables with light feta cheese,
black olives, lemon juice and balsamic vinegar

COLD MAIN COURSE   **Salmon Trio**
A medley of hot smoked, marinated and tartare salmon,
served with horseradish cream, mustard sauce and sour
cream dressing

    * *Denotes suitable for vegetarians*

Some dishes may contain nuts or traces of nut
Please contact the Maître d'Hôtel for further details

MAIN COURSES

Grilled Fillet of Butter Fish
Served on sautéed spinach, with seasonal vegetables, Château
potatoes and a parsley cream sauce

Seafood Fettuccini
A medley of clams, prawns, crab and calamari in a tomato and
pesto sauce, served on a bed of al dente fettuccini

Corn Fed Chicken Suprème
A corn fed breast of chicken presented in a creamy mushroom sauce,
served with red cabbage, green peas and duchesse potatoes filled
with tomato concasse

Beef Tenderloin
Whole roast beef tenderloin cooked to your liking, presented
in a Béarnaise sauce, with seasonal vegetables and creamed
potatoes

**VEGETARIAN
MAIN COURSES**

* **Curried Mushroom Crêpe**
A herb pancake filled with curried mushrooms and
roasted pistachio nuts

* **Vegetarian Quiche**
A delicious quiche made with seasonal vegetables, served
with a mixed salad and a creamy mustard dressing

*If you require well cooked vegetables or smaller portions
please ask your waiter*

CHEESE	**Selection of Cheese and Biscuits**
	Served with grapes and radishes
	Please ask your waiter for vegetarian cheese

DESSERTS	**Pear Belle Hélène**
	Poached pear served with vanilla ice cream, chocolate sauce and whipped cream
	Also available for diabetics

Chocolate and Cappuccino Mousse Cake
Layers of chocolate sponge cake and cappuccino mousse, served with an apricot purée and cherries

Coconut Pudding
A coconut cream pudding flavoured with Malibu, presented on a medley of tropical fruits

Ice Creams and Sorbets
Please ask your waiter for today's selection of ice creams and sorbets
Diabetic and Soya Ice Cream is also available

Some dishes may contain nut or traces of nuts
Please contact the Maître d'Hôtel for further details

Courtesy Fred Olsen Cruise Line

APPETISERS

Prawn Cocktail
with iceberg salad and light cocktail sauce

Smoked Mackerel
on a bed of lettuce,
served with horseradish sauce

THE SOUP KETTLE

Consommé "Chesterfield"
clear beef soup with mushrooms and ox tongue

V Cock-a-Leekie Soup
chicken soup with leek and pearl barley

SALAD

V Red Cabbage Salad
with apple, celery, raisins and walnuts,
served with honey mustard dressing

V Seasonal Mixed Greens
tossed green salad
served with choice of tomato vinaigrette or
herb cream dressing

SORBET Lime Sorbet

MAIN COURSES Butter Fried Fillet of Sole
with sauteed vegetables, white wine sauce
and parsley potatoes

Chicken Pie
served with gravy, mixed vegetables and roast potatoes

Roast Rack of Lamb
with peas, baton carrots, new potatoes,
mint sauce gravy

Beef Wellington
Tenderloin wrapped in puff pastry,
served with red wine sauce,
stuffed grilled tomato, broccoli and roast potatoes

VEGETARIAN CHOICE *V* Vegetable Cutlet
served with red wine butter sauce,
sauteed mushrooms, broccoli and roasted potatoes

Our Chef's Selection of Seasonal Vegetables
and Potatoes

CHEESE	**A Selection of British Cheese** with celery, grapes and cheese biscuits

DESSERTS	**Hot Apple Pie "Maria Theresa"** served with whipped cream, custard sauce and vanilla ice cream
	Bread and Butter Pudding traditional English style
	Fruit Jelly with Grand Marnier mousse and biscuits
	Butterscotch Ice Cream with toffee pieces, topped with a coffee cream

V - *Suitable for vegetarians*

Courtesy Fred Olsen Cruise Line

BLACK WATCH

GOOD MORNING

8.00am	Daily Quiz available for collection; answers posted at 5.00pm	Library & Braemar
8.15am	Walk a Mile. Meet Sherly Deck 7 aft for a brisk mile walk around the deck	Deck 7 Aft
9.00-11.00am	Library is open for the loan of Books, Videos & CDs	Deck 9
9.00-9.15am	Navigational Bridge Visit. Collect your ticket for today's visits (15 per visit)	Reception

10.00am — PORT TALK — Neptune Lounge
Join, **Dawn Ramsey** for her informative talk on the ports of **Valencia & Gibraltar**
This will be relayed at 4:30pm on Channel 4 of your Cabin TV's

10.00am — BRIDGE CLASS — Card Room
Christine will continue to talk about **"Strong Hands & Slam Bidding"**
(**Neil** will continue with Beginner's Bridge)

10.00am	Golf Putting with Nick. Meet at the Golf Nets *(Weather Permitting)*	Deck 11
10.00am	Yoga Class with Carrianne. £5.00 for 30 minutes	Fitness Centre
10.30am	Shuffleboard. Meet Amanda Port Side of Lido Deck *(Weather Permitting)*	Deck 7
10.30am	Navigational Bridge Visit. *(Weather Permitting)*	Deck 8 Fwd

10.45am — DOLPHIN RACING AUCTION — Poolside, Deck 6
An opportunity to become a Black Watch Dolphin Owner & place your 50p bets.

11.00am — BLACK WATCH PASSENGER CHOIR! — Marina Theatre
Enjoy the experience of singing all kinds of music with your fellow guests.

11.00am — ICE CARVING DEMONSTRATION - *(Weather Permitting)* — Poolside, Deck 6
Come and watch as our expert ice carver turns a 300lb block of ice into a work of art.

11.00am	Morning Quiz with Shelley. More brain teasing questions	Lido Lounge
11.00am	Darts with Julie. (Take the stairs down by the Jacuzzi on Deck 6 aft)	Deck 5 Aft

11.30am — SANGRIA DECK PARTY - *(Weather Permitting)* — Poolside, Deck 6
Join us out on deck for sangria & dancing to the music of the
Black Watch Orchestra

GOOD AFTERNOON

Noon - 1.00pm	Piano Melodies. Join Sara Leport at the Grand	Observatory
Noon- 1.00pm	Piano Melodies. Dave Johnson takes to the Grand	Lido Lounge
2.00pm	Beginners - Come & learn the basic steps with Professional Instructors **Kevin & Debbie**	Neptune Lounge

AFTERNOON BRIDGE — Card Room

2.00pm	Friendly Duplicate and Rubber Bridge with **Christine & Neil Tomkin**.	
2.30pm	Meet in the Card Room if you want a game of *Whist*.	

2.15pm	Matinee Movie 'Serendipity' Running Time: 90 mins (12)	Marina Theatre
2.30pm	Deck Quoits. Meet Amanda Port Side of Lido Deck *(Weather Permitting)*	Deck 7
2.30pm	Short Tennis Meet Julie on the Tennis Courts for a friendly game. *(Weather Permitting)*	Deck 11
2.30pm	Navigational Bridge Visit. *(Weather Permitting)*	Deck 8 Fwd.

2.30pm — HANDICRAFTS CLASS — Lido Lounge
Join your Handicrafts Instructor **Margaret Taylor** as she continues on
"Iris Ribbon Embroidery" & does
"A Demonstration Using Paper Punches & Rubber Stamping for Easter"

2.30pm — AFTERNOON LECTURE — Neptune Lounge
"From Rags to Riches" - They did it their way
Today **Barry Marcus** tells the incredible story of Henry Ford, who refused to take
over his father's farm, founded the Ford Motor Company & put the world on wheels
despite the slogan *'you can have any colour as long as it's black'*

3.00pm	Table Tennis with Joy (Take the stairs down by the Jacuzzi on Deck 6 aft)	Deck 5 Aft
3.30pm	Carpet Boules with Shelley. Roll up for a friendly game.	Star Night Club
4.00pm	Afternoon Quiz with Jon. More brain teasing questions	Lido Lounge
4.00pm	Circuit Training with Carrianne. £3.00 for 30 minutes	Fitness Centre
4.00-6.00pm	Library is open for the loan of Books, Videos & CDs	Deck 9

4.00pm — MUSIC & DANCE CONCERT — Neptune Lounge
"Melodies of the Heart"
In this programme, we celebrate *'affairs of the heart'*
with beautiful romantic music & tales of passionate love.
With **Robin & Kim Colvill**
(Music by Beethoven, Chopin, Grieg, Sibelius, Lecuona & Liszt)

5.00pm	Bingo. Join Joy & Amanda. Win cash prizes. £2 per card for 4 games	Neptune Lounge
5.30pm	Feature Film 'Time Machine' 92 mins (PG) *Repeats at 8.00pm & 10.15pm*	Marina Theatre
5.30pm	Service Clubs Meeting. An informal gathering of all Lions, Rotarians, etc.	Lido Lounge

Courtesy Fred Olsen Cruise Line

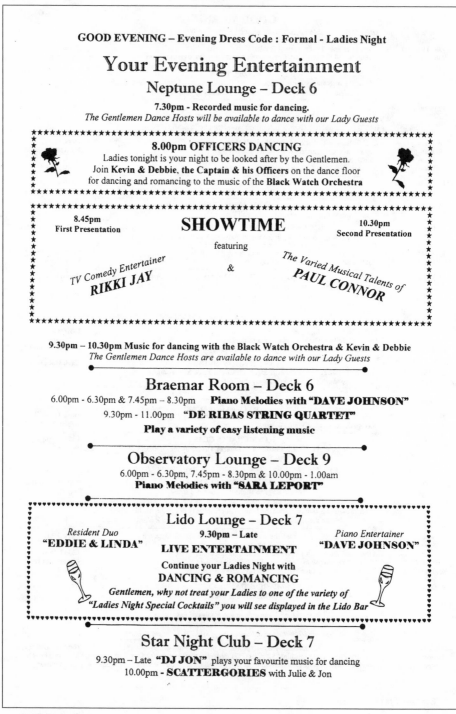

GOOD EVENING – Evening Dress Code : Formal - Ladies Night

Your Evening Entertainment
Neptune Lounge – Deck 6

7.30pm - Recorded music for dancing.
The Gentlemen Dance Hosts will be available to dance with our Lady Guests

8.00pm OFFICERS DANCING
Ladies tonight is your night to be looked after by the Gentlemen.
Join **Kevin & Debbie, the Captain & his Officers** on the dance floor
for dancing and romancing to the music of the **Black Watch Orchestra**

8.45pm
First Presentation

SHOWTIME

10.30pm
Second Presentation

featuring

TV Comedy Entertainer
RIKKI JAY

&

The Varied Musical Talents of
PAUL CONNOR

9.30pm – 10.30pm Music for dancing with the Black Watch Orchestra & Kevin & Debbie
The Gentlemen Dance Hosts are available to dance with our Lady Guests

Braemar Room – Deck 6
6.00pm - 6.30pm & 7.45pm – 8.30pm   **Piano Melodies with "DAVE JOHNSON"**
9.30pm - 11.00pm **"DE RIBAS STRING QUARTET"**
Play a variety of easy listening music

Observatory Lounge – Deck 9
6.00pm - 6.30pm, 7.45pm - 8.30pm & 10.00pm - 1.00am
Piano Melodies with "SARA LEPORT"

Lido Lounge – Deck 7

Resident Duo
"EDDIE & LINDA"

9.30pm – Late
LIVE ENTERTAINMENT

Piano Entertainer
"DAVE JOHNSON"

Continue your Ladies Night with
DANCING & ROMANCING
Gentlemen, why not treat your Ladies to one of the variety of
"Ladies Night Special Cocktails" you will see displayed in the Lido Bar

Star Night Club – Deck 7
9.30pm – Late **"DJ JON"** plays your favourite music for dancing
10.00pm - **SCATTERGORIES** with Julie & Jon

Courtesy Fred Olsen Cruise Line

FRENCH COUNTRY WATERWAYS, LTD.
P.O. Box 2195
Duxbury, Massachusetts 02331-2195
(800) 222-1236
(781) 934-9048 Fax
www.fcwl.com

ADRIENNE: entered service for cruise line 2005; 250 G.R.T.; 128'; 12-passenger capacity; 6 staterooms; French and English crew; 6-night cruises in Canal de Bourgogne in Burgundy's Cote d'Or wine-growing region. (**Category A/B— Not Rated**)

ESPRIT: converted to hotel barge 1986; refurbished 2003; 280 G.R.T.; 128'; 18-passenger capacity; 9 staterooms; French and English crew; 6-night cruises in Côte d'Or between Dijon and St. Leger-sur-Dheune. (**Category A/B—Not Rated**)

HORIZON II: converted to barge hotel 1983/1984; rebuilt for only 8 passengers in 2003; 190 G.R.T.; 128'; 8-passenger capacity; 4 suites; French and English crew; six-night cruises in historic Burgundy, Canal du Nivernais, and Canal de Bourgogne. (**Category A/B—Not Rated**)

NENUPHAR: converted to barge hotel 1979; renovated 2006; 280 G.R.T.; 128'; 12-passenger capacity; 6 suites; French and English crew; 6-night cruises in northern Burgundy between Lezinnes and Gurgy. (**CategoryA/B—Not Rated**)

PRINCESS: built in 1973; refurbished 2003; 280 G.R.T.; 128'; 8-passenger capacity; 4 suites; French and English crew; 6-night cruises in Champagne between Maizy and Chateau-Thierry as well as in the Alsace-Lorraine region. (**Category A/B—Not Rated**)

(Medical Facilities: Captains are certified in CPR and take a first-aid course. Motor vehicles travel with barge.)

French Country Waterways, Ltd., offers barge cruises designed for sophisticated active travelers who wish to explore various charming regions of France in an intimate way. Itineraries vary but include daily sightseeing excursions to medieval towns and cities, famous churches and chateaux, and renowned vineyards with wine tastings, as well as options for hot-air balloon rides. French Country Waterways is unique in that it owns, operates, and markets only its own vessels, whereas the company's competitors do not own most of the barges, but only operate and/or market them.

The exceptionally friendly, well-educated captains and crews are fluent in English and French and admirably succeed in making passengers feel as though they are guests on a private floating home.

The barges, which are also available for individual and charter bookings, are refurbished annually and each has a sun deck, comfortable, homey main salon that serves as a combination lounge, dining room, fully stocked bar, and library, and fleet of bicycles for passenger use ashore. The newest additions to the fleet are the eight-passenger *Princess* and the 12-passenger *Adrienne,* both of which boast well-appointed staterooms with king-size beds and spacious public areas.

All barges are tastefully furnished, air conditioned throughout, and suites and staterooms have private bathrooms with toilet and showers, vanities, hair dryers, heated towel bars, and adequate closet/wardrobe space, as well as various amenities. However, there are no televisions, radios, phones, refrigerators, or safes in the rooms and no Internet access aboard the barges.

All-inclusive cruise prices, ranging from $5,836 to $8,195 per person (double occupancy) depending upon the season, include all meals as well as one meal ashore at a highly rated French restaurant that has received a star rating in the *Michelin Guide,* an open bar, Premier Cru and Grand Cru wines and delicious regional cheeses at lunch and dinner, all tours and excursions, and transfers to and from Paris or another main city. Restaurant visits in 2007 included Lameloise in Chagny, Le Relais Bernard Loiseau in Saulieu, Le Cerf in Marlenheim, Les Crayers in Reims, and Auberge des Templiers in Les Bezards. (Auberge des Templiers in Les Bezards and Les Crayers are also two of the resorts included in *Stern's Guide to the Greatest Resorts of the World.*) Dining aboard the barges is exceptional, with excellent cuisine superbly prepared and presented by trained chefs who obtain fresh ingredients daily and design menus based upon what appears most appealing at the local market. The fresh croissants, baguettes, and pastries delivered each morning from a local bakery are outstanding.

There is no entertainment or organized activities in the evenings and passengers generally visit with each other over an after-dinner beverage or read a book.

A French County Waterways barge sojourn is a must for the seasoned cruiser who wishes to complete and enhance his or her cruise experiences and who can appreciate this very special type of cruise vacation.

Strong Points:

The epitome of an intimate, charming, and tranquil barge/cruise experience with fine dining and exceptional, friendly service. This is also a good option for adult families or groups of friends wishing to charter the entire barge. This is possibly the best of the barge lines exploring the waterways of France.

Horizon II *on Burgundy Canal, courtesy French Country Waterways, Ltd.*

Dining room on Horizon II, *courtesy French Country Waterways, Ltd.*

Horizon II *on Burgundy Canal, courtesy French Country Waterways, Ltd.*

Adrienne, *courtesy French Country Waterways, Ltd.*

Adrienne, *courtesy French Country Waterways, Ltd.*

Adrienne, *courtesy French Country Waterways, Ltd.*

ADRIENNE

Nemours   le 1er Septembre 2006

Foie gras de canard poêlé accompagné de ses pommes aux épices
Réduction balsamique

* * * * * * * * * * * * * *

Noix de St Jacques et sa julienne de légumes

* * * * * * * * * * * * * *

Filet de bœuf, sauce aux morilles
Pomme Paillasson et fagot de haricots verts

* * * * * * * * * * * * * *

Plateau de fromages
Salade

* * * * * * * * * * * * * *

Farandole de desserts

<u>Vin Blanc</u>   <u>Vin Rouge</u>

Alsace Sylvaner vieilles vignes 2003   Clos-Vougeot Grand Cru
1998

Corton Charlemagne Grand Cru 2000

GRAND CIRCLE CRUISES
347 Congress Street
Boston, Massachusetts 02210
(617) 350-7500
(800) 248-3737
(617) 346-6840 Fax
www.gct.com

M/S *RIVER BIZET, RIVER DEBUSSY,* and *RIVER RAVEL:* entered service 2002, 2000, and 2001, respectively; 1,900-1,952 G.R.T.; 363' x 37.6'; 120-passenger capacity; 60 cabins; international crew; up to 14-night cruises on various rivers in Europe.

RIVER CHARDONNAY: entered service 1999; 822 G.R.T.; 260' x 28'; 50-passenger capacity; 27 cabins; international crew; up to 14-night cruises on Saône and Rhône Rivers.

M/S *RIVER ADAGIO* and M/S *RIVER ARIA:* entered service 2003 and 2001, respectively; 1,935 G.R.T.; 410' x 38'; 164-passenger capacity; 82 cabins; international crew; up to 14-night cruises on various rivers in Europe.

M/S *RIVER ANUKET:* entered service 2001; 2,350 G.R.T.; 237' x 47'; 138-passenger capacity; 70 cabins; Egyptian crew; cruises on Nile River.

M/S *RIVER HATHOR:* entered service 1990; renovated 2004; 630 G.R.T.; 188' long; 32-passenger capacity; 16 cabins; Egyptian crew; Nile River cruises.

M/S *RIVER CONCERTO, RIVER HARMONY, RIVER MELODY, RIVER RHAPSODY,* and *RIVER SYMPHONY:* entered service 2000, 1999, 1999, 1999, and 1998, respectively; 1,642-1,949 G.R.T.; 361' x 38'; 140-passenger capacity; 70 cabins; international crew; 7-night cruises on various rivers in Europe.

M/S *RIVER PROVENCE:* entered service 2000; 1,000 G.R.T.; 292' x 28'; 50-passenger capacity; 27 cabins; international crew; up to 14-night cruises on Saône and Rhone Rivers.

M/S *TIKHI DON:* refurbished 2006; 3,570 G.R.T.; 425' x 54'; 220-passenger capacity; 112 cabins; Russian and international crew; 14-night cruises between Moscow and St. Petersburg along Volga and Svir Rivers and through Lakes Onega and Ladoga.

M/S *ABERCROMBIE:* built 1926; refurbished 2005; 280 G.R.T.; 128' x 17'; 22-passenger capacity; 11 cabins; European crew; 7-night cruises on River Saône and Burgundy canals.

Grand Circle Travel was launched in 1958 to serve AARP members. In 1985 the company was acquired by Alan and Harriet Lewis, who began offering Grand Circle's international itineraries to United States citizens over the age of 50. Grand Circle added a second brand, Overseas Adventure Travel, also for mature Americans, in 1993. In 2004, the company purchased Continental Waterways, adding seven barges and two riverboats.

Grand Circle Cruise Line owns and operates a fleet of 45 small ships that serves both its Grand Circle Travel (GCT) and Overseas Adventure Travel (OAT) brands. The fleet is composed of 16 river ships, eight barges, three 50-passenger ocean vessels, one expedition vessel, and various exclusively chartered vessels. GCT and OAT small ship cruise vacations take travelers to Europe, Egypt, the Red Sea, the Suez Canal, the Panama Canal, Russia, China, the Galapagos, and French Polynesia.

All of the riverboats feature air-conditioned outside cabins with closets, storage space, private bath and showers, color TV with CNN and movies, radios, direct-dial telephones, and in-room safes. Public areas include a restaurant with a single open seating, bar and lounge, and sun deck. Some have fitness rooms and saunas. The international crew all speak English and four-course dinners are featured with two choices of entrees.

The riverboats stop at cities, towns, and villages along the waterways they traverse. (See chapter 10 for description of riverboats in general.)

The barges have small air-conditioned cabins with portholes and private bathrooms with showers. Each has a main parlor/lounge with a bar and dining area that opens on to a small sun-deck area. Meals are prepared by on-board chefs, vary daily based on local produce, and include complimentary wines with dinner and tastings of cheeses from the various regions. The barges carry bicycles, allowing passengers to take short bike rides. The barges traverse inland waterways and canals, stopping daily at points of interest along the way.

Grand Circle Cruises packages these sailings with international round-trip air arrangements, all transfers, and pre- and post-land tours.

HAPAG-LLOYD

In the U.S.	In Germany
Euro-Lloyd Travel Group	Ballindamm 25 D-20095
(800) 782-3924	Hamburg, Germany
Kartagener Associates, Inc.	+49 (0) 40 3001 4580
(877) 445-7447	+49 (0) 40 3001 4849 Fax

BREMEN (formerly *Frontier Spirit*): entered service 1990; 6,752 G.R.T.; 365' x 56'; 164-passenger capacity; 82 cabins; German officers and staff (all English speaking); expedition cruises to polar regions, rivers, and remote islands. (**Category B/C—Not Rated**)

COLUMBUS: entered service 1997; 15,000 G.R.T. 472' x 72'; 410-passenger capacity; 205 cabins; German officers and staff (all English speaking); cruises in Great Lakes of U.S. and various itineraries around the world. (**Category C—Not Rated**)

EUROPA: entered service 1999; 28,890 G.R.T.; 652' x 78'; 408-passenger capacity; 204 suites; German officers and staff (all English speaking); cruises to various locations around the world.

HANSEATIC: entered service 1993; 8,378 G.R.T.; 403' x 59'; 184-passenger capacity; 92 cabins; German officers and staff (all English speaking); expedition cruises to polar regions, rivers, and remote islands. (**Category A/B—Not Rated**)

(All ships have hospitals and a physician.)

Some of these ships are rated in 11 separate categories in the second half of chapter 14.

In 1970, Hapag and North German Lloyd lines merged. Both lines date back to the 19th century and have played a role in the development of cruising during the 20th century. The company owns the *Europa, Bremen, Hanseatic,* and *Columbus.* The four ships are largely sold to the German and European markets, with German being the official language on board and the euro the official currency. The officers and staff are all multilingual, though on most cruises all announcements, programs, menus, and TV channels are exclusively in German. However, on the *Europa,* programs and menus can always be provided in English. Beginning in 2004, the cruise line has indicated that it is interested in attracting the non-German-speaking cruise market by offering select cruises on each of its ships throughout the year in different areas of the world where English, as well as German, will be the official language, thereby affording an opportunity for non-German-speaking cruisers to enjoy the special Hapag-Lloyd experience. If there is at least one English-speaking passenger aboard, announcements, etc. are bilingual.

The *Europa* is the sixth ship of the original line to receive the same name. The fifth *Europa* was sold in 1999 and the present vessel entered service the same year. Today U.S. bookings are taken through their American marketing/sales offices.

The all-suite *Europa* includes many of the technological advances and creature comforts that appear in ships built in the late 1990s; however, the design and decor are somewhat atypical of the larger ships built in recent years by other cruise lines in that there is less glitz, glamour, bells, and whistles. In many ways, the ship is more reminiscent of the vessels of the former Royal Viking Line.

Atop ship on deck 10 are 12 penthouse suites, with 14 veranda suites below, on deck 9. The remaining suites are located on decks 5, 6, and 7. All in all, 168 of the 204 accommodations have verandas, reflecting today's demand for this feature. All the suites are quite spacious, measuring 290 to 484 square feet (with 64-square-foot verandas). The two top, grand penthouse suites reach 915 square feet. In 2007, four spa suites were added close to the new Ocean Spa area on deck. The spa suites have illuminated whirlpools with ocean views, a rain shower with lateral jets, and scent lamps filled with essential oils. The comprehensive spa package comes with the option of selected in-suite treatments.

Every accommodation has two twin beds with European duvets that can be converted to a double-bed arrangement, a writing desk, a sitting area, a personal safe that can be opened with a credit card, a large walk-in closet with additional drawer space, a TV/radio with movies and music on demand, an advanced e-mail and video on-demand system with free Internet access and personal email accounts via the TV set and wireless keyboard, a hair dryer, a refrigerator stocked with complimentary soft drinks that is refilled daily, and bathrooms with terry robes and slippers, tub, and glass-enclosed shower.

The 10 484-square-foot penthouse deluxe suites are even more spacious, with an entryway, a larger lounging area, two TVs, double bathroom vanities, and Jacuzzi bathtubs. The two penthouse grand suites boast wrap-around balconies, a large living-room area with a dining table for up to six persons, giant bathrooms with saunas, and an additional guest bathroom. All of the penthouse suites enjoy extraordinarily solicitous, 24-hour butler service, free laundry and pressing, fresh fruit, canapes and caviar upon request, and free in-suite alcoholic beverages and soft drinks. In addition, there are two suites that can accommodate physically challenged passengers.

On deck 9 you will find Sansibar, an observation bar, offering a good view from the stern of the ship; a golf simulator; and a new gym. Deck 8 is the location of the unusually long swimming pool, half of which is covered with a sliding magrodome for inclement weather; a jogging track; numerous lounge chairs; an indoor/outdoor lido buffet restaurant; the Club Belvedere observation lounge, a room that can be used for movies or lectures; and a library. On deck 7 are two newly expanded children's playrooms and the Ocean Spa, which includes a beauty salon, Japanese bath, treatment rooms, solarium, steam room, sauna, and men and women's changing rooms. Deck 4 is the locale for all of the other public rooms, including the reception area, tour desk, grand show lounge, several other lounges and bars, art gallery, cigar-smoking lounge, boutique and jewelry shop, 408-seat main dining room, and Italian and Asian specialty restaurants. The main dining room seats all guests in one sitting at assigned tables for dinner and has open seating for breakfast and lunch. The two specialty restaurants are open for both lunch and dinner and require advanced reservations but exact no surcharge. Menus change daily in all three restaurants. Theme lunches with dishes typical of the region are frequently offered at the lido buffet, where a band plays on special occasions. Nightly entertainment generally includes musical performers but no production shows. There is no casino on the ship since gambling is not popular with German cruisers.

Food and service are excellent in all of the restaurants. Service throughout the ship is among the most solicitous and efficient in the industry. Cabin attendants will accommodate every reasonable request; pool attendants pamper guests with cold towels, drinks, fresh fruit, and refreshing spray; restaurant waitstaff are always available to accommodate your needs; the information desk staff is knowledgeable and anxious to assist (a rarity in the cruise industry); and the entire staff of officers and crew appear dedicated to leaving each passenger with a positive experience.

In September 2004 the ship underwent a major renovation with several additions and changes to the public areas. The lido café was redesigned with additional service stations to avoid traffic jams and in the evening offers an alternative dining venue with an open kitchen and grill stations. The size of the gym was significantly increased and moved to a more convenient location on deck 9, and state-of-the-art equipment such as treadmills with personal TVs and exercycles were added. The children's facilities also were expanded. A new observation bar, Sansibar, was constructed on deck 9 overlooking the lido café. The number of zodiacs was increased to 13. The area for nude sunbathing was moved to deck 11. Much of the carpeting was replaced and some of the walls and decor in the common areas were redone.

Itineraries generally run from two to three weeks; however, there are shorter cruises offered at different times of the year. Itineraries include the the Mediterranean, North Sea-Baltic, Southeast Asia, South America, and the South Pacific as well as other cruise grounds around the world. Passengers can book an entire world cruise if they wish. Most cruises offer a special theme ranging from gourmet cooking or classical music to arts and culture or golf.

The 15,000-ton, 420-passenger *Columbus* entered service in 1997. During the fall, when she is traversing the Great Lakes, everything on the ship is presented in English as well as in German, including announcements, menus, programs, and lectures. The rest of the year she cruises to other world destinations and German is the official language. Of the 205 cabins, eight are suites (two of which have private balconies), 140 are located outside and 63 are inside. Atop ship is a swimming pool, sunbathing area, small gym, and buffet restaurant. The cabins and suites are spread along the next five decks with the other facilities that include the single-seating restaurant, main lounge, a shop, library, photo gallery, cardroom, and several bars. Golf cruises are frequently featured. Also, there are 12 bicycles aboard ship available to passengers for shore excursions.

The 8,378-ton, 184-pasenger *Hanseatic* entered servcie in 1993. An exploration cruise vessel with the highest ice classification for passenger vessels, her ice-resistant hull and shallow draft enable her to navigate icy waters in the Arctic, Antarctic, White Russian Sea, and the Northwest Passage as well as small harbors in less-traveled waters not available to other ships, such as the Amazon River and Micronesia. She carries 14 zodiacs for shore excursions, as well as bicycles, Nordic walking, and snorkeling equipment. In polar regions, passengers are equipped with warm parkas and rubber boots. These are cruises that explore nature, history, geography, and architecture with on-board lecturers to enhance the experience.

The 88,237-square-foot, outside staterooms have either two single beds or one double bed, sitting areas, TV/radios, free personal e-mail connections, minibars, marble bathrooms with showers, hair dryers, and bathrobes. There are four 473-square-foot suites. Two cabins can accommodate the physically challenged. Seven have an additional bed, and there are also two four-bedded cabins. The suites and staterooms on bridge deck enjoy butler service.

Atop ship on the observation deck is a small pool, Jacuzzi, sauna, bar, hairdressing salon, small gym, library, and observation lounge. On the next four decks are the cabins and public facilities, which include the Columbus lounge with a bar, the Explorer lounge with a bar and dance floor, the lecture room, tour office, reception, and hospital. There is a single-seating main restaurant and a specialty restaurant serving ethnic cuisine. Snacks are available through 24-hour cabin service. The minibars in all cabins contain soft drinks and are refilled daily at no charge.

The former *Frontier Spirit,* built for expedition crusing, now sails as the *Bremen.* The ship has 80 194-square-foot outside cabins featuring sitting and bedroom areas, closed-circuit television, minibars, satellite telephone, hair dryers, and bathrobes. The two 258-square-foot suites on deck 7 and the 16 staterooms on deck 6 have private verandas. Public areas and facililtes include a library; two lounges, including a panorama lounge; sauna; gym; swimming pool; single-seating dining room; bar; beauty parlor; infirmary; and 12 exploration zodiacs. The ship went through renovations in 2007, adding additional computers and Internet connections, new carpeting, new bathrooms, and new furniture. All cabins also have been furnished with new flat-screen TVs and converted to non-smoking.

Built to cruise where other ships are unable to go (similar to the *Hanseatic* with the highest ice classification for passenger vessels), the *Bremen* visits such out-of-the-way destinations as the Arctic, Antarctic, Northwest Passage, and the deep Amazon in South America, as well as the Red Sea, the Mediterranean, the Far East, and the South Pacific.

Cruising on a Hapag-Lloyd ship offers a very typical German experience with traditional German and international cuisine, and will be appreciated most by those travelers wishing to enjoy the flavors, efficiency, excellent service, and spirit of that country.

Strong Points:

Europa: Superior accommodations in all categories; interesting, diverse dining possibilities; exceptional service; and desireable itineraries.

Columbus: The first newly built ship to offer cruises on the Great Lakes in several decades.

Hanseatic: One of the few more upscale, yacht-like cruise ships with comfortable cabins to offer expedition itineraries.

Europa, *courtesy Hapag-Lloyd*

Europa, *courtesy Hapag-Lloyd*

Europa, *courtesy Hapag-Lloyd*

Europa, *courtesy Hapag-Lloyd*

Europa, *courtesy Hapag-Lloyd*

EUROPA

Daytime activities:

07.00 h   **Pilot**
The pilot for Copenhagen arrives on board.

08.00 h   **Arrival at Copenhagen!**
MV EUROPA moors at the pier of Copenhagen.

08.30 h   **Walking**   Fitnessroom, Sport Deck
Personal Trainer Heiko Werner will meet you at the gym to start
the day with exercises.

14.00 h   **„Cruise from Hamburg to Malaga"**   TV channel 3
Our video producer Dr. Manfred Classen shows the variety of the European Atlantic
coast and dramatic scenery in this video.

16.00 - 17.00 h   **Relaxing Tea Time**   Club Belvedere, Lido Deck
Enjoy the afternoon with piano entertainment by Giorgio di Luca.
At the same time you can experience our wide variety of different teas - taste
another kind of tea each day!

16.00 - 19.30 h   **Cruising with Hapag-Lloyd**   Atrium, Europa Deck
CRUISING OFF CAPE HOORN - experience this part of the world during
Christmas time, when MV EUROPA sails from Buenos Aires to Valparaiso.
Here, in the south of Argentina the world's biggest flock of Magellan penguins can
be found. Another attraction are the beautiful glaciers of the Chilean fjords.
Ingrid Beyer-Ziegler is available for information. If you book your next cruise
on board you will be granted an additional bonus of 3%!

17.30 h   **End of Shore Leave**
We kindly ask you to be on time!

17.30, 18.30   **MV EUROPA Board TV**   TV channel 1
and 19.30 h Famous German TV presenter Babette Einstmann interviews Joan Orleans,
the Queen of Soul.

17.45 h   **Sail Away Brass music**   Bellevue Deck, Deck 9
Our New Connection Band plays when MV EUROPA leaves Copenhagen.

18.00 h   **Good Bye, Copenhagen!**
MV EUROPA leaves Copenhagen and sets course for Kiel
(172 nautical miles = 319 km).

Enjoy the evening!

18.00 - 20.00 h	**The gallery is open!** Enjoy the "Likörelle"- exhibition by german singer and Rock-Legend Udo Lindenberg! All pictures are painted with different kinds of liqueurs.	Gallery, Europa Deck
18.00 h	**Sail away** ... with melodies performed by the Rivieras Band. Enjoy the special atmosphere on deck when MV EUROPA is leaving Copenhagen. The ship's officers look forward to meet you for a glass of Champagne!	Lido Pool, Lido Deck
18.30 and 20.45 h	**Romantic tunes** ... at cocktail hour by Giorgio di Luca.	Atrium, Europa Deck
21.00 h	**Would you like to dance?** Our Rivieras Quartet invites you to dance.	Clipper Lounge, Europa Deck
21.00 h	**In the Mood** New Connection will get you in the mood for tonight's show.	Europa Lounge, Europa Deck
21.45 h	**JOAN ORLEANS: THE VOICE OF LOUISIANA** 600 appearances with standing ovations in the musical „Mahalia- Queen of Gospel" now on stage at MV EUROPA. She was discovered at the famous german TV show „Bio's Bahnhof" with Alfred Biolek. He recognized the astonishing voice of the „Souls-lady". Tonight she will be accompanied by Jo Kurzweg's New Connection- Band.	Europa Lounge, Europa Deck
22.30 h	**FAREWELL** Captain Friedrich Jan Akkermann invites you for an evening together with the crew. Enjoy the sea-chart auction with Staff-captain Peter Losinger and the crew choir with traditional German shanties. Join us afterwards in the Atrium for a sing-along with the crew.	Europa Lounge, Europa Deck

Courtesy Hapag-Lloyd

Farewell-Dinner

FROM HAMBURG TO KIEL

Thursday, 12. August 2004 · Kopenhagen

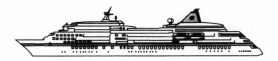

Winesuggestion

WHITEWINE

France
Burgund

2002er Chablis Premier Cru
Joseph Drouhin
48,00 €

REDWINE

Australia
Barossa Valley

1998er Cabernet Shiraz BIN 389
Penfolds
46,00 €

Russian Ossietra Caviar on Potato Fritters
Tatar of wild Salmon on Lemon-Brioche
Artichokes Tureen with Salmon Caviar

or

Black Truffle flavoured Goose Liver Mousse
presented on Beef Carpaccio

❧

Cream of sweet Potatoes and Saffron with Alaska King Crab Meat

❧

Raspberry Vinegar marinated Barbarie Duck Breast,
served in Red Bell Pepper Soup

❧

Pan fried Dover Sole with Horseradish-Hollandaise,
new Potatoes and white Asparagus

or

Symphony of Reindeer and Venison with Red Wine Espresso,
Chestnuts in Caramel, Gingerbread Polenta and Broccoli

❧

Kir Royal

❧

Selection of Tölzer Kasladen

❧

Harmony of Chocolate, fresh Strawberries
and Champagne

Courtesy Hapag-Lloyd

HOLLAND AMERICA LINE
300 Elliott Avenue West
Seattle, Washington 98119
(800) 426-0327; (206) 281-3535
www.hollandamerica.com

AMSTERDAM: entered service 2000; 61,000 G.R.T.; 780' x 105.8'; 1,380-passenger capacity; 690 cabins; European and international officers, Indonesian and Filipino crew; cruises Panama Canal, Alaska, South America, and South Pacific.

 +

EURODAM: entered service 2008; 86,273 G.R.T.; 936' x 105.8'; 2,104-passenger capacity; 1,052 cabins; European and international officers, Indonesian and Filipino crew; Caribbean cruises during winter, European cruises during summer, and East Coast of U.S. and Canada during fall.

 +

MAASDAM: entered service 1993; 55,575 G.R.T.; 720' x 101'; 1,258-passenger capacity; 629 cabins; European and international officers, Indonesian and Filipino crew; cruises the southern and eastern Caribbean, eastern Canada/New England, Canada, Panama Canal, and transatlantic.

 +

NIEUW AMSTERDAM: entered service 2010; 86,700 G.R.T.; 936' x. 105.8'; 2,106-passenger capacity; 1,053 cabins; European and international officers, Indonesian and Filipino crew; Caribbean cruises during fall/winter and European cruises during summer.

★★★★★ +

PRINSENDAM (formerly *Royal Viking Sun* and *Seabourn Sun*): entered service 1988; renovated 2008; 37,848 G.R.T.; 669' x 106'; 793-passenger capacity; 398 cabins; European and international officers, Indonesian and Filipino crew; cruises Western Europe, Mediterranean, Baltic, Norwegian fjords, Black Sea, transatlantic, Caribbean, Panama Canal, South America, and Amazon River.

★★★★★ +

ROTTERDAM: entered service 1997; 59,652 G.R.T.; 780' x 105.8'; 1,316-passenger capacity (1,605 when every berth is filled); 658 cabins; European and international officers, Indonesian and Filipino crew; cruises Mediterranean, Baltic, transatlantic, Europe, Panama Canal, and a world voyage.

RYNDAM: entered service 1994; 55,819 G.R.T.; 720' x 101'; 1,270-passenger capacity; 631 cabins; European and international officers, Indonesian and Filipino crew; cruises Alaska, Mexico, and Caribbean.

STATENDAM: entered service 1993; 55,851 G.R.T.; 720' x 101'; 1,258-passenger capacity; 675 cabins; European and international officers, Indonesian and Filipino crew; cruises Alaska, Pacific Northwest, anama Canal, and Caribbean.

VEENDAM: entered service 1996; 55,758 G.R.T.; 720' x 101'; 1,350-passenger capacity; 629 cabins; European and international officers, Indonesian and Filipino crew; cruises western Caribbean, Panama Canal, Alaska, and South America.

VOLENDAM and *ZAANDAM:* entered service 1999 and 2000, respectively; 61,396 G.R.T.; 780' x 105.8'; 1,432-passenger capacity; 716 cabins; European and international officers, Filipino and Indonesian crew; *Volendam* cruises South Pacific, Australia/New Zealand, Southeast Asia, and Alaska; *Zaandam* cruises Hawaii and Alaska.

ZUIDERDAM, OOSTERDAM, WESTERDAM, and *NOORDAM:* entered service 2002, 2003, 2004, and 2006, respectively; 81,811-82,500 G.R.T.; 935' x 105.8'; 1,916-passenger capacity on *Oosterdam, Zuiderdam,* and *Westerdam,* 1,918 on *Noordam;* 958-959 cabins; European and international officers, Indonesian and Filipino crew; *Zuiderdam* cruises the Caribbean, Alaska, and Panama Canal; *Oosterdam* cruises Mexico, Panama Canal, and Europe; *Westerdam* cruises the Caribbean, Panama Canal, and Alaska; and *Noordam* cruises the Caribbean, Mediterranean, and transatlantic.

(Medical Facilities: P-2; EM, CLS; MS; N-2to3; CM; PD; BC; EKG; TC; PO; EPC; OX; WC; ICU; X; M; CCP, D, TM, LJ; 22-23 wheelchair-accessible cabins on *Rotterdam, Volendam, Amsterdam,* and *Zaandam,* 28 on *Zuiderdam, Oosterdam, Westerdam,* and *Noordam,* 6 on *Statendam, Maasdam, Ryndam,* and *Veendam,* and 30 on *Eurodam.*)

These ships are rated in 11 separate categories in the second half of chapter 14.

Dutch owners started the Netherlands-America Steamship Company in 1872, and its first ocean liner, the original *Rotterdam,* made its maiden voyage to New York in 1873. In 1896, the company became known as Holland America Line (HAL). Westours, based in Seattle, Washington, had sold Alaskan tours since 1947 and frequently leased Holland America ships. In 1974, Holland America Line/Westours became a subsidiary of the Dutch parent company. In 1989, the line was purchased by Carnival Corporation.

Historically the cruise line's primary audience has been older, financially secure couples with an average age of 57. This has been changing and greater numbers of younger adults and couples are opting for HAL ships. Forty percent of all passengers are repeaters. The cruise line has facilities for children in order to accommodate traveling families and broaden the line's appeal to younger travelers. HAL hosts more than 25,000 children and their families aboard its ships each year. The Club HAL program is open to ages three to 12 with age-specific activities and facilities. A separate teen program is geared for ages 13 to 17 with separate venues.

All of the ships today have European or international officers holding the top jobs, with a mixed crew of Indonesians and Filipinos holding the positions of waiters, wine stewards, bartenders, and cabin attendants. Most cruisers find the crew attentive, friendly, and anxious to please, but some are disenchanted with the crew's lack of formality and lack of familiarity with European and North American tastes and needs. At times, cabin service and restaurant service can be quite slow. In past years, Holland America Line featured a "tipping not required" policy, but in practice, many cruisers elected to tip their waiters and cabin stewards. In 2004, the line changed its policy, and now tips are added to your shipboard account.

The *Rotterdam V,* built in the late 1950s, was retired from service in 1997 and subsequently sold to the now-defunct Premier Cruise Line. The sister ships *Nieuw Amsterdam* and *Noordam* were two of the more conveniently laid out, attractively designed, and tastefully furbished vessels built in the 1980s. However, with the entry of newer and larger HAL ships, these two did not fit into the fleet and were chartered long term. The *Westerdam* was built by Home Lines as the *Homeric* in 1986. She was purchased by Holland America in 1988, given an $85 million expansion in 1989, and transferred to Costa Cruise Line in 2002. This should not be confused with the new 85,000-ton *Westerdam* that entered service in 2004.

On all vessels, Holland America offers a full complement of activities and entertainment, including the aforementioned children's program, Club HAL. In recent years, the line has actively sought to increase its share in the family cruise market, as well as to appeal to younger cruisers. Guests can expect movies, numerous live nightclub shows, several orchestras, deck sports, bridge tournaments, dance lessons, gambling at the casinos, disco, romantic orchestras, wine tasting, formal teas, arts, crafts, bingo, horse racing, and audience-participation games.

Commencing in 2000, the line has been featuring an extensive golf program on Caribbean sailings, with tee times at the Caribbean's most acclaimed golf courses. Also, all of the ships are receiving expanded computer facilities permitting passengers to log on and engage in e-mail correspondence for a small charge. The *Vista-* and *Signature*-class ships are quite impressive and cabins on these ships have data ports. Wireless Internet is also available. The company has also introduced wheelchair-accessible tenders.

Although Holland America is constantly shifting its cruise grounds to accommodate the market, the ships generally sail to Alaska, Europe, the Panama Canal, Mexico, Hawaii, South America, the Caribbean, and eastern Canada/New England.

Holland America added four new modern vessels in the mid-1990s. Each of these ships is approximately 55,451 tons and carries 1,258 passengers in 629 staterooms, three-quarters of which are outside. The first of these vessels, the *Statendam,* entered service in January 1993; the second, the *Maasdam,* in December 1993; the third, the *Ryndam,* in October 1994; and the fourth, the *Veendam,* in May 1996. These ships are referred to as the "S-class" ships and are similar in layout and facilities.

The 149 deluxe cabins and suites are located on navigation and veranda decks near the top of the ships and boast floor-to-ceiling windows, private verandas, whirlpool baths and showers, hair dryers, refrigerated minibars, flat-screen TVs, plush terry-cloth robes, Aromapure bath amenities, personalized stationery, hors d'oeuvres in the suites, and maximum space and comfort. The suites also have DVD players. Most of the remaining accommodations are on the three lower decks and include two lower beds convertible to a queen-size bed, small sitting areas, decent closet space, multi-channel music systems, telephones with voice mail, flat-screen televisions, private room safes, Elemis Aromapure bath amenities, and hair dryers. Public facilities encompass eight passenger elevators; two outdoor pools; two outdoor, heated whirlpools; an elegant, dual-level dining room with tables adorned with fresh flowers, fine crystal, and Rosenthal china; a comfortable lido buffet-style restaurant with exceptional buffets; a health spa with exercise and cardiovascular machines, sauna, steam rooms, masseuse, hair salon, and daily exercise and aerobics classes; a casino; a well-stocked library with a DVD selection; card and game rooms; a comfortable movie theater; a large, two-level showroom; and numerous more intimate lounges.

The new *Rotterdam* entered service in fall 1997, when the prior *Rotterdam* was retired, and was at that time marketed as the company's flagship. The vessel was built and designed especially for luxurious European and around-the-world voyages with the capability to sustain speeds up to 25 knots (20 percent faster than today's average cruise ships) to permit more hours in ports of call and shorter sailing time between ports. Weighing in at 59,652 tons and accommodating 1,316 passengers, the *Rotterdam* incorporates abundant use of woods and darker colors for a more classic feel. She boasts an entire deck of suites with 180-square-foot verandas, including four penthouse suites that measure 1,159 square feet and 36 556-square-foot suites with special concierge lounge and concierge services. She also offers 121 additional deluxe 292-square-foot cabins with verandas, whirlpool bathtubs, refrigerators, DVDs, and other conveniences. Included on the ship are a special alternative 90-seat, reservation-only restaurant that is opulent in decor, a spectacular, two-deck main dining room, and a two-deck show lounge; expensive art; and various other tasteful public areas and lounges (as are found on all Holland America Line vessels). The layout of the ship is quite similar to the other vessels built in the 1990s. For passengers opting to partake in the "suite life" (on navigation deck), the comfort and special amenities parallel those featured on luxury-market cruises.

The line purchased the 2,400-acre Bahamian island of Little San Salvador and developed a $16 million facility, completed in late 1997, naming it Half Moon Cay. The development includes a most enviable two-mile strand of white-sand beach, snorkel area, stingray lagoon, Wave Runner park, horseback riding on the beach, tender dock, aqua park for kids, and sport area (offering kayaks, banana boats, Hobie catamarans, parasailing, Sunfish sailboats, and floating air mattresses). In addition, there are 15 private beachside cabanas (each can accommodate up to four people and costs $249), the 1,620-square foot Private Oasis (which can accommodate up to 25 people and includes a private sun deck, hot tub, water slide to a private beach area, barbeque area, wet bar, refrigerator, massage table, indoor and outdoor showers and costs $1,195 for the first 12 guests and $99 for each of the next 12, although prices are subject to change), a Bahamian straw market, a post office, a chapel for vow renewals, a food pavilion, several bars, numerous lounge chairs with umbrellas, and hiking trails. This is a major port of call for HAL ships with Caribbean itineraries and is considered by many reviewers as the best private island in the cruise industry. This is one of the only private island beaches owned by a cruise line where there are no rocks or pebbles in the water, only firm, white sand lapped by clear, aqua waters.

In 1999, the *Volendam,* and in 2000, the *Zaandam* and the *Amsterdam,* three modified sisters to the *Rotterdam,* came on line as the *Rotterdam*-class of vessels. The new ships, built by Fincantieri Shipyards in Italy at a price tag of about $300 million each, are approximately 61,396 gross tons with passenger capacities of 1,380 to 1,432 each. Technically, *Amsterdam* is a sister to the *Rotterdam* and an HAL flagship, and the *Volendam* and *Zaandam* are similar siblings. However, all four ships are quite similar in their design and facilities and there is little difference between them and the *Statendam*-class ships. *Volendam* and *Zaandam* boast an especially attractive 1,126-square-foot penthouse suite (including veranda), one of the most spacious and desirable at sea.

Joining the industry trend, "as you wish dining" was introduced on all ships of the fleet. All guests can choose between traditional, set dining times at a designated table or a flexible schedule permitting them to dine with whomever they please between 5:25 P.M. and 9 P.M. All Holland America Line ships offer dining alternatives most evenings in their lido restaurants between 6:30 P.M. and 8:00 P.M., with casual open seating, piano music, and tables set with linens, stemware, and flatware. Expanded room-service menus including items from the main dining room are also being introduced. Pinnacle specialty restaurants featuring steaks, chops, fish, and seafood (described by the cruise line as Northwest U.S. fare) were added to all ships that did not already have a specialty restaurant and replaced the prior specialty restaurants on those that did. Special wine-taster dinners with set menus will be offered at these restaurants on selected evenings. An additional specialty Pan Asian restaurant, Tamarind, was added to the new *Signature*-class ships. The casual Canaletto, an Italian-themed restaurant, is available on *Eurodam, Veendam, Noordam, Amsterdam,* and *Oosterdam.*

In 2002, the *Seabourn Sun* (formerly *Royal Viking Sun*) was transferred to Holland America and renamed *Prinsendam.* Since the acquisition, many structural renovations have been made. Of the 398 cabins, 373 have ocean views and 151 of these sport verandas. Deck 13 atop ship is the observation deck. Deck 12, the sports deck, is the location of the Crow's Nest observation lounge, eight deluxe veranda suites, the penthouse veranda suite, a golf net, and the volleyball-basketball court. On deck 11, lido deck, there are ten more veranda suites, the Neptune lounge, a concierge lounge for suite passengers, the pool, lido bar and terrace grill, and lido restaurant. Additional veranda cabins can be found on decks 9 and 10 along with the Ocean Spa/gym/beauty salon and the aft pool. The main show lounge, shopping and photo arcade, theater, cardroom, casino, Java Café, 10 newly added veranda suites, and several additional lounges are located on deck 8. On deck 7 are the outside staterooms, Internet café, Pinnacle Grill dining room, Ocean bar, and an open promenade (four times around to the mile). The remaining inside and outside cabins are located on decks 5 and 6.

In December 2002, the 82,305-ton, 1,916-passenger *Zuiderdam* entered service, the first of the line's *Vista*-class ships. She was followed by the *Oosterdam* in 2003, the *Westerdam* in 2004, and the *Noordam* in 2006. Eighty-five percent of the accommodations feature ocean views, and two-thirds sport verandas. Each ship has two penthouse veranda suites measuring 1,000 square feet with 318-foot verandas. Standard inside and outside cabins range in size from 170 square feet to 200 square feet, and deluxe veranda cabins measure 200 square feet (with 54-square-foot verandas). Veranda suites range in size from 398 to 700 square feet (including the veranda). The furnishings and facilities in the various categories of accommodations are similar to the other HAL ships with the addition of expanded veranda areas. However, storage area in the non-suite cabins and bathrooms is somewhat limited. All of the *Statendam*- and *Vista*-class ships offer concierge lounges for suite passengers, offering special services, free laundry, pressing and cleaning, priority tender boarding and other amenities, espresso, cappuccino, continental breakfasts, afternoon and evenings snacks, but no soft drinks or alcoholic beverages.

Public areas are brighter, more eclectic, less classic, with less wood and brass, and are more spread out than those on the prior generation of HAL ships, the *Oosterdam, Westerdam,* and *Noordam* being more toned down than the *Zuiderdam.* Facilities on *Vista*-class ships not found on *S*-class vessels include glass elevators on port and starboard sides of the ship with views to the sea; additional bars; a cabaret-style show lounge complementing the two-deck production show lounge; a hydrotherapy pool in the Greenhouse Spa and Salon (there is a daily or weekly charge for using the steam rooms and the pool); a new look, location, and menu for the Pinnacle Grill; reservation-only specialty restaurants; and the new Windstar Café, featuring snacks, pastries, sandwiches, and specialty coffees and cocktails.

In late 2003, the line announced a Signature of Excellence program to be completed on all ships over a 36-month period. Completed in October 2006, the innovations for the fleet include upgraded mattresses, bed linens, duvets, towels, bathrobes, and showerheads in the staterooms; DVDs; personalized stationery; fully stocked minibars; and access to the concierge lounge for all suite passengers; an Explorations Café serving coffees while guests enjoy Internet connections, the library, music, and *New York Times* crossword puzzles; additional dining times in the main dining rooms (four options); enhanced lido dining with a greater variety of international choices and table-side wait service at dinner; Greenhouse Spas to be added to all ships; expanded fitness facilities and therma-pools; additional culinary and enrichment programs, including a culinary arts center with a "show kitchen" with rotating guest chefs; upgraded children's facilities; new teen venues; a new kids/teens culinary program offering 45-minute classes on the preparation of various dishes; and early embarkation programs enabling passengers to board ship by noon.

The *Ryndam* was the first of the *S*-class ships to receive renovations while in dry dock to incorporate the full Signature of Excellence program. In addition to the aforementioned upgrades, a lounge was added that combines the library, Internet café, cardroom, and premium coffee shop; a culinary arts center was added; the HAL youth facilities were extended; new staterooms, many with verandas, were added; staterooms on lower promenade deck had windows replaced with lanai doors that open out to the deck; other staterooms were converted to spa staterooms; the aft pool on lido deck was converted to the Retreat, where guests can relax outside surrounded by an entertainment area with several bars, a pizza station, a stage for a band, and beaches running the length of each side of the pool. Similar renovations are being extended to all the *S*-class ships.

When the *Noordam* was launched, all of the Signature of Excellence program amenities and additions were already in place. The *Noordam* also features an expanded Pinnacle Grill and wine bar; expanded teen, children, and spa facilities; a combination Internet café/library/coffee bar; and four seatings in the main dining room. With this new program HAL intends to distinguish itself as the top premium cruise line.

In 2005, the cruise line announced that it had entered into contracts (through its parent, Carnival) to build two 86,700-ton, 2,104-passenger ships, to be designated *Signature* class. The first of this new class of ships, the *Eurodam,* came on line in the summer of 2008, followed by *Nieuw Amsterdam* in 2010. They have 1,052 tastefully appointed staterooms with 86 percent outside, 67 percent with balconies, and 30 wheelchair-accessible rooms. The size of all accommodations is quite generous. The 155 inside cabins range in size from 175 to 200 square feet, the 189 outside cabins are 189 square feet, the 596 veranda cabins are 200 square feet with 22- to 54-square-foot verandas, the superior and deluxe veranda suites range from 300 to 570 square feet with 89- to 130-square-foot verandas, and the two penthouse suites come in at 1,000 square feet with 318-square-foot verandas. Fifty six spa staterooms located near the Greenhouse Spa are available and offer a few special amenities, including exclusive spa and salon services (at an extra cost), direct access to the Thalasso pool (at an extra cost), and a special spa breakfast. All of the Signature of Excellence innovations described above are present in all staterooms. Bathrooms in the non-suite staterooms are small, with limited shelf space.

In addition to the main dining rooms, lido restaurant, and the elegantly appointed Pinnacle Grill, three new dining venues have been added. On top-deck, Tamarind, featuring pan-Asian fare is open for both lunch and dinner. Included in the offerings are dim sum at lunch and Rijsttafel at dinner. Across from Tamarind is The Den, an Oriental-style cocktail lounge featuring cozy cubicles for before- or after-dinner libations. The forward section of the lido restaurant converts each evening to Canaletto, tempting with a vast menu of Italian favorites. An assortment of pizzas is offered at Slice until midnight. This is the best pizza at sea. A similar Canaletto restaurant was added to the *Noordam, Oosterdam, Veendam,* and *Amsterdam.*

Other innovations include a 50-seat observation lounge featuring panoramic views; a premium wine-tasting lounge; a large Internet café atop ship with an impressive variety of books and DVDs as well as beverages and snacks; a free digital workshop; expanded shopping, spa, gym, youth, and teen facilities; and all of the Signature of Excellence features found on the other vessels. The gym is very large and offers more state-of-the-art cardio machines and equipment than the other HAL ships or ships of competing cruise lines. Guests wishing to sit out on deck with some privacy can now rent cabanas, either by the day or for the duration of the cruise. Fourteen are located on deck 12 overlooking the midship pool and eight are located on deck 9 around the pool. Each cabana comes with bathrobes, hand-held Evian spray misters, iPods, frozen grapes in the morning, and a glass of champagne and chocolate-dipped strawberries in the afternoon.

Holland America visits more than 320 ports around the world.

Strong Points:

The physical layout and décor of the vessels make the HAL vessels among the more classically attractive ships afloat; activities, facilities, dining, and itineraries make for a solid cruise experience—considered by many as one of the best in the premium market category. Luxury veranda and penthouse suites are very large and comfortable, affording a superior experience similar to ships competing in the luxury-cruise market.

Courtesy Holland America Line

Courtesy Holland America Line

Courtesy Holland America Line

Courtesy Holland America Line

Captain's Gala Dinner

APPETIZERS
Wedge of Honeydew Melon
with lime

Jumbo Shrimp Cocktail
traditional cocktail sauce

Captain's Hors d'Oeuvre Plate
goose liver pâté, bressaola, coppa with Sicilian style vegetable salad

Deep Fried Hazelnut Crusted Brie
apple cranberry chutney

SOUPS
Parisian Onion
baked with Gruyère cheese

Lobster Bisque
blended with brandy and cream

🌶 **Iced Andalusian Style Gazpacho**
chilled tomato based vegetable soup

SALADS
Our House Salad
iceberg wedge with sliced tomato, cucumber and julienne of red beet

Caesar Salad
tossed with Caesar dressing and garlic croûtons

**Your Choice of Dressing: Italian house, blue cheese, 1000 island,
ranch or fat free honey Dijon**

ENTRÉES
Halibut Fillet in Potato Spaghetti
crayfish fond, broccoli purée with a splash of Pernod and baby red beets

Roast Rack of Lamb "Aromatic"
natural jus with garlic and mint, ratatouille and dauphinoise potatoes

Peking Style Rôtisserie Duck
plum sauce, sweet & sour vegetable, Oriental fried rice

Vegetarian Sweet and Sour Tofu
basmati rice

ENTRÉES FROM THE GRILL
Beef Wellington
tenderloin wrapped in pastry dough, red wine sauce, green beans in bacon and château potatoes

🌶 **Sesame Crusted Salmon Fillet**
green peppercorn beurre blanc, carrot pearls, asparagus spears
and crabmeat mashed potatoes with dill

JEANNE JONES "IN BALANCE MENU"
"In Balance" means just that, enjoying meals that are satisfying, nutritious
and in balanced proportions. The philosophy of this cuisine is about making healthier
choices-about moderation rather than deprivation.

Tabouleh
with chopped tomato, cucumber and green onion

Creamy Lemon Chicken Fettuccini
topped with parmesan and diced tomato

Banana au Gratin

Calories 568 - Fat 14 grams

A baked potato with sour cream, bacon bits and chives is available upon request.
🌶 Means Spicy Dish
Upon request any entrée can be served without sauce.

Courtesy Holland America Line

OOSTERDAM

Holland America Line

Wednesday, February 11, 2004
ms Oosterdam

arrival 9:00 am
all aboard 5:30 pm

Eastern Caribbean · St. Maarten
sunrise 6:40 am · sunset 6:10 pm

Welcome to

In 1631 the Dutch built their first Caribbean fort, Fort Amsterdam, on the peninsula separating Great Bay and Little Bay. Invading Spaniards expanded it and added a small church. Despite its historic significance little remains of the fort other than crumbling walls and a few rusting cannons. In 1633 the Spanish (who had claimed the island but not colonized the island) invaded the island, deporting all 128 inhabitants. The Spanish reinforced a fort that the Dutch had started and then built a second fort. In 1644 an attempt to retake the island was led by the renowned Dutch colonizer Peter Stuyvesant, who lost his leg to a cannonball during the fighting.

Although the Dutch assault was unsuccessful, four years later the Spanish reassessed their interests in the region and simply left on their own. In 1733 the Utrecht Peace Treaty returned half of the island to France. Nevertheless, the Dutch and the French continued to struggle for complete control of the island for years at a time.

St. Maarten

from the navigator

Early in the morning we will pass by the island of Anguila, which is located just north of St. Maarten. Shortly thereafter we will pass the western coast of St. Maarten where we will alter course to the port and enter Grote Baai, which is Dutch for "Great Bay." Here we will pick up the local pilot who will guide us safely to our berth in Philipsburg.

weather

The weather forecast for Philipsburg, as of noon Tuesday, is a high of 27°C/80°F, with partly cloudy skies.

don't miss

Lido Barbecue and Ice Carving

Liars Club Game Show

Karaoke Hour

Brain Teasers with the Cruise Staff

Filipino Crew Show

tonight's dress: casual

Comfortable attire, but please no shorts in the dining room.

today at a glance

Wednesday, February 11, 2004

morning/afternoon

7:00am	**Walk-a-Mile** Promenade Deck, 3
8:00am	**New Body Cycle:** The best cardio spinning work out ($11) Gym, 9
8:00am	**Catholic Mass** Queen's Lounge, 2
9:00am	**The ms Oosterdam is expected to dock in Philipsburg, St Maarten**
9:00am - 10:30am	**Our Port and Shopping Ambassador Jim is available for questions** pierside
9:00am - 8:00pm	**Sports equipment is available** Outside Decks
9:00am - 9:00pm	**Surf the Internet for 10 Minutes to claim your 5 FREE Minutes** Internet Center, 3
9:00am	**New Body Fit Ball:** Abdominal conditioning ($11) Gym, 9
9:30am	**Taboo Challenge** Ocean Bar, 3
10:30am	**3-on-3 Basketball Challenge** Sports Deck, 11
11:30am	**Pictionary Fun** Piano Bar, 2
11:30am - 2:00pm	**The Wine Desk is open** Lido Deck Poolside, 9
1:15pm	**Hole In One Golf Challenge** Atrium, 1
2:00pm - 4:00pm	**Card Players Meet** (non hosted) Hudson Room, 3
2:00pm	**Ping Pong Tourney** Lido Deck, 9
3:00pm	**New Body Aerobics:** Hi/low easy to follow Gym, 9
3:00pm	**A Game of Mad Gab with the Cruise Staff** Ocean Bar, 3
3:30pm - 4:00pm	**Afternoon Tea** Explorer's Lounge, 2
3:45pm	**Afternoon Trivia** Ocean Bar, 3

afternoon/evening

4:00pm	**New Body Yoga** ($11) Gym, 9
4:30pm	**Shuffleboard Shootout** Observation Deck, 10
4:45pm	**Friends of "Bill W."** Explorer's Lounge, 2
5:00pm	**HAPPY HOUR SNOWBALL JACKPOT BINGO 2-FOR-1 DRINKS FOR ALL PLAYERS** Crow's Nest, 10
5:30pm	**All Aboard!** The gangway is raised!
6:00pm	**Oosterdam sets sail for Road Town, Tortola**
6:00pm - 8:00pm	**LIDO DECK BARBECUE** Lido Deck, 9
6:00pm - 11:00pm	**Kinkade Silent Auction** Art Gallery, 2
6:00pm	**Amber of the Seas and Faberge Style Eggs Unveiling** Shops, 3
6:30pm	**Face Up Blackjack, Tonight Only** Casino, 2
7:45pm - 8:15pm	**LIARS CLUB GAME SHOW** Vista Lounge, 2 & 3
8:00pm	**Ice Carving Demonstration** Lido Midship, 9
9:00pm - 12:00mn	**Cigars Under the Stars** Oak Room, 10
9:30pm	**The Nightclub heats up with DJ Marc** Northern Lights, 2
9:30pm - 10:30pm	**Northern Lights Happy Hour ~ All drinks 2-for-1** Northern Lights, 2
9:45pm	**Gayle Sings the blues** Piano Bar, 2
10:00pm	**BRAIN TEASERS with the CRUISE STAFF** Crow's Nest, 10
10:30pm - 11:30pm	**KARAOKE HOUR** Northern Lights, 2
11:30pm	**FILIPINO CREW SHOW** Vista Lounge, 2 & 3
12:00mn	**Midnight Madness with DJ Marc** Northern Lights, 2

vista lounge deck 2 & 3
Your Cruise Director, Dane Butcher, proudly presents

The Mikes

8:30pm First seating guests • **10:30pm** Second seating guests

Tonight, we feature five young men direct from Canada singing the best in acapella. From Do-Wop to Dave Matthews, The Mikes promise to give you a show to remember.

music & dancing

B-4 plays dance favorites
Crow's Nest, 10
7:15pm - 8:15pm
9:15pm - 12:30am

Gayle Leali tickles the ivories
Piano Bar, 2
9:15pm - close

The Alex Bellegarde Trio
keeps you dancing
Ocean Bar, 3
5:00pm - 6:00pm
7:15pm - 8:15pm

Vista Orchestra plays great hits
Ocean Bar, 3
9:15pm - 12:30am

Caribbean Breeze plays sounds of the islands
Lido Deck Poolside, 9
4:00pm - 5:30pm & 6:00pm-8:00pm

Monarchia Strings play classical and string favorites
Explorers Lounge, 2
9:15pm - 12:00 mn

DJ Marc spins the hits
Northern Lights, 2
9:30pm - close

movies

queen's lounge deck 2 • 11:00am, 2:00pm, 8:45pm & 10:45pm
Radio

starring: Denzel Washington, Eva Mendes, Sanaa Lathan, Dean Cain

1h 45mins • PG - 13 • Action/Drama

complimentary popcorn is served before each feature presentation.

---

lido barbecue
Join us for great food and terrific music at our special barbecue poolside dinner. Indulge yourself in an incredible feast of your favorite barbecue delights. This mouthwatering display of food is sure to make you come back for seconds! The fun begins at 6:00pm on the Lido Deck, poolside. Stick around for an amazing ice carving demonstration that will leave you in awe at the masterful techniques of these talented artists! Music provided by Caribbean Breeze.

filipino crew show
Tonight our Filipino crew take center stage to present a cultural show featuring music, song and dance from their homeland. Be sure to bring your cameras and videos tonight to the Vista Lounge, deck 2, at 11:30pm for a fabulous cultural adventure!

amber of the seas collection
Tonight the shops onboard will be featuring our new jewelry collection of Amber, including the Catherine the Great Collection. All pieces are handmade and set in sterling silver. Russian Faberge style eggs will also be available with prices starting at only $60.

win a cruise lottery
Take your chance at a 7-Day Caribbean cruise for 2!! Purchase your win-a-cruise lottery tickets at one of your bingo sessions, any of the bars and lounges as well as the Front Office. The drawing will be held the final night of the cruise! Time is running short, and you've got to be in it to win it!!

liars club
Looking for some great laughs this evening? Tonight, join the Cruise Staff in the Vista Lounge at 7:45pm where our panel of pathological liars take center stage...who's telling the truth? A guaranteed good time for all!

formal portraits
Professional portraits are available on formal nights at a fraction of land-based prices. Just find one of your friendly onboard photographers who are located throughout the ship to capture a lifelong memory on film. As always, there is a no purchase necessary policy.

drink of the day: lemon drops
Premium vodka, hand shaken with fresh lemon and a touch of sugar offered in adventurous stylings such as West Coast (the original lemon drop at its finest), Coral (kicked up with Absolut Mandarin and Chambord), Glacier (icy blue), and Kiwi (lemony green goodness).

food & drink

restaurants

lido restaurant, deck 9
6:30am - 10:30am
continental breakfast

7:00am - 10:00am
buffet breakfast

11:30am - 2:00pm
buffet lunch

11:30am - 1:00am
ice cream parlor

11:30am - 5:00pm
deli & salad bar

11:30am - 2:00pm
the wok stir-fry

11:30am - 1:00am
pizza & pasta bar

6:00pm - 8:00pm
lido barbecue

11:00pm - 12:00mn
south western style late night snack

coffee and tea available 24 hours in the lido restaurant.

terrace grill, lido poolside deck 9
11:30am - 5:00pm
taco bar

11:30am - 5:00pm
hamburgers and hotdogs

odyssey restaurant, deck 2
6:00pm - 9:30pm *by reservation only*
reservations accepted: 8:00am - 6:00pm in person or dial #74699 until 10:00pm
(cover charge applies)

vista dining room, deck 2 & 3
7:30am - 9:30am
breakfast, 2

6:00pm
first seating

8:15pm
second seating

doors close 15 minutes after opening of each seating

bars & lounges
10:00am - 6:00pm
atrium bar deck 1

4:30pm - 1:00am
crow's nest deck 10 forward

7:30pm - 12:00mn
explorer's lounge deck 2

9:00am - 8:00pm
lido bar deck 9

9:30pm - close
northern lights deck 2

10:00am - 12:30am
ocean bar deck 3

7:15pm - close
piano bar deck 2

9:00am - 6:00pm
seaview bar deck 9

5:00pm - close
sport's bar deck 2

7:00am - 9:15pm
windstar café

services

art gallery
lower promenade deck, 2 (open 24hrs)
kinkade silent auction
desk hours: 5:30pm - 11:30pm

casino
lower promenade deck, 2
full casino: 6:30pm - close

front office
main deck, 1 (open 24hrs)
dial 90

golf center
observation deck, 10 midship
closed

guest relations manager
main deck, 1
8:00am - 11:00am
available via the front office

greenhouse spa & salon
lido deck, 9 forward
8:00am - 8:00pm
gym: 6:00am - 9:00pm
hydropool: 8:00am - 8:00pm
dial 94 for receptionist

infirmary
deck A, forward
nurse: 8:00am - 12:00n &
            2:00pm - 6:00pm
doctor: 8:00am - 9:00am &
            5:00pm - 6:00pm
dentist: available by appointment
dial 99 for assistance

internet center
promenade deck, 3 (open 24hrs)
manager's hours: 9:00am - 12:00n &
7:00pm - 10:00pm

library
promenade deck, 3
9:00am - 5:00pm
daily quiz available 9:00am - 3:00pm

photo gallery
promenade deck, 3
8:00am - 10:00am & 5:00pm - 11:00pm

port & shopping ambassador
windstar café, 2
7:30pm - 8:30pm

pools & hot tubs
lido deck 9
pools: 7:00am - 7:00pm*
hot tubs: 9:00am - 10:00pm*
* The midship pool and hot tub will close at 5:00pm

shops on board
promenade deck, 3
6:00pm - 11:00pm

shore excursions
main deck, 1
8:00am - 9:00am
deadline for Tortola tours @ 9:00am

Courtesy Holland America Line

HURTIGRUTEN
405 Park Avenue, Suite 904
New York, New York 10022
(212) 319-1300; (800) 323-7436
(212) 319-1390 Fax
www.hurtigruten.us

MS *FINNMARKEN:* entered service 2002; 15,000 G.R.T.; 138.5 meters x 21.5 meters; 643-passenger capacity; 50 cars; Norwegian officers and crew.

MS *FRAM:* entered service 2007; 12,700 G.R.T.; 371' long; 318-passenger capacity; cruises Iceland, Greenland, and Disco Bay during summer, Antarctica during winter, and North American and European cruises during spring and fall.

MS *KONG HARALD:* entered service 1993; 11,200 G.R.T.; 121.8 meters x 19.2 meters; 490-passenger capacity; 50 cars; Norwegian officers and crew.

MS *LOFOTEN:* entered service 1964; renovated 2003; 2,661 G.R.T.; 87.4 meters x 13.5 meters; 171-passenger capacity; 4 cars; Norwegian officers and crew.

MS *MIDNATSOL* and MS *TROLLFJORD:* entered service 2003 and 2002, respectively; 15,000 G.R.T.; 135.7 meters x 21.5 meters; 674-passenger capacity; 50 cars; Norwegian officers and crew.

MS *NORDKAPP:* entered service 1996; 11,386 G.R.T.; 123.3 meters x 19.5 meters; 490-passenger capacity; 50 cars; Norwegian officers and crew.

MS *NORDLYS:* entered service 1994; 11,200 G.R.T.; 121.8 meters x 19.2 meters; 482-passenger capacity; 50 cars; Norwegian officers and crew.

MS *NORDNORGE:* entered service 1997; 11,386 G.R.T.; 123.3 meters x 19.5 meters; 464-passenger capacity; 50 cars; Norwegian officers and crew.

MS *NORDSTJERNEN:* entered service 1960; renovated 2000; 2,568 G.R.T.; 87.4 meters x 13.2 meters; 164-passenger capacity; 4 cars; Norwegian officers and crew.

MS *POLARLYS:* entered service 1996; 12,000 G.R.T.; 123 meters x 19.5 meters; 482-passenger capacity; 50 cars; Norwegian officers and crew.

MS *POLAR STAR:* entered service 1969; renovated 1988 and 2000; 3,500 G.R.T.; 86.5 meters x 21.2 meters: 100-passenger capacity; Norwegian officers and crew.

MS *RICHARD WITH:* entered service 1993; 11,205 G.R.T.; 121.8 meters x 19.2 meters; 490-passenger capacity; 50 cars; Norwegian officers and crew.

MS *VESTERALEN:* entered service 1983; renovated 1995; 6,261 G.R.T.; 108.6 meters x 16.5 meters; 318-passenger capacity; 40 cars; Norwegian officers and crew.

The cruise line also leases the 120-passenger, 6,336-ton MS *Expedition* for service in Spitsbergen.

(Medical Facilities: Generally no physicians except in Antarctica on *Fram* and *Polar Star* in Spitsbergen. No medical facilities aboard the ships.)

Hurtigruten has been operating for more than 100 years and calls at 34 Norwegian ports daily. The line has 15 ships, most of which were built since 1993, with passenger capacities between 114 and 674. Each ship has lounges, dining rooms, 24-hour cafeterias, and souvenir and sundry shops. The newer vessels have children's playrooms, conference facilities, Internet cafés, elevators, and cabins for disabled passengers. In 2005, outdoor Jacuzzis were installed on the newer vessels.

The ships offer cruises along 1,250 miles of the fjord-indented western coast of Norway. Cruises are six days southbound, seven days northbound, and 12 days round trip. Itineraries include the cultural cities of Bergen and Trondheim; small arctic towns such as Tromso, Oksfjord, and Hammerfest; and passages through narrow straits and past magnificent fjords.

The newest ship in the fleet, the MS *Fram,* is one of the most deluxe expedition ships, designed to make shore excursions easier and to offer the same amenities as upscale cruise ships, including a wellness center with saunas, a conference facility, outdoor whirlpools, and a guest bridge. She offers cruises in Antarctica and the Chilean fjords between October and March. This is a unique itinerary with unforgettable experiences to an area of the world largely undiscovered by tourists.

During the summer months, the MS *Nordstjernen,* MS *Polar Star,* and MS *Expedition* offer service in Spitsbergen. Expeditions to Greenland are also offered.

Other larger and newer ships of the line, the 15,000-ton *Trollfjord, Midnatsol,* and *Finnmarken,* entered service in 2002, 2003, and 2002, respectively. The first two ships can accommodate 674 passengers and 50 cars, whereas the *Finnmarken* accommodates 643 passengers and 50 cars. These new builds have added upscale suites for passengers willing to pay a bit more for more space and comfort. There are 32 on *Finnmarken,* 23 on *Midnatsol,* and 23 on *Trollfjord.* Five suites on *Midnatsol* and *Trollfjord* have balconies and 14 have balconies on *Finnmarken.* All accommodations on *Finnmarken* have TVs, safes, refrigerators, and telephones. Public areas include numerous dining venues, a conference area, a children's area and arcade, a library, an Internet café, shops, and several lounges. The two-story panoramic lounges provide spectacular views of the coastal scenery and even the saunas and glass elevators have sea views. The top decks contain fitness rooms, two saunas, a large sun deck, a bar, and the observation-lounge balcony. These ships cruise round trip from Bergen, Norway, to Kirkenes, close to the Russian border, and back to Bergen in 12 days.

Cruise rates range from $115 per day, per person up to $915 per day for a suite (depending on the ship, season, and cabin category). Various all-inclusive cruise programs are available, including air, train journeys, hotels, and sightseeing.

All expedition programs offer shore landings, expert guides, and lecturers.

Strong Points:

These ships offer expedition cruising as well as a definitive Norwegian fjord itinerary in a true Norwegian environment, with the potential for upscale accommodations for cruisers wishing to experience uniquely beautiful parts of the world.

Courtesy Hurtigruten

MS Fram suite, courtesy Hurtigrtuen

MS Fram, *Courtesy Hurtigruten*

METROPOLITAN TOURING'S GALAPAGOS CRUISES
Adventure Associates
13150 Coit Road, Suite 110
Dallas, Texas 75240
(800) 527-2500; (972) 907-0414
www.galapagosvoyage.com

ISABELA II: entered service 1989; 1,083 G.R.T.; 166' x 38'; 38-passenger capacity; 20 cabins; officers and crew mainly from Ecuador; 7-night cruises around Galapagos Islands. **(Category C—Not Rated)**

SANTA CRUZ: entered service 1979; refurbished 1998; 1,500 G.R.T.; 230' long; 90-passenger capacity; 43 cabins; officers and crew mainly from Ecuador; 3-, 4-, and 7-night cruises around the Galapagos Islands. **(Category C—Not Rated)**

Metropolitan Touring operates the 1,500-ton, 90-passenger *Santa Cruz* and the 38-passenger *Isabela II,* as well as five smaller vessels offering three-, four-, and seven-night pleasure cruises exploring the flora and fauna of the Galapagos Islands, 600 miles offshore from Ecuador. Cruises on the *Isabela II* sail from Baltra Island on Tuesdays and the *Santa Cruz* sails from Baltra on Mondays and from San Cristobal Island on Fridays.

On the *Santa Cruz,* which was built specifically for cruising in the Galapagos, all cabins are outside and have lower beds, toilet and shower, a closet, and storage drawers. There are two master suites with queen-size beds and private balconies, two junior suites, as well as twins, triples, and quads.

The lounge, bar, dining room, purser's office, stores, and other cabins are located on upper deck, between main and boat decks. There is also a sun deck with a bar, Jacuzzi, and observation area, but no pool.

The *Isabela II,* which began service in 1988, has 20 outside air-conditioned cabins and one owner's suite, each with private shower and toilet. This yacht-like vessel includes a large salon and bar area, a spacious dining room, separate reading and game rooms, and a sun deck with a Jacuzzi, deck chairs, and some exercise machines. She is considered more luxurious than the other ship.

The general atmosphere and dress code on all ships is casual, jackets not being required for men. There is little entertainment, and on most evenings, professional naturalists give lectures and slide presentations in order to brief passengers on the following day's activities.

The ships of Metropolitan Touring visit the islands of Barrington, Bartolome, Fernandina, Floreana, Hood, Isabela, James, North Seymour, Plaza, San Cristobal, Santa Cruz, Jervis, and Tower. Here passengers will take guided excursions and view sea lions, fur seals, penguins, flocks of flamingos, marine and land iguanas, giant tortoises, colonies of albatrosses, and such other rare birds as boobies, noddy terns, lava gulls, storm petrels, Darwin's finches, flightless cormorants, and frigates.

Prices range from $280 to $570 per person per night and include sightseeing excursions.

Strong Points:

This is heaven for naturalists and bird watchers who wish to pursue their hobby in comfort and in the companionship of other aficionados.

Courtesy Metropolitan Touring

Courtesy Metropolitan Touring

Courtesy Metropolitan Touring

MSC CRUISES
6750 North Andrews Avenue
Fort Lauderdale, Florida 33309
(800) 666-9333
(954) 776-5881 Fax
www.msccruisesusa.com

MSC *ARMONIA* (formerly *European Vision*): entered service 2002; 58,625 G.R.T.; 830 x 95; 1,554-passenger capacity (2,087 when every berth full); 777 cabins; Italian officers and international crew; 4- to 9-night cruises in South America, 10- and 11-night cruises in northern Europe, and 11-night cruises in eastern Mediterranean.

MSC *FANTASIA* and MSC *SPLENDIDA:* entered service in 2008 and 2009, respectively; 133,500 G.R.T.; 1,093'x 124'; 3,959-passenger capacity (4,100 when every berth full); 1,637 cabins; Italian officers and international crew; 7-night cruises in eastern and western Mediterranean.

MSC *LIRICA:* entered service 2003; 59,058 G.R.T.; 763' x 84.5'; 1,560-passenger capacity (2,069 when every berth full); 780 cabins; Italian officers and international crew; 10- and 11-night northern European cruises and 7-night western Mediterranean cruises.

MSC *MELODY* (formerly *Star/Ship Atlantic* and *Atlantic*): entered service 1982; refurbished 1996; 35,140 G.R.T.; 672' x 90'; 1,062-passenger capacity; 531 cabins; Italian officers and international crew; 2- to 10-night South African cruises and 7-night western Mediterranean cruises. (**Category C/D—Not Rated**)

MSC *MUSICA* and MSC *ORCHESTRA:* entered service 2006 and 2007, respectively; 92,400 G.R.T.; 963.9' x 105.6'; 3,013-passenger capacity; 1,275 cabins; Italian officers and international crew; MSC *Musica* offers 3- to 8-night cruises in South America and 7-night cruises in eastern Mediterranean; MSC *Orchestra* offers 7-night Caribbean cruises, 7-night northern European cruises, and 8-night western Mediterranean cruises.

MSC *OPERA:* entered service 2004; 59,000 G.R.T.; 763' x 84.5'; 1,712 passenger capacity; 856 cabins; Italian officers and international crew; 3- to 8-night cruises in South America, 7- to 11-night and 14-night cruises in northern Europe, and 7-night cruises in eastern Mediterranean.

MSC *POESIA* and MSC *MAGNIFICA:* entered service 2008 and 2010, respectively; 93,300 G.R.T. and 92,400 G.R.T., respectively; 963.9' x 105.6'; 3,013-passenger capacity (2,550 lower berths); 1,275 cabins; Italian officers and international crew; MSC *Poesia* offers 7-night cruises in western Mediterranean, 11-night cruises in eastern and western Mediterranean, and 3- to 10-night cruises in Caribbean and Bermuda during winter; MSC *Magnifica* sails Canada/New England in fall, Caribbean itineraries in winter and throughout 2011.

MSC *SINFONIA* (formerly *European Star*): entered service 2002; 58,625 G.R.T.; 830' x 95'; 1,544-passenger capacity; 777 cabins; Italian officers and international crew; 7-night western Mediterranean and 3- to 8-night South American cruises.

(Medical Facilities: C-2 *Armonia* and *Sinfonia;* C-6 *Lirica, Opera,* and *Melody;* C-17 on *Musica* and *Orchestra;* P-2 *Lirica* and *Opera*/P-1 on others; N-1; CM; PD; EKG; TC; OX; WC; OR; ICU; CCP; LJ.) Some medical facilities on all ships.

Some of these ships are rated in 11 separate categories in the second half of chapter 14.

MSC Cruises is part of the giant shipping group Mediterranean Shipping Company (MSC), which also operates a global fleet of container vessels with a corporate presence in Geneva, Switzerland, and Naples, Italy. In 1990, the privately owned MSC purchased an Italian cruise company, Starlauro, which owned one vessel, MV *Achille Lauro.* Between 1990 and 1995, Starlauro acquired MV *Monterey,* MV *Symphony,* and MV *Rhapsody.* In 2001, the name of the cruise line was changed to MSC Italian Cruises to take advantage of the reputation associated with the parent company. In 1997, it purchased the *Star/Ship Atlantic* from Premier Cruise Line and renamed her MSC *Melody.* The *Achille Lauro, Symphony, Rhapsody,* and *Monterey* are no longer with the cruise line.

Since 2003, MSC Cruises has taken delivery of one newly built vessel a year.

The company's first new build, the MSC *Lirica,* joined the fleet in 2003, followed by a sister ship, the MSC *Opera,* in 2004. Also in 2004, MSC purchased the 1,566-passenger *European Vision* and *European Star* from the bankrupt First European/Festival Cruises and renamed them MSC *Armonia* and MSC *Sinfonia.* Several larger new builds, the 92,400-ton, 2,550-passenger MSC *Musica,* MSC *Orchestra,* and MSC *Poesia* joined the fleet in 2006, 2007, and 2008 and sister ship MSC *Magnifica* debuts in 2010. The MSC *Fantasia* and MSC *Splendida,* two 133,500-ton sisters with 3,300 lower berths, entered service in 2008 and 2009.

In 2004, the cruise line hired industry veteran Rick Sasso to head their North American operations. Sasso, formerly CEO of Celebrity Cruises, proceeded to hire many of the people who worked with him at Celebrity with the aspiration to make MSC a major competitor in the North American as well as European markets.

Overall the line emphasizes Italian ambiance and entertainment and in past years has largely serviced the European market in the Mediterranean, South American, and South African cruise areas. During the winter, the line offers cruises in the Caribbean on the MSC *Orchestra* and MSC *Lirica* and in South America on the MSC *Armonia,* MSC *Musica,* MSC *Sinfonia,* and MSC *Opera.* Prices on the various vessels range from $90 per person per night for a minimum inside cabin with upper and lower berths to $325 for an outside suite.

In the cruise line's desire to encourage families, children 17 and under sail free when sharing a stateroom with two adults paying full fare. Special counselors organize age-appropriate activities for ages three to six in the Mini Club, seven to 12 in the Juniors Club, and 13 to 17 in the Teenagers Club. In addition, there are children's menus in the restaurants and special cruise charge cards for guests 12-17, allowing them to charge inexpensive items such as soft drinks.

In early 2009, MSC Cruises created a new position aboard all of its vessels—the guest relations manager. This person acts as a combination concierge, problem solver, and facilitator handling all guest requests.

The MSC *Melody* was formerly *Star/Ship Atlantic* with Premier Cruise Line and *Atlantic* with Home Lines. When she was acquired by Premier, she received a $10 million refurbishment, which included remodeling by interior designer Michael Katzourakis; redesigning of the cabins (increasing the ship's capacity from 1,100 to 1,500 by the addition of third, fourth, and fifth cabin berths to accommodate families); the addition of children's facilities, including teen center, recreation center, video arcade, and outdoor casual dining area; and enlargement of the main dining room, casino, and lounges.

There are 381 outside cabins, including six suites, 72 mini-suites, and 151 inside cabins. At the top of the ship, on sun deck, is the jogging track, which looks down to the terrace and pool on the pool deck. The pool deck is the location of two swimming pools (one outdoor and one indoor/outdoor), a health/fitness center, a massage room, a beauty salon, an outdoor café and buffet dining area, a piano lounge, and the ice cream parlor. The main showroom, casino, photo gallery, video arcade, shops, and lounges, including a teen center, are on lounge deck. The theater is on continental deck and the Galaxy dining room is on restaurant deck.

The children's center is on premier deck. The MSC *Melody* offers South African itineraries in the winter months and western Mediterranean itineraries during the warmer months.

The 59,058-ton MSC *Lirica* entered service in 2003, followed by a sister ship, MSC *Opera,* in 2004. Although the same exterior frame, the MSC *Lirica* has 780 staterooms, 132 of which have balconies, while the MSC *Opera* has 856 staterooms with 200 balconies. Numerous cabins can accommodate a third and/or fourth passenger, six can accommodate wheelchairs, and about half have ocean views. All accommodations on both ships have satellite television, a minibar, a private safe, a radio, a telephone, 110/220-volt electric current, and a makeup area. Average cabins measure 150 square feet with small bathrooms. The 28 accommodations sold as suites atop each ship are larger with a small sitting area, bathtub/shower combination, small walk-in closet, and additional storage. However, they would only be designated deluxe staterooms on many other cruise lines.

Public areas are traditional in décor, very tastefully designed and decorated with an Italian flare without being glitzy. They include a fitness center with several massage rooms, men and women's changing rooms, saunas and steam rooms, a relaxation area, and a medium-size gym and aerobics area; two-deck show lounge and several other nightclub venues for musical groups, including an observation lounge/disco atop the ships; two swimming pools connected by two whirlpools surrounded by two decks of lounges and a walking/jogging track; miniature golf course atop ship; supervised children's club; virtual-reality center; shopping gallery; Internet café; casino; two main dining rooms; buffet restaurant with outside grill and pizzeria and protected outside seating; and main lobby with an information desk, tour desk, and money-changing facility. In addition to nightly variety and cabaret shows, there are several listening/dancing venues and musical entertainment is outstanding throughout the ship. Activities are plentiful and could be described as Club Med style.

The majority of officers and supervisors are Italian, but the crew is a mixture of Indonesian, Eastern European, Southeast Asian, and African. Public announcements are in five languages and most of the crew speak Italian and English. Dining and entertainment on these two ships seems geared to European tastes.

The 58,625-ton MSC *Armonia* (formerly *European Vision*) and MSC *Sinfonia* (formerly *European Star*) accommodations include 132 mini-suites with balconies. Standard cabins measure 140 square feet. Public areas include two pools, a basketball court, rock-climbing wall, two-deck theater, seven lounges, a large main dining room, buffet restaurant, casino, English pub, cigar-smoking lounge, golf simulator, miniature golf course, health spa/fitness center, children's playroom, teen center, virtual-reality center and Internet café, and conference meeting space. Activities, entertainment, dining, and service are similar to that found on MSC *Lirica* and MSC *Opera* but are more geared to European tastes.

The 92,400-ton, 2,550-passenger MSC *Musica* and MSC *Orchestra* and the 93,300-ton MSC *Magnifica* and MSC *Poesia* provide sea views in 80 percent of the accommodations, and 65 percent of these have balconies. Each accommodation includes two twin beds convertible to a European king size, and many can accommodate a third and/or a fourth person. There are 17 cabins for the physically challenged. Interior and ocean-view cabins measure 150 square feet, balcony staterooms range from 164 to 191 square feet, and the 18 balcony suites are 278 square feet. All balconies measure 48 square feet.

The vessels feature a three-deck waterfall in the central foyer; 13,000-square-foot spa/beauty center; 7,000-square-foot casino; children's pool, play area, and program; LED movie screen at the main pool; two main restaurants; an à la carte Japanese restaurant and sushi bar on MSC *Musica* and MSC *Poesia*; à la carte Chinese restaurant on MSC *Orchestra;* surcharge continental steakhouse restaurant; pizza grill; wine-tasting bar; coffee bar; cigar room; two outdoor swimming pools; four whirlpools; special children and teen facilities; a solarium; golf simulator; jogging track; mini-golf; a three-deck-high theater seating 1,240; and panoramic disco. Also there is a deck tennis court on the MSC *Orchestra*.

The 133,500-ton, 3,959-passenger *Fantasia* and *Splendida* feature the MSC Yacht Club—99 suites ranging between 247 and 570 square feet in private areas accessible only to those passengers booking the most expensive accommodations. Similar to the Grill class on Cunard vessels, these passengers enjoy butlers, their own concierge service, and a VIP section in the main restaurant. Yacht Club guests also enjoy complimentary beverages in the MSC Yacht Club cafés, bars, and the ship's main restaurant. They have exclusive occupancy of their own pool, Jacuzzi, and patio sunning area; a panoramic VIP lounge; and special access to the spa. In addition to the standard stateroom amenities, these suites include WiFi, Nintendo Wii, interactive TV, luxurious linens, and a Dorelan pillow menu. The suites can sleep two to four adults and the two largest can accommodate guests with disabilities.

Standard cabins on the ship are 210 square feet, and 80 percent sport balconies. The accommodations have all of the facilities and amenities previously described for the other vessels that have premiered over the past few years.

In addition to the two main dining rooms, MSC *Fantasia* features L'Etoile, a romantic à la carte French restaurant, while MSC *Splendida* feataures L'Olivo, an à la carte Mediterranean restaurant. Both ships also offer a Tex-Mex restaurant, pizzeria, sports bar for snacks, and Italian cantina for wines and tapas. At the central piazza, there is a patisserie café and gelato stand. Dining in the special restaurants and through room service is on an à la carte basis, and you pay for each item individually rather than for the meal as a whole.

The spa complex offers a gym, Turkish bath, relaxation room, treatment rooms, spot for yoga classes, and spa bar. There are two swimming pools, one with a magradome, an Aqua Park with 150 fountains, and 12 whirlpools. The game arcade includes a four-dimensional cinema and a Formula One simulator. In a partnership with Nintendo, there are Wii consoles throughout the public areas and in the MSC Yacht Club suites.

Strong Points:

Interesting itineraries, including areas of the world not regularly visited by many other cruise lines; Italian spirit, ambiance, and regional cuisine; and a chance to mingle with passengers from other countries. Rates are reasonable, and children sail free when sharing cabin with two adults. The newer ships offer some unique and very desirable features.

MSC Orchestra, *courtesy MSC Cruises*

MSC Orchestra, *courtesy MSC Cruises*

MSC Orchestra, *courtesy MSC Cruises*

MSC Orchestra, *courtesy MSC Cruises*

MSC Orchestra, *courtesy MSC Cruises*

MSC Opera, *courtesy MSC Cruises*

Appetizers

Mosaic of tropical fruits
*pineapple, mango, papaya, cantaloupe and honeydew,
mixed into a syrup flavored with Armagnac liquor*

Smoked salmon & ricotta timbale
*smoked salmon and ricotta mousse enclosed in smoked salmon slices
served with marinated cucumbers*

Escargot Burgundy
*Escargots, shallots and mushrooms, cooked in a red wine sauce
served in a potato shell*

Soups

Lobster velouté with Champagne frothy
*lobster and vegetable cream, cooked with champagne and fish stock,
flavored with Cognac*

Onion soup
*sliced onions, sautéed in butter, cooked with white wine and beef stock,
garnished with Emmenthal cheese croutons*

Chilled strawberry soup
*strawberries cooked in red wine with spices, blend with banana and lemon juice,
finished with cream*

Salad of the day

New spinach salad
bacon bits, chopped hard boiled eggs and croutons

Dressings
creamy garlic dressing - vinaigrette

Pasta and Risotto

Florentine-style crepes
crepes stuffed with creamed spinach and cheese, served with Fontina cheese sauce

Spumante risotto with smoked Scamorza cheese
rice cooked with sparkling wine and smoked Provolone cheese

Main Courses

Sautéed shrimps "Cote d'Azur",
*king size shrimps, seasoned with herbs and flambéed with Pernod liquor,
served with saffron pilaf rice*

Veal Piccata
*thin slices of veal, dipped in eggs and parmesan cheese,
then browned and cooked in butter, served with a veal gravy*

Prime Rib of beef
*marinated with herbs and black peppercorn, roasted whole then sliced,
served with a shallot and red wine sauce*

Roasted stuffed red pepper
a whole pepper filled with saffron rice and tofu, served on a bed of spinach sauce

Cheeses

Selection of cheeses
served with crackers, grapes and orange marmalade

Desserts and Fruit

Tiramisù

Pear Belle Hélène
vanilla ice cream, pear, chocolate sauce and whipped cream

Fresh seasonal fruit

Ice cream or sorbet of the day

Sweetened with fructose

Chocolate mousse with toasted hazelnuts

Ice cream of the day

Cócteles Sugeridos Como Aperitivo

Precios indicados en la lista del bar

Apricot Gin Fizz
Gin, Licor de albaricoque,
jugo de limón, Soda

Daiquiri
Rum, jugo de limón,
azúcar

Vinos Recomendados

Greco di Tufo d.o.c. "Feudi di San Gregorio", Campania-Italia
Barbera d.o.c. Terra "Vigneti Massa", Piemonte- Italia

Precios indicados en la carta de vinos

Pan italiano

Pan con aceitunas – Focaccia - Panecillo blanco

MSC ORCHESTRA
Monday, 23rd March 2009

Sunrise 7:48am - Sunset 7:59pm

Welcome to...

COZUMEL

Expected arrival time in **Cozumel** approx **10:00am**
All aboard: **4:30pm**
Departure time for **Georgetown: 5:00pm** (334 Nautical Miles)

IMPORTANT INFORMATION
We kindly ask all our Guests to keep their watches set to ship time
even though there is a two hour difference in Cozumel (Ship time is two hours ahead).

EXCURSION MEETING POINTS

COZ09 - FURY CATAMARAN SNORKEL & BEACH	10:00am	Savannah Bar, Deck 6
COZ23 - TULUM MAYA RUINS EXPRESS	10:00am	Covent Garden Theatre, Deck 6
COZ10 - COZUMEL HIGHLIGHTS & SHOPPING	10:15am	Covent Garden Theatre, Deck 6
COZ12 - CLEAR KAYAK, SNORKEL AND BEACH SNORKEL COMBO	10:15am	Savannah Bar, Deck 6
COZ24 - PUNTA SUR ECO-PARK, MAYAN RUIN & SNORKEL	10:45am	Savannah Bar, Deck 6
COZ14 - DUNE BUGGY & BEACH SNORKEL AT PUNTA SUR	10:45am	Covent Garden Theatre, Deck 6
COZ20 - ATV JUNGLE ADVENTURE	10:45am	Savannah Bar, Deck 6
COZ21 - 3 REEF SNORKELING BY BOAT	11:15am	Savannah Bar, Deck 6
COZ22 - DOLPHIN SWIM	12:45pm	Savannah Bar, Deck 6

Passengers on excursion: Don't forget to hand your **excursion ticket** and **MSC Cruise Card**. Do you take part in the excursions? Don't forget to have mineral water, which you may purchase at the bars of the meeting point lounges. You will get 25% discount showing your excursion ticket. The bottle will cost only $ 1,50.

We inform all passengers that smoking is forbidden at the excursions meeting points.

ATTENTION!
We would like to inform our passengers that a **general emergency drill** will take place today during the morning **for crew members only**. Passengers are not required to participate. We inform you that during the drill all the services on board will be closed. Thank you for your understanding.

EXCURSION OFFICE Deck 6

We are waiting for you at the Excursion desk (Deck 6) from 4:00pm to 8:00pm to book the last available tickets for Georgetown in the Cayman Islands, the land of the stingrays!

DIAMOND POWER HOUR Take your Maps ashore!
MSC's number one recommendation for diamonds this cruise is Diamonds International, #1 on your map! If you missed them in Key West, this is your chance!! Meet Valerija at Diamonds International from **11:00am – 12:00pm Free Diamond & Sapphire Necklace Raffle!** Remember to bring your VIP card as it will guarantee you the manager's best price on jewellery and watches.
See Valerija at the gangway for last minute Tips **9:30am-10:30am**

FOLLOW THE MSC FLEET - Here's where the MSC Cruise fleet is today

MSC FANTASIA	MSC POESIA	MSC MUSICA	MSC LIRICA	MSC OPERA	MSC SINFONIA	MSC ARMONIA	MSC MELODY	MSC RHAPSODY
Naples	At sea	At sea	At sea	Ilhabela	Ilha Grande	Recife	Durban	Messina

TONIGHT'S DRESS CODE: _CASUAL_

POOLS, DECK 13
10:00am-12:00pm & 3:00pm-5:00pm
Meeting point with the Entertainment Team:
Sports equipment available: mini-golf, tennis & ping-pong, racquets, balls, table soccer, playing cards, shuffie-board decks

Morning

9:00am	Morning walk	Pools, Deck 13
9:30am	Aerobics	Pools, Deck 13
10:00am	Stretching	Pools, Deck 13
10:30am	Quiz time	Pools, Deck 13
11:15am	Aperitif game	Pools, Deck 13

Afternoon

3:00pm	Ability game	Pools, Deck 13

3:30pm Pools, Deck 13
Zankys vs Pankys– Team game

3:30pm	Shuffleboard tournament	Deck 14
4:00pm	Basketball tournament	Deck 16

4:00pm Pools, Deck 13
Towelball– Team game

4:30pm	Caribbean line dancing	Pools, Deck 13
5:00pm	Aerobics & stretching	Pools, Deck 13

Sports equipment, mini-golf, tennis & table-tennis, racquets, balls, playing cards, table soccer, will be available from **12:00pm** to **3:00pm** and from **5:00pm** to **7:00pm** at the towel distribution (**Deck 13**) showing the MSC Cruise Card.

10:15am Bar l'Incontro, Deck 5, portside
FRIENDS OF BILL W. MEETING

Our night on board

With The Entertainment Team

Savannah Bar, Deck 6

7:45pm Elvis Game

9:30pm Bachata Dance Lesson

10:30pm *Miss Orchestra*
Women: it's your moment!
With a surprise from the Entertainment Team

Shaker Lounge, Deck 7

11:15pm Karaoke

NAUTICAL INFORMATION
Around 5:20pm, once left the pilot, we will take a North East route. Keeping a distance of 3 nautical miles from the Mexican Island, we will take as a still point the Punta Molas lighthouse (Northest part of Cozumel) and around 5:50pm we will sail along the coast in direction of Georgetown.

IMPORTANT NOTICE
Please do not occupy the sun beds with towels once having left the pool area. Thank you for your co-operation.

Today Free Movie on your ITV
"CHARLIE WILSON'S WAR" Comedy
and **Tonight** at **10:00pm**
Pools, Deck 13
(on the maxi-screen)

Miniclub Activities
8:00pm R32 Disco, Deck 14
BABY CRAZY DISCO
8:45pm Cafeteria La Piazzetta, Deck 13
ICE-CREAM PARTY

Teenagers Meeting Point
(13-18 Years old)
3:30pm R32 Disco, Deck 14 **MEETING POINT**
4:00pm Barracuda Bar, Deck 13 **TABLE TENNIS**

MUSIC IN THE LOUNGES

L'Incontro Bar, Deck 5 & The Purple & Zaffiro Bar, Deck 6
5:00pm-5:45pm; 7:15pm-8:30pm; 9:00pm-10:00pm; 10:30pm-11:30pm
Latin american music with *Los Paraguayos*

The Amber Piano Bar, Deck 6
5:00pm-6:00pm; 7:00pm-8:30pm; 9:00pm-10:00pm
Evergreen with *Fabrizio e Ivana*
10:00pm-1:00am
Pianobar with *Edo*

The Savannah Bar, Deck 6
6:30pm-7:00pm; 11:45pm-1:00am
Pianobar with *Ottawa Duo*
7:15pm-8:30pm; 9:00pm-9:30pm; 10:00pm-10:30pm; 11:00pm-11:45pm International music with *Ocean Band*

The Shaker Lounge, Deck 7
8:00pm-9:00pm; 10:30pm-11:15pm
Pianobar wirh *Ottawa Duo*
9:00pm-10:30pm; 12:00am-1:00am
Music for dancing with *Popcorn Band*

La Cantinella Wine Bar, Deck 7
5:00pm-5:30pm; 7:30pm-8:15pm; 9:15pm-10:15pm; 10:30pm-11:15pm; 11:30pm-12:00am
Notes on the waves with *Igor*

DISCO DANCE - R32 Disco, Deck 14
11:45pm-... with *Dj Mike*
The entrance of underage is not reccomended.

YOUR EVENING'S EVENTS	SPECIALS TODAY

"COVENT GARDEN" THEATRE
(Entrance from Deck 6 & 7)

7:00pm 2nd Seating of Dinner
8:30pm 1st Seating of Dinner

Your Cruise Director Marco presents:

No video cameras, video telephones, drinks or food in the Theatre. The Theatre is a no Smoking Area. In some scenes, laser effects, artificial and non-toxic smoke will be used.
Seats may not be reserved.

CHEF'S SURPRISE
11:30pm   served in the lounges
FRIED FANTASIES

DAILY COCKTAIL
Served in all bars

"COSMOPOLITAN N. 2" $ 5.50
· Vodka, Cointreau, raspberry Brandy, Rose's Lime

NOT ALCOHOLIC COCKTAIL
"ALICE IN WONDERLAND" $ 3.50
Pineapple & Orange juice, grenadine, cream

DAILY COFFEE -"SPANISH COFFEE" $ 4.60
Spanish Brandy, Cointreau, coffee and whipped cream
**From 4:30pm to 8:00pm all Martini cocktails
will be available at the Savannah Bar!**
Shaker Lounge, Deck 7
Tonight you're the Bar Tender! It's your night! Our staff will bring at your table all you need and will guide you at the preparation. If you will do a good job we will hire you as Bar Tender!

Coffee Bars, Decks 5 and 6
All liqueurs will be served in a MSC glass
that you can keep as souvenir!

BODY & MIND SPA DECK 13

RELAX DAY
Today with the purchase of 3
Sun Tanning
You will pay just $ 25 instead of $ 39
3 Sessions of Press therapy
for tired legs one session $ 52; 3 for $ 126

SPECIAL OFFER !!!!!!
Only today
30 Min. Hot stones therapy massage
For two $ 139 instead of $ 178 (save $ 39)
Shampoo and Blow-dry
$ 29 instead of $ 37 (save $ 8)
Men's cut $ 25 instead of $ 31 (save $ 6)

For information and bookings, call 2732

SERVICES AND ENTERTAINMENT
AT THE PRESS OF A BUTTON
All cabins on MSC Orchestra are equipped with Interactive television (ITV). Select "Menù", and have fun! Using your remote control, you are able to book all excursions, purchase movies, order room services, and acess all the information you need. We remind you kindly to check your daily "free messages".

DUFRY SHOPS

TAX & DUTY FREE SHOPS ON BOARD, Deck 6
Discover our large selection of custom jewellery
DESIGNER COCKTAIL RINGS from only **$13.95**
R.S.Covenant's fashion is unconditionally guaranteed for life! R.S.Covenat fashion is crafted in the same manner as 14/18k gold jewellery .
Tequila tasting From 7-8 pm Get 10% discount on your Tequila purchase
COLOMBIAN EMERALDS INTERNATIONAL, deck 6
Fresh Water Pearls – Treasures form the Sea, Fantastic collection started from as little as $14.99! Take part into the game 'find the fake Amber!'.

PHOTOSHOP DECK 7

We inform you that at the Photo shop Deck 7 aft, you'll find the pictures of your cruise and all the photo-items that you may need during your vacation. My cruise DVD– We remind you that you can purchase the DVD of the MSC Orchestra translated in 5 languages with scenes of the ship and of the excursions.

TODAY'S DINING TIMES

- **BREAKFAST**

Villa Borghese Restaurant	Deck 5	7:30am-9:30am

- **BUFFET**

Self Service	Deck 13	6:30am-10:30am

- **LUNCH (OPEN SEATING)**

Villa Borghese Restaurant	Deck 5	12:00pm-1:30pm

- **BUFFET**

Self Service	Deck 13	12:00pm-3:00pm

- **GRILL**

Caffetteria la Piazzetta	Deck 13	12:00pm-4:30pm

- **TEA & SNACK**

Caffetteria la Piazzetta-right side, Deck 13		3:30pm-4:30pm
PIZZERIA	Deck 13	5:00pm-9:00pm

- **CASUAL DINNER**

Cafeteria La Piazzetta-Portside

	Deck 13	6:00pm-7:30pm

- **DINNER**

Villa Borghese Restaurant Deck 5

1st Seating	5:30pm
2nd Seating	8:00pm

Ibiscus Restaurant Deck 6

1st Seating	5:30pm
2nd Seating	8:00pm

We kindly remind you that it is not allowed to enter into the Restaurant with shorts and vests.

To offer you the finest service, please respect the above times.
Restaurant doors will close 15 min. after opening.

- **FRIED FANTASIES**

Served in the lounges	11:30pm

RESTAURANTS FOR AN UNFORGETTABLE EXPERIENCE

La Cantinella Wine Bar	Deck 7	4:00pm-1:00am

RESERVATIONS REQUIRED, CALL 99:

Shanghai Chinese Restaurant	Deck 7	12:00pm-2:30pm 7:00pm-11:00pm
Restaurant 4 Seasons (à la carte)	Deck 13	6:30pm-9:00pm

For guests with reservation, the Restaurant will be open until 10:30pm.
Extra Services

TODAY'S BAR OPENING HOURS

L'Incontro Bar (Starboard side) Coffee Bar	Deck 5	6:30am-12:00am
L'Incontro Bar(Port side) Coffee Bar	Deck 5	12:00pm-12:00am
Purple Bar - Coffee Bar	Deck 6	4:00pm-12:00am
Zaffiro Bar - Coffee Bar	Deck 6	4:00pm-12:00am
Amber Bar	Deck 6	8:00am-1:30am
Savannah Bar	Deck 6	4:30pm-1:00am
The Shaker Lounge Martini Bar	Deck 7	8:00pm-1:00am
La Cantinella Wine Bar	Deck 7	4:00pm-1:00am
La Cubana - Cigar Room	Deck 7	7:00pm-1:00am
Palm Beach Casino	Deck 7	6:00pm-...
Spa Bar - Vitamin Bar	Deck 13	9:00am-7:00pm
Barracuda Bar - Tropical Bar	Deck 13	10:00am-7:00pm
El Sombrero Bar-Ice Cream Parlour	Deck 13	8:00am-1:00am
La Piazzetta Cafeteria	Deck 13	6:30am-5:00pm
R32 Disco	Deck 14	11:00pm -...

OUR AGENT IN COZUMEL

ACS S.A. DE C.V.
*CALLE 6 NORTE ENTRE 10 Y 15 AV. APARADO
161 COZUMEL, Q. ROO MEXICO 77600*
Tel. 00 52 - 987 - 87 23779

SERVICE DIRECTORY

MEDICAL EMERGENCY NUMBER: 115

Front Desk - Reception	tel. 99	Deck 5	24 hrs
- Concierge		tel. 99	5:00pm-10:00pm
Wake up calls tel. 99			24 hrs
Room Service tel. 2720,2781			24 hrs
Medical Centre tel. 2660		Deck 5	8:00am-12:00pm 4:00pm-8:00pm
Tour Desk tel. 2804/2805		Deck 6	4:00pm-8:00pm
Accounting Desk tel. 2807		Deck 5	8:00am-11:00am 4:00pm-7:00pm
Exchange Office tel. 2806		Deck 5	8:00am-11:00am 4:00pm-7:00pm
Shops		Deck 6	5:00pm-12:00am
- Jewellery		tel. 2778	
-Cosmetics		tel. 2773	
- Duty Free		tel. 2774	
-Logo shop		tel. 2775	
- Watch shop			
Internet Cafè		Deck 7	24 hrs
Photo Shop Tel. 2706		Deck 7	5:00pm-11:30pm
Palm Beach Casino Tel. 2698		Deck 7	5:20pm-...
Slot Machines Tel. 2868		Deck 7	5:20pm-....

We remind you that only 18 and over are welcome in the Palm Beach Casino.

Art Gallery tel. 6037	Deck 7	8:00pm-10:00pm
Shopping guide	Deck 5	7:00pm-9:00pm
Library Tel. 2868	Deck 7	3:30pm-6:30pm
Swimming Pool	Deck 13	7:00am-6:30pm
Jacuzzi	Deck 13	7:00am-6:30pm
Tennis Court	Deck 16	7:00am-8:00pm

Body & Mind Spa Beauty Farm, Deck 13

Beauty Salon tel. 2732	8:00am-8:00pm
Sauna - Steam Room tel. 2732	9:00am-7:00pm
Massage Booking Desk tel. 2732	8:00am-8:00pm
Gymnasium, tel. 2875	7:00am-7:00pm

* to be allowed to workout in the gym please fill in the health form that you can find at the Fitness Centre, deck 13. Please come to the gym with sneakers.
For over 14 only

MINI, JUNIOR & TEENS CLUB

- **Mini club** (3-6 years old)
9:00am-12:00pm; 3:00pm-6:00pm; 7:00pm-11:00pm
- **Juniors club** (7-12 years old) Deck 14
10:00am-12:00pm; 3:00pm-6:00pm; 7:00pm-11:00pm
- **Teens club** (13-18 years old) R32 Disco, Deck 14
3:30pm

For information and communications
Tel. 2877 / 2879

UNFORGETTABLE DINING EXPERIENCE

We invite you to enjoy the view from a very special panoramic dinner table tonight, in the Restaurants:

	Paying Menu
4 Seasons	Deck 13 6:30pm-9:00pm
	Menu 'à la carte' $ 25.00

MSC Orchestra, *courtesy MSC Cruises*

NOMADE YACHTING BORA BORA
(formerly BORA BORA CRUISES)
B.P. 40186 Fare Tony—Vaiete
Papeete-Tahiti, French Polynesia
(689) 544-507
(689) 451-065 Fax
www.nomadeyachting.com
U.S. contact: Kurtz-Ahlers & Associates, (949) 487-0522

TI'A MOANA and *TU MOANA:* entered service 2003; 226.7' x 45.3'; 40-passenger capacity; 20 staterooms; international crew; 7-day/6-night cruises from Bora Bora to Taha'a, Huahine, Raiatea, and Bora Bora, the French Polynesian Leeward Islands of Tahiti. (**Category A—Not Rated**)

Nomade Yachting Bora Bora, formerly Bora Bora Cruises, an independent, Tahitian-family-owned company, entered the cruise market in July 2003, introducing two 40-passenger sister yachts sailing the waters and lagoons of French Polynesia.

All air-conditioned cabins face the sea and include large windows, a minibar/refrigerator, sofa or chair and table, flat-panel TV with retractable screen, individual DVD/CD players, writing desk, personal safe, hair dryer, telephone, bathrobe, and numerous amenities. Standard cabins measure approximately 166 square feet, whereas the two suites measure 330 square feet. Some accommodations have king-size beds, while others have queen or double beds. There are no balconies.

Meals are served with open seating in the indoor/outdoor main dining room. French and continental cuisine with subtle Polynesian flavors is emphasized. Guests can have their meals where and when it suits them.

Atop the ships on the sun deck are a Jacuzzi, bar, lounge chairs, and day beds. One deck below on the bridge deck are a terrace and two Bora Bora suites. On the upper deck are a library, Jacuzzi, sun pads, bar and lounge, and nine cabins. The main deck contains the reception area, restaurant and terrace, a small gym, a spa suite, and nine cabins. On the aft deck there is a floating dock for use when the ship is at anchor. The wide range of activities includes a champagne breakfast served in a lagoon, a river kayak expedition, a torch-lit dinner on the beach, local entertainers brought aboard, and movies under the stars.

Listed prices for a six-night, seven-day cruise range from 5,950 to 11,900 per person; however, there is a 10 percent discount for advance purchase of 120 days or more before departure.

Strong Points:
A casual yet elegant, self-indulgent experience exploring one of the world's most romantic and scenic areas in an opulent, yacht-like setting.

NORWEGIAN CRUISE LINE
7665 Corporate Center Drive
Miami, Florida 33126
(800) 327-7030
(305) 436-4000
www.ncl.com

NORWEGIAN DAWN: entered service 2002; 91,740 G.R.T.; 965' x 105'; 2,244-passenger capacity; 1,112 cabins; international officers and crew; Bermuda, Canada and New England, and Caribbean cruises from Miami and New York.

NORWEGIAN EPIC: entered service 2010; 150,000 G.R.T.; 1,068' x 133'; 4,200-passenger capacity; 2,100 cabins; international officers and crew; cruises from Miami to the Caribbean. **(Category C—Not Rated)**

NORWEGIAN JADE (formerly *Pride of Hawaii*): entered service 2006; 93,000 G.R.T.; 965' x 106'; 2,466-passenger capacity; 1,233 cabins; international officers and crew; cruises in Europe.

★★★★★ +

NORWEGIAN JEWEL, NORWEGIAN PEARL, and *NORWEGIAN GEM:* entered service 2005, 2006, and 2007, respectively; 93,000 G.R.T.; 965' x 105'; 2,376-, 2,394-, and 2,380-passenger capacity, respectively; 1,188 to 1,197 cabins; international officers and crew; *Jewel* cruises the Caribbean, Canada and New England, and Europe; *Pearl* cruises to Alaska, the Panama Canal, and the Caribbean from Miami; *Gem* cruises the Caribbean, Bahamas and Florida, and Europe.

★★★★★ +

NORWEGIAN SKY (formerly *Pride of Aloha* and *Norwegian Sky*): entered service 1999; 77,104 G.R.T.; 853' x 105'; 2,002-passenger capacity; 1,001 cabins; American officers and crew; 3- and 4-night cruises from Miami to the Bahamas. **(Category C—Not Rated)**

NORWEGIAN SPIRIT (formerly *Super Star Leo*): entered service 1998; rechristened 2004; 75,338 G.R.T.; 882' x 105'; 1,966-passenger capacity; 998 cabins; international officers and crew; cruises the Caribbean, Bermuda, Canada and New England. **(Category C—Not Rated)**

NORWEGIAN SUN: entered service 2001; refurbished 2004; 78,309 G.R.T.; 853' x 105'; 1,936-passenger capacity; 968 cabins; international officers and crew; cruises to the Caribbean from Port Canaveral.

NORWEGIAN STAR: entered service 2001; refurbished 2006; 91,740 G.R.T.; 935' x 105'; 2,240-passenger capacity; 1,120 cabins; international officers and crew; cruises Alaska and Mexican Riviera.

PRIDE OF AMERICA: entered service 2005; 81,000 G.R.T.; 2,138-passenger capacity; 1,069 cabins; American officers and crew; 7-night cruises in Hawaiian Islands. (**Category C—Not Rated**)

(Medical Facilities on all ships: C-0; P-1; EM; CLS; N-1; CM; PD; EKG; PO; OX; X.)

Some of these ships are rated in 11 separate categories in the second half of chapter 14.

Miami-based Norwegian Cruise Line (NCL) was formerly a subsidiary of the Oslo-based NCL Holding ASA/NRW, formerly Klosters Rederi A/S, a shipping company owned by the Kloster family since the turn of the nineteenth century. In 1996, the name of the parent company was changed to Norwegian Cruise Line, Ltd. During the period extending from late 1999 through early 2000, the stock was acquired by the Asian-based Star Cruises. In August 2007, a private equity group, Apollo Management LP, agreed to make a $1 billion cash equity investment in NCL. Under the terms of the investment, which closed in January 2008, Apollo became a 50 percent owner of NCL. Apollo Management LP also owns Oceania Cruises and Regent Seven Seas Cruises. Today, NCL has 12 ships in service and under construction and sails to approximately 140 ports around the world.

From 1968 to 1971, NCL introduced three similarly designed bread-and-butter cruise ships. First came the MS *Starward* in 1968, followed by the MS *Skyward* in 1969, and the MS *Southward* and MS *Sunward II* in 1971. All four ships were intended to bring the cruise experience to upper-middle-class and middle-class America. Passengers received numerous meals and loads of food, continuous activities and entertainment, several popular ports of call, adequate service and accommodations, and the excitement of cruising at reasonable prices. All three ships ceased being operated by NCL during the 1990s and were replaced with newer vessels.

The cabin stewards and waiters are a mixture of Filipino, Romanian, Caribbean, Asian, or Central and South American. They are generally friendly, competent, and efficient.

In 2000, NCL became an innovator for the industry by announcing its intention to eventually convert all of its vessels in order to offer Freestyle Cruising. This allows passengers to dine in any of the dining venues aboard ship whenever and with whomever they want. Although this has been the agenda on the smaller, luxury-class ships for decades, NCL is the first cruise line to offer this widely desired dining program on large, mass-market vessels. In addition to one or more main dining rooms, lido buffet, and outdoor grill areas, there are three additional on the *Pride of Aloha,* six additional on the *Sun* and *Dawn,* seven additional on the *Star,* and eight or more additional on the *Pride of America* and *Norwegian Jade, Jewel, Pearl,* and *Gem.* The dining experience on all ships has greatly improved since the takeover of the cruise line by Star Cruises. Tipping is added to the passengers' end-of-the-cruise account statement, and passengers have the option to modify it up or down.

The itineraries have shifted over the years, but when cruising in the Caribbean, the ships normally cover three or four ports, including a beach party at NCL's privately owned island paradise in the Bahamas, Great Stirrup Cay. All NCL ships feature a Dive In program, where passengers receive instruction and supervision in snorkeling, both aboard ship and while ashore. The Sports Afloat program offers a variety of exercise, aerobic, yoga, and fitness classes throughout the day, as well as organized walks both on the ships and at various ports of call.

In 1988, the 42,000-ton MS *Seaward* joined the fleet, accommodating 1,518 passengers, double occupancy. In 1998, she was renamed *Norwegian Sea,* but in 2004, she was transferred to parent company Star Cruises.

At 50,764 G.R.T. each, the MS *Dreamward* and MS *Windward* entered service in December 1992 and June 1993, respectively. In 1998, both ships were stretched and now each carries 1,747 passengers. The ships were then renamed *Norwegian Dream* and *Norwegian Wind.* In 2007, *Norwegian Wind* was transferred to parent company Star Cruises. In 2008, *Norwegian Dream* was sold to Louis Cruises along with the *Norwegian Majesty.* The 34,242-ton, 1,078-passenger *Norwegian Crown* was sold off to Fred Olsen Cruise Line in 2007.

The 77,104-ton, 2,002-passenger *Norwegian Sky* joined the fleet in August 1999, the first new ship to be built by NCL since the early 1990s. She was reflagged into the U.S. registry and renamed *Pride of Aloha* in 2004. In 2008 she was transferred to Star Cruises and then transferred back to NCL.

The *Norwegian Sun,* sister ship to *Norwegian Sky,* entered service in the fall of 2001 with numerous innovations, including larger cabins with greater storage space, more lovely and tasteful décor in the public areas, and an abundance of specialty restaurants, all with panoramic ocean views. The majority of accommodations measure 150 to 173 square feet with 48-foot balconies. The inside cabins are 145 square feet and outside cabins without balconies are 150 square feet. Suites range in size from 215 to 355 square feet with balconies from 48 to 149 square feet. The four top-of-the-line owner's suites come in at 502 square feet with 258-foot balconies sporting outdoor Jacuzzis.

Freestyle dining on this ship includes your choice of two large main dining rooms with multicourse continental menus, Le Bistro (an elegant restaurant with outstanding French/Mediterranean cuisine and attentive service with a $15 cover charge), Il Adagio (a romantic Italian restaurant with all tables and booths located either on a window or on a raised balcony immediately behind the window tables with a $10 cover charge), Pacific Heights (a calorie- and fat-count spa-cuisine restaurant with windows overlooking the sea), Las Ramblas (a tapas bar), East Meets West (a steakhouse with a $20 cover charge), and Ginza (an à la carte Japanese restaurant with a sushi bar and teppanyaki room with a $15 cover charge). The breakfast buffets at the indoor/outdoor Garden Café are among the best I have experienced on any mass-market or premium cruise ship. The occasional outdoor lunch barbeques are also outstanding, and the pizza station turns out melt-in-your-mouth thin-crusted delights. The ship also includes a lifestyle area/learning center, 10 bars and lounges, two pools, a casino, a Balinese spa, a batting cage, a basketball/volleyball court, a fitness center, and an art gallery.

In the fall of 2001, the 91,000-ton, 2,240-passenger *Superstar Libra,* originally intended to sail for Star Cruises, was transferred to NCL, named *Norwegian Star,* and positioned for Hawaiian cruises. Today she offers itineraries in Alaska, through the Panama Canal, and along the Mexican Riviera. Although not as traditionally decorated as the *Sun* and possessing a somewhat confusing traffic pattern, she boasts many alternative specialty restaurants at sea, as well as two of the largest, most indulgent courtyard villas and garden villas afloat (each suite measuring 5,000 square feet with 1,722 square feet of rooftop terrace gardens going for $3,200 per night per couple).

Average cabins are modern with ample storage but are not very large and include twin beds that convert to queens, remote-control televisions, hair dryers, writing/vanity desks, and bathrooms with magnifying mirrors and separate shower and toilet compartments. Outside cabins with balconies measure 166 square feet (with 37-square-foot balconies). In addition, there are numerous accommodations labeled "mini-suites," with small sitting areas (but not much larger than a deluxe room on other ships), and several full suites that are considerably larger and more luxurious and include balconies. Many staterooms interconnect for traveling families.

In accord with the line's Freestyle Cruising theme, passengers on the *Star* can select among the following dining options: the Versailles and Aqua (two main dining rooms offering traditional six-course meals), Ginza (a combination Chinese, Japanese, Thai restaurant with a sushi-tempura bar, teppanyaki room, and sake bar where all items are à la carte), the Soho Room (an à la carte Pacific Rim restaurant featuring a fusion of Californian, Hawaiian, and Asian dishes as well as a dramatic lobster tank with live lobsters from which passengers can select), Le Bistro (a French-Mediterranean restaurant with a $15 cover charge), Endless Summer (a

Tex-Mex restaurant overlooking the atrium lobby and incorporating a performance stage and large movie screen with a $10 cover charge), Blue Lagoon (fea-
turing hamburgers, hot dogs, fish and chips, and wok preparations), Las Rambles
(a tapas bar with a guitar player), and La Trattoria (a casual Italian restaurant
located within the 24-hour Market Café buffet venue). In addition there is an
ice-cream bar, a beer-garden bar, an outdoor grill, heart-healthy light cuisine
menus available at most restaurants, and 24-hour room service. Whatever else
one might say, no one cruising on the *Star* goes hungry.

Public facilities include a cinema; library; cardroom; photo gallery; wedding
chapel; medical center; cigar bar; wine cellar; champagne bar; coffee/pastry bar;
Internet café; observation show lounge; disco; large department-like store with a
cocktail/coffee bar; grand European, early-20th-century-style, three-deck theater
for production shows; and karaoke facilities. The more active may seek out the
fitness center and Barong Health Spa, large pool complex with giant water slides,
or jogging track atop ship. The ship also features a promenade deck attractively
decorated with murals, numerous lounges, teen club, video arcade, children's
pool and supervised children's facilities, and business meeting rooms.

A sister ship, *Norwegian Dawn,* with additional public areas and facilities,
joined the fleet in 2002. She offers itineraries to Bermuda, Canada, New England, and the Caribbean from Miami and New York.

Two additional sister ships with numerous modifications, *Norwegian Jewel* and
Norwegian Pearl, joined the fleet in 2005 and 2006. A third, *Norwegian Gem,*
joined the fleet in 2007. The *Jewel* has 68 additional cabins and can carry 2,376
passengers (double occupancy), whereas the *Pearl* and *Gem* have 2,394 lower
berths. A number of the staterooms can interconnect to create two-, three-, four-,
or five-bedroom areas. In addition to the two giant garden villas at 5,000 square
feet each, these ships offer 10 exclusive 572-square-foot courtyard villas that
include numerous amenities and share their own private pool, Jacuzzi, sun deck,
and small gym. The main accommodations include 412 143-square-foot inside
cabins, 243 161-square-foot ocean-view cabins, 360 ocean-view with balcony cabins at 205 square feet, 134 284-square-foot mini-suites, 4 460-square-foot
"Romance Suites," 10 572-square-foot penthouse suites, and 2 928-square-foot
deluxe owner's suites. Twenty-seven accommodations are equipped for the physically impaired. The full suites and villas enjoy butler service. Both the full suites
and mini-suites have a special concierge who will make arrangements for services
and dining reservations on board ship and for shore excursions.

There are 10 dining venues: two main dining rooms; an upscale steakhouse; a
French and an Italian restaurant; a Tex-Mex restaurant; an Asian complex featuring Japanese and Thai/Chinese selections, sushi and sashimi, and a teppanyaki
room; an indoor/outdoor buffet-style restaurant; and a 24-hour food-court-style
restaurant.

Public areas include a new bar central, which features a martini bar, champagne
and wine bar, and beer and whisky pub all connected but unique in their own way;
a three-story art nouveau-styled theater; a large casino; an art gallery; a library; a

cardroom; 7,000 square feet of shopping area; a sports bar/nightclub; seven additional bars and lounges; a cigar club; a chapel; a medical center; several meeting rooms; and two pools, one with a waterfall and three Jacuzzis and the other with a water slide and two Jacuzzis. Internet connections are in all staterooms and wireless Internet is available around the ship. There is also an Internet café. Guests can rent lap tops (but there is limited availability). The spas feature 20 treatment rooms, thermal suites with steam, sauna, Jacuzzis, thalassotherapy pools, and relaxation areas (all available at a surcharge for those not taking a spa treatment). The fitness centers are quite large and well equipped, and each piece of cardio equipment has its own flat-screen TV. The sports deck includes a combination full tennis court/basketball court, shuffleboard, golf nets, ping pong, and a jogging track. The Kid's Club includes a cinema, nursery, and sleep/rest areas. In addition there is a theme teen club for ages 13 to 17 and a video arcade. The *Pearl* and *Gem* also boast rock-climbing walls and bowling alleys.

The line formerly had a big presence in the Hawaiian cruise market with the *Pride of Aloha, Pride of Hawaii,* and *Pride of America* offering seven-day cruises. However, in 2008, various problems and lack of bookings resulted in the *Pride of Hawaii* being renamed and reflagged *Norwegian Jade* and transferred out of the Hawaiian market. The *Pride of Aloha* was transferred to parent Star Cruises and then back again to NCL, where it adopted its original name, *Norwegian Sky.*

Of the 1,069 cabins on *Pride of America* (the only remaining ship of the NCL America fleet), 661 sport balconies. The average cabin is 178 square feet with two lower beds that convert to queen size, a small sitting area, TV, private safe, and hair dryer. The suites are quite a bit larger and include a concierge lounge and butler service. The "best of America" theme and décor are carried throughout the ship.

There are eight restaurants, including the 496-seat Liberty and 628-seat Skyline main dining rooms, Jefferson's Bistro, Lazy J Steakhouse, East Meets West (offering Asian cuisine with a teppanyaki room), the Cadillac Diner, Aloha Café (with numerous buffet islands), and Little Italy (located in a section of the buffet restaurant and featuring Italian favorites at dinner time). Key West Bar & Grill serves up burgers and grilled chicken. A reservation service with monitors located around the ship provides waiting times and seating information.

Public facilities include the Santa Fe Spa and Fitness Center, numerous lounges, a cardroom, shops, an Internet center, children's and teen areas, a children's cinema, a conference area with breakout rooms, a large pool area with three pools, whirlpools, a bungee trampoline, and a gyro-chair.

Pride of America offers seven-day destination-oriented itineraries from Honolulu on Oahu, calling at Hilo and Kona on the Big Island of Hawaii and at the Islands of Kauai and Maui.

Norwegian Jade, originally named *Pride of Hawaii,* sister ship to the *Jewel, Pearl,* and *Gem,* has some variations in décor. Ten restaurants are featured, including Cagney's Steak House, Blue Lagoon, Le Bistro, Paniolo tapas and salsa restaurant, Papa's Italian Kitchen, buffet restaurants, and Jasmine Garden Restaurant (featuring a sushi bar and a teppanyaki table), and Pacific fusion restaurant. Like the other sister ships there are two 5,000-square-foot garden villas and 10 courtyard villas sharing a private courtyard and sun deck with interconnecting cabins to create two-, three-, four-, or five-bedroom areas. She also includes four Romance Suites that are 460 square feet with a special romantic décor. In 2008, the ship was shifted to the European market.

Pricing can be a bit confusing on all the ships since the brochure prices, though relatively high for mass-market ships, are generally heavily discounted for early bookings or during slow seasons.

NCL has announced that over the next few years, the bulk of the company will consist solely of recently constructed ships, and eventually, the older, less competitive vessels will be transferred to service less demanding markets in Europe and Asia.

Norwegian Epic, a 150,000-ton, 4,200-passenger ship with 1,415 outside cabins featuring balconies, is scheduled to be delivered in 2010, offering eastern and western Caribbean itineraries from Miami. The ship will have numerous innovative venues. POSH Beach Club at the top of the ship will offer around-the-clock activities and events ranging from morning yoga classes and body treatments in cabanas to an outdoor nightclub in the evenings. All outside cabins will have balconies.

The Epic Club is a private club comprised of 60 private suites and villas on two private decks atop ship in a courtyard villa complex featuring two whirlpools, a gym, a sauna, a sun deck, indoor/outdoor dining, a bar/nightclub, and a concierge lounge. It offers the best of everything, including upscale wines and liquors, gaming tables, and expensive art and jewelry displays.

The *Epic* introduces a new category of inside staterooms—the Studios. These staterooms maximize space and feature a large, round window that looks out into the corridor with customized changing light effects that mirror different stages of the day. These accommodations occupy two decks and have key-card access to the "Living Room," a two-story shared private lounge. The lounge has its own concierge, bar, room service, and two large TV screens.

The spa balcony, deluxe balcony staterooms and suites located within the spa, have complimentary access to the ship's thermal center and state-of-the-art fitness center.

The Ice Bar, with temperatures below 17 degrees Fahrenheit, is literally a frozen vault with walls, tables, stools, glasses, and a bar of solid ice. Passengers are given fur coats, gloves, and hats, as well as iced vodka. Spice H2O, located around the aft swimming pool, is an adults-only area. It consists of terraced decks and a giant movie screen. In the morning, spicy Bloody Marys are served accompanied by music; at noon, Asian-inspired food is served in Chinese to-go containers; and at sunset guests luxuriate with glasses of champagne to the sounds of Spanish guitars. Later the area becomes a theater with aerial performances and a water ballet. Following this entertainment, a floor covers the pool, allowing passengers to dance under the stars.

Strong Points:

The ships built since 2000 are modern, attractive ships with a plethora of facilities and are welcome additions to the mass cruise market. Freestyle Cruising, as it is executed on NCL, offers a uniquely large number of dining possibilities, with excellent cuisine, making the cruise experience akin to dining out at a different shoreside restaurant each evening. Passengers receive a good deal more for their money on NCL than on some competing cruise lines. Passengers opting for the full suites and villas enjoy the luxury and pampering offered by more expensive cruise lines. The NCL America brand, *Pride of America,* offers an ideal cruise for all members of the family wishing to visit the Hawaiian Islands. The new *Norwegian Epic* is one of the most innovative ships launched this new century.

Norwegian Pearl, *courtesy Norwegian Cruise Line*

Courtesy Norwegian Cruise Line

Pool on Norwegian Star, *courtesy Norwegian Cruise Line*

Italian Dining Room, Norwegian Sun, *courtesy Norwegian Cruise Line*

Gala Inaugural Dinner

Norwegian Sun
November 16, 2001

Appetizers

Tiger Prawns in Won Ton Ties with Cognac Mayonnaise, Curly Beets and Chives

or

Seared Hudson Valley Duck Foie Gras with Rhubarb Compote,
Fried Parsnip Slivers and Maple Syrup Drizzle

Soups

Clear Oxtail Soup with Old Spanish Sherry, Chester Stick

or

Wild Mushroom Bisque in Sourdough Bread Loaf

Salads

Cantaloupe Fan with Summer Greens, Nasturtium Flowers and Pomegranate Pearls
Champagne Dressing

or

Croûton-Crusted Goat Cheese on Mache Greens with Garlic Flakes
Walnut Oil and Balsamic Vinegar Dressing

Entrées

Baked Sea Bass with Black Truffle Shavings
in a Ring of Celery and Parsnip Mousse and Fresh Watercress Coulis

or

Broiled Caribbean Lobster Tail with Lemon Risotto on Grilled Acorn Squash
and Rosemary-Spiked Baked Garlic, Niçoise Olive and Pine Nut Tapenade

or

Skillet-Fried Veal Chop with a Forest Mushroom Ragoût,
Sorrel-Infused Veal Cream Jus, Gingered Asparagus and Grilled Polenta Crescents

or

Vegetarian — Grilled Mediterranean Vegetables in a Phyllo Crust with Feta Cheese
and Oven-Baked Tomatoes in Pesto Cream with Fried Basil Leaves

Desserts

Grappa Semifreddo Parfait with Espresso-Chocolate Sauce

or

Cinnamon-Ginger Mousse in Crisp Lavender Tuile with Fresh Blackberries

Petits Fours

With Compliments of Norwegian Cruise Line

Chardonnay, Sonoma-Cutrer, Sonoma Coast, California
Merlot, St. Francis, Sonoma County, California

Courtesy Norwegian Cruise Line

Stuff for "morning people"...

Early Morning Stretch (Free)	Fitness Center, Deck 12, Fwd	7:30am
Total Body Conditioning (Free)	Fitness Center, Deck 12, Fwd	8:00am
Tennis Play with your Fellow Guests	Sports Court, Deck 13, Aft	8:00am-10:00am
Golf Clubs Available	Great Outdoors Bar, Deck 12, Aft	8:00am-5:00pm
Common Skin & allergy problems of Cats and Dogs	Spinnaker Lounge, Deck 13, Fwd	9:00am
Service Club Meets	Whiskey Bar, Deck 6, Mid	9:00am
Library (Sudoku & Trivia Available)	Deck 12, Fwd	9:00am-11:00am
Origami with *your Host Elwyn* - bring a crisp dollar bill	Whiskey Bar, Deck 6, Mid	9:45am
Morning Trivia	Bar City, Deck 6, Mid	10:00am
Rock Climb Wall (Weather Permitting)	Deck 14, Aft	10:00am-1:00pm
Aqua Kid's Club: Port Play Group Fun ($5/hour)	Deck 12, Mid	10:00am-5:00pm
Sport Court	Deck 13, Aft	10:00am-5:00pm
2 for 1 Bowling while in port	Deck 7, Aft	10:00am-6:00pm
Bowling Alley (Must be 6 years or older to play)	Bliss Ultra Lounge, Deck 7, Aft	10:00am-Close
Board Games with your Fellow Guests	Card Room, Deck 12, Fwd	10:15am
Nintendo Wii - On the Big Screen	Crystal Atrium, Deck 7, Mid	10:30am-Noon
Golf Putting Challenge	Bar City, Deck 6, Mid	11:00am

Add pizzazz to your afternoon...

Casino Pool Deck Gaming	Deck 12, Fwd	Noon
Ping Pong Challenge	Deck 12, Fwd, Portside	12:30pm
Rock Climbing Wall (Weather Permitting)	Deck 14, Aft	1:00pm-5:00pm
Shuffleboard Challenge	Deck 7, Promenade, Starboard	1:30pm
NFL Live: Jacksonville vs. Pittsburgh	Crystal Atrium, Deck 7, Mid	Satellite Pending, 2:00pm
Library (Sudoku & Trivia Available)	Deck 12, Fwd	2:00pm-4:00pm
Bridge Play with your Fellow Guests	Card Room, Deck 12, Fwd	3:00pm
Fun Trivia	Bar City, Deck 6, Mid	4:45pm
Spin to Win Free Pull for CAS members	Pearl Club Casino, Deck 6 Fwd	4:00pm-6:00pm
Trio Los Hernandez - *Harmonies & Guitars*	Tahitian Poolside, Deck 12, Mid	4:00pm-7:00pm
Frank's Place - *Continuous Music of Sinatra*	Star Bar, Deck 13, Mid	4:00pm-Close
Bingo on the H$_2$O	Spinnaker Lounge, Deck 13, Fwd	5:00pm
NFL Live: Detroit vs. San Diego	Crystal Atrium, Deck 7, Mid	Satellite Pending, 5:15pm
Friends of Bill W.	The Chapel, Deck 13, Fwd	5:00pm
Mihail Polak - *Mellow Piano and Cocktails*	Bar City, Deck 6, Mid	5:30pm-8:45pm

Everything's hotter when the sun goes down...

Guess the Picasso	Art Gallery, Deck 7, Aft	6:30pm-9:30pm
Pearl Showband *Ballroom Dancing*	Spinnaker Lounge, Deck 13, Fwd	6:45pm-7:30pm/7:45pm-8:30pm
Aqua Kid's Club	Deck 12, Mid	7:00pm-10:00pm
Magical Showtime: featuring *Richard Burr and Josette*	Stardust Theater, Decks 6 & 7, Fwd	7:30pm
NFL Live: Washington vs. New York	Crystal Atrium, Deck 7, Mid	Satellite Pending, 9:00pm
Trio Los Hernandez - *Harmonies & Guitars*	Tahitian Poolside, Deck 12, Mid	8:00pm-10:00pm
Battle of the Sexes Game Show	Spinnaker Lounge, Deck 13, Fwd	8:30pm
Sailing Solo and Singles Mix	Star Bar, Deck 13, Mid	8:30pm
Ron Arduini - *Lyric Elegance*	Bar City, Deck 6, Mid	9:00pm-Close
Great Dance Music with *Harmony & Rhythm*	Spinnaker Lounge, Deck 13, Fwd	9:30pm-10:15pm
Magical Showtime: featuring *Richard Burr and Josette*	Stardust Theater, Decks 6 & 7, Fwd	9:30pm
Friends of Dorothy a gathering for our GLBT guests	Bliss, Port VIP section, Deck 7, Aft	9:30pm
DJ *Patrick – plays the hits*	Bliss Ultra Lounge, Deck 7, Aft	10:00pm-Close
"Name That Tune" with *Ron Arduini*	Bar City, Deck 6, Mid	10:15pm
70's Groove Party	Spinnaker Lounge, Deck 13, Fwd	10:30pm
Bliss Ultra White Party	Bliss Ultra Lounge, Deck 7, Aft	11:30pm
Paradise Lotto Drawing- Jackpot over $139,000!	Pearl Club Casino, Deck 6, Fwd	11:30pm
Double Bonus Points to be earned on slots	Pearl Club Casino, Deck 6, Fwd	Midnight-2:00am

Ok, we know this looks like a schedule (gasp!)
But, remember, you're free to whatever!

Bar Services

Java Café & Juice Bar Deck 7, Mid	7:00am-Close	
Morning Specials and Fresh Juices		
Great Outdoors Bar Deck 12, Aft	7:00am-Close	
Topsiders Bar Deck 12, Mid	8:00am-Close	
Bliss Ultra Lounge Deck 7, Aft	2:00pm-Close	
Sky High Bar Deck 13, Fwd	3:00pm-Close	
Star Bar Deck 13, Mid	4:00pm-Close	
Spinnaker Bar Deck 13, Fwd	4:00pm-Close	
Bar City Deck 6, Mid	4:00pm-Close	
Champagne Bar Deck 6, Mid	4:00pm-Close	
Maltings Bar Deck 6, Mid	4:00pm-Close	

Guest Services

Metro Video Arcade Deck 12, Mid	Open 24 Hours
Reception Desk Deck 7, Mid (#00)	Open 24 Hours
Internet Café Deck 7, Aft	Open 24 Hours
Body Waves Fitness Deck 12, Fwd	Open 24 Hours
Onboard Credit Desk Deck 7, Mid	8:00am-10:00am 6:00pm-8:30pm
Internet Manager Deck 7, Aft	8:00am-10:00am 4:00pm-6:00pm 7:00pm-10:00pm
Tahitian Pool* Deck 12, Mid	8:00am-10:00pm
Jacuzzis* Deck 12, Mid	8:00am-Midnight
South Pacific Spa & Salon Deck 12, Fwd	8:00am-10:00pm
Medical Center Deck 4, Mid	8:30am-10:00am 4:00pm-5:00pm
Photo Gallery Deck 7, Aft	8:30am-Arrival 5:00pm-11:00pm
Water Slide Deck 12, Mid	9:00am-6:00pm
Pearl Club Casino Deck 6, Fwd	2:00pmApprox-Close
Cruise Consultant Deck 7, Mid	5:00pm-9:00pm
Port Shopping Representative Deck 7, Aft	6:30pm-8:00pm
Art Gallery Deck 7, Aft	6:30pm-9:30pm
Gift Shops Deck 7, Fwd	6:00pm-11:00pm
Shore Excursions Desk Deck 7, Mid	7:00pm-9:00pm

*Pools and Jacuzzi will be open as long as it is weather permitting. Forward Jacuzzis and Pool, Deck 12, are for adults only. Please, no reserving of deck chairs. Items left on deck chairs for more than 30 minutes will be removed and placed at Reception, Deck 7, Mid

Walking & Jogging: Deck 13 is a walking/jogging track open 24/7. Deck 7 is a walking-only track; it's open 9am-9pm. Remember, all sports play is at your own risk.
Jacuzzis & Pools: Glass & bottles can't be brought into any of the pools or hot tubs; neither can children in diapers or pull-ups, including swimmers.
Casino: You have to be 18 (and have ID) to gamble or be in the casino. Sorry, but no winnings can be paid to any person or bets in violation. Also, drinks or glassware can't be taken out; pipes or cigars can't be taken in, but cigarette smoking is ok. Slot winnings of $1200 and above are subject to W2-G tax withholding.
Liquor Purchased Ashore: Any liquor purchased in our ports of call will be collected and returned to you at the end of the voyage.
Restaurant Cancellations: To ensure each of our guests receive our best service, we can only hold your dinner reservation for 15 minutes. If you need to cancel, please do so by 5:00pm on the day of your reservation to avoid having the cover charge for up to two guests applied to your account.
Smoking Policy: Smoking is only allowed inside the Casino, staterooms, Corona Cigar Club and designated outside deck areas. Cigars are only permitted in the Corona Cigar Club, Deck 6, Mid.

Freestyle Dining

Specialty Restaurants reservations can be made for the day of or the next day before dinner time. To make your reservations, call extension number 050 or visit us on the desk located at Mambo's Restaurant, Deck 8, Mid.

Getting Started-Breakfast

Early Risers Deck, 12, Mid	5:30am
Garden Café Deck 12, Mid	6:30am-10:30am
Great Outdoors (weather permitting) Deck 12, Aft	7:00am-11:30am
Summer Palace Deck 7, Aft	7:30am-9:00am
The Grill (weather permitting) Deck 12, Mid	8:00am-10:30am

Satisfy Your Afternoon Appetite-Lunch

Summer Palace Deck 7, Aft	Noon-1:30pm
Five-course meals, two-story windows	
Garden Café Deck 12, Mid	11:30am-3:30pm
Various (and delicious) Food Action Stations	

What Are You In The Mood For?-Dinner

Garden Café Deck 12, Mid	5:00pm-9:00pm
Main Dining Rooms:	
Summer Palace Deck 7, Aft	5:30pm-10:00pm
Five-course meals, two-story windows	
Indigo Deck 6, Mid	5:30pm-10:30pm
Five-courses, more intimate	
Specialty Restaurants:	
Mambo's Restaurant Deck 8, Mid	5:30pm -10:30pm
Tex Mex delights	
La Cucina Deck 12, Aft, Portside	5:30pm -10:30pm
Now that's Italian!	
Lotus Garden ($10)* Deck 7, Mid	5:30pm -10:30pm
Fusion of exotic Asian flavors	
Shabu-Shabu ($10)* Deck 7, Mid	5:30pm -10:30pm
Mongolian hot pot	
Sushi Bar ($15)* Deck 7, Mid	5:30pm -10:30pm
It doesn't get any fresher	
Cagney's Steakhouse ($20)* Deck 13, Mid	5:30pm -10:30pm
Grilled perfection, elegant setting	
Le Bistro ($15)* Deck 6, Mid	5:30pm -10:30pm
French cuisine that's magnifique	
Teppanyaki ($20)* Deck 7, Mid	5:30 / 7:30 / 9:30pm
All fresh for your enjoyment	

For Whenever You Are Hungry

Blue Lagoon Café Deck 8, Mid	Open 24 hours
Lite bites/burgers & fast wok dishes	
Great Outdoors (weather permitting) Deck 12, Aft	3:30pm-5:00pm
Topsiders Deck 12, Aft	9:00pm-11:00pm

*These restaurants charge a cover, and for what you get, you'll find it's well worth it.
Resort casual dress gets you into every bar, lounge and dining venue. Want to get all decked out? A fun choice anywhere on the ship. In the mood for casual shorts? Have a relaxing dinner in the buffet. Your favorite nice jeans? They're welcome in almost all of our restaurants. Hey, it's your vacation, so dress comfortably, and you'll find a there's venue that suits your style.

Door Decorations: Be safe – overly decorated stateroom doors can pose a fire hazard, so please keep your decorations inside your room.
Environmental Hotline: You can report environmental incidents by calling 1-877-501-5976, the ship's Reception Desk, Deck 7, Mid or via e-mail to EnvironmentalHotline@ncl.com. Reports are confidential.
Customer Advisory: Eat Smart: In case you didn't know, there's a certain level of danger to eating raw or undercooked animal products. It's also risky to drink juices that haven't been pasteurized. So if you have any immune system disorders, you should talk with your doctor.
Customer Relations: Got a service problem? We'll do our best to solve it! Dial '00' while onboard or write Norwegian Cruise Line, 7665 Corporate Center Drive - Miami, Florida 33126.
Safety Equipment: Please don't remove or meddle with any safety equipment onboard (such as smoke detectors or fire extinguishers). And, please follow safety instructions from the crew members.
Announcements: All announcements can be heard on channel 24 on your stateroom television.
Open Flames: Open flames (like burning candles and incense) are strictly forbidden.
Sharps Containers: If you've got any type of needles to throw away, please ask for a special container from the Reception Desk, your Room Steward or the Medical Center.

Courtesy Norwegian Cruise Line

OCEANIA CRUISES
8300 NW 33rd Street, Suite 308
Miami, Florida 33122
(800) 531-5658; (305) 514-2300
(305) 514-2222 Fax
www.oceaniacruises.com

REGATTA, INSIGNIA, and *NAUTICA* (formerly *R-2, R-1,* and *R-5*): entered service 1998 and 2000; refurbished 2005, 2006, and 2007, respectively; 30,277 G.R.T.; 594' x 84'; 684-passenger capacity; 342 cabins; European officers and international crew; cruises Mediterranean, Scandinavia and Baltic, Asia and the Far East, Central and South America, the Caribbean, and Panama Canal.

✭ ✭ ✭ ✭ ✭ ✭

(Note: 6 stars is the highest rating given ships in the premium-market category.)

(Medical Facilities: C-0; P-1, CLS, MS; N-1; CM; PD; BC; EKG; OX; TC; PO; EPC; WC; ICU; X; CP; TM.)

These ships are rated in 11 separate categories in the second half of chapter 14.

In 2002, two former cruise line CEOs, Joe Watters (formerly with Crystal Cruises) and Frank Del Rio (formerly with Renaissance Cruises), along with a conglomerate of other investors, created this new cruise company. Upon acquiring long-term leases on the 30,277-ton, 684-passenger former *R-1* and *R-2* of the now-defunct Renaissance Cruises, they renamed these two sister vessels *Regatta* and *Insignia* and conducted various renovations and refurbishments. Subsequently the cruise line acquired the former *R-5,* renamed her *Nautica,* and placed her in service in late 2005. In 2006, the cruise line was purchased by Apollo, a private equity firm with holdings in the travel industry. After Apollo purchased Regent Seven Seas Cruises in 2008, that cruise line and Oceania became part of Prestige Cruise Holdings but continued to operate as separate brands.

These three beauties are among the most elegantly and tastefully decorated vessels currently in service and could be described as a Ritz-Carlton or Four Seasons at sea. The traditional décor in the various public rooms is quite unique for a cruise ship. Corridors are laden with floral runner-style carpets similar to those found in grand hotels; stairways are adorned with antiques and works of art; and lounges, the main dining room, the library, and public areas are furnished with rich, dark woods as well as expensive classical-period French and English furnishings and elegant wall and window treatments. The décor throughout the vessel is ingeniously orchestrated to create a feeling of understated elegance and grand refinement without a hint of glitz or ostentation.

On each ship, there are 170 similar 173-square-foot outside accommodations with 43-square-foot verandas that include a queen or two twin beds with thick mattresses covered with posh sheets and duvets, a small sitting area, satellite TV, a hair dryer, and a bathroom with a single vanity, toilet, and shower. Of these staterooms 104 are designated concierge staterooms and have a refrigerator and minibar, a DVD player, and additional amenities. Other accommodations aboard include: 114 160- to 165-square-foot standard outside and inside cabins; 52 260-square-foot mini-suites with 72-foot verandas, larger sitting areas, and both a bathtub and shower; and six full suites ranging in size from 533 to 598 square feet with 253- to 364-foot wrap-around verandas, separate living rooms with dining areas, guest baths, and all-marble master bathrooms with whirlpool tubs. Fourteen cabins and suites can connect for families and friends traveling together, 36 can accommodate a third person, and 34 can sleep four passengers.

Atop each ship on decks 9 and 10, are the Terrace Café buffet restaurant; the centrally located swimming pool surrounded by comfortable lounges, including several built for couples; two outdoor whirlpools; the spa and fitness center; a walking/jogging path; the panoramic Observation Lounge and Bar; the library; Internet café; cardroom, and two of the specialty restaurants, Polo Club and Toscana. On all three ships, guests can book private cabanas with special services and amenities by the day for a fee. Suites and mini-suites are located on deck 8 and the remaining accommodations on decks 3, 4, 6, and 7. Conveniently located on deck 5 are the elegant Grand Dining Room, several bars and lounges, the casino, two shops, the photo gallery, and the show lounge with its comfortable traditional-style lounge chairs set around cocktail tables (unlike the theater-style arrangement on most cruise ships).

Certainly one of the strongest suits on each of the ships is the variety of superior dining experiences offered to guests. First of all, there is no assigned seating and passengers can dine where they want and with whom they want in any of the numerous dining venues without any surcharge. The elegant Grand Dining Room features a multicourse menu designed by master chef Jacques Pepin that changes daily and includes numerous gourmet specialties artistically presented and impeccably served.

In addition to the main dining facility, there are three specialty restaurants open each evening. Polo Grill is a clubby, New York-style chop house specializing in giant cuts of prime beef (16- and 32-ounce portions of prime rib, as well as porterhouse, filet, and New York strip steaks), double-cut lamb and pork chops, lobster tail, scampi, ahi tuna with all the accoutrements, as well as a nice choice of appetizers, soups, salads, and desserts. Toscana is a romantic, gourmet, multicourse Italian restaurant with a wide selection of antipasti, pastas, veal dishes, seafood, and all of your typical Italian favorites. Both Polo Grill and Toscana have their own bars. In the evening, the Terrace Café converts to a tapas restaurant featuring a variety of tapas, sushi, and sashimi, as well as most of the items offered in the main dining room. Of course guests can opt to dine in their cabins, where there is 24-hour room service and choices include items offered in the dining rooms. Suite guests can order complete course-by-course meal service from any of the dining room menus. Country club casual attire is suggested and jackets and ties are never required (although some passengers will occasionally dress for dinner).

The breakfast and lunch buffets served at the buffet-style Terrace Café and adjoining outdoor Waves Grill are outstanding and feature an enviable variety of ever-changing ethnic selections as well as high-quality more-traditional fare. Many items such as pasta, pizzas, salads, and grilled hamburgers and fish are made to order (rather than prepared in advance and left standing in steam tables).

Service in all of the restaurants is among the most solicitous and professional of any ship sailing today. We found service throughout the ships exceptional.

Although there are no lavish production shows, the ships offer superior cabaret entertainment each evening and excellent musicians for dancing and listening to in the various lounges. Each day numerous recently released movies are offered on the TV stations, as well as current cable programs, CNN, port talks, and descriptions of upcoming ports of call. Daily activities include cooking demonstrations, cultural lectures, card tournaments, exercise classes, beauty classes, art auctions, bingo, trivia, and other usual shipboard diversions.

All three ships underwent multi-million-dollar refurbishments in 2007 and 2008 wherein the top suites were rebuilt and lavishly furnished; bathrooms in the penthouse suites were completely rebuilt; the other accommodations received new carpeting, tranquility beds, and Imperial mattresses; the public areas were re-carpeted, re-upholstered, and teak decks were constructed; eight luxury cabanas were added on the top deck; the communication equipment was revamped both for high-speed Internet and to enable the use of cell phones at sea; and new flat-screen LCD TVs and DVD players were installed in all accommodations.

The three ships provide Mediterranean and Scandinavian-Baltic Sea itineraries during the warmer months and reposition to the Caribbean, Asia, the Far East, and South and Central America during the late fall and winter. The emphasis is on itineraries to the most desired destinations on somewhat longer cruises with special appeal to seasoned cruisers. The cruise line describes itself as "affordable luxury," positioning itself at the upper end of the premium-cruise market.

In 2007, the line announced that it had ordered two new 66,000-ton, 1,252-passenger ships for delivery in 2010 and 2011. These ships will have 626 cabins and suites, all of which will be 50 percent larger than those on the original three ships, 96 percent with an ocean view, and 93 percent with verandas. There will be four specialty restaurants: Polo Grill and Toscana (similar to the existing three ships) as well as a new French and a new Pan-Asian venue. The accommodations will consist of four owner's suites, six Vista Suites, 10 Oceania Suites, 120 penthouses, 440 veranda staterooms, 20 ocean-view staterooms, and 26 inside staterooms. The first ship, *Marina,* will be delivered in September 2010.

Strong Points:

Highly desirable itineraries on beautifully appointed ships with numerous fine-dining options, excellent service, and entertainment at extremely competitive prices—a top contender in the upper-premium market.

Courtesy Oceania Cruises

Courtesy Oceania Cruises

Courtesy Oceania Cruises and Carlos Munoz (Trans-Ocean Photos, Inc.)

Courtesy Oceania Cruises and Carlos Munoz (Trans-Ocean Photos, Inc.)

Courtesy Oceania Cruises

⟡OCEANIA CRUISES℠

M/S REGATTA

En Route to Oporto, Portugal
Thursday September 18th, 2003

OCEANIA SPA CUISINE MENU

Appetizer
Strawberry Cup with Black Cherry Syrup

From the Soup Kettle
Clear Chicken Consommé Bretonne

The Garden Salad
Spring Garden Lettuce with Tomato Wedges, Potato Slices and Deep Fried Onion

Main Course
Entrée
Roasted Orange Roughy Filet "Paul Bocuse" Fashion
Gratinated with Portuguese Tomatoes and Mushroom Duxelle

The Head Sommelier suggests the following wines for tonight's menu

White Wine
Pouilly Fumé "La Moynerie" Michel Redde, Loire Valley, France 2000
An elegantly fruited, dry, white wine with alluring, smoky nuances and the distinctive
fragrance of the Sauvignon Blanc grape.
$34.00

Red Wine
Barolo, Fontanafredda, Piemonte, Italy 1996
A full wine well balanced, smooth and rich.
$58.00

Dinner Menu

Appetizers

Crab Cocktail Oceania
Timbale of Crab on a Nest of Seasonal Greens, Lemon Lime Dressing
Beef Carpaccio with Balsamic and Barley Vinaigrette
Candied Red Onion and Tomato with Crispy Parmesan Tuile
Strawberry Cup with Maraschino Liquor

Hot Appetizer

Roasted New Potatoes with Reblochon Cheese Cassolette
Macaroni with Broccoli and Snow Peas

From the Soup Kettle

New England Clam Chowder, Julienne of Snow Peas
Clear Chicken Consommé Bretonne

The Garden Salad

Crisp Greens with Radicchio Lettuce Tossed with Bacon Croutons
Spring Garden Lettuce with Tomato Wedges, Potato Slices and Crispy Fried Onion

Main Courses

~ Pasta of the Day ~
Ravioli with Seafood Ragoût

~ Entrées ~
Roasted Orange Roughy Fillet "Paul Bocuse" Fashion
Gratinated with Portuguese Tomatoes, Mushroom Duxelle and Cheese Crust

Stuffed Chicken Breast with Kalamata Olive and Tomato Farce
Vegetable Spaghetti and Palet Potatoes, Natural Jus

Pink Roast Veal Rack Loin with Rosemary Jus
Sautéed Forest Mushrooms and Fondant Potatoes

Grilled New York Steak, Beurre Maitre d'Hotel
Roasted Baby Bliss Potatoes and French Beans

~ Wok of the Day ~
Malaysian Fish Curry with Lime and Coconut Milk
Steamed Basmati Rice

~ Vegetarian Dish ~
Crespelle alla Fiorentina
Fine Pancakes filled with Spinach and gratinated with Fresh Mozzarella Cheese

~ Alternative Menu Selection ~
Grilled Sirloin Steak, Broiled Chicken or Salmon Fillet – Baked or Mashed Potatoes
Pasta, Plain or with Tomato Sauce – Vegetable Bouquetiere - Béarnaise Sauce

Courtesy Oceania Cruises

THE DAILY PROGRAM

SUNDAY FEBRUARY 26TH, 2006

Good Morning

All Day	Daily Program with your Cruise Director, Shani Reay	Channel 23
8:00	Daily Quiz is available from your Social Hostess, Paula. Please turn in the quiz by 6:00 p.m.	Lobby (4)
9:30	Interdenominational Church Service hosted by your Cruise Director, Shani	Nautica Lounge (5)
10:00	Golf Putting with your Entertainment Team *(For "Big O" Player Points)*	Horizons Lounge (10)
10:00	Grand Pearl Unveiling & Presentation with Oana, your resident pearl specialist	Upper Hall (5)

10:00	Join Your Guest Lecturer, Major General Mike O'Brien, for This Morning's Lecture: *"Sudden War in the Pacific: The Japanese Attacks in 1941"*	Nautica Lounge (5)

10:30	Good Morning Coffee Chat and Needlepoint Get-Together with Paula, your Social Hostess	Horizons Lounge (10)
11:00	Ping Pong Tournament with your Entertainment Team *(For "Big O" Player Points)*	Pool Deck (9)
11:00	"Hot Lava Rock" Seminar with your knowledgeable Mandara Spa Staff	Horizons Lounge (10)

11:15	A JOURNEY INTO THE GOURMET WORLD: Cooking Demonstration with your Executive Chef, Anthony Gatherall	Nautica Lounge (5)

11:45	Everything you wanted to know about cruising and are not afraid to ask! Join your fellow guest, Steve Stern, author of "Stern's Guide to the Cruise Vacation," an annual 850+ page guide to cruise ships and ports of call; and "Stern's Guide to the Greatest Resorts of the World," who will conduct an informal Q& A for cruise buffs who wish to share their experiences.	Martini Bar (5)

Good Afternoon

12:15	Bingo on the High Seas with J.R. Please note that once the game begins, no more cards will be sold. Jackpot at least $500! Cards will be sold starting at 12:00 noon	Horizons Lounge (10)

1:45	Champagne Art Auction Preview with your Art Directors, Stu and Darice	Nautica Lounge (5)
2:00	A World Of Wine! Wine Tasting with your Head Sommelier, Moretton *(Please sign-up at Reception)*	Toscana (10)
2:00	"Eat More to Weigh Less" Seminar with your Fitness Director, Alex	Fitness Center (9)
2:15	Bridge Player Get-Together *(Non-hosted)*	Polo Grill (10)
2:30	Champagne Art Auction with your Art Directors, Stu and Darice	Nautica Lounge (5)
2:30	'O' Olympics Shuffleboard Tournament *(For "Big O" Player Points) - Weather Permitting*	Sun Deck (11)
3:00	"5 in 1 Makeover" Seminar with your knowledgeable Mandara Spa Staff	Mandara Spa (9)
3:00	Service Club Meeting hosted by your Cruise Director, Shani	Horizons Lounge (10)
4:00 - 5:00	Afternoon Tea with your Social Hostess Paula and the Royal String Quartet	Horizons Lounge (10)
4:45	Parlor Team Trivia 2006 with your Cruise Director, Shani *(For "Big O" Player Points)* Today's drink special - Champagne Cocktail *(For $4.25)*	Nautica Lounge (5)

5:45	Join Your Guest Lecturer, Dr. Michael Boll, for This Afternoon's Lecture: *"Vietnam: From Colonialism to Communism"*	Nautica Lounge (5)

Good Evening

6:15 - 7:00	The Royal String Quartet plays for your listening enjoyment	Upper Hall (5)
6:30 - 7:30	Cocktail Hour with the music of the Nautica Orchestra	Horizons Lounge (10)
6:30 - 8:00	Enjoy cocktails with Jerry Blaine at the piano	Martini Bar (5)
7:30 - 8:15	More beautiful melodies with the Royal String Quartet	Upper Hall (5)
8:30 - 9:00	The Royal String Quartet continues to play for your enjoyment	Upper Hall (5)
8:45 - 9:30	The Nautica Orchestra plays for your dancing pleasure	Nautica Lounge (5)
9:00 - 12:00	More great piano sounds with Jerry Blaine	Martini Lounge (5)
10:45	Oceania Disco. Enjoy a dance with your Entertainment Team	Horizons Lounge (10)

THE M/S NAUTICA PROUDLY PRESENTS

Australia's Award Winning Cabaret Act

Black Tie

Featuring the Performances of
Constantine, Susan, Yuri & Valerie Mavridis

9:45 P.M. NAUTICA LOUNGE (5)

10:45	**Name That Tune** with your **Cruise Director, Shani Reay, & Jerry Blaine** at the Piano	Martini Bar (5)

TODAY'S SERVICE HOURS

CONCIERGE
The Concierge is located in the Reception Foyer on Deck 4. Please contact Javier by dialing 00 for assistance with Private Parties, Dining Ashore, Hotel Reservations or any special requests.
The Concierge will be available:
8:00-12:00 noon and 4:00 - 8:00 pm

RECEPTION DESK
The Reception Desk is located on Deck 4. Please dial 00 for information & assistance.
Open 24 hours a day

MEDICAL CENTER
The Medical Center is located on Deck 4. Please dial 4400 during office hours.
Dial 00 (Reception) for after hours.
Office Hours are from:
8:00 a.m. - 9:30 a.m.
6:00 p.m. - 7:30 p.m.
Medical / nursing assistance is available 24 hours.

BEAUTY SALON & SPA
The Beauty Salon and Spa are located on Deck 9.
Please dial 2800 for an appointment.
Therapists and stylists will be in attendance today from:
8:00 a.m. - 8:00 p.m.

FITNESS CENTER
The Fitness Center is located on Deck 9.
Please dial 2800 for assistance.
Open daily from
6:00 a.m. - 10:00 p.m.

BOUTIQUE
The Boutique is located on Deck 5.
Please dial 2830/2831 for assistance.
The Boutique will be open from:
9:00 a.m - 12:00 noon
& 1:30 p.m. - 11:00 p.m.

CASINO
The Casino is located on Deck 5.
Please dial 2821 for assistance.
Slots: 10:30 a.m. - Closing
Tables: 2:00 p.m. - 5:30 pm
& 8:30 p.m. - closing

PHOTO GALLERY
Remember you can get your film, disposable cameras and batteries at the Photo Gallery, Deck 5.
Opening hours:
9:00 a.m. - 1:00 p.m.
7:00 p.m. - 11:00 p.m.

RESTAURANT HOURS

6:30 a.m. - 11:00 a.m.	Coffee Corner	Horizons Lounge (10)
6:30 a.m. - 10:30 a.m.	Suite Breakfast	Room Service
7:30 a.m. - 10:00 a.m.	Breakfast Buffet	Terrace Café (9)
10:00 a.m. - 1:30 p.m.	Brunch is served	The Grand Dining Room (5)
11:30 a.m. - 4:00 p.m.	Lunch	Waves Grill (9)
12:00 noon - 2:00 p.m.	Oriental Lunch Buffet	Terrace Café (9)
4:00 p.m. - 5:00 p.m.	Tea Time	Horizons Lounge (10)
6:30 p.m. - 9:00 p.m.	Dinner is served	Toscana Restaurant (10)
6:30 p.m. - 9:00 p.m.	Dinner is served	Polo Grill Restaurant (10)
6:30 p.m. - 9:00 p.m.	Dinner is served	Tapas on the Terrace (9)
6:30 p.m. - 9:30 p.m.	Dinner is served	The Grand Dining Room (5)

May we be of Service?
Room service is available 24 hours a day from the Suite Service Menu in your stationery folder.
Special Reservations
Please book your evening in the Polo Grill or Toscana by speaking to the Head Waiter in the Terrace Café during Breakfast or Lunch times.

TODAY'S BAR HOURS

10:00 a.m. - Closing	Pool Bar (9) (weather permitting)
10:00 a.m. - Closing	Grand Dining Room Bar (5)
7:30 a.m. - 10:00 a.m.	Terrace Cafe Bar (9)
12:00 noon - 2:30 p.m.	Terrace Cafe Bar (9)
6:30 p.m. - Closing	Terrace Cafe Bar (9)
10:00 a.m. - Closing	Horizons Bar (10)
10:00 a.m. - Closing	Martinis Bar (5)
9:30 p.m. - Closing	Nautica Lounge (5)

TODAY'S SERVICE HOURS

DESTINATION SERVICES
The Destination Desk is located on Deck 4. For any assistance please dial 2531, or see Christine, Ingrid, Brad and Juan in person **during the following hours:**
9:00 a.m. - 9:00 p.m.

Art Courtesy Desk
Darice and Stu invite all to participate in an afternoon of fun, excitement, trivia, complimentary Champagne, and a big $3,000 art giveaway while having the opportunity of obtaining some of the most sought after art in the world at pennies on the dollar.
Champagne Art Auction: 2:30 p.m. Preview: 1:45 p.m. Nautica Lounge (5)

OCEANIA @ SEA
COMPUTER CENTER OPEN HOUSE
The Computer Center is located on Deck 9 forward.
Our Computer Staff will be available to assist you with Internet and E-mail from:
Port Day: 8:00 a.m - 11:00 a.m. & 3:00 p.m.– 7:00 p.m.
Sea Day: 8:00 a.m – 7:00 p.m.

PLEASE NOTE: Guests receiving incoming shipboard email will be displayed on the information panel outside the Computer Center along with other program information. *Sign up to learn how to organize and download digital Images and for Adobe Photoshop Elements Classes.*

P & O CRUISES

In U.S.
24305 Town Center
Santa Clarita, California 91355
(800) PRINCESS; (661) 753-0000
(661) 753-1535 Fax

In U.K.
Richmond House, Terminus Terrace
Southampton, U.K. SO14 3PN
0845 3 555 333
023 80 657030 Fax

www.pocruises.com

ARCADIA: entered service 2005; 83,000 G.R.T.; 951' x 105'; 2,388-passenger capacity (1,952 double occupancy); adults only; 976 cabins; British officers and international crew; winter cruises in Caribbean and summer cruises in Mediterranean, Baltic, Canary Islands, and world cruise. (**Category B—Not Rated**)

ARTEMIS (formerly *Royal Princess*): entered service 1984; frequently renovated; 44,248 G.R.T.; 761' x 95'; 1,260-passenger capacity (1,118 double occupancy); adults only; 594 cabins; British officers and international crew; world voyages, Caribbean during winter, and Mediterranean, Canary Island, and Baltic/Arctic cruises during summer. (**Category B—Not Rated**)

AURORA: entered service 2000; 76,000 G.R.T.; 886' x 106'; 1,870-passenger capacity; 939 cabins; British officers and international crew; world voyages, Caribbean during winter, and Mediterranean, Canary Islands, and Baltic/Arctic cruises during summer. (**Category B—Not Rated**)

AZURA: entered service 2010; 116,000 G.R.T.; 290 meters x 36 meters; 3,100-passenger capacity; 1,550 cabins; British officers and international crew; Mediterranean, Baltic, and Canary Island cruises in summer and Caribbean cruises during winter.

OCEANA (formerly *Ocean Princess*): entered service November 2000; 77,000 G.R.T.; 856' x 106'; 2,016-passenger capacity; 975 cabins; British officers and international crew; Caribbean cruises during winter and Mediterranean, Canary Islands, and Baltic during summer. (**Category B—Not Rated**)

ORIANA: entered service 1995; 69,153 G.R.T.; 853' x 106'; 1,822-passenger capacity; 914 cabins; British officers and international crew; world voyages, Caribbean during winter, and Mediterranean, Canary Islands, and Baltic cruises during summer. (**Category B—Not Rated**)

VENTURA: entered service 2008; 115,000 G.R.T.; 290 meters x 36 meters; 3,597-passenger capacity (3,080 double occupancy); 1,540 cabins; British officers and international crew; European cruises in the warmer months and Caribbean cruises during winter. (**Category B—Not Rated**)

(Medical Facilities: C-0, except *Arcadia* C6; P-2; EM, CLS, MS; N-4; CM; PD; BC; EKG; TC; PO; EPC; OX; WC; OR; ICU; X; M; CCP.)

P & O (the Peninsular and Oriental Navigation Company) dates back to 1837 and is one of the oldest, most prestigious lines in the history of cruising. P & O purchased Princess Cruises in 1974 and ran most of its ships under the Princess flag during the 1980s. P & O markets the *Oriana, Aurora, Artemis* (formerly named *Royal Princess*), *Arcadia, Oceana* (formerly named *Ocean Princess*), and *Ventura* under the P & O Cruises banner, with the major promotion to British and European cruisers. Principal cruise areas between April and December include the Mediterranean, Baltic and Norwegian fjords, Atlantic Islands, Adriatic, and the Caribbean. *Aurora* and *Oriana* typically offer world voyages during the winter. *Azura, Ventura,* and *Oceana* offer Caribbean fly-cruises serviced by U.K. charter flights, while the other ships offer a variety of Caribbean or world cruise itineraries.

In 2000, P & O split the company's cruise business from its non-cruise vessels and non-cruise interests and formed a separate public company. In 2003, the shareholders of Carnival Corporation and P & O/Princess approved the formation of a new public company (which acquired all of the P & O/Princess assets, with the stock in the new corporation split up between the shareholders of Carnival and P & O/Princess) to be traded on the New York and British stock exchanges. Thereafter, P & O Cruises and Princess Cruises became brands under the Carnival corporate umbrella.

Oriana was the first P & O (non-Princess division) ship built in decades and was designed to be marketed primarily to the British as an upscale, more modern vessel than the other P & O ships. At 69,000 tons, 850 feet long, and with accommodations for up to 1,822 passengers, it debuted as the largest ship in the P & O fleet and has received a most enthusiastic reception by British cruisers wishing to sail on this more updated high-tech vessel capable of speeds up to 25 knots. The 10 passenger decks are serviced by 10 elevators and include 11 categories of cabins and suites, including eight suites measuring 400 square feet with private balconies, 16 deluxe 300-square-foot mini-suites with private balconies, and 94 cabins with twin beds that are convertible to king size. One hundred eighteen cabins have balconies, 320 are inside, and 89 can accommodate third or fourth berths. Half the cabins have bathtubs and all have color televisions, radios, refrigerators, direct-dial telephones, and personal safes—all in keeping with the ships built in the 1990s.

Atop ship is the Crows Nest observation lounge. Immediately beneath is the health spa with sauna, steam, whirlpools, massage and beauty-treatment rooms, and exercise and aerobics facilities. Adjacent are two large swimming pools, a vast sundeck area, and an indoor-outdoor lido buffet breakfast-and-lunch restaurant with an adjoining bar. The majority of cabins and suites are located on the next three decks.

Then comes D deck, where you will find the Curzon Room; Oriana Rhodes, the venue for one of celebrity chef Gary Rhodes's two fine-dining restaurants at sea; an alternate lounge for concerts, dining, and afternoon tea; the library; the cardroom;

the writing room; a 189-seat tiered cinema; a video arcade; and a children's facility, Peter Pan children's playroom, and children's pool area. On promenade deck, next below, is the 664-seat production theater, a photo gallery, several bars and lounges, a casino, a slot machine area, and a disco. E deck, below that, is the site of 81 cabins, the two dining rooms, and the bottom of the atrium area, where the shops are located. The remaining cabins and reception desk are located on F deck, and the medical center and night nursery are on G deck.

In the spring of 2000, the 76,000-ton, 1,870-passenger ship named *Aurora* entered service. The 939 cabins encompass two-deck penthouse suites, 10 suites with balconies, 18 mini-suites with balconies, 376 additional staterooms and cabins with balconies, and 22 cabins that accommodate disabled passengers. All cabins include coffee and tea-making facilities, refrigerators, private safes, color televisions, direct-dial telephones, and twin beds convertible to king-size. Among several dining options, a bistro-style restaurant is open 24 hours a day. Cafe Bordeaux offers a unique French bistro-style menu created by three-star Michelin chef Marco Pierre White. The ship also features expanded facilities for children and teens. Other facilities include a sidewalk café, a champagne bar, a coffee-chocolate-sweets bar, a virtual-reality game room, a golf simulator, a business center, a movie theater, 12 bars, a gymnasium and aerobics studio, a beauty and health service salon, and a library.

In late 2002, the *Ocean Princess* was transferred from the Princess fleet and renamed *Oceana*. She offers Caribbean cruises to the U.K. market serviced by charter flights. (A description of this ship, which is identical to the *Sun, Dawn,* and *Sea Princess* vessels, can be found in the Princess Cruises section of this chapter.) On board, Café Jardin offers a special grill-style menu with Italian-inspired dishes created by Marco Pierre White. *Sea Princess,* a sister ship to *Ocean Princess,* was transferred to the P & O fleet in 2003 and renamed *Adonia,* only to be transferred back to Princess in 2005.

The 44,348-ton, 1,200-passenger *Artemis,* formerly *Royal Princess* of Princess Cruises, was transferred to P & O Cruises in 2005 in a swap for a re-transfer of the *Sea Princess. Artemis* was one of the most innovative ships built in the 1980s. All staterooms are outside cabins with large picture windows, televisions, refrigerators, private wall safes, tubs and showers, and twin beds that can be converted to doubles. One hundred fifty of the cabins and suites have outside verandas and all are located on the top decks, whereas most public rooms are on the lower decks. There is one attractive dining room that seats all the passengers in two sittings. In addition, there is a larger-than-average swimming pool for laps, smaller wading pools, Jacuzzis, a quarter-mile jogging track, a large casino, and a 360-degree panorama lounge on the top deck that can be converted to a disco at night. The greatest weakness is the size of the standard staterooms, which come off narrow and not terribly spacious. Designing the ship so that all passengers have exterior cabins was not without its tradeoffs. This is an adults-only ship.

The 83,000-ton, 2,534-passenger *Arcadia* joined the fleet in 2005. Originally intended to be a Cunard ship named *Queen Victoria,* parent corporation Carnival decided in 2004 to send the new vessel to P & O Cruises and build another ship for Cunard for delivery in 2007. She is a child-free ship with a striking modern design, and the interior includes 3,000 pieces of modern art. Of the 976 accommodations, 758 face the sea and 685 of these include balconies. All cabins have flat-screen televisions and duvets. There are six restaurants, including Arcadian Rhodes, created by top U.K. chef Gary Rhodes, and Orchid, featuring an Asian/Oriental-fusion menu.

In the spring of 2008, *Ventura* came on line. At 115,000 tons with a maximum passenger capacity of 3,597, it is the largest ship ever built for the cruise line. The ship's design is similar to that of *Caribbean* and *Crown Princess* of Princess Cruises. Seventy-one percent of the accommodations are outside and 57 percent have balconies. The ship offers numerous dining venues, including three main restaurants (two with freestyle dining and one with traditional fixed seating); the White Room, the fine-dining restaurant created by three-star *Michelin*-rated chef Marco Pierre White with a Mediterranean menu; East, an Asian-Fusion restaurant; Ramblas, a tapas and wine bar; a pizzeria; two buffet dining rooms; room service; and balcony dining. For children and teens there are five different age group areas and programs. The 785-seat main theater features variety and cabaret shows. In addition, there is a 3-D cinema, five pools, six Jacuzzis, a large spa, five shops, a nightclub, and numerous bars and lounges offering entertainment. In the spring of 2010, a sister ship, *Azura,* came on line.

The overall experience is different from that on P & O's sister company, Princess Cruises, and dining and entertainment are more geared to British tastes. Because most of the passengers are British and there is a cross section of cruisers from other European countries and around the world, the ships offer a chance for North Americans to mix with people of other nationalities, as is the case on all P & O ships.

Strong Points:

Exceptional around-the-world itineraries at considerably better value than on the more luxurious cruise lines. The ships especially appeal to a British clientele.

Aurora, courtesy P & O Cruises

Restaurant on Oriana, *courtesy P & O Cruises*

Library on Oriana, *courtesy P & O Cruises*

Crows Nest Bar on Oriana, *courtesy P & O Cruises*

ORIANA

❀ Gravadlax of Salmon with a Light Dill and Mustard Sauce

❧ Corn on the Cob with Melted Butter

Caesar Salad

❖

❧ Cream of Asparagus

Essence of Beef with Oxtail and toasted Pine Kernels

❖

Medallions of Monkfish with Noodles
enriched with butter, lemon zest and parsley

❀ Roast Rib of Beef with Yorkshire Pudding, Gravy and Roast Potatoes

❀ Sauté of Lamb's Kidneys with Creamed Spinach and Dijon Mustard Sauce

Panfried Breast of Chicken
with ginger, spring onions and braised bok choy topped with sesame seeds

❧ Vegetable Roulade with a Tomato Coulis

Fine Beans   Panache of Vegetables   Savoyarde and Boiled Potatoes

❖

❀ Warm Apple and Cherry Strudel with Crème Anglaise
Banana and Pecan Nut Sundae
❀ Peppered Pineapple with a Sauce of Crème de Cacao with Vanilla Ice Cream
Vanilla, Mint Choc Chip and Strawberry Ice Creams
Sweet Sauces: Butterscotch Chocolate Melba
Fresh Fruit Salad
Mango Sorbet

❖

A selection of British and Continental Cheeses with Biscuits

Fresh Fruit

❖

Freshly Brewed Coffee   De-Caffeinated   Espresso   Cappuccino   Speciality Teas
After Dinner Mints

Fresh from the Bakery
White, Wholemeal, Malted Wheat and Sun Dried Tomato Rolls

D5

Courtesy P & O Cruises

ORIANA

TODAY'S EVENTS

7.55am   Navigator's Early Morning Call
Tune into TV *channel 8* for the *Navigator's* early morning broadcast with up to date weather, geographical details and other points of interest. This will also be broadcast over the open decks.

9.00am   Social Short Tennis
A chance to make a racket and have a ball. Any players wishing for a friendly game should meet in the *Sun Deck Nets* at this time.

9.45am   Choir Practice
Let's hear those harmonies. *Cathy* takes you through the hymns for this morning's service. *Theatre Royal*

9.45am   Keep Fit
No time to waste, so just make haste and lose those inches from your waist. Join *Alison* in *Harlequins.*

10.00am   Walk & Talk
Ramble as you amble around the Promenade. Meet outside the *Pacific Lounge.*

10.00am   Games Handout
A chance for you to monopolise the games cupboard as you search for your favourites. *Library*

10.00am   Hand and Nail Care Demonstration
Dry, brittle or cracked nails, or your nails simply won't grow? Join Steiner the nail care experts today and find a way to beautiful hands. *Medina Room*

10.15am
Theatre Royal
Ship's Church Service
This morning's service will be conducted by *Captain Colin Campbell.* There will a collection made for marine charities

10.30am   Coffee Chat
Thirsty for conversation. Time to relax for a while with a cuppa and a chat with some of the team in the *Curzon Room.*

10.30am   Travelling Alone Get Together
Don't sit there feeling all alone, we're here to make you feel at home. *Tiffany's*

10.30am   American Line Dancing for First Sitting Passengers
Calling all Beginner Bootscooters. Hold on to your holster and make for *Harlequins* as today *Chris* will be revising what you learnt yesterday before starting on a fun new dance. Yeehah!

10.45am   Ship in a Bottle with Ted Machin and Norman Rogers
Assembly of the ship continues with the mainsail and rigging lines being finalised and secured. *Crow's Nest*

11.00am   Wine Talk
Head Wine Steward *Bisht Santinder* will be giving an informative illustrated talk on the wine served on Oriana with particular reference to some of the interesting bin ends available. *Curzon Room*

11.00am   Deck Quoits
Make it your target to compete in this morning's game. *Deck 13 Aft*

11.00am   Shuffleboard
Shuffle along and try your luck, will yours be the winning puck. *Deck 13 Aft*

11.00am
Pacific Lounge
'Madeira Wine'
An informal lecture by *Ana Isabel Dantas* of The Old Blandy Wine Lodge Madeira Wine Company. Win a fabulous prize of some Madeira wine. Complete the quiz sheet in your cabin and return it to the *Reception Desk* by 6.00pm on the 18th October. Prizes will be announced at 10.30am on the 19th in the *Pacific Lounge.*

11.00am   Short Tennis Competition
See if you can net yourself a prize in this morning's game. Suitable footwear must be worn. *Sun Deck Nets*

11.00am   Couples Massage Demonstration
Let our experts teach you how to ease away those aches and pains. *Oasis Spa*

11.00am   Masonic Meeting
All Brethren are invited to meet at this time in the *Iberia Room.*

11.15am   American Line Dancing for Second Sitting Passengers
Calling all Beginner Bootscooters. *Chris* repeats his earlier class in *Harlequins.* Yeehah!

11.15am   Daily Tote
Come and guess how far Oriana has steamed from noon yesterday until noon today. 50p a go. Cash only please - bet you win! *Lord's Tavern*

11.15am   Port Enhancement Talk - Tenerife and Gran Canaria
Greville Rimbault gives an informative, illustrated talk on Tenerife and Gran Canaria. This will be repeated at 4.45pm and can also be seen on *channel 3* of your cabin circuits. *Chaplin's Cinema*

11.30am
Lord's Tavern
Singalong with Checkmate
The trio choose those cheery songs that'll get you humming along.

Noon   Announcement from the Bridge
Details of ship's position, present and predicted weather, and mileage report. Have you won the Daily Tote? If so collect your winnings from *Lord's Tavern.*

Noon   Golf Get Together
Crichton's

Noon
Crow's Nest
Sounds of Jazz
The Rick Laughlin Trio jazz up your lunchtime as they play for your listening pleasure.

2.00pm   Eye and Neck Care Seminar
The eyes and neck area are very delicate and unfortunately show visibly early signs of the ageing process. Join your on board therapist for the correct advice today. *Medina Room*

2.30pm   Bridge Get Together
Anyone wishing to play rubber bridge should meet in *Crichton's* at this time.

2.45pm   Adult Cricket
Don't be caught out. Join us for an afternoon game in the *Sun Deck Nets.*

2.45pm   Whist Drive
It's on the cards you'll be able to get a game in *Crichton's Aft.*

2.45pm   Make-up Made Easy with Viv Foley
Viv shows you how to do make-up easily with no fuss. *Viv* will also look at eye shapes. Please bring a lipstick with you. *Crow's Nest*

2.45pm   Advanced Line Dancing with Dawn Jordan
Dawn revises what you learnt yesterday before tackling another new dance. *Harlequins*

2.45pm   Shuffleboard
Paddle up and make your way to *Deck 13 Aft* where you can try your luck with the puck.

2.45pm   Beginner's Dance Class
If you missed yesterday's class, it's not too late. Join *Ian* and *Ruth* as they continue their light hearted instruction. Today they will revise your basic steps in the Social Foxtrot and Cha Cha Cha. Also at today's class, have fun with the Merengue. *Pacific Lounge*

3.00pm   Perfume Talk
Join *Hayley* as she describes the various perfumes available from the Knightsbridge Shop on board. *Iberia Room*

3.00pm   Deck Quoits
Make it your aim to join one of the team for this competition and you could be on target for a prize. *Deck 13 Aft*

3.15pm   Aromaspa Demonstration
The ultimate in body wraps, using the richness of seaweed combined with aromatherapy oils. This is followed by a facial and half body massage. Learn more about it with our specialist. *Oasis Spa*

3.30pm   Games Handout
All of your favourites will be available from the *Library.*

4.00pm   Social Short Tennis
See if you can meet your match and maybe net yourself a P&O prize. *Sun Deck Nets*

4.00pm   Ship in a Bottle with Ted Machin and Norman Rogers
This afternoon's class is devoted to those who require a little help. *Crow's Nest*

4.15pm   Jackpot Bingo
Hughie and the team will be calling out the lucky numbers and today it could be you. *Pacific Lounge*

4.15pm   Captain's Coketail Party
Captain Colin Campbell meets our younger cruisers in *Harlequins.* All adults are welcome to attend.

4.45pm   Port Enhancement Talk- Tenerife and Gran Canaria
Greville Rimbault repeats his informative talk on Tenerife and Gran Canaria, *Chaplin's Cinema*

5.15pm   Colours for Men and Women with Viv Foley
Viv repeats her talk on colours and how the right colours make you look healthy and successful. *Medina Room*

5.30pm   Individual Quiz
Twenty teasers to test the grey matter and if you have the highest score a prize could be yours. *Crichton's*

5.30pm   Football
Can we corner you into joining in a fun kick around in the *Sun Deck Nets?*

5.45pm   Cocktail Set
Alan Christie's music takes you to new heights in the *Crow's Nest* as you enjoy an aperitif and *Rick Laughlin* plays in *Tiffany's.*

6.00pm   Radio Oriana
The *Pete Le Gros* radio show will be playing your requests and keeping you up to date with the activities on board so tune into *channel 6* on your cabin circuits and 7317 is the number to call.

7.45pm   Cocktail Melodies
Alan Christie makes the music in the 'room at the top' as you enjoy the sounds and the views around and *Gary Jones* plays in *Tiffany's.*

8.30pm & 10.30pm
Theatre Royal
The Stadium Theatre Company presents BEST OF BRITISH

9.00pm – 12.45am
Pacific Lounge
COUNTRY MUSIC SPECIAL with Kenny Johnson & Northwind and Neon Moon

9.00pm   A Step in Time
Checkmate ask you to put on your dancing shoes and dance the night away in *Harlequins.*

9.30pm Tunes in Tiffany's
Stave off your thirst as you hear *Alan Christie* tinkle those ivories tonight in *Tiffany's*.

9.45pm With a View to Dancing
By Design will be pleased to have your company in the *Crow's Nest* whether you are dancing or enjoying their great sound.

9.45pm Boulevard Entertain
In the mood for dancing? *Boulevard* make some of the best sounds around that'll get you up on your feet dancing to the beat. *Harlequins*

10.30pm Syndicate Quiz
Get the fizz if you win the quiz. Come and join in the fun at tonight's teaser. *Crichton's*

10.45pm Checkmate
Continue dancing the night away to more great music in *Harlequins*.

10.45pm Alan Christie's Request Time
More music from our superb pianist as he plays familiar favourites in the *Crow's Nest*.

11.15pm Prepare to Party with Boulevard
Our guest band pull out all the stops to keep you up on your feet dancing to their fabulous beat in *Harlequins*. Remember the night is still young!

11.30pm Dance to the Duo
Sweet sounds from *By Design* as they take you through to a brand new day. *Crow's Nest*

12.15am Disco Dance Date
Our Debonair DJ will be spinning the discs as all you disco dollies boogie into tomorrow. *Harlequins*

12.30am Late Night Date
Scale the heights to the Room with a View where *By Design* make the midnight melodies. *Crow's Nest*

MEDICAL CENTRE

Granada Deck [4]. forward, staircase Number 1 (green carpet).
The Medical Centre will be open today from 10.00am to noon and from 5.00pm to 6.00pm **For medical attention 24 hours please dial '0' and wait for the operator. In an emergency only dial '999'.**

In the unlikely event of rough weather, effective treatment for motion sickness is available in the form of an injection.

SUPERLATIVE TRAVEL

Clive Peterson, Tour Director will be available in the Crow's Nest between 10.00am and 11.00am to answer any queries you may have.

GOLF GET TOGETHER

Although we do not officially organise golf tours, any passengers who wish to play in port or borrow any clubs should meet *Pete* at noon in *Crichton's*.

WITHOUT RESERVATIONS

'Without reservations' means you may sit at any table on either sitting in either restaurant, subject to availability. When meals are served without reservations' the port side window tables are designated smoking areas.

TOURS OFFICE

Open 8.30am to noon, and 3.30pm to 5.30pm. *Jackie* and *Nikki* will be available to assist you with bookings.

BOOKINGS FOR TOURS IN TENERIFE MUST CLOSE A T 5.30PM THIS EVENING

TENERIFE
Tour E - Taganana Village and Mercedes Forest, due to a landslide this tour has had to be cancelled.

PORT ENHANCEMENT TALKS - TENERIFE AND GRAN CANARIA
Chaplin's Cinema 11.15am and 4.45pm.
Today *Greville* will describe in his illustrated talk our visits to the Canary Islands of Tenerife and Gran Canaria. There are two large cities to explore and also some spectacular tours to consider.
These talks can also be viewed on channel 3 of the cabin TV circuit.

FOOD COMMENT FORMS

For your convenience we have installed outside the Peninsular and Oriental Restaurants passenger comment boxes and forms so that should you wish to express a concern or some satisfaction you are more than welcome. There is also a box in the Conservatory on the port side by the doors to the lifts.

WINE TALK

At 11.00am in the *Curzon Room*, Head Wine Steward *Bisht Satinder* will be giving an informative illustrated talk on some of the wines served on *Oriana*.

SPECIAL OFFER

Later in the cruise we will be offering the following special take ashore bottle offers.

Whyte & MacKay Special Scotch Whisky
£6.50 per litre

Beefeater London Gin
£6.50 per litre

Please hand a completed and signed bar chit to your Cabin Steward who will deliver the bottle to your cabin towards the end of the cruise.

CHAPLIN'S CINEMA

11.15am & 4.45pm
Port Enhancement Talk - Tenerife and Gran Canaria

2.30pm
Songwriter
Drama starring Willie Nelson and Kris Kristofferson
Running time 91 minutes, certificate 15

6.00pm
Children's Magic Show

8.30pm & 10.30pm
A Perfect Murder
Drama with Michael Douglas and Gwyneth Paltrow
Running time 105 minutes, certificate 15

DINING HOURS

CONSERVATORY

Early Bird	6.30am to 7.00am
Hot Breakfast	7.00am to 10.00am
Continental Breakfast	10.00am to 11.00am
Buffet Luncheon	noon to 2.00pm
Afternoon Tea	3.30pm to 4.30pm
Children's Tea	5.15pm to 5.45pm
	(starboard side only)

PENINSULAR & ORIENTAL RESTAURANTS
Breakfast - *without reservations*
First sitting - *Doors close at 8.15am* 8.00am
Second sitting - *Doors close at 9.15am* ... 9.00am

Luncheon - *without reservations*
First sitting - *Doors close at 12.30pm* .. 12.15pm
Second sitting - *Doors close at 1.45pm* .. 1.30pm

Afternoon Tea
Peninsular Restaurant only . 4.00pm to 4.45pm

Dinner - *with reservations*
First sitting 6.30pm
Second sitting 8.30pm

Oriana Sandwich Bar
Peninsular Restaurant only
.... 11.30pm to midnight

PIZZERIA AL FRESCO

Continuous service .... from Noon to 7.00pm

LIBRARY

9.00am - 12.30pm
2.30pm - 5.30pm
9.30pm - 10.30pm

IN THE BARS

Andersons	11.00am until 2.00pm & 5.00pm until late
Crow's Nest	11.00am until 2.00pm & 5.00pm until late
Harlequins	10.30am to noon & 8.30pm until late
Lord's Tavern	11.00am until late
Pacific Lounge	4.00pm to 5.00pm & 8.30pm until late
Riviera Bar	9.00am until 7.00pm
Splash Bar	11.00am until 6.00pm
Terrace Bar	9.00am until 7.00pm
Tiffany's	9.00am until noon & 5.00pm until midnight

Passengers under 18 years of age will not be served alcoholic beverages. Please understand that you may be requested to show identification indicating date of birth.

Cocktail of the Day
Brandy Alexander   £1.50
Smooth and creamy, with brandy, Creme de Cacao and cream.

Virgin Cocktail
Orchard Dream Fizz   90p
A blend of apple juice, grapefruit juice, a dash of Grenadine and soda.

Speciality Coffee
French Café   £1.20
Cointreau.

P & O CRUISES AUSTRALIA
203 Pacific Highway Level 7
St. Leonards NSW Australia 2065
001161 2 8424 8800
www.pocruises.com.au

PACIFIC DAWN (formerly *Regal Princess*): entered service 1991; 70,000 G.R.T.; 805' x 115'; 1,590-passenger capacity; 795 cabins; international officers and crew; cruises from Brisbane, Australia. (**Category B/C—Not Rated**)

PACIFIC JEWEL (formerly *Ocean Village Two* and *Crown Princess*): entered service 1990;70,000 G.R.T.; 805' x 115'; 1,590-passenger capacity; 795 cabins; international officers and crew; cruises from Sydney, Australia.

PACIFIC PEARL (formerly *Ocean Village, Star Princess,* and *Star Majesty*): entered service 1989; 64,000 G.R.T.; 1,600-passenger capacity; 800 cabins; international officers and crew; cruise grounds to be determined.

PACIFIC SUN (formerly *Jubilee*): entered service 1986; 47,262 G.R.T.; 733' x 92'; 1,900-passenger capacity; 743 cabins; international officers and crew; cruises from Brisbane, Australia. (**Category C—Not Rated**)

SUN PRINCESS and *DAWN PRINCESS:* See Princess Cruises. These ships sail year round in Australia but retain the Princess flag.

Formerly a division of P & O/Princess Cruises, P & O Cruises Australia became a Carnival Corporation brand following Carnival's acquisition of P & O/Princess in 2003. The division was formed to service the growing Australian cruise population.

The vessels trace their heritage to the 1980s and 1990s, when they sailed for other cruise lines. The 1,400-passenger, 35,000-ton *Pacific Star* was Carnival Cruises' first new build, debuting in 1982. As she aged, she was transferred to Carnival's Costa Line brand, and she sailed as the *Costa Tropicale* from 2003 until late 2005, when she became part of P & O Cruises Australia. In 2007 she was transferred to Pullmantur. In late 2004, the 1,900-passenger, 47,252-ton *Pacific Sun* joined the fleet. She was also transferred from Carnival, where she had sailed since 1986 as the *Jubilee*. In late 2007, Carnival transferred another of its older ships to the less demanding Australian cruise market. Princess Cruises' *Regal Princess* was transferred to P & O Cruises Australia and renamed *Pacific Dawn*. Having entered service in 1991 at 70,000 tons with a 1,590-passenger capacity, she was renovated in 2000 and is possibly the most upscale of the company's ships. Princess Cruises' more luxurious *Sun Princess* and *Dawn Princess* sail year-around from Australia, with most passengers being booked through P & O Australia. These ships still retain the Princess flag and are considered part of the premium

Princess Cruise brand, which at various times of the year offers itineraries in that part of the world while marketing to Australian cruisers as well as their usual customers. (See Princess Cruises for description of ships.)

Although different in design and layout, the two P & O Australia ships are somewhat typical of mass-market ships built from 1980 to the early 1990s, with one-third to one-half of the cabins in the interior of the ship and only a few suites sporting balconies. Public areas on each ship include main dining rooms, fine-dining specialty restaurants, casual buffet-style restaurants, pizza stations, large show lounges, casinos, nightclubs, numerous bars and lounges, Internet facilities, gyms, attractive outdoor pool areas, shops, cardrooms, hospitals, and all of the other facilities typically found aboard cruise ships of their vintage.

Upon the dissolution of Ocean Village Cruises, P & O Australia acquired the two *Ocean Village* ships and renamed them *Pacific Jewel* and *Pacific Pearl,* both originally with Princess Cruises.

Strong Points:

These are reasonably priced, full-facility vessels offering unusual itineraries in a part of the world not frequently visited by other cruise lines. A comfortable way to explore Australia, New Zealand, and nearby islands in the South Pacific.

Pacific Dawn, *courtesy P & O Cruises Australia*

PRINCESS CRUISES
24305 Town Center Drive
Santa Clarita, California 91355
(800) PRINCESS; (661) 753-0000
(661) 284-4771 Fax
www.princesscruises.com

CARIBBEAN PRINCESS, CROWN PRINCESS, EMERALD PRINCESS, and *RUBY PRINCESS:* entered service 2004, 2006, 2007, and 2008, respectively; 113,000 G.R.T.; 951' x 118'; 3,070-passenger capacities, 3,100 on *Caribbean Princess*; 1,532 cabins, 1,557 on *Caribbean Princess*; British and Italian officers and international crew; *Caribbean Princess* offers Caribbean cruises and Bermuda/Caribbean cruises; *Crown Princess* offers Caribbean cruises from San Juan as well as Canada/New England cruises and cruises northern Europe and the Baltic; *Emerald Princess* sails the Mediterranean and Baltic during summer and the Caribbean the remainder of the year; *Ruby Princess* sails the western Caribbean and Mediterranean.

☆☆☆☆☆ + +

(Medical Facilities: C-26; P-1 or 2, EM, CLS, MS; N-2 to 5; CM; PD; BC; EKG; TC; PO; EPC; OX; WC; OR; ICU; X; M; CCP; L.)

CORAL PRINCESS and *ISLAND PRINCESS:* entered service 2003; 92,000 G.R.T.; 964' x 106'; 1,970-passenger capacity; 987 cabins; British and Italian officers and international crew; cruises in Alaska and West Coast to Hawaii and Panama Canal.

☆☆☆☆☆ +

(Medical Facilities: C-20; P-2, EM, CLS, MS; N-5, CM; PD; BC; EKG; TC; PO; EPC; OX; WC; OR; ICU; X; M; TM; CCP, J.)

DIAMOND PRINCESS and *SAPPHIRE PRINCESS:* entered service 2004; 116,000 G.R.T.; 952' x 123'; 2,670-passenger capacity; 1,337 cabins; British and Italian officers and international crew; itineraries in Alaska, Mexican Riviera, Australia, New Zealand, and Asia.

☆☆☆☆☆ + +

(Medical Facilities: Same as *Caribbean Princess* except C-28.)

GRAND PRINCESS, GOLDEN PRINCESS, and *STAR PRINCESS:* entered service 1998, 2001, and 2002, respectively; renovated 2008 and 2009; 109,000 G.R.T.; 935' x 118'; 2,600-passenger capacity; 1,300 cabins; British and Italian officers and international crew; cruises Caribbean, South America, Mexican Riviera, Canada/New England, Greek Isles, Mediterranean, Scandinavia/Russia, and other European itineraries.

(Medical Facilities: C-28; P-2; EM, CLS, MS; N-5; CM; PD; BC; EKG; TC; PO; EPC; OX; WC; OR; ICU; X; M; TM CCP.)

PACIFIC PRINCESS, OCEAN PRINCESS (formerly *Tahitian Princess*), and *ROYAL PRINCESS* (formerly *R-3, R-4,* and *R-8* of Renaissance Cruises): entered service 1999, 1999, and 2001, respectively; commenced service for Princess in 2003, 2002, and 2007, respectively; 30,277 G.R.T.; 594' x 84'; 670-passenger capacity, 710 on *Royal Princess*; 334 cabins, 355 on *Royal Princess; British and Italian officers and international crew;* Pacific Princess offers various itineraries, including Alaska, Hawaii/Tahiti, South America, Europe, and world cruises; *Ocean Princess* offers 10-night cruises in French Polynesia as well as cruises to Alaska and Europe and a world cruise; *Royal Princess* sails in Europe, South America, Canada/New England, and Caribbean and offers a world cruise.

SUN PRINCESS, DAWN PRINCESS, and *SEA PRINCESS:* entered service 1995, 1997, and 1998, respectively; 77,000 G.R.T.; 856' x 106'; 1,950-passenger capacity; 975 cabins; British and Italian officers and staff, international crew; cruises to Caribbean, Panama Canal, Mexican Riviera, Hawaii, and Alaska; *Sea Princess* also offers Canada/New England in the fall and Mediterranean, northern European, and Alaskan cruises during warmer months. In the spring and summer, *Dawn Princess* and *Sun Princess* offer sailings from Australia (*Sun Princess* sales Australia year-round, while *Dawn Princess* cruises there from October to April).

(Medical Facilities: C-19; P-2; EM, CLS, MS; N-3; CM; PD; BC; EKG; TC; PO; EPC; OX; WC; OR; ICU; X; M; CCP; and TM on *Sea*.)

Note: All ships can accommodate passengers performing peritoneal dialysis, as well as hemodialysis groups accompanied by a nephrologist, dialysis nurses, and technicians.

These ships are rated in 11 separate categories in the second half of chapter 14.

The London-based Peninsular and Oriental Steam Navigation Company (P & O) dates back to the early 1800s and is one of the oldest, largest, and most prestigious lines in the history of cruising. During the first three quarters of the 20th century, numerous vessels sailed under the P & O flag. However, most of them were sold after P & O purchased Princess Cruises in 1974.

Princess was originally formed by Stanley McDonald. In 1965, he chartered the 6,000-ton *Princess Patricia* and initiated cruises from California to ports on the west coast of Mexico. Thereafter, in 1967, with the charter of the *Princess Italia,* the itineraries were expanded to include spring and summer sailings to Canada and Alaska.

The *Princess Carla* was chartered in 1968 for a short period. In 1971, a major upgrade came when McDonald chartered Flagship Line's *Island Venture,* renaming her the *Island Princess.* When P & O acquired Princess in 1974, they purchased the *Island Princess* and, soon afterward, also purchased her sister ship, the *Sea Venture,* which subsequently became famous as the *Pacific Princess*—television's "Love Boat." During the same period, P & O changed the name of its *Spirit of London* to the *Sun Princess* and designated her for seven-day cruises in the Caribbean and Alaskan markets.

The *Love Boat* television series brought cruising into the living rooms of millions of Americans whose prior nautical experience had not gone beyond a rowboat. The show not only gave a gigantic shot in the arm to the cruise industry as a whole, but also made Princess Cruises a household word. Although on most sailings passengers did not rub elbows with Captain Stubing, Julie, Gopher, Doc, or Isaac, the television series did film several segments each year on board. Ironically, over the years, I have found the real-life captains, officers, and crew on Princess ships to be among the most friendly and efficient staff sailing.

The success of the line gave rise to the addition of the popular all ocean-view accommodation, 44,000-ton *Royal Princess* in 1984. In 1988, Princess acquired Sitmar Cruises, changed the name of its vessels, and instantaneously added four new ships to its rapidly expanding empire. At the same time, the *Sun Princess* was transferred to Premier Cruise Line (not to be confused with the *Sun Princess* that entered service in 1995).

Sitmar had entered the North American cruise industry in 1971 with two refurbished Cunard ships: the *Fairsea* (*Fair Princess*) and *Fairwind* (*Dawn Princess*). Their spacious cabins, friendly and efficient Italian service, excellent cuisine, and special children's facilities and programs combined to make these two of the most popular ships of the 1970s. The 46,000-ton *Fairsky* (*Sky Princess*) was added in 1984, and in 1989, the 62,500-ton *Star Princess* became the largest vessel in the then-combined Princess-Sitmar fleets. Two new 70,000-ton vessels, the *Crown Princess* and the *Regal Princess,* were added in 1990 and 1991, respectively. All of these ships have since left the fleet.

In the mid-1990s, Princess committed more than $1 billion to the construction of its next generation of gigantic superliners. The 77,000-ton *Sun Princess, Dawn Princess, Sea Princess,* and *Ocean Princess* entered service in 1995, 1997, 1998, and 2000, respectively. The 109,000-ton *Grand Princess* commenced cruising in 1998, and two sister ships—*Golden Princess* and *Star Princess*—entered service in 2001 and 2002, respectively. Two 88,000-ton ships named *Coral Princess* and

Island Princess (not to be mistaken with the prior ship from the *Love Boat* series, which left the fleet) were delivered in 2003. Eighty percent of the outside cabins on these ships have balconies. In 2004, two 116,000-ton ships, *Diamond Princess* and *Sapphire Princess,* joined the fleet, as well as the 113,000-ton *Caribbean Princess.* The *Ocean Princess* was transferred to P & O in the fall of 2002, and *Sea Princess* followed in 2003, only to be returned in 2005. In 2006, the new *Crown Princess* and in 2007 the *Emerald Princess* entered service, ships similar in dimensions to *Caribbean Princess. Ruby Princess,* a sister ship to the others, was delivered in 2008.

Itineraries for the ships vary from year to year and include more than 280 different ports around the globe. The line offers not only Caribbean, Mexican Riviera, Panama Canal, Alaskan, Bermuda, South America/Amazon, Canada/New England, and colonial America cruises, but Mediterranean, North Sea-Baltic, Hawaii/Tahiti, South Pacific, Indian, African, Holy Land, Far East, and world cruises as well. Since Princess makes a practice of following the pulse of the marketplace, it is best to check itineraries each season.

In 2000, P & O split off the company's cruise business from its non-cruise vessels and non-cruise interests and formed a separate public company. At that time, the new company, P & O/Princess Cruises, owned and operated all of P & O's cruise ships under six separate brands: P & O Cruises, P & O Cruises Australia, Princess Cruises, Swan Hellenic, Seetours International, and Aida Cruises (these last two brands concentrate on a largely German clientele).

In 2003, the shareholders of Carnival Corporation and P & O/Princess finally approved the formation of a new public company (which acquired all of the P & O/Princess assets with the stock in the new corporation split up between the shareholders of Carnival and P & O/Princess) to be traded on the New York and British stock exchanges. Subsequently, the P & O brands were spun off and now are separate brands of Carnival.

When the sleek, 856-foot, 14-story, 77,000-ton *Sun Princess* made its debut in December 1995, it was the largest cruise ship in service. Passenger capacity was limited to 1,950 (somewhat less than its behemoth competitors), which is in keeping with Princess Cruises' intention to provide a more intimate, less crowded cruise experience aboard a large ship while still offering more dining, entertainment, and lounging options. The abundance of soft woods, brass, fine fabrics, and artwork—together with the dramatic central atrium area and design in the public rooms—made this ship and its sister ships the most attractive in the then Princess fleet.

In terms of cabins, 603 of the 975 passenger accommodations are outside, 410 have balconies, and 19 are wheelchair accessible. Standard staterooms are not large; however, they are cleverly designed and tastefully appointed and include two twin beds that convert to a queen; electronic wall safes; refrigerators; remote-control color television with CNN, in-house movies, and three music channels; hair dryers; and ample drawer and closet space. The 32 deluxe mini-suites and six ultra-deluxe full suites are considerably more spacious, have larger balconies, and include bathrooms with Jacuzzi tubs. There are self-serve laundry facilities on every stateroom deck.

The *Sun Princess* offers several dining and entertainment options, which include two elegant, formal dining rooms; a 24-hour lido café featuring breakfast, lunch, and teatime buffets and an alternative à la carte dinner menu, as well as a special children's menu; a pizzeria; a patisserie; a hamburger/hot-dog grill; an ice-cream bar; 24-hour room service; and a champagne, wine, and caviar bar that is one of the seven more intimate lounges aboard. Two 500-seat show lounges provide a diversity of evening entertainment while avoiding crowding passengers into a single multilevel facility. Other public rooms and areas adorned with $2.5 million dollars' worth of art include an attractive casino; a library; a cardroom; seven duty-free shops; five swimming pools and five whirlpools; an expansive walking/jogging track (3½ times around to a mile); and a marvelous spa/fitness area with a fully equipped gym, aerobics room, his and hers sauna and steam rooms, a variety of massage and spa treatment rooms, whirlpools, a beauty salon, and computerized golf simulator.

In its tradition of appealing to the family trade, on all of its ships Princess has built unique centers for teens and fully equipped and supervised age-appropriate fun zones and educational centers for ages three to seven and eight to 13.

The *Dawn Princess, Sea Princess,* and *Ocean Princess,* the *Sun*'s sister ships, commenced service in 1997, 1998, and 2000, respectively and are identical except for the art, decorations, and nomenclature of the various public rooms. The *Ocean Princess* was transferred to P & O in the fall of 2002 and the *Sea Princess* in 2003; however, in 2005, the *Sea Princess* was returned to the Princess fleet and the *Royal Princess* was transferred to P & O. Currently, both the *Dawn Princess* and the *Sun Princess* are offering cruises from Australia and are marketed in the Australian market as well as in the U.S. The *Dawn Princess* sails in Australia between October and April, while the *Sun Princess* cruises there the entire year.

The 109,000-ton *Grand Princess* entered service in the spring of 1998. Seven hundred and ten of the 1,300 staterooms boast private balconies and there are 28 full suites and 180 mini-suites. Twenty-eight accommodations are wheelchair accessible. The 372 inside cabins, at 160 square feet, seem a bit small, especially when they are occupied by a third or fourth passenger. Standard outside cabins vary from 165 to 210 square feet and increase by an additional 45 square feet if they have balconies. Although the cabins and bathrooms are not very large, all have twin beds that convert to queens, refrigerators, color televisions with CNN and in-house movies, hair dryers, and electronic safes. The mini-suites, measuring 325 square feet (balcony included), have a second television, larger sitting area with sofa bed, and a walk-in dressing area adjacent to a bathroom with tub and shower. For a few hundred dollars more per cruise the mini-suites are the more desirable accommodations. The full suites have separate parlors, wet bars, larger split bathrooms, and walk-in closets and, as expected, are the most desirable accommodations aboard ship.

The *Grand Princess* offers a wide range of dining venues, which include three Italian Renaissance-style main dining rooms with sitting areas divided for greater intimacy: Sabatini's, an outstanding Italian trattoria featuring an eight-course extravaganza of seafood and Italian specialties; Sterling Steakhouse; and the 24-hour Horizon Court, an alternate dining facility offering buffet breakfasts and lunches and bistro-style, full-service dinners. On lido deck, passengers can enjoy the hamburger/hot-dog grill and the pizza counter, as well as ice-cream creations. Room service is available around the clock.

Indoor and outdoor public facilities are mind-boggling and include the 748-seat Princess Theater, with lavish nightly productions, a 13,500-square-foot casino, numerous additional lounges offering entertainment, dancing, and piano music; dozens of bars; a library; a writing room; a cardroom; a business center; a wedding chapel for marriages and vow renewals; a sports bar; a coffee-champagne-caviar bar; several boutiques; three regular swimming pools (one of which has a retractable dome for inclement weather), a children's pool and playground area, a pool with infused current for exercise swimming, and several whirlpools; a golf center with a nine-hole putting green and golf simulator machine; a fitness center with cardiovascular equipment, aerobics rooms, massage and beauty treatment rooms, beauty salon, sauna and steam rooms, and locker facilities; a sport court for tennis, basketball, and volleyball; a small jogging track; youth and teen centers; an impressive virtual-reality center with motion-based simulator rides; a hospital with telemedical machines; and, atop ship, a glass-enclosed moving sidewalk ascending to Skywalkers Disco and Observation Lounge, lending the feel of entering a spaceship.

Most public areas are broken up into multiple sections in order to downplay the immensity of the vessel. In spite of multiple exits for disembarkation of the ship and tenders and numerous elevators, traffic can be heavily backed up at peak times. Many of the areas, such as the sauna-steam-shower complex, fitness center, outside deck lounges, jogging track, and outside lido dining tables, could be insufficient to accommodate all passengers on a day at sea. However, overall this is truly a resort at sea, with vast facilities and options offering something that will appeal to all age groups and a diverse segment of the cruising population.

The 109,000-ton *Golden Princess* and *Star Princess,* sister ships to the *Grand Princess,* entered service in spring 2001 and spring 2002, respectively. These ships boast wedding chapels featuring "wedding cams" enabling family and friends back home to view passenger nuptials. The *Grand*-class ships and those that were built subsequently offer sea weddings conducted by the ship's captain. Various improvements not found on the other two vessels were also made on the *Star Princess,* including an improved spa featuring the new Lotus Spa and expanded children's facilities. The three *Grand*-class ships were renovated in 2008 and 2009 with the addition of the piazza-style atrium (which includes the International Café, Vines Wine Bar, and a new Internet café/library), a 300-square-foot Movies Under the Stars screen over the pool, an adults-only sanctuary retreat, and LED flat-screen TVs in all staterooms.

The 116,000-ton, 2,670-passenger *Sapphire Princess* and *Diamond Princess* entered service in 2004. Similar to the *Grand Princess* series of ships in design, public facilities, and accommodations, these two vessels have additional features: Club Fusion (a high-tech lounge showcasing various entertainments), five main dining rooms, five pools, and eight spas. Similar to the *Grand*-class ships, standard balcony and outside cabins are not very large and the bathrooms are quite small. Passengers desiring more living and storage space are best advised to opt for a mini- or full suite. One of the most innovative features on these ships is the expanded dining possibilities. In addition to the casual, 24-hour Horizon Café and the signature specialty restaurant, Sabatini, the two main dining rooms have been divided into five different venues: one traditional two-seating, assigned-table dining room with the typical Princess continental menu and four "anytime" dining rooms. Each of these dining rooms is elegantly furnished in a décor reflecting its theme. Passengers can make dining reservations each evening through a concierge service. A reservation-only (surcharge) Sterling Steakhouse specialty restaurant, similar to that on the other Princess ships, is also available.

The 113,000-ton, 3,100-passenger *Caribbean Princess* also joined the fleet in the spring of 2004 with a magnificent décor and such innovative features as a 300-square-foot LED poolside movie screen for watching movies under the stars; expanded Internet; children and teen centers; an extended fitness area featuring 20 treadmills and numerous cardiovascular machines with personal TVs; improvements in the Lotus Spa areas with additional exotic treatments and massages; numerous premium TV channels; activities including the Scholarship at Sea program; and new entertainment venues. The ship also offers a new dining venue, Café Caribe, with nightly themed buffets of Caribbean cuisine accompanied by live island music.

The Movies Under the Stars program, which takes place in two levels around the pool, where passengers sit in comfortable lounges with blankets (if needed), popcorn, drinks, and other snacks, is also available on the *Grand Princess, Sea Princess, Crown Princess, Emerald Princess,* and *Ruby Princess.* The program has been extended to all of the ships in the fleet except the three smallest vessels.

Of the 1,557 accommodations, 1,105 face the sea, 881 have private balconies, 25 are wheelchair accessible, and 682 have additional upper berths. The square footage of the cabins and suites is similar to the other *Grand*-class ships (as described above).

Sister ships in dimension to the *Caribbean Princess,* the *Crown Princess, Emerald Princess,* and *Ruby Princess* entered service in 2006, 2007, and 2008, respectively, with numerous changes to the public areas. The atrium lobby is designed to look like a street café with a piazza-style atrium. Located here is a 24-hour international café offering specialty coffees, drinks, rotating snacks, and desserts throughout the day; a wine and seafood bar featuring an extensive list of wines by the glass and a variety of seafood; sushi and sashimi; and an Internet café. Sabatini's has been relocated to deck 16, featuring panoramic ocean views and a warm, intimate lounge, Adagio, for passengers to enjoy cocktails and live music. Crown Grill, a new specialty steak and chop restaurant with additional continental favorites located on deck 7, features a theater-style kitchen, rich leather booths, and superior cuisine. The Lotus Spa facility occupies two decks. The Sanctuary, a special adults-only, semi-shaded outdoor area offers lounges, cabanas for a private massage, healthy food and beverages, and special service at a cost of $10 per person for a half-day. The Sanctuary is to be expanded fleetwide.

When *Ruby Princess* entered service in 2008, new shipboard services were introduced, many of which are scheduled to trickle down to the other ships in the fleet. At lunch on sea days, the Wheelhouse Bar converts to an English-style pub (similar to those on Cunard's vessels), and suite passengers can enjoy an exclusive gourmet breakfast in Sabatini's. Other innovations include imported cheeses at Vines, the atrium area wine bar; additional enrichment programs, audience participation events, and children's activities; wireless and cell phone connectivity around the vessel and in the staterooms; and ship tours to back-of-the-house areas for a maximum of 12 passengers offered twice each cruise for $150 per person.

The 92,000-ton, 1,950-passenger *Coral Princess* entered service in 2003, followed by a sister ship, *Island Princess*. Of the 987 staterooms and suites, 879 have ocean views, and all but 144 of these have private balconies. The inside cabins measure 156 square feet and the outside cabins without balconies measure 162 square feet. Balcony cabins range in size from 217 to 232 square feet, mini-suites from 285 to 302 square feet, and the 16 full suites come in at 470 square feet (all measurements include the balcony). Twenty cabins are wheelchair accessible, and 616 can accommodate a third or fourth passenger. There are no ultra-deluxe grand suites as on the *Sun*-class and *Grand*-class vessels.

Public areas include three pools; five whirlpool spas; two main dining rooms; the signature Sabatini's; Bayou Café and Steakhouse, a New Orleans-style restaurant; poolside pizza; ice-cream and hamburger facilities; the main showroom; numerous lounges; a Las Vegas-themed martini bar; a casino; three duty-free shops; a fitness center and spa; children and teen centers; a library; an Internet café; a wedding chapel; an art gallery; and a golf putting green and simulator.

Princess acquired the former 30,277-ton, 670-passenger *R-3* and *R-4* of the now-defunct Renaissance Cruises and put them back into service in 2002 and 2003 after renaming them *Pacific Princess* and *Tahitian Princess*. The *Tahitian Princess* sailed year-round throughout French Polynesia, but in 2009 she was renamed *Ocean Princess* and her itineraries were changed to Alaska, Europe, and world cruises. A sister ship, the former *R-8* of Renaissance Cruises, which sailed as *Minerva II* for Swan Hellenic, was transferred to Princess in April 2007 and renamed *Royal Princess*.

These vessels are attractively designed and decorated to emulate the great ocean liners of the past with corridors laden with floral runner-style carpets similar to those found in grand hotels, stairways adorned with antiques and works of art, and lounges, libraries, and dining rooms done in rich dark woods and filled with expensive French and English furnishings, wall, and window treatments. The décor throughout the ships was ingeniously orchestrated to create a feeling of understated, old-world elegance without a hint of glitz or ostentation.

Ten suites on each ship range in size from 583 to 598 square feet with 283- to 364-square-foot private wrap-around balconies, two televisions, separate living rooms with dining areas, a guest bath, and all marble master bathrooms with whirlpool tubs. Fifty-two suites on *Pacific Princess* and *Ocean Princess* average 260 square feet with 70-square-foot balconies, and an additional 170 outside staterooms (247 on *Royal Princess*) average 173 square feet with 43-square-foot balconies.

In January 2001, Princess Cruises introduced Personal Choice Dining aboard *Grand Princess* and expanded the concept to its entire fleet over the remainder of that year. In essence, it allows passengers the choice between the traditional cruise dining, during which they sit at the same table with the same waiters and table mates each evening at a scheduled time, and the alternative, which entails dining any time between 5:30 and 10:00 P.M. at any table with anyone in the main dining room or, on certain vessels, in the specialty restaurants. Of course, the option to dine in the 24-hour buffet restaurant (which turns into an evening bistro) or through room service is always available. A steakhouse—Sterling Steakhouse on some ships and Crown Grill, featuring special cuts of Angus beef (at a surcharge), on others— is also available on all ships. We found the quality of the beef and overall dining experience at these steakhouses exceptional. Sabatini's, offering a multicourse Italian feast, is also available on all the ships. Dividing the main dining rooms into several venues was inaugurated on the *Diamond Princess* and *Sapphire Princess* ships.

An additional innovation, Internet cafés, debuted on the *Golden Princess* and were expanded to the entire fleet. With 25 computer stations open 24 hours, the facilities on these ships are among the largest and most impressive at sea. On the *Diamond* and *Sapphire Princess* there are 29 stations and coffee and pastries are available to passengers while online.

Another new program, inaugurated on *Coral Princess* and expanded to the entire fleet, is Scholarship at Sea, offering up to 20 courses per cruise ranging from ceramics, computer skills, Web design, and culinary arts to health and financial seminars. This program greatly enhances activities for days at sea.

In 2004 new amenities were added for suite passengers throughout the entire fleet and include complimentary Internet access, laundry, dry cleaning and shoe polishing, afternoon tea and before-dinner hors d'oeuvres in the suite, an initial setup of liquors and soft drinks, and a corsage on formal nights. Cell phones work aboard the *Grand Princess* and *Golden Princess,* and this feature may be extended to other ships in the future.

For $50 per person, balcony-cabin guests can opt for the "ultimate balcony dinner," wherein a multicourse dinner is elegantly served on their balcony. For $28 per cabin, a special champagne breakfast will be served in all staterooms. This is in addition to the standard room-service breakfast menu.

Commencing on the *Emerald Princess,* and eventually being introduced fleetwide (other than on *Pacific Princess, Ocean Princess,* and *Royal Princess,* the three smaller ships) is a new dining experience, the Chef's Table, where for $75 per head passengers can enjoy pre-dinner cocktails and hors d'oeuvres in the ship's galley. Hosted by the executive chef, the event is followed by a multicourse tasting dinner with special wines in the dining room and dessert and discussions with the chef that include the Princess cookbook.

Prices vary somewhat from ship to ship, being higher on European and Far East sailings. There is only a supplement for single occupancy of double cabins, and there are sizable reductions for third and fourth passengers sharing a room. Numerous air/sea packages are available, and Princess features significant discounts on early bookings (often as high as 40 to 50 percent).

All 17 ships presently in the fleet were delivered after 1995, making Princess one of the most modern lines in the market. In recent years, Princess has placed more emphasis on shore excursions with an array of air, sea, and land tours that afford opportunities to get close to the natural environs and sample the best sight-seeing in addition to numerous more active and adventurous options. Princess offers its passengers the opportunity to visit the top destinations around the globe with sailings to all seven continents ranging in length from seven to 107 days. Princess Cruises Captain's Circle program offers numerous perks for frequent cruisers on the line.

Princess competes in the premium cruise market and offers a well-rounded cruise experience for passengers of all ages. There is an overall ambiance, desire to please, and lack of stuffiness not present on many other luxury liners. All Princess ships have exceptional special facilities and programs for youngsters and a full range of activities and entertainment, making them ideal choices for families. The adult clientele is an even mix of passengers from ranging in age from 20s to 70s, making the demographics of the cruise line more diverse than that of other premium cruise lines. Most passengers are very pleased with the blend of luxury, fun, food, service, entertainment, activities, and personal-choice dining.

Strong Points:

Attractive vessels, activities, entertainment, ambiance, itineraries, good service, and varied dining choices add up to a well-rounded, upscale cruise experience. The *Grand*-class ships are extremely well appointed and among the most glamorous in the industry, offering a plethora of facilities. The innovations on the *Caribbean, Crown, Diamond, Emerald, Ruby,* and *Sapphire Princess* vessels make them some of the most desirable of the megaships presently in service.

Grand Princess, *courtesy Princess Cruises*

Lounge on Star Princess, *courtesy Princess Cruises*

Kitchen on Caribbean Princess, *courtesy Princess Cruises*

Caribbean Princess *at sea, courtesy Princess Cruises*

Gym on Caribbean Princess, *courtesy Princess Cruises*

Movies Under the Stars, Caribbean Princess, *courtesy Princess Cruises*

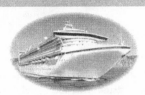

CARIBBEAN PRINCESS

CAPTAIN'S GALA DINNER

HEALTHY CHOICE MENU

Our Healthy Choice Menu reflects today's awareness of lighter, more balanced diets.
In response to these nutritional needs, Princess Cruises offers dishes that are
low in cholesterol, fat and sodium, but high in flavor.

Double Chicken Broth with Vermicelli and Scallions
Belgian Endive, Boston Lettuce and Tomato Wedges Salad
Sautéed Orange Roughy Filet with Saffron Sauce

VEGETARIAN MENU

Golden Fresh Fruit Collection Flavored with Kirsch
Roasted Garlic Velouté Enhanced with Rosemary
Belgian Endive, Boston Lettuce and Tomato Wedges Salad
Ravioli di Ricotta with Fresh Tomato Sauce
Assorted International Cheese and Crackers
Seasonal Fresh Fruit Plate

ALWAYS AVAILABLE

Classic Caesar Salad
Succulent Caribbean Shrimp Cocktail, Red American Sauce
Fettuccine all'Alfredo Original Recipe from Rome
Broiled North Sea Silver Salmon Filet
Grilled Skinless Chicken Suprême
Grilled Dry-Aged Sirloin Steak

Baked Potato and French Fries can be requested in addition to the
daily vegetable selection.

If you have any food-related allergies or special dietary requirements,
please make sure to contact only your Head Waiter or the Maître d'Hôtel.

PRINCESS
where i belong™

APPETIZERS

Pâté de Foie de Strasbourg

Liver Pâté Strasbourg Style, Garnished with Aspic Flavored with Vintage Port and Warm Brioches

Golden Fresh Fruit Collection Flavored with Triple Sec Liqueur

Baked Clams Casino with Bacon and Bread Crumbs

SOUPS

Double Chicken Broth with Vermicelli and Scallions

Roasted Garlic Velouté Enhanced with Rosemary

Chilled Apricot Purée with Toasted Almonds

SALAD

Belgian Endive, Boston Lettuce and Tomato Wedges Salad

Russian, Balsamic Vinaigrette or Low-Fat Tomato-Herb Dressing

ENTRÉES

PRINCESS FAVORITE

Ravioli con Salsa di Funghi Porcini

*Stuffed Pasta Squares of Beef, Herbs and Ricotta Cheese in a Sauce of
Wild Sautéed Mushrooms, Garlic and Cream*

Sautéed Orange Roughy Filet with Saffron Sauce

Accompanied with Snow Peas, Glazed Carrots and Crusty New Potatoes

Broiled Twin Lobster Tail

Presented on the Shell with Melted Lemon Butter and Rice Pilaf

Royal Pheasant in Pan Juices

An Oven Roast with Brussels Sprouts, Caramelized Shallots and Parisienne Potatoes

Beef Wellington

*Puff Pastry-Wrapped Tenderloin in a Black Truffle Madeira Sauce with
Baby Vegetables and Duchesse Potatoes*

Cellar Master Suggestions	Glass	Bottle
Ritz Fizz *(Sparkling Wine, Blue Curaçao and Amaretto)*	$5.00	
Moët & Chandon, Dom Perignon, Epernáy		$115.00
Chardonnay, Caliterra, Valle Central	$6.00	$24.00
Cabernet Sauvignon, Kendall-Jackson, Lake County	$7.00	$28.00
Chardonnay, Kendall-Jackson, Lake County		$28.00
Merlot, Ferrari Carano, Sonoma		$36.00

Courtesy Princess Cruises

DIAMOND PRINCESS

SUNDAY, 13TH MARCH, 2005 — AT SEA

FUN ZONE AND OFF LIMITS
9:00am to 12Noon, 2:00pm to 5:00pm & 7:00pm to 10:00pm - Fun Zone Activities
9:00am to 12 Noon, 2:00pm to 5:00pm & 8:00pm to 1:00am - Off Limits Activities
10:00pm to 1:00am - Group Babysitting (Advance Booking Required)

FITNESS CLASSES with Christo & Ian

7:30am	Pure & Simple Stretch	Aerobic studio, deck 15
8:00am	StepXpress	Aerobic studio, deck 15, fwd.
9:00am	SpinXpress 1 ($10)	Aerobic studio, deck 15, fwd.
4:00pm	Introduction to Pilates $10	Aerobic studio, deck 15, fwd.
5:00pm	Total Body Conditioning	Aerobic studio, deck 15, fwd.

LOTUS SPA SEMINAR SERIES

10:30am **No More Bad Hair Days** - Join our international hair stylists for this fun seminar. *Lifestyle Room, Deck 15*

11:00am **Eat More to Weigh Less Seminar** - Our fitness and detox specialist teaches you to use detox to eliminate those 'stubborn' areas with **Ian**. *Lifestyle Room, Deck 15*

12:00pm **The Collagen Skin Clinic** - Amazing treatment for fine lines, wrinkles and puffiness. Are there other ways to feed our skin collagen? Find out at this informative seminar. *Lifestyle Room, Deck 15*

2:00pm **Cellulite and Spider Veins Solutions** - Do you suffer from cellulite, spider veins, poor circulation? All who attend will try out some of our renowned treatment theories FREE during workshop. *Lifestyle Room, Deck 15*

3:00pm **Detoxification for Weight Loss** - Learn how to lose weight effectively and permanently with **Thys**. *Lifestyle Room, Deck 15*

ADVENTURES ASHORE
Tour Office located on Plaza Deck, Deck 5 in the Atrium Lobby
Hours: 9:00am to 5:00pm
TOUR BOOKINGS FOR PUERTO VALLARTA CLOSE MONDAY AT 10:00AM
Passengers who wish to book tours should complete a Tour Order form and place it in the 24 hour drop box beside the Tour Office. Orders placed in the drop box receive first priority over requests received at the counter. Tickets will be delivered to your stateroom.

Port & Shopping Advisor Desk Hours: 3:00pm to 5:00pm
See **Tamara** for questions on Puerto Vallarta and Mazatlan and find out **where the best buys are!** From Jewelry to Designer Watches at the Best Duty Free Prices and more! Remember to pick up your **VIP Discount Cards** before shopping ashore!

CAPTAIN'S CIRCLE HOSPITALITY DESK
10:00am to 11:00am & 3:00pm to 4:00 pm – Atrium, Deck 5
If you and your partner have traveled on the same number of cruises you should both have the same color Cruise Key Card if not, please come and see Lori.

COMPUTER COURSES With Instructor Kristoffer Wright - *Wedding Chapel, Deck 7*
9:00am – **Using a Computer for the First Time** (Complimentary)
10:00am – **Basic Digital Photo Editing** ($25.00)
11:00am – **Digital Photo Editing: Beyond the Basics** ($25.00)
1:00pm – **Windows Movie Maker** ($25.00)
2:00pm – **Uploading Digital Photographs** ($25.00)
3:00pm – **Windows Tips & Timesavers** ($25.00)

TODAY'S ACTIVITIES
Watch out for the *Reflections Video Team* wherever you see this icon!

8:00am **Brain Waves Quiz** - Pick up your daily teasers and check the answers tomorrow. *Library, Deck 5*

9:00am-6:00pm **Princess Links** - The 9 hole Putting Green is open. *Deck 16 midships*

9:00am-11:00am & 3:00pm-5:00pm **Cards & Games plus Needlepoint Kits ($5-$7)** - Are available from the Cruise Staff. *Library Deck 5*

9:15am **Tour of Diamond Princess** - Join **Sly** for an orientation and tour of the ship. Please bring your ship's pocket guide map available in your stateroom portfolio. *Skywalker's, Deck 18 Aft*

9:45am **Men's Singles Table Tennis** - Join **Paul** of the Cruise Staff. Prizes for the winners. *Conservatory, Deck 15*

9:45am **Port Shopping Talk on Puerto Vallarta, Mazatlan & Cabo San Lucas** - A must see presentation before going ashore! Your Port Shopping Advisor, **Tamara** will have vital information on the ports, best sights & Duty Free shopping! Port Maps will be available. Free raffle, for a chance to win a **Diamond Bracelet** from Diamonds International. (This talk can be seen later today on Channel 33 of your Stateroom T.V.) *Princess Theater, Deck 7 Fwd*

10:00am-Noon **Scholarship@Sea - Ceramics** - Come along and begin a project for the cruise. No special skills and talents are needed. **Hannah** of the Cruise Staff will assist you. *Conservatory, Deck 15*

10:00am-11:00am **Closest to the Pin Competition** *CyberGolf, Sports Deck 16 Fwd*

10:00am **Bridge Lecture** - With **Marilyn Wells**. *Vivaldi Dining Room, Deck 5*

10:00am-2:00pm **Easy Listening Melodies** - The Diamond Princess musicians entertain. *Atrium Lobby, Deck 5*

10:15am **Ladies Singles Shuffleboard** - with **Danny** of the Cruise Staff. *Deck 16 Aft*

10:15am **Line Dance Mania** - Join **Jo** for some popular line dances. Remember you don't need a partner! *Club Fusion, Deck 7*

10:30am **Floral Demonstration** - Join our Onboard Florist Gerry, as he takes you into his world of Bouquets, Corsages and Floral Arrangements. **Hayley** of the Cruise Staff is your host. *Atrium, Deck 5*

10:30am **Friends of Dorothy Get-Together** - All interested are invited informally. *Skywalker's, Deck 18 Aft*

11:00am-1:00pm **Virtual Golf Simulator is available** *CyberGolf, Sports Deck 16 Fwd*

11:00am-2:15pm & 3:00pm-5:00pm **Poolside Melodies** - With the sounds of **Sugar Cane**. *Neptune's Reef & Pool, Deck 14*

11:15am $$$$$ **SNOWBALL JACKPOT BINGO** $$$$$
The jackpot of **$1,000.00** could go in **50 numbers**, plus four other big cash game prizes. Cards available from 10:15am - Stateroom charge only. **Neil** and **Jo** call the numbers. *Club Fusion, Deck 7 Aft*

11:15am **Scavenger Hunt Challenge** - Join **Hayley** from the Cruise Staff. *Crooners, Deck 7*

11:30am **"Grey Zone" Get-Together** - All 18-20 year olds are invited to meet **The Cruise Staff** to discuss activities for this cruise. *Skywalker's, Deck 18*

11:30am **Morning Trivia** - **Paul** of the Cruise Staff is your Quiz Master. *Wheelhouse, Deck 7*

12:15pm **The Diamond Princess "Open" Golf Putting Championship** - How good is your short game? **Jason** from the Cruise Staff is your starter. (Over 18's only please.) *Princess Links, Deck 16*

12:30pm **Martini Madness** - Come along as our friendly bartenders show you how to prepare the perfect Martini. **Danny** is your host. *Atrium, Deck 5*

12:45pm **Arts & Crafts** - Join **Hayley** of the Cruise Staff. Today's project: **"Picture Frames"**. *Wheelhouse, Deck 7*

1:00pm – *Princess Theater, Deck 7 Fwd.*
Afternoon Movie
FINDING NEVERLAND
Starring: Johnny Depp & Kate Winslet
Duration: 1 hr. 46 mins. • Rated: PG • Drama

1:00pm **Mexican Fire Opal Seminar** - See the fire of a Mexican Sunset in these unique and beautiful genuine Opals set in 14k white & yellow gold. **Enter to Win a Free Fire Opal** valued at $175! *Wheelhouse Bar, Deck 7*

1:00pm **Singles Mingles** - All travelling singles are invited to meet **Jo** from the Cruise Staff for cocktails and introductions. *Atrium Lobby Bar, Deck 5*

1:15pm **The Weakest One** - If you would like to be a potential contestant for the popular game show, taking place later this cruise, meet **Hannah** who will explain all. *Club Fusion, Deck 7 Aft*

1:30pm **Service Club Get-Together** - **Jason** has your make up cards. *Crooners, Deck 7*

1:30pm **Photographic Seminar** - Join our onboard experts for this afternoon's presentation **"Digital Photography made Fun and Easy"**. $10 fee and receive a FREE book. *Wheelhouse, Deck 7*

2:00pm-4:00pm **Scholarship@Sea - Ceramics** - Come along and begin a project for the cruise. No special skills and talents are needed. **Hayley** or the Cruise Staff will assist you. *Conservatory, Deck 15*

2:00pm-6:00pm **Virtual Golf Simulator available** *CyberGolf, Sports Deck 16 Fwd*

2:15pm **Bridge Play** - With **Marilyn Wells** arranging the games. *Vivaldi Dining Room, Deck 5*

2:30pm **Ballroom For Beginners** - Join **Sly** for his opening class. Today: **"Merengue"**. All are welcome. *Club Fusion, Deck 7*

2:30pm - ART AUCTION – (1:30pm Preview) - *Explorer's Lounge, Deck 7*

CHAMPAGNE ART AUCTION
Do not miss the fun and excitement of viewing over 150 works of art by world famous artists at savings substantially below suggested retail prices. 100% Duty Free for U.S. residents. Art shipped anywhere in the world. **Complimentary Champagne** and $2,000.00 art giveaway.

2:30pm **Special Interest Lecture** - Join **Gil Stratton**, the Dean of Southern California Sports Broadcasters for his opening presentation of the cruise. Today's topic: **"Sports"** - a Reflection of a 40-year career, including 9 years a Pro Umpire, The NFL Voice of the LA Rams, & exclusive coverage of the Rome Olympics and the debut of Cassius Clay. *Wheelhouse, Deck 7*

3:30pm-4:30pm **Afternoon Tea** - Served in a musical atmosphere. *Pacific Moon Dining Room, Deck 6*

3:30pm **Real Live Wooden Horseracing** - Have a bunch, bet a bunch! Join Cruise Director **Billy** and the Cruise Staff and bet on the plywood ponies. *Club Fusion, Deck 7*

4:15pm $$$$$ **SNOWBALL JACKPOT BINGO** $$$$$
If not won this morning, the jackpot of **$1,250.00** could go in **50 numbers**, plus four other big cash game prizes. Cards available from 3:15pm. **Neil** and **Jo** call the numbers. *Club Fusion, Deck 7*

Courtesy Princess Cruises

REGENT SEVEN SEAS CRUISES
1000 Corporate Drive, Suite 500
Fort Lauderdale, Florida 33334
(800) 285-1835
www.rssc.com

SEVEN SEAS MARINER: entered service 2001; 50,000 G.R.T.; 709' x 93'; 700-passenger capacity; 350 suites (all with verandas); French and European officers and international crew; cruises the Mediterranean, Arabian Gulf, India, Africa, South America, and the Caribbean.

SEVEN SEAS NAVIGATOR: entered service 1999; 33,000 G.R.T.; 560' x 81'; 490-passenger capacity; 245 suites; international officers and crew; cruises in the Caribbean, South America, Alaska, Asia, Australia, New Zealand, and South Pacific.

SEVEN SEAS VOYAGER: entered service 2003; 46,000 G.R.T.; 681' x 94.5'; 700-passenger capacity; 350 suites; international officers and crew; cruises Mediterranean, Baltic, Europe, Panama Canal, and Caribbean, as well as a world cruise.

(Medical Facilities for *Mariner, Navigator,* and *Voyager:* C-4; P-1, EM, CLS, MS; N-1; CM; PD; BC; EKG; TC; PO; WC; OR; ICU; X; M; CCP.)

Note: **Six+ and six black stars are the highest ratings given in this edition to ships in the deluxe market category.**

These ships are rated in 11 separate categories in the second half of chapter 14.

In December 1994, Diamond Cruises and Seven Seas Cruise Line merged and became Radisson Seven Seas Cruises. In 1998, the cruise line embarked upon a joint venture with Monte Carlo-based Vlasof Group, which formerly owned Sitmar Cruises, to build a series of new ships. In March 2006, the cruise line was re-branded Regent Seven Seas Cruises. In early 2008, the Apollo investment group, which owns 50 percent of Norwegian Cruise Line, purchased Regent Seven Seas Cruises following an earlier purchase of Oceania Cruises. Both companies are now part of Prestige Cruise Holdings; however, they are operated as separate brands. The emphasis of the brand is luxury and service, along with destination cruising.

Radisson Hotels Worldwide made its debut into the cruise industry in May

1992 with the revolutionary $125 million, twin-hull, ultra-deluxe *Radisson Diamond.* The ship left the fleet in 2005. *Song of Flower,* which sailed for over a decade for Radisson Seven Seas, was retired from the fleet in October 2003. In January 1998, the 19,200-ton, 330-passenger *Paul Gauguin* joined the fleet, offering seven-night Polynesian cruises. The ship is now owned and operated by Grand Circle Travel.

In September 1999, the *Seven Seas Navigator* debuted. This 33,000-ton, 560-foot-long vessel accommodates 490 guests in 245 suites. All of the standard suites measure 301 square feet (add an additional five feet for suites with balconies). In addition to the main dining room, the vessel offers an alternative dining venue featuring Italian cuisine at the Portofino Grill as well as a casual pool grill. This ship includes a variety of itineraries, including a series of destination-intensive cruises in the Caribbean, the Mediterranean, and through the Middle East and around Africa.

All accommodations include extremely generous storage areas, a large walk-in closet with unattached wooden hangers, a private safe, terry-cloth robes, a makeup area with a hair dryer, an entertainment/sitting section with a writing desk, couch, small table for in-suite dining, television with DVD player, refrigerator initially stocked with soft drinks and beer (and replenished daily with soft drinks), two twin beds or a European king bed, and marble bathrooms with a separate glassed-in shower stall, separate bathtub, large vanity with abundant storage, a toilet, and various toiletries. The suites have two separate rooms with larger balconies and the four deluxe suites include a powder room and balconies that wrap around the front of the ship.

Located on decks 11 and 12, atop the ship, are the fitness center, a Carita of Paris Spa, beauty salon, jogging track, 18 suites, an observation lounge, and the romantic Galileo's Lounge, the best spot on the ship for cocktails and late-night dancing and listening. The pool, outdoor whirlpools, additional suites, and Portofino Grill can be found on deck 10. Although the Portofino Grill offers advanced-reservation Italian specialty dining along with music and singing waiters in the evening, it is also open during the day and features breakfast and lunch buffets. The remaining suites are located on decks 5 through 9 (only those on deck 5 do not include balconies).

Most of the public rooms are spread along decks 6 and 7 and include an elegant casino; a glamorous two-story show lounge; two boutiques; the central information/travel concierge area; a fully stocked library complete with books, videos, computers, printers, and e-mail/Internet capacities; a cardroom; and several other cocktail lounges. The main, single-seating Compass Rose dining room is on deck 5. Complimentary fine wines and liquor are served throughout the ship.

In 2001, the 50,000-ton, 700-passenger *Seven Seas Mariner* entered service. The ship has European senior officers, a 445-person international crew, and four different dining venues. It operates worldwide itineraries. This is the first all-suite, all-balcony vessel in the cruise industry.

Whether you opt for one of the 262 356-square-foot standard ocean-view suites or treat yourself to one of the 92 ultra-deluxe accommodations ranging in size from 449 to 2,002 square feet, you will be delighted with the large private balcony as well as the roominess, design, and tasteful furnishings. (Measurements include balconies.) Each suite features your choice of twin or matrimonial beds with down comforters, a makeup area with hair dryer, spacious walk-in closet with a private electronic safe and terry-cloth robes, separate lounging section with a writing desk, remote-control television and DVD, refrigerator stocked gratis with your choice of soft drinks and two bottles of spirits, marble bathroom with a large vanity/storage area, bathtub/shower combination (some with a large marble-accented shower stall with a seat and rain shower head), upscale toiletries, and toilets situated so that you do not crunch your knees against the door. Of course, the more expensive suites not only afford greater space but also have additional facilities and amenities. Six suites accommodate wheelchairs.

In keeping with its dedication to culinary excellence, the cruise line has provided an excellent, open-seating main dining room featuring exquisitely prepared epicurean selections as well as a nightly gourmet tasting menu and complete heart-healthy and vegetarian alternative menus.

For a change of scenery, guests can select from three additional and distinctly different dining venues. Signatures, an elegantly furnished private dining room with panoramic sea views, features haute and nouvelle French cuisine from the prestigious Le Cordon Bleu Academie d'Art Culinaire. This is one of the finest gourmet specialty restaurants at sea. Latitudes offers a variety of Indochine dishes off a fixed tasting menu in a pleasant, more intimate environment. The more casual Mediterranean bistro, La Veranda, tempts with Italian, Greek, and Middle Eastern fare. Complimentary yet excellent red and white wines from around the world are served in all four dining areas with dinner.

Public areas include a two-tiered show lounge, several observation lounges and bars, a nightclub, casino, cardroom, conference room, library, computer learning center and Internet café, health and fitness center, state-of-the-art spa operated by Carita of Paris, large outdoor swimming pool and whirlpools, shuffleboard, and golf nets. The high ratio of space-to-passenger capacity results in no area of the ship ever feeling crowded.

The 46,000-ton, 700-passenger *Seven Seas Voyager* came on line in the spring of 2003. Similar in facilities to the *Mariner,* all accommodations are balcony suites, the smallest (referred to as "Deluxe Category") measuring 306 square feet (plus a 50-square-foot balcony). The two largest master suites are a whopping 1,216 square feet, plus a 187-square-foot balcony, and the remaining suites range in size from 370 square feet to 1,403 square feet, including the balconies. Four suites can accommodate wheelchairs. All of the balconies can accommodate lounge chairs and small tables.

All accommodations feature separate lounging areas; walk-in closets; private safes; refrigerators stocked with soft drinks as well as an initial bar setup; hair dryers; telephones; cotton bathrobes; high-tech interactive television systems with free movie channels, CD and DVD players, and e-mail capabilities; and marble bathrooms with separate glass-enclosed showers and full bathtubs. Butler service is included in 88 of the most expensive suites.

Most of the public areas can be found on decks 4, 5, 6, and 11, with guest suites occupying decks 6 through 11, all with enviable ocean views. Although many of the public facilities and restaurants are similar to those described above for the *Mariner,* the Internet café and learning center have been expanded. The menu at Latitudes on *Voyager* features Indochine creations. As on the *Mariner,* Signatures, the specialty restaurant, is outstanding.

Wines and spirits are complimentary at all bars and restaurants throughout the fleet. Select shore excursions are included in the cruise fare on all voyages. Between 2008 and 2010, all three ships received extensive renovations in public areas and guest suites as well as a new pizza station and ice-cream bar.

A new grill restaurant, Prime 7, featuring steaks, chops, lobster tails, and other steakhouse fare, has been added to all three vessels. A new Dinner and Show program is featured on the *Voyager* and *Mariner.* With this program, passengers can opt for a reservation-only gourmet dinner followed by a cabaret show free of charge.

The Destination Services Department plans unusual upscale explorations such as helicopter rides, meals at luxury restaurants ashore, and pre- and post-cruise programs for passengers.

Additional ships are scheduled to enter service in the future.

Strong Points:

With the addition of new state-of-the-art vessels and continuous upgrading in dining and service, Regent Seven Seas has become one of the top contenders in the luxury-cruise market. *Seven Seas Navigator, Seven Seas Mariner,* and *Seven Seas Voyager* boast the most spacious, comfortable, and livable accommodations at sea (from the lowest to the highest category). Larger than the former Regent Seven Seas' ships, they offer exceptional cuisine, additional facilities, and entertainment without sacrificing service and concern for passenger satisfaction.

Seven Seas Mariner, *courtesy Regent Seven Seas Cruises*

Compass Rose Restaurant, Seven Seas Mariner, *courtesy Regent Seven Seas Cruises*

Seven Seas Navigator, *courtesy Regent Seven Seas Cruises*

Seven Seas Navigator, *courtesy Regent Seven Seas Cruises*

Seven Seas Navigator, *courtesy Regent Seven Seas Cruises*

LaVeranda, Seven Seas Voyager, *courtesy Regent Seven Seas Cruises*

Compass Rose Restaurant, *courtesy Regent Seven Seas Cruises*

Balcony Stateroom, Seven Seas Navigator, *courtesy Regent Seven Seas Cruises*

Dinner Selection

Appetizers

Eggplant - Tomato - Mozzarella Roll
Marinated in an olive & lemon vinaigrette

Iced Honeydew Melon Fruit Cup
Served with mint julienne

Fresh Moules Marinière
Steamed with garlic, fresh herbs and white wine

Soups

Chicken Consommé with Matzo Balls

Chilled Carrot Vichyssoise
Cool and refreshing puréed soup scented with fresh parsley

Salads

Fresh Spinach with Yellow Tear Drop Tomato, Bacon, Chopped Egg
Dill-mustard dressing

Panaché of Garden Greens with Snow Pea Julienne
Tomato-shallot vinaigrette

Pasta Dish

Linguini alle Vongole
Flat pasta noodles with clams in olive oil, garlic and chopped parsley

Main Courses

Lemon Sole à la Mode
Lemon Sole fillet marinated with Chef's choice of spices
Served with assorted garden vegetables and parsley potatoes

Pan-fried Lemon-Thyme Marinated Free Range Chicken Breast
Served on a bed of vegetable spaghetti with a lemongrass flavored chicken gravy
Saffron couscous, carrots and broccoli roses

Grilled Black Angus Filet Mignon with Sautéed Mushrooms
Served with a pink peppercorn infused natural gravy
Farmers vegetables and Duchesse potatoes

Wok Dish

Szechuan Turkey
Stir-fried small turkey cubes with green peppers and roasted cashew nuts
Presented with sticky Chinese rice

Menu Degustation

Our Executive Chef, Peter Spörndli
invites you this evening to sample a gourmet tasting menu.
These perfectly portioned dishes are designed to take you on a culinary
journey on this "Coast to Coast Panama Canal Holiday Voyage"

Salmon Rillette

Diced smoked and poached salmon marinated with Crème Fraîche and chives
Decorated with sliced cucumbers and spring lettuce bouquet

White Bean Soup Mediterranean Style

Navy beans with tomatoes, cabbage and Prosciutto ham

Linguini alle Vongole

Flat pasta noodles with clams in olive oil, garlic and chopped parsley

Refreshing Spiced Red Wine Sherbet

Roast Noisettes of New Zealand Lamb

Presented on a bed of lentil - tomato - root vegetable ragoût
Accompanied by Lyonnaise potatoes and thyme infused lamb sauce

Chocolate Charlotte with Irish Coffee Sauce

Garnished with fresh fruit

Speciality Menus

Well-being

Lean alternatives prepared to minimize fat and calories and maximize taste.

FreshMoules Marinière
Steamed with garlic, fresh herbs and white wine

Chicken Consommé with Matzo Balls

Sea Bass à la Mode
Prime sea bass fillet marinated with Chef's choice of spices
Served with assorted garden vegetables and parsley potatoes

Mango Yogurt Terrine with Orange-Lime Sauce

Vegetarian

Perfectly suitable for lacto & ovo-vegetarians

Eggplant - Tomato - Mozzarella Roll
Marinated in an olive & lemon vinaigrette

Chilled Carrot Vichyssoise
Cool and refreshing puréed soup scented with fresh parsley

Papaya with Seasonal Vegetables
Simmered in a light coconut curry sauce
Presented with Papadam bread, steamed rice and toasted cashew nuts

Apple Crumble Pie
Served with Vanilla ice cream

Simplicity

The best of the basics cooked to perfection

Freshly Cooked Pasta with Tomato Sauce

Black Angus Beef Sirloin Steak
Tender beef grilled to your preference

Boneless Breast of Chicken

Salmon Fillet
Prepared to order: plain grilled, poached, broiled or pan-fried

Courtesy Regent Seven Seas Cruises

Dessert Sensations

Chocolate Charlotte with Irish Coffee Sauce
Garnished with fresh fruit

Apple Crumble Pie
Served with vanilla ice cream

Mango Yogurt Terrine with Orange-Lime Sauce

FROZEN DESSERT
Vienna Iced Coffee
Vanilla ice cream with espresso and whipped cream

Refreshing Spiced Red Wine Sherbet

Premium Ice Creams

Amaretto – Strawberry Cheesecake – Chocolate Chips
Hot chocolate or caramel sauce

Chocolate Frozen Yogurt

Diet Peach Ice Cream

Fresh Fruit in Season

Gourmandises

INTERNATIONAL CHEESE BOARD
English Stilton – Pepper Boursin – Swiss Emmenthaler
Port Salut – French Brie
Served with assorted crackers

M/S SEVEN SEAS NAVIGATOR

En Route to Cabo San Lucas, Mexico
Friday, December 22, 2000

Evening Entertainment

STARTING WITH

A POPCORN MOVIE

"THE SANTA CLAUS"

Shown on the big screen tonight is a comedy starring Tim Allen of TV's Home Improvement as Scott Calvin in this touching tale of a divorced dad who stumbles across the chance to become Santa Claus and take his son on a magical sleigh ride. Rated PG; 97 minutes

in *Seven Seas Show Lounge* at 10:00 p.m.

"SMOOTH JAZZ & SWING CLUB"
with *The Navigator Five Orchestra*
in *Galileo's* at 10:15 p.m.

Franz Zachbauer
PASTRY CHEF

Courtesy Regent Seven Seas Cruises

SEVEN SEAS VOYAGER

PASSAGES

Regent
SEVEN SEAS CRUISES

dailyactivities

GOOD AFTERNOON

All Day	TUNE INTO THE "VOYAGER TODAY": A daily program of cruise information and shipboard personalities presented by Cruise Director Jamie Logan	TV Channel 4
All Day	INSIGHTS INTO TOURING & EXPLORING with Travel Concierge Manager Christine	TV Channels 6 & 7
12:00 - 8:00	**THE CARITA BEAUTY SALON & SPA** invites guests to book appointments by stopping by the Salon Appointment Desk for a personal consultation	**Beauty Salon & Spa (6)**
1:30 - 4:00	**RESERVATIONS FOR OUR SPECIALTY RESTAURANTS (LATITUDES AND SIGNATURES)** Meet the Maître d'Hôtel of Signatures or the Maître d'Hôtel of Latitudes restaurants to book your tables this voyage	Compass Rose Restaurant (4)
2:00 - 4:00	♥ GYM FAMILIARIZATION with Fitness Instructor, Danielle	Gymnasium (6)
2:00 - 4:00	AFTERNOON TEATIME is available	Horizon Lounge (5)
2:30 - 7:00	**THE TRAVEL CONCIERGE OFFICE** is open for reservations and assistance	**Tour Desk (5)**
4:00	**ALL ABOARD! As the *SEVEN SEAS VOYAGER* prepares to sail**	
4:15	**COMPULSORY LIFEBOAT DRILL FOR ALL GUESTS WHO EMBARKED TODAY** *In accordance with International Maritime Law, at the sound of the ship's alarm, you are asked to go to your suite, collect your lifejacket, and proceed to the Muster Station indicated on the back of your suite door. Instructions will be given to you over the public address system. Please be careful not to step on the strap of your lifejacket.*	
4:45 - 5:30	**SAIL-AWAY:** Come and make a sparkling toast to this great adventure to come! Enjoy a glass of bubbly, meet others and enjoy the music of the Seven Seas Orchestra	**Poolside (11)**
5:00	**DEPARTURE: *SEVEN SEAS VOYAGER* sails for Progresso, Mexico**	
5:00	FRIENDS OF BILL W. MEET	Latitudes Restaurant (5)
5:30 - 7:00	**PARK WEST AT SEA:** Meet Art Director Mario and collect a complimentary work or art	**Art Desk (5)**

GOOD EVENING - DRESS CODE: COUNTRY CLUB CASUAL

6:15	**ONEG SHABBAT SERVICE** Guests of the Jewish faith are invited to come and celebrate the Sabbath with **Rabbi Eli Kornreich**	**Constellation Theatre (4)**
6:15 - 7:30	EASY LISTENING MUSIC & SONG with Piano Entertainer Seana-Lee Wood	Horizon Lounge (5)
6:15 - 7:30	SUNDOWN SERENADE with Guitarist Cesar Paucar	Observation Lounge (11)
6:15 - 7:30	COCKTAIL MUSIC & DANCING BEFORE DINNER with Peter and Elisa	Voyager Lounge (4)
6:30	**SOLO TRAVELERS AND UNESCORTED GUESTS** - All guests traveling on their own or unescorted guests traveling with a group, are invited to join Ship's Hostess Louise	**Horizon Lounge (5)**
6:30	**CALLING ALL KIDS AND PARENTS (AGES 5-8 & 9-12) FOR *CLUB MARINER*:** Meet your youth leaders, Lea and Alison, who will introduce their program	**Card / Conference Room (4)**
9:00	**CALLING ALL TEENS (AGES 13-17) FOR *CLUB MARINER*:** Meet your youth leaders, Lea and Alison, who will introduce their program	**Card / Conference Room (4)**
9:00 - 10:00	**THE TRAVEL CONCIERGE OFFICE** is open for reservations and assistance	**Tour Desk (5)**
9:15 - 9:45	AFTER DINNER MELODIES with the music and songs from Peter and Elisa	Voyager Lounge (4)
9:15 - 12:00	CABARET BAR: Featuring the musical talents of Piano Entertainer, Seana-Lee Wood	Horizon Lounge (5)
9:25 - 9:40	DANCING BEFORE THE SHOW with the Seven Seas Orchestra	Constellation Theatre (4)
9:30 - 11:00	**PARK WEST AT SEA:** Meet Art Director Mario and collect a complimentary work or art	**Art Desk (5)**
9:45	**WELCOME ABOARD VARIETY SHOW: "FABULOUS PLACES"** Featuring **THE PETER GREY TERHUNE SINGERS & DANCERS** and a brief introduction of a few staff members presented by **Cruise Director JAMIE LOGAN.** Music provided by the Seven Seas Orchestra	**Constellation Theatre (4)**
10:00 onward	**TUNE INTO THE "VOYAGER TODAY" FOR TOMORROW: A daily program of cruise information and shipboard personalities presented by Cruise Director Jamie Logan**	**TV Channel 4**
10:15 - 12:15	MUSIC AND DANCING with the Peter and Elisa	Voyager Lounge (4)
10:30 - 11:30	EVENING SERENADE: Featuring Guitarist Cesar Paucar	Observation Lounge (11)
12:15 - Late	WELCOME DANCE PARTY: Come along and meet new "party" friends and dance to the music of D.J. Ray	Voyager Lounge (4)

TODAY'S SERVICE HOURS

ART DIRECTOR'S DESK
Deck 5, Main Street
Dial 805 for information & assistance
5:30pm - 7:00pm
9:30pm - 11:00pm

BOUTIQUE
Deck 5, Main Street
5:30pm - 11:00pm

CARITA BEAUTY SALON & SPA
Deck 6 Forward
Variety of Healthy Treatments,
Hair Care and Massages
12 NOON - 8:00 P.M.
Sauna and Steam Bath
12noon - 8:00pm

CLUB.COM
Deck 5
State-of-the-art computer classroom offers e-mail and access to the Internet for a nominal fee. Computer Instructor in attendance:
3:00pm - 6:00pm
9:00pm - 10:00pm

CRUISE CONSULTANT
Deck 5, Atrium
Future Cruise Information

DVD LIBRARY
Deck 5
Latest DVD releases for your viewing pleasure
Open 24-hours a day

DOCTOR'S OFFICE
Deck 3, Forward
Walk-in Surgery
4:00pm - 6:00pm
Dial "0" for Emergency Appointments
All additional medical consultation will be billed to your shipboard account.

FITNESS CENTER
Deck 6, Forward
Well-equipped Gymnasium and Aerobics Area
12noon - 8:00pm
Fitness Instructor is in attendance:
2:00pm - 4:00pm

GUEST RELATIONS MANAGER
Deck 5, Atrium
Dial "0" for information & assistance

LE CASINO
Deck 4
Wide Variety of Slot & Poker Machines, Roulette, Blackjack Tables, Craps, Stud Poker and the newest game 3 Card Poker
Slots: 5:30pm - until...
Tables: 9:00pm - until...

LIBRARY
Deck 6
Wide Selection of Books for your reading pleasure
Open 24-hours a day

PHOTO SHOP & GALLERY
Deck 6 mid-ships starboard side
9:00pm - 11:00pm

POOL & JACUZZI
Deck 11 (weather permitting)

RECEPTION DESK
Deck 5, Atrium
Dial 0 for information & assistance
OPEN 24-HOURS A DAY

SELF SERVICE LAUNDRETTE
Decks 6,7,8,9,&10 Aft
12noon - 10:00pm

SPORTS DECK
Deck 12 (weather permitting)
Shuffle board and paddle tennis courts are available
12noon - 8:00pm

TRAVEL CONCIERGE DESK
Deck 5, Atrium
2:30pm - 7:00pm
9:00pm - 10:00pm

TELEPHONE DIRECTORY

RECEPTION DESK	0
ART DIRECTOR	805
BOUTIQUE	4260
CARITA BEAUTY SALON & SPA	4500
CRUISE CONSULTANT	2480
DOCTOR'S OFFICE	4310
For emergency appointments by dialing "0"	
GIFT SHOP	4380
GUEST RELATIONS MANAGER	4270
INTERNET CAFÉ	1508
ROOM SERVICE	8888
TRAVEL CONCIERGE	2222

In-suite dining is available from the Room Service menu. In addition, items from the Compass Rose Restaurant dinner menu are also available during opening hours and can be viewed on Channel 1 of your in-suite TV.

Reservations for Latitudes and Signatures can be made in the Compass Rose Restaurant, Deck 4, during opening hours.

The following consumer advisory is in compliance with VSP Operations:
Thoroughly cooking beef, eggs, fish, lamb, pork, poultry or shellfish reduces the risk of food-borne illness. Individuals with certain health condition may be at higher risks if these foods are consumed raw or undercooked.

Smoking is not permitted during performances. No beverage service will be available during performance.

BARS & LOUNGES

COFFEE CORNER
SELF SERVICE 24 HOURS

POOL BAR *(weather permitting)*
10:00am - 6:00pm

OBSERVATION LOUNGE
11:00am - 1:00am

HORIZON LOUNGE
11:00am - 1:00am

VOYAGER LOUNGE
5:00pm - until...

CONNOISSEUR CLUB
5:00pm - until...

CONSTELLATION THEATER
9:15pm - 9:45pm

DINING OPTIONS A.M.

SNACK TIME

POOL GRILL	11:00am -	4:00pm
Snack Buffet (weather permitting)		

DINING OPTIONS P.M.

LUNCH IS SERVED

LA VERANDA	12noon	–	3:00pm

AFTERNOON TEA TIME

HORIZON LOUNGE	2:00pm	–	4:00pm

DINNER IS SERVED

COMPASS ROSE RESTAURANT	6:30pm	–	9:00pm
SIGNATURES – *By Reservation**	6:30pm	–	9:00pm
Informal Dress code applies			
LA VERANDA	6:30pm	–	9:00pm
Italian Steakhouse			
LATITUDES – *By Reservation**	7:00pm	–	8:00pm

Creating a fine dining establishment is no simple task. It requires the imagination & creativity of an inspired chef, an ambience that is both tasteful & comfortable & the commitment of a staff totally committed to offering only the best to their discerning clientele. On board *Seven Seas Voyager* we have created, not just one, but five separate restaurants that aspire to these highest of standards. Let us introduce you to them!

Superbly elegant restaurant, located adjacent to the Horizon Lounge on Deck 5, Signatures is one of two restaurants at sea (the other is aboard *Seven Seas Mariner*) operated under the auspices of chefs of the famed Le Cordon Bleu France's pre-eminent culinary academy of Paris. The menu is classic à La Carte of traditional French-accented selections enhanced by an ever changing roster of inspired delectations collected from several separate styles of cuisine pioneered by Le Cordon Bleu chefs. The menu is inspired not merely by classic favorites but also from the latest menus of France's Michelin-starred restaurants & the furthest lands bordering the Seven Seas. Classically French, of course, but also a worldly mélange of regional, nouvelle & fusion fare and therefore we are not able to accommodate alterations from this menu for special requests. This elegant venue is only open for dinner and the Dress Code is always INFORMAL. Reservations can be made today between 1:30 p.m. and 4:00 p.m. in the Compass Rose Restaurant or any other day in the Compass Rose Restaurant during breakfast and lunch hours.

Latitudes

For the first time at sea, an intimate Asian influenced restaurant featuring an open galley where our talented Chefs prepare an Indochine Menu based on Vietnamese food with modern French Cooking techniques.

Please note that in order to ensure the authenticity and quality of the recipes, we are unfortunately unable to accommodate alterations from the menus or special requests. Reservations are available for these events between 7:00 p.m. - 8:00 p.m. Please be prompt. The Restaurant is Located on Deck 5 mid-ship and is open exclusively for dinner. Guests are reminded that smoking is NOT permitted in this venue. Reservations can be made today between 1:30 p.m. and 4:00 p.m. in the Compass Rose Restaurant or any other day in the Compass Rose Restaurant during breakfast and lunch hours.

COMPASS ROSE RESTAURANT

The Compass Rose Restaurant is the principal à la carte restaurant on board *Seven Seas Voyager* and offers guests an all-enveloping range of menus at breakfast, lunch & dinner in an atmosphere that is both warmly inviting & elegant. The choices will range from traditional favorites, to dishes that are at the cutting edge of contemporary cuisine and reflect the cosmopolitan background and training of our Chef de Cuisine. In addition to the myriad of choices that will change on a daily basis the Compass Rose menu will also offer a 'Well Being' menu for the health-conscious and a daily choice of more simply prepared dishes, as well as Vegetarian dishes.

Located on Deck 4 mid-ship, this elegant restaurant offers single, open seating dining, allowing you to dine when, where and with whom you choose. Reservations cannot be accepted, all seating is assigned on a first-come, first-serve basis.

La Veranda

La Veranda offers you a buffet-style breakfast and lunch that you can enjoy either, Al Fresco on it's outside terrace or in air-conditioned comfort inside. In the evenings the port side of La Veranda is transformed into a Mediterranean Bistro or Italian Steakhouse of considerable charm and unique character. Acknowledging the current fascination with the healthy and flavorsome cuisine of the Mediterranean the chefs in La Veranda derive their inspiration for La Veranda's menus from the entire Mediterranean basin with a wide range of antipasto, cheeses and entrées from Spain, France, Italy, Greece, and North Africa. The atmosphere in La Veranda reflects the intrinsic style of the restaurant - elegantly casual and relaxed but with service standards that are uniquely Regent Seven Seas Cruises. La Veranda is located on Deck 11. Reservations are not required nor accepted and the Dress Code is Country Club Casual every evening.

The Pool Grill, located on Deck 11, Aft, is a casual area on deck where you can enjoy a selection of hamburgers, hot dogs with all the trimmings, salads and sandwiches or perhaps wander over to our barbecue where our chef will grill some skewered meat or some succulent freshly caught fish on days at sea. Lunch by the pool is a lovely way to take your noonday repast without breaking up your day. The Pool Grill is open daily, subject of course to the whims of the weather.

Regent Signature Cellars is a private wine club created exclusively for Seven Seas Society Members that gives access to the most sought after premium wines from the world's most exclusive wineries. You are automatically enrolled as a Seven Seas Society Member after taking your first voyage with Regent.

Both on board and from a special website, Members can shop from an assortment of limited production wines from top wineries, special purchases of select high-end wines, and from emerging but little known wineries. While here on board, look for the special Regent Signature Cellars icon on a limited number of wines, and once you are home, look at the website at **www.RegentSignatureCellars.com**.

REGENT signature cellars

Courtesy Regent Seven Seas Cruises

RESIDENSEA MANAGEMENT, LTD.
5200 Blue Lagoon Drive, Suite 790
Miami, Florida 33126
(305) 779-3399; (800) 970-6601
(305) 269-1058 Fax
www.aboardtheworld.com

THE WORLD: entered service 2002; 43,524 G.R.T.; 644' x 97.8'; 657-passenger capacity; 106 apartments and 59 studio apartments and veranda studios; Norwegian officers and international crew; itineraries around the world. (**Category A—Not Rated**)

A residential community at sea (i.e., a condominium-style cruise ship) offering itineraries around the world, it was conceptualized a number of years ago by Knut Kloster, Jr., whose father founded Norwegian Caribbean Line in 1966. After years in the planning stages, his vision became reality when *The World* entered service in March 2002. In 2003, the resident owners took over total ownership of the vessel. *The World* is managed by Miami-based ResidenSea Management, Ltd., which is responsible for the sales, marketing, operations, and administration of the vessel.

Sports deck and pool deck atop ship are the locations of many of the public areas, including the pool and outdoor lounging facilities; a full tennis court; paddle-tennis court; jogging track; golf club with a driving range, putting green, golf simulator, and pro shop; the Mediterranean-style Tides Restaurant; Asian-style East Restaurant; sushi bar; pool grill; and beverage bar.

Immediately below these facilities on decks 7 through 10 are the 106 luxury apartments, ranging in size from 1,106-square feet (two-bedroom, two-bath apartment) to 3,242-square feet (three-bedroom, three-bath apartment). As in any private community, a select number of apartments are available for resale. Those currently available for sale range in price from $1.45 to $7.2 million. Most of the apartments can be rented by cruise passengers at rates starting at $1,300 per night for a studio accommodation for up to two guests and $2,000 per night for a two-bed apartment. Meals, select beverages, gratuities, and port charges are included, and a six-night minimum stay is required.

The 19 one- and two-bedroom studio apartments ranging in size from 675 to 1,011 square feet and 40 veranda studios averaging 340 square feet (for the traditional cruiser) can be found on deck 6, with a few in the higher categories on deck 7. Each includes two twin beds that convert to a queen; a separate sitting area with a writing desk, dressing table, and hair dryer; a marble bath with separate tub and shower; a refrigerator and cocktail cabinet stocked with complimentary beverages; a remote-control television/VCR; a five-disc CD player; and direct-dial telephones with Internet access. Eighty-four percent have private verandas and many have walk-in closets.

In addition to the apartments located on deck 6, there is a library, gallery, Internet café, and the Garden tearoom.

Most of the remaining public areas can be found on deck 5, including the 7,000-square-foot health spa, which includes treatment rooms, a sauna, and a beauty salon operated by Clinique La Prairie; a fitness center with exercise and cardiovascular machines, aerobics classes, and personal trainers; gift boutiques; the main theater for movies and live entertainment; a cardroom; conference facility; fully equipped business center; the Marina restaurant featuring seafood, steaks, and rotisserie specialties; Fredy's Deli, which triples as a gourmet market, street café, and deli; Portraits, the most upscale dining venue offering French-fusion cuisine with themes highlighting the ship's destinations; the casino; Cigar Club; Quantum Night Club; and several lounges.

On the lowest passenger deck, deck 4, there is a medical center and retractable marina and pool.

Dinner is offered in the various venues between 7 P.M. and 10:30 P.M., and guests can dine whenever they wish and with whomever they wish. All meals, except those in Portraits, are included for cruise guests. Portraits is an á la carte restaurant where guests order from a set menu with dishes of varying prices. Evening entertainment is limited and there are no production shows or cabaret entertainers as on traditional cruise ships. Daytime activities include lectures, classes in dance, navigation, language, cooking, arts and crafts, music, computers, and photography, as well as tea service.

Representatives of the owners advise that the average occupancy is 200 residents and guests, resulting in a high service staff-to-passenger ratio. Central to *The World*'s unique concept is the flexibility afforded to residents and guests. Passengers can disembark the ship at any port and then rejoin at another, allowing extended visits ashore. A concierge is available to help with all shoreside arrangements.

ROYAL CARIBBEAN INTERNATIONAL
1050 Caribbean Way
Miami, Florida 33132
(800) 327-6700
(800) 722-5329 Fax
www.royalcaribbean.com

ENCHANTMENT OF THE SEAS: entered service 1997; lengthened 2005; 81,500 G.R.T.; 989' x 105.6'; 2,730-passenger capacity (2,252 double occupancy); 1,126 cabins; international officers and crew; 4-, 5-, and 6-night cruises in western Caribbean from Fort Lauderdale. (C-14)*

FREEDOM OF THE SEAS, LIBERTY OF THE SEAS, and *INDEPENDENCE OF THE SEAS:* entered service 2006, 2007, and 2008, respectively; 160,000 G.R.T.; 1,112' x 184'; 4,375-passenger capacity (3,634 double occupancy); 1,800 cabins; international officers and crew; 7-night eastern and western Caribbean cruises from Miami and Port Canaveral; *Independence of the Seas* offers 6- and 8-night Caribbean itineraries from Fort Lauderdale. (C-32)*

 +

GRANDEUR OF THE SEAS: entered service 1996; 74,000 G.R.T.; 916' x 105'; 2,446-passenger capacity (1,950 double occupancy); 975 cabins; international officers and crew; Caribbean cruises from Tampa during winter and 10- and 11-night Caribbean cruises and 5-night Bermuda cruises from Baltimore and Norfolk during summer. (C-14)*

LEGEND OF THE SEAS: entered service 1995; 70,000 G.R.T.; 867' x 106'; 2,074-passenger capacity (1,804 double occupancy); 902 cabins; international officers and crew; cruises in Asia and the Mediterranean. (C-17)*

MAJESTY OF THE SEAS: entered service 1992; renovated 2007; 73,941 G.R.T.; 880' x 106'; 2,744-passenger capacity (2,350 double occupancy); 1,178 cabins; international officers and crew; 3- and 4-night cruises to the Bahamas from Miami. (C-4)*

MONARCH OF THE SEAS: entered service 1991; renovated 2003; 73,941 G.R.T.; 880' x 106'; 2,744-passenger capacity (2,390 double occupancy); 1,195 cabins; international officers and crew; 3- and 4-night cruises to Bahamas from Port Canaveral. (C-4)*

⭐⭐⭐⭐

OASIS OF THE SEAS: entered service 2009; 220,000 G.R.T.; 1,180' x 151'; 5,400-passenger capacity double occupancy; 2,700 cabins; international officers and crew; 7-night eastern and western Caribbean cruises from Fort Lauderdale. **(Category C—Not Rated)**

RADIANCE OF THE SEAS, BRILLIANCE OF THE SEAS, SERENADE OF THE SEAS, and JEWEL OF THE SEAS: entered service 2001, 2002, 2003, and 2004, respectively; 90,090 G.R.T.; 962' x 106'; 2,501-passenger capacity (2,112 double occupancy); 1,056 cabins; international officers and crew; *Radiance* offers cruises to Alaska, Mexico, and South America; *Brilliance* offers cruises in the Mediterranean during summer and to the Caribbean and Panama Canal during winter; *Serenade* sails to the southern Caribbean from San Juan during winter and to Alaska and Panama Canal during summer; *Jewel* offers European cruises during summer, Panama Canal cruises during winter, and Canada/ New England cruises during fall. (C-14)*

⭐⭐⭐⭐⭐

RHAPSODY OF THE SEAS: entered service 1997; 78,491 G.R.T.; 915' x 105.6'; 2,435-passenger capacity (1,998 double occupancy); 999 cabins; international officers and crew; cruises in Hawaii, Alaska, and Australia/New Zealand. (C-14)*

⭐⭐⭐⭐⭐

SPLENDOUR OF THE SEAS: entered service 1996; 70,000 G.R.T.; 867' x 105'; 2,074-passenger capacity (1,804 double occupancy); 902 cabins; international officers and crew; South American and Mediterranean cruises. (C-17)*

⭐⭐⭐⭐⭐

VISION OF THE SEAS: entered service 1998; 78,491 G.R.T.; 915' x 105.6'; 2,435-passenger capacity (2,000 double occupancy); 1,000 cabins; international officers and crew; cruises in South America and Europe. (C-14)*

⭐⭐⭐⭐⭐

VOYAGER OF THE SEAS, EXPLORER OF THE SEAS, ADVENTURE OF THE SEAS, NAVIGATOR OF THE SEAS, and *MARINER OF THE SEAS:* entered service 1999, 2000, 2001, 2002, and 2003, respectively; 142,000 G.R.T.; 1,021' x 157.5'; 3,838-passenger capacity (3,114 double occupancy); 1,557 cabins; international officers and crew; 7-night cruises in Caribbean from Miami, San Juan, and New York as well as Bermuda cruises from New York; *Mariner* offers 7-night sailings to Mexico from Los Angeles and cruises in Europe during summer. (C-26)*

☆ ☆ ☆ ☆ ☆ +

(Medical Facilities: The wheelchair-accessible cabins [noted by *] are indicated for each ship after its listing above. For all Royal Caribbean ships, the following applies: P-2, CLS, MS; N-3; CM; PD; EKG; TC; PO; EPC; OX; WC; ICU; X; M; LJ.)

Note: Actual passenger capacity on all ships will vary and, on most cruises, is less when there are only two passengers in a cabin. Thus, doubling the number of cabins is reflective of usual passenger capacity.

These ships are rated in 11 separate categories in the second half of chapter 14.

Royal Caribbean International was founded in 1969 by three Norwegian shipping companies. In the 1990s, it became a publicly held company traded on the New York and Oslo stock exchanges under "RCL."

Its first vessel, *Song of Norway,* entered service in 1970 (sold in 1996), followed by *Nordic Prince* in 1971 (sold in early 1995), *Sun Viking* in 1972 (sold in 1998), and *Song of America* in 1982 (sold in 1998). All four ships were built in Finland and designed for cruising the Caribbean. The first of Royal Caribbean's new breed of ships, *Sovereign of the Seas,* entered service in 1988, followed by *Nordic Empress* (renamed *Empress of the Seas*) in 1990, *Monarch of the Seas* in 1991, and *Majesty of the Seas* in 1992. Commencing with *Legend of the Seas* in 1995, Royal Caribbean introduced its *Vision*-class fleet with many improvements and innovations from prior vessels. *Splendour of the Seas* and *Grandeur of the Seas* followed in 1996, along with *Enchantment of the Seas* and *Rhapsody of the Seas* in 1997 and *Vision of the Seas* in 1998. The first of its mammoth 3,114-passenger, 142,000-ton *Voyager*-class (formerly *Eagle*-class) ships, *Voyager of the Seas,* entered service in 1999, followed by *Explorer of the Seas* in 2000, *Adventure of the Seas* in 2001, *Navigator of the Seas* in 2002, and *Mariner of the Seas* in 2003. Four 90,000-ton *Radiance*-class ships came on line over the next few years. The first of this genre, *Radiance of the Seas,* entered service in the spring of 2001, followed by *Brilliance of the Seas* in 2002, *Serenade of the Seas* in 2003, and *Jewel of the Seas* in 2004. *Freedom of the Seas,* at 160,000 tons with a maximum passenger capacity of 4,370, the first of the *Freedom*-class vessels, entered service in the spring of 2006, followed by *Liberty of the Seas* in 2007 and *Independence of the Seas* in 2008. Most recently, the 220-ton, 5,400-passenger *Oasis of the Seas* made its debut in December of 2009, by far the largest cruise ship ever built. A sister ship, *Allure of the Seas,* will enter service in late 2010.

In June 1997, Royal Caribbean's parent company, Royal Caribbean Cruises, Ltd. (RCCL), acquired the highly acclaimed Celebrity Cruises, and in 2006 RCCL acquired Pullmantur, a Spanish cruise line; however, each line continues to operate as a separate brand.

The company also launched a new cruise brand, CDF Croisieres de France, tailored for the French market. The first ship for the new brand, *Bleu de France* (formerly *Europa* and *Holiday Dream*), began sailing in May 2008, following a refit. During the warmer months she sails from Marseille in the Mediterranean and during the winter from La Romana, Dominican Republic, in the Caribbean. RCCL also entered into a joint venture with TUI AG, which services the German market. The new TUI Cruises commenced operations in 2009 with one ship, the *Galaxy* from Celebrity Cruises. Two new builds are planned for 2011 and 2012. The intention is for TUI Cruises to position itself as a premium cruise line between such luxury ships as Hapag-Lloyd's *Europa* and Peter Deilmann's *Deutschland* and economy, mass-market ships of Aida Cruises.

Cruise fares vary slightly from ship to ship and for different itineraries. The brochure price for the least expensive inside cabin on all the ships goes for about $190 per person per day, graduating to $250 to $320 per day for an average cabin without a veranda and $450 to $550 per day per person for a deluxe stateroom or mini-suite with a veranda. The top-of-the-line royal suite on each ship will set you back from $650 to $1,000 per day per person. Add about $36 per day per person ($250 per week) for the air-sea packages. Additional parties sharing cabins pay about $100 per day. Prices on the *Oasis*-class, *Freedom*-class, *Voyager*-class, and *Radiance*-class ships run slightly higher, and discounts (ranging from 20 to 33 percent) are available for early bookings (nine to 12 months in advance). However, based on special promotions and other discounts, prices generally are often somewhat lower.

Unlike most cruise lines, there are numerous suites, staterooms, and cabins in each price category, and the gradual increase in price from one category to the next buys you more space and not just a more desirable location.

In recent years, Royal Caribbean has expanded its marketing program throughout the world, visiting more than 250 ports of call worldwide and providing daily programs, shore-excursion lists, and other on-board material in Spanish, German, Italian, French, and Portuguese. As a result, the line has attracted a more international mix of passengers. The number of non-U.S./Canadian cruisers will vary between 10 and 33 percent, depending upon the itinerary and port of embarkation.

In 1988, the 73,192-ton *Sovereign of the Seas* joined the fleet as the largest cruise ship then in service. Sister ships *Monarch of the Seas* and *Majesty of the Seas* followed in 1991 and 1992, respectively. These ships are capable of carrying 2,773 passengers (2,292 double occupancy) in 1,146 cabins, 722 of which are located on the outside of the ships. In 2008, *Sovereign of the Seas* was transferred to Pullmantur. *Monarch of the Seas* and *Majesty of the Seas* ship designs are similar to *Sovereign of the Seas,* with several innovations and improvements, including the addition of balconies in 62 of the suites and superior staterooms. In 2003, *Monarch of the Seas* and in 2007, *Majesty of the Seas* were renovated, adding expanded dining options, new entertainments, upgraded spa/fitness areas, and three teen-only locations, and the staterooms and bathrooms were refurbished, including upgraded bedding.

At the very top of the ship, 11 stories above sea level, is the panoramic 360-degree Viking Crown Lounge, accessible by special lift. Sorrento's Pizza, Johnny Rockets, and the Mast Bar are on deck 12. The entrance to the Windjammer Marketplace is below on deck 11, and this restaurant is the site for breakfast, lunch, and dinner buffets. Also on deck 11 are two swimming pools, a bar, the sports deck, and a teen area with three teen-only areas, i.e., the Living Room, Fuel, and the Back Deck. The fitness center and day spa are on deck 10, and immediately below is the Adventure Ocean children's center with video games and a new Aqua Tots and Aqua Babies program. On deck 8 is the Voltage Lounge. The twin-level Follies Lounge on deck 7 seats 1,050. In addition to the upper level of the main show lounge, deck 7 includes Boleros for dancing, a conference center, and business service facility. The upper level of the Windjammer Café and the Mast Bar are on compass deck. On deck 5 is the first level of the main show lounge, the casino, the Schooner Bar, Lattétudes, and the boutiques of the Centurm. The purser's desk and Mirage dining room are on deck 4, and the Illusions dining room is on deck 3. During the extensive renovation a Johnny Rockets, a pizzeria, an ice cream bar, and a Latin lounge were added.

Nordic Empress, at 48,563 tons and accommodating 1,600 passengers double occupancy (or 2,020 when all berths are filled), entered service during the summer of 1990. In 2004, she underwent a renovation and her name was changed to *Empress of the Seas.* In 2008 she was transferred to Pullmantur.

In May 1995, the 69,130-ton, 2,076-passenger *Legend of the Seas,* the first of the *Vision*-class ships, entered service with emphasis on windows overlooking the sea, a seven-deck atrium topped off by a two-deck skylight attached to a 250-seat observation lounge/nightclub, facilities that include an 18-hole miniature golf course, a state-of-the-art spa and fully equipped fitness center, a 118-foot swimming pool, an indoor-outdoor pool with sliding-glass roof, special youth and teen facilities, and public areas, with numerous innovations and improvements over the line's prior vessels. Twenty-five percent of the staterooms and suites have private verandas, and all cabins convert to queen-bed configurations. In 1996, the sister ship, *Splendour of the Seas,* joined the fleet. *Grandeur of the Seas,* which entered service in late 1996, *Enchantment of the Seas* and *Rhapsody of the Seas,* which entered service in 1997, and *Vision of the Seas,* in 1998, are all somewhat similar to *Legend of the Seas* and boast extremely exquisite designs, fabrics, and artwork.

These are attractively furnished ships. Passengers can appreciate the elegant main lobbies, stairwells, and wide corridors with their abundance of wood, brass, marble, glass, and exquisite sculptures and artwork; the spacious elevators and public washrooms; the unique casinos; the lavish spa area with its numerous facilities; the opulent shopping plaza; the selection of theme lounges and bars; the lovely, comfortable two-story dining rooms and show lounges; giant panoramic observation lounges; special facilities for children and teens; and gigantic lido-pool complexes. A standard cabin is quite adequate and includes a small sitting area, two single beds or one queen bed, a private safe, a remote-control television, a mirrored makeup area, a refrigerator, and a small bathroom. All outside staterooms and suites on decks 7 and 8 are spacious and include nice-sized balconies. The 21 grand suites, owner's suites, Royal Family suites, and one Royal Suite on deck 8 have larger sitting areas and balconies, refrigerator/minibars, and beautiful marble bathrooms with double vanities, tubs, showers, and robes. All accommodations on *Rhapsody of the Seas* and *Vision of the Seas* are a bit larger. On all of the *Vision*-class ships, the smallest inside cabin is at least 135 square feet. Average outside cabins without balconies range from 153 to 193 square feet, staterooms and regular suites with balconies from 241 to 630 square feet, and the Royal Suites over 1,100 square feet.

In 2005, *Enchantment of the Seas* was stretched, adding a 73-foot midsection; 151 additional staterooms, many with balconies; two 75-foot-long suspension bridges spanning the pool deck, and additional pool/lido areas that include a splash deck with interactive fountains for kids and four bungee trampolines. Dining attractions include a new coffee and ice-cream shop serving Ben and Jerry's ice cream and Seattle's Best coffee, Chops Grill specialty restaurant, and additional food islands in the buffet restaurant offering a more diverse range of items from different regions of the world. There is also an enhanced shopping area. The expanded spa facility added additional treatment rooms but eliminated the sauna and steam rooms. She offers four-, five-, and six-night voyages to the Caribbean from Fort Lauderdale.

All of Royal Caribbean's 69,000+-ton ships offer the same caliber of cruise experience; i.e., they are large ships lavishly furnished and boasting a multitude of activities, facilities, and entertainment options. The dining rooms feature a variety of items nightly with multi-course, rotating menus and concerned service. The Windjammer Cafés offer a casual dining alternative for all three meals, with a good selection of choices.

In November 1999, the 142,000-ton *Voyager of the Seas,* at that time the world's largest cruise ship, arrived in its home port of Miami, offering year-around cruises to the western Caribbean. Although the facilities, entertainment, and activities are similar to Royal Caribbean's other vessels, her increased size permits vastly expanded facilities and features. Public areas include the Royal Promenade, an open, four-deck atrium in the interior of the ship lined with a wide selection of shops, bars, cafés, and spontaneous entertainment; the 1,350-seat state-of-the-art theater, spanning three decks and offering nightly production shows and guest artists; the 900-seat Studio B, an ice rink featuring ice-skating by day and professional ice shows in the evening; The Vault, a unique disco off the Royal Promenade; youth facilities that include an enviable variety of video games, a teen nightclub, a children's water slide, outdoor games, supervised programs for youngsters three to 17, and more; a conference center; a fully stocked library with an abundance of computers and e-mail facilities for guests; the Spa, an upscale facility as luxurious as the finest resort spas, offering numerous beauty and body treatments, steam, sauna, hydrotherapy pool, aerobics classes, and a large, well-equipped gym, one of the most impressive at sea; unparalleled outdoor sport options including basketball, paddleball, volleyball, golf simulators, an attractive vegetated, nine-hole putting course, a rock-climbing wall, an in-line skating track, a jogging track, and several swimming pools and spas; a helipad to accommodate helicopters for emergency medical services; a fully equipped medical facility with two physicians and three nurses; a most impressive $12-million art collection disbursed throughout the ship; a chapel; and numerous lounges including a jazz club; and an observation lounge.

Nine hundred thirty-nine of the 1,557 cabins and suites spread throughout the ship have ocean views and 707 have balconies. One hundred thirty-eight of the 618 inside cabins, referred to as "promenade view" staterooms, have bowed windows overlooking the Royal Promenade, the unique four-story central area in the interior of the ship. Twenty-six staterooms are wheelchair accessible, and four cabins can accommodate families up to eight persons. Every accommodation includes twin beds that convert to a queen, a sitting area, a vanity area with a hair dryer, a refrigerated mini-bar, a radio, an interactive television, and a bathroom with screen-enclosed showers. The majority of cabins measure 160 square feet; the superior outside cabins come in at 202 feet including a balcony; and a variety of suites range from 277 to 506 feet, with the elaborate Royal Suite (with grand piano) at 1,088 feet.

The immense, yet extremely elegant, main dining room spans three decks and is connected by a dramatic grand staircase. For a $20 service charge, 88 passengers can reserve tables for dinner at the tastefully decorated Portofino, the Italian specialty restaurant. The 310-seat Windjammer Café and the 454-seat Island Grill, located near the pool area, offer buffet breakfasts and lunches and casual buffet dinners with specials from the dining rooms. Johnny Rockets, the very popular 1950s-style diner, is open around-the-clock. The sidewalk café/brasserie on the Royal Promenade is the place to enjoy a continental breakfast and specialty coffees, as well as pizza, pastries, and finger sandwiches throughout the day and evening. In addition, there is an ice-cream/yogurt parlor; a champagne bar; sports bar; the English-style pub; the Connoisseur Club selling cigars, brandies, and cordials; and 24-hour in-cabin room service.

Sisters to the *Voyager of the Seas*, *Explorer of the Seas* entered service in 2000,

Adventure of the Seas in 2001, *Navigator of the Seas* in 2002, and *Mariner of the Seas* in 2003. In addition to aesthetic and structural differences in the public rooms, *Explorer of the Seas* is the first cruise ship to boast a working oceanographic and atmospheric laboratory with research being conducted by government and academic researchers. *Navigator of the Seas* and *Mariner of the Seas,* the most recent ships to come on line, have added an interactive wine bar, expanded venues for teens, a Southeast Asian/fusion buffet restaurant adjacent to the casual multi-station Windjammer Café, a Ben & Jerry's ice-cream parlor, Chops Grill Steak House, Bolero's (a Latin jazz bar), and enhanced balconies.

The five *Voyager*-class behemoths are excellent choices for family vacations in that they offer the greatest range of activities and facilities at sea and are intended to appeal to every age group. A good number of staterooms can comfortably accommodate families, and the plethora of dining options described above are diverse enough to appeal to every family member. The demographic makeup of the passengers is quite eclectic, with passengers from diverse parts of the world, children, and young adults making up a good percentage of the population.

Although many of Royal Caribbean's competitors extol the virtues of their private islands, Labadee is the most scenic private beach destination, offering the best (and the most) beaches for swimming and the best variety of watersports. The facility added a pirate-themed water playground in 2005.

For the 21st century, Royal Caribbean introduced four 90,090-ton ships, which they refer to as *Radiance* class. Eighty percent of the accommodations have sea views, 60 percent with balconies. The first ship of this class, *Radiance of the Seas,* entered service in 2001; the second, *Brilliance of the Seas,* in 2002; the third, *Serenade of the Seas,* in 2003; and the fourth, *Jewel of the Seas,* in 2004. These elegant and beautiful ships feature nine-deck atrium lobbies and glass elevators that travel 12 decks facing out to the sea, and they are propelled by gas and steam turbine power rather than the more traditional diesel and diesel electric. These are the most luxuriously appointed of the line's cruise ships.

The smallest inside cabin measures 165 square feet and an average veranda cabin 179 square feet with a 41-square-foot veranda. The largest suite measures 1,001 square feet with a 215-square-foot veranda and includes a grand piano, wet bar, 42-inch flat-screen television with stereo and VCR, a whirlpool bath, and steam shower. Although accommodations in all categories (as well as bathrooms in the non-suites) are not particularly large, all are beautifully decorated and contain every necessary amenity.

The elegant two-level main dining room serves breakfast and lunch in an open seating and dinner in two seatings. Alternative dining includes Chops Grill, serving steaks, chops, and grilled entrées from an open kitchen, and Portofino, an upscale Italian restaurant. Both exact a $25 per person surcharge. In addition, Seaview Café replaces Johnny Rockets and features hamburgers, fish and chips, pizza, salads, and sandwiches. The Windjammer buffet restaurant serves all three meals and snacks both indoors and outdoors. The buffet restaurants on these ships have a more convenient floor plan with more service stations and better offerings than those I found in the buffet restaurants on many other ships.

Facilities aboard these ships include a state-of-the-art, attractive 15,500+-square-foot spa/fitness center; a rock-climbing wall; a golf simulator and nine-hole miniature golf course; a basketball court; a jogging track; an Internet café; a three-level theater for productions; a movie theater; a casino; a billiard club; card rooms; the Viking Crown Lounge, an observation lounge by day and a combination nightclub and disco at night; a library; a champagne bar; a conference center; and numerous other bars and lounges.

As on all of Royal Caribbean's ships, the youth program and facilities are outstanding, with different levels of activities depending on age. The age groupings are from three to five, six to eight, nine to 11, 12 to 14, and 15 to 17. Facilities include a computer lab, play stations, video games, children's pool with a water slide, and a special teen disco/coffeehouse. Activities for children are also offered on Royal Caribbean's private beach and babysitting services are available. In 2005, the cruise line entered into an arrangement with Fisher-Price, Inc. to provide interactive educational programs for children six months to 36 months old, along with their parents, known as Aqua Babies (six months to 18 months) and Aqua Tots (18 months to three years). This includes special in-cabin TV programs as well. Royal Caribbean offers some of the best all-around facilities and boasts one of the best all-around children's programs in the industry.

Royal Caribbean and its sister line, Celebrity Cruises, entered into a joint venture with Cingular Wireless Maritime Communication Network to provide a service to allow guests to receive phone calls on their own cell phones at their personal numbers while in international waters. The service was initiated on *Majesty of the Seas, Navigator of the Seas,* and Celebrity Cruises' *Summit* and was thereafter extended to all the ships of both fleets. The two cruise lines also offer an online check-in program throughout both fleets, greatly speeding up the check-in process upon boarding ship.

In 2006, *Freedom of the Seas,* the first of the *Freedom*-class ships—accommodating up to 3,634 passengers (double occupancy 4,375 with every berth full), with a tonnage of approximately 160,000 G.R.T—came on line. *Liberty of the Seas,* a sister ship, entered service in 2007, and *Independence of the Seas,* a third sister ship entered service in 2008. *Freedom of the Seas'* combined pool area is 43 percent larger than on *Voyager*-class ships and features an H2O Zone with innovative water attractions, an adults-only, jungle-themed solarium with cantilevered whirlpools that hang out 12 feet from the sides of the ship and a pool with piped-in underwater music, a dedicated sports pool, and a main pool area that transforms in the evening into an open-air nightclub. The 1,215-square-foot Presidential Family Suite, with an 810-foot patio area with an outdoor Jacuzzi and private bar, can sleep up to 14 people. Also, there is a 1,406-square-foot Royal Suite with a 377-foot balcony, and 32 accommodations are wheelchair accessible. The ship also features the first boxing ring at sea. She offers seven-night western Caribbean itineraries.

In December of 2009, the *Oasis of the Seas,* the first of the 220,000-ton, 5,400-passenger ships from Aker Yards in Finland, entered service, to be followed in 2010 by *Allure of the Seas.* The ships feature numerous innovations never seen previously on cruise ships, including a unique neighborhood concept with seven distinct areas. Central Park is an indoor/outdoor promenade area planted with tropical foliage, flowers, grass, shrubs, and trees surrounded by dining and drinking venues and shops. Included in the seven dining venues are the Chops Grill and 150 Central Park. An area for families is the Boardwalk, with a Coney Island theme, re-creating the atmosphere of a seaside-pier entertainment area. The centerpiece is the first carousel at sea. Lining the sides of the Boardwalk are a candy store, an ice-cream parlor, a Johnny Rockets diner, the Seafood Shack, teen and children's retail stores, and a temporary tattoo parlor. Suspended above is a zip line giving passengers a ride 82 feet above the Boardwalk atrium. Royal Promenade is an expanded version of the shopping mall found on other Royal Caribbean ships and includes numerous cafes, pubs, and bars. The Pool and Sports zone includes the largest swimming pool at sea: 21.9 feet wide by 51.6 feet long and 17.9 feet deep, with two diving towers. At night a music and light show features hundreds of nozzles shooting water 65 feet into the air. Other neighborhoods include the Vitality at Sea Spa and Fitness Center, the Youth Zone, and 6 Entertainment Place.

Accommodations include bi-level cabins, urban-style loft suites, two-bedroom/two-bath Aqua Theater suites, and staterooms with balconies facing Central Park and the Boardwalk. There is an increased range of dining venues located in the various neighborhoods.

In 2005, the cruise line entered into a partnership with CBS TV to provide an assortment of CBS TV programs on stateroom TVs on all 20 ships.

In 2005 and 2006, Royal Caribbean instituted a program that allows disembarking passengers to check in for their same-day flights and to check their luggage right on the ship, thereby avoiding long lines at the airport. This service, which costs from $10 to $20 per passenger depending upon the port, is available for ships arriving at Fort Lauderdale, Miami, San Juan, Seattle, and Vancouver.

In 2009, the cruise line introduced enhanced service and amenities for suite passengers throughout the fleet. Suite passengers receive a special gold "sea pass" card allowing for priority check-in and disembarkation, admittance to the Concierge club, special suite amenities, the ability to order off a full dining-room menu in their suites, and reserved seating poolside and in the theaters.

With all of the new builds, Royal Caribbean will continue to expand its itineraries around the world. Caribbean cruises depart from 10 different ports, including Miami, Fort Lauderdale, Port Canaveral, Tampa, New Orleans, Galveston, San Juan, Boston, New York, and Baltimore.

Breaking from a long tradition of assigned table dining, in 2009 the cruise line provided an option they refer to as "my time dining," allowing passengers to dine wherever and with whomever they wish during normal dining hours. In addition, "my family dining" offers expedient 40-minute dining during the first seating in the main dining room for the benefit of children ages three to 11.

Strong Points:

Beautifully appointed megaships offering spacious, attractive accommodations, a large variety of facilities, activities, and entertainment as well as fine service and enjoyable dining experiences. The *Oasis*-class, *Voyager*-class, *Freedom*-class, and *Radiance*-class ships are awesome with exquisite décor and incredible appointments. Offering some of the most activities, entertainment, and facilities at sea makes them ideal for families of all ages. Royal Caribbean is a very strong competitor in the mass cruise market, with a wide appeal to a diverse population of cruisers.

Enchantment of the Seas, *courtesy Royal Caribbean International*

Explorer of the Seas, *courtesy Royal Caribbean International*

Voyager of the Seas, *courtesy Royal Caribbean International*

Voyager of the Seas, *courtesy Royal Caribbean International*

Explorer of the Seas, *Children's Program, courtesy Royal Caribbean International*

CHEF'S SUGGESTIONS

Smoked Salmon Duet, Salmon paté in a delicious brioche crust, accompanied by a smoked salmon flower filled with caviar sour cream

Chilled Lemon Soup, With mint leaves

Red: St. Emilion, Bordeaux, France

Salade Melange, Crisp mesclun greens, bean sprouts, asparagus tips and radishes, served with French dressing

Veal Cordon Bleu, Thinly sliced veal scaloppine filled with ham and cheese, breaded then sautéed, served with roasted potatoes, carrots Vichy and sugar snap peas

Champagne: Deutz Champagne, Brut Classic, France

Explorer Chocolate Cake, Rich flourless chocolate cake served with whipped cream and chocolate shavings, complemented by liqueur-soaked berries

SHIPSHAPE

With today's active lifestyles and increased nutritional awareness in mind, our Chefs create a daily-changing ShipShape menu that is low in cholesterol, salt and fat yet highly filling and flavorful.

Onion Soup, Caramelized sweet onions simmered in beef broth

Salade Melange, Crisp mesclun greens, bean sprouts, asparagus tips and radishes, served with fat-free country Dijon dressing

Lobster Tail Royale, Broiled lobster tail complemented by a light citrus sauce, steamed potatoes and broccoli florettes

Low-fat Apple in a Jacket, A Granny Smith apple filled with raisins and cinnamon, enveloped in a light puff pastry crust, baked to a golden brown

DAILY SELECTION

Caesar Salad
Broiled Fillet of Norwegian Salmon
Grilled Chicken Breast with Rosemary
Mashed potatoes, baked potato, rice and vegetable of the day

BEVERAGES

Regular or decaffeinated coffee
Tea   Herbal Tea   Hot Chocolate
Milk   Soft Drinks   Juices

In an effort to support worldwide conservation measures, ice water is served upon request only.

WINE

Our Sommelier is available to assist you in choosing from our extensive wine list.

These fine selections are recommended and chosen specifically for today's menu

Chef's Dinner

FRESHLY BAKED BREADS

French Flute • Ciabatta

STARTERS

Sun-Ripened Pineapple Delight, A carved pineapple wedge surrounded by a tequila fruit compote

White: Puligny-Montrachet, Burgundy, France

Smoked Salmon Duet, Salmon paté in a delicious brioche crust, accompanied by a smoked salmon flower filled with caviar sour cream

Escargots Bourguignonne, Baked snails served in a sizzling garlic herb butter

SOUPS

Onion Soup, Caramelized sweet onions simmered in beef broth, topped with thinly sliced Gruyere cheese toast

Cream of Asparagus, Garnished with slivered almonds

Chilled Lemon Soup, With mint leaves

SALAD

Salade Melange, Crisp mesclun greens, bean sprouts, asparagus tips and radishes

French dressing
Hazelnut vinaigrette
Fat-free country Dijon dressing

PASTA

Garlic Rigatoni, Al dente pasta tossed with roasted garlic cream sauce, finished with Parmesan cheese

ENTRÉES

Lobster Tail Royale, Broiled lobster tail complemented by a flavorful garlic parsley butter, vegetable rice pilaf and broccoli florettes

White: Puligny-Montrachet, Burgundy, France

Veal Cordon Bleu, Thinly sliced veal scaloppine filled with ham and cheese, breaded then sautéed, served with roasted potatoes, carrots Vichy and sugar snap peas

Filet Mignon, A tender filet of beef prepared to your taste, perched on a crouton, accompanied by shallot-red wine sauce, croquette potatoes, sautéed spinach and grilled tomato

Red: St. Emilion, Bordeaux, France

Crêpes Florentine, Two delicious crêpes with a light spinach-and-cheese filling, sprinkled with Swiss cheese, served with a vegetable medley

DESSERTS

Your Waiter will present you with our menu of specially selected desserts

Courtesy Royal Caribbean International

D A I L Y   P L A N N E R

Explorer of the Seas

Compass

Day TWO

At Sea
Sunday, January 14, 2001

Dining Schedule and Afternoon Snack

BREAKFAST

6:00 am–7:30 am	Early Bird Breakfast, Windjammer Café	Deck 11
7:30 am–11:30 am	Breakfast, Windjammer Café	Deck 11
8:00 am–10:00 am	Magellan Dining Room	Deck 3

LUNCH

12 noon–2:00 pm	Magellan Dining Room	Deck 3
11:30 am–3:00 pm	Windjammer Café	Deck 11

DINNER   **FORMAL**

6:00 pm	Main Seating, All Dining Rooms	Decks 3, 4, 5
8:30 pm	Second Seating, All Dining Rooms	Decks 3, 4, 5

LIVE Dining Room Entertainment
Provided by the Magic Strings and Pianist Jim McDonough
(6:00 pm-7:30 pm and 8:30 pm-10:00 pm, All Dining Rooms)

6:30 pm–9:00 pm	Casual Dining, Island Grill	Deck 11

PORTOFINO

	Reservation Required,	
	$20 Covercharge per person applies	Deck 11
Reservations:	Please dial 3332	
	Minimum service time 2 hours	
	Guests 13 years and older are welcome	

Dress Suggestion: Smart Casual
Cancellation with less than 24 hours notice will be charged on your SuperCharge with a fee of $20.⁰⁰ per person

SNACKS

3:00 pm–5:00 pm	Windjammer Café	Deck 11
11:30 am–1:00 am	Johnny Rockets	Deck 12
	(Reserved for Youth Dining Program 6:00 pm–7:00 pm)	
24 hours	Café Promenade	Deck 5
12 midnight–1:00 am	Late Night snacks, Aquarium Bar, Schooner Bar	
	Casino Bar	Deck 4

Café Promenade will close temporarily during the Captain's Champagne Reception

Corkage Fee - An amount of $8.00 per bottle opened is charge to guests bringing their own wine & champagne into any of our dining areas to be consumed at meal times. Please note: No open liquor bottles will be permitted to be brought into the dining areas or any public spaces.

Morning Activities

24 hours	Cards & Games available,	
	Seven Hearts Card Room	Deck 14
6:00 am–8:00 pm	ShipShape Center Open	Deck 12
7:30 am–Sharp	Walk-A-Thon, Sky Bar	Deck 12
8:00 am	Stretch Class, Sports Court	Deck 13
8:00 am–8:00 pm	Beauty Salon & Spa Open	Deck 12
8:30 am	Fun Fitness, Sports Court	Deck 13
9:00 am	Step Aerobics, ShipShape Center	Deck 11
9:00 am–4:00 pm	SeaTrek Dive Program, Dive Shop	Deck 11
9:00 am	Daily Trivia, Library	Deck 7
9:00 am–Sharp	Walk-A-Thon, Sky Bar	Deck 12
9:00 am–5:00 pm	Explorations! Desk, (Questions Only)	Deck 5
9:00 am–11:00 pm	Boutiques of The Royal Promenade Open	Deck 5
9:00 am–Late	Casino Royale Slots Open	Deck 4
9:00 am–11:00 pm	Photo Gallery & Shop Open	Deck 3
9:00 am–12 noon	Business Services/Future Cruises Center Open	Deck 6
9:00 am	Advanced Free Skate, Studio "B"	Deck 3
	(Register 8:45 am)	
9:00 am–12 noon	Tuxedo Rentals, Royal Promenade	Deck 5
9:30 am	Non-Denominational Church Service, Chapel	Deck 15
9:30 am–11:30 am	**Planet Ice Tickets Available**, Studio B Lobby	Deck 3

Explorer of the Seas

Morning Activities cont...

10:00 am–LATE	Casino Royale Tables Open	Deck 4
10:00 am	Talent Show Sign Up, Library	Deck 7
10:00 am	Explorations Talk, Studio "B"	Deck 3
10:00 am	Jewish Sabbath Service Sign-Up, Library	Deck 7
10:00 am	Detox for Weight Loss Seminar, ShipShape Center	Deck 11
10:15 am–10:30 am	Sit To Be Fit, Maharajas Lounge	Deck 5
10:15 am–10:45 am	Cruise Crafts, Seven Hearts	Deck 14
10:30 am	Color Me Beautiful Workshop, ShipShape Spa	Deck 12
10:45 am	**Cash Prize BINGO,** Maharajas Lounge	Deck 5
11:00 am	**Slot Tournament,** Casino Royale	Deck 4
11:15 am–12 noon	Krooz Komics Entertain, Royal Promenade	Deck 5
11:15 am	Service Club Meeting, 19th Hole	Deck 14
11:15 am	Port Talk, The Palace Theater	Decks 3&4
11:30 am	70's Line Dance Class, Poolside	Deck 11
11:30 am	Free Skate, Studio "B"	Deck 3

Afternoon Activities

12:15 pm	Free Skate, Studio "B"	Deck 3
12:30 pm–1:30 pm	**Fine Art Preview,** Maharajas Lounge	Deck 5
12:45 pm	**Explorer LIVE Show,** Poolside	Deck 11
1:00 pm	Free Skate, Studio "B"	Deck 3
1:00 pm–5:00 pm	Business Services/Future Cruises Center Open	Deck 6
1:15 pm–1:45 pm	Mr. Sexy Legs Contest, Pool Deck	Deck 11
1:15 pm	Horse Racing Betting Windows Open, Poolside	Deck 11
1:30 pm–3:00 pm	**Fine Art Auction,** Maharajas Lounge	Deck 5
2:00 pm	Ocean Lab Presentation, Screening Room	Deck 2
2:00 pm	Adventure Family Novelquest, Sports Court	Deck 13
2:00 pm	Cellulite Myth & the Middle Age Spread Seminar, ShipShape Spa	Deck 12
2:00 pm–3:00 pm	**Planet Ice Tickets Available,** Studio B Lobby	Deck 3
2:00 pm–Sharp	Informal Bridge Pairing, Seven Hearts Card Room	Deck 14
2:00 pm	**Horseracing & Auction,** Poolside	Deck 11
3:00 pm	**Diamond & Gemstone Seminar,** Maharajas Lounge	Deck 5
3:15 pm	**Cash Prize BINGO,** The Palace Theater	Decks 3&4
3:30 pm–4:30 pm	Wine Appreciation Hour, Dining Room	Deck 3
4:00 pm	Upper Body Toning, ShipShape Center	Deck 11
5:00 pm–9:00 pm	Explorations! Desk Open For Sales	Deck 5
5:00 pm–6:00 pm	**Captain's Champagne Reception** (Main seating guests), Royal Promenade	Deck 5
5:00 pm–6:30 pm	Formal Portraits, Photo Gallery, Royal Promenade	Decks 3&5
5:00 pm–5:30 pm	Krooz Komics Entertain, Royal Promenade	Deck 5

Evening Activities

5:15 pm	Friends of Bill W. Meeting, Board Room	Deck 2
7:00 pm–7:45 pm	**Planet Ice Show** (Tickets needed), Studio "B", Center Ice	Deck 3
7:30 pm–8:30 pm	**Captain's Champagne Reception,** (Second seating guests), Royal Promenade	Deck 5
7:30 pm–8:00 pm	Krooz Komics Entertain Royal Promenade	Deck 5
7:30 pm–9:00 pm	Formal Portraits, Photo Gallery, Royal Promenade	Decks 3&5
8:00 pm–1:00 am	Cigar Aficionados, Connoisseur Club	Deck 5
9:00 pm	**History Repeating Production Show,** (Main seating guests) The Palace Theater	Decks 3&4
10:00 pm–11:00 pm	Formal Portraits, Photo Gallery, Royal Promenade	Decks 3&5
10:00 pm–11:15 pm	Karaoke Time, The Chamber	Decks 3&4
10:45 pm	**History Repeating Production Show,** (Second seating guests) The Palace Theater	Decks 3&4
11:45 pm–12:15 am	Singles' Mingle, The Chamber	Decks 3&4
12:15 am–12:45 am	**Late Night Comedy Show** (Adults Only) The Palace Theatre	Decks 3&4

SEABOURN CRUISE LINE
6100 Blue Lagoon Drive, Suite 400
Miami, Florida 33126
(800) 929-9391; (305) 463-3000
(305) 463-3010 Fax
www.seabourn.com

SEABOURN LEGEND (formerly *Royal Viking Queen* and *Queen Odyssey*): entered service 1993; refurbished 2008; 10,000 G.R.T.; 440' x 63'; 208-passenger capacity; 104 suites; Norwegian and British officers and international staff and crew; cruises the Caribbean, Mediterranean, Panama Canal, Costa Rica, Belize, and other destinations around the world.

SEABOURN ODYSSEY and *SEABOURN SOJURN:* entered service 2009 and 2010, respectively; 32,000 G.R.T.; 654' x 84'; 450-passenger capacity; 225 suites; Norwegian and British officers and international staff and crew; *Odyssey* sails a world cruise January to April 2010, then sails eastern Mediterranean and Black Sea cruises, and ends 2010 in the Caribbean. *Sojourn* debuts in northern Europe and ends 2010 in the Caribbean.

SEABOURN PRIDE: entered service 1988; refurbished 2007; 10,000 G.R.T.; 440' x 63'; 208-passenger capacity; 104 suites; Norwegian and British officers, international staff and crew; cruises Southeast Asia, China, Japan, and Korea.

SEABOURN SPIRIT: entered service 1989; refurbished 2008; 10,000 G.R.T.; 440' x 63'; 208-passenger capacity; 104 suites; Norwegian and British officers and international staff and crew; varying itineraries, including South America, the Mediterranean, Southeast Asia, the Orient, India, and Arabia.

(Medical Facilities: C-4; P-1; EM, CLS, MS; N-1; CM; PD; EKG; TC; PO; OX; WC; ICU; X; M.)

Note: Six+ black stars is the highest rating given in this edition to ships in the deluxe-market category.

These ships are rated in 11 separate categories in the second half of chapter 14.

The three all-suite vessels of Seabourn are positioned at the top of the luxury cruise market and are designed to offer the most elegant, luxurious cruise experience afloat, with spacious suite accommodations, open-seating dining with top-of-the-line service and gourmet cuisine, tasteful and elegantly appointed public rooms, excellent watersport and spa facilities, and some of the most desired destinations. Although dress during the day is casual, on most evenings gentlemen are expected to wear jackets in the dining room, and the atmosphere is more formal and sophisticated than on other ships. However, in the evening, guests may opt to have dinner at the more casual Restaurant 2, located at the Veranda Café, or at the Sky Grill on sun deck.

In May 1998, Carnival Corporation acquired Cunard Line, Ltd., merged Cunard with Seabourn Cruise Line, and transferred the two *Sea Goddesses* and the *Royal Viking Sun* from Cunard to the Seabourn brand, renaming the ships *Seabourn Goddess I* and *II* and *Seabourn Sun.* Corporate management then decided that there was little similarity between the sleek, yacht-like Seabourn vessels and the original Cunard ships. Subsequently, the two *Seabourn Goddesses* were sold to the former owner and CEO of Seabourn and the *Sun* was transferred to Holland America Line, another subsidiary of Carnival Corporation, and renamed *Prinsendam.* Presently, Seabourn is operated as an entirely separate brand from Cunard and is marketed to a somewhat different cruise population.

The original Seabourn ships, the *Pride* and *Spirit,* entered service in 1988 and 1989, respectively, and were heralded throughout the industry as the most magnificent and luxurious smaller vessels ever built. Seabourn ordered a third ship built in 1991 but exercised its option not to buy it. The shipyard, in turn, sold it to Royal Viking Line, where it entered service in 1992 as the *Royal Viking Queen.* When Royal Viking Line was dismantled by its owners, the ship was transferred to the Royal Cruise Line and renamed *Queen Odyssey.* Royal ceased operating in 1996, at which time the ship was repurchased by Seabourn and became known as *Seabourn Legend.*

Cruise-only prices in the brochure range from $400 to $2,000 per person per day (double occupancy), depending upon location of cabin and cruise area. Tips are included in the cruise fare. There is no charge for liquors or soft drinks throughout the ships, and wines are served gratis. The line also offers past passengers substantial discounts (often as high as 40 or 50 percent) and any passenger accruing 140 days on board receives a complimentary 14-day cruise on any Seabourn ship.

Itineraries for the line include northern Europe, the Orient, and the Mediterranean in the spring, summer, and early fall, and Southeast Asia, the Middle East, India, the Caribbean, South America, and Panama/Costa Rica during the remainder of the year, with several transatlantic positioning cruises. Passengers can select a variety of air and pre- and post-cruise land arrangements. Seabourn's comprehensive air program features competitively priced, negotiated tariffs with major carriers in economy, business, and first class, as well as on luxurious private jets. Land packages include prestigious hotels and custom-designed Signature Series shore excursions.

Once every cruise, guests are treated to a complimentary Exclusively Seabourn shoreside experience tailored to their personal interests. These include private visits to museums, galleries, or private homes and samples of local cuisines and local entertainment or cultural performances.

Most suites are approximately 277 square feet with a large 3' x 5' picture window looking out to the sea; twin beds that convert to a queen; flat-screen color TV with DVD player; richly appointed armchairs, sofa, and coffee table; a refrigerator and minibar (fully stocked upon embarkation free of charge); a hair dryer; large walk-in closet with private safe; and marble bathroom with twin-sink vanities (except the *Legend,* which has single-sink vanities); shower or shower/tub combination; luxurious bathroom and well-being amenities from Molton Brown; and ample storage space. There are larger suites that range in size from 400 to 575 square feet, and several have small private verandas. Small French-style balconies were added to about 35 percent of the suites in 2000, allowing passengers to peek out and enjoy the sunshine and fresh sea air. They are too small to lounge on; however, they do provide views along the side of the ship.

In 2007, the *Pride,* and in 2008 the *Spirit and Legend,* received various renovations including an expansion of the outdoor dining venues, upgraded bedding, and new carpets and furnishings.

The health spa on each vessel offers massages and herbal body wraps and includes an exercise room (recently doubled in size) with state-of-the-art equipment and treadmills with personal TVs in addition to a steam room, a sauna, three outdoor whirlpools, and an outdoor swimming pool. At the fold-out marina off the rear of the ship passengers can swim, windsurf, water-ski, banana boat, and sail.

The observation lounges at the top of each ship are glass enclosed and afford a panoramic view for passengers enjoying coffee, tea, or drinks. The club has a piano bar and is the location for evening cocktails and hors d'oeuvres as well as late-night dancing. There also is a large showroom that can accommodate all passengers; an indoor/outdoor café where imaginative buffet breakfasts, lunches, and dinners are served (possibly the best casual restaurants in the industry); a casino; hospital; boutique; Internet café with four terminals; tiny self-service launderette; and laundry and dry-cleaning service.

One of the highlights of the Seabourn experience is the elegant, open-seating dining room featuring some of the best continental cuisine at sea and an extensive wine list. Several bottles of wine are offered gratis with each meal; however, there is a charge for the other options on the wine list.

In 2002, Charlie Palmer of the renowned Aureole Restaurant in New York created 200 new dinner recipes, which he describes as "American Progressive Cuisine," to be served on board. The menus may include appetizers of flash-cooked striped bass with toasted garlic/lemon juice and capers; an extravagant entrée called "Lobster, Lobster, Lobster and Lobster Sauce"; grilled venison with aged balsamic vinegar and foie gras sauce; vegetarian delights such as soy-glazed shiitake and gingered greens, crunchy Vidalia onions, and onion soubise; and fanciful desserts such as warm lemon soufflé tart and honey-lemon sorbet or a trio of crèmes brûlée (including jasmine, cappuccino, and classic vanilla). Commencing in 2006, the Veranda Café on all the ships was transformed during the evenings to a reservation-only, casual dining venue called Restaurant 2, serving innovative, five-course tasting menus of creative, paired, small dishes. Also, a steak and seafood menu is offered a few times each week alfresco at the Sky Grill near the Sky Bar.

Service at the cafés in the main dining rooms and throughout the ships is impeccable, the most attentive at sea. This may be the ultimate cruise experience for well-heeled, sophisticated cruise aficionados. During afternoon tea, the ships feature rare estate teas and blends. In addition, there is a pre-purchase premium wine program called "Vintage Seabourn" that allows oenophiles to choose bottles from the ship's extensive wine cellars at substantial savings.

Seabourn, in connection with DHL Worldwide Express, offers a personal valet service program wherein passengers can arrange to have their personal luggage shipped directly from their homes to their suites on the ship. Although the service costs extra, passengers with a large amount of luggage may find that it is not much more expensive then paying to take extra luggage on airplanes (under the new airline regulations).

Two new 32,000-ton, 450-passenger ships were delivered in 2009 and 2010 with a third scheduled for 2011. The first, *Seabourn Odyssey*, entered service in July 2009 sailing in the Mediterranean during the summer. The second, *Seabourn Sojurn*, entered service in the summer of 2010 in northern Europe. Ninety percent of the 225 luxury suites feature verandas, and accommodations range in size from 295 to 1,682 square feet. Most suites are labeled veranda suites and measure 365 square feet. The 22 penthouse suites come in at 436 square feet and the owner's signature, "Wintergarden," and grand suites range in size from 760 to 1,682 square feet. All suites include separate living areas, walk-in closets, flat-screen TVs, fully stocked bars replenished daily, writing desks, direct-dial telephones, electronic safes, CD and DVD players, spacious granite bathrooms with separate tub and shower, twin sinks and vanities, hair dryers, and 110/220 electrical outlets.

Public areas and dining venues are somewhat similar to the original three ships but greatly expanded. There are five open-seating dining alternatives: the elegant main restaurant offering gourmet cuisine created by Charlie Palmer (jackets required on most nights and several on each cruise are black tie optional); Restaurant 2, where dishes are prepared individually by the chef in tasting portions (dress is elegant casual); Colonnade, an indoor/outdoor venue serving all three meals with changing themes for dinner (dress is elegant casual); the casual Patio Grill by the pool serving all three meals; and, of course, in-suite service, including the option to have dinner served course by course in your suite complete with fine linens and personal service.

Other public areas include five lounges and bars, an expansive pool and sunbathing area, and a spectacular two-deck indoor/outdoor 11,400-square-foot spa facility. The ship's built-in marina offers swimming, snorkeling, windsurfing, kayaking, and water-skiing off the stern of the ship. In the evenings there is musical entertainment, cabaret shows, Broadway reviews, dancing to live bands, a casino, and movies under the stars.

Although three times larger than the three earlier vessels, the *Odyssey* and *Sojourn* carry only twice the number of passengers, allowing for more room in both public areas and staterooms. They boast the highest space-per-guest ratio in the cruise industry.

Strong Points:

Top-of-the-line luxury (at top-of-the-line prices except when special offers are available on selected cruises), superb food, impeccable service, and elegant, spacious accommodations, as well as the most desired itineraries. The three original sisters are the most spacious and comfortable of the yacht-like cruise ships. The new 450-passenger ships offer the same exceptional dining, service, and accommodations with additional space, facilities, and entertainment. Most seasoned cruisers consider these the best ships in service today.

Seabourn Pride, *courtesy Seabourn Cruise Line*

Breakfast in the cabin on Seabourn Spirit, *courtesy Seabourn Cruise Line*

Main Dining Room on Seabourn Spirit, *courtesy Seabourn Cruise Line*

Award plaque in lounge on Seabourn Spirit, *courtesy Seabourn Cruise Line*

Chef presentation tasting menu on Seabourn Spirit, *courtesy Seabourn Cruise Line*

Seabourn Spirit, *courtesy Seabourn Cruise Line*

Suite, courtesy Seabourn Cruise Line

SEABOURN LEGEND

RESTAURANT DINNER MENU
MONDAY, OCTOBER 4, 2004

First Course

RUSSIAN MALOSSOL CAVIAR
potato shallot cake, remoulade, herb salad

SEARED BEEF CARPACCIO
porcini foam, brioche croutons

SAUTEED ESCALLOP OF FOIE GRAS
roasted apples, caramelized honey

□□□

DUCK BROTH WITH CONFIT
summer vegetables in a crisp pastry crust

CREAM-LESS CELERY ROOT SOUP
black truffles

□□□

YOUNG SPINACH & SHAVED FENNEL SALAD
herbed croutons, red wine vinaigrette

GRILLED PORTOBELLO MUSHROOM SALAD
aged balsamic vinaigrette, toasted walnuts

Main Course

PAN ROASTED FRESH SNAPPER
atop creamy asparagus, roasted mushroom jus

GRILLED MARINATED LOBSTER TAIL
vegetable risotto, newburg sauce, parmesan chips

ROASTED LAMB LOIN WITH CRISP LAMB BRICK
caramelized brussel sprouts and black berries

PRIME RIB OF BEEF
melted leeks, potato and carrots, crisp onion rings, shallot natural

VEGETARIAN – BARIGOULE OF ARTICHOKE
white beans, thyme roasted tomatoes, saffron potato dice

WINES

PETALUMA RIESLING, CLAIRE VALLEY 2003	$22.00
POMMARD, LOUIS LATOUR, COTE DE BEAUNE	$40.00

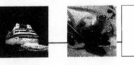

Cafe Elegant

WELCOME TO OUR ALTERNATIVE, SLIGHTLY MORE CASUAL PLACE FOR DINING OUT ON AN EVENING WHEN YOU'D REALLY RATHER NOT BOTHER WITH BLACK TIE -- OR ANY TIE AT ALL. TONIGHT WE WELCOME GUESTS FOR WHOM A JACKET OR A SIMPLE DRESS SEEMS ELEGANT ENOUGH. HERE YOU WILL ALWAYS FIND AN UNCOMPLICATED MENU OF FINE FOOD AND LIKE-MINDED, CONGENIAL COMPANY -- IN A RELAXED ATMOSPHERE OF EASYGOING ELEGANCE. WE ARE PLEASED TO BE ABLE TO OFFER YOU THE LUXURY OF CHOICE, WHICH JUST MAY BE THE GREATEST LUXURY OF ALL.

BREADS
BAGUETTE, HERB FOCACCIA, CIABATTA, GRISSINI
Virgin Olive Oil, Balsamic Vinegar, Butter

TO BEGIN WITH
TAPAS
Piemento And Chives, Humus

STARTER
RUASSIAN MALOSSOL SEVRUGA CAVIAR
Potato Cake, Remoulade, Herb Salad

SOUP
CREAM LESS CELERY ROUT SOUP
Black Truffles

SALAD
GRILLED PORTABELLO MUSHROOM SALAD
Aged Balsamic Vinaigrette, Toasted Walnuts

MAINS
GRILLED MARINATED LOBSTER TAIL
Vegetable Risotto, Newburg Sauce, Parmesan Crisp

OR

ROAST PRIME RIB OF BEEF
Melted Leeks, Potato And Carrots, Crisp Onion Rings, Shallot Natural

DESSERTS
CREME BRULLE EN PARADE
Dark, Milk And White Chocolates

OR

FRESH STRAWBERRIES
Vanilla Ice Cream

SEABOURN

Courtesy Seabourn Cruise Line

seabournherald@sea
onboard daily news

today's program at a glance

good morning

7 am......Walk your way to Civitavecchia. Register your laps at the Sky Bar (16 laps =1 mile).

9 am......Complimentary Massage Moments on deck.
(weather permitting, alternatively in the Spa) *deck #7*

10 am......Board Game and Card enthusiasts are invited to meet with Dorothy. *Card Room*

10:30 am......Enrichment Lecture Join Dr. Carlos Carmago for his second talk entitled 'The Mediterranean Diet and the French Paradox'. *King Olav Lounge*

11 am......Shuffleboard Challenge. Meet for this traditional shipboard game. *Deck #8 aft*

11:30 am....Special Interest Talk. 'Everything You Ever Wanted To Know About Cruising But Were Afraid To Ask'. Join Steve Stern, author of Stern's Guide to the Cruise Vacation' and 'Stern's Guide to the Greatest Resorts in the World' for an audience participation discussion on the world of cruising. You may win a prize in a cruise trivia quiz! *The Club*

good afternoon

12 noon......Sky Grill: Enjoy a Fajita lunch al fresco until 1:30 pm. (weather permitting) *Sky Bar*

12:15 pm......Team Trivia Challenge: Join Dorothy and Trevor for fun and prizes. *Midnight Sun Lounge*

12:30 pm......Galley Market Brunch. Chef Andre prepares his galley with special lunch items from around the world. Music provided by the Seabourn Legend Orchestra. *The Restaurant*

2 pm......Navigational Bridge Tour: Meet Dorothy at the Sky Bar. *deck #8*

2:15 pm......Fashion Show. Join Boutique Manager Daniel for this fun show featuring the fashions of our on board Boutique. *The Clu*

2:30 pm......Informal Bridge get together. Card Room

3:30 pm......Golf Putting Contest. Join Nolan and test your skill. *Meet at the Sky Bar*

4 pm......Musical Teatime. Enjoy the music and songs of Dorothy & Chad while you enjoy tea. *Midnight Sun Lounge*

4 pm......Complimentary Massage Moments on deck. (weather permitting, alternatively in the Spa) *deck #7*

good evening

	DRESS THIS EVENING AFTER 6 PM	Casual: For gentlemen, no jacket is required; a shirt with slacks is perfectly appropriate. For ladies, a blouse with skirt, or slacks.

6 pm........Early Evening Enrichment Lecture: Join Dr. Carlos Carmargo for his final talk entitled 'The Rome of Michelangelo Buonarroti'. *King Olav Lounge (cocktails will be served)*

6:30 pm......Cocktails, Soli & Andre entertain for your dancing and listening pleasure. *The Club*

9:30 pm......Soli & Andre entertain with your favorite music and song through out the evening at the Club. *The Club*

9:30 pm......Comedy Movie Time! 'Intermission' Colin Farrell and Cillian Murphy star in this faced paced, hilarious comedy about the lives of some very unique characters. *King Olav Lounge*

10 pm......Dancing Under the Stars: The Seabourn Legend Quartet invite you to dance the night away under the Mediterranean Sky. Vocals will be provided by Nolan Dean and Dorothy Bishop. *Sky Bar (weather permitting)*

..... Afterwards Soli & Andre continue the entertainment in The Club and the Seabourn Legend Quartet will continue the evening with great music at the Sky Bar.

Vol. 041003, No. 7

Saturday October 9, 2004

Captain: Geir-Arne Thue-Nilsen

Hotel Manager: Norbert Fuchs

Editor: Trevor Stephenson

Sunrise: 7:22 am

Sunset: 6:42 pm

En route to Civitavecchia, Italy

television guide

Channel 1: *CNN* (conditions permitting)

Channel 2: Satellite (conditions permitting)

Channel 1: *CNN* (conditions permitting)

Channel 2: Seabourn Legend Information

movie channels
Channel 3:
Laws of Attraction
Pierce Bronson and Julianne Moore star in this romantic comedy about two high powered New York divorce attorneys who have seen everything in love go wrong - so what are there chances?
5 am, 7:15 am, 9:30 am, 11:45 am, 2 pm, 4:15 pm, 6:30 pm, 8:45 pm, 11 pm, 1:15 pm

Channel 4:
Man On Fire
Denzel Washington stars as a government operative / soldier of fortune is hired to protect a young girl who changes his life.
5:30 am, 8 am, 10:30 am, 1 pm, 3:30 pm, 6 pm, 8:30 pm, 11 pm, 1:30 am

Channel 5:
Swimming Upstream
Judy Davis and Geoffrey Rush star in this family drama set in Brisbane during the 1950's. Based on the true story of swimming champ Tony Fingleton.
5 am, 8:30 am, 12 noon, 3:30 pm, 7 pm, 10:30 pm

Channel 6: Seabourn TV (CBS)

Channel 7: Seabourn TV (NBC)

Channel 8: Enrichment Channel
Charlie Palmer Video Highlights
5 am, 8:30 am, 12 noon, 3:30 pm,
Enrichment Lecture repeat
7 pm, 10:30 pm

Channel 9: Port Talk (replaying hourly)
Channel 11: Satellite (conditions permitting)
Channel 11: Report from the Bridge
Channel 12: View from the Bridge
Channel 13: Satellite (conditions permitting)
Channel 14: Satellite (conditions permitting)

in suite music
For your musical enjoyment throughout the cruise, a library of music CDs and audio books is available for use with the Bose® Wave® Radio/CD stereo system in your suite. Please refer to the in-suite ordering guide and request your selection either from your stewardess or from the Purser's Office (Dial 00).

special events!

11:30 am.....Special Interest Talk. 'Everything You Ever Wanted To Know About Cruising But Were Afraid To Ask'. Join Steve Stern, author of Stern's Guide to the Cruise Vacation' and 'Stern's Guide to the Greatest Resorts in the World' for an audience participation discussion on the world of cruising. You may win a prize in a cruise trivia quiz! *The Club*

6 pm........Early Evening Enrichment Lecture: Join Dr. Carlos Carmargo for his final talk entitled 'The Rome Michelangelo Buonarroti'. *King Olav Lounge (cocktails will be served)*

7- 9 pm........Ginger & Spice Dinner is served in The Veranda. (reservations required as seating is limited) *deck #7*

tonight's entertainment

6 pm........Early Evening Enrichment Lecture: Join Dr. Carlos Carmargo for his final talk entitled 'The Rome of Michelangelo Buonarroti'. *King Olav Lounge (cocktails will be served)*

9:30 pm..........Soli & Andre begins your night at the Club with great music. *The Club*

9:30 pm... ......Comedy Movie Time! 'Intermission' Colin Farrell and Cillian Murphy star in this faced paced, hilarious comedy about the lives of some very unique characters. *King Olav Lounge*

10 pm........Dancing Under the Stars: The Seabourn Legend Quartet invite you to dance the night away under the Mediterranean Sky. Vocals will be provided by Nolan Dean and Dorothy Bishop. *Sky Bar (weather permitting)*

Afterwards Soli & Andre will continue in The Club entertainment in The Club and the Seabourn Legend Quartet will continue in the evening with great music at the Sky Bar.

from the bridge

On behalf of all the Officers, Staff and Crew on board Seabourn Legend, I would like to take this opportunity to thank you for sailing with us on this cruise. It has been a pleasure to have you on board. You have had a chance to enjoy our ship and I hope you can see why we are proud of her.

We have tried to equip the Seabourn Legend with the very best facilities available. We have staffed her with the most capable crew and now we are sailing her to some of the most exciting ports in the world.

Today, we are going on separate paths, but we hope you will join us on board again very soon. Until that time, I wish you a pleasant journey home and a joyous return to your families ashore.   *Captain Geir-Arne Thue-Nilsen*

from the cruise director

On behalf of the entire entertainment team on board the Seabourn Legend, I would like to thank you for being such wonderful audiences throughout this voyage. We have thoroughly enjoyed meeting you and entertaining you over the entire cruise and although today we say farewell, we look forward to entertaining you again soon on board the Seabourn Legend.
Trevor Stephenson

The Yachts of Seabourn

Courtesy Seabourn Cruise Line

SEA CLOUD CRUISES

In U.S.	In Germany
32-40 N. Dean Street	Ballindamm 17
Englewood, New Jersey 07631	D-20095 Hamburg, Germany
(888) 732-2568; (201) 227-9404	+49(0) 403095920
(201) 227-9424 Fax	+49(0) 4030959222 Fax

www.seacloud.com

RIVER CLOUD: entered service 1996; refurbished annually; 361' x 37'; 45 cabins; 90-passenger capacity; international crew; cruises on rivers in Europe.

RIVER CLOUD II: entered service 2001; refurbished annually; 338' x 32'; 44 cabins; 88-passenger capacity; international crew; cruises on rivers in Europe. (**Category B—Not Rated**)

SEA CLOUD: entered service 1931 as private yacht; frequently renovated and refurbished; 360' x 50'; 32 cabins; 64-passenger capacity; international crew (60); cruises primarily in European waters and the Caribbean. (**Category A/B—Not Rated**)

SEA CLOUD II: entered service 2001; frequently refurbished; 384 x 52'; 47 cabins; 94-passenger capacity; international crew; cruises primarily in European waters and the Caribbean. (**Category A/B—Not Rated**)

SEA CLOUD HUSSAR V: entered service 2010; 136-passenger capacity; international crew; cruise grounds to be determined. (**Category A/B—Not Rated**)

Launched in 1931 as a private yacht, *Sea Cloud* was a home away from home for millionaires Edward Hutton and Marjorie Merriweather Post. This legendary four-masted vessel captures the elegance of the rich and famous during that period in U.S. history with its mahogany superstructure, teak decks, polished brass fixtures, and brilliant tapestry of over 32,000 square feet of sails. She was acquired in 1978 by a group of Hamburg ship owners and business executives who proceeded to install additional cabins, new rigging, and state-of-the-art navigation, communication, and safety systems. Modern amenities and upgrades notwithstanding, the ship still offers the charm and charisma of the romantic spirit in which she was conceived nearly 80 years ago.

The six original guest chambers on the main deck and the two owner's suites and two cabins (formerly crew quarters) have been skillfully restored and the furnishings recall the era of the early 1900s. Twenty-two additional staterooms were added on the two above decks.

Atop ship are the lido deck, lido bar, bridge, and eight luxury accommodations. On the promenade deck below are 10 additional staterooms, a lovely lounge, and the elegant main dining room that accommodates all passengers in a single seating with no assigned tables. There is piano music during dinner and afterwards in the lounge. When weather permits, lunch is served buffet style on the lido deck.

Although more modern in design, *Sea Cloud II* retains much of the old-world charm of her elder sister. Atop ship on sun deck is the captain's bridge. Below on lido deck are the two owner's suites, the elegant main lounge, the lido bar, and a library. On promenade deck are the single-seating dining room, boutique, purser's office, reception area, and 18 staterooms. The remaining cabins are one more deck down on cabin deck, along with a gym, sauna, hospital, and watersports deck. All accommodations include a sitting area, minibar, TV and video player, and marble baths appointed with gold fittings and inlays.

In 1996, when the 90-passenger *River Cloud* entered service with cruises on the Rhine, Main, Moselle, and Danube Rivers in central Europe, she set a high standard for riverboat travel. The four 140-square-foot double-bedded and the 35 129-square-foot twin-bedded outside cabins located on cabin deck are beautifully furnished in burled rosewoods and colorful fabrics and include ample closet space, private safes, dressing tables, a TV/video combination, and marble baths with glassed-in shower stalls, hair dryers, magnifying mirrors, and terry bathrobes and slippers. Fresh fruit and soft drinks are provided by cabin stewardesses free of charge. The six spacious, 204-foot suites on promenade deck have queen beds, separate sitting areas, a pull-down TV and video player, a writing desk, and larger bathrooms.

Atop ship on sun deck are the bridge, lido bar, putting green, and a large sunning and observation area with comfortable wood-backed lounges. The sun deck is extraordinary for a riverboat and much nicer than on competitive riverboat lines. On promenade deck are the fitness area, dining room, five suites, library, boutique, hairdresser, reception, and main lounge. It is possible to navigate around the entire outside of the boat here (7^1/$_2$ times to the mile).

The attractive, open-seating dining room with tables for four, six, and eight people is the locale for breakfast and lunch buffets featuring a vast array of regional delicacies. Multicourse dinners offer a set menu with two choices for the main course. Complimentary red and white wines are offered at all meals, as well as espresso and cappuccino. When weather permits, alfresco barbeques are offered atop ship. Soft drinks are available around the clock free of charge. A piano player entertains in the main lounge during cocktail hour and after dinner.

The 88-passenger *River Cloud II* previously cruised in Italy, up and down the Po River between Cremona and Venice. Currently, she travels the Rhine, Main, Moselle, and Danube Rivers. The overall cruise experience, as well as the layout of the boat, is very similar to the *River Cloud,* except the cabins are a bit smaller and there is no gym, sauna, or outside path along the promenade deck.

A three-masted, 28-sail new build accommodating 136 passengers and named *Sea Cloud Hussar V* will be delivered in 2010. All cabins have an ocean view and there are private verandas in two suites.

Strong Points:

Upscale sailboat and riverboat experiences on elegantly appointed vessels.

The author and the captain of River Cloud, *courtesy Sea Cloud Cruises*

Cabin on River Cloud, *courtesy Sea Cloud Cruises*

Restaurant on River Cloud, *courtesy Sea Cloud Cruises*

Sea Cloud *and* Sea Cloud II, *courtesy Sea Cloud Cruises*

Dining room on Sea Cloud II, *courtesy Sea Cloud Cruises*

————— RIVER CLOUD —————

Wednesday, August 4ᵗʰ 2004	Vienna

Sunrise: 04:51 am   Sunset: 20:04 pm

Quote of the day: "All is provided to be happy on earth – we have snow, and a new morning
every day, we have trees and rain, we have hope and dreams – we are rich!"
Friedensreich Hundertwasser – Vienniese Artist

————————————— Good Morning —————————————

06:30 am	Early Riser – Coffee, Tea and Danish Pastries	Lounge
07:00 – 09:00 am	Breakfast is served	Restaurant
08:30 pm	RIVER CLOUD arrives in Vienna. We are located at DDSG Handelskai No. 8 at the Reichsbrücke.	
09:00 am	**Departure for the Vienna City Tour** Return to ship at approx.: 12:30 pm	Gangway
12:30 pm	Lunch is served.	Restaurant
02:00 pm	**Departure for the Excursion to Schönbrunn** Return to ship at approx.: 05:00 pm	Gangway
03:30 pm	Tea time with Operetta Melodies with Geza	Lounge

————————————— Good Evening —————————————

05:00 pm	Cocktail hour with Geza	Lounge
06:00 –08:00 pm	Dinner Buffet is served in an open seating	Restaurant
07:30 pm	**Departure "Vienna Mozart Orchestra" (Hofburg Festive Hall)** The concert starts at 08:15 pm and ends at approx. 10:00 pm	Gangway
09:30 pm	Piano music by Geza	Lounge
10:30 pm	Late Night Snack	Lounge

Courtesy Sea Cloud Cruises

River Cloud
Gala - Dinner Menu

Amuse Bouche

❦

Lobster tureen
with saffron sauce and small salad

❦

Watercress soup with pike-perch

❦

Roasted goose liver
on cabbage with pepper cherries

❦

Medaillons of deer under walnut crust
with coffee-Jus on salsifies and small spinach dumplings

❦

Crème Brûlée
with forest berries and white coffee ice cream

❦

Selection of international cheese

Coffee, tea and Espresso

Courtesy Sea Cloud Cruises

SEADREAM YACHT CLUB
601 Brickell Key Drive, Suite 1050
Miami, Florida 33131
(800) 707-4911; (305) 631-6119
(305) 631-6110 Fax

SEADREAM I and *II* (formerly *Sea Goddess I* and *II* and *Seabourn Goddess I* and *II*): entered service 1984 and 1985, respectively; both redesigned in 2002; 4,250 G.R.T.; 344' x 48'; 110-passenger capacity; 55 staterooms; international officers and crew; 5-, 7-, and 9-day cruises in Caribbean and 7- to 14-day cruises in Europe.

(Medical Facilities: C-1; P-1, EM, CLS, MS; N-0; CM; PD; BC; EKG; TC; PO; EPC; OX; WC; OR; ICU; X; M; CCP; TM; LJ.)

These ships are rated in 11 separate categories in the second half of chapter 14.

SeaDream Yacht Club was launched in 2001 by Norwegian entrepreneur Atle Brynestad, founder, owner, and CEO. Mr. Brynestad was also the original founder of Seabourn Cruise Line. Robert Lepisto is the president of the company and has been part of the original SeaDream team since its inception. These twin luxury mega-yachts offer five- to 14-night Caribbean and European yachting voyages. They are sometimes under charter, so it is best to check ahead with the cruise line as to their availability on any given date.

The cruise line states that although the ships depart their first port and arrive at their last port as scheduled, the captains have authority to adjust for local opportunities and make unscheduled calls at smaller yachting ports, harbors, and secluded bays, allowing guests to indulge in watersports and unique sightseeing adventures. SeaDream offers custom-designed land adventures and other shore activities and often features overnight stays in port to enable passengers to enjoy the night life. Shoreside casual excursions are limited to a few choices in each port and are hosted by ship officers or members of the crew. The highlight of each cruise is the Champagne & Caviar Splash beach party, held at a pristine beach when in the Caribbean and usually on the vessel's pool deck when in the Mediterranean. During this event, service personnel immersed in the sea or pool offer guests champagne and caviar.

There is no formal dress code, and country-club casual attire is acceptable throughout the cruise. Guests dine in open seating either in the elegant, indoor dining salon or alfresco at the partially sheltered Topside Restaurant. In addition, there is a 24-hour simplified menu, "Small Bites," as well as elegantly prepared snacks available at the Top of the Yacht Bar and at the pool deck. It is possible to arrange a romantic tête-à-tête dinner in other areas of the ship as well. Appropriate snacks are available around the clock throughout the ship. The dining experience at all meals is exceptional, with an abundance of high-quality, gourmet preparations imaginatively presented and impressively served. Alcoholic drinks, including premium brands, are gratis throughout the ship and a nice assortment of wines is complimentary at mealtime. The wine cellar menu has a wide selection of new and old-world wines for purchase, and French champagne is available at all of the bars.

Of the 55 ocean-view guest accommodations, 54 are Yacht Club staterooms and measure 195 square feet. Sixteen of the Yacht Club staterooms can be combined to make Commodore suites, doubling their size. Travelers can opt for the 447-square-foot owner's suite with its lavishly appointed private bedroom and bath and an elegant living and dining room with a half bath. Every accommodation includes a small lounge area, closet with dresser space and a hanging area (wooden hangers provided), private safe, hair dryer, refrigerator, CD/DVD player, and flat-screen television (channels depend on the area where the ships are sailing but also include in-room movies). Guests can select queen or single beds, down or synthetic pillows, and blankets or duvets. All staterooms are Internet ready, and guests can request a laptop for use while on board. Bathrooms are quite small with little storage space but include a well-sized glassed-in shower with multiple jets and Bulgari bath amenities. There are no balconies, and standard cabins are smaller than on other luxury vessels. The new 375-square foot Admiral Suite features the same SeaDream amenities described above as well as a separate living and dining area with an en suite master bath and a half bath in the living area.

The ships were redesigned and refitted after their acquisition from Seabourn. Public areas include the SeaDream Spa with massage rooms, steam shower, and very tiny sauna; gymnasium with various equipment, including four treadmills with attached televisions, DVD players, and views looking out to sea; outdoor pool; whirlpool and pool bar; watersports marina and floating dock perfect for swimming (offering personal watercraft, snorkel gear, Sunfish, Zodiacs for water-skiing, banana boat rides, and a floating island on which to relax or sunbathe); mountain bikes available for shoreside explorations; small casino with two blackjack tables; beauty salon; boutique; 30-course golf simulator; cardroom; library with two computers for Internet access; medical facility staffed by a doctor; main dining salon; Topside Restaurant; piano bar; main lounge; and Top of the Yacht Bar with 360-degree views. The signature Balinese Dream Beds are very comfortable sun beds atop ship for sun worshippers and star gazers. There are large umbrellas for those who prefer the shade. On overnights in port, arrangements can be made to have a bed with pillows, linen, and cozy duvets made up atop ship for couples who wish to sleep under the stars.

In contrast to other cruise ships, the company describes their vessels as "yachts" and the experience as "yachting" and therefore there are no on-board organized activities and there is limited entertainment. Cocktail hour offers live piano music, lavish hors d'oeuvres, and a short talk about the next day's port of call. After dinner guests can enjoy live guitar at the Top of the Yacht Bar or starlit movies on deck or in the main salon on a giant screen. Alternatively, guests can congregate at the piano bar with their own musical requests and libations, play blackjack in the casino, or select a DVD for their staterooms from a well-stocked viewing library.

Strong Points:

A magnificent dining experience with gourmet cuisine and impeccable service, great bar service, and a lot of pampering by an award-winning crew of 95. This line will appeal most to passengers who enjoy unstructured elegance and do not require an abundance of group activities, entertainment, or a strong shore program. This is truly an intimate, yacht-like experience highly recommended for loving couples and discerning guests.

Courtesy SeaDream Yacht Club

SeaDream II, *courtesy SeaDream Yacht Club*

Dining room on SeaDream II, *courtesy SeaDream Yacht Club*

SEADREAM
YACHT CLUB

Dinner in the Dining Salon

Cruz Bay, St. John, U.S.V.I.
Monday, February 16th 2009

Our Sommelier George Simcea Recommends this Evening

White Wines:

Pouilly Fuissé, Château Fuissé	Burgundy	2002	$ 51,00
Sauvignon Blanc, Cloudy Bay , Marlborough County	New Zealand	2005	$ 89.00

Red Wines:

Echézaux Grand Cru, L. Jadot	Burgundy	2001	$134.00
Caymus "Special Selection"Cabernet Sauvignon	Napa Valley	2003	$153.00

Our Sommelier has an excellent selection of Old World and New World wines
from our cellars on the Wine List, which George will be delighted
to leave with you for your Perusal and Choice.

Executive Chef de Cuisine
Sudesh Kishore

Executive Hotel Manager
Christophe Cornu

Starters

Thai Style Beef Salad with Fresh Mango and Cilantro

•

Grilled Spiced Shrimps with Blood Orange Segments and Chili Dressing

•

Gratinated Escargots with Aubergine Compote and Champignon de Paris*

Soups

Cream of Garlic with Seven Grain Croutons

•

Lime and Coriander with Chicken Flakes

•

Chilled Raspberry Flip

Salads

Caesar Salad with Chilli Croutons and Anchovy Fillet

•

Sweet Cucumber Salad with Fresh Dill

An Assortment of Salads is always Available with your Favourite Dressings

World Flavour

Lemongrass and Ginger marinated Monkfish
on Spinach and Rocket Salad with Cherry Tomato Vinaigrette

Chef's Main Dishes

Grilled Lobster Tail on Black and White Rice, Green Vegetables,
Crispy Shallots and Crustacean Sauce*

•

Whole Roast Rack of Lamb
with Pommes Gratin, Ratatouille and Rosemary infused Demi Glace

•

Pappardelle Pasta with Parma Ham, Sautéed Spinach,
Roasted Garlic and Fresh Pesto

*SeaDream Signature Dish

This Evening's Vegetarian Alternative

Sweet Cucumber Salad with Fresh Dill

•

Cream of Garlic with Seven Grain Croutons

•

Porcini Mushroom Risotto with Arugula Lettuce and Balsamic Nage

A Selection of Steamed Vegetables and Baked Potatoes is always available

SeaDream Oriental Wellness Cuisine

In Combination with SeaDream Spa, Our Chefs have created a daily selection of dishes from the Oriental wellness Cuisine

Lemongrass and Ginger marinated Monkfish
on Spinach and Rocket Salad with Cherry Tomato Vinaigrette

•

Lime and Coriander with Chicken Flakes

•

Lean Beef Curry with Basmati Rice, Mango Chutney and Crispy Poppadum*

•

Grilled Pineapple with Coconut Frozen Yoghurt

•

Oriental Ginger Tea

À la Carte

Consommé Double with "Battonet au Fromage"

•

Caesar Salad served with Croutons and Grated Parmesan Cheese

•

Linguini al Pesto or with Chunky Tomato Sauce

•

Broiled Fillet of "Organic" Salmon with Caper Butter

•

Chicken Breast with Herbs, Lemon and Virgin Olive Oil

•

Grilled N.Y. Cut Strip-Loin Steak, Madagascar Pepper Sauce

•

Rosemary Marinated Lamb Chops

*All dishes may be ordered with your choice of French Fried Potatoes,
Baked Potato, Rice and Vegetables of the day.*

Desserts

Pastry Chef Garfield Anderson's Signature Dessert

"Fondant au Chocolat" with Vanilla Ice Cream*

∽∾

Pistachio Cheese Cake with Sour Cream Topping and Strawberry Compote
•
Grilled Pineapple with Coconut Frozen Yoghurt

Healthy and Delicious

Red Wine Poached Pear with Crème Fraîche Sorbet

Garfield's Selection of Homemade Ice Cream, Sorbets

Vanilla, Rum and Raisin, Maple Walnut Ice Cream,
Crème Fraîche Sorbet and Coconut Frozen Yoghurt

From The Cheese Board

Assorted European Cheeses
Served with Home Made Cheese Bread

SeaDream I Exclusive Selection of Herbal and Exotic Teas from "Mhai Diva Teas",
Espresso, Cappuccino, Regular and Decaffeinated Coffee accompanied by an assortment of
Homemade Petits Fours with Chocolate Truffles

SeaDream
YACHT CLUB

Courtesy SeaDream Yacht Club

Partly Cloudy
High: 79°F / 26°C
Low: 72°F / 22°C

SeaDream
YACHT CLUB

Next Port:
Sandy Ground
Anguilla, BWI
Distance:
33 Nautical Miles

Daily program
Gustavia, St. Barts, FWI
Tuesday, February 17th 2009

Sunrise: 06:39

Sunset: 18:14

07:00	Early Riser's Coffee is available at the Top of the Yacht Bar.	Deck 6
08:00 – 10:30	Breakfast is served at the Topside Restaurant.	Deck 5
07:30	SeaDream I anchors off Gustavia, St. Barts, FWI.	
	A tender service will be established and operate on a continuous basis throughout our stay.	

MORNING ACTIVITIES

08:00	**"Crew Shoreside Casual"** – Join your Club & Activities Director **Richard** for a morning hike to Fort Gustav & Fort Carl ruins; followed by swimming at Shell Beach. Please meet at the gangway and wear comfortable walking shoes and a swim suit.	Deck 3
08:00	**Yoga Session** with Khun Yuu, please meet at the SeaDream Spa.	Deck 4
09:00	A limited selection of Mountain Bikes and Snorkel Equipment is available at the gangway.	Deck 3
09:30	Yachting Land Adventure - **'The Independent Explorer'** departs from the gangway.	Deck 3
09:30 – 11:30	Yachting Land Adventure - **'Island Tour by ATV'** departs from the gangway.	Deck 3
10:15 – 12:15	Yachting Land Adventure - **'Fast & Fun'** departs from the gangway.	Deck 3
11:30 – 12:30	**Swimming** is available from the marina platform. (Port Authority & weather permitting) Please sign a waiver form and collect a wrist band from the Concierge.	Deck 2 / Marina

12:30 – 14:00	**Luncheon** is served at the Topside Restaurant.	Deck 5

AFTERNOON ACTIVITIES

13:45 – 14:45	Yachting Land Adventure - **'St. Barth Semi - Submersible'** departs from the gangway.	Deck 3
13:45 – 15:45	Yachting Land Adventure - **'Blue Cat Snorkeling'** departs from the gangway.	Deck 3
14:00 – 16:00	**Water Sports** are available from the marina platform. (Port Authority & weather permitting) Please sign a waiver form and collect a wrist band from the Concierge.	Deck 2 / Marina
15:00	**Stretch & Tai-Chi Session** with Khun Ticha, please meet at the SeaDream Spa.	Deck 4
16:00 – 16:30	**Swimming** is available from the marina platform. (Port Authority & weather permitting) Please sign a waiver form and collect a wrist band from the Concierge.	Deck 2 / Marina

18:00 – 20:00	The SeaDream Yacht Boutique is open with assistance from **Rose**.	Deck 4
18:30	**Cocktails** are served poolside.	Deck 3
19:15	A brief review of tomorrow's port of call in Sandy Ground, Anguilla with your Club & Activities Director, **Richard Jones** poolside.	Deck 3
19:30 – 21:30	**'Starlight Dinner'** is served at the Topside Restaurant.	Decks 5/6

AFTER DINNER ACTIVITIES

21:30 – 23:00	The SeaDream Yacht Boutique is open with assistance from **Rose**.	Deck 4
21:30	The **Piano Bar** is open with Chief Bartender **Jamie** serving 'After Dinner' drinks & **George** on the Piano.	Deck 4
21:30	The Top of the Yacht Bar is open with your Bartenders **Danny & Sebastian** serving your favorite Cocktails.	Deck 6
21:30	**Take 777 and win your prize!** The Casino is open with your casino dealer **Elena**.	Deck 4
21:30	*Movie under the stars* *'Mama Mia'* starring *Pierce Brosnan, Meryl Streep, and Colin Firth*	Deck 3

24:00	The last tender departs from the pier.

Early Morning SeaDream I sails for Sandy Ground, Anguilla.

In the Family – SeaDream II is in San Juan, Puerto Rico.
DRESS CODE THIS EVENING IS 'YACHT CASUAL' AFTER 18:30

Concierge Desk	08:00 – 23:00	Deck 3		SeaDream Spa	08:00 – 20:00	Deck 4
Gymnasium	07:00 – 20:00	Deck 4	**ON BOARD RECREATION**	Hospital	09:00 – 10:00	Deck 5
Golf Simulator	08:00 – 22:00	Deck 6		Hospital	17:00 – 18:00	Deck 5
Boutique	18:00 – 20:00	Deck 4		Casino	From 21:30	Deck 4
Boutique	21:30 – 23:00	Deck 4		Future Bookings	see Richard or Dial 9	

>>>SeaDream I telephone number: + 47 23 67 59 30<<<

Courtesy SeaDream Yacht Club

SILJA LINE

Erottajankater 19   (In US) SeaEurope Holidays Inc.
00130 Helsinki, Finland   2500 Quantum Lakes Drive, Suite 203
                                     Boynton Beach, Florida 33426
+358(0)9-18041   (800) 533-3755
+358(0)9-1804-402 Fax   (561) 491-5156 Fax
www.silja.us

SILJA EUROPA: entered service 1993; 59,914 G.R.T.; 662' x 105'; 3,013-passenger capacity; 1,152 cabins; Finnish officers and crew; day and night cruises between Turku and Stockholm. (**Category D—Not Rated**)

SILJA FESTIVAL: entered service 1986; refurbished 1992; 34,419 G.R.T.; 551' x 90.5'; 2,023-passenger capacity; 588 cabins; Finnish officers and crew; day and night cruises between Turku and Stockholm. (**Category D—Not Rated**)

SILJA SERENADE: entered service 1990; 58,376 G.R.T.; 660' x 130'; 2,852-passenger capacity; 986 cabins; Finnish officers and crew; day and night cruises between Helsinki and Stockholm. (**Category D—Not Rated**)

SILJA SYMPHONY: entered service 1991; 58,376 G.R.T.; 660' x 130'; 2,852-passenger capacity; 986 cabins; Finnish officers and crew; overnight cruises between Helsinki and Stockholm. (**Category D—Not Rated**)

(Medical Facilities: No information was provided by the cruise line.)

Silja Line is part of the Silja Group, owned by Tallink, a Baltic ferry operator.

The *Silja Europa* and *Silja Festival* offer either day or night sailings between Turku, Finland, and Stockholm, Sweden (taking nine to 12 hours), and range in price. Cars are additional.

The *Silja Europa* is the world's largest cruise ferry. All cabins are air conditioned and include telephone, radio alarm clocks, television (except in the lowest category), and toilets with showers. Cabins are small and storage space is limited. I would not recommend anything less than a Silja-class cabin for cruisers requiring a modicum of comfort.

Dining options aboard the *Europa* range from a self-serve café, a McDonald's at sea, an all-you-can-eat Food Market with up to a 670-seat smorgasbord-style buffet, and à la carte steak, seafood, and gourmet restaurants. The Bon Vivant, the most upscale and expensive dining room, offers continental cuisine and fine wines.

After dinner, cruisers can enjoy a movie, mediocre live entertainment, disco and pop dancing, a music pub, gambling at a casino, or duty-free shopping. The facilities aboard include a small indoor swimming pool, sauna, three whirlpools, a children's pool, conference rooms and VIP meeting facilities, and a children's playground.

The voyage between Helsinki and Stockholm offered on the *Symphony* and *Serenade* departs at 5:30 P.M. and arrives at 9:30 A.M. the next morning.

On all the ships, Scandinavians make up the majority of the passengers, with a smattering of travelers from other European countries, Asians, and North Americans. Announcements are in numerous languages. There is an abundance of families with small children.

The above sailings offer an economical alternative means of transportation between the countries they service and are especially ideal for travelers with automobiles. The seasoned cruiser must be prepared to make many allowances. Overall comfort, food, and service are not comparable to that found on typical cruise ships.

Courtesy Silja Line

Sun Flower Oasis Spa, courtesy Silja Line

Silja-class cabin on the Silja Europa, *courtesy Silja Line*

SILVERSEA CRUISES, LTD.
110 E. Broward Boulevard
Fort Lauderdale, Florida 33301
(800) 722-9955
(954) 356-5881 Fax
www.silversea.com

PRINCE ALBERT II (formerly *Delfin Clipper* and *World Discoverer*): entered service 1989; totally renovated and refurbished 2008; 6,072 G.R.T.; 132-passenger capacity; 66 cabins; European officers and staff and international crew; expedition cruises in Arctic Circle, Iceland, and Greenland during summer and Antarctica and South America during winter. **(Category A—Not Rated)**

SILVER CLOUD: entered service 1994; refurbished 2004; 16,800 G.R.T.; 514' x 71'; 296-passenger capacity; 148 suites; Italian officers, European staff, and international crew; cruises the Mediterranean, northern Europe, Baltic, the Caribbean, South America, and other worldwide destinations.

SILVER SHADOW and *SILVER WHISPER:* entered service 2000 and 2001, respectively; 28,258 G.R.T.; 610' x 82'; 382-passenger capacity; 194 suites; Italian officers, European staff, and international crew; *Silver Shadow* cruises to Alaska, the Panama Canal, Mexican Riviera, and Far East; *Silver Whisper* cruises to the Baltic, northern Europe, the Arabian Peninsula, Indian Ocean, South Pacific, Far East, South America, and other worldwide destinations.

SILVER SPIRIT: entered service 2009; 36,000 G.R.T.; 642'x 86'; 540-passenger capacity; 270 suites; Italian officers and international crew; 91-day voyage around South America; varied worldwide itineraries, including the Mediterranean and the Caribbean.

SILVER WIND: entered service 1995; refurbished 2008; 16,800 G.R.T.; 514' x 71'; 296-passenger capacity; 148 suites; Italian officers, European staff, and international crew; cruises the Mediterranean, Africa, the Seychelles, Arabian Peninsula, India, and other worldwide destinations.

(Medical Facilities: C-all; P-1; EM, CLS, MS; N-1; CM; PD; BC; EKG; TC; PO; EPC; WC; OR; ICU; X on *Whisper* and *Shadow* only; M; CCP; LJ.)

Note: Six+ black stars is the highest rating given in this edition to ships in the deluxe market category.

These ships are rated in 11 separate categories in the second half of chapter 14.

In 1994, the Lefebvre family of Rome, previously a co-owner of Sitmar Cruises, entered the deluxe cruise market with two new 16,000+-ton vessels that compete with Seabourn, Cunard, Crystal, and Regent Seven Seas. *Silver Cloud* and *Silver Wind* entered service in 1994 and 1995, respectively. Every accommodation on these ships is a suite, and three-quarters of them feature spacious teak verandas. Although the majority of the line's staterooms are veranda suites (295 square feet in size, including the veranda), other suites on these two ships range in size from 240 to 1,314 square feet. Air-sea fares are among the industry's most inclusive and are somewhat less than many of the line's competitors.

The intent of Silversea Cruises was to create the optimum ship—small enough to sail intriguing waterways unavailable to most of the larger vessels while also providing a smooth, comfortable ride in deep-water cruising. In addition, these ships offer the intimacy, service, and nuances found on many of the smaller deluxe cruise ships while also affording all of the facilities, amenities, and activities available on the larger cruise ships.

These ships have the most advanced nautical architecture and maritime equipment, which renders them very steady at high speeds and highly maneuverable. Design and decor were conceived by Norwegian architects whose credits include most of the other small luxury cruise ships, as well as Royal Caribbean's mega-liners. In addition to glass doors leading out to verandas in 75 percent of the suites and large picture windows in the remaining 25 percent, each suite features spacious storage; a walk-in closet; mirrored dressing table; writing desk; twin beds (convertible to queen); a separate sitting area; stocked refrigerator; electronic wall safe; remote-controlled television with videocassette player; a large umbrella; all-marble bathrooms with tub, shower, hair dryer, and 110- and 220-volt outlets; and plush terry-cloth robes and slippers. Guests desiring more space than the standard vista or veranda suites can opt for a silver suite (541 square feet), the two-bedroom owner's suite (827 square feet), a two-bedroom royal suite (1,031 square-feet), or a two-bedroom grand suite (1,314 square feet).

During 2008, extensive refurbishments were completed on the *Silver Wind*. Included among these additions are new carpeting and some new furnishings in the public areas; a new ocean-view spa and fitness center; a new observation lounge; eight new larger suites on decks 7 and 8; and reduction of some vista suites on deck 4. All suites received new flat-screen TVs, sofas, armchairs, desks, vanities, night tables, headboards, carpeting, drapes, and bed coverings, as well as new fixtures, bathtubs, and marble countertops, walls, and flooring in the bathrooms.

Featuring the highest space-to-guest and crew-to-guest ratios of any ship in the industry, the 28,258-ton, 382-passenger *Silver Shadow* was launched in 2000, followed in the summer of 2001 by its sister ship, *Silver Whisper.* Every suite on these newer vessels includes the facilities described above for the *Cloud* and *Wind*, plus a few innovations, such as double marble vanities in the bathrooms. Except for 26 vista suites measuring 287 square feet, all other accommodations sport verandas. These include nine additional vista suites with shared verandas, 128 veranda suites measuring 345 square feet, and 23 larger suites ranging in size from 521 square feet up to 1,435 square feet for one of the grand suites with an optional second bedroom. The six largest suites sell for considerably more than the vista or veranda suites and feature additional amenities, such as whirlpool tubs, greater private veranda space, CD player/stereo systems, comfortable dining areas, deluxe bathroom amenities, guest powder rooms, giant closets, flat-screen televisions, and complimentary laundry and butler service.

The line offers one of the most inclusive cruise packages available in the ultra-luxury cruise market. Air-sea fares include all gratuities, alcoholic and non-alcoholic beverages (both in your suite and throughout the ship), fine wines with lunch and dinner, round-trip air transportation, a deluxe pre-cruise hotel stay, as well as transfers, porterage, and complimentary shuttle-bus service to the city center in many ports of call. Although there is a charge for shore excursions, select sailings feature a special complimentary Silversea Experience—a customized shore event available only to Silversea guests—which can range from a traditional street party in Mykonos with wine, dancing, and singing to a formal soirée in one of St. Petersburg's lavish 19th-century palaces. Also included in the fare are special in-suite touches such as fresh fruit and flowers, personalized stationery, lunch and dinner menus and satellite newsletters delivered daily, and a bottle of chilled Pommery Brut Royal champagne to greet you upon arrival. In addition, your cruise tickets, baggage tags, and itineraries arrive before the cruise in a handsome leather portfolio. Another innovation for passengers is the option to board or disembark at any port they choose during every cruise itinerary.

Dining options range from casual to elegant, with open seating in both the more casual indoor/outdoor La Terrazza and in the more formal restaurants, including the ultra-gourmet Le Champagne Wine Restaurant by Relais & Chateaux. Twenty-four-hour in-suite dining is also offered, with course-by-course dinner service available. Both the more formal restaurant and La Terrazza are elegantly furnished and afford a good deal of space between tables, a well-controlled sound level, and fine food and service. La Terrazza takes on an Italian accent for dinner, offering an innovative à la carte menu showcasing classic Italian and rustic Tuscan cuisine.

The main dining rooms on each ship feature selected menu items created in conjunction with the famed chefs of Relais & Chateaux. The alternative specialty restaurants on all four ships are Relais & Chateaux wine-themed restaurants, featuring a collection of dishes designed specifically to compliment great wines. Gratuities are not expected in any of the restaurants.

Special theme parties and dinner dancing are featured on each sailing, and mature gentlemen hosts are available as dance and bridge partners on selected sailings. Public areas also offer guests a great variety of choices and include a multi-level show lounge with full-scale entertainment throughout the cruise; a panorama lounge; a library stocked with books, computers with Internet access, periodicals, and reference materials as well as videos and DVDS; a bar/nightclub; a full casino with roulette, blackjack, and slots; a health spa with masseuse, beauty salon, sauna, and well-equipped exercise facility; a cardroom; an outdoor pool and two heated whirlpools; and a sun deck observation area.

Public areas on the *Shadow* and *Whisper* are similar to those on the *Cloud* and *Wind,* with various innovations available due to their increased size, including a larger casino; a larger, more fully equipped exercise facility and spa; a poolside grill; the Humidor, a cigar bar by Davidoff; and a scenic observation lounge atop ship.

Worldwide itineraries offer cruises that can be booked from six to 126 days. Frequent cruisers can earn points resulting in significant savings when booking future cruises.

Officers and staff on board Silversea ships are highly experienced, and many have extensive tenure with other upscale and premium cruise lines. Italian officers create a warm and friendly on-board ambiance, Asian butlers provide efficient and hospitable suite service, and a northern European hotel staff, together with an international support staff, provide gracious on-board dining.

A partnership with Wireless Maritime Services allows passengers to use their mobile phones and other wireless devices aboard ship. Silversea also offers remote wireless Internet access (Wi-Fi) in designated locations aboard its ships.

Notable guest lecturers on each voyage offer definitive views of the history, culture, and geography of the countries the ships visit. The line will also continue its Wine Cruises, hosted by some of the world's finest vintners, as well as its Culinary Arts cruises, featuring renowned chefs from the Relais & Chateaux-Relais Gourmands, the prestigious association of boutique hotels and restaurants.

In 2007, the cruise line purchased the former 6,072-ton, 132-passenger *World Discoverer,* upgraded and refurbished her, and commenced operating her as *Prince Albert II* in June 2008. The expedition ship has a strengthened hull and can operate in remote locations around the world such as the Arctic and Antarctica. All accommodations have ocean-view rooms ranging in size from 175 to 675 square feet and flat-screen TVs with DVD players, and many also have balconies. Included in accommodations are two owner's suites, two grand suites, and six silver suites similar to the cruise line's other vessels. There is Wi-Fi and cell phone access throughout the ship. The main restaurant features single-seating dining. Other public areas include a cigar lounge, library/Internet café, theater for shows and lectures, boutique, beauty salon, fitness center, full-size spa, two Jacuzzi pools, and the Panorama and Observation lounges.

A new 36,000-ton, 540-passenger new build named *Silver Spirit* joined the fleet late in 2009. This vessel offers 270 ocean-view suites (all but 12 with verandas), 26 silver suites, six grand suites, two owner's suites, a new supper club featuring live music, dancing, and cabaret entertainment, an Asian-theme restaurant, 8,300 square feet of expanded spa facilities, four whirlpools (three attached to the outdoor pool and one in the spa), a fitness center with two aerobics studios and a kinesis wall, a beauty salon, three boutiques, a library, an Internet café, a casino, the Observation Lounge, the show lounge, the Panorama Lounge, a pool bar, a humidor bar, and a lobby bar serving Italian coffees, champagne, wine, and spirits gratis.

In 2009, butler service for all suites was extended to every ship in the fleet.

Strong Points:

Silversea offers the ultimate in a luxury, yacht-like cruise experience with imaginative gourmet cuisine, sumptuous accommodations, and impeccable service on vessels somewhat larger than its competitors, with more public area space and expanded facilities, activities and entertainment, and exotic itineraries. Many critics rate Silversea as the best.

Courtesy Silversea Cruises

Courtesy Silversea Cruises

Courtesy Silversea Cruises

Silver Whisper, *courtesy Silversea Cruises, Ltd.*

Courtesy Silversea Cruises, Ltd.

Courtesy Silversea Cruises, Ltd.

*A*PPETIZERS

STACK OF SMOKED STURGEON
Grapefruit and Greens, Lime and Dill Dressing
per serving: 126 calories; 8g fat; 6g carbohydrates

BABY CARROT AND FOREST MUSHROOM TERRINE ❦
Carrot Reduction and Ginger Yoghurt Dressing

PIMM'S MELON COCKTAIL ❦
with Pear and Cucumber

ESCALOPE OF FOIE GRAS WITH CANDIED APPLE AND FIG CHUTNEY
Raspberry Vinegar and Port Wine Reductions

*I*NTERMEZZO

TRUFFLE CONSOMMÉ
with Truffle Shavings
per serving: 52 calories; 2g fat; 4g carbohydrates

CREAMY CRAB AND CORN CHOWDER
with Crab Chunks

CANNELLONI AL FORNO ❦
Ricotta Cheese and Spinach-stuffed Pipe Noodles with Béchamel, Mozzarella and Tomato Gratin

STILTON AND PEAR SALAD ❦
Cashews and Chives with Blue Cheese Dressing

*E*NTREES

BROILED FILLET OF FRESH CARIBBEAN SWORDFISH WITH RED WINE REDUCTION
Wilted Arugula and Extra Virgin Olive Oil
per serving: 256 calories; 8g fat; 10g carbohydrates

TEMPURA TIGER PRAWNS WITH PRAWN COULIS
Sun-dried Tomato, Wild Mushroom and Saffron Risotto

BEEF 'WELLINGTON'
Herb and Vegetable Bouquet, Port and Cognac Jus

VEAL CHOP WITH TOMATO BÉARNAISE
Sautéed Portobello Mushrooms and Garlic Mousseline

GRATINATED POLENTA GNOCCHI ❦
Grilled Marinated Vegetables and Tomato Sauce

Executive Chef Carsten's Recommendation

ESCALOPE OF FOIE GRAS WITH CANDIED APPLE AND FIG CHUTNEY
Raspberry Vinegar and Port Wine Reductions

CREAMY CRAB AND CORN CHOWDER
with Crab Chunks

BROILED FILLET OF FRESH CARIBBEAN SWORDFISH WITH RED WINE REDUCTION
Wilted Arugula and Extra Virgin Olive Oil

ALASKA FLORIDA
Ice Cream Dome on a Sponge Base with a Baked Meringue Crust

All-day selection

Shrimp 'Martini'
with American Cocktail Sauce
per serving: 90 calories; 5g fat; 2g carbohydrates

Silversea Spring Roll
with Asian Slaw and Sweet Chili Sauce

Crispy Corn Cakes
with Baby Leaves and Garlic Dip

Chicken Consommé
with Matzo Balls

Crispy Greens
with your Choice of Dressing

Penne Pasta
with Fresh Herbs and Tomato Sauce

Poached or Broiled Salmon Fillet
with your Choice of Light Lemon Dressing
or Hollandaise Sauce

Grilled Chicken Breast
Garden Vegetables and Pan Gravy
per serving: 90 calories; 5g fat; 2g carbohydrates

Sirloin Steak
with your Choice of Béarnaise, Green Peppercorn or Mushroom Sauce

---

VEGETARIAN FARES

WELLNESS OPTIONS (the average nutritional values provided are based on the standard Silversea recipes. These may vary slightly.)

At Silversea Cruises, we take maximum food precautionary measures to ensure the safest quality product is offered to our Guests; United States Public Health advises that consuming raw or undercooked meat, poultry, seafood, shellfish or eggs may increase your risk of food-borne illness.

Courtesy Silversea Cruises

SATURDAY, DECEMBER 13, 2008

Sunrise 6:19am • Sunset 5:37pm

GOOD MORNING

7:30	Sunrise Chi Walk with Fitness Instructor Daiane	Walking Track (9)
8:00	THE SILVER SHADOW IS SCHEDULED TO DOCK IN CASTRIES, ST. LUCIA	
	Good Morning from the Bridge by your Cruise Director Martin	Public Address System
	Guests staying onboard are advised that games, books, music CD's and DVD's are available in the... Library (8)/Observation Lounge (10)	
8:00	Internet Point Host Paul is in attendance to assist you until 11:00am	Computer Centre (8)
8:00	International Hostess Roxana is available to assist non English-speaking Guests until 9:00am	Tour Desk (5)
8:30	Silversea Quiz. Points for prizes will be awarded for the first most correct sheet returned before 3:00pm	Tour Office (5)
8:30	Today's Crossword Puzzle and Sudoku are available	Library (8)
8:30	Aerobics with Fitness Instructor Daiane	Aerobics Room (10)
9:30	Social Bridge Play with your fellow guests	Card Room (7)
10:00	Italian Class with International Hostess Roxana	The Bar (5)
10:30	Coffee Chat. Join the Cruise Staff for a morning chat!	Panorama Lounge (8)
11:30	Shuffleboard Tournament with the Cruise Staff *(weather permitting)*	Shuffleboard Court (10)

GOOD AFTERNOON

2:00	Social Bridge Play with your fellow guests	Card Room (7)
3:00	Table Tennis with the Cruise Staff	Poolside (8)
4:00	Afternoon Tea is served to the piano music of Jose (until 5:00pm)	Panorama Lounge (8)
4:00	Internet Point Host Paul is in attendance to assist you until 7:00pm	Computer Centre (8)
4:45	Team Trivia for Prize Points! Join your Cruise Director Martin and the Cruise Staff	The Bar (5)
5:00	"Sundowners Bar" Relax at this special time of day with old and new friends until 7:00pm	Poolside (8)
5:30	Golf Putting with your Golf Pro Gordon	Outside The Terrazza (7)
5:30	Pathway to Yoga with Fitness Instructor Daiane	Aerobics Room (10)
5:30	ALL GUESTS ARE REQUESTED TO BE BACK ON BOARD / THE SILVER SHADOW IS SCHEDULED TO SET SAIL FOR ROSEAU, DOMINICA	

GOOD EVENING - DRESS CODE: FORMAL

6:45	Enjoy a pre-dinner cocktail to the fine music of the Joy Duo	The Bar (5)
6:45	CAPTAIN IGNAZIO TATULLI *invites Guests for* WELCOME ABOARD COCKTAILS	Athenian Lounge (6)
	International Hostess Roxana will introduce Guests to the Captain	
9:45	The Joy Duo plays for Guests' listening and dancing enjoyment	The Bar (5)
10:00	Late Night dance to the fine sounds of the Silver Shadow Quartet	Panorama Lounge (8)
10:00	SHOWTIME! SILVERSEA PRODUCTIONS PROUDLY PRESENTS	Athenian Lounge (6)

Broadway Rocks

Singers: Jessica Kaiser and Theo Wishhusen.
Ballroom Dancers: Natallia Korsak and Dmitry Svirydau.
Silversea Dancers: Lisa Jayne Heath, Lucie Payne and Rebecca Schick.
A breakaway from the "My Fair Lady" syndrome of "Phantom", this show will include music, costume, dance from such Stars as Abba, Queen, Elton John, etc. Songs everyone will know no matter from what part of the world you are from and what language you speak. Also... make sure you are in good voice as who knows...the chorus may belong to you!

Courtesy Silversea Cruises

SONESTA NILE CRUISE COLLECTION
c/o Sonesta Collection Hotels-Resorts-Cruises
116 Huntington Avenue
Boston, Massachusetts 02116
(800) 766-3782
www.sonesta.com/Nilecruises/

MOON GODDESS: entered service 2000; renovated 2010; 220' x 43'; 112-passenger capacity; 50 staterooms; Egyptian crew; 4- and 6-night cruises up and down the Nile. (**No Category—Not Rated**)

NILE GODDESS: entered service 1989; renovated 2008; 118-passenger capacity; 57 cabins; Egyptian crew; 4- and 6-night cruises up and down the Nile. (**No Category—Not Rated**)

ST. GEORGE I: entered service 2006; 74.5 meters long; 118-passenger capacity; 59 cabins; Egyptian crew; 3-, 4-, and 7-night cruises between Luxor and Aswan. (**No Category—Not Rated**)

STAR GODDESS: entered service 2006; 72 meters long; 66-passenger capacity; 33 cabins; Egyptian crew; 3-, 4-, and 7-night cruises between Luxor and Aswan. (**No Category—Not Rated**)

SUN GODDESS: entered service 1993; 124-passenger capacity; 62 cabins; Egyptian crew; 4- and 6-night cruises up and down the Nile. (**No Category—Not Rated**)

(Medical Facilities: C-4; P-1; EM; CLS; MS; N-O; OX; LJ.)

Nile Goddess was built in 1989 and totally renovated in 1995 and 2008. Its five decks include a pool with an adjoining lounge, recreation area, barbecue area, show lounge, bar, game room, shop, disco, and restaurant. The one-sitting restaurant provides buffet meals.

There are 49 cabins, four junior suites, and four full suites. All cabins are air conditioned and feature panoramic windows to view the Nile and passing scenery. All accommodations include private direct-dial telephones, hair dryers, safety-deposit boxes, minibars, music, wireless Internet access, plasma televisions with movies, and bathrooms with full-size bathtubs.

The *Sun Goddess* was built and added to the fleet in 1993. The public areas are similar to the *Nile Goddess* and include a Turkish bath. The ship has 58 cabins and four suites with the same facilities and amenities as its sister ship.

The *Moon Goddess* came on line in 2000 and offers 48 junior suites, each with sliding-glass doors opening to a private balcony, and two presidential suites with private lounges. All staterooms feature private direct-dial telephones, in-room safes, hair dryers, remote-control television and video, and bathrooms with bathtubs. Amenities on board include an outdoor pool, pool bar, lounge, casino, disco, jogging track, table tennis, and gym.

All three ships sail between Luxor and Aswan, Egypt, on alternate four- and six-night cruises. Shore excursions visit the Temples of Karnak and Luxor, the Valley of Kings and Queens, the Temple of Queen Hatshepsut, the Colossi of Memnon, the Temple of Dendera in Kena, the Temple of Horus in Edfu, the Temple of Sobek and Harocies in Kom Ombo, the Agha Khan Mausoleum, the High Dam granite quarries, and the Temple of Philae in Aswan.

In 2006, two new ships joined the fleet, *Star Goddess* and *St. George I*. They operate three-, four-, and seven-night cruises between Luxor and Aswan with the same shore excursions as those listed above.

The *Star Goddess* has four decks and 33 suite accommodations that feature private direct-dial international telephone lines, Internet access, individual climate control, hair dryers, minibars, safety-deposit boxes, television and movie programs, and bathrooms with full-size tubs. Facilities include an outdoor swimming pool with bar service, jogging track, spa offering massage, sauna, and Jacuzzi, gym, dining room and outdoor barbecue area, discotheque, main lounge, and several bars. On each cruise there are theme nights, shows, and a captain's welcome cocktail party.

The *St. George I* has five decks, 49 cabins, nine presidential suites, and one royal suite. All accommodations feature double-glassed open panoramic windows, private direct-dial telephones, wireless Internet access and laptops, safety-deposit boxes, hair dryers, minibars, 21-inch LCD televisions with satellite programming, and bathrooms with Jacuzzis and showers with music and water massage. Facilities and entertainments are similar to those described for *Star Goddess*.

Strong Points:

New, modern riverboats offering in-depth Nile cruises. The two newest ships are especially upscale for Nile riverboats.

Nile Goddess, *courtesy Sonesta International Nile Cruises*

Cabin, Star Goddess, *courtesy Sonesta International Nile Cruises*

Sun Goddess, *courtesy Sonesta International Nile Cruises*

STAR CLIPPERS
7200 NW 19th Street, Suite 206
Miami, Florida 33126
(800) 442-0551
www.starclippers.com

ROYAL CLIPPER: entered service 2000; 5,000 G.R.T.; 439' x 54'; 227-passenger capacity; 114 cabins; European officers and international crew; 7-day Caribbean cruises during winter from Barbados and 7-, 10-, and 11-day Mediterranean cruises during summer from Athens and Venice.

STAR CLIPPER: entered service 1992; 2,298 G.R.T.; 360' x 50'; 170-passenger capacity; 85 cabins; European officers and international crew; 7-, 10-, and 11-day Mediterranean cruises from Cannes during summer and winter cruises in Thailand and Malaysia.

STAR FLYER: entered service 1991; 2,298 G.R.T.; 360' x 50'; 170-passenger capacity; 85 cabins; European officers and international crew; 7-, 10-, and 11-day cruises in French Polynesia and Mediterranean cruises during summer.

(Medical Facilities: C-0; P [on trans-ocean cruises only]; N-1—Medical facilities and equipment are very limited.)

These ships are rated in 11 separate categories in the second half of chapter 14.

In 1991, Mikael Krafft, a Swedish shipping and real-estate entrepreneur and the founder and managing owner of Star Clippers, embarked on bringing to the cruise market yacht-like sailboats that sail more than they operate their engines. The cruise line emphasizes enjoying a sailing vessel, being close to the sea, participating in watersports, and visiting great beaches in a casual yet comfortable shipboard environment.

When *Star Flyer* and *Star Clipper* entered the cruise market in 1991 and 1992, they were (and still are) the tallest sailing ships afloat, with 36,000 square feet of Dacron sail flying from four towering masts, the highest rising to 226 feet. The ships feature a unique anti-rolling system designed to keep them upright and stable for sailing and while at anchor.

Eighty-five air-conditioned staterooms accommodate 170 passengers. Six are small inside cabins with upper and lower berths. The remainder measure about

120 square feet and are outside, with two twin beds that convert to a double bed, television that plays in-house DVDs, radios, lighted dressing table with mirror and stool, small closets with shelving and built-in personal safes, cellular satellite telephone with direct dialing, and small bathrooms with showers, toilets, hair dryers, and mirrors. The eight more-expensive cabins located on main and sun decks are a wee bit larger and include refrigerators, full windows, and larger bathrooms with Jacuzzi tubs and shower attachments.

Public areas, entertainment, and on-board activities are very limited. However, every day the officers permit passengers to participate in hoisting and lowering the sails and steering the vessel. In the evening there are audience-participation events and dancing. Atop ship on sun deck, surrounded by the sails, are two small swimming pools and the lounge chairs. Main deck, below, is the location of six of the larger cabins, the piano bar lounge, the library, and the sheltered outdoor tropical bar—the hub of activity on the ship. The dining room and half of the remaining cabins are on clipper deck; the other cabins are located on commodore deck.

The attractive dining room seats all passengers at an open sitting. Breakfast and lunch are served buffet style, and a five-course dinner features a choice of four entrees, including a vegetarian offering. The diverse selection of ethnic and continental cuisines is excellent and the service is warm, friendly, and efficient. The atmosphere is casual, and jackets are never required. At midnight, the chef prepares a special snack that is served in the piano bar.

At least once each cruise, there is a barbecue lunch and beach party at a private, secluded beach with watersports and games. An extensive watersport program is available daily as well, at no extra cost. The watersport staff supervises kayaking, snorkeling, small-craft sailing, and scuba (for a small supplement).

The ships are sometimes under charter to private groups, and you must check in advance to be certain the cruise date you select is open to the general public. Itineraries for the two ships are not written in stone; however, historically the ships cruise in the Caribbean or southeast Asia during the winter months and in the Mediterranean or Caribbean during the summer. I have found the sailings in southeast Asia from Phuket, Thailand, to be spectacular, calling at small, pristine scenic islands seldom visited by the average tourist. This is a beach, snorkel, and watersport lover's paradise. Currently the *Star Flyer* offers cruises in French Polynesia.

Rates run from approximately $240 per person per day for a standard outside cabin with double or twin beds up to $370 per person per day for one of the larger cabins on main or sun decks. A third passenger sharing a cabin pays only $53 per night. The cruise line will arrange air from most U.S. cities for an average cost of $865 to the Caribbean, $1,290 to the Mediterranean, $1,285 to Asia, and $1,095 to Tahiti. Star Clippers is also marketed throughout Europe, so you can expect a large percentage of the travelers to be European, even in the Caribbean. Announcements are in English, followed by German and French, depending on the passenger mix of each cruise.

The 5,000-gross-ton, 227-passenger, 42-sail *Royal Clipper* entered service in spring 2000 as the largest sailing ship afloat. A total of 56,000 square feet of sails fly from her five great steel masts. Considerably larger and more elegantly appointed than the other vessels, she offers two 355-square-foot owner's suites and 14 215-square-foot deluxe suites with verandas. The remaining standard cabins measure 108 to 145 square feet and include marble bathrooms with shower stalls, remote-control televisions, radio channels, satellite telephones, private safes, and elephant-trunk hair dryers. (Six of these are interior accommodations, and two are somewhat larger and open onto the deck.) The seven-day itineraries cover the Caribbean from Barbados during the late fall and winter, and the ship offers seven-, 10-, and 11-day cruises from Rome and Venice throughout the remainder of the year. Overall, the accommodations and public areas are a great deal more upscale than on the two smaller vessels and are enhanced by the use of brass, rich dark woods, attractive fabrics, mirrors, and nautical art and accents.

Public areas include an indoor main lounge with a piano bar midship; an observation lounge; an outside, but protected Tropical Bar; and a library, all similar to those on the two smaller ships but on a much larger scale. In addition there is a two-level, paneled dining room (accessible from staircases that descend from a dynamic atrium) featuring open seating, with buffet offerings for breakfast and lunch and dishes served at the table for dinner; a lower-deck complex that includes a gym with antiquated equipment; a spa offering various massage and body treatments; a Turkish bath; a sun deck with three tiny pools and scattered lounge chairs; and a hydraulic platform at the rear of the ship for watersports and access to the tenders. Rates range from approximately $200 to $400 per person per night for the six categories of standard cabins, up to $500 to $600 for the 16 deluxe suites, and $630 to $690 for the two owner's suites.

The cruise line is building a new 7,400-ton, 296-passenger, five-masted, 37-sail barque that will be 518 feet long by 61 feet wide and come on line in 2010. She will be 50 percent larger than the *Royal Clipper* and have an ice-class hull. The 10 inside cabins will measure 129 square feet, while the 140 standard outside cabins will measure 162 square feet. For more space and amenities, there are 30 323-square-foot deluxe suites, two deluxe 215-square-foot deck cabins, and two 592-square-foot owner's suites. All deluxe accommodations have balconies. Public areas include a two-level, one-seating main restaurant, a piano lounge, a two-level tropical bar, a dive/spots bar, an observation room, a multi-purpose room that can convert to a 160-person conference room, a library, a spa, a gym, three pools, a swim tube for scuba training in the aft swimming pool that extends down through the dive/sports bar into the library, and a retractable marina at the stern of the ship for watersports.

Strong Points:

A more intimate, hands-on sail/cruise experience to great beach destinations and offbeat small ports in a casual environment at middle-market prices and enviable dining and service—but with less entertainment, service, creature comforts, and amenities than those found on the other, more traditional smaller cruise ships. A must for real sailors and beach/watersport lovers! The *Royal Clipper* offers more space, facilities, pampering, and comfort, as well as several more upscale deluxe suites with verandas.

Courtesy Star Clippers, Inc.

Courtesy Star Clippers, Inc.

The author aboard Star Flyer, *courtesy Star Clippers, Inc.*

Courtesy Star Clippers, Inc.

Courtesy Star Clippers, Inc.

STAR CLIPPERS

Les Entrees

Bresaola et sa salade d'orge
Thinly sliced dried beef served with a barley salad
Bresaola, luftgetrocknetes Rindfleisch, mit Graupensalat

Crêpes au saumon, sauce au safran
Salmon pancakes with saffron sauce
Crepes gefüllt mit Lachs in Safransauce

Le Potage

Velouté de carottes á l'orange
Cream of carrot soup with Orange slices
Karottencremesuppe mit Orangenspalten

Le Sorbet

Sorbet Tomate Vodka
Tomato - Vodka sorbet
Tomatensorbet mit Vodka

Les Plats

Queue de homard grillée, beurre aux fines herbes
Grilled lobster tail with herb butter
Gegrillter Hummerschwanz mit frischer Kräuterbutter

Filet de bœuf « Chateaubriand »
Filet of beef "Chateaubriand" with truffle sauce
Rinderfilet "Chateaubriand" mit Trüffelsauce

Le Vegetarien

Quiche aux Champignons
Mushroom quiche
Champignon Quiche

Caribbean Chef Special

Magret de canard au curry
Duck breast with curry sauce
Entenbrust mit Currysauce

Vous pouvez également commander un Consommé, des Pâtes ou une Entrecôte, Pommes frites
If you wish, you may order a Consommé, a Pasta dish or a Sirloin steak with French Fries
Auf Wunsch servieren wir Ihnen eine Kraftbrühe, ein Nudelgericht oder ein Entrecote mit Pommes frites

Convient aux Végétariens / Suitable for Vegetarians / Empfehlung für Vegetarier

Courtesy Star Clippers, Inc.

STAR CLIPPERS

La Salade

Salade de Radicchio aux pignons, vinaigrette à la crème
Radicchio salad with pine nuts and cream dressing
Radicchiosalat mit Pinienkernen und Rahmsauce

Le Fromage

Une sélection de fromages, accompagnée de fruits et biscuits salés
A selection of international cheeses served with fresh fruit and biscuits
Kleine Käseauswahl mit frischem Obst und Salzgebäck

Les Desserts

Omelette Norvégienne
Baked Alaska
Flambierte Eistorte "Alaska"

~ * ~

Le Conseil du Sommelier

Louis Jadot, Puligny Montrachet AOC, Burgundy 2004.
Fresh, clean citrussy nose - still quite closed.
Rounded and medium-bodied with ripe, warm citrus and toasted oak flavors.
75 cl € 48.00

Château La Chapelle de Calon, St. Estephe AOC 2004, Bordeaux.
Appealing ripe prune fruit, spicy oak bouquet. Full bodied,
balanced tannins and good finish.
75 cl € 36.00

Star Clippers a consulté le chef Jean Marie Meulien, honoré de trois étoiles au
guide Michelin, pour la création de ces menus.

For the creation of these menus Star Clippers has consulted the chef Jean Marie Meulien
who has been awarded 3 stars in the Michelin guide throughout his career.

Star Clippers konsultierte den mit drei Michelin Sternen ausgezeichneten
Chef Jean Marie Meulien zur Gestaltung der Menus

Rodolfo Soledad	**Francesco Mazzoni**	**Emmanuel Abella**
Executive Chef	Hotel Manager	Maitre d' Hotel

Courtesy Star Clippers, Inc.

SPV Royal Clipper

Barbados – Union Island – Grenada – <u>Tobago Cays</u> – St. Vincent/Bequia – Martinique – St. Lucia – Barbados

08:00 – 08:30	**Morning Gymnastics** *with Tanja*	*Tropical Bar*
08:00 – 20:00	**Captain Nemo Lounge** *(Spa / Wellness / Fitness Centre) is open for you!*	
09:00	**Port Information on Tobago Cays** *with Timoteo*	*Bridge*

> *09:30*　　**SPV Royal Clipper anchors off the Tobago Cays !**
> *A continuous tender service will be at your disposal to the beach and back.*
> *Do not forget to take some money (EC$ or US$) for the local t-shirts!*

South of Canouan and West of Mayreau lie the Tobago Cays Islands like giant turtle shells rousing from the crystal clear water. The white sand beaches and the turquoise blue water are withstanding for those who like swimming, snorkelling and diving. The coral reefs are an unforgettable experience for all visitors!

> *09:30*　　**„Southern Grenadines by Powerboat"**　　　　　*Meet at the **Tropical Bar***
> *(do not forget to put your swimsuit & to take towel, hat, sun lotion and camera!)*
> **Tour ends at +/- 13:00 on the beach for the beach barbeque**

10:00 – 15:30	**The Sports Team** *awaits you* **at the Beach** *with water sports activities (weather permitting)*	
10:30	**Certified Dive** *with the Dive instructors*	*Marina Platform*
13:00	**Discover Scuba Dive** *with the Dive instructors*	*Beach*
14:00	**Aqua Gymnastics** *with Tanja*	*Beach*

> <u>*15:30*</u>　　**Last tender back to the SPV Royal Clipper ! All guests back on board !**
> *16:00*　　**SPV Royal Clipper sets sail for St Vincent !**
> *Join Captain Sergey and Crew for the sail away maneuvers by the bridge.*
> *Enjoy the afternoon sailing on deck !*

16:45	**Captain Sergey's Story time following by Sailing maneuvers**　*Bridge*	
	(weather permitting)	
19:00 – 20:30	**Piano melodies** *with Laszlo*	*Piano Bar*
21:30 – 22:00	**After-dinner music** *with our musician Laszlo*	*Tropical Bar*

> *22:00*　　　**𝒩𝒾𝑔𝒽𝓉 𝑜𝒻 𝓂𝓊𝓈𝒾𝒸**　　　　　　　*Tropical Bar*

AFTERWARDS DANCING UNDER THE STARS...

Captain Sergey and the entire Crew wish you a fantastic day in Tobago Cays!

Courtesy Star Clippers, Inc.

STAR CRUISES

9 Penang Road
#11-08, Park Mall
Singapore 238459

65-6226-1168
65-6220-6993 Fax

Star Cruise Terminal
Pulau Indah Pelabuhan Barat
42009 Pelabuhan Kelang
Selangor Darul Ehsan, Malaysia
(603) 31011313
(603) 31011406 Fax

www.starcruises.com

MEGASTAR ARIES and *MEGASTAR TAURUS* (formerly *Aurora II* and *I*): entered service 1991; 3,300 G.R.T.; 82.2 meters x 14 meters; 74-passenger capacity; 36 cabins; Scandinavian officers and international crew; cruises in Far East for private charters. **(Category B—Not Rated)**

SUPERSTAR AQUARIUS (formerly *Norwegian Wind* and *Windward*): entered service 1993; stretched 1998; 50,760 G.R.T.; 754' x 94'; 1,748-passenger capacity; 874 cabins; Scandinavian officers and international crew; cruises from Hong Kong. **(Category C—Not Rated)**

STAR PISCES (formerly *Kalypso*): entered service 1990; 40,000 G.R.T.; 579' x 97'; 2,000-passenger capacity; 700 cabins; Scandinavian officers and international crew; cruises from Hong Kong. **(Category D—Not Rated)**

SUPERSTAR LIBRA (formerly *Norwegian Sea*): entered service 1988; 42,000 G.R.T.; 713' x 93'; 1,480-passenger capacity; 740 cabins; Scandinavian officers and international crew; cruises from Mumbai, India. **(Category C—Not Rated)**

SUPERSTAR VIRGO: entered service 1999; 76,800 G.R.T.; 880' x 106'; 1,960-passenger capacity; 980 cabins; Scandinavian officers and international crew; cruises from Singapore. **(Category B/C—Not Rated)**

(Medical Facilities: all ships equipped with a clinic and medical personnel.)

Formed in 1993 by Tan Sri Lim Goh Tong, Star Cruises is the first major cruise line concentrating on meeting the needs and satisfying the tastes of the cruise market in Asia. Although the top ship officers are Scandinavian and the crew is from all over the world, the passenger mix is 70 percent Asian. The main language spoken on board is English, while second languages, such as Mandarin, would depend upon the area of operation.

The line offers three categories of cruise experiences. The *Star Pisces,* a converted ferry liner, is designed to appeal to the Asian mass market of first-time cruisers, vacationing families, and the young-at-heart seeking a less-expensive cruise on a no-frills ship with an abundance of activities and facilities. *MegaStar Aries* and

MegaStar Taurus are generally booked by private charter groups (up to 74 passengers) seeking a more elegant, yacht-like cruise experience. *SuperStars Libra* and *Virgo* are geared to the more traditional, seasoned traveler seeking a more typical cruise experience on longer voyages to multiple destinations, with international standards for food, service, facilities, etc. *SuperStar Libra,* formerly *Norwegian Sea* of Norwegian Cruise Line, joined the Star Cruise fleet in 2005, while *Virgo* is a 76,800-ton new build that entered service in 1999.

Star Pisces was converted from ferry service and offers cruises from Hong Kong. All cabins have small private bathrooms, televisions, and telephones. The junior and executive suites have additional facilities and amenities and would be my recommendation for those requiring more space and comfort. Passengers can dine in a variety of ethnic restaurants serving both Asian and Western cuisine. Public facilities include a cinema, show lounge, several smaller lounges and bars, a Karaoke lounge, an indoor pool, a small gym and health spa, numerous shops, a sun deck, jogging track, video arcade, and child-care center.

MegaStar Aries and *MegaStar Taurus* are the former *Aurora II* and *I* of Classical Cruises. These small, yacht-like vessels—which feature more traditional, rather than nautical, decor—are used for private groups and business charters and do not offer regular itineraries.

The second of the line's new builds, *SuperStar Virgo,* debuted in the summer of 1999. The first, *SuperStar Leo,* has been transferred to Norwegian. *SuperStar Virgo* weighs in at 76,800 G.R.T. and can accommodate a maximum of 1,960 passengers (lower berths only) in 980 cabins. This ship offers destination cruises along the Straits of Malacca and is based in Singapore. There are seven 627- to 629-square-foot executive suites on decks 9 and 10 with private balconies, lounging areas, separate bedrooms, master bathrooms with whirlpool tubs and separate shower, guest powder rooms, and two interactive color televisions. There are also 11 474- to 510-square-foot junior suites. All of the 331 inside cabins have four berths.

Public areas include an atrium spanning six decks; the two-story, 824-seat lido show lounge; the 370-seat Galaxy of the Stars observation lounge and disco; an English-style pub with darts and billiards; karaoke rooms; young children's and teen facilities that rival the Disney ships; and Apollo spa and fitness center with pools and Jacuzzis. There are multiple dining venues composed of the 560-seat, three-meal-a-day Bella Vista; the 330-seat, family-style Pavilion Room, serving Chinese; the 516-seat Mediterranean Buffet Terrace, offering international food; the 94-seat á la carte Chinese Noble House; the 26-seat á la carte Italian Palazzo; the 110-seat á la carte Japanese Samurai Restaurant with teppanyaki and tatami rooms; the 132-seat, casual, 24-hour Blue Lagoon Café; the Taj Indian buffet; and the Taverna.

SuperStar Libra was transferred from Norwegian Cruise Line in 2005. When based in Mumbai, she offers cruises to Lakshadweep and Goa. When based in Taiwan, she offers cruises to Ishigaki and Naha in Japan as well as Penghu Island, Taiwan. Public facilities include a variety of restaurants, a pool bar, ice-cream bar, karaoke lounge, discotheque, show lounge, pool, Jacuzzi, sport deck, beauty salon, fitness center, video arcade, and Internet café.

Presently the ships are based in Singapore, Hong Kong, India, China, and Taiwan. Key markets are Singapore, India, China, Malaysia, and Australia.

SuperStar Aquarius, formerly *Norwegian Wind* and *Windward* of Norwegian Cruise Line, joined the fleet in Hong Kong in June 2007 and offers one-night gambling cruises.

In late 1999 through early 2000, Star Cruises acquired control of Norwegian Cruise Line. Subsequently, 50 percent of Norwegian was acquired from Star Cruises by the Apollo group, which also owns Oceania and Regent Seven Seas Cruises. In 2008, Star Cruises sold its remaining 50 percent.

Strong Points:

Star Cruises offers a variety of cruising styles that are gauged to appeal to Asian and international cruisers.

Balcony Stateroom on SuperStar Virgo, *courtesy Star Cruises*

Bella Vista on SuperStar Virgo, *courtesy Star Cruises*

Grand Piazza, SuperStar Virgo, *courtesy Star Cruises*

Parthenon Pool on SuperStar Virgo, *courtesy Star Cruises*

BELLA VISTA

Western Gala Dinner Set Menu

APPETIZER

Smoked Salmon Tatare
on bed of cucumber salad finished with raspberry vinaigrette

or

Duck and Chicken Terrine
served with white truffle walnut dressing and rocket lettuce

or

Gala Salad
mesculin leaves with papaya and mango dressed with
Champagne vinaigrette

SOUP

Clear Oxtail Broth
scented with dry sherry

or

Cream of Fresh Garden Herbs
finished with sour cream

MAIN COURSE

Beef Wellington
pink roasted tenderloin wrapped in puff pastry, rich red wine
jus and garden vegetables

or

Duo of Pan - fried Seabass Fillet & Grilled Tiger Prawn
set on wok fried vegetables with a sake - lemon grass sauce

or

Grilled Chicken Breast
set on casserole of leek, mushroom and artichoke accompanied with
potato gratin and peppercorn cream sauce

or

Gratinated Shitake Mushrooms Stuffed with Beancurd
served on crispy taro root roesti with asparagus tips and coriander cream

DESSERT

Semi Frozen Blueberry and Baileys Parfait
served with caramelized orange sauce

Coffee or Tea
Petit Fours

Courtesy Star Cruises

SUPERSTAR VIRGO

Today At A Glance

Time	Activity	Venue	Deck
Morning	(Staying onboard? Port Stay Activities)		
7:00am - 7:30am	Early Morning Walk: A perfect way to start your day	Track Oval	13 Fwd
7:30am - 8:00am	Rise and Stretch* (Pre-registration required. Pls call 12310)	Universal Gym	12 Fwd
9:30am - 10:00am	Phobia Quiz Challenge	Galaxy of the Stars	12 Fwd
10:00am - 10:45am	Scrabble Battle & Jenga Challenge	Galaxy of the Stars	12 Fwd
11:00am - 11:30am	Daytona USA Race Challenge	Video Arcade	10 Aft
Afternoon			
1:00pm - 2:00pm	Boardgame Mania - Please borrow your favorite boardgames at...	Activity Centre	12 Fwd
	(Boardgames are to be played in the Card Room only, Deck 12 Fwd)		
2:00pm - 4:00pm	English Blockbuster Movie: **Ocean's Twelve** (Rating - U)	The Lido	7 Aft
2:30pm - 3:00pm	**Single's Club:** Giant Chess Challenge	Amphitheatre	11 Aft
2:30pm - 3:00pm	Boot Scooting Line Dancing	Galaxy of the Stars	12 Fwd
2:30pm - 3:30pm	Activity-On-Request - Please register at...	Activity Centre	12 Fwd
3:00pm - 3:30pm	Table Tennis-Double's Competition - Pre-registration required at	Activity Centre	12 Fwd
3:00pm - 3:45pm	The Art of Cartoon Drawing	Galaxy of the Stars	12 Fwd
3:00pm - 3:45pm	Coconut Bowling Competition	Parthenon Pool	12 Mid
3:45pm - 4:15pm	Country & Western Musical Trivia	Galaxy of the Stars	12 Fwd
5:00pm - 5:45pm	Step Aerobics* (Pre-registration required. Pls call 12310)	Universal Gym	12 Fwd
Evening			
5:50pm - 6:05pm	'Gala Fashionista' - A tribute to Costumes of Asia and more!	Grand Piazza	7 Mid
6:00pm - 9:00pm	Fancy Costume Party (for registered kids only)	Child Care Centre	10 Aft
6:15pm & 8:30pm	Captain's Gala Cocktail	Grand Piazza	7 Mid
7:15pm - 8:30pm	Gala Showtime: **SORPRESA - A New Season** (Part 2)	The Lido	7 Aft
	(For Late Seating Dinner)		
8:00pm - 11:00pm	SSV CNY Lottery :Ticket Promotion	Activity Centre	12 Fwd
	Buy 6 Get 1 FREE Topless Show ticket, available at...	Galaxy of the Stars	12 Fwd
8:45pm - 9:30pm	Ballroom Dance Music with the SuperStar Virgo Lounge Band		
9:15pm - 10:30pm	Gala Showtime: **SORPRESA - A New Season** (Part 2)	The Lido	7 Aft
	(For Early Seating Dinner)	Bellini	8 Mid
9:15pm - 1:00am	Continuous Entertainment with the SuperStar Virgo Musicians	Galaxy of the Stars	12 Fwd
9:30pm - 10:15pm	Gala Party for Teens and Kids	Out of Africa	7 Fwd
10:00pm - 10:45pm	Karaoke "Singles" Challenge		
	Pre-registration required at 9:45pm, Maximum of 10 participants only.		
10:15pm - 11:00pm	Live Music Entertainment with the SuperStar Virgo Big Band	Galaxy of the Stars	12 Fwd
10:30pm - 11:15pm	MEGA JACKPOT $24,000 BINGO	The Lido	7 Aft
10:15pm - 11:00pm	DJ Mix Class for Teens	Celebrity Disco	13 Fwd
11:00pm - 11:45pm	Adult Funtime: **NEWLY WED NOT SO NEWLY WED**	Galaxy of the Stars	12 Fwd
11:45pm - 2:00am	Live Music Hits with the SuperStar Virgo Big Band	Galaxy of the Stars	12 Fwd
12:00mn - 12:40am	Las Vegas Style Topless Revue: **DESIRE**	The Lido	7 Aft

Galaxy of the Stars: For the comfort of others, guests below the age of 18 years shall not be allowed entry after 11:00pm

*Universal Gym: A mininimum of 3 participants must be in attendance for all classes to be held. Pre-registration is required for all classes.

Courtesy Star Cruises

UNIWORLD
"Boutique River Cruise Collection"
Uniworld Plaza
17323 Ventura Boulevard
Los Angeles, California 91316
(800) 733-7820
(818) 382-2709 Fax
www.uniworld.com

DOURO QUEEN: entered service 2005; 254' x 37'; 126-passenger capacity; 63 cabins; European officers and crew; 10-night cruise/tours in Portugal and Spain along the Douro River. **(Category B—Not Rated)**

GISELLE: entered service 1996; refurbished 2005; 120-passenger capacity; 56 cabins; 12- and 13-night cruises/tours on Nile and Lake Nasser (to Abu Simbel) in Egypt. **(Category B—Not Rated)**

LITVINOV: entered service 1991; refurbished 2001/2002; 423' x 55'; 210-passenger capacity; 109 cabins; Russian officers and crew; 14-, 16-, and 17-night cruise/tours along the Volga and waterways and lakes of Russia and to Rostov/Black Sea. **(Category B—Not Rated)**

RIVER AMBASSADOR: entered service 1996; refurbished 2006; 360' x 38'; 128-passenger capacity; 70 cabins; European officers and crew; 7-night cruises along the Rhine, Main, and Danube Rivers. **(Category B—Not Rated)**

RIVER BARONESS: entered service 1997; refurbished 2005; 360' x 38'; 140-passenger capacity; 70 cabins; European officers and crew; 7-night cruises along Seine and Rhône Rivers and 7-night cruises in Netherlands, Belgium, Germany, France, Austria, Slovakia, and Hungary along the Rhine, Main, and Danube Rivers. **(Category B—Not Rated)**

RIVER BEATRICE: entered service 2009; 410' x 37.5'; 160-passenger capacity; 80 cabins; European officers and crew; cruises on the Danube River. **(Category B—Not Rated)**

RIVER COUNTESS: entered service 2003; 360' x 37.5'; 134-passenger capacity; 68 cabins; European officers and crew; 7- to 21-night cruises along the Rhine, Main, and Danube Rivers. **(Category B—Not Rated)**

RIVER DUCHESS: entered service 2003; 360' x 37.5'; 134-passenger capacity; 68 cabins; European officers and crew; 7- to 14-night cruises along the Rhine, Main, and Danube Rivers. **(Category B—Not Rated)**

RIVER EMPRESS: entered service 2002; refurbished 2005; 360' x 37.5'; 134-passenger capacity; 68 cabins; European officers and crew; 7- to 14-night cruises along the Rhine, Main, and Danube Rivers. **(Category B—Not Rated)**

RIVER PRINCESS: entered service 2001; refurbished 2005; 360' x 37.5'; 132-passenger capacity; 68 cabins; European officers and crew; 7- to 11-night cruises in Germany, Austria, Hungary, and Slovakia along the Rhine, Main, and Danube Rivers. **(Category B—Not Rated)**

RIVER QUEEN: entered service 1999; refurbished 2003; 360' x 37.5'; 132-passenger capacity; 68 cabins; European officers and crew; 9- and 12-night cruises along the Rhine and Moselle Rivers.

RIVER ROYAL: entered service 2006; 360' x 37.5'; 132-passenger capacity; 66 cabins; European officers and crew; 7-night cruises in France on Rhône and Sâone Rivers. **(Category B—Not Rated)**

Uniworld commenced operations in 1976 and has expanded to become one of the largest river cruise and tour companies servicing North American travelers. Its diverse and continually expanding product lineup features deluxe river cruises, escorted land tours, and combined cruise/tours to some of the world's most exciting destinations, including the rivers of Europe, Russia, China, and Egypt. In 2006, a luxury hotel company and Trafalgar Tours purchased Uniworld.

Uniworld programs are designed for the North American audience and include such customized features as all outside cabins with panoramic windows aboard hotel-style river cruise ships, English-speaking on-board and shoreside staffs, a nonsmoking environment inside the ship, classic cuisine and international specialties, first-class hotel accommodations, round-trip flights aboard major airlines, guided sightseeing opportunities, and the services of an experienced cruise or tour manager throughout the trip. Daily guided shore excursions are included in the pricing. Other additional shore excursions are also available. Select pre- and post-cruise hotel packages are featured as well.

On my most recent cruise, I noted that in addition to U.S. and Canadian passengers, there were also passengers from Australia, Spain, Germany, and other parts of the world. The most outstanding features of the cruise experience were the dedication of the staff to varying passenger comforts and needs and the complimentary shore excursions.

The European-based riverboats are designed on the generic European model but are customized to American tastes. Each ship is outfitted as a fine hotel, offering somewhat larger cabins than those on some of the other riverboats. On the

River Countess, Duchess, Empress, Princess, Queen, and *Royal* standard cabins are approximately 151 square feet; whereas, suites are 215 square feet. On the newest vessel, *River Beatrice,* in addition to the standard cabins, there are 14 225-square-foot suites and a 300-square-foot owner's suite. Eighty percent of the cabins and suites have French balconies. On *River Ambassador,* all cabins are 117 square feet; on *River Baroness,* 128 square feet; and on *Douro Queen,* 135 square feet.

All staterooms feature a picture window and beds that can be arranged as one large double or two twins with European-style comforters and duvets with choice of pillows, flat-screen televisions with CNN, hair dryers, direct-dial telephones, and private safes. There are ice buckets in the rooms as well as ice machines in public areas but no refrigerators or minibars. On the newer vessels magnetic key cards provide added security; Internet stations are available to receive and send e-mails; and each has a fitness center, steam room, and sauna.

Staterooms are located on upper and lower decks. Atop the ships are a sun deck and the bridge. Public areas generally include the main restaurant, four lounges, the reception area, a small shop, a beauty salon, and gymnasium-spa area (on the recent new builds).

All programs include round-trip air transportation from the United States and Canada (unless the passenger elects to book his or her own air); cruise accommodations; all on-board meals and complimentary wines at dinner; all shore excursions; and all transfers. Many of the itineraries offer additional features such as hotel accommodations, select meals on land, and a variety of local entertainment. Theme cruises are offered on select European sailings. Providing a more extensive study of the art, music, and wine defining the regions visited, these theme-cruise voyages include bonus excursions to museums, cathedrals, and vineyards. Special concerts, on-board guest lecturers, and performers are also featured from time to time.

The China/Yangtze River cruises are offered on riverboats owned and operated by Victoria Cruises, the only U.S.-managed operation on that river. Uniworld, however, has offices in China and a full staff to assist customers taking these cruise/tour packages. Victoria Cruises is described later in this chapter.

Commencing in 2006, a 13-day program in Egypt was added with seven-day cruises along the Nile and an optional six-day land extension to Petra in Jordan. The program is offered on the 120-passenger, 60-cabin *Giselle.* This riverboat features all outside cabins with satellite television, minibars, and music systems; a swimming pool; a gift shop; and international cuisine.

Strong Points:

Comfortable riverboat cruise experience along some of Europe's most scenic waterways, packaged and geared toward North Americans who prefer a more familiar cruise experience than that offered by the European riverboat lines. Outstanding complimentary shore excursions and attentiveness to passenger comforts and needs.

River Queen, *courtesy Uniworld*

River Queen, *courtesy Uniworld*

River Queen, *courtesy Uniworld*

River Royal, *courtesy Uniworld*

River Royal, *courtesy Uniworld*

River Royal, *courtesy Uniworld*

River Empress, *courtesy Uniworld*

MS River Queen

Tuesday, August 05, 2008

Menu

Carpaccio of beef with salad on truffle-tomato vinaigrette

Essence of tomatoes with semolina dumplings **v**

Sword fish medallion on sautéed cucumber vegetables

White Wine - Cousiño - Macul - Maipo Valley - Chile
2006 Gran Vino Chardonnay

*Grilled veal tenderloin with almond broccoli, carrots and béchamel potatoes
served on balsamic-red wine sauce*
or
Vegetable & feta cheese quiche served with white tarragon sauce **v**

Red Wine - Markus Molitor Vinery - Germany
2004 Molitor Spätburgunder

Chocolate tart with mixed berries
or
Ice Coupe "Dutch Dream"
with cognac biscuit, orange sorbet and blueberry sauce

Coffee or tea

Restaurant Manager : Borislav Asenov   Executive Chef : Martin Koscelnik

Please note that certain dishes may contain traces of nuts
You are kindly asked to advise your restaurant manager if you have an allergy which may react adversely to this ingredient

River Queen, *courtesy Uniworld*

UNIW⊜RLD

Daily Programme
Cologne
Tuesday, 5th of August 2008

06:00 – 07:30 am	Coffee & pastries for our early risers in the Patio
07:30 – 09:30 am	Enjoy our sumptuous Breakfast Buffet in the Restaurant
Morning	Enjoy a leisurely morning whilst sailing
10:30 am	**German lesson with Hildegard in the Lounge**
12:00 – 01:30 pm	The Lunch Buffet is open in the Restaurant, enjoy it!
Approx. 01:00 pm	MV River Queen arrives in Cologne,
02:00 pm	**Cologne Walking Tour & Cathedral Visit**
04:00 – 05:00 pm	Tea Time with piano music played by our musician Laszlo
06:00 – 07:00 pm	Cocktail Hour with Zlati, Maria and music by Laszlo in the Lounge
06:45 pm	Port Talk by our Cruise Manager Hildegard in the Lounge
07:00 – 09:00 pm	Dinner is served in the Restaurant, bon appétit!
09:00 pm	**The Cologne Shanty choir is singing for you in the Lounge**
Afterwards	Laszlo is playing for you
11:30 pm	All on board, please!
Midnight	Ship sets sail to Koblenz
DVD CHANNEL:	**Screening at** 07:00 am, 09:00 am, 11:00 am, 01:00 pm, 03:00 pm, 05:00 pm, 07:00 pm, 09:00 pm, 11:00 pm
	<u>Channel 14:</u> **Ray** **(Biography)**
	<u>Channel 15:</u> **Because I Said So** **(Starring Mandy Moore & Diane Keaton)**

The Crew from the MV River Queen wishes you a wonderful day!

Expected Weather for today:
23°C/74°F – Mostly sunny

Board shop Hours:
10:00 am – 12:00 noon

Cocktail of the Day:
White Russian

River Queen, *courtesy Uniworld*

VICTORIA CRUISES, INC.
57-08 39th Avenue
Woodside, New York 11377
(800) 348-8084; (212) 818-1680
(212) 818-9889 Fax
www.victoriacruises.com

VICTORIA ANNA: entered service 2006; 6,200 G.R.T.; 308-passenger capacity; 153 cabins; Chinese officers and crew with American, European, or Australian cruise directors; cruises on Yangtze River. (**No Category—Not Rated**)

VICTORIA EMPRESS: rebuilt 2002; renovated 2008; 3,868 G.R.T.; 198-passenger capacity; 99 cabins; Chinese officers and crew with American, Australian, or European cruise directors; cruises on Yangtze River. (**No Category—Not Rated**)

VICTORIA JENNA: entered service 2009; 8,000 G.R.T.; 378-passenger capacity; 209 cabins; Chinese officers and crew with American, Australian, and/or European cruise directors; cruises on Yangtze River. (**No Category—Not Rated**)

VICTORIA KATARINA: entered service 2004; renovated 2008; 5,780 G.R.T.; 98 meters x 15 meters; 266-passenger capacity; 133 cabins; Chinese officers and crew with American, Australian, or European cruise directors; cruises on Yangtze River. (**No Category—Not Rated**)

VICTORIA PRINCE: rebuilt 2004; 4,587 G.R.T.; 208-passenger capacity; 104 cabins; Chinese officers and crew with American, Australian, or European cruises directors; cruises on Yangtze River. (**No Category—Not Rated**)

VICTORIA QUEEN: rebuilt 2003; renovated 2008; 4,587 G.R.T.; 206-passenger capacity; 103 cabins; Chinese officers and crew with American, Australian, or European cruise directors; cruises on Yangtze River. (**No Category—Not Rated**)

VICTORIA ROSE: rebuilt 2001; renovated 2008; 2,428 G.R.T.; 130-passenger capacity; 65 cabins; Chinese officers and crew and American, Australian, or European cruise directors; cruises on Yangtze River. (**No Category—Not Rated**)

VICTORIA STAR: rebuilt 2003; 4,587 G.R.T.; 206-passenger capacity; 103 cabins; Chinese officers and crew and American, Australian, or European cruise directors; cruises on Yangtze River. (**No Category—Not Rated**)

(Medical Facilities: P-1, EM, MS; OX; WC; L)

Note: The China National Tourism Administration rates these ships 5 stars, except for the *Victoria Rose,* which is unrated by that organization; however, these riverboats are not rated for this book.

Victoria Cruises is an American company that operates downstream and upstream cruises between Chongqing and Yichang on the Yangtze River and Yichang/Chongqing round-trip cruises, with extended cruises to Shanghai, all of which pass by the picturesque Three Gorges region.

The single-seating dining room features Chinese cuisine as well as western selections. Breakfast and lunch are buffet style, whereas dinner is served family style. Except for the *Victoria Rose* and *Victoria Prince,* the ships also feature an à la carte dining room with western and Chinese cuisine at a $45 surcharge per day.

While passengers are not on shore excursions, on-board activities include lectures and demonstrations relating to Chinese culture. There is also some form of entertainment nightly.

Standard cabins on the *Anna* measure 226 square feet, on the *Prince, Queen,* and *Star,* 211 square feet, on the *Katarina,* 206 square feet, on the *Empress,* 157 square feet, and on the *Rose,* 145 square feet. (Measurements include balconies on all ships except the *Rose,* which does not have balcony cabins.) Suites on the various ships range in size from 237 square feet to 646. Each accommodation has lower twin berths, private bathroom with shower and bathtub (on all ships but the *Victoria Rose*), and televisions with HBO, CNN, and feature films. Most ships also offer three categories of suites with sitting areas. Ships are smoke free except for the outside observation deck. Facilities on the various vessels include dining halls, cocktail lounges, business centers, gift shops, libraries, fitness rooms, beauty salons, saunas, mah-jongg rooms, and observation decks.

One of the newer and larger ships, *Victoria Anna,* entered service in 2006 carrying over 300 passengers. She includes two dining rooms, two elevators, and an entertainment center on the top deck. In 2009, the 8,000-ton, 378-passenger *Victoria Jenna* entered service as the largest cruise/riverboat on the Yangtze.

Itineraries offered include three-night/four-day downstream and four-night/five-day upstream cruises between Chongqing and Yichang, ranging in price from $710 to $2,410. The seven-day downstream/nine-day upstream cruises that continue to Shanghai range in price from $1,470 to $3,850, and the eight-day Chongqing/Yichang/Chonqing round-trip cruises range in price from $1,260 to $4,070.

Cruises that depart Chongqing at 9 P.M. with a shore excursion to Fengdu, or alternatively to Shibaozhai or Wanzhou, continue through the Qutang Gorge, Wu Gorge, the Xiling Gorge, and the Three Gorges Dam and offer an excursion on a tributary through the Small Three Gorges before disembarking in Yichang. The upstream cruise from Yichang reverses the itinerary. The round-trip cruise includes different shore excursions in each direction and adds tours of Yichang and New Zigui. An optional excursion to White Emperor City at Fengjie may be offered on select sailings. Cruises that extend to Shanghai include excursions to Wuhan, Mt. Huang, and Nanjing.

Pacific Delight, Ritz Tours, Uniworld, and other tour operators utilize these ships for their cruise/tour packages in China.

Strong Points:

The vessels are geared for a western clientele, yet offer a Chinese environment and a comfortable alternative to explore the Yangtze River.

Victoria Anna, *courtesy Victoria Cruises, Inc.*

Victoria Anna, *courtesy Victoria Cruises, Inc.*

Victoria Anna, *courtesy Victoria Cruises, Inc.*

Victoria Anna, *courtesy Victoria Cruises, Inc.*

Dinner Menu 晚宴

冷菜 Cold Dishes
泡菜 Yangtze Pickles
闷豆腐 Flavored Bean Curd
蒜泥黄瓜 Cucumber in Garlic Sauce
芝麻肉丝 Shredded Pork With Sesame
夫妻肺片 Chicken & Beef Slices With Hot Sauce

汤 Soup
维多利亚西湖汤 Victoria Beef Soup

热菜 Hot Dishes
宫保鸡丁 Diced Chicken with Peanuts
蒜香仔排 Garlic Spare Ribs
西芹炒牛肉 Stir-Fried Beef With Celery
菊花鱼 Sweet & Sour Fish
清炒菠菜 Stir-Fried Chinese Spinach
炸土豆饼 Deep-Fried Potato Cakes
什菜拌饭 Fried Rice & Vegetables

甜点 Dessert
南瓜饼 Pumpkin Cake
法式煎饼 French Puff-Crepes
新鲜水果 Seasonal Fruit Plate

欢送宴会

冷菜 Cold Dishes
叉烧肉 Barbecued Pork
开心牛肉 Beef Slices
香油西芹 Celery With Sesame Oil
珊瑚雪莲 Lotus Roots
雀翅黄瓜 Cucumber

汤 Soup
什锦海鲜汤 Sea Food Soup

热菜 Hot Dishes
干烧武昌鱼 Dry Fried Wuchang Fish
芝士鸡排 Cheese Chicken with Eggplant
百花雀巢 Chicken, Beef & Shrimp in Bird's Nest
八宝石榴鲜 Egg Rolls with Pork & Vegetable
富贵肘子 Roast Pork Knuckle
香菇菜心 Mushrooms With Bok Choy
兰花烩香菇 Country Style Broccoli
菠萝炒饭 Fried Rice With Pineapple
剌猬金瓜 Pumpkin & Sticky Rice Buns

甜点 Dessert
苹果派 Apple Pie
冰淇淋 Ice Cream
新鲜水果 Seasonal Fruit Plate

Courtesy Victoria Cruises, Inc.

Fengdu 丰都

	Saturday, Oct. 13, 2007	Day / Night	Prec. %
Day 4	Rainy Periods	(°C) 25°/20° (°F) 77°/68°	70%

6:00 AM	Early Bird **coffee & tea** service.
	Yangtze Club, Deck 4
7:15 AM	Dr. Liu teaches the art of **Tai Chi** – shadow boxing.
	Yangtze Club, Deck 4
7:45 AM	**Buffet breakfast** service begins.
	Dynasty Dining Room, Deck 1
8:45 AM	*Shore Excursion: The* ship is docked at **Fengdu**. Passengers go ashore to visit the **"City of Ghosts"**, the #1 tourist attraction on the upper reaches of the Yangtze. The temple area on top of Ming Mountain pays tribute to the "King of the Underworld". A local guide introduces the legends surrounding Fengdu, as well as the many displays portraying interpretations of the Afterlife.
Please Note:	There is a chair lift that can take you to near the top of the hill. (There are close to 100 stairs in stages after that). Return trip fare is 20 Yuan for the chair lift. If you prefer to walk, there are over 400 stairs in total, just let your local guide know. Wear good walking shoes, and beware of ghosts!
11:30 PM	Passengers return to the ship.
12:00 PM	Chinese Tea Culture Display.
	Yangtze Club, Deck 4

"BLOODY MARY TIME!!!"

☺ 30% off this popular cocktail any time before lunch ☺ YANGTZE BAR, Deck 4 ☺
Special Drinks of the Day "Black Russian" and "Screwdriver " only 25 Yuan all day!

12:15 PM	**Buffet lunch** is served. **Dynasty Dining Room, Deck 1**
1:30 PM	**MAHJONG LESSON** Learn the basics of China's favorite pastime in the deck 3 meeting room.
2:45 PM	*DUMPLING MAKING CLASS* – Learn the basics and watch live vegetable carving demonstrations with our chef in the Yangtze Club.
3:15 PM	*Afternoon Tea Time* – Tea & biscuits are served for one hour in the Yangtze Club.
3:45 PM	**"ARTISTS BAZAAR"** – Live demonstrations of traditional Chinese arts together in the Yangtze Club.
5:00 PM	*"China Through the Eyes of a Resident Foreigner"*– Join Kevin for an informal Q&A session regarding life in a changing society. **Yangtze Club, deck 4**
6:00 PM	DVD SCREENING – Videographer Vincent plays the **voyage DVD** in the Yangtze Club.

6:00 PM – 7:00 PM
☺ **"HAPPY HOUR" in the Yangtze Club** ☺   **All Drinks 30% off!!!** ☺

7:00 PM   Victoria Cruises Farewell Banquet is Served in the Dynasty Dining Room

(formal attire requested but not required)

9 to 10 PM, its...   Open Floor Dance Nite!
Choose your favorite dance music with our DJ and dance to your heart's content!

Also, don the attire of the EMPRESS & EMPEROR of the Qing Dynasty and take home a photo souvenir!
We bring the costumes, you bring the camera! (8:30 – 9:30 PM, deck 3 meeting room)

(9:30 PM): In-house Movie – **"Curse of the Yellow Flower"** (Channel 13)

Please note that all arrival and departure times, shore excursions & lectures are subject to change due to weather, river condtions, and permission from navigational authorities.

Courtesy Victoria Cruises, Inc.

VIKING RIVER CRUISES, INC.
5700 Canoga Avenue, Suite 200
Woodland Hills, California 91367
(877) 66VIKING
(877) 668-4546
(818) 227-1237 Fax
info@vikingrivercruises.com
www.vikingrivercruises.com

Ships Cruising in Europe	Year Entered Service	Passenger Capacity
Viking Burgundy	2000	154
Viking Danube	1999	150
Viking Europe	2001	150
Viking Fontane	1991, refurb. 2002	124
Viking Helvetia II	2006	198
Viking Legend	2009	189
Viking Neptune	2001	150
Viking Pride	2001	150
Viking Primadonna	1998	78
Viking Schumann	1991, refurb. 2009	124
Viking Sky	1999	150
Viking Spirit	2001	150
Viking Sun	2005	198

Ships Cruising in Russia and Ukraine

Viking Kirov	1989, refurb. 2009	212
Viking Lavrinenkov	1989, refurb. 2003	212
Viking Lomonosov	1975, refurb. 2003	202
Viking Pakhomov	1989, refurb. 2003	212
Viking Peterhof	1990, refurb. 2003	212
Viking Surkov	1984, refurb. 2008	210

Ships Cruising in China

Viking Century Sky	2005	306

✮✮✮✮✮

Viking Century Sun	2006	306

✮✮✮✮✮

Viking River Cruises was formed in 1997 by a Scandinavian and Dutch consortium. At that time, it purchased four Russian ships. Purchases continued, and by the end of 1999, the fleet had grown to 14 ships. In March 2000, the company announced the purchase of KD River Cruises of Europe, adding an additional nine river vessels. At the same time, the company established U.S. headquarters in Los Angeles to meet the growing demand of U.S. travelers wishing to experience a cruise on one of Europe's colorful waterways. Subsequently, the company introduced eight all-new, modern river vessels, each accommodating about 150 passengers, and sold off some of the older ships. Today, the line operates 19 river-cruise vessels.

The cruise line offers passengers a variety of all-inclusive eight- to 17-night cruise and cruise/land packages on many of Europe's, Russia's, Ukraine's, and China's scenic rivers, including the Rhine, Danube, Elbe, Main, Moselle, Rhône and Saône, Seine, Holland's waterways, Russia's waterways, Ukraine's Dnieper, and the Yangtze. There is a land-based Egypt itinerary that includes a Nile cruise. Also available are land-based extensions to major cities. English is the on-board language and is spoken by the staff. Dining is always in an open, single-seating dining room with panoramic river views.

One of my more recent cruises with Viking River Cruises was on the *Viking Neptune,* an identical sister ship to the *Viking Pride, Viking Spirit,* and *Viking Europe.* These four ships entered service in 2001 and feature 150-square-foot outside cabins attractively appointed with a generous wardrobe and storage space, writing desks, televisions with CNN and BBC news, hair dryers, 115- and 220-watt electrical outlets, twin beds convertible to queens with European duvets, and small bathrooms with shower, toilet, and vanity. Sixty-three of the 75 cabins on each ship have large picture windows that open. There are no refrigerators or filled ice buckets; however, there are ice machines down the hall available to the passengers.

All three meals are served open-seating in the main dining room with buffet options at breakfast. Lunch features a salad and sandwich bar, or you can order from a menu with at least two options for each course. Dinner is a multicourse meal, sometimes with a fixed menu and other times with two choices for a starter, main course, and dessert. Always offered are grilled steak, chicken, or Caesar salad. The wine list is quite limited and passengers are allowed to bring their own bottles into the dining room; however, they are charged a $10 corkage fee. Although coffee and ice tea are available around the clock near the reception area, there is a significant charge for soft drinks, wines, alcoholic beverages, and espresso. Viking offers a Silver Spirits beverage package that covers soft drinks and alcoholic beverages for one fixed price, which varies by length of the itinerary.

Public areas are limited and include the main lounge and bar; a venue for all port lectures, socializing, and nightly piano music; a small, not-very-well-stocked library; and an extensive sun deck with lounges, a covered area, and a few tables. There is a partial promenade deck around the ship and some e-mail facilities. Commencing in 2009, all European, Russian, and Ukrainian ships offer free Wi-Fi service onboard. There is an Internet café on Chinese ships. On most of the riverboats, there is no pool, Jacuzzi, sauna, or gym and no deck towels or bicycles. Many of these items were sorely missed by the passengers and one would hope some additions will be made in the future.

The highlight of Viking River Cruises is the numerous well-organized, daily shore excursions that are included in the cruise fare. They include wine tastings and visits to world-renowned museums and historical sites.

Viking Sky, which entered service in 1999, is similar to the four newer vessels except four double cabins have bathtubs and there is a small whirlpool and an elevator between the middle and upper decks.

The layout of *Viking Burgundy,* built in 2000, is quite similar to the *Viking Neptune*-category of ships; however, the other European Viking river ships were built in the 1980s and 1990s and the cabins are smaller and more in the style of that generation of vessels.

In 2009, the cruise line's newest, state-of-the-art river vessel, *Viking Legend,* entered service sailing the Rhine, Main, and Danube Rivers. She carries 189 passengers in 98 staterooms, cabins, and suites. All have hotel-style beds, 26-inch flat-screen TVs, and refrigerators.

In 2004, the cruise line began offering cruises on China's Yangtze River and now offers four Chinese itineraries that combine exceptional land tours with six- to 10-night Yangtze River cruises. The first vessel to offers cruises on that river, the *Viking Century Star,* is no longer with the fleet. In 2005, the cruise line launched a second ship to cruise on the Yangtze, the 306-passenger *Viking Century Sky,* featuring five decks with two elevators; an observation lounge and bar; a site for entertainment, lectures, and cocktail hour; a large, open-seating dining room serving excellent western and Chinese cuisine (the ship carries both a European and Chinese head chef); a marble lobby/information area at the bottom of a five-deck atrium; a tiny gym (with only Exercycles and no treadmills or other equipment); a sauna (where passengers are charged $18 per hour for its use); a massage room; a doctor's office (with a Chinese doctor and no western medicines); four computers with Internet connections (however, on the Yangtze they are extremely slow and often passengers cannot access a connection); a small boutique; a tailor; a hairdresser; a smoking lounge (otherwise smoking is not allowed inside the ship); and a partially covered sun deck and bar, the best location from which to view the scenery.

There are 153 all-balcony, air-conditioned cabins, each with a private bathroom with a shower, toilet, and sink; hotel-style beds; TV with CNN, BBC, and movies; phone; hair dryer; small complimentary bottles of water and tea; and a coffee maker. (Since you are not supposed to drink the tap water, guests must purchase additional bottles of water from the housekeeping staff and additional bottles are available for shore excursions.) All accommodations open up through glass doors to balconies with two chairs. The 141 standard cabins measure a generous 221 square feet. Four junior suites are a wee bit larger at 241 square feet, and the six full suites measure 332 square feet.

In 2006, *Viking Century Sun,* an identical sister ship to *Viking Century Sky,* joined the fleet. For 2010, the cruise line offers Yangtze River land and cruise packages from 12 to 17 days and visits Beijing, Xian, Shanghai, and the Yangtze. An alternative itinerary features three nights in Lhasa, Tibet. In addition, on any Chinese cruise tour, travelers can add a four-night shoppers' paradise extension to Hong Kong and Guilin.

On my cruise in 2006, I found the preparation, presentation, and imagination of the kitchen exceptional. Service throughout the ship is very attentive and friendly; however, passengers must make allowances for the staff's somewhat limited familiarity with English and requests of western passengers. The Chinese tour escorts are also exceptional and stay with their group of passengers from the moment they disembark the plane until they return home, assisting with baggage, tours, and all special requests. The ships are very modern, spotlessly clean, and far more comfortable than those of the other riverboats that cruise the Yangtze.

Strong Points:

Scenic riverboat experience on some of Europe's, Russia's, Ukraine's, and China's most desired rivers and waterways on comfortable vessels. The more recently built river ships offer larger accommodations and a more modern décor.

Courtesy Viking River Cruises

Courtesy Viking River Cruises

Courtesy Viking River Cruises

Courtesy Viking River Cruises

Courtesy Viking River Cruises

VIKING
RIVER CRUISES

C A P T A I N ' S   D I N N E R
Viking Century SKY
Monday, April YX, 2006

Smoked Peking Style Duck
Pork Su Mai
Cream Golden Crab Puffs
Five Spice Cucumber Salads with Garlic
Glass Noodles Salad with Sesame and Chilli
Marinated Eggplant Salad with Sichuan Peppercorn

❦

Mandarin Hot and Sour Soup

❦

Black Pepper Beef with Tree Peppers
General Tso's Chicken
Beijing Pots tickers
Sichuan Fried Jumbo Prawns with Sweet Chilli Sauce
Braised Bean Curd "Sichuan Style"
Emerald Fried Rice with Golden Pine Nuts

❦

Golden Pan-cake Sweet Bean Paste

❦

Chinese Tea with Ginger Cookies

Courtesy Viking River Cruises

VIKING
RIVER CRUISES

WELCOME DINNER
Viking Century SKY
Saturday, March XVIII, 2006
Selection of Appetizer
Smoked Duck Breast with Salad Greens & Raspberry-Orange
Vinaigrette

or

Caesar Salad with Quail Eggs and Parmesan Cheese

Selection of Soup
Double Chicken Consommé with Truffle Dumplings

or

Potato Cream with Roasted Garlic, Marjoram and Chives

Selection of Main Course
Sliced Striploin of Beef with Bourbon Jack Sauce,
Baked potatoes with Sour Cream and a trio of Beans

or

Salmon and Leeks in Pasty Weaves
with Shrimps Bisque Sauce and
Sesame Garden Vegetables

Selection of Dessert
Chocolate-lavender Pot de Crème with French Straw

or

Honey-Nut Stuffed Apple with Carmel Sauce and Pistachio Cracker

or

International Cheese Selection with assorted Fruits and Biscuits

Courtesy Viking River Cruises

VIKING
RIVER CRUISES

VIKING NEWS

YOUR PROGRAM FOR WUSHAN 21/03/06

6:00-7:00 AM	**'Early Bird' Breakfast:** Coffee, juice and pastries are served at the coffee station for early risers in the Observation Lounge.
7:30-8:00 AM	Practice **Tai Chi** with Master Huang on the Sun Deck.
7:00-9:00 AM	**Breakfast:** Start your day with a generous breakfast buffet served in the Dining Room.
8:00-8:30 AM	**Scenic Cruising:** *Viking Century Sky* sails through the Qutang Gorge. Join your Cruise Manager Thomas on the Sun Deck for informative landscape narration.
10:00 AM	*Viking Century Sky* arrives in Wushan. **Shore Excursion: Lesser Three Gorges.** You will change to a smaller excursion boat at the port. A picnic lunch will be served during the excursion ashore.
3:30 PM	**Anchors Aweigh!** *Viking Century Sky* leaves Wushan and sets sail for the Three Gorges Dam at a distance of 85 miles away.
3:30-4:15 PM	**Scenic Cruising:** *Viking Century Sky* sails through the Wu Gorge. Join your Cruise Manager Thomas on the Sun Deck for informative landscape narration.
3:30–5:30 PM	**Margarita Party:** Join us on the Sun Deck or in the Sun Deck Bar

4:00-5:00 PM	**Tea Time:** Have a cup of tea or coffee while listening to piano music in the Observation Lounge.
5:00 PM	A **Lecture on "The Three Gorges Dam"** is given by your Cruise Manager Thomas in the Observation Lounge.
6:00 PM	**Daily Briefing:** Join fellow passengers in the lounge for an information briefing by your Cruise Manager Thomas on the next day.
6:30-7:30 PM	**Cocktail Hour:** Try one of our specials and listen to live music in the Observation Lounge.
7:30 PM	**Dinner:** Chef de Cuisine Olaf Grams and Maître d'Hotel Florian Fedeli invite you for Dinner in the Dining Room. Bon appétit!
9:00 PM	**"East meets west":** enjoy a music performance where our onboard bands perform traditional Chinese music and western music in the Observation Lounge.
approx. 9:00 PM	*Viking Century Sky* sails through the Three Gorges Dam ship locks (estimated duration 3 and 1/2 hours).
10:00 PM	**Evening Snack** is served in the Observation Lounge.
	Viking Century Sky docks overnight in Maoping.

DRESS SUGGESTIONS

During the day: casual
For cocktail and dinner: casual chic

COCKTAILS OF THE DAY
Misty Forest
Rum, Blue Curacao,
Orange Juice
48 RMB

The Viking Century Sky team wishes you an unforgettable day!

Courtesy Viking River Cruises

VIKING
RIVER CRUISES

VIKING NEWS

YOUR PROGRAMME FOR TODAY 18/08/2004

6:00-7:00 AM	**'Early Bird' Breakfast:** Coffee, juice and pastries are offered at the coffee station for early risers.	**5:30 PM**	**Daily Briefing:** Join fellow passengers in the lounge for an information briefing by your Cruise Manager Carin van der Sloot.
7:00 AM	*Viking Neptune* arrives in Vienna.	**5:45 PM**	**Dinner:** Chef de Cuisine Kunj Bihari and Maître d'Hotel Zoltan Felgyöi invite you for a special Austrian dinner in the restaurant. Bon appétit!
7:00-9:00 AM	**Breakfast:** Start your day with a generous breakfast buffet served in the restaurant.		
8:30 AM-12:00 PM	**Shore Excursion:** City sightseeing tour of Vienna.	**7:30-10:15 PM**	**Optional Excursion:** Mozart and Strauss Concert.
12:00 PM	**Lunch:** Our restaurant team welcomes you for lunch in the restaurant. Enjoy!	**8:00 PM**	**Live Music:** Mingle with fellow passengers for an after dinner drink while enjoying soft musical entertainment up on the sundeck.
1:45-5:00 PM	**Optional Excursion:** Visit of Schönbrunn Palace.		
3:30-4:00 PM	**Tea Time:** Have a cup of tea or coffee and enjoy a variety of cakes or pastries up on the sundeck.	**10:00 PM**	**Late Night Snack:** To satisfy your evening appetite, a snack is served up on the sundeck.
4:45-5:45 PM	**Cocktail Hour:** Try one of our specials and listen to live music in the Viking lounge.	**midnight**	*Viking Neptune* departs Vienna and sets sail to Dürnstein.

SHIP'S CONTACTS

Reception: +49 (0)174 303 51 02
Cruise Manager: +49 (0)172 307 45 39

COCKTAIL OF THE DAY

Exotica	€ 5.50
Kiss Me Tender	€ 5.00

The Viking Neptune team wishes you an unforgettable day!

Courtesy Viking River Cruises

WINDSTAR CRUISES
2101 Fourth Avenue, Suite 210
Seattle, Washington 98121
(800) 258-7245
www.windstarcruises.com

WIND SPIRIT: entered service 1988; renovated 2007; 5,703 G.R.T.; 440' x 52'; 4 masts 204' high; 6 sails and 3 engines; 148-passenger capacity; 74 cabins; British officers, Indonesian and Filipino crew; 7-day cruises in the Caribbean from St. Thomas during winter, and in the Mediterranean and Greek Islands during summer and early fall, plus two transatlantic repositioning cruises.

WIND STAR: entered service 1986; renovated 2007; 5,703 G.R.T.; 440' x 52'; 4 masts 204' high; 6 sails and 3 engines; 148-passenger capacity; 74 cabins; British officers, Indonesian and Filipino crew; 7-day cruises of Costa Rica and the Panama Canal during winter and the Mediterranean and Greek Islands during summer and early fall, plus two transatlantic repositioning cruises.

WIND SURF (formerly *Club Med I*): entered service 1990; renovated 2006; 14,745 G.R.T.; 617' x 66'; 312-passenger capacity; 156 cabins; British officers, Indonesian and Filipino crew; 7-day cruises in the Mediterranean during summer and early fall and in the Caribbean during winter and spring, plus two transatlantic repositioning cruises.

(Medical Facilities: C-0; P-1; EM, CLS; N-0; BC; CM; PD; EKG; TC; PO; EPC; OX; WC; ICU; LJ, except *Wind Surf,* which also carries a nurse.)

These ships are rated in 11 separate categories in the second half of chapter 14.

Windstar Cruises was founded in 1984 by Finnish-born Karl Andren, who put the uniquely designed *Wind Star* into Caribbean service in 1986. Thereafter, *Wind Star* was joined by her two identical sister ships, *Wind Song* in July 1987 and *Wind Spirit* in 1988. In 1997, Windstar purchased *Club Med I* from Club Med Cruises, renamed the ship *Wind Surf,* and conducted extensive renovations, including the addition of 31 new suites, a 10,000-square-foot spa, and a bistro-style restaurant. *Wind Surf* commenced service for its new owners in the Mediterranean in the spring of 1998. In late 2002, the *Wind Song* was destroyed in an unfortunate fire. The line decided not to rebuild the ship and has since discontinued itineraries in French Polynesia.

Windstar Cruises was purchased by Holland America Line in 1988, and Holland America was subsequently purchased by Carnival Cruise Line. In February 2007, Carnival sold the cruise line to Ambassadors International, Inc.

The unique feature of these vessels is the computer-monitored and -directed sailing systems with diesel-electric back-up propulsion. However, the ships are not under sail the duration of the cruise.

All of the 74 cabins on the two original ships are outside, virtually identical, and located on the lower two decks. (There is also one larger suite.) They are 188 square feet in area and are designed in a modern interpretation of the nautical tradition, with mixed woods and rich fabrics. Each includes a flat-screen color television, DVD player, lock box, three-channel radio, CD player, desk and sitting area, fully stocked refrigerator, minibar, terry-cloth robes, L'Occitane bath amenities, a direct-dial ship-to-shore telephone, two twin beds that convert to queen size, and a nice-sized bathroom with separate toilet compartment, sink, shower, and generous cabinet space. All cabins have portholes, and none have verandas. Room service is available around the clock. Several cabins offer a third berth. All rooms also have a Bose SoundDock speaker for docking Apple iPods and wireless Internet.

The public areas are located on the top two decks, but the small gym, sports shops, and watersports platform are on the third deck down from the top (designated deck 2). The public areas include a sun deck with a small pool and hot tub, a small casino, an intimate yet elegant wood-paneled dining room, a lounge and bar, a hairstylist, a boutique, an infirmary, and a library. Breakfast and a buffet lunch are served partially buffet style and partially with table service in the glass-enclosed veranda lounge. Dinner takes place in the romantic main dining room from 7:30 to 9:30 P.M. without pre-assigned seating. The line describes its cuisine as a combination of French, European, and New American. Previously there was a no-tipping policy; however, today $12 per person per day is added to your shipboard account in lieu of personal tipping. Guests do have the right to adjust this amount up or down if they so choose.

In the evening, dance music and (once per cruise) a gala deck barbecue under the stars are offered. A large selection of DVDs and CDs are available in the library and can be aired in individual cabins. There is also a small casino with two blackjack tables and 13 slot machines. Guests can send e-mails on a computer in the library or they can rent laptops at reception. Wireless Internet is available throughout the ship.

During the winter, the itineraries for the *Wind Spirit* include some of the more picturesque islands in the Caribbean. The ships sail to a number of French, Italian, Greek, and other Mediterranean islands and ports during the spring, summer, and fall. The unique ability of these vessels to navigate shallow waters and to tender passengers to beaches and harbors permits these ships to call on more unusual destinations that the larger cruise ships cannot negotiate.

The emphasis of all three vessels is on beaches; watersports; small, quaint ports; and making the most of the beauty of the natural surroundings. Each ship is equipped with Zodiac-type inflatable motor launches for water-skiing and transportation to shallow beaches as well as water skis, snorkel equipment, kayaks, wind-surfing boards, and small sailboats. A watersport platform extends from deck 2 (second deck from the bottom of the ship).

The most enjoyable features of cruises on this line are the impressive comfort, special features, and storage space in all cabins; the intimate dining experience that permits passengers to dine alone or with other passengers of their choice and alfresco for breakfast and lunch (with waiters rather than cafeteria style); the option to dress casually and comfortably; the relaxed and unregimented program; and the ability to visit numerous exotic ports seldom offered by other cruise lines. The Indonesian and Filipino service staff is friendly but somewhat limited in imagination and understanding of the needs and requirements of North American and European travelers.

The line offers attractive air-sea packages. Cruise fares are the same for every cabin, ranging from about $285 per day per person to $665, depending on the ship, cruise grounds, and season. Special discount values are available on various cruises throughout the year.

Wind Surf offers two recently constructed 495-square-foot suites, 31 suites that measure 376 square feet, twice the size of the 123 deluxe, 188-square-foot cabins. All accommodations are outside with queen beds that convert to twins, flat-screen color televisions with DVDs, CDs, safes, minibar/refrigerators, international direct-dial telephones, wireless Internet, cell phone service, Bose SoundDock speakers, L'Occitane bath amenities, hair dryers, and terry-cloth robes. The 31 suites are actually double cabins where one has been converted to a parlor while retaining its storage space and bathroom, affording exceptional space and comfort for its occupants.

Following a second refit completed in December of 2000, the *Wind Surf* has an intimate, small-ship feel like the other members of the fleet. The most visible change is found in the lounges and casino, where the innovative new design creates a more comfortable and sociable gathering place. In addition to the single-seating main dining room, there is Degrees, the alternate-dining bistro, which has been expanded to seat 124 guests. Four nights each week a steakhouse menu is offered, and on the other three nights the menu alternates between Italian, French, and Indonesian cuisines. A similar steakhouse specialty restaurant, Candles, is now available on all three ships.

Breakfast and lunch are served atop ship at the Veranda restaurant or alfresco immediately outside. Most items appear on the buffet but additional items from the menu will be served at your table. Hot appetizers are served each evening in the lounges and snacks, pastries, and special treats are served late each afternoon at Compass Rose, the indoor/outdoor lounge/bar overlooking one of the pools.

The 10,000-square-foot spa features treatment rooms for body wraps, facials, and massages. The locker room and sauna are shared by both sexes and are inconveniently located near the marina. A well-stocked, glassed-in fitness center sits atop ship, permitting those exercising to enjoy interesting panoramas. Complimentary watersports, including water-skiing, sailboating, kayaking, windsurfing, and snorkeling, are available off the marina deck, and the ship has two outdoor swimming pools, two Jacuzzis, and several lido/lounge/bar areas. Meeting facilities can accommodate up to 60 people with special audiovisual equipment. Other public facilities include a large main lounge; a signature boutique, the Yacht Club; a new lounge with an espresso bar; eight computers with Internet access; DVDs, CDs, and books that can be checked out; a casino; and an infirmary. *Wind Surf,* being almost three times the size of the other three vessels, offers more indoor public areas and far more generous outdoor deck space.

Between 2006 and 2007, the ships underwent a multi-million-dollar fleet enhancement project with improvements to public areas, soft goods, and pool and deck areas. Known as the "Degrees of Difference" incentive, new additions include Apple iPod nanos, Bose SoundDocks, personal laptops and wireless connectivity throughout public areas, new flat-screen TVs and DVD/CD players in all staterooms as well as luxury soft goods and mattresses, an array of bathroom amenities by L'Occitane, and hammocks built for two located on deck under the sails. The *Wind Surf* received major renovations in 2006, and the other two ships received similar renovations in 2007.

Wind Surf will offer seven-day cruises in the Mediterranean during the spring and summer and Caribbean cruises from Barbados the remainder of the year.

Strong Points:

Unique, beautiful design; attractive staterooms; watersports; casual, tasteful atmosphere; a more intimate dining experience; and super itineraries for beach and watersports lovers wishing to travel in comfort and luxury. The newly renovated *Wind Surf* offers an attractive suite option for the more affluent traveler and greater indoor and outdoor public areas.

Wind Spirit, *courtesy Windstar Cruises*

Wind Spirit, *courtesy Windstar Cruises*

Wind Spirit, *courtesy Windstar Cruises*

Wind Surf, *courtesy Windstar Cruises*

Wind Surf, *courtesy Windstar Cruises*

Wind Surf, *courtesy Windstar Cruises*

$\mathscr{A}$PPETIZERS

Escargots with Roasted Shallots, Potatoes and Red Wine Sauce

Chilled Artichoke Stack with Vegetable Spaghetti, Shrimps and a Tomato Coulis

$\mathscr{S}$OUPS

Traditional French Onion

Chilled Carrot Lemongrass with Coriander Crème Fraiche

$\mathscr{S}$ALADS

Chinese Chicken Salad with Crispy Wontons Strips

Wind Song House Salad with Hearts of Palm, Avocado and Fresh Greens with
an Herb Vinaigrette

with your choice of Dressing:

French, Italian, Thousand Island, Blue Cheese and Hot Honey Mustard
Light dressings available on request

$\mathscr{E}$NTREES

Pan Fried Fish of the Day with Slivered Potatoes and a Garlic Chive Nage

Farm Raised Chicken Breast with Creamy Polenta, Crispy Parmesan Chips and Truffle Oil

Roasted Rack of Lamb with a Marinated Vegetable Tart and Lamb Jus

Oven Roasted Beef Striploin "English Cut" Served with Sauce Choron,
Green Beans and Potato au Gratin

$\mathscr{V}$EGETARIAN

Moroccan Sweet Potato Stew
Calories: 377 Fat Grams: 2.0

Baked Potato and Vegetables of the Day upon Request

Special thanks to Chef Joachim Splichal of Patina and Pinot of Los Angeles
for taking us in new culinary directions. "180° From Ordinary".

$\mathscr{C}$HEF $\mathscr{S}$TEPHAN`S
$\mathscr{D}$INNER $\mathscr{R}$ECOMMENDATIONS

*The suggested wines have been specifically chosen
to complement the Chef's recommendations.
They are served in degustation glasses for an attractive total price of $12.00*

Chilled Artichoke Stack with Vegetable Spaghetti, Shrimps and a Tomato Coulis
White Wine: Sauvignon Blanc Santa Rita, Chile

~

Traditional French Onion

~

Chinese Chicken Salad with Crispy Wontons Strips

~

Pan Fried Fish of the Day with Slivered Potatoes and a Garlic Chive Nage
Red Wine: Mouton Cadet Rothschild, France

~

Classic Morjolaine
Dessert Wine by the Glass: Quady Essencia, California

$\mathscr{S}$AIL $\mathscr{L}$IGHT $\mathscr{M}$ENU

Cucumber and Peanut Salad

~

Thai Country Style Chicken

~

Tart Tatin with a Light Crème Fraiche
Total Calories: 761 Total Fat Grams: 27.2

$\mathscr{W}$INES BY THE GLASS

White Wine

Chardonnay Nathanson Creek
California $4.00

Sauvignon Blanc Santa Rita
Chile $4.00

Mouton Cadet Rothschild
France $4.00

Red Wine

Cabernet Sauvignon Nathanson Creek
California $4.00

Merlot Louis Eschenauer
France $3.50

Mouton Cadet Rothschild
France $4.50

𝒟ESSERTS

Strawberry Crumble Cake

Chocolate Croissant Pudding with a Wild
Turkey Sauce

Individual Caramelized Flan with
Coconut Sauce

Assorted French Pastries

International Cheese Tray

𝒞OUPE 𝒲IND 𝒮ONG

Vanilla and Coffee Ice Cream with
Caramelized Bananas

𝒮AIL 𝓛IGHT

Baklava
Total calories: 246   Total fat grams: 10

𝒥CE 𝒞REAM

Of the Day

𝒮HERBET

Of the Day

ℬEVERAGES

Espresso, Cappuccino, Café au Lait,

Chocomilk, Hot Chocolate,

Tea and Herbal Teas,

Regular or Decaffeinated Coffee

𝒞ORDIALS & 𝓛IQUEURS

Louis XIII, Remy Martin $75.00

Remy Martin X.O. $10.00

Courvoisier V.S.O.P. $6.75

Deluxe Grand Marnier $29.00
(Cûvée du Cent Cinquantenaire "150 years")

Super Premium Grand Marnier $15.00
(Cûvée du Centenaire "100 years")

Premium Grand Marnier $7.50
(Cûvée Louis Alexandre Marnier-LaPostolle)

Grand Marnier Cordon Rouge $5.00

Tia Maria $5.00
Cointreau $5.00
Drambuie $5.00
Sambuca $5.00

𝒞OFFEE 𝒟RINKS

Coffee Specialties $6.50

Captain's Coffee
with Grand Marnier and Tia Maria

Irish Coffee
with Irish Whiskey

French Coffee
with Cognac

Italian Coffee
with Sambuca

Mexican Coffee
with Kahlua

Almond Dream
with Amaretto and Bailey's

French Chocolate
with Hot Chocolate and Brandy

Courtesy Windstar Cruises

GOOD DAY

Captain Tim Roberts
Hotel Manager Robert De Carlo

Mayreau, Grenadines

Saturday, January 6, 2007
Please have your Ship ID with you when going ashore.

Win a Windstar Bathrobe!
As a "thank you" for your time in completing our Comment Form, all forms submitted to Reception by 7:00pm Saturday, will be eligible for a drawing. The winner will receive a Windstar Bathrobe!

Please visit Reception Desk if you have queries regarding your Preliminary onboard account. As well, please do not forget to claim your passports and to bring your receipts with you. Phone, fax and Email services will be inaccessible from 10:00pm this evening onwards.

Shore Excursions

In consideration of your fellow passengers please meet in the **Lounge 5 minutes before** the tour departure. Do not forget to bring your snorkeling gear if you signed up for an aquatic tour.

8:55am   Sailing and Snorkeling tour

Today's Highlights

Join us for some Caribbean Fun in the Sun "Wind Surf's BBQ on the Beach" Lunch is served 12:00noon to 1:30pm

4:00pm-5:00pm at the Marina Deck 2, Snorkel Gear Return

4:00pm-5:00pm Crepe Suzette in the Compass Rose

6:30pm-7:00pm Please join Captain Tim Roberts in the Lounge for his Farewell Address, followed by your Host Jean-Michel with important information and tips about disembarkation. We recommend that at least one person from each cabin attend.

Entertainment Tonight

Enjoy the Music of "Nice & Easy"
6:30pm – 8:15pm & 9:30pm – Closing in the Lounge

Enjoy the Music from " Talisman Duo "
6:30pm–8:15pm & 9:30pm – Closing in the Compass Rose

Weather

Sky   Sunny
Temp   83F
Sunrise 6:30am
Sunset   5:53pm

Arrival (Anchor)   8:00am
All aboard   3:30pm

The Wind Surf prepares to sail for Barbados

In case of emergency, please contact Corea & Co Phone: 1784-456-120.

Places to lounge

Pool Bar
11:30am – 6:00pm

Lounge
6:00pm – Closing

Compass Rose
9:30am – Closing

Terrace Bar
9:30pm – Closing

Yacht Club
7:00am-12:00pm, 3:30pm-5:00pm & 9:00pm-Midnight

Cocktail of the Day: Azuluna
Mocktail of the Day: Virgin Daiquiris
Martini of the Day: Beautiful Tini

The dress code for cocktail & dinner hours is elegantly casual (shorts, T-shirts & Jeans are not permitted)

Places to eat

Continental Breakfast
6:00am –11:00am, Compass Rose.

Breakfast
7:30am – 9:30am, Veranda.

Snacks
11:30am – 4:00pm, Pool Bar.

BBQ Lunch on the beach
12:00noon – 1:30pm
Limited Lunch – Veranda
12:30pm – 2:00pm

Crepe Suzette at Afternoon tea
4:00pm-5:00pm, Compass Rose

Appetizers
6:30pm – 7:15pm in the Lounge and Compass Rose.

Dinner
7:30pm – 9:30pm, Restaurant
The restaurant has an open seating policy.
No reservations required or accepted.

Dinner
7:30pm – 9:30pm, Degrees
Reservations for Degrees are taken starting at 8:00am at the Reception Desk, or dial"0".

Room Service - until 12:00 Midnight
Please dial "3450".

WINDSTAR
CRUISES

WC 30742170 (6296)

Printed on Recycled Paper

Signature Shop (Main Deck, aft) – Dial 3702

Shop open   4.30pm – 11.00pm

Amber world event unveiling, prices start from $25.00, join the raffle to find out whom was the winner of the spot the fake competition at 6.00pm.

Wind Spa (Deck 2, aft) – Dial 3253

Spa & Sauna   8:00am-10:00pm

Join us today for **massage on the beach**, there is nothing better than to relax on the beach and be massaged by professional massage therapist. Treat yourself today! We will be situated near the BBQ area.

Park West At Sea (Art Hall, Main Deck)

Final Art Sale!   5pm – 8pm

Your last chance to acquire that special artwork you've been admiring all cruise! Internationally-acclaimed Artists. Up to 40% Savings. Shipping included. Treat Your Home this Vacation!

Photo & Video Gallery (Main deck, Aft) - Dial 3700

Gallery Open for viewing & ordering: 24 hours per day
Gallery staffed from: 5:30pm – 6:30pm
                                                          9:00pm – 10:00pm

Do not leave for home without them - Today is the last opportunity to purchase the wonderful photographs & unique cruise video Paola & Paula have taken during your Wind Surf Caribbean Sailing cruise.

Casino (Main Deck, forward)– Dial 3441

Slots and Tables   4:30pm-Close

You Could Win Up To $1000 Instantly!!!
Scratch Cards Available. Just $1 each at the casino cage.

News & info

Channel 78	Discovery Channel
Channel 80	Instant! Text News: 24 hours
Channel 82	CNN – Reception permitting
Channel 86	BBC World – Reception permitting
Channel 84	ESPN - Reception permitting
Channel 88	Windstar Cruises Channel
Channel 90	World Leading Cruise Lines

Movies today

Channel 72 **Da Vinci Code:**
9:00am, 12:00 noon, 3:00pm, 6:00pm, 9:00pm, 12:00 midnight

Channel 74 **Break up:** 9:00am, 11:00am
1:00pm, 3:00pm, 5:00pm, 7:00pm, 9:00pm, 11:00pm,1:00am

Channel 76 **Over the Edge:** 9:00am, 11:00am
1:00pm, 3:00pm, 5:00pm, 7:00pm, 9:00pm, 11:00pm,1:00am

For Suite Cabins, bedroom side TV, channels are 1 to 9.
DVD'S are available in the library and can be checked out at the Reception Desk.

Reception Desk (Main Deck, aft.)

Reception is the information center of the ship.
If you have any questions, please stop by.
Open 24 hours   Dial "0"

Infirmary (Deck 1, aft) – Dial 3152

Opening hours: 8:00am – 9:00am
                                          4:30pm – 5:30pm
Dial "3152" during opening hours.

For emergencies dial "0".
If you are using syringes/needles, please call at the Infirmary for a free disposal container. Please do not break off needles or dispose of your capped needles in the trash. Automatic Sanitizing Dispensers are located at the Gangway and throughout the ship and are provided to kill bacteria and viruses that may be prevalent in this area of the world. Please take advantage of these devices.

Staying in touch

To call the Wind Surf from the United States:
Tel: 011 + (874) 330 824 216
Fax: 011 + (874) 330 824 217

To call the shore from your cabin:
USA/Canada:
9 – Wait for dial tone - 1 – area code - number
To call Other Countries:
9– Wait for the dial tone – 011 – country code – area code – number

The charge per minute is US $7.95 and will be billed on your shipboard account, If you experience problems please call reception. Dial "0".

To call another cabin:
Please dial "2" followed by the cabin number.

Internet Access (Yacht Club - Main Deck)

Opening Hours: 6:30am - **10:00 pm**
Supervisor on duty   6.30pm-7.00pm

Fitness (Nautilus Room, Star Deck)

Fitness Center   6:00 am –10:00pm
Pools and Jacuzzi   6:00 am – 10:00pm

7.30 am   Stretch class-free terrace bar
8.00 am   Pilates $10 – terrace bar
2.00 pm   **Eat more weigh less seminar**
3.00 pm   Aerobics $10 - windsurf lounge
4.30 pm   Yoga $10 - windsurf lounge

Diving & Watersports (Marina, Deck 2, Aft)

7:30am-8:00am   Snorkel Gear Handout- Marina

10:30pm-2:30pm   Kayaking, Windsurfing and Sailing from the Beach

4:00pm-5:00pm   Snorkel Gear Return - Marina

7:45pm   Diver Logbook Signing meets in the Nautilus Room

Courtesy Windstar Cruises

MISCELLANEOUS ADDITIONAL CRUISE LINES

BLUE LAGOON CRUISES
(877) 252-3454
www.bluelagooncruises.com

MV *FIJI PRINCESS:* 196' long; 34 cabins.

MV *LYCIANDA:* 128' long; 21 cabins.

MV *MYSTIQUE PRINCESS:* 184' long; 36 cabins.

MV *NANUYA PRINCESS:* 160' long; 26 cabins.

Blue Lagoon Cruises was founded in 1950 by a New Zealand stockbroker and an Australian aviator in hopes of establishing a tuna-fishing industry. The venture failed and both men having fallen in love with Fiji went on to establish Fiji Airways (the forerunner of Air Pacific) and Blue Lagoon Cruises, offering cruises to the picturesque Yasawa Island group. In 1966, the cruise line was sold to a New Zealand ship owner and the line acquired various vessels over the years.

Presently the four boutique ships offer three-day/two-night, four-day/three-night, and seven-day/six-night cruises from Lautoka on Viti Levu, Fiji, to the Manuka Islands and the Yasawa Islands, truly some of the most pristine island paradises to be found anywhere in the world. Cruise rates fluctuate depending upon length of cruise and ship. In general they range from approximately $410 per cabin per night to $1,264 per cabin per night for the largest suite on sky deck. The vessels can also be chartered.

On the flagship of the line, MV *Mystique Princess,* there are 36 air-conditioned staterooms ranging in size from 179 square feet to the 296 square-foot owner's suite on sky deck. Some staterooms have twin beds and others, king-sized beds. Many have convertible day beds for additional passengers. Each accommodation has an ocean view, a minibar, a sofa, an international self-dial telephone, a personal safe, a TV/DVD/audio system, a vanity table, and a hair dryer. Public areas include a 100-seat dining salon, a lounge, two cocktail bars, a guest laundry, a well-stocked boutique, a spa, and three decks for sunbathing.

The accommodations on the other ships are somewhat smaller: 117' to 142' on MV *Fiji Princess;* 95' to 110' on MV *Nanuya Princess;* and 94' to 101' on MV *Lycianda.* All vessels have dining saloons, lounges, bars, and sun decks.

The main attraction of these cruises is the destinations. Pristine beaches, blue lagoons, swimming, snorkeling, fish feeding, windsurfing, outdoor island feasts, and other activities taking advantage of the unique geography of this region are featured.

CAPTAIN COOK CRUISES
No.6 Jetty Circular Quay
Sydney NSW 2000, Australia
+61 2 9206 1122
+61 2 9251 4725 Fax
www.captaincook.com.au

MV *REEF ESCAPE:* 1,850 G.R.T.; 68 meters x 13.5 meters; 120-passenger capacity; 60 cabins; cruises in Fiji to Yasawa Islands.

MV *REEF ENDEAVOR:* 3,125 G.R.T.; 73 meters x 14 meters; 150-passenger capacity; 75 cabins; cruises to Great Barrier Reef and Cape York from Australia.

PS *MURRAY PRINCESS:* 1,500 G.R.T.; 67 meters x 15 meters; 120-passenger capacity; 60 cabins; riverboat offering river cruises on Murray River in Australia.

CDF CROISIERES DE FRANCE
0891 362 233
www.cdfcroisieresdefrance.fr

BLEU DE FRANCE (formerly *Holiday Dream, SuperStar Aries,* and *Europa*): entered service 1981; renovated 2008; 37,000 G.R.T.; 658' x 95'; 1,006-passenger capacity; 316 cabins; Mediterranean and Caribbean cruises for French passengers. **(Category C—Not Rated)**

Royal Caribbean Cruises, Ltd. created this new cruise line aimed at the French market. The new company began operations in May 2008 with *Bleu de France,* formerly Pullmantur Cruises' *Holiday Dream.* Originally built in 1982 as Hapag-Lloyd's *Europa,* the ship was also with Star Cruises as *SuperStar Aries* before being bought by Pullmantur. Before entering service with CDF, the ship underwent a complete 30 million refit. The onboard experience of *Bleu de France*'s guests is totally French, from cuisine to entertainment to decor. French is the language used on the ship as well. The ship operates Mediterranean cruises from Marseille and repositions to La Romana, Dominican Republic, for Caribbean cruises during the winter.

CELEBRATION CRUISE LINE
(800) 309-5934; (954) 414-1336
www.bahamascelebration.com

BAHAMAS CELEBRATION (formerly *Princess Ragnhild*): entered service in 1981; refurbished 2009; 1,500-passenger capacity; international officers and crew; 2- and 3-night cruises to Nassau from Port Everglades. (**Category D—Not Rated**)

This ship replaced the *Regal Empress,* which entered service in 1953. *Bahamas Celebration* offers a casino, pub, piano bar, karaoke lounge, two-level nightclub, three levels of supervised children's activities for ages three to 10, 11 to 14, and 14 to 17; and a pool with a water slide. Dining options include a classic American restaurant, an all-you-can-eat Brazilian-style steakhouse and buffet, and a casual Italian restaurant. A specialty, reservation-only restaurant is open for dinner at a $25 surcharge. Two- and three-night cruises to the Bahamas from Port Everglades in Fort Lauderdale range in price from $119 to $199 per person.

CRUCEROS AUSTRALIS
4014 Chase Avenue, Suite 215
Miami Beach, Florida 33140
(877) 678-3772; (305) 695-9618
(305) 534-9276 Fax
www.australis.com

MARE AUSTRALIS: entered service 2001; 233' x 42'; 129-passenger capacity; 63 cabins.

VIA AUSTRALIS: entered service 2001; 233' x 42'; 136-passenger capacity; cruises in South America and Straights of Magellan.

EASYCRUISE
362 Syngrou Avenue
176 74 Kallithea
Athens, Greece
(866) 335-4975
www.easycruise.com

EASY CRUISE LIFE (formerly *Jasmine* and *Farah*): renovated 2008; 12,711

G.R.T.; 134 meters long; 550-passenger capacity; 250 cabins; cruises Greek Islands, the Aegean, and Turkey. (Category D—Not Rated)

EasyCruise is a division of the Easy Group that operates ultra-budget air, car, and hotel packages. Originally, fares started at $32 per night per cabin and at $60 for a suite. All food, entertainment, housekeeping, etc. cost extra on a pay-as-you-go basis, as on some of the ferry boats traversing the North Sea and Baltic. However, now half-board is compulsory and the fares have risen. The original *Easy Cruise I* (the former *Renaissance 2*) has left the fleet, and the only ship remaining is a bare bones ship with no activities or entertainment and far from the normal cruise experience. Basically it offers passage to the various islands and ports in the eastern Mediterranean and passengers spend little time aboard. The line markets to budget-minded passengers from Great Britain and elsewhere in their 20s, 30s, and 40s.

HEBRIDEAN ISLAND CRUISES
Kintail House, Carleton New Road,
Skipton, North Yorkshire BD23 2DE
(800) 659-2648
www.hebridean.co.uk

HEBRIDEAN PRINCESS: entered service 1964; refurbished 2001; 2,112 G.R.T.; 50-passenger capacity.

HEBRIDEAN SPIRIT: entered service 1991; refurbished 2001; 4,200 G.R.T.; 79-passenger capacity.

This British company offers cruises around the British Isles, northern Europe, the Mediterranean, and the Indian Ocean. This is more of an upscale, yacht-like experience visiting scenic ports.

IBEROCRUCEROS CRUISES
+902282221
www.ibercruceros.es

GRAND CELEBRATION (formerly *Celebration*): entered service 1987; 47,262 G.R.T.; 733' x 92'; 1,486-passenger capacity; 743 cabins; Italian officers and international crew; 7-night cruises from Barcelona. (Category C/D—Not Rated)

GRAND VOYAGER (formerly *Olympia Voyager*): entered service 2000; 25,000 G.R.T.; 593' x 84'; 420 cabins; 920-passenger capacity; 7-night cruises between Piraeus to Venice. **(Category C/D—Not Rated)**

GRAND MISTRAL (formerly *Mistral*): entered service 1999; 47,900 G.R.T.; 708' x 95'; 598 cabins; 1,715-passenger capacity; 7-night Baltic and Norwegian fjord cruises from Copenhagen. **(Category C/D—Not Rated)**

This Spanish cruise line caters mostly to passengers from Spain. In 2007, Carnival entered into a joint venture with Iberojet and now owns 75 percent of the renamed cruise line. Carnival transferred the *Celebration* in 2008, and it is expected that Carnival will transfer additional ships from its other holdings to IberoCruceros Cruises.

LINBLAD EXPEDITIONS
96 Morton Street
New York, New York 10014
(800) 397-3348; (212) 765-7740
(212) 265-3770 Fax
www.expeditions.com

NATIONAL GEOGRAPHIC ENDEAVOR: entered service 1966; rebuilt 1998; 3,132 G.R.T.; 295' long; 110-passenger capacity; 62 cabins; cruise grounds in Galapagos Islands.

NATIONAL GEOGRAPHIC EXPLORER (formerly *Lyngen* and *Midnatsol*): entered service 1982; renovated 2007; 356' long; 148-passenger capacity; 81 cabins; cruise grounds include Arctic, Iceland, Greenland, Arctic Canada, Antarctica, South America, North America's Atlantic Coast, Newfoundland, the Baltic, and North Cape.

ISLANDER: entered service 1994; 164' long; 48-passenger capacity; 24 cabins.

SEA BIRD and *SEA LION:* entered service 1981 and 1982, respectively; 100 G.R.T.; 151' x 31'; 70-passenger capacity; 36 cabins.

SEA VOYAGER: entered service 1982; 354 G.R.T.; 174' long; 64-passenger capacity; 32 cabins.

The cruise line commenced operations in 1979 as a division of Linblad Travel. In 2005, it formed a partnership with National Geographic. All meals are single seating at unassigned tables. A naturalist and/or historian gives lectures and leads expeditions. All vessels have kayaks, snorkel equipment, underwater video cameras, and Zodiacs. Cruise areas include Baja California, Galapagos Islands, Antarctica, Falkland Islands, Patagonia, Chilean Fjords, Panama, Costa Rica, the Arctic, Coastal Norway, Baltic, Canary Islands, and the Columbia and Snake Rivers. The two major vessels are the *National Geographic Explorer* and the *National Geographic Endeavor.* Published per diem rates for these two ships start at $460 to $850 and go as high as $790 to $1,600.

LOUIS CRUISE LINE

Sterling Vacations
5213 Doc Valley Line
Austin, Texas 78759

2 Nikis 3-5
Karagiordi Servias St.
10563 Athens, Greece

(512) 345-7755
(512) 345-7722 Fax
www.louiscruises.com

AQUA MARINA (formerly *Nordic Prince*): entered service 1971; 23,149 G.R.T.; 637' x 79'; 1,158-passenger capacity; 525 cabins. **(Category D—Not Rated)**

AUSONIA: 12,609 G.R.T.; 159 meters x 21.3 meters; 701-passenger capacity; 254 cabins. **(Category D—Not Rated)**

CORAL (formerly *Cunard Adventurer, Sunward II,* and *Triton*): entered service 1971; refurbished 2005; 14,000 G.R.T.; 491' x 71'; 945-passenger capacity; 378 cabins. **(Category D—Not Rated)**

CRYSTAL: 25,611 G.R.T.; 162 meters x 25 meters; 1,200-passenger capacity; 480 cabins; cruises from Greece. **(Category D—Not Rated)**

IVORY: entered service 1957; 12,609 G.R.T.; 690-passenger capacity; 259 cabins. **(Category D—Not Rated)**

LOUIS MAGESTY (formerly *Norwegian Magesty* and *Royal Magesty*): 38,000 G.R.T.; 680' x 91'; 1,462 passenger capacity; 731 cabins. **(Not Rated)**

ORIENT QUEEN: 15,781 G.R.T.; 160 meters x 23 meters; 912-passenger capacity; 364 cabins; cruises from France and Italy. **(Category D—Not Rated)**

PERLA: 16,710 G.R.T.; 163 meters x 23 meters; 1,095-passenger capacity; 395 cabins; cruises from Greece. **(Category D—Not Rated)**

PRINCESA CYPRIA: built 1968; refurbished 1990; 9,984 G.R.T.; 124.9 x 19 meters; 733-passenger capacity; 274 cabins. **(Category D—Not Rated)**

SAPPHIRE: 12,163 G.R.T.; 149 meters x 21.5 meters; 650-passenger capacity; 300 cabins.

SUNBIRD (formerly *Song of America*): entered service 1982; 37,584 G.R.T.; 214.8 meters long; 1,611-passenger capacity; 725 cabins. **(Category D—Not Rated)**

This is a Cyprus-based company operating budget cruises on older ships, but the cruise line is in the process of building new ships and may eventually sell off some of the older vessels. In the spring of 2008, the cruise line acquired the 1,460-passenger *Norwegian Majesty* and 1,750-passenger *Norwegian Dream* from Norwegian Cruise Line. Several of the ships they own are frequently on charter to other companies. Louis Cruises also owns the *Calypso, Emerald, Thomson Destiny,* and *Thomson Spirit,* which are all under lease to Thomson Cruises.

LUEFTNER LUXURY RIVER CRUISES
Amraser See Strasse 56, Menardi Center
6020 Innsbruck, Austria
+43512365781
+43512365781-6 Fax
www.lueftner-cruises.com

MS *AMADEUS I:* entered service 1997; 1.56 G.R.T.; 110 meters x 11.4 meters; 146-passenger capacity; 73 cabins; international officers and crew. **(Category C—Not Rated)**

MS *AMADEUS CLASSIC:* entered service 2001; 1.56 G.R.T.; 110 meters x 11.4 meters; 142-passenger capacity; 71 cabins; international officers and crew. **(Category C—Not Rated)**

MS *AMADEUS DIAMOND:* entered service 2009; 2 G.R.T.; 295' x 148'; 148-passenger capacity; 77 cabins; international officers and crew. **(Category B—Not Rated)**

MS *AMADEUS PRINCESS:* entered service 2006; 1.56 G.R.T.; 110 meters x 11.4 meters; 166-passenger capacity; 83 cabins; international officers and crew. **(Category B—Not Rated)**

MS *AMADEUS RHAPSODY:* entered service 1998; 1.56 G.R.T.; 110 meters x 11.4 meters; 142-passenger capacity; 71 cabins; international officers and crew. **(Category C—Not Rated)**

MS *AMADEUS ROYAL:* entered service 2005; 1.56 G.R.T.; 110 meters x 11.4 meters; 144-passenger capacity; 72 cabins; international officers and crew. **(Category B—Not Rated)**

MS *AMADEUS SYMPHONY:* entered service 2003; 1.56 G.R.T.; 110 meters x 11.4 meters; 146-passenger capacity; 73 cabins; international officers and crew. **(Category C—Not Rated)**

MS *DANUBIA:* joined cruise line in 2007 and totally renovated and redecorated; 102 meters x 11.4 meters; 71 cabins; international officers and crew. **(Category C—Not Rated)**

Since this riverboat line entered the market in 1997, it has been increasing its fleet, with each new entry more modern and more luxurious than the previous vessel. The three most recent riverboats, MS *Amadeus Diamond* (2009), MS *Amadeus Princess* (2006), and MS *Amadeus Royal* (2005), are considered premium ships with very elegant décor, large floor-to-ceiling windows opening with French balconies in most staterooms, and more spacious public areas.

All the vessels have well-appointed cabins 161 square feet in size. A limited number of suites on each ship are actually double cabins, 323 square feet with one cabin devoted to a lounging area with additional storage.

Public areas on the vessels include a foyer/reception area, panoramic lounge and bar, panoramic dining room, fitness center, observation deck with lounges (some with whirlpools), library, and hairdresser.

Itineraries include the various rivers of Europe, including the Rhine, Moselle, Main Canal, Danube, Rhône, Saône, Seine, and waterways of Holland and Belgium.

PAGE AND MOY
Compass House, Rockingham Road, Market Harborough
Leicester, LE167QD, U.K.
0800 0430 234
www.pageandmoy.com

OCEAN MAJESTY (formerly *Homeric*): 10,417 G.R.T.; 535-passenger capacity; 273 cabins. **(Category D—Not Rated)**

OCEAN MONARCH (formerly *Daphne*): 15,739 G.R.T.; 420-passenger capacity; 211 cabins. **(Category D—Not Rated)**

BLACK PRINCE: entered service 1966; renovated 1998; 11,209 G.R.T.; 451-passenger capacity; 241 cabins. **(Category D—Not Rated)**

Page and Moy is a large British cruise agent active in the cruise charter business. Cruise grounds include the Mediterranean, Black Sea, and northern Europe.

PONANT CRUISES
408 avenue du Prado
13008 Marseilles, France
+33 4 88 66 64 00
www.ponant.com

LE DIAMONT (formerly *Song of Flower*): entered service 1986; 8,282 tons; 407' x 52'; 198-passenger capacity; 99 cabins. **(Category B/C—Not Rated)**

LE LEVANT: entered service 1999; 3,504 G.R.T.; 328' x 46'; 90-passenger capacity; 45 cabins. **(Category B/C—Not Rated)**

LE PONANT: entered service 1991; 1,489 G.R.T.; 289' x 39'; 3-mast sail cruiser; 67-passenger capacity; 32 cabins. **(Category B/C—Not Rated)**

Cruise grounds include Adriatic, Black Sea, Aegean Sea, Indian Ocean, Red Sea, South America, North Sea, and Norwegian jjords. The cruise line is building two new 130-cabin ships for delivery in 2010.

PULLMANTUR CRUISES
C/Orense 16
Madrid, Spain
00 34 91 418 88 91/92
00 34 91 418 87 79 Fax
www.pullmantur.es

MS *EMPRESS* (formerly *Empress of the Seas*): entered service 1990; renovated 2004; 48,563 G.R.T.; 692' x 100'; 1,840-passenger capacity; 801 cabins. **(Category C— Not Rated)**

MOON EMPRESS (formerly *Sovereign of the Seas*): transferred from Royal Caribbean and to be renamed; entered service 1988; renovated 2004; 73,192 G.R.T.; 880'x 106'; 2,773-passenger capacity (2,292 double occupancy); 1,146 cabins; international officers and crew. **(Category C—Not Rated)**

MS *OCEAN DREAM* (formerly *Tropicale, Costa Topicale,* and *Pacific Star*): entered service 1982; renovated 2001; 35,000 G.R.T.; 1,400-passenger capacity; 511 cabins; international officers and crew. (Category D—Not Rated)

MS *ISLAND STAR* (formerly *Horizon*): entered service 1990; 47,000 G.R.T.; 682' x 95'; 1,875-passenger capacity; 753 cabins; international offices and crew. (Category C—Not Rated)

SKY WONDER (formerly *Fairsky, Sky Princess,* and *Pacific Sky*): to be renamed; entered service 1984; 46,314 G.R.T.; 189' x 91'; 1,550-passenger capacity. (Category D—Not Rated)

ZENITH: transferred from Celebrity Cruises and to be renamed; entered service 1992; refurbished and renovated 1999; 47,255 G.R.T.; 682' x 95';1,375-passenger capacity; 687 cabins. (Category C—Not Rated)

Pullmantur is a subsidiary of Royal Caribbean International servicing the Spanish cruise market. The largest Spain-based cruise line, it began operations in the 1990s. Royal Caribbean has transferred several of their older vessels, as well as *Zenith* of Celebrity Cruises, to this cruise line. Subsequently, it acquired *Horizon* from Island Cruises, also a former Celebrity ship. Formerly it owned three of the Renaissance Cruises *R*-class ships but they were sold to Oceania and Azamara. Most itineraries are in the Mediterranean; however, some are in the Caribbean and Baltic.

QUARK EXPEDITIONS
47 Water Street
Norwalk, Connecticut 06854
(866) 961 2961; (203) 803-2888
(203) 857-0427 Fax
www.quarkexpeditions.com

LYUBOV ORLOVA: 4,251 G.R.T.; 90 meters x 16 meters; 110-passenger capacity; 54 outside cabins and 5 suites.

CLIPPER ADVENTURER: entered service 1975; 4,364 G.R.T.; 110 meters x 16 meters; 122-passenger capacity; 58 outside cabins and 3 suites.

OCEAN NOVA: 73 meters x 11 meters; 68-passenger capacity; 37 outside cabins.

KAPITAN KHLEBNIKOV: 122.5 meters x 26.5 meters; 108-passenger capacity; 47 outside cabins and 7 suites.

AKADEMIK SHOKALSKY: 48-passenger capacity; 24 outside cabins.

AKADEMIC IOFFE: 117 meters x 18 meters; 110-passenger capacity.

AKADEMIC SERGEY VAVILOV: 117 meters x 18 meters; 105-passenger capacity.

This expedition and adventure cruise line offers cruises to the Canadian Arctic, the Arctic Islands, Spitzbergen, the Northeast Passage, Greenland, Antarctic, South Georgia, and the Falkland Islands. Most of the vessels have dining rooms, bars and lounges, small gyms, libraries, observation decks, and zodiacs. Brochure prices range from roughly $400 to $800 a night per person.

SAGA CRUISES
The Saga Building, Folkestone
Kent CT20 3SE, England
0800 096 0079
44-1303 771190
800-343-0273
www.sagacruises.com

SAGA RUBY (formerly *Vistafjord* and *Caronia*): entered service 1973; refurbished 1999; 23,492 G.R.T; 763-passenger capacity. (**Category C—Not Rated**)

SPIRIT OF ADVENTURE (formerly *Berlin*): entered service 1980; 9,570 G.R.T.; 458' x 56', 470-passenger capacity. (**Category C—Not Rated**)

A British tour operator, Saga Cruises specializes in cruise-tour packages for mature British cruisers (over 60). Cruise grounds include northern Europe, the Mediterranean, the Caribbean, South America, the Indian Ocean, Australia, and the Canary Islands.

SWAN HELLENIC
Lynnem House, 1 Victoria Way, Burgess Hill
West Sussex, Great Britain R1415 9NF
+44 (0) 845 246 9700
44 (0) 845 017 0126 Fax
www.swanhellenic.com

MV *MINERVA* (former *Explorer II*): entered service 1996; 12,500 G.R.T.; 435' x 65.5'; 300-passenger capacity; 197 cabins; British and European officers; international crew.

Swan Hellenic entered the cruise business in 1954 and has owned and operated various ships over the years. P & O purchased the company in 1983. After Carnival Corporation acquired P & O/Princess, Swan Hellenic became a brand of Carnival. Thereafter, in 2006, Carnival decided to drop this brand; however, a former CEO of P & O/Princess, Lord Sterling, reacquired the original *Minerva* that had been sailing as *Explorer II,* and the cruise line lives again. The ship is targeted at the British cruise market.

THOMSON CRUISES
Greater London House, Hempstead Road
London NW1 7SD, England
0870 0602277
www.thomson-cruises.co.uk

CALYPSO: 11,162 G.R.T.; 486-passenger capacity; cruises Black Sea and eastern Mediterranean (adults only); leased from Louis Cruise Lines.

EMERALD: entered service 1958; refurbished 1992; 26,431 G.R.T.; 1,198-passenger capacity; leased from Louis Cruise Lines.

THOMSON DESTINY (formerly *Song of America*): entered service 1981; 37,000 G.R.T.; 705' x 93'; 1,522-passenger capacity; 701 cabins; leased from Louis Cruises Lines.

THOMSON DREAM (formerly *Westerdam, Homeric,* and *Costa Europa*): entered service 1986; lengthened 1990; refurbished 2003 and 2005; 55,000 G.R.T.; 798' x 101'; 1,494-passenger capacity; 733 cabins.

THOMSON SPIRIT (formerly *Nieu Amsterdam*): entered service 1983; refurbished 2003; 33,900 G.R.T.; 1,254-passenger capacity; 627 cabins; leased from Louis Cruise Lines.

THOMSON CELEBRATION (formerly *Noordam*): entered service 1884; refurbished 2004; 33,930 G.R.T.; 1254-passenger capacity; 627 cabins.

Thomson is Britain's largest tour operator. The ships offer seven- to 14-day itineraries in the Mediterranean and Canary Islands. The *Spirit* and *Celebration* formerly sailed as Holland America ships and have very attractive interiors and public facilities.

VANTAGE TRAVEL
90 Canal Street
Boston, Massachusetts 02114
(800) 322-6677
www.vantagetravel.com

MS *RIVER DISCOVERY:* entered service 2007; 360' long; 166-passenger capacity.

MS *RIVER EXPLORER:* entered service 2001; refurbished 2006; 410' long; 170-passenger capacity.

MS *RIVER NAVIGATOR:* entered service 2000; refurbished 2007; 360' long; 140-passenger capacity.

MS *RIVER ODYSSEY:* entered service 2000; refurbished 2007; 410' long: 170-passenger capacity.

These ships offer riverboat cruises on the waterways of Holland and Belgium and on the Rhine, Danube, and Moselle Rivers and the Main-Danube Canal. Prices include round-trip air from select U.S. cities.

The newest ship, *River Discovery,* boasts French balconies in 83 percent of the staterooms; all cabins are outside, have twin beds that can convert to doubles, and include flat-screen TVs with in-room movies and CNN, hair dryers, and in-room safes. There are 14 junior suites and one owner's suite. The *River Navigator* has similar accommodations, but only 21 cabins have French balconies and beds that convert to doubles, and the vessel has only four junior suites. All of the ships have three passenger decks, a restaurant, an observation lounge, and a sun deck with lounges.

VOYAGES OF DISCOVERY
DISCOVERY WORLD CRUISES
1800 SE Tenth Avenue, Suite 205
Fort Lauderdale, Florida 33316
(866) 623-2689; (954) 761-7878
(954) 761-7768 Fax
www.voyagesofdiscovery.com

MV *DISCOVERY* (formerly *Island Princess*): entered service 1971; 20,186 G.R.T.; 553' x 80'; 796-passenger capacity; 355 cabins; cruises the Panama Canal, Galapagos Islands, South America, Antarctica, Falkland Islands, Patagonia, transatlantic, Azores, South Africa, Indian Ocean, India, Persian Gulf and Red Sea, eastern Mediterranean and Black Seas, Turkey, and Greek Islands. (**Category C—Not Rated**)

This cruise line specializes in longer cruises, including a 108-day voyage to exotic places around the world. Although this is a vintage ship, the cabins are air-conditioned, have TVs, hair dryers, and safes. The upper category cabins have minibars/refrigerators, bath and shower, and picture windows. There are five suites. Many cabins can accommodate a third and/or fourth passenger.

Public areas include two pools, one with a magradome roof, a Jacuzzi, restaurant, theater for shows, health and beauty spa, buffet restaurant, Internet center, library, and wireless access at specified locations aboard ship. Lectures by historians and experts on the cruise areas are featured. The line offers a full cruise experience. Rates range from $270 to $660 per night; however, there are early booking discounts from 20 percent to 50 percent.

Chapter Twelve

Rooms at the Top,
or the Suite Life at Sea

Most fine hotels around the world provide at least one presidential or ultra-grand suite or villa where visiting dignitaries, wealthy clientele, or special VIPs can be accommodated with facilities that can house a small entourage, entertain guests, and provide extra services and amenities. In my research for *Stern's Guide to the Greatest Resorts of the World*, I have encountered many awesome accommodations, some measuring up to 5,000 square feet and with price tags as high as $6,000 per night.

Therefore, it is not surprising that "fine hotels at sea" would offer similar luxury accommodations. Historically, the existence of ultra-grand suites on ships has undergone a metamorphosis. During the era of the legendary superliners such as the *Titanic, Normandie,* and *Queen Mary,* offering extremely large, ultra-deluxe accommodations was *de rigueur*. However, during the period from 1970 to 1990, when cruising gained popularity with the mass market of vacationers, expensive suites were not a priority, and cruise lines considered a 400- to 600-square-foot stateroom more than sufficient for important clientele.

The final decade of the 20th century and the early years of the 21st century have been periods of unprecedented growth for the cruise industry, during which small companies were gobbled up by the major leaguers, who raised funds to acquire and/or build new ships by selling shares of stock to the public. Millions of dollars were spent annually on advertising and publicity in an attempt to stay afloat with the competition and to create the image of having the most prestigious vessels. Savvy cruise operators—seeking top ratings among ship reviewers as well as wishing to appeal to high-profile personalities and a wealthy clientele who could afford and demand the very best—wisely included at least one or two special ultra-deluxe suites in the 800- to 1,400-square-foot range on their new vessels, at fares ranging from $750 to $1,500 per person per night (for those who pay the published rate).

It is not uncommon for these grand suites at sea to include a master bath with a separate glassed-in shower stall; a large Jacuzzi tub; double vanities; toilet and bidet compartments; a second guest bathroom; an entryway; a large, elegantly furnished living room with a dining area; several giant televisions with VCR, DVD, and CD attachments; a full-facility, fully stocked pantry where a chef can prepare meals; and one or more large verandas for alfresco entertaining or relaxing. Of course, rooms at the top vary from ship to ship, and some are neither "at the top" (of the ship) nor much more inviting than the deluxe category of suites otherwise available on the ship.

In order to provide my readers with information on options for the "suite life," the following charts and photos may prove helpful.

CODE TO SPECIAL FACILITIES

A. Second connecting bedroom at no additional charge.
B. Second connecting bedroom option at additional charge.
C. Guest bathroom.
D. Large walk-in closet.
E. Kitchen or pantry where meals can be prepared.
F. Large-screen television.
G. CD player.
H. Jacuzzi in bathroom.
I. Jacuzzi on patio.
J. Dining room or separate dining area.
K. Separate shower stall and separate bathtub..

CODE TO SPECIAL AMENITIES

A. Private butler service.
B. Complimentary soft drinks, liquors, and wines.
C. Free laundry, dry cleaning, and pressing.
D. Complimentary shore excursions.
E. Automatic invitation to Captain's table.
(*) Designates that there has been no verification as to whether square footage represented by cruise line includes or excludes the veranda.

Cruise Line	Azamara	Carnival	Carnival	Carnival	Celebrity	Celebrity	Costa
Ship(s)	Quest & Journey	Spirit Class	Conquest Class	1) Destiny Class 2) Freedom Class	Century & Mercury	1) Millennium, Infinity, Summit, & Constellation 2) Solstice Class	1) Atlantica & Mediterrenea 2) Victoria 3) Romantica & Classica 4) Fortuna & Magica 5) Concordia & Serena
Name/Number of Suites	Penthouse Suite	Penthouse Suite	Penthouse Suite	Penthouse Suite	Penthouse Suite	Penthouse Suite	N/A
Square Footage of Suite w/o Veranda	660'	300'	345'	345'	1,101'	1) 1,432' (including veranda) 2) 1,290'	1) 367' 2) 430' 3) 580' 4) 450' 5) 313'
Square Footage of Veranda	340'	115'	85'	85'	118'	1) N/A 2) 389'	1) 282' 2) N/A 3) N/A 4) 84' 5) 88'
Special Facilities (Per Code)	B, C, D, E, F, G, H, I, J, K	G, H	G, H	G, H	B, C, D, E, F, G, H, I, J, K	B, C, D, E, F, G, H, I, J, K, & piano	D, F, H, K, J
Special Amenities (Per Code)	A				A	A	A & B (on embarkation only)

Cruise Line	Crystal	Cunard	Peter Deilmann	Disney	Hapag-Lloyd	Holland America	Holland America
Ship(s)	1) Symphony 2) Serenity	1) QV 2) QM2	Deutschland	Magic & Wonder	Europa	Amsterdam, Rotterdam, Zaandam, Volendam, Zuiderdam, Oosterdam, Westerdam, Noordam, & Eurodam	Veendam, Statendam Maasdam
Name of Suite	Penthouse Suite	1) Mauretania & Laconia Suites 2) Balmoral & Sandringham Suites	Owner's Suite	Walt Disney & Roy Disney Suites	Grand Penthouse Suite	Penthouse Suite	Penthouse Suite
Square Footage of Suite w/o Veranda	1) 983' 2) 1,345'	1) 965' 2) 1,506'	382'	845'	915'	846' to 1,000'	946'
Square Footage of Veranda	1) 93' 2) 112'	1) 886' 2) 624'	100'	145'	307'	280' to 318'	180'
Special Facilities (Per Code)	C, D, F, G, H, I, J, K	B, C, D, E, F G, H, I, J, K	F, G, K	A, C, D, E F, G, H, J, K	B, D, E, F G, H, J, K	B, D, E, G, H	B, D, E, G, H, J
Special Amenities (Per Code)	A, B, & C (pressing only)	1) A, B 2) private elevators A, B	A, E	A & piano	A, B, C, E	A, C, E	A, C, E

Cruise Line	MSC	Norwegian	Oceania	P & O	P & O	Paul Gaugin	Princess
Ship(s)	Fantasia & Splendida	Star, Dawn, Jewel, Gem, Pearl, & Jade	Regatta, Insignia, & Nautica	1) Aurora 2) Artemis	1) Ventura 2) Oriana 3) Oceana 4) Arcadia	Paul Gaugin	Ocean, Royal, & Pacific
Name of Suite	Royal Suite	Garden Villa	Owner's Suite	1) Piano Suite & Library Suite 2) Oriana Suite & Canaberra Suite	Suites	Owner's Suite	Owner's Suite
Square Footage of Suite w/o Veranda	571'	4,300'	660'	1) 865' (bi-level) 2) 769' (bi-level)	1) 534' 2) 424' 3) 683' 4) 398'	531'	660'
Square Footage of Veranda	172'	720'	340'	1) 40' & 48' (2 balconies) 2) 79'	1) 126' 2) 90' 3) 293' 4) 134'	57'	340'
Special Facilities (Per Code)	D, E, G, H, K	A, B, C, D, E, F, G, H, I, J, K	C, D, F, G, H, J, K	D, F, G, H, K	D, F, G, H, K	F, G, J, K	D, F, G, H, K
Special Amenities (Per Code)	A, B	A, B, C, E	A, C (pressing only)	A	A	A, B	A, B, (initial set up)

Cruise Line	Princess	Princess	Princess	Princess	Princess	Regent Seven Seas	Royal Caribbean
Ship(s)	1) Grand 2) Golden 3) Star	Sun, Dawn, & Sea	Coral & Island	Diamond & Sapphire	1) Caribbean 2) Crown 3) Emerald 4) Ruby	1) Navigator 2) Mariner 3) Voyager	Sovereign Class
Name of Suite	Grand Suite	Monaco Suite	16 Full Suites	Grand Suite	1) Grand Suite 2, 3, 4) Owner's Suite	Master Suite	Royal Suite
Square Footage of Suite w/o Veranda	1) 613' 2) 977' 3) 977'	447'	353'	980'	1) 942' 2, 3, 4) 513'	1) 1,067' 2) 1,204' 3) 1,216'	670'
Square Footage of Veranda	1) 117' 2) 337' 3) 337'	248'	117'	340'	1) 335' 2, 3, 4) 174'	1) 106' 2) 798' (2 balconies) 3) 187'	145'
Special Facilities (Per Code)	D, F, G, H, J, K	D, G, H, J, K	D, E, H, J, K	A, D, H, J, K	A, D, H, J, K	1) C, D, F, G, K 2, 3) A, C, D, F, G, H, I, K	D, F, G, H, J, K
Special Amenities (Per Code)	A, B (initial set up)	A, B, C (initial set up)	A, B (initial set up)	B, C (initial set up)	B, C (initial set up)	A, B	A

Cruise Line	Royal Caribbean	Royal Caribbean	Silversea	Seabourn	Victoria
Ship(s)	Freedom Class	Radiance, Vision, & Voyager Classes & Oasis of the Seas	1) Silver Cloud & Silver Wind 2) Silver Shadow & Silver Whisper 3) Prince Albert II	1) Pride, Spirit, & Legend 2) Odyssey	Victoria Jenna
Name of Suite	Presidential Family Suite	Royal Suite	Grand Suite	Grand Wintergarden Suite	Shangri-La
Square Footage of Suite w/o Veranda	810'	1,001' to 1,188'	1) 1,314' 2) 1,435' (2 bedrooms) 3) 626'	1,182'	587'
Square Footage of Veranda	810'	131-215'	1) 89' 2) 178' (2 balconies) 3) 158'	215' (2 balconies)	215'
Special Facilities (Per Code)	B, C, D, F, G, H, J, K (piano)	B, C, D, F, G, H, J, K (piano)	B, C, D, F, G, H, J	1) C, D, F G, J, K 2) A, C, D, E, F, G, H, I, J, K	F
Special Amenities (Per Code)	A	A	A, B, C (no dry cleaning), E		A, B, C

Owner's suite, Nautica, *courtesy Oceania Cruises*

Sea Cloud, *courtesy Sea Cloud Cruises*

Rotterdam VI, *courtesy Holland America Line*

Prinsendam, *courtesy Holland America Line*

Carnival Destiny, *courtesy Carnival Cruises*

Seabourn Pride, *courtesy Seabourn Cruises*

Penthouse suite, Millennium, *courtesy Celebrity Cruises*

Crystal Symphony, *courtesy Crystal Cruise Line*

Dawn Princess, *courtesy Princess Cruises*

Royal suite, Explorer of the Seas, *courtesy Royal Caribbean International*

Silver Wind, *courtesy Silversea Cruises*

Roy Disney suite, courtesy Disney Cruise Line

Deluxe suite, Seven Seas Navigator, *courtesy Regent Seven Seas Cruises*

Deutschland, *courtesy Peter Deilmann Cruises*

Owner's suite, Norwegian Sun, *courtesy Norwegian Cruise Line*

Garden Villa, private garden on Norwegian Star, *courtesy Norwegian Cruise Line*

Queen Mary 2, *courtesy Cunard Line*

Chapter Thirteen

Specialty Restaurants at Sea

Passengers on cruise ships generally do not have the option of leaving the ship for dinner as they do when vacationing ashore at a hotel or resort. Therefore, the challenge for cruise operators has been keeping the dining experience sufficiently interesting and diverse to prevent guests from becoming bored or dissatisfied.

The various lines attempt to vary the menus each day of the cruise and to provide theme nights in an effort to make each dinner seem special. However, experienced cruisers soon realize that the environs, the style of preparation and one's table companions (except on open-seating vessels) are the same and often feel that a change would be welcome.

The existence of an alternate dining venue with a new decor, separate kitchen, different style of cuisine and an option for a dining companion or companions of your choice becomes a welcome plus, enhancing the cruise experience.

In recent years, a competition has developed among cruise lines to boast the very finest alternative, reservation-only, gourmet, specialty restaurant at sea. During the 1990s, pizza venues, casual evening dinners at the pool-side buffet restaurant, ice cream parlors and hamburger/hot dog grills near the pool became the rigueur, available on most major cruise lines. However, discerning cruisers, tired of the ennui of dining night after night in the main dining room quickly became enamored with alternative specialty restaurants offering more upscale cuisine and service, as well as the opportunity to dine when you want and with whom you want.

The first ships to introduce fine-dining specialty restaurants as an alternative to the main dining room were the Crystal Cruise Line ships offering both elegant Italian and atmospheric Asian restaurants. Not to be outdone, the other cruise lines followed suit. Today, Azamara, Carnival, Celebrity, Costa, Cunard, Peter Deilmann, Disney, Hapag-Lloyd, Holland America, MSC, Norwegian, Oceania, P & O, Princess, Regent Seven Seas, Royal Caribbean, Seabourn, Silver Sea, Star, Victoria, and Windstar all offer guests one or more alternative dining possibilities.

Initially, alternative Italian restaurants sprung up since Italian cuisine was considered the most universally popular ethnic fare. This was followed by steak and chop houses, Asian-style restaurants including Sushi and Teppanyaki specialty areas, and more formal French and Continental-style dining rooms.

The different cruise lines have varying policies on exacting a surcharge for these restaurants. On some there is no additional charge; on others there is a minimal charge of $5 to $10 largely to cover tips to the waiters; and on the more up-scale French-Continental dining rooms, the tariff can reach from $22 to $35 per person. However, the multi-course repast (with impeccable service) in these dining rooms is well worth the price and could easily run two to four times as much in a comparable restaurant in Europe or the U.S.

Since more and more cruise lines are experimenting with alternative specialty restaurants, as well as keeping their buffet restaurants open for dinner, those readers who find these features important would be well advised to check with the cruise line at the time of booking.

The following charts, photos, and menus are offered to afford my readers a rough idea of the alternative dining possibilities as they exist at the time of publication on cruise ships that feature these options. Only "fine-dining," alternative specialty restaurants are covered. Casual dining venues that are also open for breakfast and lunch, as well as dinner, are not described.

Code:
FR—French
ITL—Italian
CTL—Continental
SCH—Steak/Chop house

JP—Japanese;
C—Chinese
A—Asian
MX—Mexican or Tex Mex.

Alternative Dining Restaurants

Cruise Line	Azamara	Carnival	Celebrity	Costa	Crystal	Cunard	Peter Deilmann
Ships (s)	Quest & Journey	1) Spirit 2) Pride 3) Legend 4) Miracle 5) Conquest 6) Glory 7) Valor 8) Liberty 9) Freedom	1) Millenium 2) Infinity 3) Summit 4) Constellation 5) Century 6) Mercury 7) Solstice	1) Victoria 2) Atlantica 3) Mediterranea 4) Fortuna 5) Magica 6) Concordia 7) Pacifica 8) Luminosa	Symphony & Serenity	QM2 & QV	Deutschland
Restaurant(s)	1) Prime C 2) Aqualina	1) Nouveau 2) David's 3) Golden Fleece 4) Nick and Nora's 5) The Point 6) Emerald Room 7) Scarlett's 8) Harry's Supper Club 9) Supper Club	1) Olympic 2) United States 3) Normandie 4) Ocean Liners 5, 6) Murano 7) Murano, Tuscan Grill, & Silk Harvest	1) Magnifico 2) Club Atlantica 3) Club Medusa 4) Club Grand Conte 5) Club Magica 6) Club Concordia 7) Club Blue Moon 8) Club Luminosa	1) Prego 2) Silk Road	Todd English	Four Seasons
Cuisine	1) SCH 2) CTL	SCH	1-6) CTL/FR 7) CTL/FR, SCH, & A	ITL	1) ITL 2) A	CTL	CTL/FR
Surcharge	N	Y	Y	S	N but gratuity expected	S	N

Cruise Line	Disney	Hapag-Lloyd	Holland America	MSC	Norwegian	Oceania	P & O
Ship(s)	Magic & Wonder	Europa	All ships	1) Orchestra 2) Musica 3) Magnifica 4) Poesia	1) Dawn 2) Jewel 3) Pearl 4) Gem 5) Jade 6) Sun 7) Star 8) Pride of America	Regatta, Insignia, & Nautica	1) Arcadia 2) Oceana 3) Aurora 4) Oriana 5) Artemis 6) Ventura
Restaurant(s)	Palo	1) Venezia 2) Oriental	1) Pinnacle Grill 2) Tamarind 3) Cavaletto	Varies by ship	1-5) Le Bistro, Teppanyaki, Lotus Garden, Cagney's, La Cucina, & Mambos 6-7) Le Bistro, Ginza, East Meets West, Il Adago, & Teppanyaki 8) Jefferson's Bistro, Lazy J, East Meets West, & Little Italy	1) Polo Grill 2) Toscana	1) Arcadian Rhodes & Orchid 2) Horizon & Café Jardin 3) Café Bordeaux 4) Oriana Rhodes 5) Horizon Grill 6) White Room & East
Cuisine	ITL	1) ITL 2)A	1) CTL 2) A 3) ITL	1-4) SCH 2-4) JP 1) A	1-5) FR/J/A/ SCH/ITL/MX 6-7) FR/J/CTL ITL/J 8) FR/SCH/ CTL/ITL	1) SCH 2) ITL	1) CTL/A 2) SCH/ITL 3) FR 4) CTL 5) SCH 6) CTL/A
Surcharge	Y	N	1-2) Y 3) N	Y	Y/N	N	Y

Alternative Dining Restaurants

Cruise Line	Princess	Regent Seven Seas	Royal Caribbean	Seabourn	Silversea	Victoria	Windstar
Ship(s)	1) Coral & Island 2) Diamond & Sapphire 3) Golden, Grand, & Star 4) Caribbean, Crown, Emerald, & Ruby 5) Ocean, Pacific, & Royal	1) Mariner 2) Voyager 3) Navigator	1) Voyager Class 2) Radiance Class 3) Freedom Class	All ships	Cloud, Wind, Shadow, & Whisper	Jenna	All ships
Restaurant(s)	1) Sabatini & Bayou Café 2-3, 5) Sabatini & Sterling 4) Sabatini & Sterling or Crown Grill	1-2) Signatures & Prime 7 3) Portofino & Prime 7	1-2) Portofino & Chops 3) Portofino, Chops, & Jade	Restaurant 2	1) La Terrazza 2) Le Champagne	Top of the Yangtze	Candles
Cuisine	ITL & SCH	1-2) FR/CTL & SCH 3) ITL & SCH	1-2) ITL/SCH 3) ITL/SCH/A	Bistro-style Theme Dinners	1) ITL 2) FR/CTL	CTL/A	SCH & Themes
Surcharge	Y	N	Y	N	1) N 2) Y	Y	N

4 Seasons, MSC Orchestra, *courtesy MSC Cruises*

Cagney's, Norwegian Pearl, *courtesy Norwegian Cruise Line*

Il Adagio, Norwegian Sun, *courtesy Norwegian Cruise Line*

Le Champagne, Silver Whisper, *courtesy Silverseas Cruises*

Scarlett's Supper Club, Carnival Valor, *courtesy Carnival Cruises*

Polo Grill, courtesy Oceania Cruises

Prego, Crystal Serenity, *courtesy Crystal Cruises*

Pinnacle Grill, Oosterdam, *courtesy Holland America Line*

Trattoria Sabatini, Grand Princess, *courtesy Princess Cruises*

Olympic Restaurant, Millennium, *courtesy Celebrity Cruises*

Latitudes, Seven Seas Voyager, *courtesy Regent Seven Seas Cruises*

Signatures, Seven Seas Mariner, *courtesy Regent Seven Seas Cruises*

Palo, Disney Magic, *courtesy Disney Cruise Lines*

Chops Grill, Radiance of the Seas, *courtesy Royal Caribbean International*

Todd English Restaurant, QV, courtesy Cunard Line

Chef's Galley on QM2, courtesy Cunard Line

Four Seasons, Deutschland, *courtesy Peter Deilmann Cruises*

Club Medusa, Costa Mediterranea, *courtesy Costa Cruises*

aboard the M/v Silver Shadow

THE BEST OF BURGUNDY

Cuvée Louise, Pommery, 1998

MINI DÉLICES BOURGUIGNONS
A Bite-size Taste of Burgundy

Chablis "Grenouilles" Grand Cru, Maison Champy, 2003

PETITS GRIS À LA PERSILLADE AVEC FONDUE DE TOMATE
Burgundy Snails with Herb Butter and Tomato Fondue

Puligny-Montrachet, Louis Latour, 2005

POULET DE BRESSE AUX ECREVISSES
Whole-roasted Bresse Chicken with Shrimps

Pommard Louis Latour, 2005

BRIOCHE D'EPOISSES AUX RAISINS DE BOURGOGNE
Burgundy Cheese Brioche with Fresh Grape Coulis

St. Amour Domaine Barbelet, 2004

TOUR EIFFEL EN FANTAISIE
Chocolate Eiffel Tower Fantasy

Paradis Hennessy Extra

DÉGUSTATION DE CAFÉ AVEC BOCAUX GOURMANDS
Coffee Degustation with Sweet Regional Delights

Le Champagne, courtesy Silversea Cruises

ASSORTED SATAY

SATE SAPI, SATE AYAM, SATE IKAN, SATE BABI
BEEF, CHICKEN, SEAFOOD OR PORK SATÉ WITH PEANUT SAUCE
SATÉ VAN RUNDVLEES, KIP, VIS OF VARKENSVLEES

VEGETABLES

GADO GADO
STEAMED VEGETABLES & FRIED TOFU WITH PEANUT SAUCE
GESTOOMDE, GEMENGDE GROENTEN EN
GEBAKKEN TOFU MET PINDASAUS

TUMIS BUNCIS
STIR FRIED GREEN BEANS
ROER GEBAKKEN GROENE BOONTJES

POULTRY

OPOR AYAM
CHICKEN BRAISED IN COCONUT MILK BROTH
EEN CASSEROLE VAN KIP IN EEN KOKOSBOUILLON

BEBEK BEBANAM
ROASTED DUCK WITH A SAUCE OF TOMATO AND PALM SUGAR
GEROOSTERDE EEND GESERVEERD MET EEN TOMAAT EN
PALMSUIKER SAUS

MEATS

TONGSENG
STIR FRIED LAMB IN SWEET SOY SAUCE
LAM GEBAKKEN IN KECAP MANIS

EMPAL DAGING
JAVANESE FRIED BRAISED BEEF SQUARES
GESTOOFD JAVAANS RUNDVLEES

SEAFOOD

BRENGKESAN IKAN
SNAPPER GRILLED IN A BANANA LEAF
SNAPPER GEGRILD IN BANANENBLAD

IKAN ASEM MANIS
DEEP FRIED TILAPIA SERVED WITH SWEET & SOUR SAUCE
GEFRITUURDE TILAPIA GESERVEERD MET ZOETZURE SAUS

SIDE DISHES

NASI KUNING/NASI PUTIH
STEAMED YELLOW RICE/WHITE RICE
GESTOOMDE GELE RIJST/WITTE RIJST

SAMBAL GORENG KENTANG
STIR FRIED SWEET & SPICY POTATO CUBES
ROER GEBAKKEN, PITTIG GEKRUIDE ZOETE AARDAPPELBLOKJES

ACAR CAMPUR
SWEET & SOUR VEGETABLE PICKLES
ZOETZURE GROENTEN

KRUPUK UNDANG
SHRIMP CRACKERS
GARNALEN KROEPOEK

SERUNDENG
LIGHTLY STIR FRIED CHILI, PEANUTS AND SHREDDED COCONUT
LICHT GEBAKKEN, GERASPTE KOKOSNOOT, PINDA'S EN EEN
VLEUGJE PEPER

BAWANG GORENG
FRIED ONIONS
GEFRITUURDE UITJES

Tamarind, Courtesy Holland America

MSC Orchestra

presents

4 Seasons

Gastronomic Restaurant

Menu at
US$ 25.00 p.p.

Appetizers

Duck Foie Gras terrine with gingered fig compote
served with a raisin brioche

*Terrina di Foie Gras d'anatra e composta di fichi allo zenzero
servita con la sua brioche all'uvetta sultanina*

"Armonia di sapori italiani"
A medley of scallops, saffron-marinated swordfish,
smoked duck breast and Arnad lard

*Composizione di cappesante, pesce spada marinato allo zafferano,
petto d'anatra affumicato e lardo d'Arnad*

Scrambled egg with salmon roe
enhanced with a chive's sour cream and asparagus tips

*L'uovo strapazzato con uova di salmone
panna acida all'erba cipollina e punte di asparagi*

Soups

Onion soup au gratin

Zuppa gratinata di cipolle

Cream of Cannellini bean soup
with warm scampi and mussels

Crema di cannellini con cozze e scampi tiepidi

Chilled cucumber and mint velouté

Vellutata fredda di cetriolo e menta

Main Courses

Seared monkfish medallions
with light citrus sauce

Medaglioni di pescatrice alla piastra
salsa leggera agli agrumi

Rack of lamb with pistachio crust
served with whole-grain mustard sauce

Carré di agnello in crosta di pistacchi
salsa ai grani di senape

Beef tenderloin on a crispy potato tartlet
with caramelised apples and Modena balsamic vinegar

Filetto di manzo su tortino croccante di patate
con mele caramellate e riduzione all'aceto balsamico di Modena

Gragnano "Vermicelli"
with clams and Cherry tomatoes

"Vermicelli" di Gragnano con vongole e pomodorini

Pumpkin and Amaretti ravioli,
served with melted butter, Parmesan and fried sage

Ravioli al ripieno di zucca e Amaretti, con burro fuso, parmigiano e salvia fritta

Our Special Cuts

Grilled Veal Chop
grilled on the bone, lightly flavored with oregano

*Squisita costoletta di vitello con l'osso cucinata ai ferri,
delicatamente profumata all'origano*

New York Strip Steak
the king of steak, thick and juicy, grilled to perfection as you like it and
served with your favorite choice of sauce

*La bistecca per eccellenza, spessa e succosa, grigliata a piacere
ed accompagnata dalla vostra salsa preferita*

"Filet Mignon"
without a doubt, our most tender choice of meat,
grilled to your liking and served with your favorite sauce

*Senza dubbio la nostra carne alla griglia più tenera cotta a piacere
ed accompagnata dalla vostra salsa preferita*

Rib Eye Steak
mouth watering rib eye, grilled as you prefer, best served with "Café de
Paris" butter

*Succulenta costata di manzo alla griglia cotta a piacere,
perfetta accompagnata da burro "Café de Paris"*

| VORSPEISEN/APPETIZERS |

KALIFORNISCHER CAESAR SALAT . . . . € 4,50
Römersalat mit einem Dressing aus Sardellen, Olivenöl,
Zitrone, Knoblauch Croutons und Grana Padano

CARPACCIO VON DER GARNELE . . . . € 8,60
mit Zitrusfrüchten

GEBRATENE ENTENSTOPFLEBER . . . . € 12,10
mit Mangochutney

STEAKHOUSE SALAT . . . . € 3,50
Knackiger Salatmix mit Tomaten, Mais und roten Bohnen

| SUPPEN |

NEW ENGLAND CLAM CHOWDER . . . . € 3,60
Muschelsuppe

SUCCOTASH . . . . € 2,80
Indianischer Bohneneintopf mit Mais

UNSERE STEAKMENÜS ENTHALTEN EINEN FRISCHEN SALAT VORWEG
UND BAKED POTATO MIT SOUR CREME ZUM HAUPTGERICHT

| SURF & TURF |

DAS BESTE VOM RIND UND DAS BESTE AUS DEM MEER

½ HUMMERSCHWANZ UND EIN FILET MIGNON .... € 29,90
vom Grill inklusive Beilagen Ihrer Wahl

| STEAKS VOM BISON |

BISON - RIB-EYE STEAK .... 240 g (8,5 Oz)   € 24,50

BISON - FILET STEAK .... 240 g (8,5 Oz)   € 29,50

| AMERICAN BEEF |

DELMONICO STEAK – RIB-EYE STEAK .... 240 g (8,5 Oz) € 17,00
Rib-Eye Steak wird aus dem mageren Kern der Hochrippe 400 g (14 Oz)
€ 22,00
geschnitten. Es zeigt einen deutlichen Fettkern, das „Auge"
(Eye).

NEW YORK STRIP STEAK .... 180 g (6,4 Oz) € 14,50
Strip Steak – auch New York Strip Steak 480 g (17 Oz) € 12,90
Ein gut marmoriertes Stück vom Rinderrücken.

PORTERHOUSE STEAK .... 750 g (26,5 Oz) € 39,00
T-Bone Steak – Steak mit T-förmigem Knochen, auf einer
Seite das Roastbeef, auf der anderen Seite das Filet.

FILET MIGNON .... 180 g (6,5 Oz) € 16,50
Filet Steak aus dem besten Teil des Filets. 240 g (8,5 Oz) € 21,00

| SPEZIALITÄTEN |

JERK CHICKEN .... € 12,80
scharf gewürztes Huhn

HAMBURGER XXL .... € 8,50
aus reinem Rindfleisch

RACK OF LAMB .... € 17,80
Lammkrone – bestes Fleisch aus Patagonien

GEGRILLTER HUMMERSCHWANZ .... € 26,90
das Genusserlebnis aus dem Meer

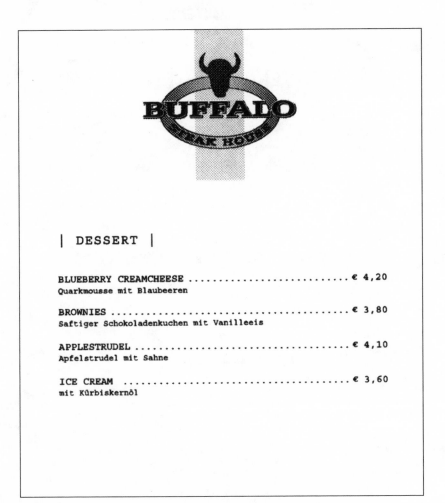

| DESSERT |

BLUEBERRY CREAMCHEESE .... € 4,20
Quarkmousse mit Blaubeeren

BROWNIES .... € 3,80
Saftiger Schokoladenkuchen mit Vanilleeis

APPLESTRUDEL .... € 4,10
Apfelstrudel mit Sahne

ICE CREAM .... € 3,60
mit Kürbiskernöl

Buffalo Steak House, courtesy AIDA Cruises

Steakhouse Favorites
(The beef cuts like butta' here, Dahling.)

Starters

Colossal Shrimp Cocktail
Jack Daniel's Cocktail Sauce

Jumbo Lump Crab Cakes
Creole–rémoulade Dip

Oysters Rockefeller

Soups and Salads

Lobster Bisque with Lobster Custard

New England Clam Chowder

Cardini's Original Caesar Salad
Created in 1924 in Tijuana, Served Tableside

The Wedge Iceberg Lettuce
Crumbled Blue Cheese, Tomato, Bacon Bits, Red Wine Vinaigrette

Sliced Beefsteak Tomato and Bermuda Onion
Balsamic Dressing

Main Courses

Darne of Atlantic Salmon Oscar,
Alaskan King Crab Leg
Chive Beurre Blanc

Grilled Rare Ahi Tuna Steak
Scallions, Teriyaki Sauce

Corn Fed Half Rotisserie Chicken
Lemon–pepper, Fortified–garlic Gravy

Double Cut Domestic Lamb Chops
Rosemary Sauce

12 oz. Milk Fed Veal Chop
Foie Gras Croutons, Madeira Demi–glace

Slow Roasted Prime Rib of Beef
Petite Cut 10 oz.
King Cut 14 oz.
Au Jus, Horseradish Crème

Filet Mignon
Mate's Cut 5 oz.
Captain's Cut 8 oz.

14 oz. Rib Eye Steak
Cajun Blackened

10 oz. New York Strip Steak

16 oz. T-bone Steak

Sauces to Choose From:
Béarnaise, Green Peppercorn, Port Wine Demi–glace, Café de Paris Butter

Your Choice of Sides
Served for Two Persons

Cagney's Fries
French Fries, White Truffle Oil,
Parmesan, Sea Salt, Parsley

Baked Jumbo Idaho Potato

Mashed Potatoes

Gratin Potatoes

Creamed Spinach

Sautéed Mushrooms

Onion Shoestrings

Steamed Fresh Asparagus

Sweet Corn

Cover charge applies

Steakhouse Specials

Whole Lobster
Approximately 1.5 lb. per Piece

Surf & Turf
Filet Mignon and ½ Lobster

24 oz. Porterhouse Steak

Each of the dishes require an additional per person above the normal Cover Charge.
The special includes as many choices as you desire of
Appetizers, Soups, Salads, Accompaniments and Desserts from the Main Steakhouse Menu.

Cover charge applies
If you have any type of food allergy, please advise your Server before ordering

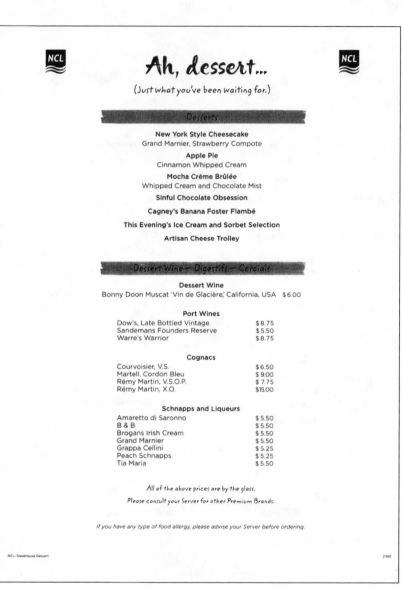

Ah, dessert...

(Just what you've been waiting for.)

Desserts

New York Style Cheesecake
Grand Marnier, Strawberry Compote

Apple Pie
Cinnamon Whipped Cream

Mocha Crème Brûlée
Whipped Cream and Chocolate Mist

Sinful Chocolate Obsession

Cagney's Banana Foster Flambé

This Evening's Ice Cream and Sorbet Selection

Artisan Cheese Trolley

Dessert Wine – Digestifs – Cordials

Dessert Wine
Bonny Doon Muscat 'Vin de Glacière,' California, USA $6.00

Port Wines
Dow's, Late Bottled Vintage	$8.75
Sandemans Founders Reserve	$5.50
Warre's Warrior	$8.75

Cognacs
Courvoisier, V.S.	$6.50
Martell, Cordon Bleu	$9.00
Rémy Martin, V.S.O.P.	$7.75
Rémy Martin, X.O.	$15.00

Schnapps and Liqueurs
Amaretto di Saronno	$5.50
B & B	$5.50
Brogans Irish Cream	$5.50
Grand Marnier	$5.50
Grappa Cellini	$5.25
Peach Schnapps	$5.25
Tia Maria	$5.50

All of the above prices are by the glass.

Please consult your Server for other Premium Brands.

If you have any type of food allergy, please advise your Server before ordering.

Cagney's, courtesy Norwegian Cruise Line

"SOMMERTAGE VOLLER LEBENSLUST"

*

Arrividerci

Donnerstag, 12. August 2004 · Kopenhagen

Duetto di Caviale con Cetrioli
Mille Feuille von Sevruga und Keta-Kaviar
auf Spiegel von Gurkenschmand

Carpaccio d'Agnello
Lammcarpaccio mit mariniertem Salat von Fenchel und Äpfeln

*

Zuppa Chiara al Pomodoro
Helles Tomatensüppchen mit Basilikumklösschen

*

Lasagne al Forno
Lasagne mit Kalbfleisch und Gemüse im Töpfchen serviert

*

Coda di Rospo in Padella
Gebratener frischer Seeteufel mit Safranrisotto und Barolojus

oder

Involtini di Vitello con Carciofi
Kalbfleischröllchen gefüllt mit Hirse und Schafskäse
auf einer Artischockentapenade

*

Carello dei Formaggi
Käseauswahl vom Wagen abgerundet mit edlen Olivenölen

*

Mille Foglie con Cioccolata
Schokoladen Mille Feuille mit Balsamicoerdbeeren und Vanilleschaum

Venezia, courtesy Hapag-Lloyd

EUROPA

„SOMMERTAGE VOLLER LEBENSLUST"

Farewell Dinner

Donnerstag, 12. August 2004 · Kopenhagen

Unter Berücksichtigung der Euro-Asiatischen Geschmacksrichtung

Türmchen von zweierlei Kaviar im Wan Tan Blatt,
dazu gebratene Jacobsmuscheln

✹

Thailändischer Rindfleischsalat mit Zitrusfrüchten
und Mirin-Chilimarinade

✹

Kürbis-Galgant-Suppe mit Baumpilzen

✹

Gebratene Garnelen mit
warmem Fenchelsalat und rotem Reis

✹

Tandoori gewürztes Lammkarree mit Knoblauch-Bergpfeffersauce,
dazu gedämpfter Kokosmais und Sojagemüse aus dem Wok

✹

Ingwer Charlotte
mit asiatischen Früchten im Pflaumenweinsirup

Oriental, courtesy Hapag-Lloyd

M/S SEVEN SEAS NAVIGATOR

En Route to Cabo San Lucas, Mexico
Friday, December 22, 2000

Ristorante

Portofino

CHEF'S SPECIAL FRESH FROM THE MARKET

CALAMARI FRITTI SERVITI CON INSALATA VERDE CON ACETO E OLIO DI AMALFI
Deep-fried Squid with Lemon
Served with leaf lettuce tossed in garlic and oil Amalfi vinaigrette

FETTUCCINE AI FUNGHI
Pasta Ribbons in a Creamy Mushroom Sauce

ASTICE E VERDURE NOVELLE ALLA GRIGLIA
Grilled Lobster and Seasonal Vegetables
Served with carrots, broccoli and zucchini

DOLCI E FORMAGGI AL CARRELLO
Assortment of Italian Desserts and Cheeses
From the trolley

SELECTED FROM THE SEVEN SEAS WINE CELLAR

White Wine: Pinot Grigio, D.O.C., Santa Margherita, Valdadige, Italy, 1999
With its delicately fruity bouquet and lightly refreshing acidity it is little wonder that Pinot Grigio has always been one
of Italy's most favored wine exports. A traditional favorite in Italian restaurants throughout the United States.

Red Wine: Barbera d'Asti, Michele Chiarlo, Piemonte, 1998
The Barbera grape is native to Piedmont, and Barbera from Asti is generally considered to be Italy's finest, yielding wines of
superior fruit intensity and fragrance. Michele Chiarlo Barbera d'Asti is a supple, medium-bodied wine of velvety texture
and depth.

*For those with a taste for rare vintages, our experienced, professional Head Sommelier is available at any time,
should you wish to purchase premium wines from our cellar.*

Mike Römhild
PORTOFINO CHEF

Beppe Castino
PORTOFINO HOST

Antipasto al Carrello
Affettato Misto - Mozzarella alla Caprese
Selected Italian Cold Cuts - Buffalo Mozzarella & Sliced Tomato

Vitello Tonnato
Thinly Sliced Veal Served with Tuna in a Caper Sauce

Zuppa
Zuppa di Fagioli alla Toscana
Tuscany Bean Soup

Stracciatella alla Romana
Chicken Broth with Egg, Grated Parmesan and Nutmeg

Pasta
Spaghetti al Pomodoro, Bolognese e Pesto
Select one of the following sauces for your Spaghetti
Beef bolognese - pesto - tomato sauce

Insalata
Insalata Fiorentina
Baby Spinach with Mushrooms and Cherry Tomatoes
Aged balsamic vinegar and extra virgin olive oil

Secondi
Trancio di Pesce Spada Fresco ai Ferri alla Palermitana
Sicilian Grilled Swordfish Steak
Accompanied by roast potatoes with fresh herbs

Pollo al Limone
Broiled Marinated Breast of Chicken with Lemon Sauce
Served with vegetable couscous

Scaloppine di Vitello con Mozzarella e Tartufo Nero
Veal Scaloppini with Mozzarella Cheese and Sliced Black Truffle

Melanzane alla Parmigiana
Baked Eggplant with Layers of Mozzarella Cheese
Accompanied by tomato sauce

Dolci
il Tiramisù in terrina
Drenched Lady Fingers Flavored with Espresso and Marsala Wine
Layered with Mascarpone cheese and sprinkled with cocoa powder

Torta di Fragoline
Wild Strawberry Tart

Frutta Fresca - Formaggi Italiani
Fresh Fruit Salad - Selection of Italian Cheeses

Portofino, courtesy Regent Seven Seas Cruises

Welcome to Prego where we offer our Guests an alternative choice of dining. Our Prego chef prepares your Italian meals individually upon request. This "a la minute" style cooking may require a slightly longer preparation, but allow us to provide our Guests with the freshest and finest Italian cuisine.
Buon Appetito!

PIEDMONTE

In this lushly wooded countryside at the foot of the Alps are the great delicacies of the region's cuisine: pheasant and hare, tiny sweet strawberries and delicately flavored snowy white truffles. The result is elegant, flavorful and beautifully presented. The vine-covered hillsides produce robust full-bodied Barolo, gentler Barbaresco, and Barbera.

ANTIPASTI

ANTIPASTO MISTO
Italian Appetizer Plate with Marinated Seafood, Prosciutto Ham, Marinated Vegetables, Mozzarella-Tomato, Olives, Anchovies, and Grilled Scampi

CARPACCIO DI MANZO
Thinly Sliced Raw Beef Tenderloin with Mustard Sauce and Capers
FROM PIEMONTE

PROSCIUTTO E MELONE
Sweet Melon Slices with Italian Prosciutto
FROM PERUGIA

TORRE DI VEGETALI ALLA GRIGLIA CON FETTE DI ARAGOSTA, GAMBERONI E CAPOSANTE SALTATI
Tower of Grilled, Marinated Vegetables with Slices of Lobster, Sautéed Prawns and Scallops in Truffle Vinaigrette
FROM SICILY

ASSAGGI DI PASTA A VOSTRA SCELTA
All Pasta Dishes are Available as Appetizers

TRE VENEZIE

Risotto, hearty soups and cool seafood salads accented by fresh lemon may be found on tables in this fertile region crisscrossed by rivers. Wine glasses hold pale white wines with overtones of ripe pear. The region also cultivates red wines of French transplants such as rich Cabernet, velvety Merlot and the lighter Malbec.

INSALATA

INSALATA MISTA
Chopped Seasonal Salad with Olive Oil and Balsamic Vinaigrette

INSALATA "CESARE"
Caesar Salad Prepared by Your Head Waiter

INSALATA CAPRESE
Sliced Roma Tomatoes and Mozzarella Cheese, Topped with Mesclun of Greens, Tossed in Basil Vinaigrette

ZUPPE

CREMA DI FUNGHI SERVITA NEL PANE ALL'ORIGANO
Cream of Selected Italian Mushrooms: Porcini, Morel, and Champignons, Served in an Oregano Bread Cup
FROM CALABRIA

ZUPPA DI LENTICCHIE CON PETTO D'ANATRA
Country Style Lentil Soup with Duck
FROM VENETO

ZUPPA DI POMODORO CON TORTELLINI RIPIENI DI PATATE
Light Cream of Tomato, Served with Potato Tortellini
FROM LIGURIA AND LOMBARDIA

EMILIA-ROMAGNA

Parma. Simply uttering the name of the culinary capital of this region brings to mind the region's nickname, la grassa—the "fat one". Highlights of the sumptuous cuisine feature tangy Parmesan cheese, creamy fresh mozzarella, fragrant basalmic vinegar and prosciutto di Parma, the satiny, rose-pink ham celebrated worldwide.

PIATTO VEGETARIANO

RISOTTO PRIMAVERA
Traditional Italian Vegetable Risotto

PIATTI PRINCIPALE

LASAGNE ALLA CASALINGA
*Layers of Pasta with Ground Beef, Porcini Mushrooms, Tomato,
Béchamel, and Mozzarella Cheese*
FROM EMILIA ROMAGNA

RAVIOLI AL CARCIOFI' FATTI IN CASA CON BURRO ALLE
ERBE E PESTO DI RUCOLA
*Homemade Artichoke Ravioli, Tossed in a Light Herb Butter Sauce,
Sprinkled with Arrugula Pesto*
FROM LAZIO

SPAGHETTINI AI FRUTTI DI MARE
AL VERDE DI PREZZEMOLO
*Freshly Cooked Spaghetti with Assorted Seafood,
Garlic, Red Chili, Parsley, and White Wine*
FROM PUGLIA

PASTA INTEGRALE CON VERDURA E ERBE ALL' OLIO D'OLIVA
*Whole Wheat Linguine with Seasonal Vegetables,
Extra Virgin Olive Oil, and Herbs*
FROM LAZIO-TOSCANA

SPAGHETTI O PENNE RIGATE A PIACERE
*Spaghetti or Penne Rigate with Your choice of Bolognese, Puttanesca,
Arrabiata, or Tomato-Basil Sauce*

GAMBERONI MARINATI ALLA GRIGLIA CON
CAPPELLINI SALTATI CON VERDURA MISTA
E SALSA AL POMODORO E LIMONE
*Grilled Marinated Tiger Prawns, Served on Capellini, Tossed in
Eggplant, Zucchini, Artichoke, and Lemon Flavored Tomato Sauce*
FROM CAMPAGNA

SALMONE "DOLCE E FORTE"
*Broiled Fresh Salmon Fillet on a Carmalized Green Peppercorn Sauce,
Served with New Potatoes and Grilled Vegetables*
FROM PUGLIA

SCALOPPINE DI VITELLO CON CAPELLI D'ANGELO
*Sautéed Veal Scaloppine with a Light Lemon Sauce, or Mushroom
Sauce, Served with Angel Hair Pasta and Summer Vegetables*
FROM LOMBARDIA

FILETTO DI MANZO AL "BAROLO"
*Grilled Filet Mignon of Black Angus Beef, Served with
Barolo Red Wine Sauce, Grilled Polenta, and Seasonal Vegetables*
FROM TOSCANA

COTOLETTE D'AGNELLO ARROSTO ALL'AGLIO E ERBE,
SERVITE CON PURE DI PATATE ALL'AGLIO
E ZUCCHINE ALLA GRIGLIA
*Roasted Rack of Baby Lamb with a Herb Crust,
Served with Garlic Mashed Potatoes and Grilled Zucchini*
FROM MOLISE-MARCHE-ABRUZZO

TOSCANA

*Raise a glass of Chianti to this
home of Italy's world-renowned
wine. Its blend of four grapes
from vineyards rolling over the
hills from Florence to Siena dates
back to the nineteenth century.
Enjoy it with food that is rusti-
cally simple and full of flavor:
veal and pasta accented by silky
Tuscan olive oil and herbs, fresh
vegetables and golden-crusted
breads.*

UMBRIA

*The treasure of Umbria's moun-
tain villages is the black truffle.
Its big, dense flavor make it a
luxurious addition to simply
roasted meats and fish, or as the
jewel crowning a dish of buttery
fettucine. The perfect accompaniments to Umbria's hearty fare
are the bold reds and dry whites.*

SICILIA

*Ripe, red Sicilian tomatoes are
enjoyed year round, either fresh
and plump or dried in the bright
sun that warms the island. This
is Italy's produce basket—mellow
artichokes, crisp endive, fragrant
fennel, olives and figs are planti-
ful. The region is famous for
intense white wines and especially
for its dessert wines, Moscato and
the famous Marsala.*

WINE SUGGESTIONS

VINO BIANCO

Pinot Grigio, Santa Margherita 1997	$7.00 *per glass*
Orvieto Classico, Villa Antinori, Umbria 1996	$5.00 *per glass*

VINO ROSSO

Centine, Rosso di Montalcino, Castello Banfi,	
Toscano 1996	$5.50 *per glass*
Chianti Classico Riserva, Villa Antinori, Toscano 1994	$6.50 *per glass*
Brunello di Montalcino, Villa Banfi, Toscano 1992	$11.50 *per glass*

Prego, courtesy Crystal Cruises

CRYSTAL SERENITY

Silk Road Restaurant (Nobu) Menu

Appetizers

Nobu Style Miso Chips
Scallop and Tuna Marinated with Two Different Miso Served on Crisp Potato Chips

Matsuhisa Shrimp
Broiled Butterfly Shrimp with Osetra Caviar, Shiitake Mushroom and Yuzu Juice

Pan-Seared Diver Scallops
On Stir Fried Brussels Sprouts Leafs, Topped with Jalapeno Relish

Broiled Eggplant
Topped with Nobu-style Saikyo Miso Sauce

Grilled Marinated Squid
On Seasonal Vegetable Salad with Jalapeno Dressing

Lobster Spring Roll with Caviar
Filled with Lobster Meat, Shiitake Mushrooms and Shiso Leafs
Served with Maui Onion Salsa

Tempura
Rock Shrimp or King Crab Claw or Vegetable Tempura
Served on Tossed Lettuce with Spicy Creamy Sauce and Traditional Tipping Sauce

Assortment of Nobu Style Sushi and Sashimi from our Sushi Bar

Soups

Mushroom Soup
Assorted Seasonal Mushrooms Cooked in its Own Broth
Served in a Japanese Tea Kettle

Miso Soup
Traditional Japanese Miso Soup with Tofu and Scallions

Spicy Seafood Soup
Assorted Seafood Simmered in a Light Spicy Clear Broth

Salads

Tomato Ceviche, Nobu Style
Sun Ripened Tomatoes, Tossed with Nobu Ceviche Dressing, Cilantro and Red Onions

Nobu Style Sashimi Salad
Seared Ahi Tuna, Field Greens Tossed with Matsuhisa Dressing

Mushroom Salad
a Variety of Seasonal Mushrooms Sautéed with Yuzu Dressing, Served over Mesclum Lettuce, Garnished with Chives and Lime

Entrees

Cold Soba Noodles
Served with delicious Soup and your choice of Tempura

Hot Soba Noodles
Served with Stir Fried Vegetables or delicious Soup and your choice of Tempura

Nobu Style Lobster with Truffle-Yuzu Sauce
Stir Fried Lobster with Garlic, Asparagus, Shiitake, Snap Peas Finished with Nobu Style Truffle-Yuzu Sauce

Spicy Sour Shrimp
Pan Sautéed Shrimps with Broccoli Florets and Young Onions in a Light Spicy Sour Sauce

Nobu Style Black Cod with Miso
Nobu-Style Saikyo Miso Marinated and Broiled Black Cod Lemon and Hajikami

Nobu Style Sea Bass with Black Bean Sauce
Steamed Sole Fillet Topped with Chinese Bean Sauce Garnished with Hamabofu Leaves

Chicken with Teriyaki Balsamic
Grilled Chicken Breast with Teriyaki Balsamic Sauce and Sautéed Assorted Vegetables

Grilled Beef Tenderloin Filet Steak
With Your Choice of Anticuccho or Nobu Style Wasabi Pepper Sauce

*Steamed Japanese Rice * Vegetable Fried Rice * Brown Rice
Stir Fried Seasonal Vegetables * Steamed Vegetables*

Desserts

Trio of Crème Brulées
Ginger and Truffle and Green Tea and Crème Brulée

Bento Box
Chocolate Soufflé Cake with Shiso Syrup and Sesame Ice Cream

Silk Road, courtesy Crystal Cruises

T R A T T O R I A.

ANTIPASTI

PROSCIUTTO E MELONE
*Imported from Italy with
Sweet Melon*

PERLE DEL MAR CASPIO
*Sevruga Caviar on
Potato Latkes and Chive Cream*

INSALATA DI GAMBERI E CARCIOFI
*Tender Shrimp and Marinated Artichoke
with White Truffle Oil*

POLPETTINE AL GRANCHIO
*Deviled Crab Cakes
with a Salmon Roe Rouille*

PORCINI ALL'OLIO VERGINE
*Porcini Mushroom in Extra Virgin
Olive Oil and Fresh Tarragon*

BRESAOLA DELLA VALTELLINA
*Air Cured Beef Fillet,
Grilled Vegetables and Sun Dried Tomatoes*

COZZE ALLO ZAFFERANO
*Steamed Black Mussels
with Garlic, Fennel and Saffron*

OSTRICHE IMPANATE E FRITTE
*Batter Fried Oysters
on a Mediterranean Tapenade*

❦

PIZZA

NORDICA
*Topped with Wild Smoked Salmon, Fresh Tomato,
Garlic, and Sprinkled with Capers and Dill*

TROPICALE
*With a Tropical Touch of Hawaiian Pineapple, Baked Prosciutto Cotto and
Marinated Goats Cheese*

SABATINI
*Topped with Cured Parma Ham, Buffalo Mozzarella,
Fresh Tomato Sauce and Sweet Basil*

CAMPAGNOLA
*A Combination of Mozzarella and Cheddar Cheese with Tomato Sauce,
Red and Yellow Bell Pepper, Avocado, Zucchini and Fresh Mushrooms*

S A B A T I N I

ZUPPE E INSALATA

HEARTY MINESTRONE ALLA MILANESE
Served with Garlic Bread Bruschetta

SEAFOOD CIOPPINO
Shellfish, Tomato, Garlic and Chickpeas

FRESH MESCLUN GREENS
Tossed Tableside with Homemade Balsamic Dressing

❧

PASTA

SPAGHETTI ALLO SCOGLIO
*Pasta Noodles Tossed in a Fresh Tomato Sauce,
Accompanied with Mussels and Clams*

GNOCCHI AL FORMAGGIO
Asiago Stuffed Gnocchi in a Smoked Fontina Cheese Fondue

CANNELLONI ALLA NIZZARDA
*Baked Fresh Homemade Pasta,
Filled with Ground Sirloin, Eggplant and Ricotta Cheese*

❧

SECONDI PIATTI

BRANZINO CILENO
*Grilled Chilean Sea Bass with a Lemon and Pinot Grigio Sauce
Served with Risotto al Nero di Seppia*

GRIGLIATA DI SCAMPI
*Langoustines with Fresh Squeezed
Lime and Cilantro*

CAPESANTE AL PEPE
*Jumbo Sea Scallops
Seasoned with Pepper and Galliano*

ARAGOSTE ALLO CHAMPAGNE
*Cold Water Lobster Tail
Brushed with Champagne Butter*

GAMBERONI ALL' AGLIO
*Tiger Prawns
Glazed with a Garlic Peri-Peri*

GALLINELLE AL ROSMARINO
*Rosemary Spring Chicken
with a Truffle Demi Glace*

VITELLO ALLO SCALOGNO
Shallot Crusted Veal Chop

Sabatini, courtesy Princess Cruises

S T A R T E R S

FRAGRANT CHICKEN THAI SOUP
Coconut Milk & Lemon Grass

ULTIMATE NORTHWEST CLAM CHOWDER
Double Smoked Bacon, Clams, Tender Red Potatoes

VINE RIPE BEEFSTEAK TOMATO SALAD
Balsamic Vinaigrette, Extra Virgin Herb Oil

SEASONAL GREENS
*Fresh Northwest Pear, Warm Pecan Crusted Oregon Blue Cheese
Dried Cherries & Cider Pear Vinaigrette*

DUNGENESS CRAB CAKES
Spiral Shaved Cucumbers & Sweet Chili Sauce

SEARED DUCK BREAST
Pickled Walla Walla Onions, Blackberry Relish

GERARD & DOMINIQUE'S SMOKED PLEASURES
*Black Cod, Salmon, Scallops
Wasabi Cream*

ENTREES

FROM THE GRILL

The Odyssey Restaurant features hand selected Sterling Silver Beef, unsurpassed in tenderness and taste, its flavor is enhanced by our own special seasoned rubs and the juices are sealed in by our 1600 degree grill.

FILET MIGNON
Petite Cut or Odyssey Cut

BONE-IN RIB EYE STEAK ~ PORTERHOUSE
Served with our selection of our hand crafted sauces:
Sun Dried Tomato Steak Sauce ~ Classic Béarnaise ~ Horseradish Mustard Sauce

HALIBUT ~ KING SALMON
Our fish selection is troll caught in Alaskan waters, quick seared on our grill served with your choice of Lemon Garlic Herb Splash or Sesame Soy Kalbi

SIGNATURES

PAN SEARED ROSEMARY CHICKEN
Cranberry Chutney

LAMB RACK CHOPS
Apple Spice Chutney, Drizzled Mint Sauce

SEAFOOD CIOPPINO
Mussels, Clams, King Crab, Halibut

GRANDE WILD MUSHROOM RAVIOLI
Pesto Cream Sauce

SIDE DISHES

SCALLOPED POTATOES

OVERSIZED BAKED WASHINGTON POTATO

GRILLED ASPARAGUS WITH BÉARNAISE SAUCE

SAUTÉED BUTTON MUSHROOMS

CREAMED SPINACH

HONEY MAPLE THREE BEAN RAGOUT

LEMON-WHEAT BERRY BASMATI RICE

SWEET ENDINGS

NOT SO CLASSIC BAKED ALASKA

WARM GRAND MARNIER CHOCOLATE VOLCANO CAKE

LEMON BERRY ANGEL SHORTCAKE

ASSORTMENT OF CHEESES

Pinnacle Grill, courtesy Holland America Line

MILLENNIUM

SOUPS, SALADS AND APPETIZERS

Iced Tropical Paradise
Chilled Exotic Fruit Soup garnished with Kiwi
Sauvignon Blanc, Pouilly Fumé "Baron de L" 1996 - Domaine de Ladoucette   Bottle $96   Glass $24

Lobster Velouté
A creamy lobster broth
Chardonnay, Meursault "Les Narvaux" 1998 - Olivier Leflaive   Bottle $112   Glass $28

Caesar Salad
A classic; tossed and served at your table
Pinot Gris, Collio Pinot Grigio 1997 - Marco Felluga   Bottle $41   Glass $11

Russian Salad
A salad of diced vegetables, ham, tongue, a creamy mayonnaise, lobster and truffle
Chardonnay, Cervaro Castello Della Sala 1999 - Marchesi Antinori   Bottle $81   Glass $21

Chilled Asparagus, Sauce Gribiche
Asparagus spears with a sauce of finely chopped capers, eggs, gherkins and parsley
Sauvignon Blanc, Poggio alle Gazze 1999 - Tenuta dell Ornellaia   Bottle $43   Glass $11

Tartare of Salmon Garnished with Quail Eggs
Potted fresh and smoked salmon seasoned with herbs, lemon and fromage blanc
Chardonnay, Hess Collection 1998   Bottle $53   Glass $13.50

Shredded Smoked Chicken with Oriental Salad
Sliced smoked breast of chicken served on ribbons of Chinese cabbage,
toasted almonds and crispy rice noodles
Arneis, Roero Arneis Neive 1998 - Bruno Giacosa   Bottle $43   Glass $11

Stuffed Quail Glazed with Port Jelly
Boned quail with a forcemeat of veal, chicken and pork flavored with green peppercorns
Pinot Noir, Savigny-Lès-Beaune 1er Cru Les Bourgeots 1997 - Domaine Simon Bize   Bottle $67   Glass $17

Goat Cheese Soufflé with Tomato Coulis
Delicate warm goat cheese soufflé served with a creamy sauce and tomato coulis
Sauvignon Blanc, Delatite Mansfield 1998   Bottle $29   Glass $7.50

ENTREES

Risotto Primavera
Risotto of baby spring vegetables
Chardonnay, Rossj BASS Langhe D.O.C. 1998 - Angelo Gaja   Bottle $67   Glass $17

Grilled Fillet of Sea Bass
Fillet of Sea Bass, brushed with tapenade and served with grilled vegetables
Chardonnay, Savigny-Lès-Beaune Blanc 1997 - Simon Bize   Bottle $68   Glass $17

Boston Scrod with Sauce Nantua
Medallions of young cod with a rich shellfish sauce
Chardonnay, Puligny Montrachet 1997 - Louis Jadot   Bottle $90   Glass $23

Flambéed Scampi
Prawns, wrapped in pancetta, flamed in Armagnac and served on a bed of rocket leaves
Chardonnay, Chassagne Montrachet 1996 - Colin Deléger   Bottle $110   Glass $28

Farm Raised Spring Chicken a L'Etouffée
Farm chicken, cooked "en cocotte" with vegetables and the cooking juices
finished with a thyme and tarragon butter
Pinot Noir, "Cuvée Laurenne" 1997 - Domaine Drouhin   Bottle $85   Glass $21

Saltimbocca alla Romana
Escalopines of veal with prosciutto, pan fried
and served with a Marsala Sauce
Barbera, Sitorey Barbera "D.O.C." 1996 - Angelo Gaja   Bottle $98   Glass $25

Rack of Lamb en Croûte
Rack of lamb coated with a mushroom duxelle,
wrapped in puff pastry and baked until golden
Cabernet Sauvignon, Château Lynch Bages 1990   Bottle $365   Glass $91

Steak Diane
New York steak cooked to your liking and served with garlic,
parsley, Cognac and Worcestershire sauce
Zinfandel, Ravenswood Sonoma 1998   Bottle $48   Glass $12.50

CHEESE

A Selection of Cheeses served with Grapes and Apples
Graham's Malvedos 1987   Bottle $98   Glass $14

DESSERTS

Crêpes Suzette
A classic dessert of fine crepes flavored with orange and Grand Marnier
Muscat, Vin de Glacière 1999 - Bonny Doon   ½ Bottle $30   Glass $9

Zabaglione flavored with Marsala
A fluffy delicate Marsala flavored sabayon
Tawny Port, Taylors 10 years old   Bottle $77   Glass $11

Waldorf Pudding served on the R.M.S. Olympic in 1914
A creamy vanilla pudding flavored with a hint of nutmeg, diced apples and sultana grapes
Vin de Constance 1996 - Klein Constantia   Bottle $75   Glass $18

Chocolate Soufflé
The most classic and well-known light souffle
Château Coutet 1986 - Barsac   Bottle $98   Glass $19

Michel Roux's Favorite Bite Size Surprise Desserts
Recioto della Valpolicella 1994 - Romano Dal Forno   ½ Bottle $127

Selection of Ice Creams and Sorbets
Freshly churned ice creams and sorbets

Antipasti dello Chef
APPETIZERS

ANTIPASTI ASSORTITI
A flavorful selection of traditional Italian appetizers, all on one plate

RISOTTO AL GAMBERETTI
Sauteed prawns in creamy Arborio rice, scented with safron and garnished with fresh rosemary

INSALATA DEL 'ORTO
Seared sea scallops served on a bed of grilled vegetables, mixed baby greens and sun dried tomatoes drizzled with citrus vinaigrette

CARPACCIO CON SCAGLIE DI PARMIGIANO
Tenderloin of beef thinly sliced, served with shaved Parmesan, capers and arugola lightly drizzled with your choice of homemade pesto or traditional lemon vinaigrette

MOZZARELLA DI BUFALA POMODORA E BASILICO
Buffalo mozzarella and wine-ripened tomatoes garnished with fresh basil

Zuppe
SOUPS

CACCIUCCO ALLA LIVORNESE
Seafood and vegetables simmered in a flavorful tomato garlic broth

Zuppa del Giorno
Soup of the Day

Inasalate
SALADS

Mista
Butter lettuce, cherry tomatoes, sweet onion rings and roasted peppers, served with balsamic vinaigrette or fat free Italian dressing

Cesare
Crisp romaine lettuce with shaved Parmesan cheese and herb croutons, tossed with Caesar dressing prepared table side

Paste
PASTA

RAVIOLI BICOLORI DI ASTICE
Lobster and asparagus stuffed pasta in a delicate tarragon-cream sauce sprinkled with fresh herbs

PENNE CON SALSA DI POMODORO
Penne in sun-dried tomato and basil sauce finished with shaved Pecorino Romano

SPAGHETTI ALLE VONGOLE
Baby clams and spaghetti in a fresh del tomato and red pepper sauce

FETTUCCINE AI FUNGHI
Fettuccine with porcini and portobello mushrooms tossed in a white wine cream sauce

Piatti principali
MAIN COURSES

Served with mixed seasonal Italian vegetables, Gnocchi Romaine and truffle oil scented mashed potatoes and Chef's daily starch

GAMBERONI FRITTI AL PROFURMO DI MARE
Sauteed tiger shrimp enhanced with roasted garlic and fresh herbs

ARAGOSTA AL FORNO IN SALSA DI ERBE AROMATICHE
Succulent baked lobster tail served with savory garden herb emulsion

SOGLIOLA
Pan-seared sole paired with a tomato, lemon and caper salsa

POLLO ALLA PARMIGIANA
Tender breaded chichen breast sauteed and finished with rich tomato sauce and fresh mozzarella

SALTIMBOCCA ALLA ROMANA
A Roman classic-tender veal medallion topped with thinly sliced prosciutto and fresh sage, served with natural jus

FILLETO DI MANZO AL FERRI
Grilled filet mignon drizzled with smokey pepper coullis

Dolci
DESSERTS

TIRAMISU
Espresso and Kahlua cake filled with light mascaporne cream and dusted with cocoa powder

TORTA DI ZABAGLIONE AL CIOCCOLATO
A two layer cake white wine chocolate mousse cake

FRUTTI DI BOSCO
Marinated berries with Marsala zabaliogne

FANTASIA DI GELATI E SORBETTI
Ask your waiter about today's selection of Italian ice cream and sorbets

Formaggi
CHEESES

Scelta Di Formaggi Assortiti
A sampling of Italian cheeses

Portofino, courtesy Royal Caribbean International

Le Cordon Bleu Restaurant

FEATURED FROM THE SEVEN SEAS WINE CELLAR

CHABLIS PREMIER CRÛ, DOMAINE LAROCHE, BURGUNDY, FRANCE

As with all classic white Burgundies, the wine is made from 100% Chardonnay grapes. This strikingly beautiful wine combines crispy acidity, along with steely minerality and smoky aromas, coming from the unique soil of the region. The color is pale straw with green tinges; flavors of pears, green apples and white peaches delight the nose.

CHÂTEAUNEUF-DU-PAPE "LES CLOSIERS", OGIER CAVES DES PAPES, RHONE VALLEY, FRANCE

The regions most famous red wine from the southern Rhone Valley is Châteauneuf-du-Pape, which is considered to be among the world's finest wines. A big wine, composed of grenache, syrah, mouverde and cinsault with generous aromas of black berries, mint, licorice, sweet tobacco.

For those with a taste for rare vintages, our experienced, professional Head Sommelier is available at any time, should you wish to purchase premium wine from our cellar.

STEPHANE MOENCH	VERONIQUE RADOS
SIGNATURES CHEF	**MAITRE D' HÔTEL**

La Carte

Le Cordon Bleu Académie D'Art Culinaire

Entrées

MARINADE DE NOIX DE PÉTONCLES À L'HUILE D'HERBES, POMMES DE TERRE DE DEUX FAÇONS
Scallops marinated in herb oil, spring onions and mashed potato

SALADE DE HOMARD AUX EPICES ET SA CRÈME DE YAOURT À LA MANGUE,
PLACE DE LA BASTILLE
Salad of Lobster with Spice and Mango Fondue

CASSOULET D'ESCARGOTS SIGNATURES
Cassoulet of snails Signatures Dish

CHARLOTTE DE CRABE ET D'ASPERGES VINAIGRETTE AUX HERBES
Crabmeat and asparagus with fresh herb vinaigrette

CAVIAR SEVRUGA SUR RÉMOULADE DE CÉLERI AU FOIE GRAS, SAUCE CITRONNÉE
Sevruga caviar on celeriac and Foie Gras remoulade finished in lemon sauce

NOIX DE FOIE GRAS RÔTI AUX FIGUES À L'AIGRE DOUCE
Nutmeg Roasted Foie Gras with Sweet and Sour Figs

GATEAU DE LEGUMES SURMONTÉ D'UNE CROUSTILLADE AROMATIQUE (**V**)
Layered Provencal Vegetable Gateau with Toasted Aromatic Crust

Soup

BISQUE DE CRUSTACÉS AVEC GARNITURE D'AVOCAT, MIETTES DE CRABE ET TOMATE FRAÎCHE
Crustacean Bisque with avocado-crabmeat-tomato garnishes

CONSOMMÉ PERIGORD
Beef consommé with truffle and foie gras quenelles

CRÈME DE CHAMPIGNONS À L'AIL CONFIT (**V**)
Creamy mushroom soup with candied garlic

Plats Principaux

ESCALOPE DE SAUMON SAUTÉE ET SA BARIGOULE DE LÉGUMES BRAISÉS, SAUCE BEURRE BLANC
Sautéed salmon fillet with a mixture of vegetables Barigoule Style and butter sauce

FLÉTAN BRAISÉ À LA BETTERAVE ET AU RAIFORT
Braised Halibut Fillet with Beetroot and Horseradish

SAUTÉ DE GAMBAS ÉPICÉS AUX ASPERGES VERTES, Á LA CRÈME DE CHAMPIGNONS
Sautéed prawns with curry and green asparagus with mushroom cream

FILET DE VEAU, TOMATES FARCIES AU CAVIAR D'AUBERGINE
ÉCHALOTES BRAISÉES AU VIN ROUGE
Tenderloin of veal, tomatoes stuffed with eggplant caviar
and shallots braised in red wine

TOURNEDOS ROSSINI, BOUQUETIÈRE DE LÉGUMES GLACÉS, SAUCE PERIGUEUX
Beef tournedos Rossini with glazed vegetable Bouquetiere, Sauce Perigueux Style

POITRINE DE CANARD SAUTÉE CÔTE BASQUE, CAROTTES AU CUMIN,
NAVETS LONGS FARCIS AU BEURRE D'HERBES
Côte Basque sautéed duck breast, carrots with cumin,
daikon radish stuffed with herb butter

CARRÉ D'AGNEAU ROTI, CHAMPIGNONS SAUTÉS ET POMME FONDANTE, JUS DE CUISSON
Rack of lamb with mushrooms and melted potato garnishes, and lamb juice

PITHIVIERS DE POMMES DE TERRE, SALADE DE POUSSES D'ÉPINARDS (**V**)
Potato Pithiviers, spinach leaf salad

Desserts

CRÈME BRÛLÉE À LA VANILLE DE TAHITI, AUX FRAISES MARINÉES ET SON COULIS
Tahitian Vanilla Crème Brûlée with Strawberries
coated with strawberry coullis

TIRAMISU EN PANIER ACCOMPAGNÉ DE BANANE CARAMALISÉE
Harlequin Basket of Tiramisu and Caramelised Bananas

BABA AU VIEUX RHUM, CRÈME PISTACHE ET FRUITS ROUGES
Baba with aged rum, pistachio cream and red berries

TARTE TIÈDE AU CHOCOLAT ET AUX FRAMBOISES
Warmed chocolate tart with raspberries

NOTRE CHARIOT DE FROMAGE FRANCAIS AFFINÉS
Our Selection of Fine French Cheeses from the Trolley

(V) Vegetarian Dishes

Signatures, courtesy Regent Seven Seas Cruises

M/V SEVEN SEAS MARINER

Docked in Hamilton, Bermuda
Thursday, April 12, 2001

Mediterranean Bistro

Classic Alternatives

Chicken Paillard with Basil Pistou

Thinly pounded chicken breast garnished with a pesto-style sauce
of basil, garlic, olive oil and Parmesan cheese

Baked Vegetable Lasagne

Baked bell peppers, aubergine, zucchini and pasta sheets
layered together and served with a rich tomato sauce

Pan-fried Chilean Halibut Fillet

Served with lemon and extra virgin olive oil

Beef Medallions with Balsamic Reduction

Cooked to your preference and served with crisp Arugula and Parmesan cheese

Selected from the Seven Seas Wine Cellar

White Wine: Pinot Grigio, D.O.C., Santa Margherita, Valdadige, Italy, 1999
With its delicately fruity bouquet and lightly refreshing acidity it is little wonder that Pinot Grigio has
always been one of Italy's most favoured wine exports. A traditional favourite in Italian restaurants
throughout the United States.

Red Wine: Chianti Classico, D.O.C.G., Fattoria Ormanni, Tuscany, Italy, 1998
The tradition of winemaking in the Chianti region dates back centuries but Chianti in its modern form
was essentially 'invented' by Baron Ricasoli in 1872 who laid down the formula, which synthesised
generations of tradition. Winemaker, Giulio Gambelli, has fashioned a superb wine from the 1997
vintage relying on the traditional Chianti blend of Sangiovese and Canailo to produce a medium-bodied
wine with a deliciously, lingering finish.

For those with a taste for rare vintages, our experienced, professional Head Sommelier is
available at any time, should you wish to purchase premium wines from our cellar.

Evan Cavanagh
LA VERANDA CHEF

Paolo Vercelli
MÂITRE D'HÔTEL

Tapas - Mezze - Antipasti
Kindly take your selection from the buffet table
Tablouleh Salad
Eggplant Rolls
Marinated Artichokes
Tomato Mozzarella
Tapenade
Cold cuts from Spain, France and Italy
Marinated Olives
Hummus Tahini
Baba Ghannauj

Soup Tureen
Fasoulaatha Mavromatika
Greek Black-Eyed Bean Soup

Salad
Freshly prepared by the Head Waiter
Panzanella Salad
Italian bread salad with cucumber, tomatoes, peppers, capers, basil, olive oil
and balsamic vinegar

Pasta
Cavatappi con Frutti di Mare
Pasta with seafood, fresh herbs and olives

Main Course
Greek Moussaka
Combination of ground lamb, eggplant, potatoes topped with feta cheese

Dessert Trolley
Tiramisu
Sponge Lady Fingers moistened with espresso and Amaretto liqueur
Finished with whipped Mascarpone cheese and heavy cream, vanilla and cocoa powder

Cannoli alla Palermitana
Sweet Palermo rolls filled with Mascarpone cream and candied fruit

Assortment of Mediterranean Cheeses

Fruit Salad

Sliced Fruits in Season

Mediterranean Bistro, courtesy Regent Seven Seas Cruises

LE BISTRO

APPETIZERS

Norwegian Seafood Timbale
Smoked Salmon with Avocado, Shrimp and Scallops Filling on Dill and Chervil Cream Sauce

Warm, Green Asparagus
with Hollandaise Sauce

French Escargots in Garlic Butter
Braised in Fresh Herbs and Vegetables Brunoise, Oven-Baked with Le Bistro Garlic Butter

SOUPS

Traditional French Onion Soup
Baked with a Gruyère-Parmesan Cheese Croûton

Cream of Forest Mushroom
Served in a Crusty Sour Dough Loaf

Beef Consommé with Julienne of Vegetables en Croûte
Sealed with a Golden Pastry Dome

SALADS

"Niçoise Style" Seared Yellow-Fin Tuna
with Green Beans, Red Bliss Potatoes, Boiled Eggs and Roma Tomatoes

Spinach Salad with Warm Goats Cheese Crouton
Crispy Onion Rings and Pine Nuts, Sun-Dried Tomato Vinaigrette

Caesar Salad
Romaine Lettuce and all the Classical Ingredients Tossed Tableside

ENTRÉES

Filet Mignon
Rossini Style with Foie Gras and Truffled Veal Jus
Merlot, Meridian, Paso Robles, California, USA   Glass: $6.25 Bottle: $25.00
or
Bèarnaise Barigold on a Red Wine Jus
Château Le Bourdieu, Medoc, Bordeaux, France   Glass: $6.25 Bottle: $25.00

Salmon à L' Oseille
Salmon Fillet in Sorrel Cream Sauce
Sauvignon Blanc, Concannon, San Francisco Bay, California, USA   Glass: $6.00 Bottle: $24.00

Steamed Chicken Breast filled with a Tiger Prawn Mousse
on a Bed of Wild Rice, Cognac-Thyme Beurre Blanc
Mâcon-Villages, Georges Duboeuf, Burgundy, France   Glass: $ 5.75 Bottle: $23.00

Mille-Feuille of Seabass with Tomato Concassé and Mushroom Duxelles
Oven-Glazed with a Chardonnay Mousseline, Parsley Potatoes
Sancerre, Barton & Guestier, Loire Valley, France   Glass: $7.00 Bottle: $28.00

Vegetarian Four Seasons
Gratin Dauphinoise in Baked Potato, Sautéed Mushrooms in Grilled Tomato,
Creamy Spinach in Roasted Onion and Ratatouille in Courgette
Gewürztraminer, Navarro, California, USA   Glass: $5.50 Bottle: $22.00

DESSERTS

Trolley du Jour
Our Pastry Chef's Selection of Sweet Delights from the Trolley

Chocolate Fondue
The House Specialty
Muscat "Vin de Glaclère", Bonny Doon, California   Glass: $6.50

Apple Tart Tatin á la mode
Vanilla Ice Cream and a Dollop of Whipping Cream
Harvey's Bristol Cream   Glass: $4.25

Tart au Citron
The Classical French Lemon Tart
Sandemans Founders Reserve Glass: $ 4.25

Cover Charge US $ 10 per Person

Le Bistro, courtesy Norwegian Cruise Line

COSTA MEDITERRANEA

APPETIZERS

Tortino di gamberi con verdure
Shrimp Pie with vegetables

Salmone all'aneto, salsa dolce-forte alle pere
Marinated Fillet of Salmon accompanied with a Sweet Pear sauce

Insalata di capesante allo zenzero e pepe rosa
Scallop Salad with ginger and pink peppercorns

Filetto di vitello, salsa leggera al tonno e maionese
Fillet of Veal, light Tuna Sauce and Mayonnaise

Gazpacho in gelatina con mozzarella
Jellied Gazpacho with Mozzarella cheese

PASTA AND RICE

Cannelloni di Dentice
Cannelloni filled with Snapper

Corzetti al pesto leggero e pinoli
Corzetti Pasta with a light Pesto sauce and pine nuts

Riso zafferano con salamella mantovana saltata
Saffron Rice with Italian salami

Penne, asparagi e polpa di granchio
Pasta enhanced with asparagus and crabmeat

MAIN COURSES

Crespelle di melanzane con fonduta al tartufo nero
Aubergine Crepes with black truffle fondue

Navarin d'agnello con polenta croccante
Lamb with crispy Polenta

Filetto di manzo, spinaci, pinoli e uvetta, salsa al vino rosso
Fillet of beef with spinach, pine nuts, raisins with a red wine sauce

Scaloppe di tonno, fagioli cannellini all'uccelletto
Baked Tuna Steak with stewed cannelloni beans

Filetto di merluzzo, fonduta ai porri, limone candito
Fillet of Cod, Leek Fondue and candied Lemon

DESSERTS

Semifreddo allo zabaione, cioccolato gran cru, salsa al cioccolato
Egg-nog Parfait and Grand Cru Chocolate with Chocolate Sauce

Tortino al Lampone e crema al limone
Raspberry Tartlet and Lemon Cream

Zuccotto fiorentino, salsa all'arancia
Sponge Cake covered Iced Mousse, orange sauce

Pere ai due vini con mousse alla cannella
Pear with two wines served with cinnamon mousse

Club Medusa, courtesy Costa Cruises

TODD ENGLiSH

Dinner

Starters

Lobster and Baby Corn Chowder
with whipped parsnip, black truffle & potato

Oven Fried Asparagus and Morel Tart
with caramelized onions, double smoked bacon & creamy fontina cheese

Fig Rosemary and Prosciutto Flatbread
with sweet and sour fig jam, gorgonzola cheese & prosciutto di parma

Potato and Truffle Loveletters
Madeira jus burofusco shaved truffles

Cucumber Spun Yellow Fin Tuna Tartare
with crispy fried rock shrimp, warm sesame dressing & whitefish caviar

Golden Beet Carpaccio
with warm roquefort drizzle, white balsamic syrup & walnut tuille

Grilled Squid and Octopus
with warm chick pea vinaigrette, roasted tomatoes, toasted garlic & parsley

Tender Lettuce of Boston Bibb and Mache
with shaved white onions, toasted walnut dressing & a 'shower' of
blue cheese

Hand Cut Wide Papardelle Noodles
with shaved asparagus, seared porcini mushrooms & country ham

Entrees

Seared Jumbo Sea Scallops in Crispy Oxtail Glaze
served with silky cauliflower puree, seared chanterelles & frisee salad with
oven dried tomato

Braised Prime Beef Short Rib
En casserole of baby vegetables, whipped potatoes & fresh horseradish
cream

Lemon and Herb Roasted Free Range Chicken
served with roasted garlic jus, country mashed potato & cake haricot vert

Sesame Grilled Atlantic Salmon Steak
served with tomato braised mussels, toasted farro & herb salad

Grilled Sirloin served over Tuscan Bruschetta
with vidalia onion roquefort cream, peas and country ham

Rack of Lamb with Confit of Shanks Crepinette
served with assorted salads of roasted red pepper, chickpea,
cucumber & rouille black olive sauce

Butter Poached Lobster and Crispy Sweetbreads
served with ham hock, risotto & mild yellow curry broth

Crispy Duck with Ginger Scallion Glaze
with sweet and sour cabbage & root vegetable mash

Paella Olivacious an Untraditional-Tradition
Braised lobster, clams, mussels, assorted fish & chicken in a
chorizo broth with saffron short grain rice

Brown Butter Sauté Turbot Filet
served with spinach and fingerling potato salad, garlic shrimp & citrus
vinaigrette

Dessert

Chocolate Fallen Cake
in a sauce of raspberries & vanilla ice cream

Roasted Pineapple Upside-Down Cake
with a macadamia nut crisp, vanilla passion fruit ice cream & coconut cream

Classic Vanilla Soufflé
with creamy vanilla custard & tahitian vanilla ice cream

Thai Iced Coffee Tiramisu
Layers of creamy mascarpone, chocolate & Thai coffee sorbet

Mandarin Orange Crème Brulee
with berry salad & citrus short bread

Warm Chocolate Pudding Cake
Chocolate sorbet, manjari pudding & chocolate sugar wafers

Panache of Seasonal Sorbet
on a minted mango citrus salad

Selection of Ice Creams
milk chocolate, dark chocolate, vanilla, butter pecan
vanilla passion with vanilla shortbread

Warm Cookies and Biscotti

Selection of Cheese

Todd English, courtesy Cunard Cruise Line

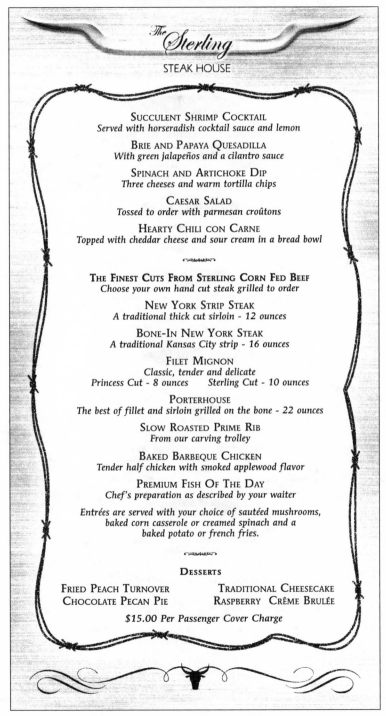

The Sterling STEAK HOUSE

SUCCULENT SHRIMP COCKTAIL
Served with horseradish cocktail sauce and lemon

BRIE AND PAPAYA QUESADILLA
With green jalapeños and a cilantro sauce

SPINACH AND ARTICHOKE DIP
Three cheeses and warm tortilla chips

CAESAR SALAD
Tossed to order with parmesan croûtons

HEARTY CHILI CON CARNE
Topped with cheddar cheese and sour cream in a bread bowl

THE FINEST CUTS FROM STERLING CORN FED BEEF
Choose your own hand cut steak grilled to order

NEW YORK STRIP STEAK
A traditional thick cut sirloin - 12 ounces

BONE-IN NEW YORK STEAK
A traditional Kansas City strip - 16 ounces

FILET MIGNON
Classic, tender and delicate
Princess Cut - 8 ounces   Sterling Cut - 10 ounces

PORTERHOUSE
The best of fillet and sirloin grilled on the bone - 22 ounces

SLOW ROASTED PRIME RIB
From our carving trolley

BAKED BARBEQUE CHICKEN
Tender half chicken with smoked applewood flavor

PREMIUM FISH OF THE DAY
Chef's preparation as described by your waiter

Entrées are served with your choice of sautéed mushrooms,
baked corn casserole or creamed spinach and a
baked potato or french fries.

DESSERTS

FRIED PEACH TURNOVER   TRADITIONAL CHEESECAKE
CHOCOLATE PECAN PIE   RASPBERRY CRÈME BRULÉE

$15.00 Per Passenger Cover Charge

Sterling Steak House, courtesy Princess Cruises

Polo Grill

APPETIZERS

Jumbo Shrimp Cocktail with Spicy Cocktail Sauce
Goat Cheese and Roasted Red Pepper Terrine
Smoked Norwegian Salmon
Potted Smoked Pork with a Sweet Corn Salsa
Skewer of Monkfish and Bresaola Wrapped Sea Scallops
Escargots in Freuillete Crust with Garlic and Brandy Sauce

SOUPS

New England Clam Chowder
French Onion Soup with Gruyere Gratinéted Crouton
Lobster Bisque

SALADS

The "Wedge" with Bleu Cheese and Crumbled Bacon
Tomato and Sweet Onion Salad
Hearts of Palm Salad
Caesar Salad prepared Tableside

MAIN COURSES

All Beef Cuts are Aged Black Angus Beef

Broiled New York Striploin Steak
Grilled Filet Mignon
Porterhouse Steak
Grilled Rack of Lamb
Grilled Veal Chop
Roasted Chicken with Herbs and Olive Oil
Mesquite Grilled Double Cut Pork Chop
The following sauces are always available:
Balsamic Vinegar, Bearnaise, Hollandaise, Creamy Horseradish, and Au Poivre

SEAFOOD

The Polo Surf & Turf - Lobster Tail with Filet Mignon
Grilled Shrimp Scampi over Roasted Tomatoes
Grilled Ahi Tuna Mediterranean
Grilled Mahi Mahi Filet

Please Ask Your Waiter for the Special Fish of the Day

SIDE DISHES

Creamy Garlic Mashed Potatoes
Baked Potato with Trimmings
Fried Ranch Potatoes
Creamed Spinach
Wild Mushrooms Ragout
Seasonal Fresh Vegetables

Polo Grill, courtesy Oceania Cruises

TOSCANA

Antipasti Freddi
Carpaccio di Manzo
Thinly Siced Prime Beef Tenderloin Topped with Arugula, Aged Parmigiano Reggiano Shavings and Drizzled
with Extra Virgin Olive Oil and Lemon Infusion

Mozzarella di Bufala Caprese
Tower of Fresh Bufala Mozzarella and Vine Ripened Tomatoes, Basil and Extra Virgin Olive Oil Emulsion

Fantasia di Vegetali Marinati con le Spezie Fiorentine
Florentine Spiced Marinated Grilled Seasonal Fresh Garden Vegetables

Antipasti Caldi
Involtini di Melanzane alla Ghiotta
Sliced Eggplant Rolled and Sautéed with Roasted Minced Veal Stuffing and Basil, Baked in Fresh Tomato Sauce

Code di Scampi Avvolte nel Prosciutto Crudo di Parma
Sautéed Jumbo Shrimp Tenderly Wrapped in Prosciutto di Parma Ham and Served with Candied Cherry Tomato

Fritto di Calamari con Salse a Scelta
Lightly Breaded Baby Calamari Served with Spicy Marinara or Aioli Sauce

Le Zuppe
Minestrone Alla Genovese
Genovese Northern Italian Vegetable Soup Finished with Fresh Pesto and Chopped Potatoes

Zuppa di Fagioli alla Toscana
Hearty Tuscan Bean Soup with Homemade Quadrucci Pasta

Pasta E Risotti
Gnocchi di Patate al Pesto
Hand Rolled Potato Dumplings in a Creamy Pesto Sauce

Farfalle al Salmone Affumicato e Vodka
Bow Tie Pasta Sautéed with Wild Scottish Smoked Salmon, Flambéed with Grey Goose Vodka
and Folded in a Light Creamy Tomato Sauce

Vulcano di Spaghetti alla Sorrentina
Volcano of Spaghetti with a Herb Infused Fresh Tomato Sauce Topped with Sorrento Bufala Mozzarella

Risotto ai Funghi Porcini
Traditionally Prepared Arborio Italian Rice with Porcini Mushrooms, Caramelized Shallots and Fresh Thyme

Ravioloni di Ricotta e Spinaci al Burro Fuso, Salvia e Cuore di Pomodoro
Giant Handmade Raviolis Stuffed with Ricotta Cheese and Spinach, Tossed with Chopped Roma Tomatoes and Laced in Sage Butter

Trio Toscana
Gnocchi di Patate al Pesto, Fettuccine Fresche alla Carbonara and Risotto ai Funghi Porcini

Rigatoni alla Campagnola
Country Style Rigatoni with Sautéed Neapolitan Sausage, Yellow Bell Peppers, Zucchini and Baby Artichokes,
Tossed in a Light Cherry Tomato and White Wine Sauce and Topped with Crumbled Tuscan Goat Cheese

Risotto ai Gamberoni e Punte di Asparagi
Delicate Arborio Rice Slowly Simmered in White Wine and Saffron Infused Stock with Sautéed Shrimp and Asparagus Tips

Lasagne al Forno alla Toscana
A Hearty Dish of Handmade Fresh Pasta Layered with Minced Beef Tenderloin, Béchamel Sauce and Grated Parmigiano Reggiano

Special Pasta of the Day as described by your waiter

TOSCANA

Le Insalate

Insalata Mista
Farm Fresh Field Greens with Tomatoes, Cucumbers and Aged Modena Balsamic Vinegar Dressing

Insalatine di Campo con Formaggio di Capra, Pomodori e Olive Nere
*Baby Field Greens with Crumbled Goat Cheese, Tomatoes and Kalamata Olives in a Delicate
Lemon Oregano Vinaigrette*

Classic Caesar Salad Prepared Tableside
*Tender Romaine Lettuce Tossed in Homemade Caesar Dressing Served with Anchovies,
Toasted Croutons and Topped with Reggiano Parmesan Shavings*

I Secondi

Filetto di Manzo con Carciofi e Mozzarella Affumicata
Filet Mignon Topped with Sauteed Artichokes and Smoked Mozzarella in a Piedmonte Truffle Sauce

Costata di Vitello alla Griglia con Porcini Trifolati
A Tender Bone In Milk Fed Veal Chop Grilled to Perfection and Topped with Sautéed Piedmonte Wild Porcini Mushrooms

Osso Buco alla Milanese
Tender Veal Shank Slow Oven Braised in a Porcini Enhanced Stock Served with Saffron Infused Risotto

Scaloppine di Vitello alla Parmigiana
Sautéed Breaded Scallops of Veal Tenderloin Gratinated with Bufala Mozzarella and Fresh Tomato Concasse

Costolette d'Agnello con Pomodori Secchi, Olive e Aglio
Braised Double Cut Lamb Chops Served in a Sun-Dried Tomato, Black Olive and Roasted Garlic Sauce

Pollo Arrosto al Rosmarino e Chianti
*Free Range Half Rotisserie Chicken Marinated in Tuscan Herbs, and Brushed with Extra Virgin Rosemary Infused Olive Oil
Served with Truffle Mashed Potatoes and Vintage Chianti Sauce*

Filetto di Branzino Dorato con Limoni di Sorrento E Capperi
*Pan Seared Sea Bass Filet Topped with an Emulsion of Sorrento Lemons, Capers, and Chardonnay Wine Served with Steamed
New Potatoes, Sprinkled with Parsley and Fresh Summer Garlic Infused Extra Virgin Olive Oil, and Grilled Vegetables*

Aragosta Fra Diavolo con Linguine
*Succulent Lobster Tail Sautéed with Fresh Garlic, Spicy Crushed Chili Peppers, Italian Parsley and Vine Ripened
San Marzano Tomatoes, Served Over Linguine Pasta*

Toscana Side Dishes

*All Entrées are served with Rustic Rosemary Roasted Potatoes and Gratinated Vegetable Tower.
In addition, Garlic Mashed Potatoes or Creamy Polenta with Sautéed Italian Sweet Sausage are always available.*

Toscana, courtesy Oceania Cruises

Starters

TRIO OF ESCARGOTS
Baked in Brioche, Wrapped in Rice Paper and
Classic Bourguignonne

BEEF CARPACCIO
Sliced Raw Beef Tenderloin with Shaved Parmesan Cheese
Marinated Mache Lettuce

SUSHI PLATTER
Ahi Tuna, Salmon, Shrimp and Unagi with Pickled Ginger and Wasabi

ICED RUSSIAN CAVIAR
1 oz. of Sevruga Caviar with Traditional Condiments and Buckwheat Blinis
An Extra $29.00 Charge will Apply

SHRIMP COCKTAIL
Colossal Black Tiger Prawns with American Cocktail Sauce

NEW ENGLAND CRAB CAKE
On Roasted Pepper Rémoulade

LOBSTER BISQUE WITH VINTAGE COGNAC
Fleuron and Fresh Cream

BAKED ONION SOUP "LES HALLES"
A Parisian Classic

Salads

CLASSIC CAESAR SALAD
Hearts of Romaine Lettuce, Traditionally Prepared

BABY LEAF SPINACH AND FRESH MUSHROOMS
With Bleu Cheese, Warm Bacon Dressing

TOSSED GARDEN SALAD
Greens, Radicchio, Tomato Wedges, Purple Onion Rings and Watercress
Choice of House, Ranch or Bleu Cheese Dressing

Side Dishes

BAKED POTATO WITH TRIMMINGS
SAUTÉED MEDLEY OF FRESH MUSHROOMS
YUKON GOLD MASH WITH WASABI HORSERADISH
SPAGHETTI WITH FRESH TOMATO SAUCE
GRILLED FRESH VEGETABLES IN SEASON
CREAMED SPINACH WITH GARLIC

Entrées

Our Steaks are Hand-Selected and Aged for 30 Days to Our Specifications.
Carefully Handled and Perfectly Cooked.

BROILED NEW YORK STRIP LOIN STEAK
14 oz. of the Favorite Cut for Steak Connoisseurs

CLASSIC PORTERHOUSE STEAK
Combines the Full Flavor of the Strip Loin with the Tenderness of the Tenderloin
24 oz. of the Best from Both Worlds

BROILED FILET MIGNON
9 oz. for the True Gourmet

SURF & TURF
Seared Lobster Tail over Tomato Confit, Grilled Filet Mignon over
Cardamom Braised Carrots, Pumpkin Ravioli

CHILEAN SEA BASS
Lobster Nage Braised Sea Bass over Young Spinach and Mango Salad

BROILED LOBSTER TAIL
Served with Drawn Butter

BROILED SUPREME OF FREE RANGE CHICKEN
With Blackberry — Port Wine Reduction

GRILLED LAMB CHOPS
Double-Cut Lamb Chops
Served on Five Bean Cassoulet and Rosemary Jus

BROILED PROVIMI VEAL CHOP
Center-Cut from the Highest Grade Milk-Fed Veal

Sauces Available

THREE PEPPERCORN SAUCE

WILD MUSHROOM SAUCE

SAUCE BÉARNAISE

Desserts

CITRUS CHEESECAKE WITH HAZELNUT BISCUIT
Burnt Basmati and Mango Ravioli with Almond and Mascarpone Jam

WASHINGTON APPLE TARTE TARTIN
Served with Chocolate and Lemon Balm Salad

CHOCOLATE TARTE WITH BITTER CHOCOLATE PÀTÉ
Raspberry and Pineapple Croquant, Tiramisu Notre Façon

FRESH FRUITS
*Assembly of Tropical Fruit and Berries in Season,
Served with Homemade Sherbet*

SELECTION OF INTERNATIONAL CHEESES

Beverages

FRESHLY BREWED COFFEE
Regular or Decaffeinated

TEA AND HERBAL TEAS

Dessert Wines

QUADY ELECTRA, *California*
WEISSER RIESLING, *South Africa*

After-Dinner Drinks

GRAHAM'S SIX GRAPE
DOW'S 20 YEAR TAWNY
DE MONTAL ARMAGNAC SPECIAL RESERVE
HARDY, V.S.O.P.
HARDY, X.O.
CLES DES DUCS ARMAGNAC, V.S.O.P.
PINAR DEL RIO, GAUTIER X.O.
HENNESSY, X.O.
MARTELL CORDON BLEU
HENNESSY PARADIS
COURVOISIER, X.O.
REMY MARTIN LOUIS XIII

Scarlett's Supper Club, courtesy Carnival Cruise Line

Chapter Fourteen

Star Awards and Ship Ratings
in Specific Categories

Because the quality of food, service, and entertainment, as well as the general physical condition of ships, is constantly changing, it is risky to attempt to compare or rate cruise ships. Any such attempt must reflect a great deal of personal preference and may be somewhat undependable inasmuch as quality can vary from cruise to cruise on the same ship due to a change in chefs, staff, or company policy. In fact, the quality can even change between the date of this writing and the time you are reading this book.

However, travel agents, potential cruisers, and the cruise industry in general have come to rely upon travel writers' ratings and personal opinions. Having a profound desire to make this guide the most helpful and most valuable cruise guide available, I have succumbed to peer pressure and attempted to rate the ships as definitively as possible.

A system of "Star Awards" (overall ratings) will be found below and after each ship listed previously in chapter 11. In addition, ratings in 11 specific categories will be found for at least one ship from each major cruise line. Again, I must emphasize that these are my personal, subjective opinions, and you may disagree with them after you have cruised on the ships being rated. An intelligent traveler should not take the ratings of any guide as gospel. Obviously, every reviewer has his personal preferences and prejudices that may or may not coincide with your own.

Explanation of Star Awards

Since all ships are not competing for the same potential passengers, it would be unfair to make overall comparisons of ships with vastly different price structures. Obviously, a ship charging $600 to $1,000 per day per person for an average cabin can afford to give its affluent customers more than one charging $150. Therefore, the various vessels have been divided into four major market categories. As was pointed out in chapter 2, pricing policies of cruise lines are confusing, if not deceptive.

Courtesy Silversea Cruises

Therefore, my division into major market categories is not only based upon published fares, but also upon on-board costs, air-sea packages, the economic passenger market the line seeks to attract, and the market it actually does attract.

CATEGORY A—DELUXE

"Black star awards" are given to ships competing for business at the top of the market for the affluent, mature traveler whose prime consideration is not cost: minimum cabin in excess of $400 per person per day; average cabin about $500 to $700 per person per day; and top suites may go from $750 to $1,500 per person per day.

CATEGORY B—PREMIUM

"Crisscrossed star awards" are given to ships competing for business between the middle- and top-priced cruise markets for the upper-middle-class segment: minimum cabin in excess of $300 per person per day; average cabin about $350 to $450 per person per day; and suites may go from $450 to $750 per person per day.

CATEGORY C—STANDARD/MASS MARKET

"Diagonal star awards" are given to ships competing for business in the middle-priced cruise markets for travelers looking for bargains without sacrificing the total cruise experience: minimum cabin in excess of $175 per person per day; average cabin about $200 to $275 per person per day; and suites may go from $350 to $600 per person per day.

CATEGORY D—ECONOMY

"White star awards" are given to ships competing for business in the economy cruise market for singles, younger cruisers, and bargain hunters wishing to experience a good time on a cruise but willing to sacrifice comfort, food, and service for price savings: minimum cabin about $100 per person per day; average cabin about $150 to $200 per person per day.

Note: **Rates referred to above are based on published prices. In reality, almost every cruise line offers an array of discounted fares that may average considerably less than the official published fare.**

Some ships and cruise lines overlap categories and therefore have been assigned "split designations." An "A/B" (black star/crisscross star) category reflects a ship that provides a product geared to travelers who prefer a luxury vessel at a lower price without some of the amenities or bells and whistles as are included on the pure luxury vessels. A "B/C" (crisscross star/diagonal star) category is reserved for ships that cannot quite be described as premium because of condition, age, décor, or facilities, yet provides passengers a higher-level cruise experience than those in the mass-market division.

An award of six stars in any given market category—A, B, C, or D—represents overall excellence in dining, service, accommodations, entertainment, facilities, itineraries, condition of the ship, and creature comfort relative to the particular market category. We have given a rating of six-plus stars to a limited number of luxury ships where the attention to passenger comfort and satisfaction is so extraordinary as to entitle these vessels to special recognition. Five stars represent that the vessel is very good in most areas, although it may be excellent or average in some. Three to four stars denote a ship that is average to mediocre in most areas. Two stars are reserved for those ships that are well below average in most areas, and one star suggests readers should have second thoughts before booking passage.

Because the ships have first been divided into market categories based on price and clientele, it would not be accurate to compare ratings for ships in different market categories. A five-star award given a ship in Category A does not necessarily mean that the ship offers less overall than a six-star award given vessels in Categories B, C, or D. Be certain you compare apples with apples.

A deluxe-category ship is expected to perform at a higher level than a premium or mass-market category vessel; therefore, the standard of excellence required to receive high ratings for the latter category is less stringent. Be careful not to compare our ratings with those in other cruise guides. Some authors have chosen to utilize anywhere from three to ten stars, ribbons, anchors, etc., or opt for a hundred-point evaluation system. The reader must be aware of the range of categories utilized by each reviewer in order to make a valid comparison. (Be advised that most of the smaller riverboats and barges that do not offer a full cruise program have not been rated in this chapter; some ships that have recently changed ownership or that are not marketed in the United States also have not been rated.)

Note: **"N/A" indicates that the tonnage was not made available by the cruise line. "N/R" indicates that ship was not rated due to changes that have occurred since most recent investigation of ship or author has not recently sailed on ship.**

Alphabetical listing of cruise ships with tonnage, market category, and ratings:

Name of Ship	Cruise Line	Tonnage (G.R.T.)	Market Category	Ratings
Abercrombie	Grand Circle Cruises	280	N/R	N/R
Actief	European Waterways	N/A	N/R	N/R
Adrienne	French Country Waterways	250	A/B	N/R
Adventure of the Seas	Royal Caribbean	142,000	C	5+
AidaAura	Aida Cruises	43,289	C	N/R
AidaBella	Aida Cruises	68,500	C	N/R
AidaCara	Aida Cruises	38,600	C	N/R
AidaDiva	Aida Cruises	68,500	C	N/R
AidaVita	Aida Cruises	42,289	C	N/R
Akademik Ioffe	Quark Expeditions	N/A	N/R	N/R
Akademik Shokalsky	Quark Expeditions	N/A	N/R	N/R
Akademik Sergey	Quark Expeditions	N/A	N/R	N/R
Alouette	European Waterways	N/A	N/R	N/R
Amabella	AMA Waterways	N/A	B	N/R
Amacello	AMA Waterways	N/A	B	N/R
Amadagio	AMA Waterways	N/A	B	N/R
Amadante	AMA Waterways	N/A	B	N/R
Amadolce	AMA Waterways	N/A	B	N/R
Amadouro	AMA Waterways	N/R	N/R	N/R
Amalegro	AMA Waterways	N/A	B	N/R
Amalyra	AMA Waterways	N/A	B	N/R
Amadeus I	Luftner River Cruises	1.56	C	N/R
Amadeus Classic	Luftner River Cruises	1.56	C	N/R
Amadeus Danubia	Luftner River Cruises	N/A	C	N/R
Amadeus Diamond	Luftner River Cruises	2.0	B	N/R

Ship	Cruise Line			
Amadeus Princess	Luftner River Cruises	1.56	B	N/R
Amadeus Rhapsody	Luftner River Cruises	1.56	C	N/R
Amadeus Royal	Luftner River Cruises	1.56	B	N/R
Amadeus Symphony	Luftner River Cruises	N/A	C	N/R
Amadouro	AMA Waterways	N/A	N/R	N/R
Amaryllis	Abercrombie & Kent	N/A	N/R	N/R
American Eagle	American Cruise Line	N/A	B/C	N/R
American Glory	American Cruise Line	N/A	B/C	N/R
American Spirit	American Cruise Line	N/A	B/C	N/R
American Star	American Cruise Line	N/A	B/C	N/R
Amsterdam	Holland America Line	61,000	B	5+
Anacoluthe	Abercrombie & Kent	N/A	N/R	N/R
Anjodi	European Waterways/Abercrombie & Kent	N/A	N/R	N/R
Anni	Sheraton Nile Cruises	N/A	N/R	N/R
Aqua Marina	Louis Cruise Line	23,149	N/R	N/R
Arcadia	P & O Cruises	83,000	B	N/R
Arkona	Arkona Touristik	18,519	N/R	N/R
Artemis	P & O Cruises	44,248	B	N/R
A'Rosa Bella	Arosa River Cruises	3,500	N/R	N/R
A'Rosa Donna	Arosa River Cruises	3,500	N/R	N/R
A'Rosa Mia	Arosa River Cruises	3,500	N/R	N/R
Asuka	NYK Cruises	28,717	B	N/R
Asuka II	NYK Cruises	49,400	A	N/R
Atbos	European Waterways	N/A	N/R	N/R
Aton	Sheraton Nile Cruises	N/A	N/R	N/R
Aurora	P & O Cruises	76,000	B	N/R
Ausonia	Louis Cruise Line	12,609	D	N/R

Ship	Cruise Line	Tonnage		
Avalon Affinity	Avalon Waterways	N/A	B	N/R
Avalon Artistry	Avalon Waterways	N/A	B	N/R
Avalon Creativity	Avalon Waterways	N/A	B	N/R
Avalon Scenery	Avalon Waterways	N/A	B	N/R
Avalon Imagry	Avalon Waterways	N/A	B	N/R
Avalon Tranquility	Avalon Waterways	N/A	B	N/R
Avalon Tapestry	Avalon Waterways	N/A	B	N/R
Avalon Poetry	Avalon Waterways	N/A	B	N/R
Awani Dream 2	Awani Cruises	17,593	D	N/R
Azamara Journey	Azamara	30,277	B	5
Azamara Quest	Azamara	30,277	B	5
Azura	P & O Cruises	116,000	B	N/R
Bahamas Celebration	Celebration Cruises	35,000	D	N/R
Bali Sea Dancer	Classical Cruises	4,000	N/R	N/R
Balmoral	Fred Olsen Cruise Line	34,242	C	N/R
Black Prince	Fred Olsen Cruise Line	11,209	C/D	N/R
Black Watch	Fred Olsen Cruise Line	28,000	C/D	N/R
Bleu De France	CDF Croisieres de France	37,000	C	N/R
Boudicca	Fred Olsen Cruise Line	25,000	C	N/R
Braemar	Fred Olsen Cruise Line	19,089	C	N/R
Bremen	Hapag-Lloyd	6,753	B/C	N/R
Brilliance of the Seas	Royal Caribbean	90,090	C	5
Caledonian Star	Special Expeditions	3,095	N/R	N/R
Calypso	Louis Cruise Line/Thomson Cruises	11,160	D	N/R
Caribbean Princess	Princess Cruises	113,000	B	5++
Carnival Conquest	Carnival Cruise Lines	110,000	C	5
Carnival Destiny	Carnival Cruise Lines	101,353	C	5

Carnival Dream	Carnival Cruise Lines	130,000	C	5+
Carnival Ecstacy	Carnival Cruise Lines	70,367	C	4
Carnival Elation	Carnival Cruise Lines	70,367	C	4+
Carnival Freedom	Carnival Cruise Lines	110,000	C	5
Carnival Fantasy	Carnival Cruise Lines	70,367	C	4
Carnival Fascination	Carnival Cruise Lines	70,367	C	4+
Carnival Glory	Carnival Cruise Lines	110,000	C	5
Carnival Imagination	Carnival Cruise Lines	70,367	C	4+
Carnival Inspiration	Carnival Cruise Lines	70,367	C	4+
Carnival Legend	Carnival Cruise Line	88,500	C	5
Carnival Liberty	Carnival Cruise Line	110,000	C	5
Carnival Miracle	Carnival Cruise Line	88,500	C	5
Carnival Paradise	Carnival Cruise Line	70,367	C	4+
Carnival Pride	Carnival Cruise Lines	88,500	C	5
Carnival Sensation	Carnival Cruise Lines	70,367	C	4+
Carnival Spirit	Carnival Cruise Lines	88,500	C	5
Carnival Splendor	Carnival Cruise Lines	113,300	C	5
Carnival Triumph	Carnival Cruise Lines	102,000	C	5
Carnival Valor	Carnival Cruise Lines	110,000	C	5+
Carnival Victory	Carnival Cruise Lines	102,000	C	5
Celebrity Century	Celebrity Cruises	70,606	B	5+
Celebrity Constellation	Celebrity Cruises	91,000	B	5+
Celebrity Infinity	Celebrity Cruises	91,000	B	5+
Celebrity Mercury	Celebrity Cruises	77,713	B	5
Celebrity Millennium	Celebrity Cruises	91,000	B	5+
Celebrity Solstice	Celebrity Cruises	122,000	B	N/R

Celebrity Summit	Celebrity Cruises	91,000	B	5+
Celebrity Xpedition	Celebrity Cruises	2,329	B	N/R
Cinderella	Euro Cruises (Viking Line)	46,398	D	N/R
Clelia II	Classical Cruises	4,077	B	N/R
Clipper Adventurer	Quark Expeditions	4,364	N/R	N/R
Clipper Odyssey	Abercrombie & Kent	5,200	C	N/R
Club Med 2	Club Med Cruises	14,000	B	4+
Colibri	Abercrombie & Kent	N/A	N/A	N/R
Columbus	Hapag-Lloyd	15,000	C	N/R
Colibri	American Waterways	N/A	N/R	N/R
Coral	Louis Cruises Line	14,000	D	N/R
Coral Princess	Princess Cruises	92,000	B	5+
Costa Allegra	Costa Cruise Lines	28,500	C/D	N/R
Costa Atlantica	Costa Cruise Lines	85,000	C	5
Costa Classica	Costa Cruise Lines	53,000	C	4
Costa Concordia	Costa Cruise Lines	112,000	C	N/R
Costa Europa	Costa Cruise Lines	53,872	C	4
Costa Fortuna	Costa Cruise Lines	105,000	C	5
Costa Luminosa	Costa Cruise Lines	92,700	C	5
Costa Magica	Costa Cruise Lines	105,000	C	5
Costa Marina	Costa Cruise Lines	25,500	C/D	3+
Costa Mediterranea	Costa Cruise Lines	85,000	C	5
Costa Pacifica	Costa Cruise Lines	114,500	C	5
Costa Romantica	Costa Cruise Lines	53,000	C	4
Costa Serena	Costa Cruise Lines	112,000	C	N/R
Costa Victoria	Costa Cruise Lines	75,000	C	4

Ship	Cruise Line	Tonnage		
Crown Princess	Princess Cruises	113,000	B	5++
Crystal	Louis Cruise Line	25,611	D	N/R
Crystal Serenity	Crystal Cruises	68,000	A	6+
Crystal Symphony	Crystal Cruises	51,044	A	6+
Dawn Princess	Princess Cruises	77,000	B	5
Deltastar	Luftner Cruise Line	1,550	N/R	N/R
Deutschland	Peter Deilmann Cruises	22,400	A/B	5+
Diamond Princess	Princess Cruises	116,000	B	5++
Discovery	Voyages of Discovery	20,186	N/R	N/R
Disney Magic	Disney Cruise Line	83,000	B	5+
Disney Wonder	Disney Cruise Line	83,000	B	5+
Donaustar	Luftner Cruise Line	1,550	N/R	N/R
Douro Queen	Uniworld	N/A	B	N/R
East King	Abercrombie & Kent	N/A	N/R	N/R
Easy Cruise Life	Easy Cruise	12,711	D	N/R
Eclipse	Abercrombie & Kent	N/A	N/R	N/R
Elizabeth	Abercrombie & Kent	N/A	N/R	N/R
Emerald	Thomson Cruises	26,431	D	N/R
Emerald Princess	Princess Cruises	113,000	B	5++
Empress	Pullmantur	48,563	C	N/R
Enchante	Abercrombie & Kent	N/A	N/R	N/R
Enchantment of the Seas	Royal Caribbean	81,500	C	5
Esprit	French Country Waterways	280	A/B	N/R
Eurodam	Holland America Line	86,700	B	5+
Europa	Hapag-Lloyd	28,890	A	6
Explorer II	Saga Cruises	12,500	N/R	N/R

Ship	Cruise Line			
Explorer of the Seas	Royal Caribbean	142,000	C	5+
Fiji Princess	Blue Lagoon Cruises	N/A	N/R	N/R
Finnmarken	Hurtigruten	15,000	N/R	N/R
Fleur de Lys	Abercrombie & Kent	N/A	N/R	N/R
Fram	Hurtigruten	12,700	A/B	N/R
Freedom of the Seas	Royal Caribbean	160,000	C	5+
Fuji Maru	Mitsui OSK	23,340	N/R	N/R
Galapagos Explorer	Galapagos Cruises	3,990	C	N/R
Giselle	Uniworld	N/A	B	N/R
Golden Princess	Princess Cruises	109,000	B	5+
Grand Celebration	IberoCruceos	47,262	C/D	N/R
Grand Princess	Princess Cruises	109,000	B	5+
Grand Mistral	IberoCruceros	47,900	N/R	N/R
Grand Voyager	IberoCruceros	25,000	N/R	N/R
Grande Caribe	Am. Canadian Carib. Line	98	C/D	N/R
Grande Mariner	Am Canadian Carib. Line	98	C/D	N/R
Grandeur of the Seas	Royal Caribbean	74,000	C	5
Hanseatic	Hapag-Lloyd	8,378	A/B	N/R
Hebridean Princess	Hebridean Island Cruises	2,112	N/R	N/R
Hebridean Spirit	Hebridean Island Cruises	4,200	N/R	N/R
Hirondelle	European Waterways/Abercrombie & Kent	N/A	N/R	N/R
Holiday	Carnival Cruise Lines	46,052	C	4
Horizon II	French Country Waterways	190	A/B	N/R
Hotp	Sheraton Nile Cruises	N/A	N/R	N/R
Illich	Euro Cruises	8,000	D	N/R
Independence of the Seas	Royal Caribbean	160,000	C	5+

Ship	Line			
Insignia	Oceania Cruises	30,277	B	6
Isabela II	Metropolitan Galapagos Cruises	1,083	C	N/R
Island Princess	Princess Cruises	92,000	B	5+
Island Star	Pullmantur	47,000	C	N/R
Islander	Linblad Expeditions	N/A	N/R	N/R
Ivory	Louis Cruise Line	12,600	N/R	N/R
Jewel of the Seas	Royal Caribbean	90,090	C	5
Kapitan Khlebnikov	Quark Expeditions	N/A	N/R	N/R
Kong Harald	Hurtigruten	11,200	N/R	N/R
La Belle Epoque	European Waterways/Abercrombie & Kent	N/A	B	N/R
La Bonne Amie	Independently Owned	N/A	A	N/R
La Dolce Vita	European Waterways	N/A	N/R	N/R
La Margerite	AMA Waterways	N/A	B	N/R
La Reine Pedaque	European Waterways	N/A	N/R	N/R
L'Arte de Vivre	European Waterways/Abercrombie & Kent	N/A	N/R	N/R
La Nouvelle Etoile	Abercrombie & Kent	N/A	N/R	N/R
Le Bon Vivant	Independently Owned	N/A	A	N/R
Le Diamont	Ponant Cruises	8,282	B/C	N/R
Le Levant	Ponant Cruises	3,500	B/C	N/R
Le Phenicien	Abercrombie & Kent	N/A	N/R	N/R
Le Ponant	Ponant Cruises	1,489	B/C	N/R
Legend of the Seas	Royal Caribbean	70,000	C	5
Libellule	Abercrombie & Kent	N/A	N/R	N/R
Liberty of the Seas	Royal Caribbean	160,000	C	5+
L'Impressionniste	European Waterways/Abercrombie & Kent	N/A	N/R	N/R
Litvinov	Uniworld	N/A	B	N/R
Lofoten	Hurtigruten	2,661	N/R	N/R

Lorraine	Abercrombie & Kent	N/A	N/R	N/R
Lycianda	Blue Lagoon Cruises	N/A	N/R	N/R
Lyubov Orlova	Quark Expeditions	N/A	N/R	N/R
Maasdam	Holland America Line	55,451	B	5+
Magna Carta	European Waterways/Abercrombie & Kent	N/A	N/R	N/R
Majesty of the Seas	Royal Caribbean	73,941	C	4
Mare Australis	Abercrombie & Kent/Cruceros Australis	N/A	N/R	N/R
Mariella	Euro Cruises	37,799	D	N/R
Mariner of the Seas	Royal Caribbean	142,000	C	5+
Marjorie II	Abercrombie & Kent	N/A	N/R	N/R
Maxim Gorki	Black Sea Shipping	25,000	D	N/R
Meanderer	Abercrombie & Kent	N/A	N/R	N/R
MegaStar Aries	Star Cruises	3,264	B	N/R
MegaStar Taurus	Star Cruises	3,264	B	N/R
Midnatsol	Hurtigruten	15,000	N/R	N/R
Minerva	Swan Hellenic/Abercrombie & Kent	12,500	N/R	N/R
Monarch of the Seas	Royal Caribbean	73,941	C	4
Moon Empress	Pullmantur	73,192	C	N/R
Moon Goddess	Sonesta Nile Cruise Collection	N/A	N/R	N/R
MSC Armonia	MSC Cruises	58,500	C	4+
MSC Fantasia	MSC Cruises	133,500	C	5
MSC Lirica	MSC Cruises	59,000	C	4+
MSC Melody	MSC Cruises	36,500	C/D	N/R
MSC Musica	MSC Cruises	86,600	C	5
MSC Opera	MSC Cruises	59,058	C	4+
MSC Orchestra	MSC Cruises	89,600	C	5
MSC Poesia	MSC Cruises	92,400	C	5

Ship	Cruise Line			
MSC Sinfonia	MSC Cruises	C	58,625	4+
MSC Splendida	MSC Cruises	C	133,500	5
Murray Princess	Captain Cook Cruises	N/R	1,500	N/R
Mystique Princess	Blue Lagoon Cruises	N/R	N/A	N/R
Nanuya Princess	Blue Lagoon Cruises	N/R	N/A	N/R
Napoleon	Abercrombie & Kent	N/R	N/A	N/R
National Geographic Endeavor	Linblad Expeditions	N/R	3,132	N/R
National Geographic Explorer	Linblad Expeditions	N/R	N/A	N/R
Nautica	Oceania Cruise Line	B	30,277	6
Navigator of the Seas	Royal Caribbean	C	142,000	5+
Nemphar	French Country Waterways	A/B	280	N/R
Niagra Prince	American Canadian Line	D	99	N/R
Nile Adventurer	Abercrombie & Kent	N/R	N/A	N/R
Nile Goddess	Sonesta Nile Cruise Collection	N/R	N/A	N/R
Noordam	Holland America Line	B	82,000	5+
Nordkapp	Hurtigruten	N/R	11,386	N/R
Nordlys	Hurtigruten	N/R	11,200	N/R
Nordnorge	Hurtigruten	N/R	11,386	N/R
Nordstjernen	Hurtigruten	N/R	2,568	N/R
Norwegian Dawn	Norwegian Cruise Line	C	91,740	5
Norwegian Dream	Norwegian Cruise Line	C	50,764	N/R
Norwegian Gem	Norwegian Cruise Line	C	93,502	5
Norwegian Jade	Norwegian Cruise Line	C	93,502	5
Norwegian Jewel	Norwegian Cruise Line	C	93,502	5
Norwegian Majesty	Norwegian Cruise Line	C	40,876	N/R
Norwegian Pearl	Norwegian Cruise Line	C	93,502	5
Norwegian Spirit	Norwegian Cruise Line	C	75,338	N/R

Norwegian Star	Norwegian Cruise Line	91,000	C	5
Norwegian Sun	Norwegian Cruise Line	78,309	C	5
Nymphea	European Waterways	N/A	N/R	N/R
Oasis of the Seas	Royal Caribbean	220,000	C	N/R
Oceana	P & O Cruises	77,000	B	N/R
Ocean Dream	Pullmantur	35,000	D	N/R
Ocean Majesty	Page and Moy	10,417	D	N/R
Ocean Monarch	Page and Moy	15,739	D	N/R
Ocean Nova	Quark Expeditions	N/A	N/R	N/R
Ocean Princess	Princess Cruises	30,277	B	5+
Oceanic Odyssey	Spice Island Cruises	5,218	N/R	N/R
Oosterdam	Holland America Line	82,000	B	5+
Oriana	P & O Cruises	69,153	B	N/R
Orient Queen	Louis Cruise Line	15,781	D	N/R
Orient Venus	Venus Cruises	21,884	N/R	N/R
Pacific	Pullmantur	20,000	N/R	N/R
Pacific Dawn	P & O Cruises Australia	70,000	B/C	N/R
Pacific Explorer	Cruise West	N/A	N/R	N/R
Pacific Jewel	P & O Cruises Australia	70,000	C	N/R
Pacific Pearl	P & O Cruises Australia	64,000	C	N/R
Pacific Princess	Princess Cruises	30,277	B	5+
Pacific Sun	P & O Cruises Australia	47,262	C	N/R
Pacific Venus	Venus Cruises	26,518	N/R	N/R
Panorama I	Classical Cruises	599	N/R	N/R
Paul Gauguin	Paul Gauguin Cruises	18,800	N/R	N/R
Perla	Louis Cruise Line	16,710	D	N/R
Poesia	MSC Cruises	89,600	C	N/R

Ship	Line			
Polaris	Linblad Expeditions	2,214	N/R	N/R
Polarlys	Hurtigruten	12,000	N/R	N/R
Polar Star	Hurtigruten	3,500	N/R	N/R
Pride of Aloha	Star Cruises	77,104	C	N/R
Pride of America	Norwegian Cruise Line	81,000	C	N/R
Prince Albert II	Silversea Cruises	6,072	A	N/R
Princesa Cypria	Louis Cruise Line	9,984	D	N/R
Princesa Marissa	Louis Cruise Line	10,487	D	N/R
Princess	French Country Waterways	280	A/B	N/R
Princess Danae	Classic International Cruises	17,074	D	N/R
Prinsendam	Holland America Line	37,848	B	5+
Prosperite	Abercrombie & Kent	N/A	N/R	N/R
Queen Mary 2	Cunard Line	150,000		
	(Queens Grill)		A	6+
	(Princess Grill)		A	6
	(Britannia)		B	5+
Queen Victoria	Cunard Line	90,000		
	(Grill Rooms)		A	6+
	(Britannia)		B/C	5
Radiance of the Seas	Royal Caribbean	90,090	C	5
Reef Endeavor	Captain Cook Cruises	3,125	N/R	N/R
Reef Escape	Captain Cook Cruises	1,850	N/R	N/R
Regatta	Oceania Cruises	30,277	B	6
Reine Pedaque	European Waterways/Abercrombie & Kent	N/A	N/R	N/R
Renaissance	European Waterways/Abercrombie & Kent	N/A	A	6
Rhapsody of the Seas	Royal Caribbean	78,491	C	5
Richard With	Hurtigruten	11,205	N/R	N/R

River Adagio	Grand Circle Cruises	1,935	N/R	N/R
River Ambassador	Uniworld	N/A	B	N/R
River Anuket	Grand Circle Cruises	2,350	N/R	N/R
River Aria	Grand Circle Cruises	1,935	N/R	N/R
River Bizet	Grand Circle Cruises	1,950	N/R	N/R
River Baroness	Uniworld	N/A	B	N/R
River Beatrice	Uniworld	N/A	B	N/R
River Chardonnay	Grand Circle Cruises	822	N/R	N/R
River Cloud	Sea Cloud Cruises	N/A	B	5
River Cloud II	Sea Cloud Cruises	N/A	B	N/R
River Concerto	Grand Circle Cruises	1,935	N/R	N/R
River Countess	Uniworld	N/A	B	N/R
River Debussy	Grand Circle Cruises	1,950	N/R	N/R
River Discovery	Vantage Travel	N/A	N/R	N/R
River Duchess	Uniworld	N/A	B	N/R
River Empress	Uniworld	N/A	B	N/R
River Explorer	Vantage Travel	N/A	N/R	N/R
River Harmony	Grand Circle Cruises	1,935	N/R	N/R
River Hatbor	Grand Circle Cruises	630	N/R	N/R
River Melody	Grand Circle Cruises	1,935	N/R	N/R
River Navigator	Vantage Travel	N/A	N/R	N/R
River Odyssey	Vantage Travel	N/A	N/R	N/R
River Princess	Uniworld	N/A	B	N/R
River Provence	Grand Circle Cruises	1,000	N/R	N/R
River Queen	Uniworld	N/A	B	N/R
River Ravel	Grand Circle Cruises	1,950	N/R	N/R
River Rhapsody	Grand Circle Cruises	1,935	N/R	N/R

Ship	Operator	Tonnage		
River Royal	Uniworld	N/A	B	N/R
River Symphony	Grand Circle Cruises	1,935	N/R	N/R
Road to Mandalay	Abercrombie & Kent	N/A	N/R	N/R
Roi Soleil	Abercrombie & Kent	N/A	N/R	N/R
Royal Princess	Princess Cruises	30,227	B	5+
Rotterdam	Holland America Line	59,652	B	5+
Rousse	Luftner Cruises	1,295	C	N/R
Royal Clipper	Star Clippers	5,000	B	4+
Royal Princess	Princess Cruises	30,277	B	5+
Royal Star	Star Lines/Sea Air Holidays	5,360	D	N/R
Ruby Princess	Princess Cruises	113,500	B	5++
Ryndam	Holland America Line	55,819	B	5+
Safari Explorer	Abercrombie & Kent	N/A	N/R	N/R
Safari Quest	Abercrombie & Kent	N/A	N/R	N/R
Safari Spirit	Abercrombie & Kent	N/A	N/R	N/R
Saga Ruby	Saga Cruises	23,492	C	N/R
Saint Louis	European Waterways	N/A	N/R	N/R
Santa Cruz	Metropolitan Galapagos Cruises	1,500	C	N/R
Sapphire	Thomson Cruises/Louis Cruises	12,183	D	N/R
Sapphire Princess	Princess Cruises	116,000	B	5++
Saroche	Abercrombie & Kent	N/A	N/R	N/R
Savoire Faire	European Waterways	N/A	N/R	N/R
Scottish Highlander	European Waterways/Abercrombie & Kent	N/A	N/R	N/R
Sea Bird	Linblad Expeditons	100	N/R	N/R
Seabourn Legend	Seabourn Cruise Line	10,000	A	6+
Seabourn Odyssey	Seabourn Cruise Line	32,000	A	6+
Seabourn Pride	Seabourn Cruise Line	10,000	A	6+

Ship	Line			
Seabourn Sojourn	Seabourn Cruise Line	32,000	A	6+
Seabourn Spirit	Seabourn Cruise Line	10,000	A	6+
Sea Cloud I	Sea Cloud Cruises	N/A	A/B	N/R
Sea Cloud II	Sea Cloud Cruises	N/A	A/B	N/R
Sea Cloud Hussar	Sea Cloud Cruises	N/A	A/B	N/R
SeaDream I	SeaDream Yacht Club	4,250	A	5+
SeaDream II	SeaDream Yacht Club	4,250	A	5+
Sea Lion	Linblad Expeditions	100	N/R	N/R
Sea Princess	Princess Cruises	77,000	B	5
Sea Voyager	Linblad Expeditions	354	N/R	N/R
Serenade	Louis Cruise Line	37,584	N/R	N/R
Serenade of the Seas	Royal Caribbean	90,090	C	5
Seven Seas Mariner	Regent Seven Seas	50,000	A	6+
Seven Seas Navigator	Regent Seven Seas	33,000	A	6
Seven Seas Voyager	Regent Seven Seas	46,000	A	6+
Shannon Princess II	European Waterways/Abercrombie & Kent	N/A	N/R	N/R
Silja Europa	Silja Line	59,914	D	N/R
Silja Festival	Silja Line	34,419	D	N/R
Silja Serenade	Silja Line	58,376	D	N/R
Silja Symphony	Silja Line	58,376	D	N/R
Silver Cloud	Silversea Cruises	16,800	A	6+
Silver Shadow	Silversea Cruises	28,258	A	6+
Silver Spirit	Silversea Cruises	36,000	A	6+
Silver Whisper	Silversea Cruises	28,258	A	6+
Silver Wind	Silversea Cruises	16,800	A	6+
Sky Wonder	Pullmantur	46,314	D	N/R
Sovereign of the Seas	Royal Caribbean	73,192	C	4

Spirit of Adventure	Saga Cruises	9,570	C	N/R
Spirit of Alaska	Cruise West	97	N/R	N/R
Spirit of Columbia	Cruise West	98	N/R	N/R
Spirit of Discovery	Cruise West	94	N/R	N/R
Spirit of Endeavor	Cruise West	95	N/R	N/R
Spirit of Glacier Bay	Cruise West	1,471	N/R	N/R
Spirit of '98	Cruise West	96	N/R	N/R
Spirit of Oceanus	Cruise West	4,500	N/R	N/R
Spirit of Yorktown	Cruise West	2,352	N/R	N/R
Splendour of the Seas	Royal Caribbean	69,130	C	5
St. George I	Sonesta Nile Cruise Collection	N/A	N/R	N/R
Star Clipper	Star Clippers	3,025	C	4+
Star Flyer	Star Clippers	3,025	C	4+
Star Goddess	Sonesta Nile Cruise Collection	N/A	N/R	N/R
Star Pisces	Star Cruises	40,000	D	N/R
Star Princess	Princess Cruises	109,000	B	5+
Statendam	Holland America Line	55,851	B	5+
Sun Bird	Louis Cruise Line	37,584	D	N/R
Sun Boat III	Abercrombie & Kent	N/A	N/R	N/R
Sun Boat IV	Abercrombie & Kent	N/A	N/R	N/R
Sun Goddess	Sonesta Nile Cruise Collection	N/A	N/R	N/R
Sun Princess	Princess Cruises	77,000	B	5
SuperStar Aquarius	Star Cruises	50,760	C	N/R
SuperStar Libra	Star Cruises	42,000	C	N/R
SuperStar Virgo	Star Cruises	76,800	B/C	N/R
Swiss Pearl	AMA Waterways	N/A	N/R	N/R
Thomson Celebration	Thomson Cruises	33,900	N/R	N/R

Ship	Cruise Line	Tonnage		
Thomson Destiny	Thomson Cruises	37,000	N/R	N/R
Thomson Spirit	Thomson Cruises	33,900	N/R	N/R
Tikhi Don	Grand Circle Cruises	3,570	N/R	N/R
Terra Australis	Odessa America	1,899	N/R	N/R
Ti'a Moana	Bora Bora Cruises	N/A	A	N/R
Tolstoy	AMA Waterways	N/A	N/R	N/R
Trollfjord	Hurtigruten	15,000	N/R	N/R
Tu Moana	Bora Bora Cruises	N/A	A	N/R
Tut	Sheraton Nile Cruises	N/A	N/R	N/R
Veendam	Holland America Line	55,758	B	5+
Ventura	P & O Cruises	115,000	B	N/R
Vesteralen	Hurtigruten	6,261	N/R	N/R
Via Australis	Cruceros Australis	N/A	N/R	N/R
Victoria Anna	Victoria Cruises, Inc.	6,200	N/R	N/R
Victoria Empress	Victoria Cruises, Inc.	3,868	N/R	N/R
Victoria Jenna	Victoria Cruises, Inc.	10,000	N/R	N/R
Victoria Katarina	Victoria Cruises, Inc.	5,780	N/R	N/R
Victoria Prince	Victoria Cruises, Inc.	4,587	N/R	N/R
Victoria Queen	Victoria Cruises, Inc.	4,587	N/R	N/R
Victoria Rose	Victoria Cruises, Inc.	2,428	N/R	N/R
Victoria Star	Victoria Cruises, Inc.	4,587	N/R	N/R
Viking Burgundy	VikingRiver Cruises	N/A	N/R	N/R
Viking Century Sky	Viking River Cruises	N/A	B	5
Viking Century Sun	Viking River Cruises	N/A	B	5
Viking Danube	Viking River Cruises	N/A	N/R	N/R
Viking Europe	Viking River Cruises	N/A	N/R	N/R
Viking Fontaine	Viking River Cruises	N/A	N/R	N/R

Ship	Cruise Line			
Viking Helvetia II	Viking River Cruises	N/R	N/A	N/A
Viking Kirov	Viking River Cruises	N/A	N/R	N/R
Viking Lavrinenkov	Viking River Cruises	N/A	N/R	N/R
Viking Lomonosov	Viking River Cruises	N/A	N/R	N/R
Viking Neptune	Viking River Cruises	N/A	N/R	N/R
Viking Pakhomov	Viking River Cruises	N/A	N/R	N/R
Viking Pride	Viking River Cruises	N/A	N/R	N/R
Viking Princess	Palm Beach Cruise Line	6,422	N/R	N/R
Viking Schumann	Viking River Cruises	N/A	N/R	N/R
Viking Seine	Viking River Cruises	N/A	N/R	N/R
Viking Sky	Viking River Cruises	N/A	N/R	N/R
Viking Spirit	Viking River Cruise	N/A	N/R	N/R
Viking Sun	Viking River Cruises	N/A	N/R	N/R
Viking Surkov	Viking River Cruises	N/A	N/R	N/R
Vision of the Seas	Royal Caribbean	78,491	C	5
Volendam	Holland America Line	61,396	B	5+
Volga Dream	Abercrombie & Kent	N/A	N/R	N/R
Voyager of the Seas	Royal Caribbean	142,000	C	5+
Westerdam	Holland America Line	82,000	B	5+
Wind Spirit	Windstar Cruises	5,350	B	5
Wind Star	Windstar Cruises	5,350	B	5
Wind Surf	Windstar Cruises	14,745	B	5
World	ResidenSea Management, Ltd.	40,000	A	N/R
Yangzi Explorer	Abercrombie & Kent	N/A	N/R	N/R
Zaandam	Holland America Line	61,396	B	5+
Zenith	Pullmantur	47,255	C	N/R
Zuiderdam	Holland America Line	85,000	B	5+

Explanation of Ship Ratings _____

All ships are not excellent, good, or bad across the board; and some excel in one area and fall short in others. For example, there are several Category A—Deluxe Ships that are known for impeccable food and service and fine accommodations, yet offer little entertainment and activities and could be poor choices for younger singles or children. On the other hand, some Category D—Economy Ships have only passable food and service, numerous small or inadequate cabins, yet provide so much fun and entertainment that less demanding, budget-minded, younger cruisers would have a more rewarding experience.

For the purpose of these more detailed ratings, I chose ships from each major cruise line upon which I most recently cruised. The vessel rated is not necessarily the best in the line, and its ratings may not be identical to those of the cruise company's other ships.

I have used a simple five-point system:

*****   excellent (the best available at sea)

**** very good   (one notch below the best, but better than most)

***   good   (average)

**   fair   (below average)

*   poor   (a rose by any other name)

Explanation of Categories _____

The ships are ranked according to how they measure up in the following eleven categories:

1)   *Casual/Buffet Facility*—quality of food presentation and preparation

2)   *Dining Rooms & Specialty Restaurants*—gourmet quality of food, preparation, presentation, caliber of wines, tableside preparations, and availability of special orders

3)   *Service in Dining Rooms*

4)   *Service in Cabins*

5)   *Activities and Entertainment*—quantity and quality

6)   *Average Cabin*—spaciousness, decor, and facilities included

7)   *Outside Deck Area*—spaciousness for passenger capacity, condition, decor, and facilities available

8)   *Inside Public Area*—spaciousness for passenger capacity, condition, decor, and facilities available

9)   *Physical Condition of Ship, Public Areas, and Cabins*

10)   *Special Activities and Facilities for Children*

11)   *Good Ship for Singles*

	Casual/Buffet Facility	Dining Rooms & Specialty Restaurants	Service in Dining Rooms	Service in Cabins
Azamara Cruises *Journey* *Quest*	****+	****+	****	****
Carnival Cruise Lines *Conquest* *Destiny* *Freedom* *Glory* *Legend* *Liberty* *Miracle* *Pride* *Spirit* *Triumph* *Valor* *Victory*	***** (lunch & dinner) *** (breakfast)	**** (dining room) ***** (specialty restaurant)	***+	****+
Carnival Cruise Lines *Elation* *Imagination* *Inspiration* *Fascination* *Paradise* *Sensation*	***** (lunch & dinner) *** (breakfast)	****	***+	****+
Celebrity Cruises *Constellation* *Infinity* *Millennium* *Summit*	****	**** (dining rooms) *****+ (alternative specialty restaurant)	***** (dining rooms) *****+ (alternative specialty restaurant)	*****
Celebrity Cruises *Century* *Mercury*	****	**** (dining rooms) *****+ (Murano)	**** (dining rooms) *****+ (Murano)	*****

Activities and Entertainment	Average Cabin	Outside Deck Area	Inside Public Area	Physical Condition of Ship, Public Areas, and Cabins	Special Activities and Facilities for Children	Good Ship for Singles
***	****	****	*****	*****	*	*
*****	****+	****	*****	*****	*****	***** (young) *** (mature, over 60)
****+	****+	****	****	*****	*****	***** (young) *** (mature, over 60)
****+	*****	*****	*****	*****	****	***
****	*****	*****	****+	*****	****	***

	Casual/Buffet Facility	Dining Rooms & Specialty Restaurants	Service in Dining Rooms	Service in Cabins
Costa Cruise Lines *CostaVictoria* *CostaRomantica*	***	***+	***	***+
Costa Cruise lines *CostaAtlantica* *Costa Concordia* *Costa Deliziosa* *Costa Fortuna* *Costa Luminosa* *Costa Magica* *CostaMediterranea* *Costa Pacifica* *Costa Serena*	***	***+ (dining rooms) ***+ (specialty restaurant)	***+	***+
Crystal Cruises *Crystal Symphony* *Crystal Serenity*	*****	***** (dining room) ***** (specialty restaurants)	*****	*****
Cunard Line *Queen Victoria*	***+	***** (grill rooms) ***+ (other rooms)	***** (grill rooms) ***+ (other rooms)	****
Cunard Line *Queen Mary 2*	****	***** (grill rooms) **** (other rooms) ***** (specialty restaurant)	***** (grill rooms) ****+ (other rooms) ***** (specialty restaurant)	*****

Activities and Entertainment	Average Cabin	Outside Deck Area	Inside Public Area	Physical Condition of Ship, Public Areas, and Cabins	Special Activities and Facilities for Children	Good Ship for Singles
****	****	*****	****+	*****	****	****
*****	*****	*****	*****	*****	****+	****
*****+	*****	*****	*****	*****	**	** (young) **** (mature, over 60)
****+	****	*****	*****	*****	*	*** (mature, over 60) * (young)
****+	****+	****	*****	*****	****	****

	Casual/Buffet Facility	Dining Rooms & Specialty Restaurants	Service in Dining Rooms	Service in Cabins
Peter Deilmann Cruises *Deutschland*	*****+	****+ (dining rooms) ***** (specialty restaurant)	****	****+
Disney Cruise Line *Disney Magic* *Disney Wonder*	****	**** (dining rooms) *****+ (specialty restaurant)	****	****
Hapag-Lloyd *Europa*	*****	*****	*****	*****
Holland America Line *Amsterdam* *Maasdam* *Rotterdam VI* *Ryndam* *Statendam* *Veendam* *Volendam* *Zaandam*	***+	**** (dining rooms) ****+ (specialty restaurant)	****	****
Holland America Line *Eurodam* *Noordam* *Oosterdam* *Westerdam* *Zuiderdam*	***+	**** (dining rooms) ****+ (specialty restaurants)	****	****
MSC Cruises *Lirica* *Opera*	***	***+	***+	****

Activities and Entertainment	Average Cabin	Outside Deck Area	Inside Public Area	Physical Condition of Ship, Public Areas, and Cabins	Special Activities and Facilities for Children	Good Ship for Singles
** (U.S. Pass.) *** German Pass.)	***+ **** ****+ ***** (some of each)	****	*****	*****	*	**
****	*****	*****	*****	*****	*****+	**
**	*****+	****	****	*****	**	**
****	****	*****	*****	*****	****+	*** (young) ***** (mature, over 60)
****	****	*****	*****	*****	****+	*** (young) ***** (mature)
*****	***+	****	****	*****	***+	***

	Casual/Buffet Facility	*Dining Rooms & Specialty Restaurants*	*Service in Dining Rooms*	*Service in Cabins*
MSC Cruises *Orchestra* *Musica* *Poesia*	**+	***+ (dining rooms) ** (specialty restaurant)	****	****
Norwegian Cruise Line *Norwegian Sun*	*****	****+ (dining rooms) ****+ (specialty restaurants)	****+	****+
Norwegian Cruise Line *Norwegian Star* *Norwegian Dawn* *Norwegian Jewel* *Norwegian Gem* *Norwegian Pearl*	***** (food) *** (service)	**** (dining rooms) ***** (specialty restaurants)	****	***
Oceania *Insignia* *Regatta* *Nautica*	*****	***** (dining rooms) ***** (specialty restaurants)	*****	*****
Princess Cruises *Caribbean Princess* *Crown Princess* *Emerald Princess* *Ruby Princess*	*****	****+ (dining room) ****+ (specialty restaurants)	*****	*****
Princess Cruises *Diamond Princess* *Sapphire Princess*	*****	****+	****+	*****

Activities and Entertainment	Average Cabin	Outside Deck Area	Inside Public Area	Physical Condition of Ship, Public Areas, and Cabins	Special Activities and Facilities for Children	Good Ship for Singles
*****	***+	*****	*****	*****	****	****
****+	****+	****	****	*****	****+	****+
****+	****	*****	*****	*****	*****	***+
****+	****	*****	*****	*****	*	**
*****	**** ****+ (some of each)	*****	*****	*****	*****	****
*****	**** ****+ (some of each)	*****	*****	*****	*****	****

	Casual/Buffet Facility	Dining Rooms & Specialty Restaurants	Service in Dining Rooms	Service in Cabins
Princess Cruises *Dawn Princess* *Sun Princess* *Golden Princess* *Grand Princess* *Sea Princess* *Star Princess*	*****	**** (dining rooms) ****+ (specialty restaurants)	*****	*****
Regent Seven Seas **Cruises** *Seven Seas Mariner* *Seven Seas Voyager*	*****+	*****+ *****+ (Signatures)	*****	*****
Regent Seven Seas **Cruises** *Seven Seas Navigator*	*****+	*****	*****	*****
Royal Caribbean *Adventure of the Seas* *Enchantment of the Seas* *Explorer of the Seas* *Freedom of the Seas* *Grandeur of the Seas* *Independence of the Seas* *Legend of the Seas* *Liberty of the Seas* *Mariner of the Seas* *Navigator of the Seas* *Rhapsody of the Seas* *Splendour of the Seas* *Vision of the Seas* *Voyager of the Seas*	****+	***+ (dining rooms) **** (specialty restaurants)	****	****
Royal Caribbean *Brilliance of the Seas* *Jewel of the Seas* *Radiance of the Seas* *Serenade of the Seas*	****+	***+ (dining room) **** (specialty restaurants)	****	****

Activities and Entertainment	Average Cabin	Outside Deck Area	Inside Public Area	Physical Condition of Ship, Public Areas, and Cabins	Special Activities and Facilities for Children	Good Ship for Singles
****+	****	*****	*****	*****	*****	****
****	*****+	****+	*****	*****	**	**
****	*****+	****	****+	*****	**	**
*****	****	*****	*****	*****	*****+	****+
*****	****	*****	*****	*****	*****+	****+

	Casual/Buffet Facility	Dining Rooms & Specialty Restaurants	Service in Dining Rooms	Service in Cabins
Seabourn Line *Seabourn Legend* *Seabourn Pride* *Seabourn Spirit*	*****+	*****+ (dining room) *****+ (specialty restaurant)	*****+	*****
SeaDream Yacht Club *SeaDream I* *SeaDream II*	*****	*****+	*****+	*****
Silversea Cruises, Ltd. *Silver Cloud* *Silver Wind*	*****	*****	*****	*****
Silversea Cruises, Ltd. *Silver Shadow* *Silver Whisper*	*****	*****	*****	*****
Star Clippers, Inc. *Star Clipper* *Star Flyer*	****+	****+	****+	***
Star Clippers, Inc. *Royal Clipper*	****	****	***	***
Windstar Cruises *Wind Spirit* *Wind Star*	****	****	****	****
Windstar Cruises *Wind Surf*	****	*** (dining room) **** (specialty restaurant)	***+	***

Activities and Entertainment	Average Cabin	Outside Deck Area	Inside Public Area	Physical Condition of Ship, Public Areas, and Cabins	Special Activities and Facilities for Children	Good Ship for Singles
****	*****	****	*****	*****	*	**
*	****	****	****	****	*	*
***	*****+	*****	*****	*****	*	*
****	*****+	*****	*****	*****	*	*
*	***	**	***+	***	*	**
*	***	***	***+	****	*	**
**	****	***+	***+	****	*	*
**	****+	****	****+	*****	*	*

VESSEL SANITATION INSPECTION REPORT

Cruise Ship	Date	Score	Cruise Ship	Date	Score	Cruise Ship	Date	Score
Adventure Of The Seas	01/04/2009	100	Disney Wonder	04/19/2009	99	Pacific Venus	06/08/2008	89
AIDAaura	09/17/2008	99	Ecstasy	11/15/2008	99	Palm Beach Princess	02/25/2009	95
Amadea	04/04/2008	84	Elation	05/03/2009	99	Paradise	02/23/2009	96
Amsterdam	06/24/2009	100	Emerald Princess	04/09/2009	96	Pride of Aloha	12/21/2007	78
Arabella	05/03/2009	97	Empress Of The North	08/18/2007	90	Prince Albert II	08/31/2008	98
Arcadia	02/01/2008	95	Enchantment Of The Seas	05/02/2009	97	Prinsendam	04/30/2009	95
Artemis	01/03/2009	93	Eurodam	04/07/2009	100	Queen Elizabeth 2	04/10/2008	95
Asuka II	06/09/2008	97	Europa	02/01/2008	97	Queen Mary 2	04/14/2009	100
Aurora	03/24/2009	100	Explorer Of The Seas	04/08/2009	99	Queen Victoria	01/10/2009	97
Azamara Journey	03/16/2009	98	Fantasy	04/27/2009	95	Radiance Of The Seas	05/19/2009	99
Azamara Quest	04/12/2008	94	Fascination	06/04/2009	96	Regatta	03/09/2009	100
Bahamas Celebration	05/20/2009	92	Freedom Of The Seas	02/01/2009	99	Rhapsody Of The Seas	04/28/2009	99
Balmoral	04/29/2009	99	Golden Princess	06/27/2009	97	Rotterdam	05/16/2009	98
Braemar	03/05/2009	95	Grand Princess	04/06/2009	98	Ruby Princess	04/11/2009	100
Bremen	05/19/2008	98	Grande Caribe	10/21/2008	93	Ryndam	01/09/2009	95
Brilliance Of The Seas	04/04/2008	92	Grande Mariner	10/08/2008	95	SagaRuby	10/07/2007	95
C. Columbus	11/05/2007	94	Grandeur Of The Seas	04/18/2009	97	Sapphire Princess	03/21/2009	100
Caribbean Express	02/18/2009	96	Holiday	03/23/2009	93	Sea Bird	04/28/2009	100
Caribbean Princess	04/05/2009	100	Imagination	03/06/2009	94	Sea Lion	05/17/2009	91
Carnival Conquest	11/16/2008	99	Independence of the Seas	03/01/2009	96	Sea Princess	09/30/2008	96
Carnival Destiny	04/20/2009	97	Inspiration	11/08/2008	97	Seabourn Legend	04/03/2009	97
Carnival Freedom	04/25/2009	100	Island Adventure	08/07/2008	93	Seabourn Odyssey	05/18/2009	
Carnival Glory	06/06/2009	99	Island Princess	04/23/2009	95	Seabourn Pride	12/20/2008	89
Carnival Legend	03/08/2009	97	Jewel Of The Seas	03/02/2009	98	Seadream I	04/03/2009	97
Carnival Liberty	03/21/2009	94	Liberty of the Seas	02/16/2009	95	Seadream II	04/05/2009	96
Carnival Miracle	01/24/2009	100	Maasdam	05/30/2009	97	Sensation	02/26/2009	98
Carnival Pride	02/22/2009	98	Majesty Of The Seas	04/24/2009	98	Serenade Of The Seas	05/05/2009	97
Carnival Spirit	01/07/2009	98	Mariner Of The Seas	02/19/2009	93	Seven Seas Mariner	07/27/2008	94
Carnival Splendor	06/14/2009	100	Monarch Of The Seas	06/05/2009	96	Seven Seas Navigator	12/29/2008	97
Carnival Triumph	04/19/2009	88	MS Royal Princess	01/20/2009	100	Seven Seas Voyager	12/18/2008	92
Carnival Valor	03/22/2009	94	MSC Lirica	01/06/2009	100	Silver Cloud	04/04/2009	95
Carnival Victory	02/15/2009	95	MSC Orchestra	05/05/2009	96	Silver Shadow	01/03/2009	94
Celebrity Century	04/20/2009	96	MV Clipper Pacific	07/14/2008	84	Silver Wind	03/08/2008	95
Celebrity Constellation	02/23/2009	94	MV Explorer	12/14/2008	100	Spirit Of Columbia	07/20/2007	97
Celebrity Galaxy	04/07/2008	97	MV Fram	10/13/2008	96	Spirit Of Endeavor	05/18/2009	93
Celebrity Infinity	12/03/2008	85	National Geographic Explorer	10/15/2008	92	Spirit of Glacier Bay	07/21/2007	92
Celebrity Mercury	03/08/2009	94	Navigator Of The Seas	11/22/2008	98	Spirit Of Oceanus	05/19/2009	99
Celebrity Millennium	04/27/2009	95	Nippon Maru	06/27/2008	86	Stad Amsterdam	03/25/2009	91
Celebrity Solstice	04/12/2009	100	Noordam	03/04/2009	99	Star Princess	11/20/2008	99
Celebrity Summit	04/04/2009	98	Norwegian Dawn	03/07/2009	100	Statendam	05/06/2009	89
Club Med 2	04/02/2009	82	Norwegian Dream	10/12/2008	97	Sun Princess	08/10/2008	94
Coral Princess	05/21/2009	97	Norwegian Gem	11/29/2008	98	Tahitian Princess	01/14/2009	99
Costa Fortuna	01/18/2009	97	Norwegian Jewel	03/06/2009	100	The World	06/23/2009	100
Costa Luminosa	05/15/2009		Norwegian Majesty	10/11/2008	95	TSS Topaz	08/09/2007	93
Costa Mediterranea	04/05/2008	99	Norwegian Pearl	05/07/2009	100	Veendam	02/08/2009	98
Crown Princess	04/26/2009	99	Norwegian Sky	02/06/2009	98	Vision Of The Seas	10/26/2008	97
Crystal Serenity	05/23/2009	99	Norwegian Spirit	05/29/2009	96	Volendam	05/22/2009	95
Crystal Symphony	03/09/2009	98	Norwegian Star	02/21/2009	98	Voyager Of The Seas	03/15/2009	99
Dawn Princess	05/05/2009	99	Norwegian Sun	04/30/2009	100	Westerdam	05/24/2009	100
Diamond Princess	05/20/2009	100	Oosterdam	03/14/2009	99	Wind Spirit	03/15/2009	97
Discovery Sun	03/03/2009	96	Oriana	02/01/2009	94	Zaandam	03/22/2009	99
Disney Magic	02/18/2009	98	Pacific Princess	02/27/2009	99	Zuiderdam	06/25/2009	98

*Inspections scores of 85 or lower are NOT satisfactory

Index

CRUISE LINES

CRUISE SHIPS

PORTS OF CALL